# 100 YEARS OF THE AMERICAN AUTO

BY THE AUTO EDITORS OF CONSUMER GUIDE®

Publications International, Ltd.

Louis Weber, CEO
Publications International, Ltd.
7373 North Cicero Avenue
Lincolnwood, Illinois 60712



Manufactured in China.

8 7 6 5 4 3 2 1

ISBN: 0-7853-9625-X

Library of Congress Catalog Card Number: 2003105299

# ACKNOWLEDGMENTS


## PHOTOGRAPHY

The editors gratefully acknowledge the cooperation of the following people who supplied photography to help make this book possible.

Scott Baxter; Ken Beebe/Kugler Studio; Les Bidrawn; Tom Bigelow; Joe Bohovic; Terry Boyce; Scott Brandt; Michael Brown; Robert Burrington; Chan Bush; Tom Cannell; Michael Carbonell; Joseph Caro; J. Cavallo; Henry Austin Clark, Jr.; William Cornelia; Jim Frenak; Mitch Frumkin; Mark Garcia; H. Russ Garrett; Thomas Glatch; Ed Goldberger; David Gooley; Sam Griffith; Lloyd Grotjan; Jerry Heasley; Alan Hewko/De Christopher's; Bill Hill; S. Scott Hutchinson; Reed Hutchison; Bert Johnson; Joe Joliet; Bud Juneau; Bill Kanz; Laurel H. Kenney, Jr.; Tim Kerwin; Milton Gene Kieft; Bill Kilborn; Rick Lenz; Randy Lorentzen; Dan Lyons; Vince Manocchi; Mark McMahon; Doug Mitchel; Photos by Morton; Mike Mueller; Jerry Naunheim; Jay Peck; Greg Price; Rob Van Schaick; William J. Schintz; Rick Simmons; Gary D. Smith; Robert Sorgatz; Richard Spiegleman; David Talbott; David Temple; Bob Tenney; Jim Thompson; Joe Wherry; Willoughby Photos; Hub Willson; Nicky Wright.

**Special thanks to:** Larry Gustin, Buick Motor Public Relations; Brandt Rosenbush, Barbara Fronczak, Chrysler Historical Collection; Brooks Stevens, Ron Grantz, National Automotive History Collection; Detroit Public Library; Leslie Lovett, NHRA; Daniel F. Kirchner, Peggy Dusman; American Automobile Manufacturers Association; Tom Downey, Studebaker National Museum; Jim Wren.

## OWNERS

Special thanks to the owners of the cars featured in this book for their enthusiastic cooperation.

**CHAPTER 2:**
Bob & Loni Babcock; Gene Baldwin; Art Banducci; Crawford Collection; Bob Fruehe; Frank Iaccino; Panhandle Plains Museum; Carl M. Riggins; Carroll Studebaker; Harold Walters, Sr.

**CHAPTER 3:**
Dewayne Adams; Fred Bausch; Richard Bayer; Briggs-Cunningham Museum; Ron Dehler; Dells Auto Museum; Dennis Fink; Gilmore Museum; Elmore Goehring; Frank Gonsalves; Dan & Carol Hansen; Harrah National Auto Museum; Ken Havekost; Owen Hoyt; Jonnie Keller; William Lyon Collection; Darrell A. Rader; Carl M. Riggins; Bob & Karyn Sitter; Stan Sokol; William E. Stever; Ernest J. Toth, Jr.; Earl White; Mike Young.

**CHAPTER 4:**
William S. Abbott; Daniel Allen; Farnum Alston; Armand Annereau; Norm Anselment; Robert Atwell; Barbara Atwood; Les Aubol; Auburn-Cord-Duesenberg Museum; Robert Babcock; Ed Barwick; Richard Bayer; M. D. Belden; Spencer L. Bing; Norman & Joyce Booth; James H. Bowersox; Ron Bransky; Bob Briggs; Howard A. Bring; Brooks Stevens Museum; Donald Burkholder; Canton Classic Car Museum; Joe Cimmino; James L. Carlson; Mrs. Benjamin R. Caskey; J.F. Cassan; Bob Clarke; Bill Cline; Edward & Arlene Cobb; Debbie Colaniro; Joe Consalvo; Briggs Cunningham; Fraser Dante; Annette & Dan Darling; James Day; Charles Deaubl; Harry & Virginia DeMenge; Dick Dennis; Larry Desenville; Donald E. Dessing; Richard DeVecchi; Gerald Dewey; Harold Dinger; Harvey Doering; Alex & Beverly Dow; Michael Doyle; Donald D. Duffy; Ken & Stephanie Dunsire; Jerry Emery; Alfred Ferrara; Fred C. Fischer; Jim Flicek; Joseph B. Folladori; Francis Frisch; Gilmore Car Museum; Wayne R. Graefen; L.D. Grandey; Lee Greer; Bud Greist; Peter Guido; Ed Gunther; David L. Guthery; Tom Hall; Jack Harbaugh; John F. Hare; Jacques Harguindeguy; Wm. F. Harrah Museum; David R. Harriman; Shel Harriman; Dick & Nancy Harvey; Dr. Frank Hayward; Earl Heintz; Robert R. Hekfenstein; Harold Hofferber; Philip & Nancy Hoffman; David Holls; Bill & Bertha Honey; Tom Hrudka; Ray Hunter; Julius Ironhart; Jim Jeram; G. Johnson; Terry Johson; Press A. Kale; George D. Kanaan; Craig Karr; Bruce Kennedy; John Kepich; Knox Kershaw; Frank Kleptz; James Kozbelt; Evertt A. Kroeze; Darvin & Becca Kuehl; Phil Kuhn; Ron & Debbie Ladley; William Lauer; Warren & Sylvia Lauridsen; Mike Laureno, Jr.; Larry Lawyer; Basil Lewis; John Librenjac; Ron Lipsey; James Lockwood; Maurice W. Ludwig; William Lyons Collection; John Madison; Jerry Malecki; James P. Manak; Sam & Emily Mann; James Martin; Mr. & Mrs. Norman Martin; Paul & Peg Mather; Gerard & Lorraine May; Robert McAtee; Jim McGrew; Dick McKean; Frank O. McLiesh; Paul Mehes; Ray Menefee; Paul Miller; S. Ray Miller, Jr.; Chuck Mitchell; Armin F. Mittermaier; Erville W. Murphy; Marshall R. Nelson; Ralph Neubauer; Clay Nichols; Jack Passey; Gene Perkins; B. Perrou; John Poochigian; Ester Price Candies Corp.; Jack Pufall; Terry Radey; Ted & Jo Raines; Vito Ranks; Glen & Vera Roberts; Philomena Ronco-Cohan; Eric & Molly Rosenau; Joseph Rotar; Fran Roxas; Eugene Roy; Jess Rupp; John Sanders; Sandy Sanger; Ralph Schmidt; Ronald N. Schneider; William and Joseph Schoenbeck; Sam H. Scoles; Walter G. Serviss; Ed Siegfried; R.C. & Virginia Simmons; Harv Sjaarda; Thomas B. Smiley; William Snyder; Peter A. Spear; Samuel Spedale; Thomas P. Spenny; Walt Sprague; Carroll Studebaker; Bruce R. Thomas; Mike Thraser; Eric Thurstone; Mr. & Mrs. Jack Tiechel; Ed & Eleanor Todd; Ernest J. Toth, Jr.; Bill Trnka; Gene Troyer; Ed Wachs; Craig Watrous; W. Wauer; John Webber; Billy F. Wilson; Larry Wilson; William L. Wilson; Harry Wynn; Ron Yori; William Young; Marvin E. Yount, Jr.; Robert Zaitlin; P. Alvin Zamba.

**CHAPTER 5:**
Arnie Addison; Thomas Barratt; Norman & Joyce Booth; Terry Davis; William Lauer; James R. Lauzon; Joseph Leir Memorial Auto Collection; Bill Leonhardt; Dr. Gerald M. Levitt; Charlie Montano; Robert Reeves; Raymond J. Reis, Sr.; Al Wilkiewicz; Harry Wynn.

**CHAPTER 6:**
Joe Abela; Al Adams; Jim Ashworth; Samuel R. Barone; Jack Bart; Sharon Bielefeldt; Neil S. Black; Gordon Blixt; Robert Bradley; Elmer F. Brawn; Dave Cammack; Robert Carlson; Tom L. Carver; Joseph Clampitt; Dr. Steven Colson; Donald W. Curtis; Raymond E. Dade; Vince Daul; Gary L. Faulk; Bev Ferreira; Fraser Dante, Ltd.; Terri Gardner; Ed Gunther; Harrah National Auto Museum; Ken Havekost; Harvey Hedgcock; Chris & Pete Jakubowski; Blaine Jenkins; Dick Johnson; Ralph Johnson; Bud Juneau; Roger Kash; Bill Knudsen; Peter Krakowski; William. H. Lauer; Jerry & Adell Laurin; Dr. Roger K. Leir; Thomas F. Lerch; David Marshall; Richard Matson; Robert L. McAtee; Dick McKean; Ralph G. McQuoid; Robert Messinger; Mike Moore; Tom Morgan; Michael Morris; Rod Morris Classic Cars; Harry Nicks; Louis & Inez Noose; John Otto; Donald Passardi; Dick Pyle; Ken Rathke; Steve Sim Roberts; William Rohley; Arthur Sabin; Roy A. Schneider; H. Robert & Katheryn Stamp; Suburban Motors; Ron Szymanowski; Chip Turtzo; Unique Motor Cars; Burt Van Flue; Alan West; John White; Jerry Windle; Bob Zarnowsky.

**CHAPTER 7:**
Jim Bauldauf; Bob Brelsford; Donald & Phyllis Bueter; Tony Capua; Dick Choler; Myron Davis; Harry & Virgina DeMenge; David Doyle; Glenn Eisenhamer; Bob Getsfried; Sonny & Maci Glasbrenner; Ken Griesemer; Bill Halliday; Bob Hill; David Hill; Victor Jacobellis; Bud Juneau; Press & Janet Kale; Russel A. Liechty; Verl D. Mowery; Tenny Natkin; Charles Newton; Rader's Relics; Myron Reicheret; Bill Reinhardt; Tom Rohrich; Art Sabin; John Segedy; Raymond Silva, Jr.; John Spring; Danny L. Steine; Sam Turner; Bob Ward; Anthony Wells.

**CHAPTER 8:**
Bob Adams Collectibles, Ltd.; William D. Albright; Edward George Allen; Donald Baldwin; Nancy L. Beauregard; Joseph E. Bortz; R. G. Brelsford; Bill Burgun; Bonnie Carey; Steve Carey; Earl J. Carpenter; Bob & Brad Chandler; Dick Choler; Phil & Louella Cruz; Keith Cullen; James E. Dinehart; James L. Dowdy; Robert Frumkin; Anthony J. Gullatta; Dix Helland; George S. Jewell; Alan & Wilma Jordan; Jack Karleskind; John Keck; John & Minnie Keys; Gary J. Kistinger; Larry K. Landis; Paul A. Leinbohm; Bud Manning; Paul & Peg Mather; Richard Matson; Mike & Nancy McCutcheon; Steve Megyes; George W. Mills; Ken Netwig; Greg Pagano; Donald W. Peters; Peter's Motorcars; John Pollack; Lewis E. Retzer; Robert Rocchio; Homer Jay Sanders, Sr.; John Sanders; Robert G. Seals; Charles O. Sharpe; Henry Smith; Bonnie & Dennis Statz; Jerry Tranberger; Charles Watson, Jr.; Keith Zimmerman.

**CHAPTER 9:**
Bob Aaron; Robert & Diane Adams; Mervin Afflerbach; Albie Albershardt; William D. Albright; J. Alexander; Andrew Alphonso; Eldon Anson; Christopher Antal; Len Antrim; Mark Apel; Lynn Augustine; Robert Babcock; John Baker, Sr.; Barry & Barb Bales; Tom & Karen Barnes; David Barry; Paul Bastista; Bob Baumgardner; Charles R. Bell; Raymond & Marylin Bendy; Michael L. Berzenye; Patrick Billy; Neil S. Black; Bill Bodnarchuck; Pete Bogard; Ernest Bollerud; Clayton E. Bone; Pete Bose; James Bottger; Bob Brannon; Charles R. Breed; Brooks Stevens Museum; Dr. Douglas Bruinsma; Joseph R. Bua; David Burkholder; Vern Burkitt; Dr. Art Burrichter; Paul A. Buscemi; Jim Cahill; Stephen Capone; Richard Carpenter; Dwight Cervin; Chicago Car Exchange, Inc.; Dick Choler; Gordon Christl; Jerry Cinotti; Steve & Dawn Cizmas; Jim Clark; Classic Car Center; Roger Clements; Community Trading; Kathy Crasweller; Arthur & Suzanne Dalby; Gail & John Dalmolin; Richard Daly; T. Davidson; Charles Davis; Myron Davis; Deer Park Car Museum; Ray & Nancy Deitke; Harry & Virgina DeMenge; Tom Devers; Jim Digreborio; Orville Dopps; Harry E. Downing; Jeff Dranson; Stanley & Phyllis Dumes; Dale & Marilyn Dutoi; Sherry Echols; William B. Edwards; Galen & Fay Erb; Stan

Farnham; Everett Faulkner; Don & Sue Fennig; David Ferguson; Al Ferreira; Don & Barbara Finn; Bob Flack; Edsel Ford; Robert C. Fox; J. Franklin; Tom Franks; Kurt Fredricks; Ted Freeman; John M. Galandak; F. James Garbe; Ray Geschke; Sal Gianfriddo; Harold Gibson; G.R. Good; Roger & Connie Graebar; Wayne R. Graefen; Art Gravatt; Tim Graves; Jim D. Gregorio; Greg Gustafson; Tim & Sharon Hacker; Robert Hallada; S. Halloran; Sam Harpster; Jay Harrigan; Bill & Dorothy Harris; Ralph Harsock; Dennis Hauke; Maurice B. Hawa; Henry T. Heinz; Paul Hem; Dr. Ernie Hendry; Carl Herre; Charles Hilbert; Bill Hill; Roger Hill; Bob Hoffmann; S. Holloran; Lester H. Hooley; David D. Horn; Mac Horst; Tom Howard; Dick Hoyt; Virgil Hudkins; Dennis L. Huff; Fritz Hugo; Melvin R. Hull; Fred & Diane Ives; Robert D. Jaehnig; Blaine Jenkins; Roger & Betty Jeriel; Gary Johns; Dennis & Cathy Johnson; Arron Kahlenberg; Sherwood Kahlenberg; Thomas L. Karkiewicz; Glendon & Betty Kierstead; William R. Kipp; Edwin C. Kirstatter; Gerry Klein; Bill Knudsen; Norb Kopchinski; Don R. Kreider; John Krempasky; Andrew Krizman; David & Anne Kurtz; Edward S. Kuziel; David Lawrence; Donald R. Lawson; William Lauer; Steve Lefevre; Dr. William H. Lenharth; Ken G. Lindsey; William R. Lindsey; Brian Long; Tom Lorek; George Lucie; Andrew & Bonita MacFarland; Joe Malta; Thomas R. Matthews; Gene Mauburger; R. McAtee; Michael D. McCloskey; Virgil & Dorthy Meyer; Cal & Lori Middleton; Gary Mills; Dennis B. Miracky; Bob Montgomery; Bob Moore; Jack E. Moore; Guy Morice; Jim Mueller; M. Randall Mytar; Jim Nagel; Richard Nassar; Gerald Newton; Bob & Janet Nitz; Paul F. Northam; Tom Null; Pat & Marge Oglesby; Dale Osten; Ray Ostrander; Robert W. Paige; Alan Parker; John E. Parker; John W. Petras; Robb Petty; Richard & Janice Plastino; Norman Plogge; A. La Rue Plotts; Michael Polsinelli; Joel Prescott; Richard V. Presson; Priceless Classics; Norman W. Prien; Leonard Quinlin; Ramshead Auto; Vito S. Ranks; Larry & Annis Ray; Jerry Retka; Gary Richards; George Richards; John Riordon; Gary Robinson; Philomena Ronco-Cohan; Bob Rose; Otto T. Rosenbush; Dick Rosynek; H. Rothman; Charles G. Roveran; Glyn & Jan Rowley; Jess Ruffalo; Al & Alice Russell; Jim Scarpitti; Al Schaefer; Peter & Jan Schlacter; Bill Schwelitz; John Scopelite; Robert W. Seiple; Robert Sexton; Bob & Roni Sue Shapiro; David Showalter; Don Simpkin; Frank & Gene Sitarz; Karl Smith; Walter J. Smith; Don & Bonnie Snipes; Ray Somers; Allan Spethman; Tom Stackhouse; David L. Stanilla; Dennis M. Statz; Dan Streick; Bob Strous; John Struthers; Studebaker National Museum; David Studer; Duane & Steven Stupienski; Neil W. Sugg; Robert G. Swanstrom; George Swartz; Frank Tallarico; Ed Tolhurst; Kris Trexler; William E. True; Kennedith & Wayne Turner; Joel Twainten; Kenneth Ugolini; Dean Ullman; Bill Ulrich; Roy Umberger; Charles Vander Velde; James & Susan Verhasselt; Christine & Robert Waldock; Bob & Wendi Walker; Marvin Wallace; Glen Warrick; Edward E. Wassmann; Bob Weber; Herbert Wehling; Michael Wehling; Ron Welch; Jim & Pat Welker; Jeff & Aleta Wells; Tim Wenzlowski; H.H. Wheeler; John White; Lee Willett; Brian H. Williams; William M. Witt; John Wood; Frank Wrenick; Charles & Veronica Wurm, Jr.; Dennis Yauger; Eugene Yaughn; Dr. Roy V. Yorns; Richard Zeiger.

**CHAPTER 10:**
Arnie Addison; Rich Antonacci; Carolyn & Mark Badamo; Barry & Barb Bales; Joseph Barrera; Ron & Claudia Bjerke; Dave Brown; Bob Burroughs; Kenneth J. Caswell; Robert & Karen Christanell; Mike Congelose; Virgil K. Cooper; Mike Cowles; Thomas Crockatt; Claud E. Daniel, Jr.; Jim Davidson; Myron Davis; John Deved; Jack Driesenga; Roger Eberenz; Mike Elward; Fred Engle; Greg & Doug Englin; Phil Fair; Robert & Gene Fattore; John & Jeanne Finster; Bob French; Paul Garlick; Andy Gartzman; John Gaylord; Gary Girt; Stephen Gottfried; Alden Graber; Jack Gratzianna; Wanda Habenicht; Robert Hallada; Ron & Kate Hanaway; Rex Harris; Ken Havekost; Phil Hayenga; Chuck Henderson; David Hooten; Andy Hotton; Bill Jackson; Vic Jacobellis; Bruce Jacobs; Blaine Jenkins; Chuck Jenkins; John Karaway; Michael & Patricia Kelso; Bobbie Kincaid; George Kling; William Korbel; Melvin Lewis; Harold Lee Lockhart; Terry Lucas; Guy Mabee; Don Maich; Ed Meurer; Lloyd W. Mill; S. Ray Miller; Amos Minter; Frank J. Monhart III; Bob Montgomery; Dean Moroni; Jim Mueller; Jon B. Myer; Bob Newman; Jack Nichols; Jim Noel; Barry Norman; Ed Oberhaus; Anthony Patane; Bob Patrick; Thomas J. Patterson; Joseph A. Pessetti; Roger Porep; George W. Rappeyea; Les Raye; Vivian Riley; Nick Schafsniti; Charles Schnetlage; Sam Scoles; Doug Scott; M.J. Shelton; Ray Shinn; Roy Sklarin; Joseph Smiesko; Mike Spaziano; Specialty Sales; Frank Spittle; Dean Stansfield; Larry Stumpf; Joe Sutter; Rusty Symmes; Dick Tarnuter/Dells Museum; Gary Thobe; Steve Thompson; Keith Thomson; Robert Thornton; Marion & Lindy Van Wormer; Harold Von Brocken; John Wacha; Alois Peter Warren II; Janet Wright; Lou Zandn.

**CHAPTER 11:**
Sam & Char Adams; Roger Adkins; Norman Andrews; David Arent; Jim Ashworth; Doug & Judy Badgley; Trever Badgley; Howard L. Baker; Jeffery Baker; Ray & Dolores Banuls; Ray Banuls; John Baritel; Larry Barnett; David Bartholomew; Larry Bell; Tom Bigelow; John Breda; David L Briebling; Scott Brubaker; Rodney Brumbaugh; Jerry Buczkowski; Joe Burke; Richard L. Burki; Bill Bush; Frank Capolupo; Ken Carmack; Richard Carpenter; Ed Catricala; Vince Cesena; Classic Auto Showplace; Charles & Marie Cobb; Dave Cobble II; Mike Cohen; James E. Collins; Gordon Coman; Community Trading Center; John Cook; Ed Coughlin; Dr. Mike Cruz; Allen Cummins; Nick D'Amico; Sandy D'Amico; Connie Davis; Don & Linda Davis; David Dawes; Harry & Virgina DeMenge; Rock DiOrio; Patrick & Barbara Dugan; Keith Duncan; Donald F. & Chris Dunn; Jay Dykes; Joseph Eberle; Neil Ehresman; Glenn Eisenhammer; Ray & Lil Elias; Ron Embleton; Howard S. Engerman; James & Mary Engle; The Beechy Family; Eugene Fattore; Mark E. Figliozzi; Robert G. Finley; Christina Finster; John T. Finster; Bob H. Firth; John Fobair; Frank Frandsen; Al Fraser; Irene A. Galier; Charles P. Geissler; Tony & Suzanne George; Louise Gibino; G. Grams; Michael S. Gray; Tom Griffith; Dennis Guest; Mike Guffey; Tom Haase; Pete Haliman; Jerry Hammer; Earl F. Hansen; James Harris; Ralph Hartsock; Michael E. Hatch; Ken Havekost; Jon F. Havens; Grady Hentz; Ray Herman; Fred Hicks; Brad & Barb Hillick; Steve Hinshaw; Jim & Trish Holmes; Steven Jenear; William John; Aaron Kahlenberg; Jack Karleskind; Lawrence Keck; Dave & Cindy Keetch; Don & Karen Kerridge; Michele King; Robert Kleckauskas; Robert & Ann Klein; Frank Kleptz; Scott R. Koeshall; William W. Kramer; Steve & Sally Kuss; Mark Kuykendall; Jim Labertew/RPM Motors; William G. Lajeunesse; Leroy Lasiter; Norman & Peggy Llewellyn; James Lojewski; Dan & Joyce Lyons; George Lyons; John L. Maciejewski; Richard Martindale; Ralph M. Mathiot; Steve Maysonet; Donald C. McCallum; Tom McGann; Bryan McGilvray; Paul McGuire; Michael Mennella; Sue & Horace Mennella; Greg & Rhonda Meredyk; Bruce Meyer; Larry & Karen Miller; Rick Mitchell; Thom Moerman; Manny Montgomery; David R. Mullett; Allan B. Murray; M. Randall Mytar; Yoshio & Eric Nakayama; Ken Nelson; Rich Neubauer; Burt & Lynda Neuner; Ed Oberhaus; Ben Oliver; Alfred L. Olson; Jay F. Painter; Samuel Pampenella, Jr.; Dan Parilli; Patricia & Rexford Parker; Lawrence Pavia; Lee Pawilratz; Andrew Peterson; Paul D. Pierce; Sam Pierce; Joseph Pieroni; Chris Plylar; Thomas & Carol Podemski; Edwin Putz; Ed Radek; Ramshead Auto Collection; John & Shirlee Rasin; Les Raye; Jim Regnier; Greg Reynolds; Bruce Rhoades; Jim Riley; David L. Robb; Si Rogers; Dennis D. Rosenberry; Darryl A. Salisbury; Joe L. Saunders; Walter Schenk; Tom Schlitter; Owen Schlmacher; Howard Schoen; Lou Schultz; Han Schumacher; Robert & Mary Lu Secondi; Steve Shuman; Duane & Carol Silvius; Larry Simek; Russ Smith; David Snodgrass; Roy L. Spencer; Frank Spittle; Vince & Helen Springer; Tom & Katherine Stanley; Charles E. Stinson; Nate Struder; Tom & Nancy Stump; Steve Sydell; David Temple; Michael Tesauro, Jr.; Gary R. Thalman; Brian & Elvira Torres; David A. Ulrich; Dennis A. Urban; Charles A. Vance; Volo Museum; Ron Voyes; Bob Weggenmann; Jeff Wentz; Doug West; William E. Wetherholt; Sherman Williams; Walter P. Wise; Stephen Witmer; Patrick Wnek; Ron Wood; Bill Woodman; David Yordi; Rich & Joan Young; Dr. Richard Zeiger; C.L. Zinn.

**CHAPTER 12:**
Kirk Alexander; Mark Alter; Fernando F. Alvare; Sam Bardic; Tom Berthelsen; James H. Carson; Gordon & Dorothy Clemmer; Rick Cybul; Leonidas Demopoulos; J. Glenn Dowd; Tony & Betty Fabiano; G. Benjamin Graves; Alan L. Gray; Gregg Gyurina; David L. Hargrove; Bud Juneau; Charles M. Kerr; Kevin Kloubec; William Korbel; Bob Masi; Don McLennon; Ralph Milner; Dolores Ann Mitchell; Ed Oberhaus; Steven S. Pasek; Steven L. Pegler; John Phillips; Thomas & Carol Podemski; Dennis W. Riley; Doug Schliesser; Sheryl Sommers; Frank Trummer; Roseanne Winney; Peter Zannis; Larry Zidek.

**CHAPTER 13:**
Gina Biciunas; Lloyd Bradbury; Bill Daubney; Dennis Helferich; James Marino; Dale Shetley; Bill & Sherry Souther; Zimmer Motors.

# CONTENTS


INTRODUCTION
An American Odyssey...7

CHAPTER ONE
In the Beginning: 1893-1902...8

CHAPTER TWO
Up and Running: 1903-1919...32

CHAPTER THREE
Anything Goes: 1920-1929...90

CHAPTER FOUR
Survival of the Fittest: 1930-1941...138

CHAPTER FIVE
Detroit Goes to War: 1942-1945...190

CHAPTER SIX
The Postwar "Seller's Market": 1946-1948...202

CHAPTER SEVEN
A New Era Begins: 1949...230

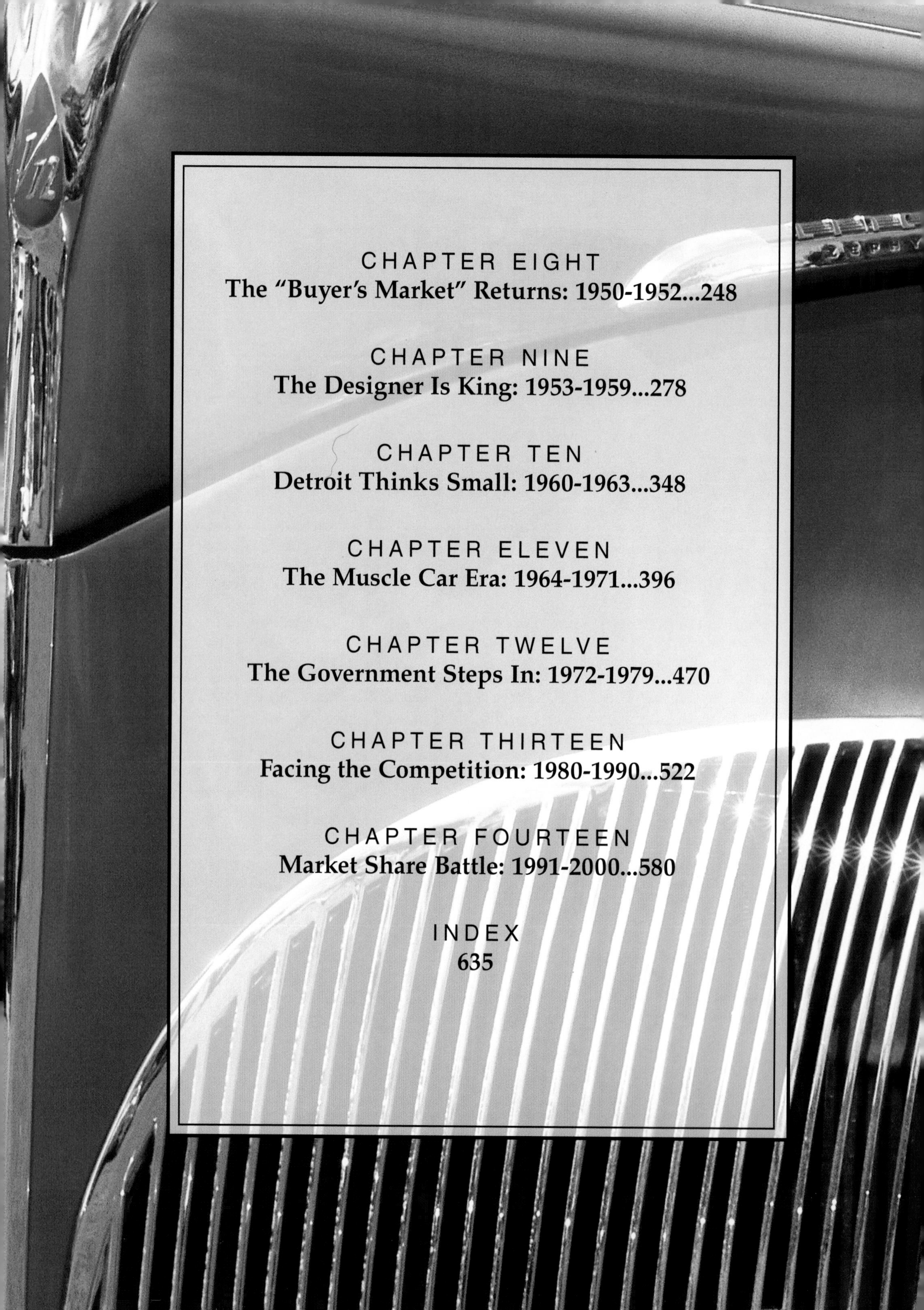

CHAPTER EIGHT
**The "Buyer's Market" Returns: 1950-1952...248**

CHAPTER NINE
**The Designer Is King: 1953-1959...278**

CHAPTER TEN
**Detroit Thinks Small: 1960-1963...348**

CHAPTER ELEVEN
**The Muscle Car Era: 1964-1971...396**

CHAPTER TWELVE
**The Government Steps In: 1972-1979...470**

CHAPTER THIRTEEN
**Facing the Competition: 1980-1990...522**

CHAPTER FOURTEEN
**Market Share Battle: 1991-2000...580**

INDEX
**635**

# AN AMERICAN ODYSSEY

Welcome to a great story well told. The American automotive saga is rich in color and variety, and if there's a better way to convey its pace, scope, and excitement than with more than 4000 photos and captions, we haven't seen it. Think of *100 Years of the American Auto* as a "family album" of the American automobile: a scrapbook of the major and minor, the good and ghastly, the memorable and forgettable.

Actually, it's a tale that spans more than 100 years, so this album does, too. But the automobile is the quintessential Twentieth Century device, and its story is the story of the American Century. Indeed, our chronicle is divided according to historical periods, with highlights of significant events and trends included in the introduction to each chapter. As for the automotive subject matter itself, the editors have striven to portray as many representative models as possible. If we have omitted things you think should have been included, we can only plead that there's never enough room for-everything—except maybe in the Smithsonian Institution.

We've designed this book to inform and entertain readers of every age in every land, and there's a good reason why it should. Just as America is like no other country and Americans like no other people, American automobiles have a unique character.

Although born in Europe, the automobile really "grew up" in America, becoming an expression of the nation's values and technology, as well as an engine of economic and social change. In fact, nowhere else has the automobile been a more pivotal player on a national stage. We were quick to adopt the "horseless carriage" as our own. We paved landscapes so we could drive the machines everywhere (to the ultimate decline of our railroads). We perfected interchangeable parts so we could build cars consistently, then made Detroit the Motor City by devising the mass-production assembly line to turn automobiles out so efficiently that everybody could afford one—the very essence of democracy.

Americans made cars bigger and heavier than Europeans did, if only for comfort and durability in a large nation full of wide open spaces. The cars were also made to be as fast and powerful as possible. And why not, when gasoline was so much cheaper and more plentiful here? Historically cheap gas not only hastened America's acceptance of the internal combustion engine over steam and electricity, it made Detroit the home of horsepower—all the better for covering, say, 500 miles in a day. The typical European road trip doesn't cover half that distance.

One thing you may glean from these pages is the way American automobile design still reflects the can-do flamboyance of Americans. This holds true not only for appearance, which Americans tend to alter more often and capriciously than Europeans, but also for technical features, which have often been something less than advertised. Yet if Detroit was once ridiculed for gaudy gimmicks and faddish "planned obsolescence," it was only because Americans most always believed that "new" really was "better." Besides, how else to encourage people to buy from an industry that came to account directly or indirectly for one of every three American jobs?

Not that the American car industry hasn't done its share to advance the state of automotive art. The modern high compression engine, safety-rim wheel, power steering and brakes, automatic transmission, air conditioning, and the air bag were all invented here. These innovations deserve due credit, if only to balance more dubious Detroit achievements, such as tailfins and wraparound windshields. Then again, "styling" was invented here, too.

To browse though this book is to be struck by how far the automobile has come in only a hundred years—from the crude, costly, slow, and smoking rattletrap at the turn of one century to the clean, quiet, safe, and sophisticated conveyance at the turn of another. It's been a remarkable ride. And it's only just begun.

The Auto Editors of Consumer Guide®

CHAPTER ONE

1893-1902

# IN THE BEGINNING

Though first in countless technical developments, America came late to the automobile. By the time the Duryea brothers took their horseless carriage for a spin in 1893, such European motorcars as Benz and Panhard et Levassor had been marketed for several years.

Clearly, American inventors had the engineering skills to have created an automobile earlier. Many were aware of European developments. Nevertheless, the American auto industry lagged at the starting gate.

Roads presented one major obstacle. America was a vast land of muddy ruts—where any pathway existed at all. Besides that, potential backers feared the financial risk, so countless automakers would fail due to lack of sufficient capital.

Three power sources vied for attention: steam, electricity, and gasoline. Steam locomotives had helped tame the American West. Couldn't a steam-powered conveyance also run on roads? Oliver Evans had proposed such a wagon in 1801. Sylvester Roper had built a steam carriage in 1863. Finally, by 1897, the Stanley twins were producing steam-powered automobiles. Though powerful, steamers demanded skilled maintenance. Stanleys lingered through the mid-Twenties, but their heyday was over long before then.

Electric motors powered carriages by the early Nineties. Despite their short range, electrics were genteel: clean, silent, perfect for ladies. At the turn of the century, electrics grabbed an impressive 38 percent of the market, but their share soon plummeted. Nearly a century later, the long-expected battery "breakthrough" still remains elusive.

No single inventor earns credit for the internal-combustion engine, first patented in 1826. Etienne Lenoir patented a two-cycle motor in France, in 1860. George Brayton's American-built gasoline engine ran at the 1876 Centennial in Philadelphia. Inspired by Brayton's two-cycle motor, George Selden applied for a patent on a "road engine." Years later, Selden's patent would cause American automakers grave consternation.

In 1885, Karl Benz and Gottlieb Daimler, of Germany, independently created the world's first vehicles with internal-combustion engines, operating on the four-cycle principle devised by Nicholas Otto. Charles and Frank Duryea read about the Benz in the *Scientific American* and—on September 21, 1893—drove their motorized phaeton. Was theirs really the first in America? No one knows for sure. Charles Lambert, for instance, claimed to have produced one in 1891.

If any one event paved the way for gasoline power it was Chicago's *Times-Herald* race, held in November 1895. The grueling contest, run in the snow, was won by a two-cylinder Duryea.

By 1895, *Horseless Age* magazine estimated that 300 Americans had attempted to build a motorized carriage. Like Daimler and Benz, nearly all worked alone, unaware of others' efforts.

In March 1896, Charles King drove his car in Detroit. Three months later came Henry Ford's Quadricycle. Before the year was out, Ransom Olds and Alexander Winton had cars ready for production. By 1897, the auto industry was rolling full steam—or gasoline—ahead.

An impartial observer might have pronounced the gasoline engine's prospects limited. The operator had to start it with a crank, tinkering with various controls. It shook and clattered, smoked and stank. Shifting gears was no picnic. Farmers were angered, horses frightened. Genteel, it was not. Soon, though, the trend narrowed to the water-cooled, four-cycle gasoline engine.

Many of the visions of our pioneer automakers faltered quickly. Others carried on for several years. A handful, like the Curved-Dash Runabout named for Ransom Olds, and the soon-to-arrive Buick and Ford, have persisted into modern times.

---

**Pre-1893**

Credit for the first self-propelled land vehicle goes to the 1770 French Cugnot, a steam-powered artillery tractor

By 1865, Sylvester Roper mounts a steam engine on a carriage to create a self-propelled runabout

Even earlier, in 1862, Jean Joseph Etienne Lenoir experiments with a gasoline-powered road vehicle in Europe

Ransom Eli Olds begins experiments with three-wheeled steam vehicles as early as 1886

An improved Olds steamer of 1891 earns a mention in *Scientific American* magazine

Lucius D. Copeland builds a steam-powered bicycle in the early 1880s and experiments with electric power; steam tricycles are produced later in the decade

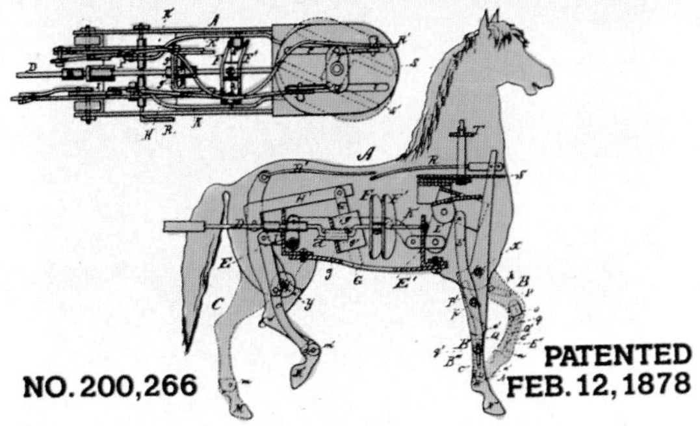


◀ Ideas for self-propelled vehicles proliferated late in the 19th century. This 1878 patent included both the conveyance and a "horse" with an internally mounted motor.

▲ Wheeled motorcars already dotted Europe, but this 1891 patent was basically for a six-legged mechanical horse.

▲ The popularity of bicycles in the 1880s led various inventors to envision mechanization. Lucius D. Copeland attached a small boiler to his Star bicycle's front frame tube, and a small steam engine below the saddle. His steam bicycle was exhibited in 1884 in Arizona.

◀ Henry Ford began work on a motorized bicycle in 1893, in a little brick shed behind his Detroit home. Completed in 1896, his Quadricycle used belt and chain drive and a two-cylinder, water-cooled engine. This replica of Ford's workshop may be viewed at Greenfield Village in Dearborn, Michigan.

---

DeLamarre De Bouteville patents a carburetor in 1884

Two German motor vehicles appear by 1886: Benz three-wheeler and Daimler sidewheeler cycle

Benz obtains a German patent for a gasoline-powered "Motorwagon" in January 1886

Karl Benz and Gottlieb Daimler earn credit as developers of the first workable gasoline-powered vehicles; their creations attract little attention in America

European automobiles are in regular production by the early 1890s

William Morrison drives his electric vehicle in Chicago in 1888

Early vehicles that claim title to the first American car include Lambert and Nadig, both built in 1891

The three-wheeled, surrey-topped Lambert runabout gets a price tag of $550, but fails to sell

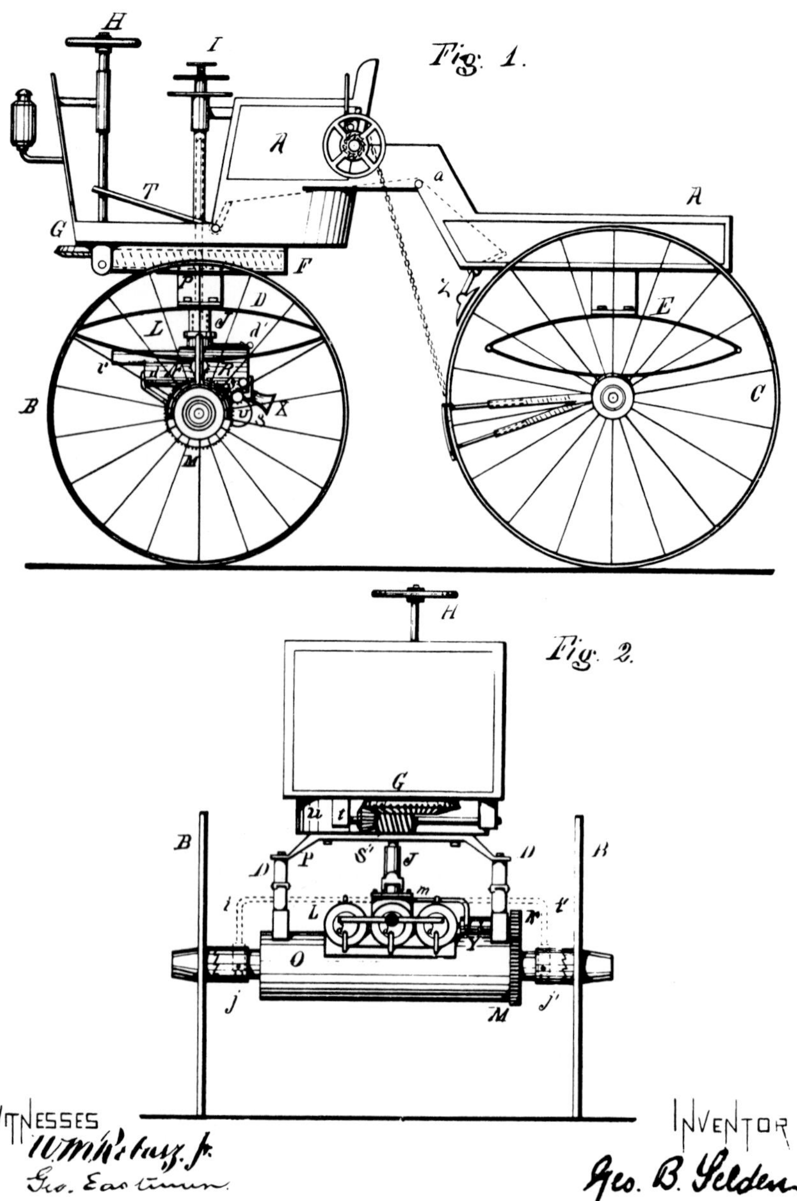


▲ Few grasped the ultimate significance of the "Road Engine" patent granted to George B. Selden on November 5, 1895. Later, Selden would demand royalties from infant automakers, claiming that his patent covered their efforts.

▲ Elwood P. Haynes tends the tiller of his first motorcar, which he drove in Kokomo, Indiana, in 1894. Haynes bought a single-cylinder, two-stroke Sintz engine, then asked the Apperson brothers to build a vehicle around it.

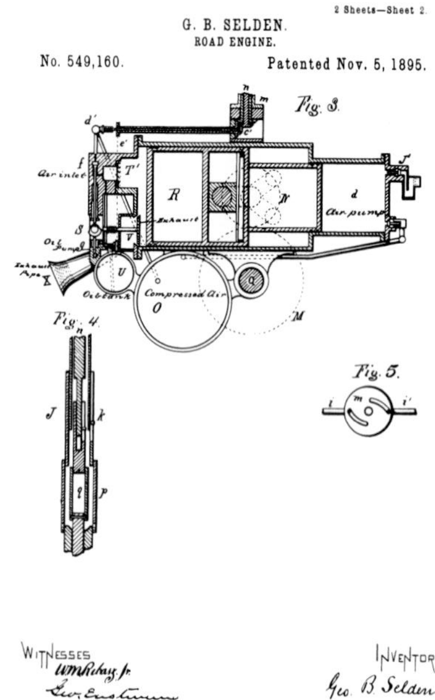


▲ The Selden patent specified a modified Brayton-type engine. No vehicle had been built at the time of issuance, but Selden had one constructed years later.

---

The Nadig carriage uses a one-cylinder gasoline engine and belt drive—but is never patented by creator Henry Nadig

Andrew L. Riker designs an electric three-wheeler in 1884, but none are built; his experiments with electric power result in an actual motorcar in the mid-1890s

Francis E. and Freelan O. Stanley, owners of a photographic equipment company, attempt in 1884 to build a steam car based on the Field steamer. They fail, but later will produce the fabled Stanley Steamer

A sliding-gear transmission debuts in France in 1891; created by René Panhard/Emile Levassor, it foretells modern stick-shift gearboxes

Panhard, produced in France, is the first vehicle with a front-mounted internal-combustion engine driving rear wheels via gearbox and driveshaft, circa 1891

◀ Charles Duryea sits in the machine used in a court case as "Deft's Exhibit-7." Duryea and his brother, J. Frank, built what most authorities consider the first American gasoline-powered car, driven in 1893. They formed a company in 1895, the same year a Duryea driven by J. Frank won the *Times-Herald* race in Chicago on a snowy Thanksgiving day.

▲ Years later, many Americans would incorrectly believe that Henry Ford invented the automobile. Ford was an engineer at the Edison Illuminating Company when he started work on his first vehicle.

▲ Henry Ford's Quadricycle drew scant attention when he drove it around Detroit on June 4, 1896, at 2:00 a.m. Its two-cylinder engine made about four horsepower.

▲ Ford's 1896 Quadricycle used a buggy-type chassis, bicycle wheels, and gas-pipe hubs. The primitive vehicle had two forward speeds, of 10 and 20 mph, but no reverse.

**1893-94**

J. Frank Duryea and brother Charles operate the one-cylinder "Buggyaut" on September 21, 1893, at Springfield, Massachusetts—it's considered the first successful gas-engine vehicle built in the U.S.

An early Duryea advertisement explains to incredulous readers that the vehicle "actually operated under its own propulsion"

Elmer and Edgar Apperson and Jonathan Maxwell build the single-cylinder Haynes; conceived by Elwood Haynes, it is tested in fall 1893 and operating by July 4, 1894

Henry Ford builds his first working engine in 1893, then starts on his first vehicle

The U.S. Office of Road Inquiry is established in 1893, a result of the "good roads" movement initiated by cycling fans

▲ Beating Ford by three months, Charles B. King drove a gasoline-powered carriage on Detroit streets on March 6, 1896. The historic vehicle was reconstructed in 1946.

▲ Charles Brady King grasps the tiller of his first automobile, in 1896. Beside him is assistant Oliver E. Barthel, who was later associated with Henry Ford.

► Ransom E. Olds (*rear*) formed the Olds Motor Vehicle Company in 1897. His passenger in the one-cylinder '97 model, M.F. Bates, claimed to have built the first internal combustion engine in Michigan.

▲ Ransom Eli Olds experimented with steamers in 1887, and then built his first gasoline-powered vehicle in 1896.

---

The first brick-surfaced rural road is laid on Wooster Pike, Ohio, fall 1893

Henry G. Morris and Pedro G. Salom apply for a patent on the Electrobat electric motorcar in early 1894

Early gearboxes are "progressive"—the driver must move a shifting lever one step forward at a time to go between gears, not unlike a motorcycle transmission

Rather than adopt the noisy sliding-gear unit, many pioneer American automakers will turn to the planetary transmission, with constant-mesh gears and clutches to change ratios

▲ Dr. Carlos G. Booth, of Youngstown, Ohio, may have been the first American physician to use a motorcar in his practice. Booth assembled his own vehicle.

▼ After building 13 vehicles in 1896, the Duryea brothers were definitely in business as the Duryea Motor Wagon Company. Note the early use of the term "automobile" in this ad for their 1897 model.

DAIMLER MOTOR CO., Steinway, Long Island City, N. Y.

**Duryea Motor Wagon Company,**

SPRINGFIELD, MASS.

MANUFACTURERS OF

**Motor Wagons, Motors,** and

**Automobile Vehicles of all kinds.**

▼ Henry Ford built his second Quadricycle in 1898-99, with a far more finished appearance than the 1896 model. Note the tiller handgrip.

**1895**

Durvea Motor Wagon Company is the first American firm established to build gasoline autos

U.S. Patent Office grants a patent on a motorcar to George B. Selden; it covers the principal features of the gasoline automobile

J. Frank Duryea wins the *Times-Herald* Race in Chicago on Thanksgiving Day, traveling 54 miles at an average 7.5 mph—the first U.S. race in which *any* entrants finish

The first four-wheeled Riker Electric is built, but no vehicles are sold until 1897

Hiram Percy Maxim opens a motor carriage department for Pope Mfg. Company, a Connecticut bicycle maker

Two automotive trade journals debut: *The Horseless Age* and *The Motocycle*

▶ Built by the Detroit Automobile Company in 1899, this delivery van was the first Ford-related truck intended for sale. Henry Ford had left his job at Edison and was named superintendent at Detroit Automobile, but serious production never happened. The company collapsed late in 1900.

▲ Cadwallader W. Kelsey had built a four-wheeled vehicle in 1897, at age 17, then teamed with college friend Sheldon Tilney on this three-wheeled, single-cylinder "Autotri."

▲ Alexander Winton turned from bicycle production to an experimental auto in 1896, then formed Winton Motor Carriage Company. A total of 22 were sold in 1898.

*The Horseless Age* claims more than 300 people or firms have built motorcars

Early inventors don't all concentrate on gasoline, steam, and electricity for propulsion: The Burdick Spring Motor, described in *The Horseless Age,* uses more springs to gain extra power

The American Motor League, the first U.S. automotive association, is formed in Chicago

Despite the fact that the first macadam-paved road in America had been laid in 1785, roads are notoriously primitive (where they exist at all)

**1896**

Charles B. King drives his water-cooled, four-cylinder, four-cycle vehicle in Detroit on March 6, 1896

Track races are held for the first time on September 7 at Narragansett Park, Rhode Island; a Riker Electric is the winner.

▲ An electric wagon leads the Detroit-built 1899 Olds Electric that carries Ransom Olds and his finely attired wife.

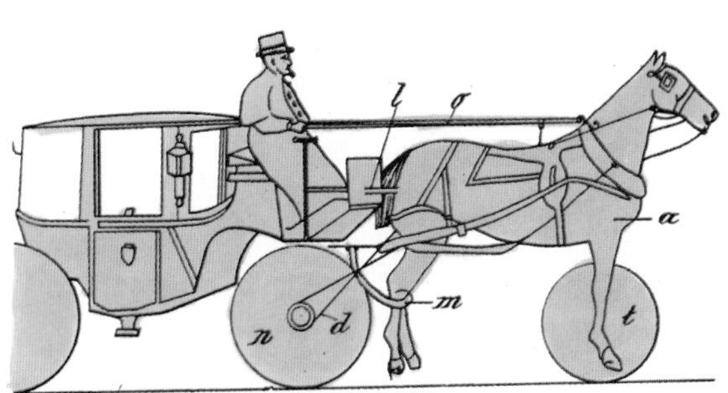

▲ Some inventors just couldn't get away from the horse. This patent for a mechanical "Automotor Horse" pulling an elegant carriage was granted on September 19, 1899.

▲ Francis E. and Freeland O. Stanley produced their first steam car in 1897. Stanley Steamers, including this 1899 runabout, scored well in racing and endurance events.

◀ Kelsey & Tilney's 1899 experimental three-wheeler ultimately went to the U.S. National Museum. Kelsey's father forbade him to put it into production, but a decade later he developed a Motorette, aimed to rival Ford's new Model T.

---

Alexander Winton builds an experimental two-seat, single-cylinder motor carriage

The American Electric Vehicle Company offers its first wares

Ransom E. Olds drives a one-cylinder, six-horsepower, gasoline-engined motorcar in Michigan

J. Frank Duryea produces his third car, followed by 13 more—the first time the same design is used for multiple cars

Nadig, contender for the title of "first" American car (in 1891), launches another, with a two-cylinder gasoline engine

Frank Stearns constructs his first auto, at age 17, in a home machine shop provided by his father

Henry Ford drives his two-cylinder "Quadricycle" in Detroit on June 4

▲ Noisy, smoky, gasoline-powered carriages tended to frighten live horses. But Uriah Smith had a calming solution in his 1899 patent for a "Vehicle Body," which included a life-size horse's head up front. Haynes-Apperson used it for their Horsey Horseless Carriage in 1900.

► In 1900, the first electric ambulance rolled through New York City to St. Vincent's Hospital. A year earlier, Akron, Ohio, police had acquired an electric patrol wagon.

"OLDSMOBILES"

ELECTRIC AND GASOLINE.



Can be Operated by the Inexperienced.

PRICE, $600.00 AND UPWARD.

Write for Catalogue.

OLDS MOTOR WORKS, 1299 Jefferson Ave., DETROIT, MICH.

▲ The first White Steamcar, a Stanhope model, appeared in 1900. Former sewing-machine maker Thomas White adopted the newly invented semi-flash boiler for his motorcars.

▲ Ransom Olds had planned both electric and gasoline vehicles for 1901, but when a fire gutted the Detroit plant in March, only a gasoline-engined runabout was saved.

---

Hiram Percy Maxim, of Pope Mfg. Company, builds an electric motor carriage

American publications start to use the word "automobile"—a French term—to describe the new horseless carriages

**1897**

The Olds Motor Vehicle Company is formed in Lansing on August 21 to begin motorcar production; it's Michigan's first auto company

The first Oldsmobile buggies have a one-cylinder engine, two-speed planetary transmission, and tiller steering—and will soon evolve into the famed "Curved Dash"

Studebaker Brothers, a carriage building firm since 1852, starts motor vehicle experiments

▲ Photographed in 1900 near his Kenosha, Wisconsin, shop, Thomas B. Jeffery's experimental vehicle—forerunner to the Rambler—had been completed three years earlier. The basic-looking runabout featured a one-cylinder engine.

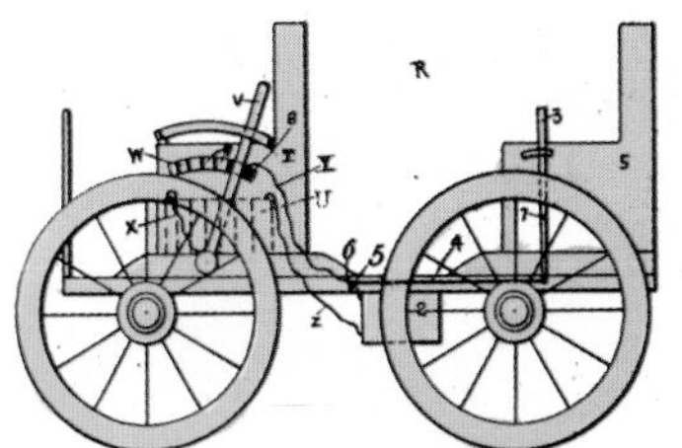

O. 659,121 PATENTED OCT. 2, 19(

▲ Nervous back-seat drivers would have adored this "safety device," patented in 1900 by E.W. Ayres. By simply pulling a lever, the passenger could cut the power to the vehicle at any moment.

The "Motor Age" of Chicago thus describes the Perfect Automobile:

"A handsome, stylish vehicle which can be started instantly and without previous laborious or lengthy preparation, can be stopped promptly, can be run at any speed up to twenty-five miles an hour, can be perfectly controlled by any person without special training, can travel over rough streets hnd roads, can climb stiff grades, can, in short, do anything and everything that a horse or span of horses attached to a vehicle can do, and do it more satisfactory, do it at a fraction of the expense and at the same time have none of the inherent faults of the horse, and no new ones of its own at the present time." There are vehicles that combine some of these advantages, but none that combine them all except

**THE PORTER STANHOPE, price $750.00.**

We make only one grade, and that the best, and the best only will be found satisfactory in the long run.

**THE PORTER STANHOPE is the Perfect Automobile.**

It is handsome and elegant in its lines and conforms in design to the modern horse carriages.

Safe, simple and durable.

Boiler is absolutely non-explosive and water-feed automatic.

It is free from all complications in its mechanism, so that an engineer is not necessary in its use.

Fuel is cheap and obtainable everywhere.

It is noiseless and free from all odor and vibration.

The Burner (or engine fire) is of low draft and so protected from the air as to be unquenchable in all weathers.

It is controlled by one lever only, as in times of danger several levers arè confusing. The methods of lighting the burner at first are so simple that anyone can do it quickly and in a manner that is not complicated.

Before you buy an Automobile mention this magazine and write to the } **Write Now!**

PORTER MOTOR CO.,

950 Tremont Building, . . . . . . . Boston, Mass.

▲ Modesty obviously wasn't a virtue at the Porter company, yet its steam-powered "perfect automobile" lasted only through 1900-01. The light runabout featured an aluminum body.

◀ In 1900, New York's Madison Square Garden hosted the first national American automobile show. Here, a family tests the maneuverability of one of the 300 cars exhibited by 40 makers.

---

Pope Mfg. markets Columbia Mark III Electric Phaetons, and on May 13 holds the first auto press preview in America

The first Stanley Steamer is completed by bearded identical twins Francis E. and Freelan O. Stanley—three are built by spring 1898

Bicycle manufacturer Thomas B. Jeffery builds his first auto; with a single-cylinder gasoline engine, it will evolve into the Rambler

Winton automobiles enter production, following formation of the Winton Motor Carriage Company

A Winton car travels a mile in one minute and 48 seconds—33.64 mph—on Memorial Day; that summer, it travels from Cleveland to New York in 10 days

Earle C. Anthony builds a crude electric runabout at age 17; later he'll open one of the world's first gasoline stations

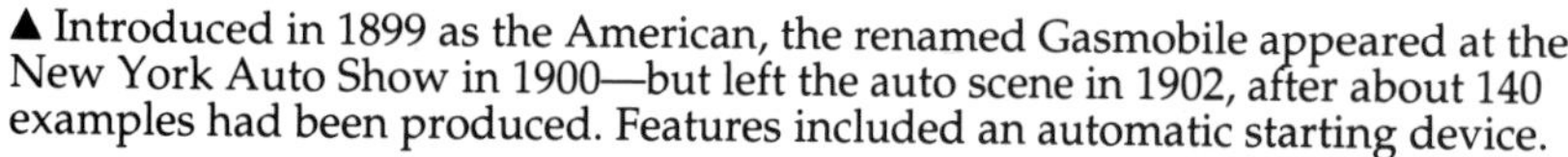

▲ Introduced in 1899 as the American, the renamed Gasmobile appeared at the New York Auto Show in 1900—but left the auto scene in 1902, after about 140 examples had been produced. Features included an automatic starting device.

▲ The Mobile Company of America acquired rights from the Stanley Brothers for the 1900 Mobile steamer.

▲ A.L. Moore, head of the Cleveland Machine Screw Company, had sold electric cars but preferred gasoline. Production began in 1902. Unlike many rivals, this firm built its own engines.

▶ Back in 1900, a filling station had to come to the motorist, carrying barrels of fuel. Not until 1901 was the first storage tank installed, in New York. Early that year, the "Spindletop" oil gusher came in, slashing prices to a mere nickel a barrel.

---

**1898**

New makes this year include General Electric and Waverley Electric

F.B. Stearns & Company is organized; several dozen motor buggies are built through 1901, when serious production commences

Alexander Winton sells his first car. Agent H.O. Keller, Reading, Pennsylvania, is believed to be the first franchised dealer for American automobiles

In Detroit, William E. Metzger establishes the first independent auto dealership in the U.S.

The Empire State Motor Wagon Company operates one of the first American used-car lots at Catskill, New York

John Wilkinson builds an air-cooled, four-cylinder engine with valve-in-head configuration, which leads to the motor used in Franklin motorcars

▲ After buying steam-car rights from the Stanley Brothers, John Brisben Walker and partner Amzi Barber split up. Walker offered the Mobile; Barber produced the Locomobile. By 1901, seven versions were built, including this Locosurrey. An 1899 ad had promised "no noise, jar, or odor;" by the end of 1903, 5000 Locomobiles had been built.

**New Makes: 1899**

Baker Electric, Baldwin Steam, Chicago Electric, Dyke (kit car or assembled), Grout, Gurley, Holyoke, Kensington, Kidder, Leach Steamer, Locomobile, Media, Oakman-Hertel, Orient, Packard, St. Louis, Strathmore (gas or steam), Victor Steam, Waltham Steam, and Woods Electric

▲ Favorable response to the exhibition of a $900 Runabout at auto shows in 1900 prompted Thomas Jeffery to sell his successful bicycle business and focus on Rambler motorcars.

► Production of Model A Rambler runabouts began in 1901. A steering wheel (left-hand drive) and front engine were planned, but cars introduced for 1902 had a right-hand tiller and one-cylinder engine located under the seat.

▲ The Waverley Electric was a product of the American Bicycle Company, of Indianapolis, Indiana. In 1900, this 1050-pound Model 22 Road Wagon carried a $925 price tag, including top.

---

Electric taxis take to the streets of New York City

Genevra Delphine Mudge—one of the first woman drivers—pilots a Waverly Electric around New York City, later races a Locomobile

**1899**

Olds Motor Works, Ransom's second company, is established and moves from Lansing to Detroit

James Ward Packard constructs his first automobile and runs it on November 6 in Warren, Ohio

Until 1903, all Packards are single-cylinder machines

Henry Ford finishes his second Quadricycle; the Detroit Automobile Company is formed

Pittsburgh Motor Vehicle Company becomes the Autocar Company

▲ Henry Ford's third car, sporting fancy fenders and a steering wheel (no tiller), was built by the Detroit Automobile Company while he was superintendent there in 1901.

▲ Soon after Ford's third car emerged, the Detroit Automobile Company folded. The Henry Ford Company was organized in November, but Ford himself soon departed.

▲ A modest crowd watches a 1901 Oldsmobile climb the State Capitol steps in Lansing, Michigan. Many such stunts took place to demonstrate the prowess of early motorcars. Note the big blocks on the rear wheels for traction.

◀ John Maxwell pilots a 1901 Oldsmobile up a harsh hill. Rough roads served as "proving grounds" in the early years. Mass production of gasoline-engined cars began in 1901—425 "Curved-Dash" Model R runabouts were built.

---

The first Locomobile, a steam runabout, is produced. This New England company will produce motorcars through the Twenties

Percy Owen opens the first automobile salesroom in New York City to sell Wintons

Mrs. John Howell Phillips, of Chicago, gets a driver's license—the first American woman known to obtain one

A.L. Dyke establishes the first American auto parts business, in St. Louis

Boston bans automobiles from its park from 10 a.m.–9 p.m. to avoid accidents with runaway horses

The U.S. Army buys its first electric vehicles

The U.S. Post Office experiments with motor vehicles for postal collections

▲ In this demonstration, three 1901 Oldsmobiles ride a see-saw-like contraption to prove their agility. The Curved-Dash Olds used a horizontal single-cylinder, 4.5-bhp engine.

◀ Drivers (and passengers) had to bundle up, but early automobiles could brave the toughest blizzards, as this circa-1901 Olds runabout demonstrates. Even so, flat tires and mechanical problems were inevitable on most trips.

▼ Not every car fared as well on snowy roads as did a 1901 Oldsmobile. Roy Chapin's daunting drive from Michigan to New York boosted interest in the $650 Curved-Dash model.

Electric vehicles are used for deliveries by stores in New York and Boston

The American Motor Company of New York claims that it offers "competent mechanics always on hand to make repairs when necessary"

Uriah Heep patents a motorcar body with a horse's head up front, to prevent scaring live horses; Haynes-Apperson's "Horsey" horseless carriage of 1900 will wear one

*Motor Age* magazine begins publication

The Automobile Club of America is formed

A Stanley Steamer driven by Freelan O. Stanley (built by him and twin brother Francis E.) climbs Mount Washington in New Hampshire

**New Makes: 1900**

Akron, American De Dion, Auburn, Automobile Fore-Carriage, Baker Electric, Bolte (prototype), Boston (steam), Buffalo, Canda, Clark Steam, Collins Electric, Crest, Crowdus Electric, Eclipse Steamer, Friedman, Gasmobile, Hasbrouck, Hewitt-Lindstrom, Holley, Imperial, International, Keene Steamobile, Keystone, Klock, Knox, Lane Steam, Marlboro (steam), Milwaukee (steam), Peerless, People's, Remington, Robinson, Searchmont, Skene Steam, Springfield Steam, Strong & Rogers Electric, Triumph (electric or steam), and White Steamer

▲ Ransom E. Olds (*left*) and friend John Maxwell (founder of Maxwell Motors) lean forward, as though riding horses, while testing the climbing ability of a 1901 Olds. It used a two-speed planetary gearbox and semi-floating rear axle.

◀ Henry Ford sits in his first racing car, powered by a 26-bhp, two-cylinder engine. On October 10, 1901, it averaged 43.5 mph over a 10-mile course at Grosse Pointe, Michigan, beating a Winton.

Alexander Winton drives his own automobile from Cleveland to New York City in 47 hours, 37 minutes (actual driving time)

Engine emissions gain attention by the turn of the century, including the concept of a catalytic converter

**1900**

A total of 4192 automobiles are produced in America this year

Some 48,000 fans attend the first National Automobile Show in November in New York; 40 auto companies exhibit products, as do 11 parts/accessory firms

Seven cars at the first auto show are steam-powered

Car prices at the show range from $280 to $4000 (about 300 types are on exhibit)

◀ Henry Ford experimented with this two-cylinder runabout in 1901-02. By early '02, his short stay with the Henry Ford Company was over. Barney Oldfield set an American speed record in the Ford "999" racer in October: 5 miles in 5 minutes, 28 seconds.

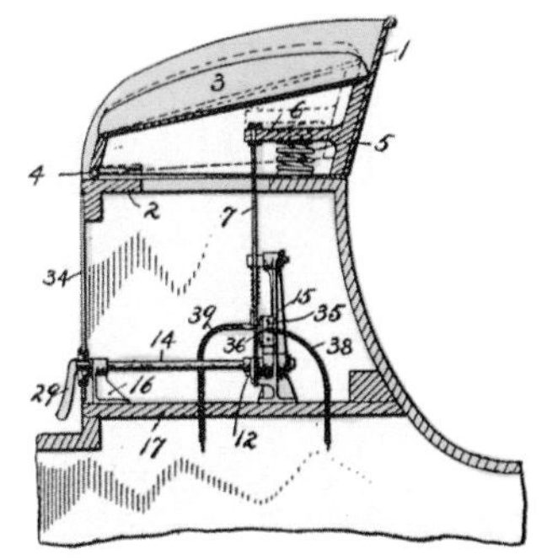

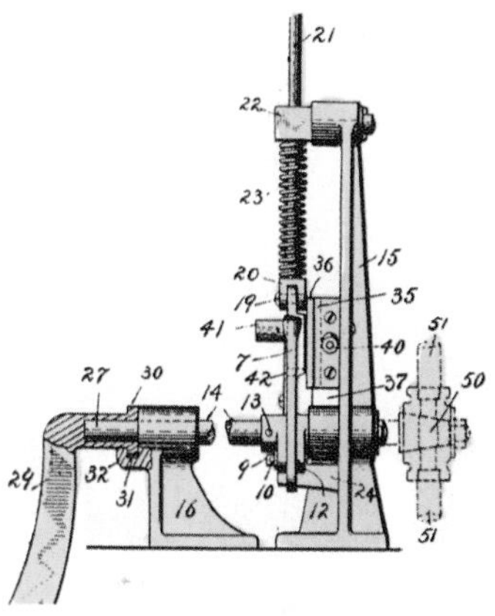

▲ Some auto patents were serious, others frivolous. This "Safety Stop," patented by Arthur Stevens in 1901, aimed to prevent runaway vehicles. A movable seat responded to the "motorman's" weight. If he fell out of the car, the engine would die, stopping the car.

◀ Racing dominated Henry Ford's mind at the time, but he nonetheless built a third Quadricycle in 1901. After Henry left the Detroit Automobile Company, this car would evolve into the Cadillac.

---

The Mobile Company of America builds a 200-foot ramp (53 feet high) at the show to demonstrate the hill-climbing and braking ability of steam vehicles

The Auburn and Peerless makes appear, along with the Knox three-wheel runabout and the first few White Steamers

The Baker Electric makes its formal debut early in the year

**Sample Production Figures: 1899-1900**

|  |  |
|---|---|
| 1. Columbia (1900) | 1,500 |
| 2. Locomobile (1900) | 750 |
| 3. Winton (1899) | 100 |
| 4. Packard (1900) | 49 |
| 5. Stanley (1899) | 30 |
| 6. Stearns (1899) | 20 |
| 7. Knox (1900) | 15 |
| 8. Oldsmobile (1899-1900) | 11 |

*Some figures are estimates*

▲ A "hedgehog" engine, nicknamed for the appearance of its air-cooled cylinder, powered this 1901 Knox, pictured at a 1934 parade. The initial three-wheeled Knoxmobiles soon were joined by four-wheeled runabouts. In this one, passengers sat up front.

▲ Production of the 1901 Locomobile Steamer was limited to four cars per day, implying that the car was built with precision. An early Locomobile might hit 40 mph, but couldn't travel far—usually about 20 miles—before it needed more water.

▲ In 1901, company president George N. Pierce posed in a Pierce Motorette, whose one-cylinder engine developed 2¾ horsepower. About 150 were built through 1902.

▲ Like many start-up ventures, the Niagara car, built at Niagara Falls, quickly failed: begun in 1901, gone a year later. The little runabouts used a four-bhp gasoline engine.

---

The newest Packard, introduced late in the year, features a steering wheel to replace the usual tiller

Several makes have gasoline engines under a hood—the first such installation on American vehicles

Automobile advertising appears in *The Saturday Evening Post* for the first time

The National Association of Automobile Manufacturers is formed

William McKinley is the first U.S. President to ride in an automobile—first a steamer, and then an electric

R.E. Dietz Company introduces special kerosene lamps with a clear white flame that cast a 200-foot beam and remain steady on rough roads

**New Makes: 1901**

Ajax Electric, Autocar, Automotor, Brecht, Buckeye, Buffalo Electric, Buffum, Century (electric and steam), Conrad (steam), Cotta Steam, Crestmobile, Darling, Desberon, Empire Steamer (some built in 1899-1900), Essex, Fanning, Foster, Geneva Steam, Halsey Steam, Hoffman (steam), Hudson Steamer, Lewis, Long Distance, Moncrief Steam, Murdaugh, National Electric, Norton, Pawtucket Steam, Prescott Steam, Reading Steamer, Rogers & Hanford, Steamobile, Stearns, Storck Steam, Taunton Steam, Thompson (steam), Thompson Electric, Toledo (steam), Wall, and Warwick

▲ Nattily dressed occupants of this "double-seated" 1901 Locomobile enjoyed the benefits—and failings—of steam power. Early Locomobiles used tiller steering and chain drive; frames were welded together.

◀ Ads for the 1901 Reading Steam Carriage optimistically promised that it "runs indefinitely without attention." This Model B sold for $750 with a four-cylinder engine—most steamers used only two.

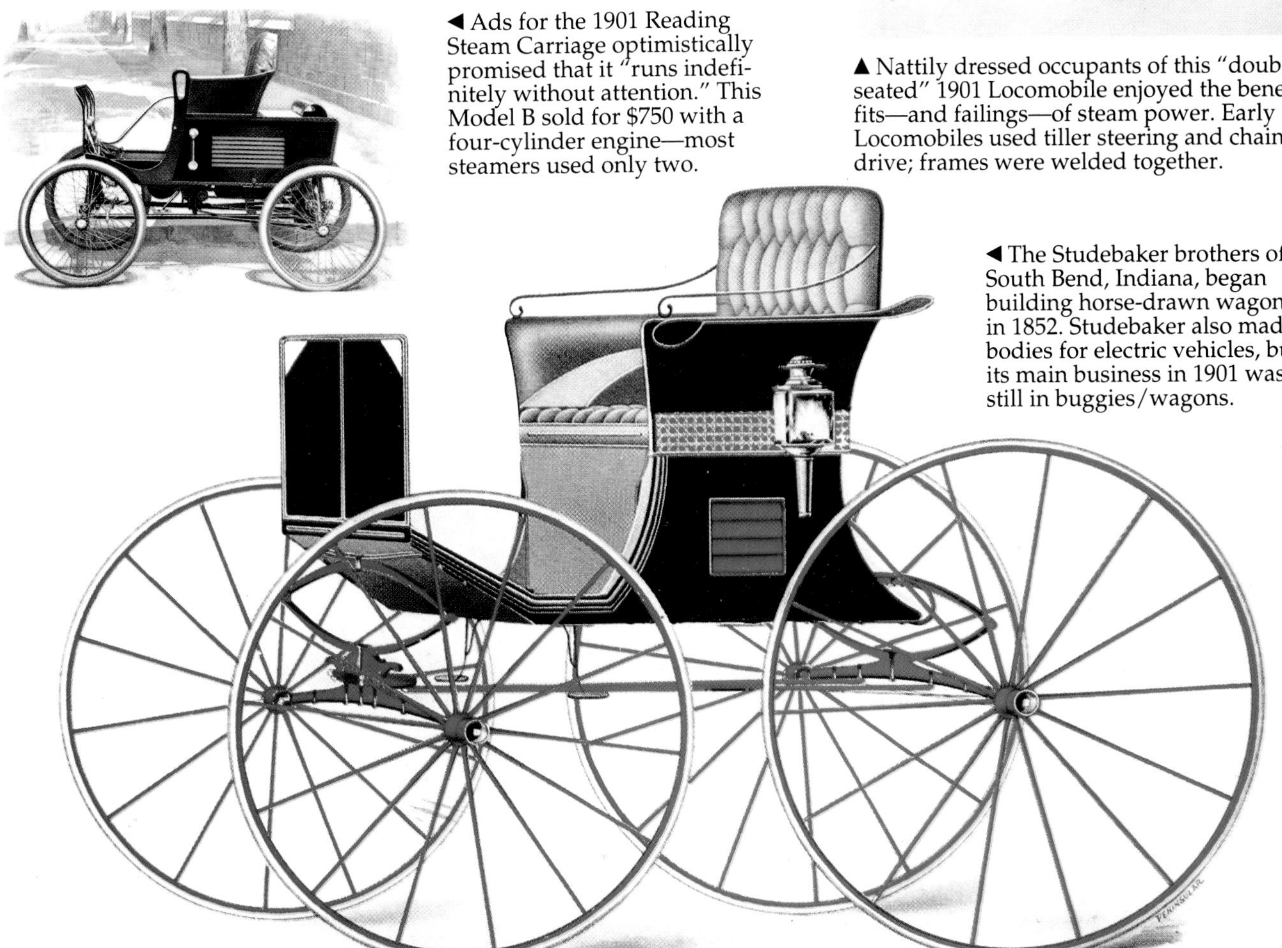

◀ The Studebaker brothers of South Bend, Indiana, began building horse-drawn wagons in 1852. Studebaker also made bodies for electric vehicles, but its main business in 1901 was still in buggies/wagons.

Theft is a problem, even in the early days, so the Leach Motor Carriage has a removable steering lever—an early anti-theft device

Alexander Winton is the first American to participate in foreign auto competition: The Gordon Bennett Race, in France

**1901**

Approximately 7000 automobiles are built in the U.S. this year

Some 88 exhibitors display products at the Second National Automobile Show in November, again at Madison Square Garden

Most engines in cars at the show are water-cooled, with multiple cylinders; many models have removable tires

In an October 31 *Motor Age* ad, Packard urges buyers to "Ask The Man Who Owns One"

▲ The 1901 Toledo Steam Carriage, whose engine used 3 x 4-inch piston valves, came from the American Bicycle Company. This $900 Módel A runabout was joined in 1902 by a gasoline-engined model.

▲ Thomas M. Galey luxuriates in a 1901 Winton Surrey. Single-cylinder Wintons started at $1200, and one was driven 810 miles to the New York show in 38 hours. Sales in 1901 reached 700 units.

▲ Displayed at the First National Automobile Show in New York, this 1901 Winton was driven there from Cleveland—the longest known drive at the time.

---

A steering wheel is now employed on most cars, instead of a tiller

The Electric Vehicle Company, holder of the Selden Patent, threatens legal action for infringement by unlicensed auto manufacturers

The short-lived Henry Ford Company is organized

Autocar develops a shaft-driven motor vehicle

R.E. Olds builds 425 Curved Dash models this year, making them the first "mass-produced" gasoline-engine autos in the world

Olds parts and subassemblies are supplied by other Detroit shops

The first White automobile is sold

Buffalo's George N. Pierce Company announces the Pierce Motorette

Stearns goes into full production with a single-cylinder car

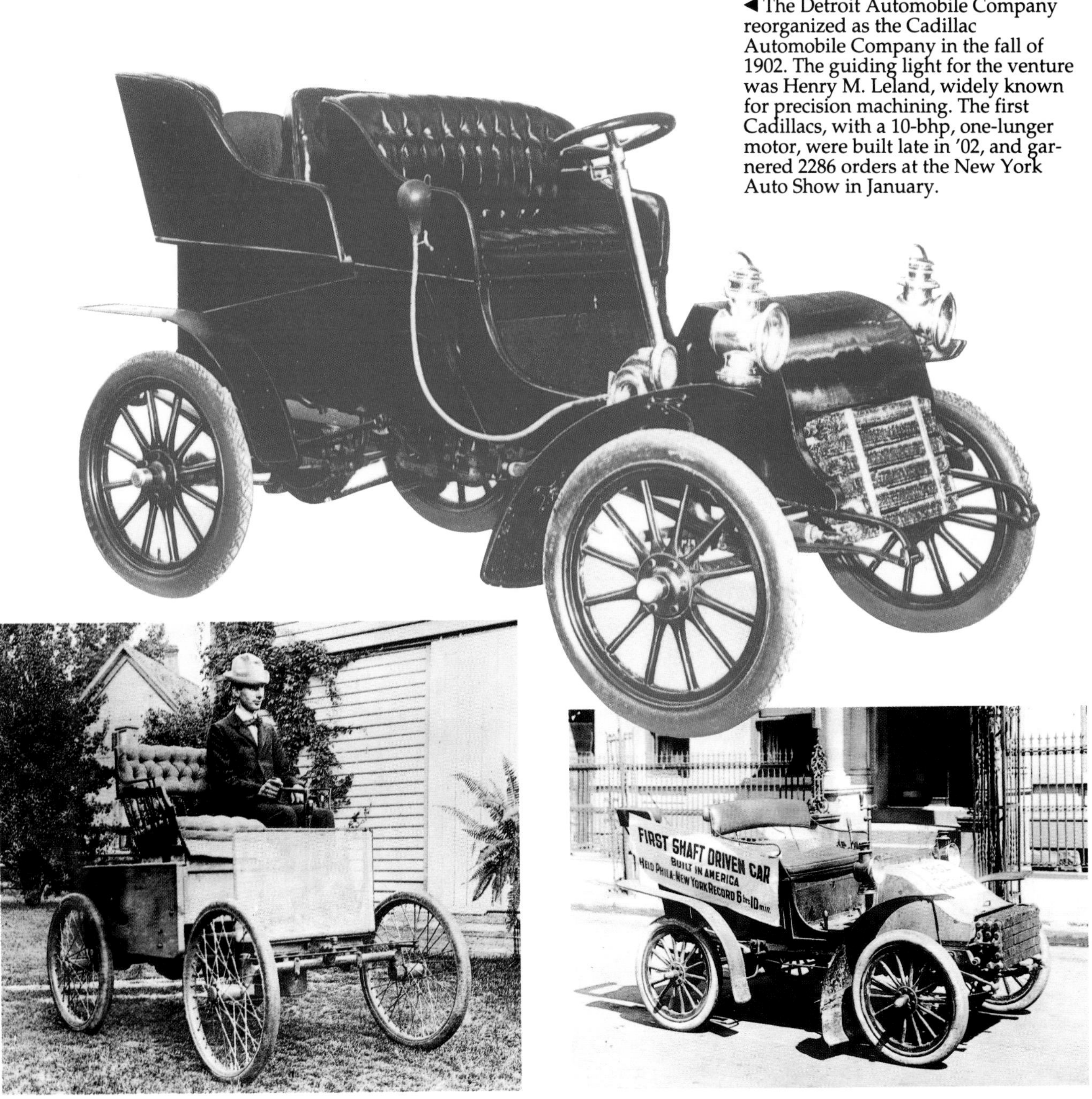


◀ The Detroit Automobile Company reorganized as the Cadillac Automobile Company in the fall of 1902. The guiding light for the venture was Henry M. Leland, widely known for precision machining. The first Cadillacs, with a 10-bhp, one-lunger motor, were built late in '02, and garnered 2286 orders at the New York Auto Show in January.

▲ W.K. Ackerman's car, an experimental model built before 1900, had window-screen cowling, but no springs to smooth the ride. Ackerman later joined Cadillac's engineering department.

▲ Proclaimed as the "first shaft driven car," a six-bhp, two-cylinder 1902 Autocar traveled from Philadelphia to New York City in a record 6 hours, 10 minutes. The runabout cost $800.

---

Roy Dikeman Chapin drives an Oldsmobile from Detroit to New York City in 7½ days, averaging 14 mph

"Spindletop" gusher comes in near Beaumont, Texas, sinking the price of crude oil below five cents per barrel

The Automobile Club of America starts a roadside touring sign program between New York and Boston

New York State begins to license motor vehicles, and earns nearly $1000 the first year

**Sample Production Figures: 1901**

|  |  |
|---|---|
| 1. Locomobile | 1,500 |
| 2. Winton | 700 |
| 3. Oldsmobile | 425 |
| 4. White | 193 |
| 5. Autocar | 140 |
| 6. Knox | 100 |
| 7. Packard | 81 |
| 8. Stanley | 80 |

*Some figures are estimates*

▲ Edgar and Elmer Apperson enjoy a spin in the first Apperson car, built in 1902. Their venture followed a split from Haynes in 1901. A Sintz two-cylinder, 16-bhp gas engine powered the Model A.

▲ Even after Edgar and Elmer Apperson departed for their own auto venture, the Haynes-Apperson name remained for a couple of years. Here, the brothers are pictured in a two-passenger 1902 Haynes-Apperson, whose engine was a horizontal twin.

▲ Locomobiles hailed from Bridgeport, Connecticut. The $1600 1902 Model A Touring held four people above a 73-inch wheelbase. Its steam engine had a 42-gallon water tank and a 16-inch boiler/burner.

**1902**

Some 9000 automobiles are built in America this year; output is rising steadily, if gradually

Studebaker is now in production with electric cars

The Detroit Automobile Company becomes Cadillac Automobile Company; the first car is completed in October

The Apperson brothers, formerly with Haynes, begin production of their own automobile, initially with two-cylinder engines

Rambler is launched by the Thomas B. Jeffery Company in Kenosha, Wisconsin; 1500 are built this year

Franklin and Holsman make their debut, the latter a highwheeler produced through 1910

**New Makes: 1902**

Apperson, Baldner, Binney & Burnham Steam, Blomstrom, Brazier, Bristol, Centaur, Cloughley, Covert, Davenport Steam, Decker, Flint Steam, Franklin, Fredonia, Gaethmobile, General, Graham Motorette, Holsman, Ideal, Kunz, Model, Murray, Northern, Pomeroy, Rambler, Reber, Rockaway, Sandusky, Santos-Dumont, Studebaker Electric, Toledo (gas), Tourist, Union, Upton, Walter (also known as American Chocolate), Wick (prototype only), Wildman, and Yale

▲ Begoggled and single-mindedly intent on victory, Dan Wurgis wields the tiller of the '02 racing Olds Pirate. Note how he leans over as he rounds the turn, as if driving a motorcycle. The one-cylinder Pirate, whose twin "rockets" are fuel tanks, ran in the first race at Daytona Beach, Florida, in April 1902 against Winton's four-cylinder Bullet 1. The Olds, renamed Flyer in 1903, set a light-weight one-mile record over the sand: 54 mph.

◀ With the exception of Henry Ford's Model T later in the decade, few automobiles earned the popularity of the Curved-Dash Oldsmobile. In fact, the 1901 fire at the factory proved providential, letting Olds focus on a single model. This 1902 Runabout carried a single-cylinder, 95.4-cubic-inch engine with a 4½ x 6-inch bore and stroke. The motor, turning at a leisurely 500 rpm, was said to emit "one chug per telegraph pole."

---

Franklin will become the best-known manufacturer of cars with air-cooled engines

The Packard firm changes its name from Ohio Automobile Company to Packard Motor Car Company

Locomobile is the first U.S. gasoline automobile with a four-cylinder, front-mounted, water-cooled engine

Henry Ford and Alexander Y. Malcomson agree to develop a car

Jonathan Dixon Maxwell joins Charles Brady King to build the Northern (sometimes called Silent Northern); it introduces an integral engine/transmission, three-point suspension of power unit, and running boards

▲ Dos-a-Dos (2+2) seating was a $25 option on the 1902 Rambler Model C Runabout, which sold for a modest $750.

▲ Everyone on this family outing looks grim, despite the virtues of their 1902 Rambler Dos-a-Dos. Wheelbase measured a compact 72 inches; wheel size 28 x 2½ inches.

▲ The 1902 Ramblers steered with a tiller—a steering wheel became standard in 1904—and had chain drive. Production came in third, with 1500 built for 1902.

---

Packard patents the "H" gearshift slot pattern, which will soon become commonplace

Louis S. Clarke, of Autocar, designs the porcelain spark plug insulator and patents double-reduction gearing for rear axles

While attending Cornell University, Clarence W. Spicer builds a car to test U-joints and shaft drive, leading to the formation of the Spicer Manufacturing Company

The 112-member National Association of Automobile Manufacturers adopts a 60-day guarantee for new automobiles

T.H. Shevlin is fined $10 in Minneapolis for traveling more than 10 mph faster than the speed limit

▲ Long after it was built, top executives of the successor company enjoyed an occasional outing in a 1902 Rambler. George W. Mason, president of Nash-Kelvinator by 1937, holds the tiller, joined by sales manager H.C. Doss.

▲ Dr. George B. Crissman and his bride-to-be guide their 1902 Rambler Model C Runabout through a public park in Fort Collins, Colorado. The 1902 model was the first production Rambler; its one-lung engine developed four bhp.

▲ "It starts from the seat," boasted the catalog for the 1902 Stevens-Duryea. J. Frank Duryea joined with the J. Stevens Arms & Tool Company to produce this five-bhp flat-twin runabout for $1200.

▲ By 1902, Studebaker was producing a wagon-like Electric Runabout with a "stick seat" and tubular frame. Ads promised it "can be run any day in the year by any member of the family."

Motor Mart is established in New York City to buy and sell used cars

A Chicago ordinance allows drivers to wear spectacles (but not eyeglasses)

The American Automobile Association is formed in Chicago to oversee racing

A Pierce Motorette is victorious at the Automobile Club of America's endurance run

Ford's "999" racing car sets a speed record: five miles in five minutes, 28 seconds

**Sample Production Figures: 1902**

| | |
|---|---|
| 1. Locomobile | 2,750 |
| 2. Oldsmobile | 2,500 |
| 3. Rambler | 1,500 |
| 4. White | 385 |
| 5. Knox | 250 |
| 6. Packard | 179 |
| 7. Stanley | 170 |
| 8. Union | 60 |

*Some figures are estimates*

CHAPTER TWO
1903-1919

# UP AND RUNNING

Not much time passed before the trickle of pioneering automobiles turned into a steady flow. Buyers had countless cars to choose from—though most were too costly for the middle class. In addition to the companies that prospered and grew into giants, hundreds more turned out a handful of vehicles, then disappeared.

Because most early cars were assembled, not built from scratch, entry into manufacturing wasn't terribly difficult. Automakers typically bought components on credit, and then sold finished automobiles for cash.

In 1903, seven years after driving his first Quadricycle, Henry Ford founded the Ford Motor Company. By 1906, Ford ranked first in sales. Henry Leland focused on precision craftsmanship with the first Cadillac, also in 1903. The adoption of interchangeable parts was a giant leap forward from the practice of hand-fitting every piece.

The Electric Vehicle Company, having acquired George Selden's "road engine" patent, claimed that it covered nearly all motorcars. Most manufacturers fell in line, paying royalties to the Association of Licensed Automobile Manufacturers. Henry Ford was one of the few who resisted.

Detroit quickly grew into an automotive power, but cars were built all over the nation. Studebaker turned to gasoline cars in 1904, when Ransom E. Olds launched Reo (or REO). William C. Durant gained control of Buick, then founded General Motors. In 1908 came Hupmobile; then Hudson, Chevrolet, and the Dodge Brothers. Higher up the scale, sportsmen might have preferred a Stutz Bearcat or Mercer Raceabout.

Taking an early day spin wasn't exactly a picnic. Gearboxes were balky; steering required muscle. Drivers faced hand throttles, spark levers, drip oilers—each unit demanding attention. Carbide and kerosene lamps gave little illumination.

Farmers might threaten—or even aim a gun at fast-moving machines. Motorists needed special apparel, and one had to expect a succession of flat tires, if not more serious troubles. Owners (or their chauffeurs) were expected to do their own repairs.

By 1908, nearly 400,000 vehicles were registered. Charles Duryea (no longer an industry force) estimated that 515 companies had entered production—but more than half had failed. Then, Ford announced the car that would alter America: the Model T, destined to live for two decades and sell more than 15 million copies. Adoption of the moving assembly line in 1913 helped make Ford's "flivver" easily affordable, the first "car for the masses."

Innovations were many, but the gasoline engine had elbowed aside electrics and steamers, and cars took a standardized form. Still, plenty of inventors thought they had a better idea, such as the Charter Water-Gasoline car of 1903. A decade later came a short-lived fad of fragile "cyclecars." Air-cooled engines had their proponents. Highwheelers came and went. Friction drive and electric transmissions were tried. Among the strangest: the eight-wheeled Octoauto.

Few technological advances would change the automobile's future as much as the electric self-starter, installed in 1912 Cadillacs. Elimination of the dangerous hand crank meant more Americans, particularly women, could drive.

In the Teens, the "Sunday drive" took hold. Vacationers were turning to autocamping. Automobiles carried comedians to their destinies in silent films, and played a major role as America finally entered the Great War. After the Armistice, American women won the right to vote, and were ready for their own flirtation with the automobile.

---

**1903**

A total of 11,235 automobiles are built in America this year

New features include mechanical valves (Olds and Rambler), compensating carburetors, square "bonnets," honeycomb radiators

Tonneau bodies (with rear seats) are evident at the show; some closed cars display "glass front" design

T-head engines appear in various cars; so do mechanically actuated intake valves, sliding-gear transmissions, and shock absorbers

Ford Motor Company is incorporated on June 16, 1903, with $28,000 capital. The company earns money immediately, pays a 10-percent dividend in November

Henry Ford is the company's vice president and chief engineer, with 25.5-percent interest; John S. Gray is president

▲ Chief engineer Walter Marr (*at wheel*) and Thomas Buick—son of David Dunbar Buick, the company's founder—drive the first Buick built in Flint, Michigan. The Model B Runabout had a two-cylinder, 21-bhp valve-in-head engine.

▲ William Crapo Durant, co-owner of the Durant-Dort Carriage Company, took over Buick on November 1, 1904.

▲ Production of the Buick Model B began in the summer of 1904, after the company passed from David Buick and Benjamin Briscoe to James Whiting, of the Flint Wagon Works. The Flint plant had been known as a maker of carriages and farm wagons before the arrival of motorcars.

▲ Ford Motor Company began life in 1903 in this modest factory on Mack Avenue in Detroit, with John Gray serving as president. Ford paid $75 a month rent for the building, which initially had a single floor. A second story soon was added. Note the sign identifying a former resident.

---

Initial Ford stockholders include John and Horace Dodge, Albert Strelow, Alex Y. Malcomson, and James Couzens

The first Ford Model A runabout is sold in July; its L-head engine has twin opposed cylinders displacing 100.5 cubic inches

The Association of Licensed Automobile Manufacturers (ALAM) is formed, including the Electric Vehicle Company and eight other automakers

Until 1911, nearly all manufacturers of gasoline automobiles pay royalties through ALAM

Rejected as an ALAM licensee, Ford is sued by George Selden for patent infringement. Selden claims to have invented the automobile, as currently produced, back in 1877

▲ Ford's first production auto, the $850 1903 Model A, had a two-cylinder, 100.5-cid engine under the seat, yielding eight horsepower. A removable tonneau was a $100 option.

▲ Three daring travelers had to squeeze to fit into a 1903 Ford Model A "turtleback" runabout. One ad promised that a Ford was "so simple that a boy of 15 can run it."

▲ Light and efficient, Ford's 1250-pound Model A rode a 72-inch wheelbase and could do 30 mph, via a two-speed planetary gearbox. Right-hand steering was typical of the day.

▲ Oldsmobile production rose to 4000 units in calendar-year 1903. The popular Curved-Dash runabout continued with a tiller and a seatside crank for the 4¼-horse engine.

◀ Two Oldsmobile runabouts, "Old Scout" (*left*) and "Old Steady," line up in New York City for the start of the first transcontinental auto race in the spring of 1905. Destination: Portland, Oregon, traversing 4000 miles of crude roads. Old Scout won, arriving after 44 days, to help open the Lewis & Clark Centennial Exposition.

---

A single-cylinder, 7.3-horsepower Cadillac appears at the National Automobile Show; the first Cadillac automobile goes to a customer

The Overland automobile goes into production

Some 88 new auto companies begin in 1903, 15 of them in Michigan

The Buick Company is formed, with funds advanced by Benjamin Briscoe, Jr., and Frank Briscoe, to build cars with a valve-in-head engine. The first Buick is tested

The Jackson Automobile Company issues both a gasoline runabout and the Jaxon steamer

A four-cylinder Packard Model K debuts, joining the single-cylinder model

◀ The first car to travel a mile in less than a minute (42 seconds) was the 1903 Oldsmobile "Pirate," at Daytona Beach. Torpedo-like tanks suggest the Olds "Rocket" of the Fifties. Early race drivers were dangerously exposed—note his shoe at the axle.

▼ Detail refinements for the 1903 Packard Model F runabout included a sloped hood, longer 88-inch wheelbase, and lower $2000 price tag. Note the white tires and right-hand steering wheel. Packard also offered a costly, $7300 four-cylinder Model K.

**New Makes: 1903**

Austin, Bates (late 1903), Berg, Blackhawk, Buckmobile, Cadillac, Cameron, Cincinnati Steam, Clarkmobile, Columbus Electric, Commercial Electric, Country Club, Eldredge, Ford, Glide, Graham Electric, Greeley, Hall, Hammer-Sommer, Howard (some made in 1901-02), Iroquois, Jackson, Jaxon Steam, Jones-Corbin, Lyman & Burnham, Mackle-Thompson, Marble-Swift, Marr, Matheson, Mercury, Mitchell, Mohawk, Monarch, Moyea, Niagara, Overland, Parkin, Phelps, Pope-Robinson, Pope-Toledo (late 1903, as '04 model), Premier, Randall Three-Wheeler, Rapid, Regas, Rotary, Russell, Shelby, Smith, Springer, Star, Thomas, Tincher, Warner (Muncie), Waterloo, Welch Tourist, and Zentmobile

▲ Mom and Pop occupy the center seat of a one-cylinder 1903 Rambler; kids go up front. Wheelbase: 78 inches.

▲ Barely a dozen single-cylinder, tiller-steered Overland runabouts were built in 1903. They cost just $595.

Peerless adopts a pressed-steel frame; three others follow shortly

Power steering, operated by a separate electric motor, is installed in a Columbia Electric Motor Truck

Bicycle racer Berner Eli "Barney" Oldfield races the Ford "999"

White Steamers attain perfect scores during 650-mile reliability trials in Great Britain and Ireland

C. Harold Wills joins Ford as chief engineer and factory manager

Packard moves to Detroit, occupying the world's first factory made of reinforced concrete

**1903 Model Year Production**

|  |  |
|---|---|
| 1. Oldsmobile | 4,000 |
| 2. Cadillac | 2,497 |
| 3. Ford | 1,708 |
| 4. Pope-Hartford | 1,500 |
| 5. Rambler | 1,350 |
| 6. Winton | 850 |
| 7. White | 502 |
| 8. Knox | 500 |

*Some figures are estimated or calender-year*

▲ Riding an 87-inch wheelbase, and sporting curved fenders, the 1904 Buick Model B touring car used a right-hand steering wheel. A 159-cid, two-cylinder engine gave 22 bhp. Price was $950, but only 37 were built.

▲ In Ford's second year, a Model C replaced the A. Its two-banger had 10 horses. Price was $950 with tonneau.

▲ Henry Ford dreamed of a cheap car, but this 1904 four-cylinder Model B touring went for a hefty $2000.

◀ Cadillac's Model B succeeded the Model A in 1904, with a one-cylinder "Little Hercules" Leland & Faulconer engine and two-speed planetary transmission. Advertised at 8¼ horsepower, the motor displaced 98 cubic inches and used a new pressure-fed oiler.

▼ The roots of the Orient make can be traced to 1893, and Orient bicycles. Car production began in 1902. The 1904 Orient Buckboard rode on a wooden platform without springs, and could reach 30 mph with its one-cylinder, four-horsepower engine. Note the steering tiller.

▲ Henry Ford topped 91 mph when he piloted the 1904 Arrow "999" racer (left) on icy Lake St. Clair in January of that year.

**1904**

Industry output totals 22,130 cars and 700 trucks

The Fourth National Automobile Show is the largest yet, with 87 of the 185 exhibitors showing automobiles

The all-weather touring car with a glass-sided "California top" is considered the first "convertible"

Autocar and other makes feature automatic lubrication

Various cars utilize a fan to cool water pipes

Many new models feature quick-demountable wheel rims as standard equipment

The first Buicks go on sale, with a two-cylinder valve-in-head engine under the floor, plus planetary transmission

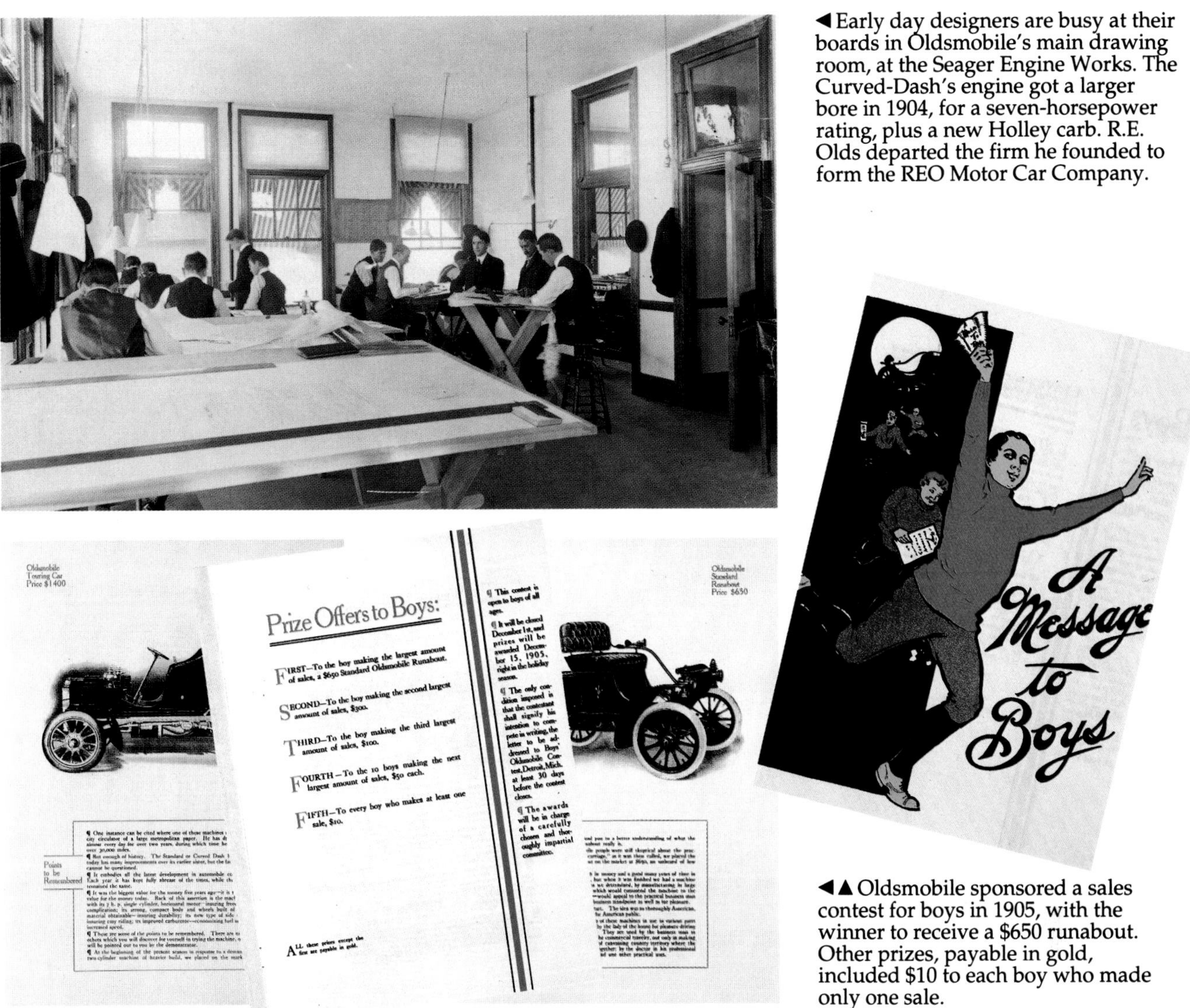



Prize Offers to Boys:

FIRST—To the boy making the largest amount of sales, a $650 Standard Oldsmobile Runabout.

SECOND—To the boy making the second largest amount of sales, $300.

THIRD—To the boy making the third largest amount of sales, $100.

FOURTH—To the 10 boys making the next largest amount of sales, $50 each.

FIFTH—To every boy who makes at least one sale, $10.

ALL these prizes except the first are payable in gold.

¶ This contest is open to boys of all ages.

¶ It will be closed December 1st, and prizes will be awarded December 15, 1905, right in the holiday season.

¶ The only condition imposed is that the contestant shall signify his intention to compete in writing, the letter to be addressed to Boys' Oldsmobile Contest, Detroit, Mich. at least 30 days before the contest closes.

¶ The awards will be in charge of a carefully chosen and thoroughly impartial committee.

◀ Early day designers are busy at their boards in Oldsmobile's main drawing room, at the Seager Engine Works. The Curved-Dash's engine got a larger bore in 1904, for a seven-horsepower rating, plus a new Holley carb. R.E. Olds departed the firm he founded to form the REO Motor Car Company.

◀▲ Oldsmobile sponsored a sales contest for boys in 1905, with the winner to receive a $650 runabout. Other prizes, payable in gold, included $10 to each boy who made only one sale.

**New Makes: 1904**

Acme, American Napier, Beverly, Black Diamond, Brew-Hatcher, Buick, Cantono Electric, Chadwick, Christie, Compound (E.H.V.), Courier, Dawson, De Motte, Detroit, Dolson, Duquesne, Four Wheel Drive, Frayer-Miller, Gibbs Electric, Hill, Logan, Luverne, Mahoning, Marion, Marmon, Michigan, Moline, Ormond Steam, Pierce-Racine, Pope-Hartford (tested in 1903), Pope-Tribune, Pope-Waverley Electric, Pungs-Finch, Reliance, Queen, Quinlan, Richmond, Roberts, Royal Electric, Royal Princess, Royal Tourist, Schacht, Smith, S&M Simplex, Standard (New Jersey), Stoddard-Dayton, Studebaker (gas-engine), Sturtevant, Synnestvedt Electric, Walworth, Wayne, and Wolverine

Sturtevant is one of the first American cars with an automatic transmission, using a centrifugal clutch with high and low ranges; it also has an airbrake

Studebaker sells its first gasoline vehicle, a two-cylinder; the cars are called Studebaker-Garford at first

Leland & Faulconer Manufacturing Company merges with Cadillac Automobile Company to become Cadillac Motor Car Company

A huge factory fire delays Cadillac production, forcing the company to return dealer deposits on 1500 autos

Ransom E. Olds sells his interest in Olds Motor Works, then organizes Reo Motor Car Company; production begins for 1905

▲ On January 3, 1904, Charles Schmidt drove a Packard Gray Wolf racer to new one- and five-mile records at Daytona Beach, Florida.

▲ The smallest of Colonel Albert Pope's four makes was this Pope-Tribune runabout, launched in 1904 on a 65-inch wheelbase. It carried a six-bhp, one-cylinder engine.

▲ A total of 2342 Rambler motorcars left the T.B. Jeffery plant in 1904, all with steering wheels. Three models had a single-cylinder engine; others boasted a 235.6-cid, front-mounted two-cylinder motor.

► A rural family prepares for an outing in a 1904 Rambler Model L canopy touring car. The two-cylinder motor developed 16 bhp. Lamps, horn, and baskets were included. Note the square grille.

---

Moline and Stoddard-Dayton automobiles enter production

The first few Maxwells are built

Marmon is in minimal production with a V-4 model, after experimental cars in 1902-03; output truly begins in 1905

An air-cooled Ford engine is announced, but a water-cooled four debuts as the Model B

Single-cylinder Packards fade away, leaving only fours through 1911

The National Association of Retail Automobile Dealers is established

Rivals criticize the Pope-Hartford firm for including lamps as standard equipment

The Prest-O-Lite Company is formed, with the goal of perfecting a safe method of using acetylene gas for headlights

▲ Buick output rose to 750 cars in 1905. Billed as "The Car of Quality," the $1200 Model C touring car differed little from the Model B, but wore a new Royal Blue body and used a foot brake. Wheelbase was again 87 inches.

◀ Engine and wheelbase of Ford's Model C grew in 1905, to 113.4 cid and 78 inches. In addition to the tonneau (*shown*) and runabout, a Model E panel-delivery debuted. Windshield, headlights, and top cost extra.

---

The Hartford Shock Absorber is announced

On January 12, Henry Ford drives his "Arrow" racer to a world-record 91.37 mph; the feat is topped a week later by William K. Vanderbilt doing 92.307 mph in a Mercedes

**1904 Model Year Production**

|  |  |  |
|---|---|---|
| 1. | Oldsmobile | 5,508 |
| 2. | Cadillac | 2,457 |
| 3. | Rambler | 2,342 |
| 4. | Ford | 1,695 |
| 5. | White | 710 |
| 6. | Stanley | 550 |
| 7. | Franklin | 400 |
| 8. | Packard | 250 |

*Some figures are estimated or calender-year*

**1905**

Industry output totals 24,250 cars and 750 trucks

Rear-entry tonneaus are giving way to longer bodies with side doors

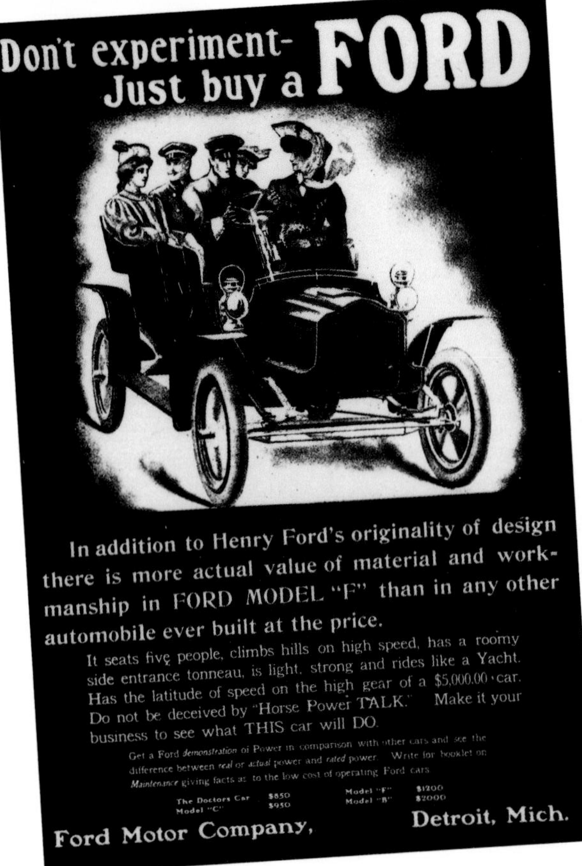


▲ Ford's *Field and Stream* ad pushed the new $1200 Model F touring car, with its 127.2-cid, 16-bhp two-cylinder engine. Ford boasted that the five-seater "rides like a yacht."

▲ Elegant it was, but the 1905 Ford Model B touring car, carrying a 283.6-cid, 24-bhp four-cylinder engine, was heavy—and at $2000 cost too much to attract many buyers.

▲ A 77-cid, two-cylinder engine went into the curious-looking 1905 Overland Model 17 runabout ($750). Also available: a $1500 four-cylinder Model 18 with side-entrance tonneau.

◀ Sporting gents in 1905 could have quite a time tooling around the countryside in a $750 one-cylinder Oldsmobile Touring Runabout. This one is driven by Howard Coffin, who later co-founded Hudson. Gus Edwards and Vincent Bryan wrote the famous tune, "In My Merry Oldsmobile," but R.E. Olds himself had turned to the REO automobile.

---

Big gasoline-engined cars are the trend at the Fifth National Automobile Show. Exhibits include 177 gasoline-powered cars, 31 electrics, four steamers

Innovations this year include Goodyear universal rims, an ignition lock, power tire pump, Gabriel exhaust horn, Weed tire chains

Emphasis this year is on comfort, more than strictly speed

Several makes feature cape or folding tops

Maxwell is in full production with two-cylinder models

First-year production begins for the friction-drive Cartercar, Lozier, Moon, and Reo

**New Makes: 1905**

A.B.C. High-Wheeler, Adams-Farwell, American Mercedes, Ardsley, Ariel, Aurora, Banker, Berkshire (debut in late 1904), Boss, Breese & Lawrence, Cartercar, Corbin, Crawford, Culver, Eagle Air Cooled, Forest City (prototype), Fritchle Electric, Gale, Gas-Au-Lec, Halladay, Hammer, Johnson, La Petite, Leader, Lozier, Maxwell, Monarch, Moon, Morse Steam, Oxford, Parsons Electric, Pullman, Rauch & Lang, Rainier, Reeves, Reo, Speedway, Victor, Walker, and Watrous

▲ Road signs were still rare when the occupants of this 1905 Rambler Type One Surrey, with two-cylinder, 18-bhp engine, needed directions on a rural byway. This was the final year for one-cylinder Ramblers, as total output hit 3807 units.

▼ The first automobile with an automatic transmission was the $5000, six-cylinder 1905 Sturtevant. High- and low-speed clutches worked by centrifugal force, based on engine rpm.

The engine in the new Ariel car is air-cooled in winter, water-cooled in summer

Adams-Farwell boasts a rotary three-cylinder engine

American Mercedes issues an exact copy of its German-built motorcar

The Crawford Automobile Company is organized by Robert S. Crawford, known for bicycles

A four-cylinder Cadillac debuts, with three-speed planetary transmission

Oldsmobile adds a side-entrance, two-cylinder touring model

Overland produces two- and four-cylinder cars, abandoning the one-lunger powertrain

Packard adopts a larger 265.7-cid, 28-bhp four-cylinder engine

▲ A modest revision of Buick's Model C, including a recirculating radiator, yielded the $1250 Model F touring, again a two-cylinder. The 1906 F weighed 1850 pounds; 1207 were sold.

▲ Shoppers took kindly to Ford's dashing $500 "boattail" Model N runabout, introduced in 1906—predecessor of the legendary Model T. A front-mounted, 134.2-cid four-cylinder engine developed 15 bhp, good enough for 45 mph.

**New Makes: 1906**

Aerocar, American (Underslung), American Mors, American Simplex, Autocycle (Vandegriff), Babcock Electric, Bliss, B.L.M., Brunn, Chalfant, Colburn, Deere-Clark, DeLuxe, Dorris, Dragon, Essex Steam, Fostoria, Frontenac, Harrison, Hawley, Heine-Velox, Hewitt, Jewell, Kansas City, Kissel Kar, Kobusch, Lambert, MacNaughton (electric), Mason, Maumee, Moore, Mora, Nielson, Page, Palmer (highwheeler), Paragon, Pontiac, Postal (highwheeler), Reliable Dayton, Shawmut, Shoemaker, Single Center, Steel Swallow, Success Auto Buggy, and Thomas-Detroit

▲ Henry Ford sits at the wheel of a Model K, powered by a 405-cid, 40-bhp six-cylinder engine. Priced at $2500 (soon $2800), the big roadster with "mother-in-law" seat was guaranteed to hit 60 mph—for anyone foolhardy enough to try.

The final single-cylinder Ramblers are built; two-cylinder models will be continued through 1909

A 20-bhp, four-cylinder Studebaker debuts

The Society of Automobile Engineers is formed

The first cars are sold on an installment plan

The American Motor Car Manufacturers Association is launched

A White Steamer leads President Theodore Roosevelt's inaugural parade

**1905 Model Year Production**

| | |
|---|---|
| 1. Oldsmobile | 6,500 |
| 2. Cadillac | 3,942 |
| 3. Rambler | 3,807 |
| 4. Ford | 1,599 |
| 5. Franklin | 1,098 |
| 6. White | 1,015 |
| 7. Reo | 864 |
| 8. Maxwell | 823 |

*Some figures are estimated or calender-year*

◄ Henry Ford loved racing, but his company soon left that domain. This racing version of the massive Model K set a 24-hour speed record, traveling 1135 miles at an average of 47.2 mph at Ormond Beach. Henry never liked the K—he thought it was too expensive.

▼ Ford's Model K touring car looked taller—and plainer—than the roadster. Luxury-league rivals ranged from Marmon to Thomas Flyer.

**1906**

Vehicle production this year consists of approximately 33,200 passenger cars and 800 trucks

By this time, an estimated 41,696 cars have been built in accordance with the Selden patent

Vehicles at the Sixth National Automobile Show feature stronger materials, such as chrome-nickel and high-carbon steel

Lighter-weight autos gain popularity, including Marmon with its cast aluminum body

Six-cylinder engines gain favor, with models from Ford, Franklin, Pierce-Arrow, National, and Stevens-Duryea

Ford introduces the low-priced ($500-$600), 45-mph Model N, forerunner of the Model T

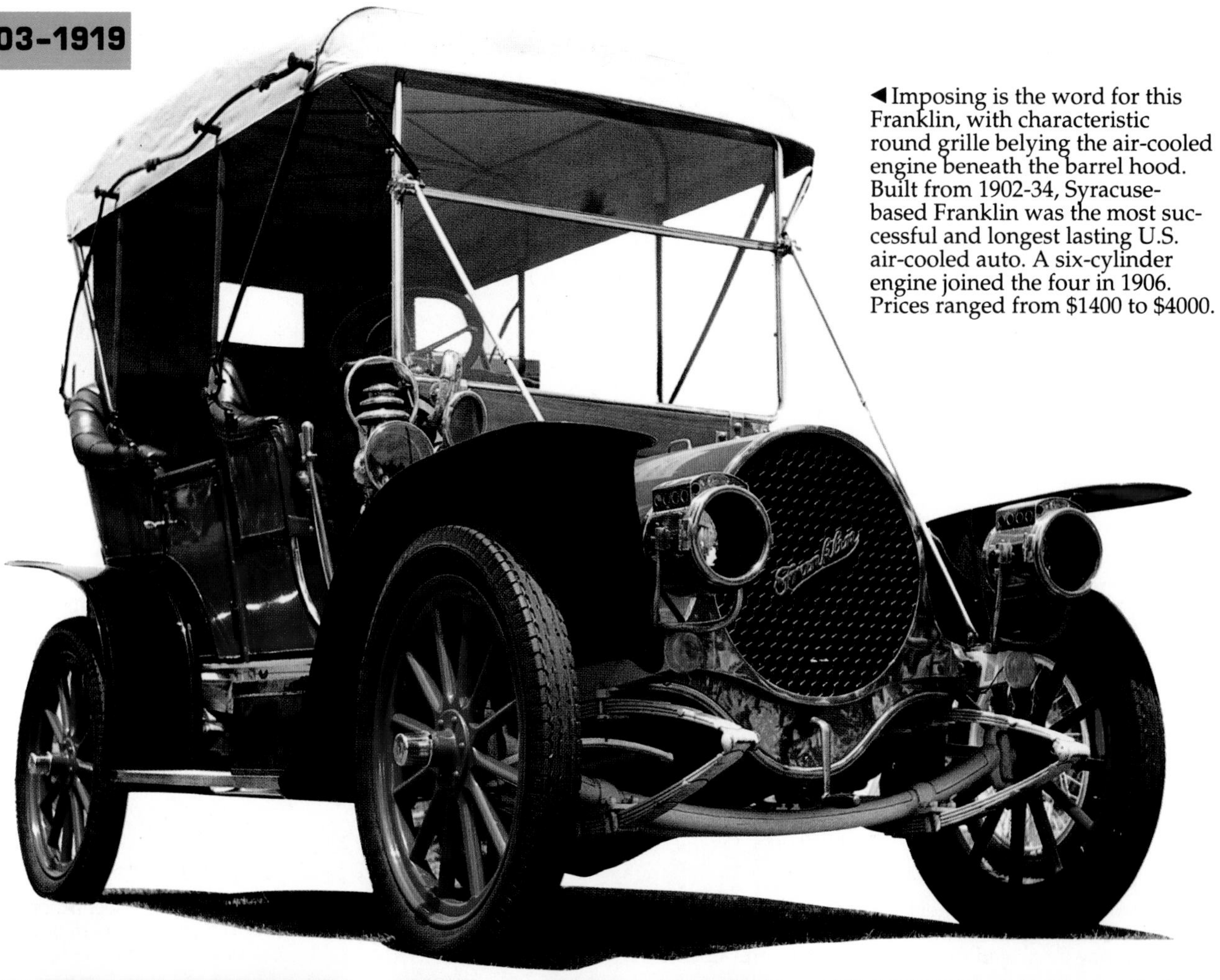

◀ Imposing is the word for this Franklin, with characteristic round grille belying the air-cooled engine beneath the barrel hood. Built from 1902-34, Syracuse-based Franklin was the most successful and longest lasting U.S. air-cooled auto. A six-cylinder engine joined the four in 1906. Prices ranged from $1400 to $4000.

▲ After leaving Buick, Benjamin Briscoe joined Jonathan Maxwell to produce the Maxwell. This is the 20-bhp 1906 Model H. Note the standup windshield. Also offered: 40-bhp four-cylinder Model M.

▲ The 1906 model year brought this Packard roadster, and the first of the marque's T-head engines, which incorporated magneto jump spark ignition. The T-head, a four, displaced 349.9 cubic inches and produced 24 bhp.

▲ Four-cylinder engines were available in Ramblers for the first time in 1906, in 226- and 432-cid sizes (25 and 35/40 bhp). Seen here is a two-cylinder, 100-inch-wheelbase Type II Surrey. Rambler prices ranged from $800 to $3000.

---

Ford's huge, plush, six-cylinder Model K ($2500) is guaranteed to do 60 mph; it will be built through 1908

Production of the Kissel Kar touring begins in Hartford, Wisconsin, aimed at the 1907 season

Buicks come with a storage battery as standard equipment

Buick launches the 30-bhp, four-cylinder, T-head Model D as a 1907 model—at twice the price of prior models ($2000)

For 1906 only, Cadillac offers a more costly four-cylinder model: 392-cid, 40 horsepower

A four-cylinder Model M joins the Maxwell two-cylinder; Reo also offers its first four

▲ From 1906 to 1909 the St. Louis Car Company built the French Mors under license, calling it the American Mors. This 1907 American Mors limousine sold for $4500.

▲ No roof was included in the $800 base price of a one-cylinder 1907 Cadillac Model K runabout. An extra $40 bought a rubber top; $70, a leather top; $100, a Victoria top.

▲ Buick built 535 1907 Model G "turtle back roadsters," which had a tilt steering column and optional $70 top. A belly pan now enclosed the engine and transmission.

▲ Buick output rose to 4641 units in 1907—second only to Ford—as four-cylinder models joined the line, including this Model H touring. The 255-cid T-head yielded 30 bhp.

◀ Four-cylinder Cadillacs, with L-head engines rated at 20 horsepower, were far more posh than the one-cylinder models. This 1907 Model G touring car sold for $2000, $2120 with "Cape Cart Top"; 1030 Model Gs were produced in four models for 1907. Cadillac was already well known for precision manufacture, as well as easy maintenance.

---

The $2250 four-cylinder Model S joins the Oldsmobile line, billed as the "best thing on wheels"

Rambler Models 15 and 16 employ a 431.9-cid, 40-bhp four-cylinder engine

Optional front bumpers are offered on some makes

Henry Ford buys out Alexander Malcomson's share, takes over as company president after the death of John S. Gray

**1906 Model Year Production**

|  |  |  |
|---|---|---|
| 1. | Ford | 8,729 |
| 2. | Cadillac | 3,559 |
| 3. | Rambler | 2,765 |
| 4. | Reo | 2,458 |
| 5. | Maxwell | 2,161 |
| 6. | Oldsmobile | 1,600 |
| 7. | White | 1,534 |
| 8. | Buick | 1,400 |

*Some figures are estimated or calender-year*

▲ A $750 Model R Ford (*shown*) and less-equipped S joined the cheaper N in 1907. Each had a 15-bhp four.

▲ Sales of Ford's Model K roadster never took off. Near the end of its 1906-08 run, prices plunged $1000.

▲ Driving was no picnic in the early days of motoring. Here, a 1907 Packard roadster bogs down in goo.

▲ Rambler's Model 24 touring car had a 286.3-cid four-banger good for 25/30 bhp.

▲ A 20-percent graduated incline tested the prowess of an '07 Rambler.

▲ The 1907 Rambler Models 24 (*shown*) and 25 had four-cylinder engines, but two-cylinder cars also were offered. Wheelbase on the $2000 Model 24: 108 inches.

**New Makes: 1907**

Albany, Anderson, Atlas, Aurora, Bailey Electric, Barnes, Bay State, Belden, Brush, Bugmobile, C-F (Cornish-Friedberg), Chase, Colt, Conover, Continental, Corbitt, Cosmopolitan (highwheeler), Craig-Toledo, Crescent, Cunningham, C.V.I., Detroit Electric, Diamond T, Duer (highwheeler), Durocar, Earl, Euclid, Eureka, Everybody's, Falcon, Fee-American, Four Traction (Kato), Gearless, Gifford-Pettitt, Great Smith, Griswold, Harper, Hatfield, Hay-Berg, Haydock, Ideal, International (highwheeler), Jenkins, Kermath, Kiblinger (highwheeler), Kingston, Klink, Lauth-Juergens, Lorraine, Marvel, Maryland, Miller, Monarch, Oakland, Pennsylvania, Perfection, Ranger, Regal, Selden, Senator, Simplex, Simplicity, Speedwell, Staver, Stilson, Trebert, Triumph, and Wolfe

**1907**

Industry production totals 43,000 cars and 1000 trucks in a year of economic depression

Total U.S. auto registrations pass the 140,000 mark

Selective transmissions are a major trend at the Seventh National Automobile Show

Cars at the show feature bigger brakes, bodies with up to 30 coats of paint, and more six-cylinder engines

The Oakland Motor Car Company is formed by buggymaker Edward M. Murphy; its two-cylinder car is designed by Alanson P. Brush

At $700-$750, Models R and S join the plainer Model N as the final right-hand-drive Fords

◀ This Rambler Model 21 torpedo-deck runabout rode a 100-inch wheelbase, and had a 20/22-bhp two-cylinder engine. Tank on the running board fueled lights—a common sight.

▼ Elegance marked Studebaker's all-black Electric runabout, with tiller steering and chain drive. Studebaker was focusing on gasoline automobiles by 1907, but sold 1841 electrics from 1902 to 1912, both cars and trucks.

---

Cadillac is now focusing on four-cylinder models

The last of the famed one-cylinder Curved Dash Oldsmobiles is built

Once again, Packard's T-head four has greater displacement: 431.9-cid, good for 30 horsepower

Buick adopts a T-head four-cylinder engine with a three-speed, sliding-gear transmission

Various engines have enclosed timing gears, and include mud aprons below

The $4500 Hewitt V-8 touring car is claimed to be the first V-8-powered American car, but Buffum also offers one this year

Oldsmobile begins nickel-plating trim components that had formerly been brass

▲ The Apperson Jack Rabbit made its debut in 1908. Its eye-opening (and guaranteed) top speed was 75 mph.

▲ A 255-cid, 30-bhp T-head four again powered the 2000-pound 1908 Buick Model D touring car. Price: $1750.

▲ Restyled for 1908 on a longer 92-inch wheelbase, Buick's Model F kept its 159-cid, 22-horse two-cylinder engine.

▲ The 1908 Buick Model G roadster had far fewer sales than the Model F touring—219 versus 3281.

▲ Buick's popular new car for 1908 was the $900 Model 10 runabout; 4002 were produced. It had a 22.5-bhp four.

▲ A Buick Model 10 runabout could have a two-passenger rear seat. Price included acetylene headlights.

▲ Cadillac Model G limo (*top*) was new for 1908; Model S runabout cost $850.

▲ William Durant incorporated General Motors on September 16, 1908, in New Jersey.

▲ Named GM's second president was William M. Eaton. He served from October 1908 to November 1910.

The Association of Licensed Automobile Manufacturers offers a formula for calculating engine horsepower, later to be used by many states for tax purposes

Humps are installed on some streets in Glencoe, Illinois, to discourage speeders

Despite a depressed economy, Ford and Packard both earn $1-million-plus profits

President William Howard Taft orders a White Steamer—the first official White House automobile

**1907 Model Year Production**

|  |  |  |
|---|---|---|
| 1. | Ford | 14,887 |
| 2. | Buick | 4,641 |
| 3. | Reo | 3,967 |
| 4. | Maxwell | 3,785 |
| 5. | Rambler | 3,201 |
| 6. | Cadillac | 2,884 |
| 7. | Franklin | 1,509 |
| 8. | Packard | 1,403 |

*Some figures are estimated or calender-year*

▶ J. Frank Duryea (*near right*) and Charles Duryea earned credit for producing the first true working automobile in America in 1893, but the brothers went their own ways before the turn of the century. J. Frank helped issue the Stevens-Duryea, while Charles produced vehicles under the Duryea nameplate as late as 1917.

**New Makes: 1908**

Allen-Kingston, Bendix, Benner, Bertolet, Black, Browniekar, Chalmers-Detroit, Chicago Motor Buggy, Chief, Clark-Hatfield, Clymer (highwheeler), Crown (highwheeler), Davis, Deal, DeSchaum, De Tamble, Duplex, Economy (highwheeler), E-M-F, Fairbanks-Morse, Famous, Fuller, Garford (debut in October 1907), Hobbie, Imperial, Jeannin, Lincoln, Marathon, Midland, Mier, Owen-Thomas, Palmer-Singer, Paterson, Pittsburgh, Rider-Lewis, St. Joe, Stafford, Sears (highwheeler), Sharp Arrow, Sultan, Viking, Waldron, Webb Jay (steam), and Zimmerman

▲ This 1908 Ford Model S roadster sold for $700 as a two-seater, or $750 with tonneau. Curb weight was about 1400 pounds. Even with a top, weather was a problem.

▲ Oakland began in 1908 with two-cylinder power, but sold only 300 cars, so a new 40-horsepower, four-cylinder Model 40 seen here was introduced in time for 1909.

**1908**

Annual production rises to 63,500 cars and 1500 trucks

Nearly all autos at the Eighth National Automobile Show have four-cylinder, vertical engines and sliding-gear transmissions

Most new models feature longer wheelbases, with rear seats positioned closer to the center of the car for improved ride comfort

Mechanical improvements include easier component access, larger brakes, better-enclosed clutches, and easier-to-use controls

This year's innovations include left-hand steering (to be popularized by the Ford Model T), Stewart magnetic speedometers, silent timing chains, baked-enamel paint, and motor-driven horns

▲ This 1908 Oldsmobile four-cylinder Series M carries a limousine body. A six-cylinder Series Z bowed this year.

▲ Like other 1908 cars, the Olds limo made ample use of wood construction.

▲ This Model M touring car was one of 1145 cars built by Oldsmobile in 1908.

▼ In 1908, Overlands used a 173-cid, 20/22-bhp four-cylinder engine and 96-inch wheelbase. Sizes soon grew.

◀ Overland began a comeback in 1908, with 465 cars built. Crude bodywork belied the car's mechanical qualities.

---

The General Motors Company is incorporated in New Jersey by William Crapo Durant; William Eaton is named president

Buick and Oldsmobile join the GM team, as does the Rapid Motor Vehicle Company, a truck builder

Ford launches the Model T on October 1, 1908, New York's Grand Central Palace hosts the formal debut on December 31

Studebaker enters into an agreement with the Everitt-Metzger-Flanders Company to sell Studebaker-EMF cars

C. Harold Wills develops vanadium steel, for use by Ford

Charles Y. Knight invents the sleeve-valve engine, which eliminates troublesome poppet valves

The Fisher Body Company is formed by Fred J. and Charles T. Fisher

▲ Buick's 1909 Model 16 Tourabout, which sold for $1750, featured "modern" rounded fenders and a 318-cid four.

◀ The 1909 American Simplex seven-passenger touring car had a two-stroke four-cylinder engine with 50 bhp.

▲ Bob Burman raced a stripped Buick against a plane at Daytona Beach in 1909.

▲ Famed racer Bob Burman and mechanic look ready, as does their modified Buick Model 16.

▲ Is the natty passenger in this racing Buick Model 10 trying to escape, threatened by those huge exposed exhaust pipes?

---

A four-cylinder, 60-bhp Thomas Flyer wins the 170-day New York-to-Paris race, traveling 13,341 miles in 88 days; the rest of the journey was by sea

John North Willys becomes Willys-Overland President

Cadillac is the first U.S. automaker to win the Dewar Trophy, presented by Britain's Royal Automobile Club for the development of interchangeable components

During the model year, Oldsmobile adds its first six, a 505-cid Series Z touring, priced at $4500

**1908 Model Year Production**

|  |  |
|---|---|
| 1. Ford | 10,202 |
| 2. Buick | 8,820 |
| 3. Studebaker | 8,132 |
| 4. Maxwell | 4,455 |
| 5. Reo | 4,105 |
| 6. Rambler | 3,597 |
| 7. Cadillac | 2,377 |
| 8. Franklin | 1,895 |

*Some figures are estimated or calender-year*

▲ Destined to lead America into motoring, the Model T Ford offered such innovations as transverse springs. Oil lamps were standard on the $850 touring car.

▲ Ford's 176.7-cid Model T engine delivered 22 bhp. The water pump yielded to thermo-syphon cooling.

**New Makes: 1909**

Abbott-Detroit, Alco, Babcock, Black Crow, Broc Electric, Coates-Goshen, Cole, Correja, Croxton-Keeton, Cutting, Detroit-Dearborn, Emancipator, Empire, Enger, Everitt, F.A.L., Firestone-Columbus, G.J.G., Herreshoff, Hudson, Hupmobile, Illinois, Inter-State, Jonz, Kauffman (Advance), Kearns, Keystone, Lexington, McCue, McIntire, Metz, Ohio, Paige-Detroit, Petrel, Pickard, Pilot, Planche, Pratt-Elkhart, Ricketts, Roebling, Salter, Sellers, Spoerer, Sterling, Toledo, Velie, Washington, and Westcott

**1909**

Total industry output: 123,900 cars (17,771 Fords) and 3255 trucks

By year's end, more than 290 makes are built in America, in 24 states: 45 from Michigan, 44 from Indiana, 39 from Ohio

The Ninth National Automobile Show focuses on customer satisfaction, not merely on taking orders from dealers

Some 71 percent of gasoline-engined cars exhibited are four-cylinder, 27 percent six-cylinder

Some steering wheels have a corrugated underside to prevent hand slippage

A U.S. District Court holds that the Selden patent is valid—and that Ford has infringed upon it

▲ Two Fords entered the 1909 New York-Seattle race. Number 1, driven by Frank Kulick, got lost along the way.

▲ The St. Louis-built Moon lasted from 1905-1929. Here, the 1909 Model D: 32.2-bhp four; 121-inch chassis; $3850.

◀ A peek inside the Oakland Motor Company factory, in 1909, reveals an intriguing crop of nearly finished automobiles. Many notable cars that emerged in the 1900-10 period would last into the '20s or beyond: Auburn, Moon, Hudson, Hupmobile, Mercer. Dozens of companies made high-wheelers for rural folks who preferred down-to-earth transportation.

▲ This $2750 Model DR, one of Oldsmobile's four-cylinder models, helped 1909 output reach 6575 units.

▲ Overland production rose sharply in 1909 to 4907; this Model 34 four-passenger roadster had the firm's first six.

Cadillac, Oakland, and other automakers enter the General Motors fold

The new Hupmobile places the transmission and multiple-disc clutch integral with the engine

The Hudson Motor Car Company is formed, with the first cars produced in July (as 1910 models)

Ford's Model T is modified for a three-pedal transmission; by May, production lags far behind demand

White, known for steamers, builds a gasoline-engine automobile

Buick's four-cylinder Model 7 is huge, with 5 x 5-inch bore and stroke for 392.6 cid; only 85 are sold for 1909-10

▲ Not even a roof protected the driver of the '09 Overland Model 31 taxicab. This four-cylinder model sold for $1400.

▲ The 31's 226-cid four powered this 1909 Overland Model 30 tonneau touring, with bucket-like seats. Price was $1400.

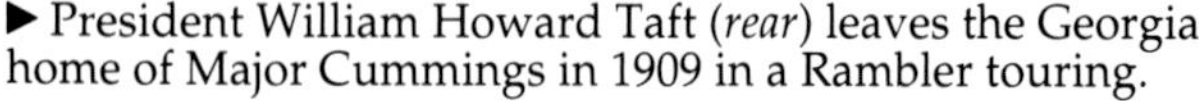

► President William Howard Taft (*rear*) leaves the Georgia home of Major Cummings in 1909 in a Rambler touring.

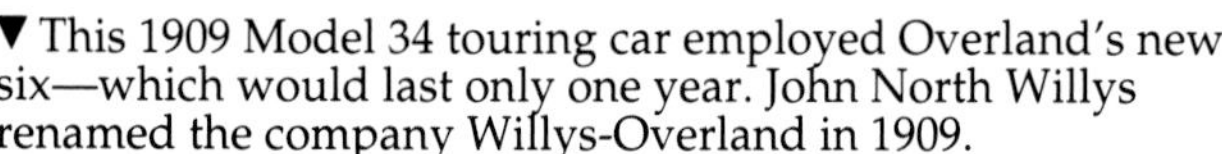

▼ This 1909 Model 34 touring car employed Overland's new six—which would last only one year. John North Willys renamed the company Willys-Overland in 1909.

Mrs. John R. Ramsey is the first woman to drive across America, in a Maxwell touring car

Packard launches a smaller, less expensive Model Eighteen with a 265.7-cid, four-cylinder engine

Race driver Louis Chevrolet starts work on a six-cylinder automobile

This year's manufacturing trends include larger numbers of cellular-type radiators, greater use of magnetos, more chrome-nickel steel and vanadium steel

High-tension ignition systems replace make-and-break setups on most cars

This year's Glidden Tour is the longest ever at 2636 miles; the Indianapolis Speedway is finished

The first rural section of concrete pavement, a one-mile stretch, opens on Woodward Avenue, near Detroit, on July 4

▲ The 1910 American Simplex touring car had a 117-inch wheelbase.

▲ Apperson Jack Rabbits raced frequently. This is a 50-bhp 1910 model.

▲ A Detroit publicity stunt pitted a 1910 Brush runabout against a horse.

▲ Among the 11,000 Buick Model 10s built for 1910 were many roadsters.

▲ New at Buick for 1910 was this $1400 Model 19 touring, with a 255-cid four.

▲ Buick's 92-inch-wheelbase Model 10 used a planetary gearbox.

▲ Buick had its 622-cid "Bugs" ready when the Indianapolis Speedway opened in 1910. Bob Burman drove a time trial record 105.87 mph.

| 1909 Model Year Production | |
|---|---|
| 1. Ford | 17,771 |
| 2. Buick | 14,606 |
| 3. Maxwell | 9,460 |
| 4. Studebaker/EMF | 7,960 |
| 5. Cadillac | 7,868 |
| 6. Reo | 6,592 |
| 7. Oldsmobile | 6,575 |
| 8. Willys-Overland | 4,907 |

*Some figures are estimated or calender-year*

**1910**

Industry production reaches approximately 181,000 cars and 6000 trucks

Ford's output jumps to 32,053, for a market share of 17.8 percent

Featured at the 10th National Automobile Show is a new Torpedo body—called a "bathtub on wheels" by some wags

This year's trend is standardization

**New Makes: 1910**

American Fiat, Ames, Amplex, Anchor, Anhut, Bergdoll, Borland Electric, Burg, Continental, Courier, Demot, Dispatch, Everitt, Flanders, FWD Truck, Great Eagle, Great Western, Henry, Kenmore, Kimball Electric, Kline Kar, K-R-I-T (debut in late 1909), Lion, McFarlan, Mercer, Morse, Norwalk, Ohio Electric, Otto, Owen, Parry, Plymouth, Republic, Sebring, Spaulding, Warren, White (gas), and Wilcox

▲ Mass-production techniques had not yet been very highly developed at General Motors plants in 1910, when this chassis/body assembly line was photographed.

▲ The Everitt was a 1910 outgrowth of EMF (Everitt-Metzger-Flanders). This is the 1910 Model 30 touring car.

▲ This Ford Model T, with a dapper fellow in the "mother-in-law" seat, participated in the 1910 Munsey Tour. Ford's market share neared 18 percent, with 32,053 cars built.

◀ Oldsmobile boasted that its huge and powerful 1910-12 Limited set a "new standard of luxury." Limiteds rode a 130-inch chassis powered by a 60-bhp, 505-cid six.

Some cars are now available fully equipped

Ford markets a $700 chassis that can accommodate bodies from outside suppliers

Clutches still come in a variety of forms: contracting-band type, leather-faced cone (with cork insert), Borg & Beck single-plate, and multiple-disc

Buick offers its first closed body, a limousine

James J. Storrow is named president of General Motors

Charles W. Nash becomes head of Buick, succeeding William C. Durant

Packard adopts a dry multiple-disc clutch

▲ A 226-cid four powered the 1910 Chalmers-Detroit. Renamed Chalmers for 1911, it was popular in the Teens.

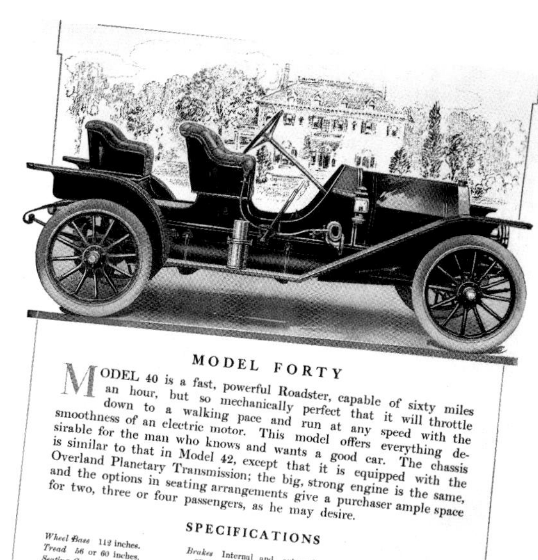


▲ A 35-bhp, four-cylinder Overland Model 40 roadster, with a two-speed planetary gearbox, could do 60 mph.

▲ Eight wheels on the huge 1910 Reeves Octoauto promised a smoother ride and longer tire life. The firm also created a six-wheel Sextoauto. Neither ultimately went on sale.

▲ Best known (if not the most sophisticated) of the steam cars, Stanley offered four 1910 models. This one cost $1150.

Overland's "38" is marketed as a fully-equipped car, the first in the $1000 class with standard top, windshield, lamps, and magneto

Patents are issued for the Knight sleeve-valve engine principle

Alvan Macauley is named Packard's general manager

Ford initiates production at its new Highland Park plant, the world's biggest under one roof

The four-cylinder Reo earns a perfect score in the James Gordon Bennett reliability contest

| 1910 Model Year Production | |
|---|---|
| 1. Ford | 32,053 |
| 2. Buick | 30,525 |
| 3. Willys-Overland | 15,598 |
| 4. Studebaker/EMF | 15,020 |
| 5. Cadillac | 10,039 |
| 6. Maxwell | 10,000 |
| 7. Brush | 10,000 |
| 8. Reo | 6,588 |

*Some figures are estimated or calender-year*

▲ Hill-climbing was still a popular means of evaluating a car's potential in 1911-12. Here, a $900 Buick Model 34 roadster with a 165-cid four scampers up a steep slope.

▲ The American was most commonly known as American Underslung—named for a frame that hung below the axles. This 1911 American was snapped on Detroit's South Blvd.

▲ Model 39 was Buick's designation for the touring-car version of the 38, priced identically at $1850; 905 found buyers.

▲ New to Buick for 1911 was the Model 38 roadster, with a 48-bhp, 318-cid four, and 116-inch chassis; 153 were sold.

▲ A new 25.6-bhp, 201-cid four with sliding-gear transmission drove Buick's $1050 Model 26 roadster; 1000 were sold.

**1911**

Industry volume totals 199,319 cars and 10,681 trucks

Nearly every automaker at the 11th National Automobile Show in New York exhibits a four-door model

A truck show, held in conjunction with the National Automobile Show, draws 286 exhibitors

Several self-starting mechanisms emerge, including the Amplex compressed-air starter and the Geiszler Starting Device, which works with an electric charge

Chevrolet Motor Company is organized in November 1911; production quickly gets underway with a handful of cars

Little, a low-priced companion to Chevrolet, is announced on October 30, but doesn't go into production until 1912

▲ Cadillac promoted the precision of its four-cylinder "Thirty" engine, which had grown to 286.3 cid by 1911.

▲ The wheelbase of Cadillac's "Thirty" coupe grew to 116 inches in 1911. This closed three-seater sold for $2250.

▲ The first open Cadillac with a front door was the $1800 "Thirty" Fore-Door touring. Note the windshield supports.

◀▲ A prototype of the Chevrolet Classic Six was finished early in 1911. The first Chevrolet, a large car, used a cone clutch and three-speed gearbox on the rear axle. Its 299-cid, six-cylinder T-head engine gave up to 40 bhp.

▶ Louis Chevrolet and his prototype car looked quite colorful in this rendering. Because Louis was well-known throughout America for his racing exploits, Billy Durant formed Chevrolet Motor Company, certain that a car with a Chevrolet badge would sell. The problem was that Louis designed a prestigious upmarket car, while Billy wanted a cheaper car that would sell in large volume. Louis soon left the fledgling venture to build the Frontenac; Billy went on to use Chevrolet as a foundation for regaining control of General Motors.

---

Studebaker acquires full control of the Everitt-Metzger-Flanders Company

Stutz goes on sale after an 11th-place finish at the Indianapolis 500 race (averaging 68.25 mph); the production car virtually duplicates the racer

Mercer's Model 35 Raceabout will become one of most-craved sporty motorcars

The U.S. Court of Appeals reverses the U.S. District Court decision on the Selden Patent, holding it "valid but not infringed" by Ford and others; payment of royalties stops

Hudson's fluid-cushioned clutch rotates in a blend of oil and kerosene; "wet" clutches will be a company "trademark" into the Fifties

▲ Ford touring cars adopted sheet steel over wood framing in 1911, instead of wood construction. Metal running boards displayed the famous "Ford" script.

Studebaker Corporation is formed; electric vehicles are dropped so the firm can focus on gas-engine automobiles

The Knight sleeve-valve engine is introduced in the U.S. by Stearns, followed by Stoddard-Dayton and Columbia

Ford's Model T gets a new body and prices are cut to as low as $680—sales double, market share hits 35 percent

Buick's Model 10 successor employs a three-speed sliding-gear transmission, replacing the planetary unit on prior low-cost models

Hudson's new Model 33 gets a bigger 226.2-cid four; the touring car costs $1250

The 1911-12 Oldsmobile Limited, now on a 138-inch wheelbase, boasts one of the biggest six-cylinder engines ever built: 706.9 cubic inches, 5x6-inch bore and stroke

◀ Intended as a rival to Ford's Model T, this 1911 Flanders 20 was named for Walter Flanders, but built by Studebaker. Roadster, Suburban, and coupe bodies joined the original four-cylinder runabout and touring this year. More than 31,000 cars were built from 1910-12, when the company was melded into Studebaker.

**New Makes: 1911**

Alpena, ArBenz, Atterbury, Carhartt, Case, Chevrolet, Colby, Crow-Elkhart, Dalton, Gaylord, Havers, Hupp-Yeats, King, Lenox, Mighty Michigan, Motorette, Nyberg, Penn, Rayfield, R.C.H. (for 1912), Roader, Rogers, S.G.V., Standard Electric, Stutz, Stuyvesant, Virginian, and W.F.S.

▲ A dusty duo in a Ford Model T navigate the 1911 Glidden Tour. Extra spare tires were vital to make it the distance.

▲ In 1911, Ramblers came in a choice of three wheelbases: in this case, 112 inches for the 34-horsepower Model 63 coupe.

---

William S. Knudsen joins Ford—later to head Chevrolet

Thomas Neal is named third president of General Motors

Automaker securities are now listed on the New York Stock Exchange

Painted center lines first appear on highways near Detroit

Ford Model Ts score major victories in hill-climbing events

International Motor Company (Mack) is formed; Diamond T Motor Car Company abandons passenger cars to concentrate on trucks

General Motors Truck Company is organized, combining the Rapid and Reliance companies

▲ The biggest 1912 Buick was the Model 43 touring, on a 116-inch wheelbase with a 318-cid four-cylinder engine and sliding-gear transmission. Buick stood fourth in sales.

▲ The first car to use C.F. Kettering's self-starter was the 1912 Cadillac, which won the make a second Dewar Trophy in 1913. A new slogan said it all: "Standard of the World."

▲ A combination starter motor-generator (*above*) was installed on 1912 Cadillacs, freeing drivers from cranking the engine. A 1983 5-MT cranking motor is also shown.

▲ The 1912 Cadillac roadster had a steel body; closed cars wore aluminum.

► Charles W. Nash served as GM's fifth president, from late 1912 to 1916.

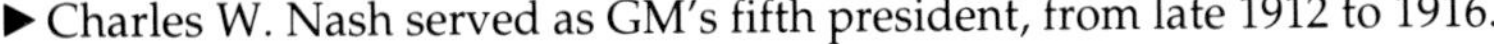

Buick sets a speed record, traveling 20 miles in just over 13 minutes

Ray Harroun wins the first 500-mile Indianapolis Speedway Race in a six-cylinder Marmon Wasp, taking 6 hours, 42 minutes, 8 seconds. The car employs the first rear-view mirror used in the U.S.

**1911 Model Year Production**

|  |  |
|---|---|
| 1. Ford | 69,762 |
| 2. Studebaker/EMF | 26,827 |
| 3. Willys-Overland | 18,745 |
| 4. Maxwell | 16,000 |
| 5. Buick | 13,389 |
| 6. Cadillac | 10,071 |
| 7. Hudson | 6,486 |
| 8. Chalmers | 6,250 |

*Some figures are estimated or calender-year*

**1912**

The industry produces a total of 356,000 cars and 22,000 trucks

A new Automobile Board of Trade sponsors the 12th National Automobile Show

▲ Louis Chevrolet (*far right*) poses with a 1912 Chevrolet touring car. Initial examples used a compressed-air starter.

▲ Henry Ford sits at the wheel of a Model T "Fore-Door" Touring. Despite the name, the driver's "door" didn't open.

▲ The final year for this tall Flanders 20 coupe with sliding windows was 1912; after that, Studebaker took over fully.

▲ The driver's door of Ford's Model T Touring was fake, but both front doors could be removed for a sporty look.

▲ The 20-bhp Little was built from 1912-13, when the Durant-launched make merged into Chevrolet.

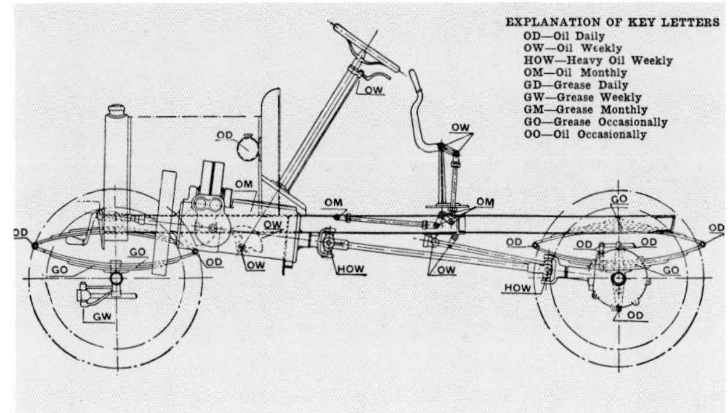


▲ Like other early cars, the 1912 Maxwell had many points to be oiled or greased frequently, as this lube chart reveals.

A wide variety of self-starters appear at the show, including 13 acetylene-operated units, six using compressed air, seven electric, 14 mechanical, two gasoline-powered, plus one that operates from exhaust gases

Cadillac adopts an electric self-starter developed by Charles F. Kettering, accompanied by generator-battery lighting and ignition systems

A total of 3000 Chevrolets are built; the six-cylinder touring car sells for $2150

Ford Model T prices are slashed by $80; Ford claims each dollar's reduction attracts a thousand new buyers

Ford production rises to 78,440, but market share skids to 22 percent as competition increases

▲ In 1911-12, Oldsmobile produced this brash, low-slung Autocrat Speedster, a $3500 two-seat roadster with twin-barrel gas tanks. Underhood lurked a 471-cid, T-head four.

▲ Ransom E. Olds called the 1912 "Reo the Fifth" his "Farewell Car," the culmination of his efforts. A top and extras added $100 to the $1055 price tag, a self-starter $25.

▲ In 1912, a 30-bhp, 106-inch-wheelbase Overland 59-R cost $900; Fords began at $590. Overland was second in output.

▲ The $2000 45-bhp Overland 61-C coupe featured Bosch duplex ignition, gas lamps, and electric pillar lamps.

▲ Even the model names of some 1912 Ramblers—Gotham, Country Club, Valkyrie—suggested fancy traveling. Four-cylinder engines with 38 or 50 bhp had 286 and 432 cid.

Edward Gowen Budd invents the all-steel car body. Oakland and Hupmobile take an interest, and Dodge Brothers orders Budd bodies for its forthcoming car

The Boyce Moto-Meter is introduced to monitor engine temperature

A short-lived cyclecar craze begins—the low-cost, often-fragile vehicles draw scorn from some, purchase agreements from others

Charles W. Nash is named president of General Motors; Walter P. Chrysler goes to work under him, as Buick plant manager

Packard introduces its first six-cylinder series, with a 525-cid T-head engine

Hudson moves into the medium-price field at mid-year with the 1913 Model 54, its first six-cylinder

▲ Studebaker abandoned electric autos in 1912, but battery-powered makes, such as Baker, still hung on. Detroit Electrics endured well into the '30s.

◀ Production of the tall, stubby, and stately Studebaker Electric coupe would cease by 1912, but some drivers—especially city women—still liked their silence and tiller steering.

**New Makes: 1912**

Argo Electric, Atlas-Knight, Car-Nation (cyclecar), Chevrolet (production models), Chicago Electric, Church-Field Electric, Crane, Detroiter, Dodo (cyclecar), Edwards-Knight, Great Southern, Grinnell Electric, Henderson, Little, Marquette, Modoc, Omaha, Pathfinder, Perfex, Pratt, Stoddard-Dayton Knight, and Touraine

---

Hudson's Mile-A-Minute Roadster is guaranteed to do—what else?—60 miles an hour

The City of Chicago enacts an ordinance limiting horn blowing

White traffic-separation lines are painted on the streets of Redlands, California

The Stewart Motor Corporation is formed to produce cars and trucks

A loaded Packard is the first truck to make a westbound transcontinental crossing, in 46 days

**1912 Model Year Production**

|  |  |
|---|---|
| 1. Ford | 78,440 |
| 2. Willys-Overland | 28,572 |
| 3. Studebaker/EMF | 28,032 |
| 4. Buick | 19,812 |
| 5. Cadillac | 12,708 |
| 6. Hupmobile | 7,640 |
| 7. Reo | 6,342 |
| 8. Oakland | 5,838 |

*Some figures are estimated or calender-year*

▲ Buick's rakish $950 Model 24 roadster found 2850 buyers. Buick sales rose from 19,812 to 26,660 in 1913.

▲ At $1050, Buick's 1913 Model 25 touring attracted 8150 buyers. This five-passenger model weighed 2335 pounds.

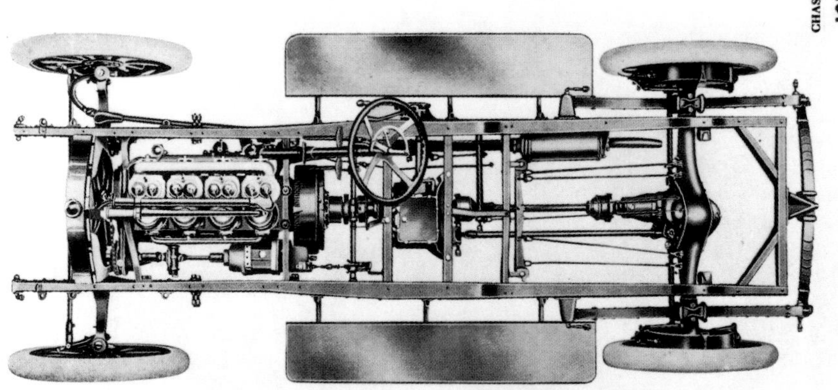


◀ All 1913 Buicks used four-cylinder engines and a three-speed gearbox with cone clutch. Brakes worked on two wheels. Three series were sold—24/25, 30/31, 40—on three wheelbases. Electric lighting was available.

▼ Charles F. Kettering tinkers with a self-starter, which evolved from his NCR cash register motor. Eliminating the dangerous hand crank would bring the blessings of motoring to more Americans, but electric starters took a while to become universal.

▲ Charles F. Kettering sits at the wheel of a 1913 Buick, testing the self-starter that had debuted on the 1912 Cadillac.

**1913**

Industry output spurts to 461,500 cars and 23,500 trucks

Cadillac earns its second Dewar Trophy, this time for the electric starter

The 13th National Automobile Show is held in two locations: Madison Square Garden for luxury and high-powered cars, Grand Central Palace for modestly priced cars

Many of this year's cars display sloping fronts and hoods, with smoother body lines and longer curves

Mass production of the Ford Model T begins, using an overhead body drop

▲ This $1975 Torpedo touring was one of seven Cadillac body styles offered for 1913. All controls were now inside.

▲ The $2500 Chevrolet Classic Six sported a European flair. Only the windshield mount changed for 1913.

▲ In mid-1913, Chevrolet launched the Series H, with a 171-cid, 24-bhp four. This "Baby Grand" touring cost $875.

▲ "Royal Mail" was Chevrolet's $750 104-inch-wheelbase Series H roadster. It came with top and windshield.

◀ Closed bodies in various states of completion are being readied for installation on Chicago Electrics at the Seaman body company in 1913. Note how much wood was used. Scores of U.S. manufacturers still turned out vehicles, but the total was beginning to decline. Electrics were fading fast, but the short-lived "cyclecar" craze was about to begin.

---

Annual Ford output more than doubles to 168,220 cars; production reaches 1000 per day

Chandler automobiles debut; they're produced in Cleveland

New on the market are the Imp and Twombly cyclecars, continuing a short-lived trend that began a year earlier

The Bendix electric-starter drive appears

A new six-cylinder engine and a bigger four-cylinder are found under Hudson hoods; the four departs after this season

The first six-cylinder Maxwell is introduced

▲ A winter roundup of Fords en route to a New York dealership pauses for a photo. Brass had nearly disappeared from Fords by 1913, as bodies received another revamping. Soon, as mass production really took hold, far more Fords would be built each day.

▲ At $800, the most costly Ford of 1913 was the seven-passenger Model T Town Car. A runabout cost only $525. Ford output more than doubled to 168,220.

**New Makes: 1913**

Chandler, Coey, De Soto (cyclecar), Grant, Holly, Howard, Imp (cyclecar), Lyons-Knight (late 1913), Monarch, Partin-Palmer, Read, Tribune, Twombly (cyclecar), Vulcan, and Wahl

---

Oakland debuts a six-cylinder model; fours remain in production into 1916

Kissel Kar sports a primitive form of a wraparound windshield

Packards use forced-feed lubrication and worm bevel gears

Pierce-Arrow cars sport "frog-eye" headlamps mounted on the mudguards (fenders), a patented design feature that will continue until the marque's demise in 1938

Studebaker engines get cast *en bloc* construction

Chevrolet moves to Flint, Michigan, and merges with Little Motor Car Company

The Little/Chevrolet line consists of the Little Four and Six, plus a six-cylinder Chevrolet Model C; the Little line is dropped by the end of 1913

▲ Delco electric starting/lighting was available on 1913 Oldsmobiles, including this Model 53 touring car, on a long 135-inch wheelbase. Its 380-cid six-cylinder engine made 50 horsepower. Olds hoped it would sell better than the now-extinct Limited. Four-cylinder Defenders also were offered.

◀ Overlands came in two series for 1913: Model 69, on a 110-inch wheelbase; and Model 71, at 114 inches. Touring (*shown*), roadster, and coupe bodies were sold. Overlands were practical and well-built, but sporting folks had other choices, such as a Mercer Raceabout or Stutz Bearcat.

◀ Only one car from the Pope empire remained in 1913: the Pope-Hartford, here as a $2250 Model 31 touring.

▶ Steam engines had powered Whites since 1900, but by 1912 the firm sold only four- and six-cylinder gasoline autos. Here, a 1913 touring car.

---

Dealers, fretting over the impact of used-car sales on the new-car market, ask the National Association of Automobile Manufacturers to investigate

Automobiles are increasingly being financed by installment loans

The Automobile Board of Trade and National Association of Automobile Manufacturers merge into the National Automobile Chamber of Commerce, which recommends a standard 90-day new-car warranty

Gulf Oil Company is the first to offer free road maps

**1913 Model Year Production**

| | |
|---|---|
| 1. Ford | 168,220 |
| 2. Willys-Overland | 37,422 |
| 3. Studebaker | 31,994 |
| 4. Buick | 26,666 |
| 5. Cadillac | 17,284 |
| 6. Maxwell | 17,000 |
| 7. Hupmobile | 12,543 |
| 8. Reo | 7,647 |

*Some figures are estimated or calender-year*

▲ Buick's first overhead-valve six, rated at 48 bhp, went into this $1985 1914 B-55, on a 130-inch chassis.

▲ The first of Buick's closed coupes was the 1914 Model B-38, with a 35-bhp four, and 112-inch wheelbase.

▲ Rounded hoods gave the '14 Buicks Series 36/37/38 a more modern look. They also now had left-hand drive.

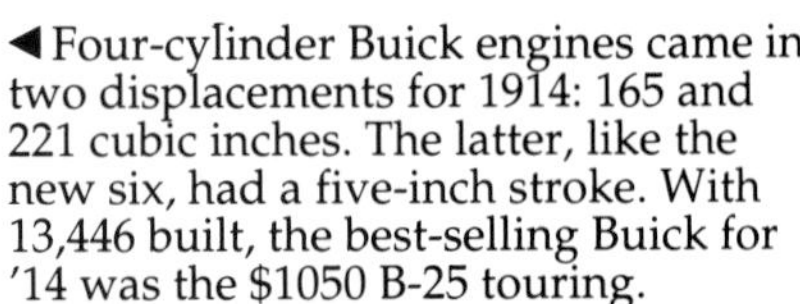

◀ Four-cylinder Buick engines came in two displacements for 1914: 165 and 221 cubic inches. The latter, like the new six, had a five-inch stroke. With 13,446 built, the best-selling Buick for '14 was the $1050 B-25 touring.

▼ General Motors would never have enjoyed its worldwide success without the talents of such luminaries as Henry Leland (*second from right*), who soon would leave Cadillac and a half-dozen years later would initiate the Lincoln, and electrical wizard Charles F. Kettering (*far right*), who later founded the GM Research Laboratories.

**New Makes: 1914**

Benham, Briscoe, Dile, Doble Steamer, Dodge, F.R.P., Hercules, Jeffery, Jones, Lewis, Milburn Electric, Moline-Knight, Monroe, Saxon, Singer, Sphinx (as 1915 model), Vixen, and Willys-Knight

**1914**

The "Great War"—World War I—begins in Europe; the Dow Jones stock average falls 24.4 percent on December 12

Industry output rises again, to 548,139 cars and 24,900 trucks

Construction of the Lincoln Highway—the first transcontinental road, stretching from New York to San Francisco—begins

The National Automobile Chamber of Commerce sponsors the 14th National Automobile Show

Cyclecars for one or two passengers, introduced in 1912-13, are the fad of the season, including the $295 Argo

Five show exhibits help cyclecars rise from the status of "toy" to relative popularity, though the trend will soon evaporate

◀ Innovations on the 1914 Cadillac included a new Timken two-speed rear axle, plus a hinged steering wheel and driver's cushion to ease entry/exit. All Cadillacs, like this $1975 roadster, had a 365.8-cid four-cylinder engine and rode a 120-inch wheelbase.

▼ A fully loaded Chevrolet "Baby Grand" climbs the State Capitol steps at Des Moines, Iowa. This feat, up a 45-degree grade, was achieved at 18 mph. The touring car sold for $875.

▲ Louis Chevrolet was well-known as a racing driver before his name went on a production auto. Here, he wields the wheel of a Buick at Atlanta.

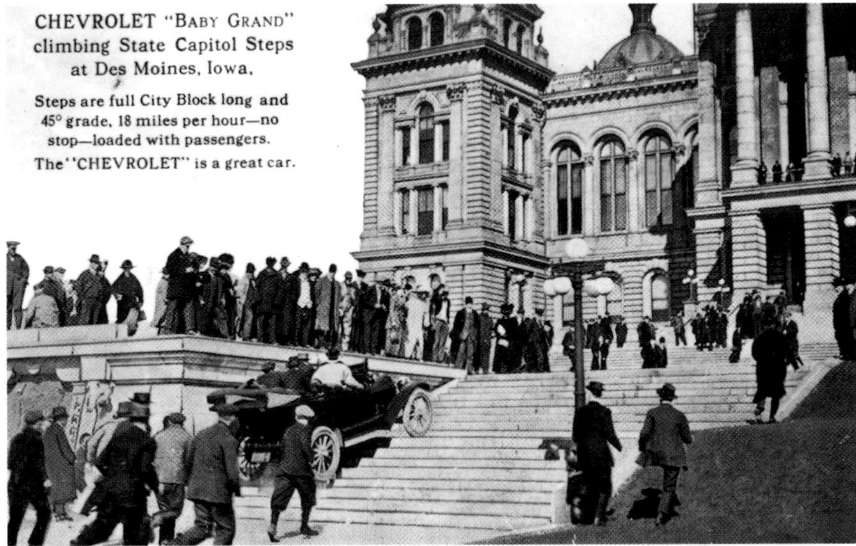

▲ A 1914 Chevrolet "Royal Mail" flat-deck roadster could be ordered in plum color or basic gray. Price: $750.

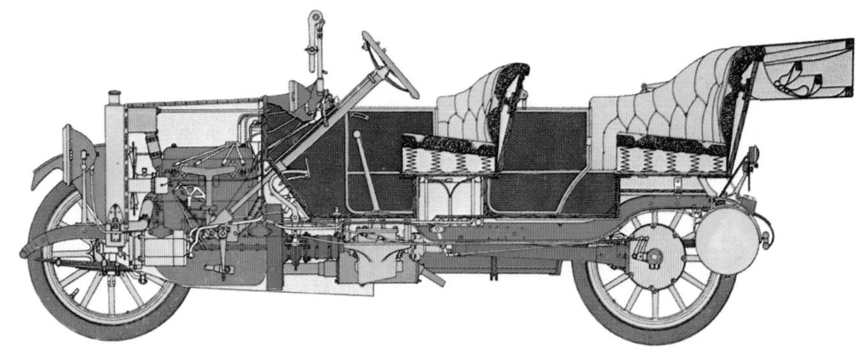

▶ Chevrolet's Series H used a three-speed gearbox with a leather cone clutch, and a 24-bhp four. An Auto-Lite electrical system cost $125 extra.

Dodge cars, produced by brothers Horace and John Dodge, debut late in the year

Notable new nameplates include Briscoe (with a single "cyclops-eye" headlight), Doble Steamer, and Willys-Knight

Rambler cars, still made by the Thomas B. Jeffery Company (though founder Thomas B. had died in 1910), are renamed Jeffery

Cadillac introduces a high-speed V-8 engine in September 1914 for the '15 model year

Henry Ford announces an eight-hour day with a $5 minimum daily wage (as part of a profit-sharing plan) for certain adult workers; 15,000 qualify. The investigative Ford Sociological Department's duty is to see that workers make "proper" use of the wage

▶ Outside builders produced the wooden bodies for Ford's Depot Hack back in 1914. Ford wouldn't get around to producing its own station wagons until years later. Riders got plenty of fresh air in the Depot Hack, or the vehicle could carry cargo. A bare Model T chassis, of which Ford sold many tens of thousands over the years, weighed in at about 960 pounds.

▲ John and Horace Dodge launched their first car in 1914.

▲ By 1914, black was the Ford Model T's only color.

▲ Women eagerly took to Ford Model Ts, including the driver of this new "turtle deck" runabout.

▲ The Rambler was gone, but Thomas Jeffery's son Charles replaced it with the Jeffery in 1914—both cars and trucks.

---

Ford's $5 daily wage is intended to reduce worker turnover, keep Industrial Workers of the World (IWW, the "One Big Union") out, and boost productivity

Ford output of 308,162 cars sets a calendar-year record

The Ford Model T is now sold "in any color so long as it's black"

Buick's first six-cylinder car, Model B55, appears with 331 cubic inches and 48 horsepower

Cadillac's final four-cylinder model has a Timken two-speed rear axle with an electro-magnetic shifting mechanism

Chevrolet drops its six-cylinder car to focus on four-cylinder models; the new four is considered the ancestor of subsequent Chevrolets

◀ Dozens of automotive legends had started—or advanced—their careers at Oldsmobile in Curved-Dash days. This photo of 56 Olds Pioneers, taken in January 1914, includes such dignitaries as Howard E. Coffin and Roy D. Chapin (now at Hudson), B.F. Everitt, and William Metzger. Charles Nash now served as Olds president.

▼ Vehicles don't get much more impenetrable-looking than this 1914 armored car, which betrays little of its Jeffery basis. As World War I began in Europe, Jeffery focused on trucks, even though the United States steered clear of the conflict.

▲ This rakish two-seater—with a 348-cid, 48-bhp six-cylinder engine—was one of 10,417 1914 Jefferys.

▲ One of the higher-quality cyclecars was this 1914 Scripps-Booth Rocket, which featured belt drive and tandem seats.

▲ An air-cooled, 70-cubic-inch Spacke vee-twin engine drove the Scripps-Booth Rocket to a top speed of 45 mph.

A new 288.6-cid, six-cylinder engine is available in Hudsons—it remains in production through 1929

The first sleeve-valved Willys-Knights are four-cylinder models

Electric stoplights are installed in Cleveland

Ford announces a $40-$60 rebate to buyers of a new Model T—if more than 300,000 are sold in a one-year period. The refund actually comes to $50

The first stop sign appears on Detroit streets; a city ordinance prohibits curbside gasoline pumps

**1914 Model Year Production**

|  |  |  |
|---|---|---|
| 1. | Ford | 308,162 |
| 2. | Willys-Overland | 48,461 |
| 3. | Studebaker | 35,374 |
| 4. | Buick | 32,889 |
| 5. | Maxwell | 18,000 |
| 6. | Reo | 13,516 |
| 7. | Jeffery | 10,417 |
| 8. | Hupmobile | 10,318 |

*Some figures are estimated or calender-year*

▶ Belts and pulleys drove an assortment of machinery in this General Motors plant. By 1914, Ford had turned to full mass production at his Highland Park, Michigan, plant, building upon ideas that had been employed by Oldsmobile years earlier.

▼ This was no ordinary 1915 Buick, but ranks as one of the earliest special-bodied "dream cars," created to flaunt fresh ideas. A total of 43,946 conventional Buicks were built, featuring a new ventilating windshield.

▲ One of Buick's popular 1915 cars was this $1235 Model C-37 touring, with a 37-bhp, 221-cid four. Like other mid-priced cars, Buicks were owned by relatively affluent families.

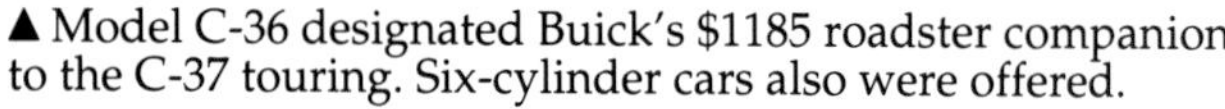

▲ Model C-36 designated Buick's $1185 roadster companion to the C-37 touring. Six-cylinder cars also were offered.

▲ Notice the old-style exposed gas tank on this 1915 Buick C-24 roadster, with the final 165-cid engine; 3256 were sold.

**1915**

Materials shortages begin as a result of World War I, even though the U.S. is not yet an active participant

Industry volume leaps to 895,930 cars and 74,000 trucks

The usefulness of trucks in the European war boosts their sales at home

More than a half-million Fords are built this year

Eight-cylinder engines—all V-8s—are featured at the National Automobile Show in Cadillac, King, Briggs-Detroiter, and Remington cars

The Ford Model T is restyled with curved rear fenders and electric headlights; a Coupelet and Center-Door Sedan are added

▲ All Cadillacs, designated Model 51 in 1915, boasted a brand-new L-head V-8 engine. The touring cars came in both five- and seven-passenger versions.

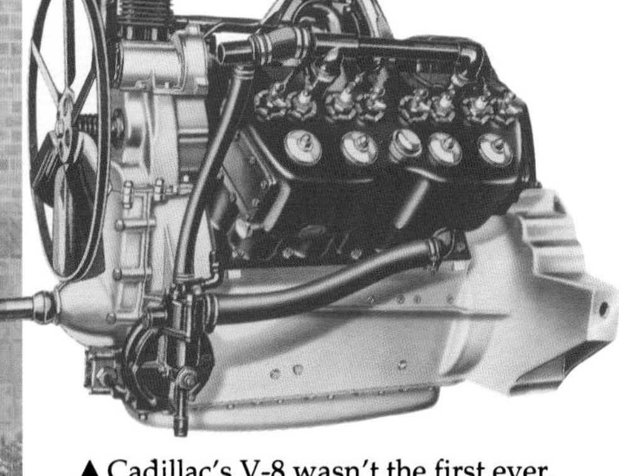

▲ Cadillac's V-8 wasn't the first ever, but was the first to go into serious production in the U.S. Displacing 314 cubic inches, it developed 70 bhp.

▲ This $2800 1915 Cadillac center-door "Sedan for Five Passengers" boasted a three-piece "rain vision" windshield.

▲ The side curtains of the one-man top on this $1975 Cadillac touring car opened with the doors. This was the first Cadillac series with left-hand drive.

**New Makes: 1915**

Alter, Biddle, Crane-Simplex, DeKalb, Dort, Farmac, Harvard, Herff-Brooks, Hollier, Madison, Mecca (cyclecar), Menominee Electric, Meteor, Milburn Electric (debut late 1914), Monitor, Monroe (debut late 1914), Ogren, Owen Magnetic, Pilgrim, Pilliod, Richard, Ross, Scripps-Booth, and Yellow Cab

---

Cadillac's new engine ranks as the first successful V-8 built in America. Initially developing 60 horsepower from 314 cubic inches, it lasts into 1927

Packard announces a V-12, appropriately called "Twin Six," in May, as a 1916 model

Standard-size Scripps-Booth cars appear, designed by William B. Stout. The company had formerly built the "Rocket" cyclecar

Dodges go on sale, with a 35-bhp four and cone clutch—it's the first mass-produced car with an all-steel body (by Budd)

Packard, Winton, Kissel, and Kline autos offer a "sociable" body with an aisle between the front seats, so passengers can move between front and rear

The Gadabout cyclecar roadster features a wicker body on a wood frame

▲ The $750 Chevrolet Royal Mail cut a dashing figure in 1915, with shapely fenders and a rear-of-seat gas tank.

▲ In 1915, a young woman's fancy might turn to Chevy's Amesbury Special, a dolled-up Royal Mail costing $985.

▲ Louis Chevrolet (*at wheel*), who could barely fit inside the unibodied Cornelian, nonetheless raced it at Indianapolis.

▲ The $975 Ford center-door sedan, which soon exchanged aluminum body panels for steel, came with electric lights.

▲ A special Seaman formal body graced this 1915 Jeffery. Eight models were priced from $1450 to $2900.

▲ The 1915 Olds Model 42, offered as a touring car (*shown*) or roadster for $1285, had a 194.2-cid, 30-bhp four.

Demountable rims replace clincher-style wheels on most cars

Cadillacs come with tilt-beam headlamps

Oldsmobiles are fitted with a standard top and windshield—still extra-cost items on most cars

Prism headlamp lenses appear for the first time

The Detroit-built Saxon, priced at $395, is one of the light cars that is gaining in popularity

General Motors declares its first dividend, $50 per share

**1915 Model Year Production**

|  |  |  |
|---|---|---|
| 1. | Ford | 501,462 |
| 2. | Willys-Overland | 91,904 |
| 3. | Dodge | 45,000 |
| 4. | Maxwell | 44,000 |
| 5. | Buick | 43,946 |
| 6. | Studebaker | 41,243 |
| 7. | Cadillac | 20,404 |
| 8. | Saxon | 19,000 |

*Some figures are estimated or calender-year*

▲ Buick's first sedan, the 1916 center-door Model D-47, boasted a new 45-bhp ohv six. At $1800, 881 were sold.

▲ With 73,827 built, the most popular 1916 Buick was the $1020 D-45 touring car. Its ohv six was cast *en block.*

▲ Buick output hit 124,834 in 1916. The Model 55, with its 130-inch chassis and 331-cid ohv six, was in its last year.

▲ The 1916 Cole touring had a 39.2-bhp eight built by GM's Northway division.

▼ Neat lines on Buick's D-6-44 roadster featured a squared-off rear deck.

**1916**

Industry output shoots up to 1,525,578 cars and 92,130 trucks

Car and fuel prices rise during the year, prompting an increase in the number of fuel-economy tests

Low prices and more power are trends at the 16th National Automobile Show, with most cars priced below $1250

Five automakers display V-12 models at the show: Packard, Enger, Haynes, National, and Pathfinder

Some 18 cars now offer V-8 engines: Abbott, Apperson, Briscoe, Cadillac, Cole, Daniels, Hollier, Jackson, King, Monarch, Oakland, Oldsmobile, Peerless, Pilot, Ross, Scripps-Booth, Standard, and Stearns-Knight

▲ Cadillac dubbed its 1916 touring a "Seven-Passenger Car." Total Cadillac output: 13,002 units.

▲ Chevrolet launched the 490 roadster and touring (*shown*) as '16 models, both priced at $490; 70,701 were built.

▲ Ford cut 1916 Model T prices to combat Chevy's new 490. This $590 Coupelet sold 3532 copies.

THE SATURDAY EVENING POST

WATCH THE SIGNS

*They Give Momentous Meaning to the*

HUDSON SUPER-SIX

**Don't make the mistake of under-rating this Super-Six invention. It is not one of the passing sensations. It is not one of those claims to motor supremacy which yields in a year to another. Learn the realities of it. Mark what its records mean. There is plenty of evidence now to convince you that it cannot be superseded**

*An 80 Per Cent Advance*

Here is a motor—a standard light Six—which creates about 84 horsepower. In our best former types, that size at limit delivered about 42 horsepower. Thus half the power was lost in vibration, in the best motor we knew up to this one.

The Super-Six, in the same size, delivers full 76 horsepower. It has increased motor efficiency by 80 per cent, by lessening vibration. Thus it comes within 10 per cent of an absolutely frictionless motor.

In a perfect motor there would be no vibration. But that is impossible. It is not very likely that anyone will ever get closer than that 10 per cent.

*Look Facts in the Face*

In choosing a car for years to come, don't minimize the Super-Six advantage.

You may not care for the speed it makes. You may not need its power. You will rarely, it is true, utilize half its capacity. But it is good for a motor to be always undertaxed.

Why buy a fine car without the finest motor? The Super-Six means smoothness. It means vast reserve capacity. It means almost doubled endurance. It means pride in your car. You surely cannot think it wise to sacrifice such things.

*All Promises Came True*

The Super-Six, in official tests, has outperformed all other types of stock cars. In speed, in endurance, in hill-climbing—in flexibility and quick pick-up—it has proved itself supreme.

Now there are 18,000 owners who find themselves the masters of the road.

In beauty, quality and luxury, there is no way known to excel this car. So it marks, in our opinion, about the apex in a high-grade motor car.

We are preparing to build the same model indefinitely. Parts and material are here or ordered for 27,000 more.

Consider these things when you buy a car to keep. The gap between the Super-Six and others is widening month by month. The lack of the Super-Six motor in time will seem a vital lack.

The Super-Six output has quadrupled since April. Men no longer wait months for delivery. So there exists no reason nowadays for not getting the car you want.

*No Feats Like These Ever Before Performed*

HUDSON MOTOR CAR COMPANY, DETROIT, MICHIGAN

▲ Many companies issued elegant limousines; shown here, the 1916 Jeffery.

◀ Hudson debuted the Super-Six for 1916, with a powerful 76-horsepower engine.

▶ Save for the Chesterfield Six, Jefferys were four-cylinder cars, such as this Special Touring model.

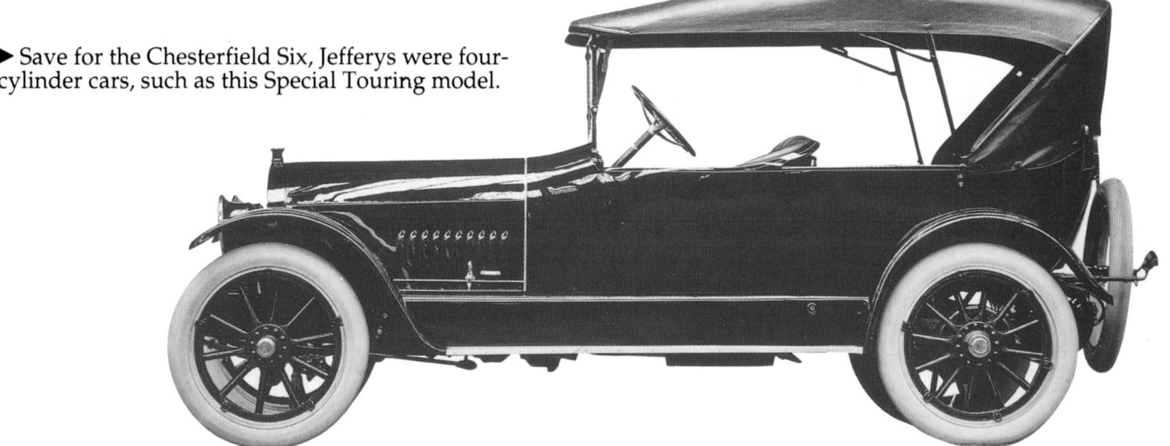

Design trends include slanted windshields and dual-cowl bodies, as well as wider availability of wire wheels

Packard's Twin Six, the first American V-12, is the first engine to use aluminum pistons

Cadillac becomes a Division of General Motors

A new Doble Model C, America's most sophisticated steamer, introduces the "uniflow" principle (steam moving in one direction only)

Ford cuts Model T prices again: The Runabout dips to $345

A lower-cost four-cylinder Chevrolet "490" lists at just $490

Hudson's Super Six is the first American car with a balanced, counterweighted crankshaft

▼ Sleeve-valve engines powered all 1916 Willys-Knights. Wraparound glass added elegance to this $1500 coupe.

▲ By 1916, six-cylinder Reos joined the fours, which rode a shorter 115-inch wheelbase. Prices went from $875 to $1250.

**New Makes: 1916**

Anderson, Bell, Birch, Bour-Davis, Brewster-Knight, Bush, Columbia, Daniels (debut late 1915), Dixie Flyer, Drummond, Economy, Elcar, Elgin, Fergus, H.A.L., Hatfield, Homer-Laughlin, Jordan, Kent, Laurel, Liberty, Maibohm, Marion-Handley, Mecca (standard-size), Moore, Murray, New Era, Riddle, Roamer, Stephens (as a '17 model), Sun, Waco, and Yale

---

Oaklands may have a four- or six-cylinder engine, or a new V-8

Oldsmobile launches a V-8 engine: 246.7-cid and 40 horsepower

Packard abandons its six-cylinder engine (temporarily) after 1916, producing only the Twin Six until 1921

Charles W. Nash leaves General Motors to take over the Thomas B. Jeffery Company, which will soon become Nash Motors Company

William C. Durant succeeds Nash as General Motors president

Alvan Macauley is named president of Packard Motor Car Company

The Federal Road Aid Act, passed by Congress and approved by President Wilson, paves the way for an interstate highway system

▲ For $1040, the '17 Buick D-44 roadster provided a 224-cid, 45-bhp six.

▲ After extensive tests in 1917, the Cadillac V-8 was chosen as a "standard model" for service in WWI.

▲ Not many ads used color in 1917—surely not pink, as in this pitch for the $2480 Chalmers Town Car.

▲ Chevrolet's new 1917 Series D—$1385 for touring car or roadster—boasted a 288-cid ohv V-8 and lush interior. Note the tiny round portholes in the top.

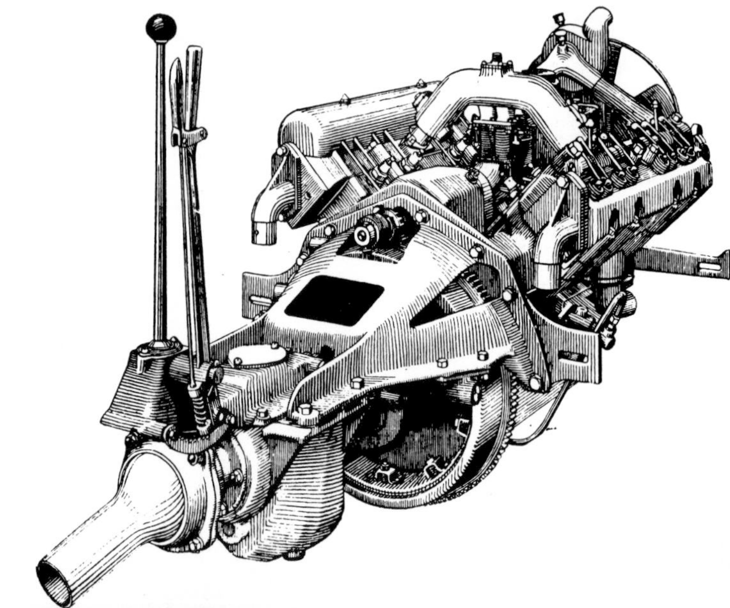

▲ The short-lived 1917-18 90-degree Chevrolet V-8 had vertical overhead valves and detachable cross-flow cylinder heads. Bore/stroke was 3.375 x 4.00, for a displacement of 288 cubic inches and 55 horses. Only 6350 (some say less) were produced. Not until 1955 would Chevy build another V-8. By 1916, Packard offered a V-12 "Twin-Six" with aluminum pistons.

▲ Though not overly impressive to look at, Chevrolet's V-8 was advanced inside—yet it was gone by 1919.

Cross-licensing agreements, which allow for sharing the benefits of patents, take effect throughout the auto industry

United Motors Corporation is established; Alfred P. Sloan, Jr., is named president

**1916 Model Year Production**

|  |  |  |
|---|---|---|
| 1. | Ford | 734,811 |
| 2. | Willys-Overland | 140,111 |
| 3. | Buick | 124,834 |
| 4. | Dodge | 71,400 |
| 5. | Chevrolet | 70,701 |
| 6. | Maxwell | 69,000 |
| 7. | Studebaker | 65,536 |
| 8. | Saxon | 27,800 |

*Some figures are estimated or calender-year*

**1917**

American automakers offer their full cooperation as the U.S. enters World War I on April 6

Auto manufacturers help in the development and production of Liberty aircraft engines

▲ Peak production year for the mid-priced Crow-Elkhart was 1917: 3800 units, touring car or roadster.

▲ The Wisconsin-built "All-Year" Kissel had a detachable top. A V-12 "Double-Six" joined the sixes in 1917.

▲ Continental six-cylinder engines powered the mid-priced 1917 Liberty, built from 1916-23 in Detroit.

▲ A V-8 had been offered, but the 1917 Mitchell ran with a six. A power tire pump came with this Racine-built car.

▲ The driver of a 1917 Premier changed gears via pushbuttons, which actuated a magnetic gearshift.

**New Makes: 1917**

Amco, American Piedmont, Ben Hur, Comet, Commonwealth, Cruiser, Disbrow, Eagle-Macomber Rotary, Fageol, Geronimo, Ghent, Hackett, Harroun, Napoleon, Nash, Nelson, Olympian, Pan-American, Pennsy (debut late 1916), Phianna, Sayers, Seneca, States, Tulsa (as a 1918 model), and Woods Dual Power

---

Trucks prove their worth during the war in Europe

A total of 1,745,792 cars and 128,157 trucks are produced this year

The first true Ford truck is launched, and 39,000 go to the Allied forces by the end of the war

Ford's Model T gets a modern facelift, including crowned fenders; output slips to 622,351 units, market share shrinks to 36 percent

The first Nash car appears in the summer—initially as a renamed Jeffery, then for 1918 as a "true" Nash

Notable new nameplates include Oklahoma-built Geronimo, Harroun (designed by Ray Harroun, winner of the first Indy 500), and the short-lived $12,000 Fageol luxury car

The National Automobile Dealers Association (NADA) is established

▲ Oldsmobile listed sixes and V-8s in 1917, the latter a two-main-bearing, 58-bhp unit. This $1185 Light Eight touring car rode a 120-inch wheelbase.

▲ Studebaker pitted its "Value" against costlier cars in this 1917 ad, but mentioned no rivals. Fours and sixes were offered from $1025 to $2750.

▲ Since 1913, Pierce-Arrows had come with fender-mounted "frog-eye" headlights, but this 1917 limousine has the optional separate drum headlamps.

▲ Illinois/Michigan-based Roamer built cars from 1916 to 1929. The 1917 touring model was available with a 23- or 38-horsepower six.

▲ Cars and trucks shared billing in this 1917 Reo ad, touting the make as "The Gold Standard of Values." The four-cylinder models began at $875.

▲ The V-8 engine powering this 1917 Willys-Knight 88-8 cape-topped Victoria was rated at 65 bhp. A sedan, limo, and town car were sold at $2800-$2900.

---

Henry M. Leland, former head of Cadillac, forms the Lincoln Motor Company

Late in the year, Chevrolet introduces a long-stroke, overhead-valve V-8, the $1550 Series D; only 2781 are built, and it will be extinct by 1919

The Essex Motor Car Company is formed by Hudson in October to produce a light automobile; production will begin late in 1918

Columbia cars feature an exclusive: built-in radiator shutters, developed by Frederick Furber

**1917 Model Year Production**

|  |  |  |
|---|---|---|
| 1. | Ford | 622,351 |
| 2. | Willys-Overland | 130,988 |
| 3. | Buick | 115,267 |
| 4. | Chevrolet | 111,877 |
| 5. | Dodge | 90,000 |
| 6. | Maxwell | 75,000 |
| 7. | Studebaker | 39,686 |
| 8. | Oakland | 33,171 |

*Some figures are estimated or calender-year*

▲ A uniquely bodied $4250 Town Landaulet joined the Cadillac line in 1918, featuring tilting headlights.

▲ General John J. Pershing steps out of a specially built Cadillac sedan. More than 2000 served in World War I.

▲ Still called the 490, Chevrolet's cheapest model jumped to $685 for 1918. Closed cars now had rear-mounted gas tanks; open models kept gravity fuel feed.

---

**1918**

Industry output sinks to 943,436 cars and 227,250 trucks, partly due to steel shortages and production for the military

Shortages of coal and petroleum develop

Americans endure "heatless days" and "gasless Sundays" to conserve fuel, and automobiles are excise-taxed as luxury items

Manufacturers offer various devices to prolong car life, as well as carburetors designed to run on low-grade fuels or kerosene

Women enter factories as men march off to war; the auto industry produces shells, caissons, tanks, anti-aircraft guns, aircraft engines, and military vehicles

Ford's civilian volume drops to 436,000 as the war sends car prices upward

### New Makes: 1918

Cleveland (really a small Chandler), DuPont (which will last through 1932), and a tiny Briggs & Stratton Flyer (a buckboard runabout)

► A 212.3-cid four drove the Dodge Bros. Model 30 roadster, which was priced at $985. Leather upholstery came standard, as did a speedometer. As the fifth-ranked automaker, Dodge produced some 62,000 cars in 1918.

◄ The police had special requirements for their "screenside" Ford Model T trucks, often called Police Wagons.

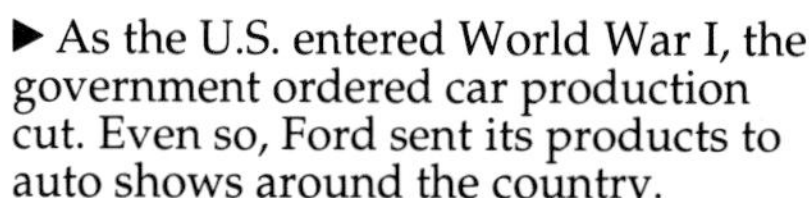

► As the U.S. entered World War I, the government ordered car production cut. Even so, Ford sent its products to auto shows around the country.

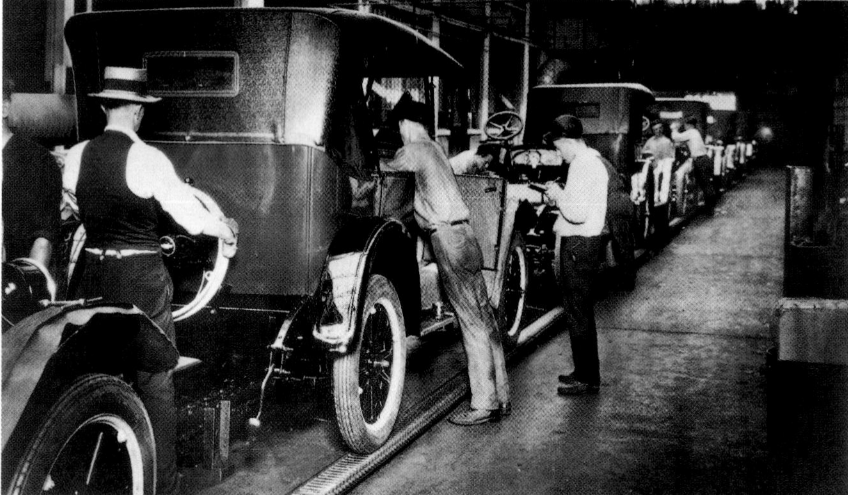

▲ Brand-new Chevrolet touring cars get a final inspection at the assembly plant in Flint, Michigan. Workers often wore hats—even vests—on the job.

▲ Olds said that Pacemaker prices were "cheerfully quoted" by dealers.

---

Despite American participation in the war, the 18th National Automobile Show is held in New York as usual

Borrowing from military designs, four cars come equipped with steel wheels; other cars display straight lines and taller hoods

Nash becomes the world's biggest truck producer, the result of an Army contract for 11,494 four-wheel-drive "Quads"

An all-new Nash arrives, with an overhead-valve six-cylinder engine and three-speed gearbox

The Chicago-built Deering Magnetic features an Entz electric transmission, licensed from the makers of the Owen Magnetic. Various automakers continue to search valiantly for ways to eliminate onerous gearshifting

▲ After offering two four-cylinder series and a six in 1918, Overland issued only a Light Four the next year. Prices rose industry-wide after the Great War.

▲ For business or fun: the 1918 Overland 90 roadster, whose 179-cid Light Four was rated at 32 bhp. Price: $780.

▲ With side pillars removed, Overland's Model 85 Big Four Touring Sedan foretold the hardtop craze of the '50s.

---

Chevrolet becomes a member of the General Motors group

The first short section of highway under the Federal Road Aid Act is finished, in California

White abandons passenger-car production, focuses on trucks

Malcolm Loughead develops four-wheel hydraulic brakes; they will soon see use under the "Lockheed" name

An armistice is signed on November 11, 1918, but car prices fail to drop as anticipated

**1918 Model Year Production**

|  |  |
|---|---|
| 1. Ford | 435,898 |
| 2. Willys-Overland | 88,753 |
| 3. Chevrolet | 88,717 |
| 4. Buick | 77,691 |
| 5. Dodge | 62,000 |
| 6. Maxwell | 34,000 |
| 7. Oakland | 27,757 |
| 8. Oldsmobile | 19,169 |

*Some figures are estimated or calender-year*

▲ All 1919 Buicks, like this $1595 H-44 roadster, used a 60-bhp, 242-cid six.

▲ Buick's heaviest and costliest 1919 model was the $2585 seven-seat H-50.

▲ The most popular '19 Buick was the H-45 touring car; 44,589 were built.

▲ This seven-passenger Cadillac was billed as the "Standard Seven-Passenger Car of the United States Army."

▲ Chevrolet's $1110 FB touring car of 1919 rode a 110-inch chassis and wore flowing "reverse-curve" front fenders.

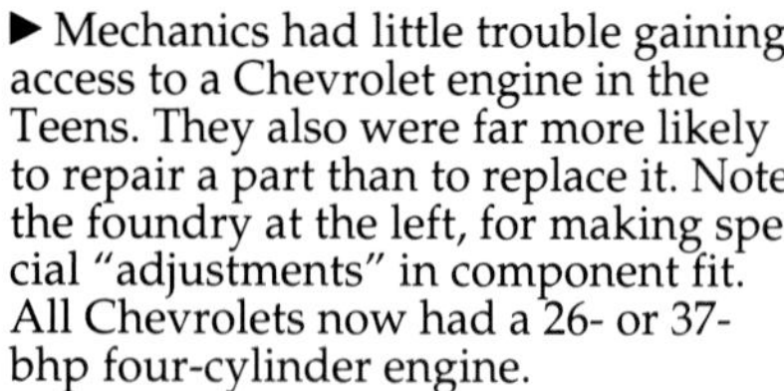

► Mechanics had little trouble gaining access to a Chevrolet engine in the Teens. They also were far more likely to repair a part than to replace it. Note the foundry at the left, for making special "adjustments" in component fit. All Chevrolets now had a 26- or 37-bhp four-cylinder engine.

**1919**

Coal shortages and strikes worry industry leaders, who aren't sure they can meet the surprisingly strong postwar demand for automobiles

Dealers demand new models, but cars are in short supply—partly due to strikes and rising wages, partly because of materials shortages

A total of 1,651,625 passenger cars are built, nearly double the 1918 figure, plus 224,731 trucks

Ford produces 820,445 cars, including the three-millionth Model T

The four-cylinder Essex, the only new car at the 19th National Automobile Show, will almost immediately make the low-cost closed sedan popular

▲ An electric starter finally became standard on Ford's Model T, but only on closed cars like this center-door sedan. The added equipment helped explain a price hike from $645 to $875 for this model in 1919. Demountable rims were also standard on closed models; open cars gained both later.

◀ Essex debuted in 1919, with an F-head four that produced an impressive 55 horses. Seen here is the two-door roadster, which sold for $1595.

---

The Hudson-built Essex employs a four-cylinder F-head engine with rocker-actuated intake valves and 55 bhp

Auburn's "Beauty Six" wears a streamlined body and windshield vent wings

An electric starter finally becomes available on the Ford Model T, as do demountable rims to ease tire-changing

Even now, nine out of 10 cars built are open models, mainly touring cars

**New Makes: 1919**

Argonne Four, Briggs & Stratton, Champion, Cleveland, Climber, DuPont, Essex, Highlander, Lone Star, Meteor, Noma, Pan, Porter, Rock Falls, and Spacke

▶ Though not the most graceful Ford design, the tall $750 coupe had its share of fans—including women—especially with electric starter and demountable rims. Fords with a self-starter also got an instrument panel.

▲ Hudson's rugged Super Six boasted a tougher-yet chassis for 1919.

---

General Motors Acceptance Corporation is formed

After 67 years, Studebaker drops carriage-building to focus solely on motor vehicles

Auto repair shops try a flat-rate pricing system, an idea that will gradually gain acceptance

The first tri-color stoplight is installed, in Detroit

General Motors buys a majority interest in the Fisher Body Company; Nash acquires interest in the Seaman Body Company

Henry Ford announces a cheap (non-Ford) car, a ruse to buy out minority stockholders. After payments of $75 million, the Ford family becomes sole owner of Ford Motor Company, with Edsel named president

▲ After leaving GM, Charles W. Nash bought out Jeffery in 1916 and launched the Nash auto. This $1395 1919 Model 681 was one of four six-cylinder touring models listed.

▲ An Entz electric gearbox, shifted via hand lever, was the foremost feature of the big, expensive Owen Magnetic, "Car of a Thousand Speeds." The firm failed in 1920.

▲ Forerunner of Pontiac, the Oakland was built in this Pontiac, Michigan, plant. Oakland offered a V-8 engine for a while, but all 1919 models were "Sensible Sixes."

▲ Hyped as the "Most Beautiful Car in America," the six-cylinder Paige was known for clean, graceful styling.

▲ This 1919 Oldsmobile four-door sedan was the one-millionth car built by General Motors. Both a Pacemaker V-8 and Sixth-Series Six were marketed at $1395-$1895.

---

Oregon, opening a floodgate, enacts the first state gasoline tax

NADA sponsors the National Motor Vehicle Theft Act to curtail movement of stolen vehicles across state lines

Ralph de Palma drives Packard "905" to a world speed record: 149.8 mph

A Duesenberg racing car with *two* straight-eight engines sets a land-speed record at Daytona Beach, reaching 158 mph

**1919 Model Year Production**

|  |  |  |
|---|---|---|
| 1. | Ford | 820,445 |
| 2. | Chevrolet | 129,118 |
| 3. | Buick | 119,310 |
| 4. | Dodge | 106,000 |
| 5. | Willys-Overland | 80,853 |
| 6. | Oakland | 52,124 |
| 7. | Maxwell | 50,000 |
| 8. | Oldsmobile | 39,042 |

*Some figures are estimated or calender-year*

CHAPTER THREE

# 1920-1929

# ANYTHING GOES

Novelist F. Scott Fitzgerald called it "the greatest, gaudiest spree in history." Newspaperman-philosopher H.L. Mencken coined the term "boobus Americanus" to describe provincial adherents of the booming consumer society.

Either way, this was the "Jazz Age"—a decade of silliness and sophistication; of evangelists and literary giants; of fads from marathon dances to flagpole-sitting. Bobbed-haired "flappers" cavorted to the aptly named shimmy. Prohibition was the law, speakeasies the rule. Broadcast radio was born by 1920, "talking" movies a few years later.

Despite the boisterousness, conformism was the "American Way." Except for the 1920-21 depression, prosperity seemed permanent. Canny politicians promised such goodies as a "car in every garage." Salesmanship ruled the business world, bolstered by small-town boosterism. Money gained unprecedented importance.

An automotive culture was emerging, as the car shifted from frivolous plaything to virtual necessity. Roadside stands, tourist camps, and gasoline stations spread throughout the land. Affluent families began their migration to suburban subdivisions, linked by automobile to downtown businesses. Young blades did their courting in cars. Chain stores were displacing independent retailers.

Ford remained king of the automotive pack, but the faithful flivver wouldn't long remain the vehicle of choice—not for those who could hustle the bucks to select from the fast-unfurling array of consumer goods. By late 1927, something fresh from Ford awaited: the perky Model A.

Alfred P. Sloan ushered in an era of efficiency at General Motors. GM also cleverly pioneered "planned obsolescence," introducing new models designed to make customers dissatisfied with the cars they'd recently loved so much.

Those fortunate enough to possess wealth often elected to flaunt it. What better way than a flamboyant automobile? Duesenberg, Lincoln, Marmon, Cadillac, Pierce-Arrow, Packard Twin Six—for the well-heeled, a cornucopia of choices awaited. And with such expert coachbuilders as Derham and LeBaron to create the bodywork, the fine machinery wore a cloak to match its inner magnificence.

For less-affluent folk, mid-decade saw the founding of Chrysler Corporation, then its addition of Dodge, DeSoto, and Plymouth.

Automotive technology was moving forward. Closed bodies were displacing the open roadster and touring car, using less wood and more steel. Hydraulic brakes began to replace mechanical units, stopping four wheels instead of two. Introduction of synchromesh soon would make gear clashing a distant memory. Driving was becoming easier and safer.

Ned Jordan's essay, "Somewhere West of Laramie," changed the face of automotive advertising, but not everyone was able to join the automotive whirl just yet. Even when the Model T bottomed at $260 in 1925, the average worker earned just $1434 per year. As many as three-fourths of new cars were bought on installments, however, as automakers urged customers to "pay as you ride."

One Indiana resident told researchers Robert and Helen Lynd that the dominant force changing America amounted to "just four letters: A-U-T-O." Others were more direct, insisting they'd "rather do without clothes," or even food, "than give up the car."

All the ballyhoo came crashing down in October 1929, as Wall Street responded to the speculation and overproduction of the Twenties. A slimmed-down America was coming, but the automobile had already cut too deep a path to retreat.

---

**1920**

The "Roaring Twenties" begin, with Prohibition in force and American women now eligible to vote

Postwar fuel shortages are rumored during the year

America now has 191 miles of federally assisted highways

Production for the year totals 1,905,560 passenger cars (a quarter million more than 1919) and 321,789 trucks

Despite the industry gain, Ford output drops by half, yet leads the production race by far (as usual). Dodge, Chevrolet, Buick, and Oakland follow behind

▲ Critics acclaimed the arrival of the revised Type 59 Cadillac for 1920, like this $4750 four-door sedan.

▲ As it had in the Teens, the new Cadillac featured a 314.5-cid V-8 and tilt steering. This is the $3590 roadster.

▲ Except for new reverse-curve front fenders, the Chevrolet 490 and costlier FB changed little for 1920.

▲ A popular extra in the Twenties was the Boyce MotoMeter, a temperature gauge mounted on a radiator cap.

▲ Ray Lampkin sits at the wheel of a stripped Essex, which won a series of southern races in 1920. The Essex four, built by Hudson, debuted in 1919.

THE SATURDAY EVENING POST

This is the Chalmers on which there is a $56,000,000 "Run"

Quality First

First, 18,000 of these cars were built. Then, 10,000 more. And now we have put through a factory work order for 20,000 more.

48,000 in all. A $56,000,000 "run" on this one Chalmers car. Always the demand is for more, more of the 3400 r. p. m. Chalmers. Therefore the model must be continued into next season. There's no time limit set. So you're dead safe in getting a car which has yet to reach its peak of popularity.

The reason for this huge demand is quality. Quality which expresses itself day after day in Performance. Performance made this 3400 r. p. m. Quality Chalmers famous in a week, and now is causing a $56,000,000 "run" on the factory.

If the thing you want is Performance, and if at the same time price interests you, get your name down on the dotted line. Buy Quality and get the benefit of the price which big production enables us to quote, $1090 Detroit, $1475 Walkerville, Ont.

▲ Despite lavish claims, the "quality" Chalmers wouldn't survive past 1923.

▲ Henry Ford—one of the wealthiest men in the world—poses here in his modest office.

The Duesenberg Model A is introduced late in 1920—the first American production car with all-wheel hydraulic brakes and a straight-eight engine (with a single-overhead cam)

The Kurtz Automatic, made in Cleveland, uses a preselector gearshift, with shift levers at the steering wheel

The St. Louis-built Gardner debuts, initially with a four-cylinder Lycoming engine

LaFayette, a V-8 luxury make, goes into production late in the year; prices start at $5025

Slanted windshields are gaining favor, as are wire wheels

Essex ranks as the first low-priced closed car, courtesy of a sedan model added late in 1919

▲ The Indiana-built Lexington survived from 1909-27. This "Convertible Sedan" was among 6000 six-cylinder cars built in 1920. A pair of others ran first and second at Pikes Peak.

▲ At $3400, a 1920 Hudson sedan was fairly costly. The Super Six—with 76 bhp, 289 cid—came in three series.

▲ Note the strapped hood on this Hudson "Pikes Peak" Special. Even on stock Hudsons, bumpers cost extra.

▲ Dubbed the "Sensible Six," Oakland carried a 44-horse, 177-cid engine. Sun visors were common in 1920.

▲ The 1920 Oldsmobile Sixth Series came with a 44-bhp, 177-cid, ohv six; the Thorobred with a 58-bhp V-8.

**New Makes: 1920**

Ace, Adelphia, Alsace, Beggs, Bradley, Cyclomobile, Duesenberg, Economy-Vogue, Ferris, Gardner (late 1919), Gearless Steam, Globe, H.C.S., Huffman, Innes (prototypes), Kelsey, Kenworthy, Kessler, Kurtz Automatic, LaFayette (in August as a '21 model), LaMarne ('19 debut), Leach-Builtwell, Lorraine, Manexall, Marshall, Moller, Parenti, Premocar, R&V Knight, Ranger, Severin, Shaw (Colonial), Simms, Skelton, Southern Six, Stanwood, Texan, and Wasp

▲ Though exposed, the chauffeur got some shelter in this 1920 Packard Twin Six limousine with a 424-cid V-12. Wheelbase could be either 128 or 136 inches.

---

William C. Durant loses control of General Motors for the second and last time; Pierre S. duPont becomes president

Walter P. Chrysler takes charge at Willys-Overland via a two-year contract and a $1-million-per-year salary

Three important industry pioneers depart this earth: John and Horace Dodge, and Elmer Apperson

Heaters are becoming standard, usually built in the car floor to make use of exhaust-gas heat

The General Motors Research Corporation is formed, directed by Charles F. Kettering

A committee of bankers takes over Maxwell's facility

Ford Model T prices are cut drastically—averaging $148—in September, but sales fail to rise

▲ A narrower, taller radiator marked the 1921 Buicks, here a $3295 Model 50. It used a 60-bhp, 242-cid six.

▲ The first Checker Cabs were built in Illinois in 1921, a variation of the Commonwealth, which was gone by 1922.

▲ Chevrolet production dropped to 130,855 units in 1921. A firm of engineers advised GM to drop the make.

▲ Chevrolet's first *Saturday Evening Post* ad touted the 490 Touring Car.

▲ Traffic congestion was a growing problem, as this 1921 scene on New York City's Fifth Avenue reveals. Some 4500 vehicles used the Avenue every hour.

▲ Essex was a lower-priced, four-cylinder mate to Hudson. This 1921 Essex roadster sold for $1595.

**New Makes: 1921**

Adria, Ambassador, Automatic Electric, Birmingham, Bowman, Carroll Six, Checker Cab, Colonial, Commodore, Curtis (debut during 1920), Drake, Driggs, Durant, Fox, Fremont, Friend, Hamlin-Holmes (experimental), Handley-Knight, Hanover, Heine-Velox, Henney, Lincoln, McGill (4WD), Merit, Murray-Mac Six, Northway, Peters, Raleigh, Rees, Reese Aero-Car (prototype), Rodgers, Rolls-Royce, Romer, Sheridan, Spencer, Sperling, Washington, Wills St. Claire, Winther, and Wizard (debut in late 1920)

**1920 Model Year Production**

| Rank | Make | Units |
|---|---|---|
| 1. | Ford | 806,040 |
| 2. | Chevrolet | 146,243 |
| 3. | Dodge | 141,000 |
| 4. | Buick | 115,176 |
| 5. | Willys-Overland | 105,025 |
| 6. | Studebaker | 48,831 |
| 7. | Hudson/Essex | 45,937 |
| 8. | Chandler | 45,000 |

*Some figures are estimates*

**1921**

Auto sales sag badly due to the brief, but serious, economic depression

Total passenger-car production dips to 1,468,067; truck output sinks by nearly half, to 148,052

Big price cuts stimulate Ford Model T sales, helped by the eventual upturn in the U.S. economy

Ford production more than doubles to a record-setting 1,275,618 units; market share triples to 61.5 percent

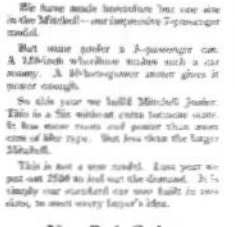

▲ Built in Wisconsin, the six-cylinder Mitchell adopted this ill-fated, sloped-down front in 1920, then turned out a quick restyle for '21.

▲ Priced at $395 early in 1921, the Ford Model T Runabout dropped to $370—then $325. Sales lagged well behind the roomier $450 touring car.

▲ Angular styling marks this 1921 New Improved Essex Cabriolet, which rode a 108.5-inch wheelbase. Its 179-cid, F-head four developed 55 horses.

▲ Cars didn't have to be costly to wear custom-built bodywork. Bodies for Ford's Depot Hack came from outside suppliers. A Model T chassis alone cost $360 ($455 for heavy-duty).

► Ford's Center Door Sedan dropped sharply in price, from $975 in 1920 to $795—then lower yet. Rear-quarter panels were now an integral part of the bodysides, not split in two.

---

Chevrolet output runs a distant second, followed by Buick, Dodge, and Studebaker

Lincoln Model L automobiles go on sale—after a September 1920 introduction—powered by an 81-bhp, 357.8-cid V-8. The connection to Ford comes later

Henry M. Leland, who'd launched the first Cadillac, is responsible for the new Lincoln, selling for $4600 in touring-car form

Durant Motors is organized by William C. Durant after his retirement from the General Motors board; the four-cylinder Durant car debuts

The new Wills St. Claire uses an automatic back-up light in conjunction with the taillight. Its advanced V-8 engine has an overhead-cam, with extensive use of molybdenum and aluminum

▲ A padded roof and side windows made this 1921 Nash seven-seat touring car, with a 249-cid six, look almost impenetrable. Four-cylinder models debuted this year.

► A slightly smaller 234-cid V-8 went into the $1825 Model 47 Oldsmobile in 1921. Also new: a four-cylinder Olds.

▲ One of the best known—and most coveted—sporty autos was the Stutz Bearcat, still with right-hand drive in 1921. A 361-cid four gave lots of oomph.

► Walter P. Chrysler had taken charge of the Willys empire for a time, but John North Willys regained control. A $2195 Model 20 sleeve-valve Willys-Knight touring car for 1921 is shown.

---

Checker Cab goes into production; there had been an earlier version in 1920 made by Commonwealth Motors

Glass wind wings, long popular in Southern California, are introduced in the East

Hydraulic brakes are installed on several makes

Nickel-plating appears on some radiators and headlamps

Cadillac carburetors gain thermostatic control

Three consulting engineers join forces to design a car: Fred M. Zeder, Owen R. Skelton, and Carl Breer. Chrysler will soon be one of their products

William S. Knudsen leaves Ford for Chevrolet, in the wake of policy battles with Henry Ford

▲ Four-cylinder models returned to Buick in 1922, among them this $975 Model 22-4-35 five-passenger touring car with a new 170-cid, 35/40-bhp four; 22,521 were built.

▲ Buick's overhead-valve, 242-cid six-cylinder engine with multi-disc clutch powered the $1495 22-6-44 roadster. New sport roadster and touring models had wire wheels.

▲ Closed coupes, like this $1475 Buick Model 22-4-136, kept a tall profile. Some 2225 were sold. Four-cylinder Buicks rode a 109-inch wheelbase; sixes, 118/124-inch.

▲ At $2435, this Buick Model 22-6-47 six-cylinder sedan (4878 built) had many rivals in the mid-price closed-car field, including Auburn, Case, Chalmers, Elcar, and Reo.

▲ Buick's Model 22-4-37 four-door sedan cost $1650, versus $975 for a touring car, so only 3118 were sold. Buick also built commercial vehicles, but they wouldn't last.

▲ Open touring cars, such as this $1735 Buick 22-6-49, continued to sell well, but their era soon would end as Americans discovered the comforts of closed bodies.

---

Warren G. Harding is the first American President to ride to inauguration in an automobile, a Packard Twin Six

The $19 million General Motors Building opens, on Grand Avenue in Detroit

The nation's first drive-in restaurant opens—in Dallas, Texas

Detroit police try synchronized traffic lights and raised-platform safety zones

Tetraethyl lead is proven effective as a gasoline additive by Dr. Thomas Midgley, Jr.

**1921 Model Year Production**

| | |
|---|---|
| 1. Ford | 1,275,618 |
| 2. Chevrolet | 130,855 |
| 3. Buick | 82,930 |
| 4. Dodge | 81,000 |
| 5. Studebaker | 65,023 |
| 6. Willys-Overland | 48,016 |
| 7. Hudson/Essex | 27,143 |
| 8. Nash | 20,850 |

*Some figures are estimates*

▲ A year after this 1922 taxi was built by Checker Cab Manufacturing Company in Illinois, the firm moved to production facilities in Kalamazoo, Michigan.

▲ Big price cuts—to $510 for the 490 roadster—boosted 1922 Chevy sales.

▲ Not every home had one yet, but a Westinghouse radio could be installed in the 1922 Chevrolet for $200. The antenna covered the entire sedan roof.

---

**1922**

Passenger-car output rises smartly to 2,274,185 units; trucks total 269,991

Model T Ford output nears 1.2 million—over half the U.S. total

Far behind, with 152,653 units built, is Dodge; next come Chevrolet and Buick

The roadster-coupe—a roadster body with a fixed top, intended for business use—appears at the National Automobile Show

Rickenbacker, a new make built in Detroit, is named for the racing driver and World War I flying ace

The budget-priced Star ($319 for a roadster) is launched by William C. Durant, ready to rival Ford's Model T; 100,000 are produced in less than a year

▲ Wooden station wagon-type bodies generally came from outside suppliers. This 1922 Dodge hailed from J.T. Cantrell & Company. Called a Suburban, it had three doors and three rows of seats, the rear units removable.

▲ This Essex cabriolet looked sharp in 1922, but the big news was the new coach—with low height and an equally low $1245 price tag, it speeded the demise of open cars.

▲ As before, a 55-bhp, F-head four also powered the '22 Essex touring car.

Dagmar serves as a sporty companion to the Crawford; its home is Hagerstown, Maryland

A mid-priced six, the new Jewett is issued as a subsidiary of the Paige-Detroit Motor Car Company

A one-piece windshield is installed on the short-lived Earl touring car, which is basically a reworked Briscoe

Balloon tires are introduced

Various carburetors begin to breathe through air cleaners

Nash adopts rubber mounts to reduce engine vibration

Fuel gauges appear on several instrument panels

▲ Three six-cylinder and V-12 Haynes series vied for sales in 1922. Shown is a $1785 Model 55 touring, with 50-bhp six. Haynes would survive into 1925.

▲ Introduced a year earlier by Henry Leland, the Lincoln became a Ford product in 1922. Under the hood was a 357.8-cid V-8 rated at 90 horsepower.

◀ Henry Ford (*left*) and Henry M. Leland stand behind their sons, Edsel and Wilfred, as Henry purchases the ailing Lincoln Motor Company on February 4, 1922, for $8 million. Edsel Ford was named president.

---

Studebaker employs molybdenum steel

Ford Model T prices are cut again; the touring car dips as low as $298

Ford buys the Lincoln Motor Company out of receivership for $8 million

The Essex closed two-door coach sells for as little as $1245—just $200 more than the touring car

Durant buys Locomobile

Charles M. Schwab takes the helm at Stutz; Harry Stutz had left the firm in 1919

William S. Knudsen serves as vice-president in charge of operations at Chevrolet

▲ Beneath the hood of this $1045 Nash Model 41 sat a four-cylinder engine, but Nash also produced sixes in 1922.

▲ Three-seat Oldsmobile coupes, with a four or V-8, had this angled windshield. Olds output for '22: 21,499.

▶ Launched in 1921, the Wills Sainte Claire made ample use of molybdenum. Perfectionism demanded by C. Harold Wills led to its demise in '27.

**New Makes: 1922**

American Steamer, Bay State, Coats Steam Car, Commander (prototype), Corinthian, Crane-Simplex, D.A.C. (Detroit Air Cooled), Dagmar, Earl, Falcon, Farner, Frontenac, Goodspeed, Gray, Gregory (debut during 1920), Harrigan (prototype), Jewett, McCurdy, Metropolitan, Richelieu, Rickenbacker, St. Louis, Star, Stratton-Bliss, Tarkington, Trask Steam, Waltham, and Wharton

▶ Willys-Knight sales rose in the early '20s. The L.F. Kuehne Co. of Chicago produced a taxi body for this 1922 Model 20A, on a 118-inch wheelbase. Willys claimed the four-cylinder sleeve-valve engine "improves with use. . . . Carbon only makes it better."

---

Henry Ford publishes *My Life and Work,* which is translated worldwide

About 73 percent of cars are now bought on time, but Henry Ford still disapproves of installment payments

George Selden dies; he claimed to have developed the first automobile, but lost his patent suit to Henry Ford

An electrically interlocked traffic signal system is installed in Houston, Texas

Car insurance policies, formerly based on purchase price, are revised to reflect actual values

The first suburban shopping center opens near St. Louis

NADA starts used-car value study, at government request

▲ A big car with an old name: the 1923 Apperson V-8, here the $2620 touring, had a remote-controlled gearshift.

▲ The sleeker '23 Buicks sported rounded window frames and crowned fenders. This four-cylinder coupe cost $1175.

▲ Six-cylinder Buicks rode a 118- or 124-inch wheelbase. This $2195 Model 23-6-50 sedan saw 10,279 copies built.

▲ Cole, previously known as the Aero Eight, built just 1522 cars for 1923. This $2685 touring car had an 80-bhp V-8.

▼ In addition to this low-cost ($865) four-cylinder model, Buick added a big-chassis roadster in 1923, with the 242-cid six-cylinder engine. More than 201,000 Buicks were built in calendar-year '23.

An Oldsmobile sets a record by traveling 1000 miles in 15 hours, a 67-mph average

Elwood Haynes earns the John Scott Medal for work in stainless steel and chrome iron

| 1922 Model Year Production | |
|---|---|
| 1. Ford | 1,147,028 |
| 2. Dodge | 152,653 |
| 3. Chevrolet | 138,932 |
| 4. Buick | 123,152 |
| 5. Studebaker | 105,005 |
| 6. Willys-Overland | 95,410 |
| 7. Durant makes | 55,300 |
| 8. Maxwell/Chalmers | 44,811 |

*Some figures are estimates*

**1923**

Industry production zips upward again, to 3,624,717 passenger cars and 409,295 trucks

More than two million Fords are built this year, including more than 1.8 million cars—half the industry total

▲ All Type 61 Cadillacs for 1922-23 rode a 132-inch wheelbase. Horns went underhood. Cadillac's immodest crest still proclaimed it the "Standard of the World."

▲ DeLuxe Chevrolets, introduced during 1923, came with disc wheels, bumpers, step plates, and other fancy extras. Wind wings were popular on open models.

▼ Kettering's "Copper-Cooled" (air-cooled) engine was to replace the regular Chevy four, but the disastrous overhead-valve, 134.7-cid four overheated severely.

◀ The Dort Motor Car Company was a 1915 outgrowth of the Flint Road Car Company, formed in 1886 by Josiah Dort and William Crapo Durant. By 1923, nearly 100,000 Dorts had been produced. The '23 Dort Sport Touring ran with a 45-bhp six. The example seen here, one of four known to exist, was in storage for 55 years.

---

Chevrolet output increases to 323,182 cars—well above third-place Buick's volume. Willys-Overland ranks fourth

The fixed-top phaeton (with removable or lowerable windows) and closed five-seat car are popular at the 23rd National Automobile Show

Dodge is first to offer all-steel closed bodies (except for the roof), developed by Edward G. Budd

Short-lived Eagle prototype and show cars appear, made by Durant

The Durant organization launches the Flint nameplate, referred to by some as the "junior Locomobile" (another Durant-owned company)

The Doble Steamer is revived after a several-year absence

▲ The 1923 Essex coach carried the last of the company's four-cylinder engines: 179-cid and 55 horsepower. At $1145, a coach cost just $100 more than a touring car.

▲ By 1923, the Dorris was a big, powerful car, with a 132-inch wheelbase and 377-cid six. Dorris survived from 1906-26, building about 3100 cars and 900 trucks total.

▲ Restyling gave Ford's 1923 Model T a lower profile with sloped windshield.

The first production station wagon, styled at the factory, is offered by Star, Durant's low-priced car line

Jordan Motor Car Company changes the pattern of automobile advertising with themes such as "Somewhere West of Laramie. . ."

Four-wheel brakes, power wipers, and foot-controlled dimmer switches become standard on several makes

Most cars wear drum-type headlights, introduced on a few models in 1922

The Springfield Body Corporation offers factory-installed car radios

Ethyl gasoline, developed by the General Motors Research Corporation, goes on sale in February; Standard Oil Company agrees to distribute the fuel

**New Makes: 1923**

Barley, Cardway, Courier, Deemster, Delling Steamer, Detroit Steamer, Eagle, Flint, Harris Six, Leon Rubay, MacDonald, Princeton, Rollin, Sekine, and Sterling-Knight

◄ Differences between Hudson's 1923 seven-passenger phaeton (*left*) and Speedster aren't evident at a glance. Both Super Six models gave excellent performance with a 75-bhp, 289-cid six. They rode a 125.5-inch wheelbase.

▲ Peak year for Hupmobile's Series R was 1923, when 38,279 cars were built. This Special Roadster Model RRS sported nickel plating and drum headlights.

▲ Charles Nash initiated the luxurious LaFayette, shown here in 1923 touring sedan form. This 4200-pound Model 134 with its 348-cid V-8 engine cost a whopping $5500.

▲ Edsel and Eleanor Ford enjoy their Lincoln. Model L wheelbase grew to 136 inches in 1923. Sales rose, too.

▲ The 1923 Moon Sport Touring Model 6-58 cost $1985 and rode a 128-inch chassis. Lesser Moons were also sold.

▲ When "Cannon Ball" Baker drove this Olds coast-to-coast in 12½ days, all gears except high had been removed.

---

Floor-type heaters are losing favor, due to the dangers of exhaust gases

Buick produces its one-millionth car

Nash introduces a vacuum-powered windshield wiper motor; Buick and Cadillac follow suit in 1924-25

The Model T Ford is restyled with front-hinged doors; "Fordor" and "Tudor" sedans debut

Ford announces a weekly purchase plan; over 300,000 cars are sold this way in two years. The customer gets the car only after the full amount is paid, in $5 installments

▲ Wartime ace Captain Eddie Rickenbacker, with the car that bore his name and featured a dual-flywheel engine.

▲ Challenging Ford, William Durant built 100,000 Stars—like this $443 1923 touring car—during the first year.

◀ This square-rigged 1923 Nash Model 694 seven-passenger sedan listed at $2190. It rode a long 127-inch chassis, and like most cars of the day, placed the rear passengers atop the axle.

▼ Willys-Knight was one of various makes enlisted for taxi or limousine service, with special bodies mounted. Several other manufacturers had also tried the Knight sleeve-valve engine, but none lasted as long as Willys.

Ford advertising resumes after a six-year lapse; ads push quality and price—as low as $295 for the touring car

Chevrolet abandons its larger four-cylinder engine, but keeps the 170.9-cid version through 1928

Alfred P. Sloan, Jr., is named president of General Motors

Walter P. Chrysler, chairman of Maxwell-Chalmers Corp., joins with Zeder, Skelton, Breer Engineering Company to develop the Chrysler automobile

Participants in the Chrysler venture include Fred M. Zeder, Owen Skelton, Carl Breer, and B.E. Hutchinson

Roy D. Chapin retires as Hudson's president, becomes chairman of the board

▲ Bigger and roomier, this '24 Buick Model 50 six saw 9561 copies built.

▲ Four-wheel brakes went into Buicks and several other makes for 1924.

▲ New for 1924 was Chevrolet's Coach—a bargain at $695. Some DeLuxe models had disc wheels and bumpers. Ads promoted "economical transportation."

▲ Hydraulic brakes and a high-compression six marked the new 1924 Chrysler.

E.G. "Cannon Ball" Baker drives an Oldsmobile cross-country in 12½ days using nothing but high gear; refueling is accomplished by raising the rear wheels off the ground to keep the engine running

**1923 Model Year Production**

| | |
|---|---|
| 1. Ford | 1,831,128 |
| 2. Chevrolet | 323,182 |
| 3. Buick | 201,572 |
| 4. Willys-Overland | 196,038 |
| 5. Durant makes | 172,000 |
| 6. Dodge | 151,000 |
| 7. Studebaker | 146,238 |
| 8. Hudson/Essex | 88,914 |

*Some figures are estimates*

**1924**

For the first time, all cars at the National Automobile Show have gasoline engines

Maxwell-Chalmers Corp. introduces the Chrysler, with four-wheel hydraulic brakes and a high-compression (4.7:1) engine

▲ Essex adopted a longer, lower profile for '24, though not quite as radical as this prototype. A tiny 130-cid L-head six (bhp not released) replaced the tough 180-cid F-head four.

▲ The little Essex six was quickly bored and stroked to 144.5 cid and an estimated 40 horses. Note the "suicide" (rear-hinged) door—common in 1924—on this $975 coach.

▲ An integral deck replaced the removable "turtleback" on Ford's new five-window coupe. Demountable rims were standard. Closed cars had rotary window regulators.

▲ In Speedster form, a Model T Ford looked swift—even with its top up. Sloped windshields gave all open Fords a sporty nature. Note the fuel tank behind the seat.

◀ Tough and ready, a Ford Model T (or truck TT) chassis could be ordered stripped or with a cab, able to accept a variety of special bodies from myriad outside suppliers. Ford also built its own steel bodies.

**New Makes: 1924**
Balboa (prototype), Chrysler, Kleiber, Luxor, S&S, Schuler, and Traveler

---

The initial six-cylinder Chrysler 70 draws admiration at the 1924 show; features include a replaceable-cartridge oil filter and air cleaner, plus instruments grouped behind an oval glass panel

Passenger-car output dips to 3,185,881 units; trucks rise slightly to 416,659

Model T production slips to 1.75 million, yet Ford hangs on to half the market

Dodge ousts Buick from third place in output; Chevrolet volume drops sharply, but still retains second spot

Oakland cars are now sprayed with quick-drying Duco lacquer

▶ Franklin "Desert Camels" relax at Scotty's Furnace Creek Ranch in Death Valley, California, in May 1924. Treks through the blazing California-Nevada desert tested the stamina of the air-cooled engine—and passengers. Later Franklins adopted fake radiators.

▼ The last LaFayette was built in '24, shown here in dapper two-seat, $5000 roadster form. Total 1921-24 output: 2267. Nash clung to the name, and would use it again in the '30s.

▲ Two Nash series were sold in 1924: a six-cylinder 690 and four-cylinder 40 (final year for fours). Landau bars, as on this Brougham, decorated many '20s cars.

▲ Only six-cylinder engines went into 1924 Oldsmobiles: 42-bhp and 169-cid. This 30-B Series coupe, listing at $1075, attracted 8839 customers. Note the tire chains.

---

Packard issues a 357.8-cid, L-head straight-eight, the first one to be truly mass-produced, and adopts four-wheel mechanical brakes

A straight-eight engine is introduced by Hupmobile, and also offered by Auburn, Duesenberg, Hupmobile, Jordan, Rickenbacker, and others

The last four-cylinder Buicks are produced; only sixes will be offered until 1931. Four-wheel mechanical brakes are introduced

Oakland drops its overhead-valve six, replacing it with a new L-head of the same dimensions. A single-disc clutch replaces the cone unit

Balloon tires and four-wheel brakes are standard on a number of makes

Twin-filament headlight bulbs appear

Baked-enamel paint is used on various low-priced automobiles

▲ A 191-cid six-cylinder engine replaced the four for Standard Series Buicks in 1925, but this $2125 Master Six coupe, which sold 6799 copies, kept its 255-cid six.

▲ New "enclosed" touring cars, with a permanent top and sliding windows, joined the '25 Buick line. This $1475 Master Six was one of 160,411 Buicks built for the year.

▲ In 1925, the $735 Chevrolet closed Coach, with wooden wheels and balloon tires, was a popular family car.

► Chevrolet ran color ads touting "Economy" in 1925. New quick-drying Duco paint helped boost output to 306,479 units. The year brought a new radiator and cadet visor, and a single-disc clutch replaced the old cone unit.

▲ The Aluminum Corporation of America joined with Pierce-Arrow in 1925 to produce 10 experimental aluminum cars, powered by a 75-horsepower six.

Ford builds its 10-millionth automobile, begins production of factory accessories

Ford prices drop to $265 for the Runabout, $295 for the Touring. The average employed American earns $1293 annually

William S. Knudsen is named Chevrolet's president

Nash Motors purchases LaFayette Motors Corp., then drops it after only 2267 cars have been built in three and a half years

Chandler adopts a "traffic transmission" with constant-mesh gearing, a forerunner of the forthcoming synchromesh

The General Motors Proving Ground is completed at Milford, Michigan

▲ Body meets chassis at the body drop in a Chevrolet assembly plant.

◀ This Series R one-ton truck, with vestibule front delivery body, was the 100,000th Chevrolet assembled at Chevy's Janesville, Wisconsin, plant.

Two Millionth Chevrolet

▶ Chevrolet's two-millionth car was a coach. Assistant general sales manager C.E. Dawson (*left*) poses with Chevy president William S. Knudsen.

**New Makes: 1925**
Ajax, Barbarino, Bauer (taxi), Diana, Julian (experimental), Majestic (taxi), and Mayfair

◀ Workers are busy with the new Chevrolet engine for 1925. Series K looked similar to the prior F, but was better mechanically. The engine had a new block, heavier crankshaft, drop-forged rods with bigger bearings, and an enclosed flywheel.

---

Ethyl Corporation is formed by GM and Standard Oil of New Jersey. Ethyl (leaded) "anti-knock" gasoline goes on sale

The Winton Company drops out of auto production, concentrates on diesel engines

**1924 Model Year Production**

|  |  |
|---|---|
| 1. Ford | 1,720,795 |
| 2. Chevrolet | 264,868 |
| 3. Dodge | 193,861 |
| 4. Willys-Overland | 163,000 |
| 5. Buick | 160,411 |
| 6. Hudson/Essex | 133,950 |
| 7. Durant makes | 111,000 |
| 8. Studebaker | 105,387 |

*Some figures are estimates*

**1925**

Passenger-car output rises to 3,735,171; truck volume reaches 530,659 units

Ford output skids to 1,669,847 cars, but truck output sets a record at 268,411

▶ Americans weren't ready for compacts in 1925, but Fabio Sergardi (*at wheel*) designed this experimental small car for the General Motors Research Staff. Though considered for export, it was never produced.

▲ As elsewhere, closed bodies gained favor at Ford. For example, this $580 Tudor sedan attracted 195,001 buyers.

▲ Even though the '25 Ford Fordor sold for $660—more than twice the price of a touring car—81,050 were sold.

▶ Ford dealers grew worried as Chevrolet and other rivals gained strength. Even with a weekly payment plan available to bolster sales, many had trouble meeting sales quotas. A mid-1925 facelift didn't help much.

The 25-millionth American motor vehicle is produced

More closed cars than open models are sold this year, a first

Safety and comfort draw customers: Most automobiles now boast four-wheel brakes and balloon tires, and many even carry standard bumpers

Companion makes appear: the $865-$995 Ajax is introduced by Nash, the $2000 Diana by Moon, but neither will last long

Ajax has a six-cylinder L-head engine rated at 40 horsepower

Lighter steering is featured on several car models with balloon tires, including the new Diana, which aims at women drivers

▲ Landau bars had no function, but they looked good on a 1925 Hudson Special.

▲ Model 48, Locomobile's biggest 1925 car, had a 142-inch chassis, 525-cid six, and $7400 price tag for the Sportif.

▲ In addition to this Model 48, Locomobile offered a new Junior Eight, on a shorter 124-inch wheelbase. Built in Bridgeport, Connecticut, the marque survived into 1929.

◀ Angular styling didn't harm the appeal of the Nash Special Six, which replaced the four-cylinder line. This Model 133 two-door sedan, with its 207-cid engine, cost $1225. Also new: a cheaper Ajax series.

---

The trend toward straight-eight engines is evident at the 25th National Automobile Show

Other notable trends include rumble seats, one-piece windshields, mohair upholstery, and crank-type window lifts

The last Stanley Steamers are smaller and cheaper, with hydraulic brakes; the well-known make fades away after 1925

Quick-drying synthetic pyroxylin paints permit wide color choices—and can be sprayed and baked

A Fisher ventilating windshield for GM cars retracts vertically, allowing a watertight seal when closed and no-draft ventilation when opened

A chain of national drive-it-yourself (rental-car) stations is established

▲ Oakland had been the first car to adopt new Duco paint with its 1924 "True Blue" model. A larger 185-cubic-inch six powered this $1095 Greater Six roadster in 1925.

▲ No, reel-to-reel tape recorders hadn't been invented yet. Performance of this 1925 Model 30 Oldsmobile coach is being evaluated by a primitive "fifth wheel."

◀ Conventional poppet-valve engines powered the Willys-Overland, which cost considerably less than Willys-Knight models. This $850 Overland Model 91 Standard sedan featured a 154-cid four and 100-inch wheelbase. The Model 93 sixes rode a longer 113-inch chassis. Automakers were starting to worry about market saturation.

▲ Following years of sleeve-valve fours, Willys-Knight added a six-cylinder version, with 60 horses and 236 cid. Shown here is the $1750 Model 66 roadster for 1925.

▲ Both a coupe and a coupe-sedan were listed by Willys-Knight. So were touring cars, roadsters, sedans, and Broughams. Total Willys sales in 1925 topped 200,000.

---

Auto accessories marketed at this time include stop signals, mirrors, ashtrays, cigar lighters, heat indicators, locking radiator caps, trunk racks, all-weather tops for touring cars, balloon tire jacks

The "improved Ford" gets a major facelift during the summer, the first since 1917

Model T prices are cut again, to an all-time low: $260 for the Runabout, $290 for the Touring car

Lawrence P. Fisher is named president of the Cadillac Motor Car Division

Fisher Body acquires the Pennsylvania-based Fleetwood custom-body firm

▲ Buick's six was boosted to 75 bhp for 1926. This $1795 Master Six four-passenger coupe sold 10,028 copies.

▲ To lengthen the life of this $1925 Master Six Brougham Touring Sedan, Buick now fitted oil and air filters.

▲ This 1927 ad proclaimed that the Chevy Sport Cabriolet was in "vogue."

▲ In 1926, Chevy touted "Economical Transportation," showing the coach.

▲ This Landau coupe, priced at a modest $645, helped push total Chevrolet production to 588,962 units for 1926.

▲ Chevy's $510 roadster—with rear storage—challenged Ford for sales.

▲ Accessories—such as a front bumper, step plates, and MotoMeter (temperature gauge)—added dash to the '26 Chevrolet Superior two-passenger coupe.

---

GM acquires the Yellow Truck and Coach Manufacturing Company

Maxwell-Chalmers Corp. is reorganized as Chrysler Corp.

Motor buses are in use by over 150 electric railway systems across the country

Auto pioneer Elwood Haynes dies

Uniform markings for federally aided highways are adopted: even numbers for east/west roads, odd for north/south

A trade paper, *Automobile Daily News,* is established and commences publication

▲ Walter P. Chrysler (*right*) and C. Walrich pose with the new, distinctively styled, $2885 Chrysler Imperial E-80 roadster, which paced the Indianapolis 500 race in 1926.

▲ New Hudson-built steel coach and sedan bodies and a nickel-plated radiator highlighted the '26 Essex, here the $735 coach. Output this year totaled 157,247 units.

▲ This stunt illustrated the Essex's rugged construction, particularly the piano-hinge doors adopted late in '26.

▲ Edsel Ford sits at the wheel of the 15-millionth Ford, built in May 1926; his father Henry sits alongside.

▲ Closed Fords now sported a nickel-plated radiator shell. This $660 Fordor ($545 after May) posted 102,732 sales.

▲ Accessories, like wire wheels, added pizzazz to the $345 Ford Model T Runabout, which appealed to 342,575 buyers.

---

Ralph Mulford drives a Chandler automobile 1000 miles in a record-setting 689 minutes

The Lincoln Highway is completed—the first transcontinental highway

Miller front-wheel-drive racing cars appear at the Indianapolis 500 race, foretelling a front-drive production model of 1929

**1925 Model Year Production**

| | |
|---|---|
| 1. Ford | 1,669,847 |
| 2. Chevrolet | 306,479 |
| 3. Hudson/Essex | 269,474 |
| 4. Willys-Overland | 215,000 |
| 5. Dodge | 201,000 |
| 6. Buick | 192,100 |
| 7. Studebaker | 133,104 |
| 8. Chrysler/Maxwell | 132,343 |

*Some figures are estimates*

▲ A Brougham with Biddle & Smart body joined Hudson's line in mid-1925.

▲ Hudson was durable and its 76-horse Super Six was fast, so a $1650 seven-passenger sedan made sense as a taxi.

▲ Two new Hupmobile series arrived for '26: A-1 Six on a 114-inch wheelbase, and E-2 Eight on a 125-inch chassis.

► Despite little change, Oldsmobile sold 53,015 cars for '26, among them 3296 copies of this $990 landau coupe. Reo, the second marque started long before by Ransom E. Olds, continued to turn out six-cylinder passenger cars and soon would launch the fast and impressive Flying Cloud.

**1926**

U.S. vehicle output remains relatively stable at 3,692,317 passenger cars and 608,617 trucks

Chevrolet edges closer to Ford in the production battle, but is still far behind with 547,724 cars to Ford's 1,426,612

Narrower windshield pillars improve visibility of various models displayed at the 26th National Automobile Show

The new Pontiac, first seen at the National Automobile Show, is a low-priced companion to the Oakland, but is offered only as a closed coupe or sedan

Rubber mounts hold Pontiac's six-cylinder L-head engine in place

▲ In addition to the cars issued under its own name, Nash offered the lower-priced Ajax (*right*) for one year only. It was replaced by the Nash Light Six by 1927, with the same 40-bhp, 170-cid L-head engine. "True" Nashes used overhead-valve sixes.

◄ The first Pontiacs rolled off the line in 1926, lower-priced mates to the long-established Oakland. This Pontiac is enduring a test run inside the plant, its front tires blocked. Pontiacs featured a 40-bhp, 187-cid L-head six and rode a 110-inch wheelbase.

▲ Only a coach (*shown*) and coupe, both $825, were offered in Pontiac's first year. Sales were an amazing 76,742.

▲ Landau bars were included with the '26 Pontiac coupe, which also featured cowl lamps and automatic wipers.

Both Oakland and Pontiac models are produced through 1931, with different bodies and engines

The Willys-built Whippet debuts in the fall as the smallest American automobile; it has a 134-cid, four-cylinder engine

The Maxwell nameplate disappears; the four-cylinder car is renamed Chrysler 58 and marketed alongside the six-cylinder Model 70

Chrysler's new distinctively styled, higher-priced Imperial ($2645-$3695) carries a more powerful six-cylinder motor and bullet-shaped headlamps

Stutz adopts an overhead-cam "Vertical Eight" engine with silent chain drive, automatic tension adjustment, and 92 horsepower

▲ All '26 Willys-Knights had a six: 178 or 236 cid, 53 or 60 horses. This is a $2295 Great Six sedan. In the '20s, Willys generally sold more than 50,000 Knights a year.

▲ Five- and seven-passenger touring cars, both $1750, were offered in the Model 66 Willys-Knight line, on a 126-inch wheelbase. The Model 70 rode a 113-inch chassis.

▲ The Willys-Knight Model 70, here the $1525 roadster, was new for 1926.

▲ The '27 Buick Standard Six two-door sedan had 63 horses. At $1195, it was Buick's best-seller: 33,190 units.

▲ Buick's engines for 1927 were hyped as "vibrationless beyond belief." Here, the $1275 coupe; 7178 were built.

Cadillac introduces shatter-resistant safety glass; Stutz and Rickenbacker offer "shock-proof" windshield glass, using internal wires or celluloid laminate

GM opens the first styling studio, the impressively titled Art & Colour Section, directed by soon-to-be-legendary Harley J. Earl

Packard develops hypoid gears for the rear axle, for use in '27 models

Glass "eyes" at the rear of some headlights let the driver see if the lights are on

Chandler offers a one-shot lubrication system, a setup that soon will appear on many higher-priced cars

Hot-water heaters become available; safer than the old exhaust-type heaters, they won't become standard in most models until the 1940s

▲ Ads promoted 1927 Buicks as "one of the good things of life." This $1495 Master Six sedan had a 274-cid engine.

▲ Opera windows and landau bars marked the Buick Model 51 Brougham, a $1925 sedan that snared 13,862 customers.

▲ The top-selling '27 Chevrolet was the $695 coach: 239,566 units. Closed cars were rapidly growing in popularity.

▲ Chrysler was turning out 4000 cars a week by 1927, including this '27 Series 60 touring phaeton.

◀ All seven Fisher brothers attended groundbreaking ceremonies for the Fisher Building in Detroit, in August 1927. Each of the brothers except Howard (*second from right*) was in the automobile business. GM had bought all the remaining stock in the Fisher Body Company in 1926, but the Fisher name remained on GM cars for many years afterward.

**New Makes: 1926**

Cavalier, Hertz, Pontiac, Saf-T-Cab (taxi), and Whippet (late in year)

---

Oldsmobile introduces chrome plating of parts

The low-slung, boattailed Rickenbacker Super Sport lacks running boards, features brass-bound mahogany bumpers—and is guaranteed to hit 90 mph

GM acquires the Fisher Body Corporation

The one-millionth Studebaker is built

Ford initiates the five-day work week, announces its intent to drop the Model T, but denies rumors that it soon will be replaced

Model T Fords come in a choice of colors for the first time since 1913, though fenders are still black (a common industry practice)

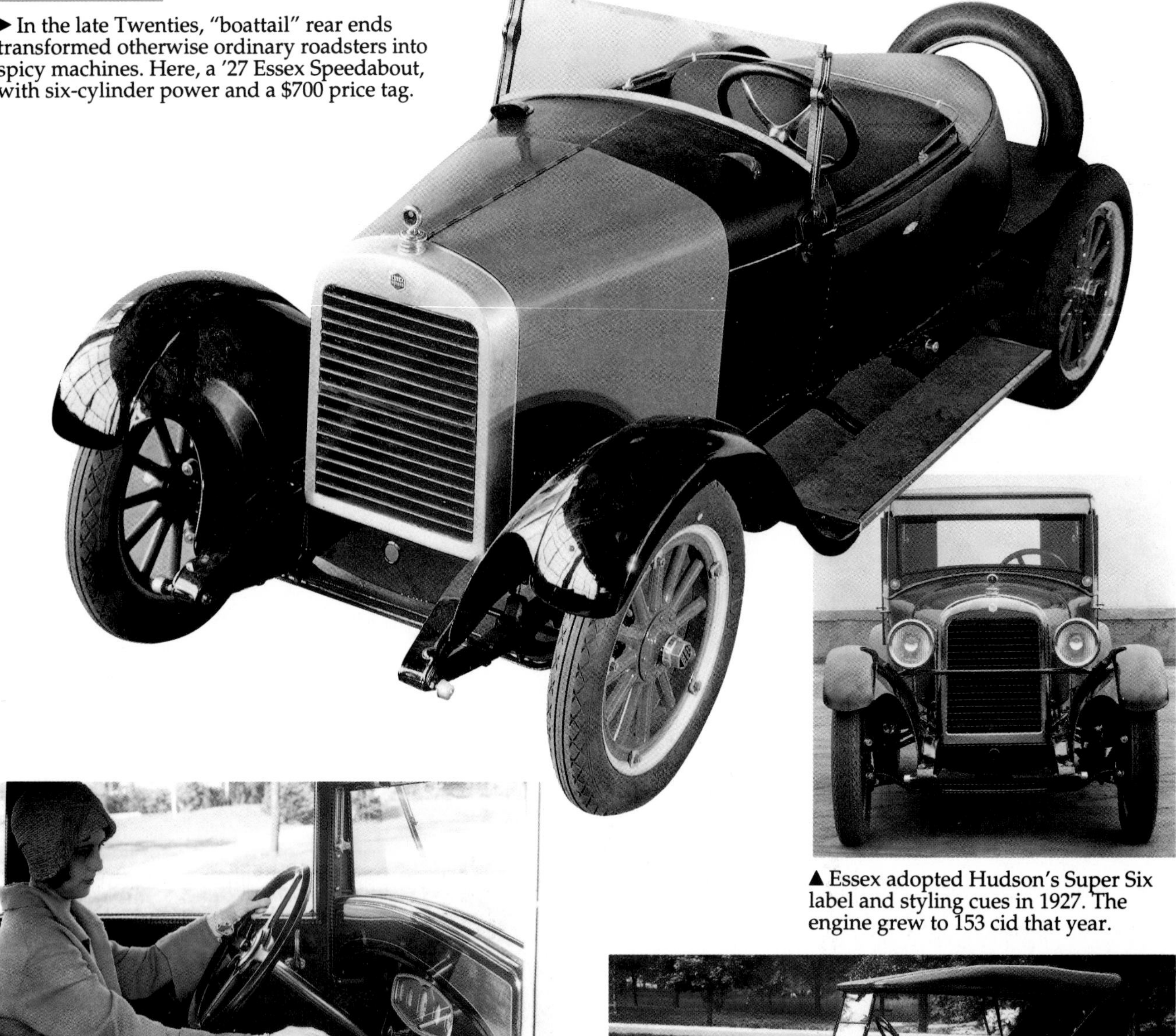

▶ In the late Twenties, "boattail" rear ends transformed otherwise ordinary roadsters into spicy machines. Here, a '27 Essex Speedabout, with six-cylinder power and a $700 price tag.

▲ Essex adopted Hudson's Super Six label and styling cues in 1927. The engine grew to 153 cid that year.

▲ Most 1927 interiors, like this Hudson's, had central gauges. An F-head engine replaced the L-head Super Six.

▲ Last of an era: the 1927 Model T Ford. More than 15 million had been built. Ford was preparing a successor.

---

An electric starter is finally standard on open Model T Fords

Chryslers feature rubber engine mounts, rubber spring shackles, adjustable front seats

E.G. "Cannon Ball" Baker drives a loaded GM truck cross-country in 5 days, 17½ hours

The *Encyclopedia Britannica* contains a Henry Ford article on "mass production" (formerly referred to as "Fordism")

**1926 Model Year Production**

|  |  |
|---|---|
| 1. Ford | 1,426,612 |
| 2. Chevrolet | 547,724 |
| 3. Buick | 266,753 |
| 4. Dodge | 265,000 |
| 5. Hudson/Essex | 227,508 |
| 6. Willys-Overland/Whippet | 182,000 |
| 7. Chrysler | 135,520 |
| 8. Pontiac/Oakland | 133,604 |

*Some figures are estimates*

▲ Legendary stylist Harley Earl earned credit for the new 1927 LaSalle, which had a 75-bhp, 303-cid L-head V-8. GM slotted it between Buick and Cadillac.

▲ Prince William of Sweden (*at wheel*) visited the Nash plant in Kenosha, Wisconsin, in 1927. Scandinavian workers presented him with this newly available Nash Ambassador Six (Model 267) four-door Brougham sedan.

▲ Capacity of the $1475 Nash Advanced Six roadster for '27 was four, but two had to squeeze into the rumble seat. Wheelbase measured 127 inches; power came from a 69-bhp, 278-cid six. Special and Light Six Nashes were smaller.

**1927**

GM president Alfred Sloan leads the trend toward the annual model change, heralding what will become known as "planned obsolescence," whereby motorists will be encouraged to grow dissatisfied with their cars—and eager to obtain the very latest model

Passenger-car volume skids to 2,936,533; trucks dip to 464,793 units

Chevrolet outproduces Ford by a whopping margin, but only because the Model T era finally draws to a close

A small-car trend is evident at the 27th National Automobile Show

The Studebaker-built, $995 Erskine—"The Little Aristocrat"—debuts with a 146-cid Continental six; it lasts only into 1930

▲ The Hudson Motor Car Company's office building is alit on a snowy night.

▲ Automobiles produced for export had to be crated like other cargo for the ocean voyage. Here, a $1385 Hudson Standard four-door sedan is being readied for the trip.

▲ Idle at the moment, this array of cutters at the Hudson axle plant produced ring gears. A single-disc, oil-filled clutch replaced the multi-disc unit in 1927.

▲ Dramatic restyling lowered Hudson bodies, led by bullet-shaped headlamps and a taller radiator. A new 289-cid F-head six made 92 bhp. Sales for 1927 totaled 66,034.

▲ Long known for massive cars, the Marmon company added a Little Marmon 8 in 1927—but it lasted only one season. Shown is a Locke-bodied four-passenger Victoria.

---

The Little Marmon ($1795 and up) and Little Custom Playboy join the Marmon and Jordan lineups, but Americans aren't ready for costly compact models

The LaSalle V-8 is introduced as a companion to Cadillac: lower in price ($2496 and up), but comparable in quality

LaSalle helps establish the reputation of Harley Earl's Art & Colour Section, giving it a status separate from GM's engineering department

Reo launches the Flying Cloud series—the first car to use Lockheed's newly developed internal-expanding hydraulic brakes

The $1195 Wolverine is introduced by Reo as a lower-cost companion to the Flying Cloud

**New Makes: 1927**
Brooks Steamer, Calvert, Erskine, Falcon-Knight, LaSalle, New York Six (with "Parkmobile" device), and Wolverine

◀ For 1927, Oldsmobile bored its little six to 185 cubic inches, upping output to 47 horses. Deluxe equipment for this $975 30-E roadster included front/rear bumpers; 2342 were sold.

◀ The "Safety Stutz" with hydraulic brakes and available safety glass emerged in 1926, and was "improved" for '27. The overhead-cam "Vertical Eight" grew from 287 to 299 cid.

▶ Ads promoted the roadability of the '27 Stutz. Lush, low Weymann Flexible Bodies enhanced its appeal. Thin wires in the safety glass could actually be seen. Black Hawk Speedsters earned 1927 AAA stock-car honors.

▼ Crossing the continent with minimal fuel was no problem for the little 1927 Willys-built Whippet four. A Whippet six set a 24-hour endurance record for its class at Indianapolis.

▲ A notable feature of the $1635 '27 Velie 60 Royal Sedan was its front door, slanted to match the windshield. Built in Illinois, Velie lasted for two decades: 1909-29.

---

Hudson's six-cylinder engine, an L-head, adopts overhead intake valves, making it an F-head

The Nash Light Six replaces the abandoned Ajax

A six-cylinder "Senior" Dodge joins the four-cylinder models late in the year

Nearly all cars now have four-wheel brakes; many have air cleaners, oil and gas filters, crankcase vents, mirrors, and automatic windshield wipers

Packard and the Little Marmon employ hypoid rear axles, which permit a lower body profile

Carl Breer begins to study auto-related aerodynamics, which will lead to Chrysler's Airflow design and monocoque construction

▲ Gear clashing was a common sound until Cadillac launched the synchromesh transmission in 1928, as on the Fisher-bodied Imperial sedan.

◀ New Lovejoy hydraulic shock absorbers and a double-drop frame altered the ride and stance of this $1765 Buick Country Club coupe, which sported new bullet-shaped headlamps; 6555 were sold.

◀ The best-looking '28 Chevrolet sedan was this Imperial Landau. At $715, 54,998 buyers couldn't resist it. This was the first Chevy styled by Harley Earl's Art & Colour Section.

▲ Colorful ads hyped the '28 Chevy's size, operating ease, and popularity.

◀ Service work at a Chevrolet dealer's shop required mainly hand tools. Chevy's first true convertible arrived in mid-1928, with a rumble seat as standard equipment.

▶ Even though Chevrolet was selling nose-to-nose with Ford's new Model A, salesmen weren't always busy with customers. Engine output rose from 26 to 35 bhp.

---

Graham-Paige Motor Corporation supersedes the Paige-Detroit Motor Car Company

Studebaker celebrates its 75th Anniversary

GM stockholders receive nearly $135 million in dividends; Chrysler stockholders get $10 million

Workers now own $20 million in Nash stock

The final Model T Fords are built, ending a 19-year era

Rarely—if ever—has any commodity had such an impact on American life as the Model T

▲ The five-millionth Chevrolet was a coach—Chevy's top '28 seller by far.

▲ Top GM men visited Delco-Remy manager C.F. Wilson (*center, front*) in 1928. Flanking Wilson are GM president Alfred Sloan and vice-president W.S. Knudsen.

▲ Maurice Lichtenstein of Chicago won this flashy, two-tone Essex Speedabout in a "*College Humor*" art contest.

▲ The $700 Essex Speedabout was dropped in late '27. Essex set an all-time production record for '28: 229,887 cars.

▲ Although Essex was considered a fairly small car, this woman looks tiny at the wheel of the $750 '28 phaeton.

---

A total of 15,007,033 "Tin Lizzies" were built through May 1927 (plus 477,748 that summer)—a record finally beaten by the Volkswagen Beetle

An all-new Model A Ford is announced on May 25, 1927, but is unveiled in December as a 1928 model

Hudson develops a single-disc, cork-insert clutch, and keeps that design into the 1950s

A Studebaker travels 25,000 miles averaging more than a mile-a-minute

Packard builds a 500-acre proving ground in Utica, Michigan

Charles Lindbergh flies solo, non-stop from New York to Paris

▲ Customers clamored to see the new Model A Ford, like this $480 roadster.

▲ Ford's 40-horsepower, 200.5-cid L-head four included a water pump. Battery ignition replaced the old magneto.

▲ Safety glass, three-speed gearbox, and four-wheel brakes were standard in the Model A; here, the $460 phaeton.

▲ The $550 Tudor shows the Model A's sweeping hoodline and crowned fenders—much like a scaled-down Lincoln.

▲ Ford business coupes came with a fabric or rubberized roof. Ford built 607,592 Model As during calendar 1928.

| 1927 Model Year Production | |
|---|---|
| 1. Chevrolet | 1,001,820 |
| 2. Ford | 367,213 |
| 3. Hudson/Essex | 276,414 |
| 4. Buick | 255,160 |
| 5. Pontiac/Oakland | 188,168 |
| 6. Willys-Overland/Whippet | 188,000 |
| 7. Chrysler | 182,195 |
| 8. Dodge | 180,000 |

*Some figures are estimates*

**1928**

The new Model A Ford has a conventional three-speed gearbox; 40-bhp, L-head four; four-wheel brakes; standard shatterproof glass

An estimated 10 million people flock to see the Model A within 36 hours of its unveiling

Horsepower and compression-ratio increases are evident at the 28th National Automobile Show

▲ This $1295 Hudson Model S Custom Roadster sported a taller, slimmer radiator and bullet headlamps in '28.

▲ Aircraft developer Eddie Stinson poses with his plane and a brand-new $735 Essex Coach. Celebrity endorsements gained favor during the Twenties.

▲ Spare tires moved to front fenders during the Twenties, giving this 1928 LaSalle convertible coupe a dashing air. Model year LaSalle production came to 14,806 units.

▲ A taller radiator distinguished this 1928 Nash two-door sedan. Nash production was up sharply to 138,137 units for the calendar year—and wouldn't be topped until 1949.

▲ The top-line 1928 Nash, as before, was the Advanced Six, on a 121- or 127-inch chassis with a 70-bhp, 279-cid six. This $1775 rumble-seat coupe sports two-tone paint.

▲ In addition to the Advanced Six (*shown*), Nash sold a 52-bhp, 224-cid Special Six. At the budget end of the lineup, a 45-bhp Standard Six replaced the Light Six.

---

Car prices are falling; eight-cylinder engines are growing in popularity

Passenger-car output rebounds to 3,775,417; trucks reach 583,342 units

Chevy leads again: 1,193,212 cars to 607,592. But its Number One spot will be short-lived as Ford Model A production increases

Chrysler Corporation launches Plymouth in July, DeSoto in August—both as 1929 models

Plymouth is the only four-cylinder model from Chrysler

Chrysler Corporation takes over Dodge Brothers on July 30, with K.T. Keller at the helm

▲ Folding down the windshield enhanced the sporty flavor of the patriotically named Oakland All-American Six Sports Roadster. At $1075, it boasted a bigger 211-cid six.

▲ Riding in the rumble seat of the '28 Oldsmobile Sport Coupe wasn't so joyous if the weather turned sour. The $1145 base price included a larger 197-cid, 55-bhp six.

▲ Studebaker president A.R. Erskine (*sixth from left, front*) hosted top auto men when the National Automobile Chamber of Commerce met in South Bend, Indiana. Front-row guests included R.E. Olds (*second from left*), C.W. Nash (*third*), Roy Chapin (*fourth*). Studebaker sold Dictator, Commander, and President models.

► European styling touches flavored the 1928 Stutz "BB" line, with such fancy model names as Versailles and Biarritz. The fastest U.S. production car was the Blackhawk Speedster.

---

Chrysler Corporation turns out 360,398 cars, up from 137,668 in 1928

Graham-Paige automobiles emerge, with four-, six-, or eight-cylinder engines; most have a four-speed transmission

Chandler adopts a Westinghouse vacuum brake system that cuts pedal pressure by two-thirds

Cadillac introduces synchromesh transmission—no more need for tiresome double-clutching to change gears

Cadillacs offer all-around safety glass

Auto radios begin to appear

▲ Bulging side panels on the restyled '29 Buick quickly caused it to be dubbed "pregnant." Closed cars, such as this $1525 Sport Sedan, featured twin electric wipers.

▲ Buick would remedy its 1929 styling misjudgment after one season. This $1875 DeLuxe Convertible Coupe was just one of 196,104 Buicks produced for the model year.

▲ The rarest '29 Chevrolet (300 built) was the $725 Landau Imperial sedan, with fold-down rear quarter.

▲ Under the hood of the '29 Chevrolet lurked a new 46-bhp "Stovebolt Six." The $525 roadster sold 27,988 copies.

▲ A '29 Chevy undergoes testing at GM's Proving Ground. It was advertised as "A Six for the Price of a Four."

▲ Twin-beam headlamps were new to Chevrolet. Stepping on a floor button changed the beam angle, so the driver could keep both hands on the wheel.

◀ Dubbed the "cast iron wonder," Chevy's new six would last through 1936.

---

Dodge offers a pair of six-cylinder engines to replace the former four: 208 cid in Standard and Victory models, 224 cid in the Senior model; the latter is soon enlarged to 241.6 cid

Hudson is first with a hard-rubber, steel-core steering wheel, containing finger scallops around the rim

LaSalle has a 303-cid V-8, Cadillac turns to a 341-cid version

Lincoln's V-8 grows to 384.8-cubic inches, delivering the same 90 horsepower as its smaller predecessor

The new President boasts Studebaker's first eight-cylinder engine: 313-cid, 100 horsepower

▲ For 1929, Chrysler debuted its first major styling change, led by a new 75 series: 75 horsepower, 75 mph. This is the $1550 roadster, of which 6414 were built.

▲ Chrysler launched a new marque for 1929: DeSoto. This sharp Roadster Espanol sold for $845. DeSoto's first-year output topped 80,000—a record for a new make.

▲ Like many automakers, DeSoto put the gauges in the center of the dash.

▶ Introduced on August 4, 1928, DeSoto offered seven models on a 109.75-inch wheelbase. This $845 phaeton had hydraulic brakes.

▲ DeSoto's 175-cid, L-head six-cylinder engine cranked out 55 horsepower.

▶ DeSotos receive final inspection at the Highland Park, Michigan, plant.

---

Ford assets are nearly a billion dollars; switchover to the Model A costs $250 million

Studebaker gains control of Buffalo-based Pierce-Arrow

Studebaker adopts a mechanical fuel pump, replacing the vacuum tank

Coast-to-coast bus service begins

Industry pioneer James Ward Packard dies

Buick celebrates its 25th Anniversary

A one-off Miller speedster is produced

Martin minicar prototypes appear, aiming to be the smallest practical car on the market (60-inch wheelbase). Production never happens

▲ Amorous couples enjoy a $895 Essex convertible, named Challenger for '29. Its 160-cid six produced 55 bhp.

▲ Essex offered a Town Sedan in 1929, but this Town Car with open driver's compartment was custom-bodied.

▲ A "Rumble Roof" gave some shelter to rear occupants in a '29 Essex coupe. Exiting gracefully wasn't easy.

**New Makes: 1929**
Blackhawk, Cord, Fargo, Marquette, Roosevelt, Ruxton, Viking, and Windsor

▼ Leather (or leatherette) went on the back and top of Ford's Briggs-bodied Fordor "leatherback" sedan. Far more complex than the primitive Model T, the Model A cost more, $625 in this case—but most buyers were satisfied.

Herbert Hoover is elected President

Penicillin is discovered

| 1928 Model Year Production | |
|---|---|
| 1. Chevrolet | 1,193,212 |
| 2. Ford | 607,592 |
| 3. Willys-Overland/Whippet | 315,000 |
| 4. Hudson/Essex | 282,203 |
| 5. Pontiac/Oakland | 244,584 |
| 6. Buick | 221,758 |
| 7. Chrysler | 160,670 |
| 8. Nash | 138,137 |

*Some figures are estimates*

**1929**

The year starts strong, but the curtain closes on the prosperity of "The Roaring Twenties" in autumn

▲ At $695, the Town Sedan cost $70 more than a regular Fordor Model A. Four new body styles debuted in 1929.

▲ Small rear side windows identified the Murray-bodied Ford Town Sedan; other Fordors had blank quarters.

▲ The most popular Model A was the $525 Tudor: 523,922 in 1929. Conversely, only 913 Town Cars were sold.

▲ Over-the-shoulder visibility was better in the five-window Model A coupe than in some of its Ford mates.

▲ Bright colors added glamour to the new $670 Model A cabriolet—Ford's first true convertible since the Model T Coupelet. External trunks were a popular add-on.

▲ Henry Ford's son Edsel created the formal-looking Town Car, with an open chauffeur's compartment. At $1400, it cost more than twice as much as any other Ford Model A.

---

Wall Street "crashes" on "Black Thursday," October 29, 1929. The Great Depression begins, and will last—with sporadic upturns—until the outbreak of World War II

Passenger-car output rises again, to 4,455,178 units; truck volume leaps to 881,909. The overall total will not be beaten until 1949

The millionth Model A Ford is built, followed by the two-millionth in July

Ford's production and market share doubles to 32 percent of the market, well ahead of Chevrolet; Hudson-Essex is third

Chevrolet counters Ford's Model A with a six-cylinder engine; the 194-cid, overhead-valve six develops 46 horsepower

◀ A 322-cid, L-head straight-eight engine powered this '29 Model 827 rumble-seat cabriolet, but Graham-Paige also offered six-cylinder cars. The marque had bowed a year earlier.

▼ Even in sedan form, the 1929 LaSalle exhibited graceful lines. Series 328 borrowed the synchromesh transmission and safety glass from big-brother Cadillac, and added chrome trim. Bodies came from Fisher or Fleetwood.

▲ Dietrich supplied the body of this $6900 '29 Lincoln convertible sedan, riding the usual 136-inch wheelbase.

▲ A coupe body accentuated the massive lines of the 1929 Model L Lincoln. The 385-cid V-8 developed 90 bhp.

Oldsmobile introduces an upmarket companion, the $1595 Viking V-8; it lasts only two seasons

Buick launches the $1000 Marquette at mid-year; it's an early '30 model with an L-head six

Duesenberg announces the Model J, with a 265-horsepower, dual-overhead-cam, straight-eight engine; it's huge, fast, powerful, and impressive

A Duesenberg J hits 116 mph in tests at the Indianapolis Speedway

Even low-income motorists who can barely fantasize about owning a Duesenberg soon appreciate the meaning of the phrase, "It's a Duesy"

▲ Magnificent is the word for a 1929 Lincoln dual-cowl phaeton.

▲ Each coachbuilder had its own notions of good looks on a '29 Lincoln chassis. This is a LeBaron Aero Phaeton.

▲ Twin Ignition added horsepower and speed to the $1550 Nash Advanced Six (*shown*) and Special Six for 1929.

▲ The Nash Standard Six kept single ignition for its L-head engine, standard on the $935 phaeton.

▲ Oldsmobile issued a costlier companion make for 1929: the Viking V-8. This is the $1595 convertible.

▲ This view shows the nearly identical 1930 Viking convertible with the top down. Its 259-cid V-8 made 80 horses.

The new luxurious Cord L-29 features front-wheel drive; so does the new, equally luxurious, Ruxton

The $3095-$3295 Cord has a 298.6-cid, 125-horsepower Lycoming straight-eight

Ruxton's developers have trouble finding a production facility; it will eventually be built by Moon

Ruxton, one of few cars to lack running boards, is soon known for its narrow Wood-Lite headlights (actually an option)

The Marmon-built Roosevelt and Stutz-built Blackhawk appear, both less powerful and expensive than their big brothers

▲ The biggest '29 Packard: the 645 DeLuxe Eight, in dual-cowl phaeton form.

▲ Familiar built-in headlamps made Pierce-Arrows easy to spot in 1929, the first year for P-A straight-eights. This Town Car wears a Willoughby body.

▲ Packard's 385-cid straight-eight boasted 105 horses. Wheelbase of the 645 Series was 145½ inches.

▲ Pontiac's restyling for 1929 echoed the British Vauxhall, owned by GM.

▲ Marmon issued a lower-cost ($995), straight-eight Roosevelt in 1929-30.

▲ Early '29s had horizontal hood louvers, but overheating led Pontiac to switch to vertical openings.

---

DeSoto is officially on the market with a 174.9-cid, L-head six that cranks out 55 bhp

The Franklin "le Pirate" models have concealed running boards under the doors

Radios are available in many car models

Dual taillights begin to appear, but some makes keep single lights well into the '30s

Chrysler adopts downdraft carburetors for improved fuel distribution

Auburn exhibits a streamlined aluminum Cabin Speedster with an aircraft-inspired interior

▲ This dashing 1929 Stutz Series M roadster wears a LeBaron-designed body. The 322-cid, overhead-cam straight-eight drove through a four-speed gearbox.

▲ Note the unusual cut-down door on this 1929 Stutz M dual-cowl phaeton. Known for sport and luxury, Stutz offered an appetizing selection of bodies.

---

More than 80,000 DeSotos are sold—a first-year record for a new make

The Fargo commercial sedan/wagon is launched by Chrysler

Kleiber Motor Company experiments with diesel truck engines

An Aerocar house trailer is launched; autocamping has become a popular pastime and will continue into the 1930s

Nearly 90 percent of all cars sold are closed models—the opposite had been true a decade earlier

Nash develops a 100-bhp straight-eight for 1930

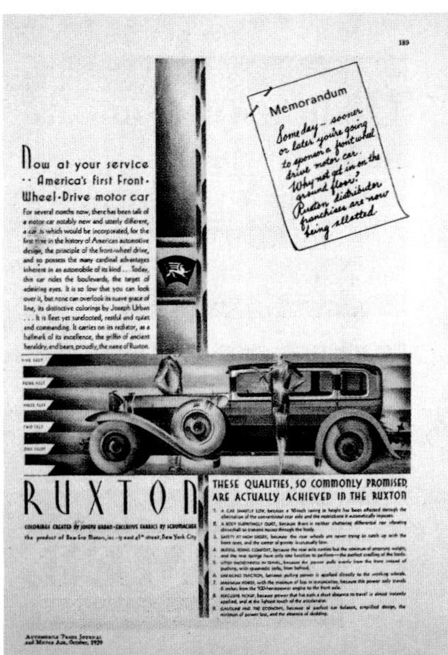


▲ Launched in 1929, the sleek Ruxton had a straight-eight engine and fresh idea: front-wheel-drive. This made possible the low overall height.

▲ In addition to its regular big-car line-up, Stutz launched a new make for 1929: the lower-priced Blackhawk, with six or eight cylinders.

▲ Stutz built many stylish motorcars, but this 1929 Series M Versailles sedan, on a 134.5-inch wheelbase with body by Weymann, looks formidable.

▲ The low-roofed fabric body by Weymann on this '29 Stutz Monte Carlo hints at chopped hot rods of later vintage. Wheelbase was a lengthy 145 inches.

▲ Oldsmobile produced the Viking only in 1929-30, on a 125-inch wheelbase. Sedan, close-coupled sedan, and convertible coupe bodies were sold.

▲ Willys-Knight six-cylinder sleeve-valve engines came in two sizes in 1929: 178- or 255-cid. Two-tone paint flattered this Great Six coupe.

---

Nash initiates volume production of its "Twin-Ignition" system for overhead-valve sixes and eights, using two spark plugs per cylinder

Two auto pioneers die this year: David Dunbar Buick and Walter C. White

Gangland violence peaks with Chicago's St. Valentine's Day Massacre—like other Americans, criminals make extensive use of automobiles

**1929 Model Year Production**

|  |  |  |
|---|---|---|
| 1. | Ford | 1,507,132 |
| 2. | Chevrolet | 1,328,605 |
| 3. | Hudson/Essex | 300,962 |
| 4. | Willys-Overland/Whippet | 242,000 |
| 5. | Pontiac/Oakland | 211,054 |
| 6. | Buick | 196,104 |
| 7. | Dodge | 124,557 |
| 8. | Nash | 116,622 |

*Some figures are estimates*

CHAPTER FOUR

# 1930-1941

# SURVIVAL OF THE FITTEST

"Brother, can you spare a dime?" Those words became a veritable anthem of the Great Depression, as millions of workers hit the street.

Americans were confused, downhearted, downtrodden. After three rough years, voters ousted President Hoover in favor of Franklin Delano Roosevelt's "New Deal." Industrial output sank to half the 1929 level, and one-fourth of the workforce was jobless. Soup lines fed the hungry.

Even as the Civilian Conservation Corps (CCC) and Works Progress Administration (WPA) provided government-sponsored jobs, the Great Depression lingered on. In 1937, FDR still saw "one third of the nation ill-housed, ill-clad, ill-nourished."

Movies and radio tried to boost morale. "Art deco" design added brightness to daily life. Such utopian concepts as "technocracy" and Huey Long's "share our wealth" campaign drew legions of followers.

The Dust Bowl of mid-decade added more misery, sending thousands of "Okies" on the road. Labor strife culminated in a bitter sit-down strike at GM's Fisher Body plant in 1936-37. Then a heated battle between Ford-employed thugs and strikers erupted a few months later.

Hard times made the *used* car king, and an astounding number of families somehow did manage to keep a motor running. The Depression notwithstanding, car ownership was still a big part of the "American Dream." Cowboy-philosopher Will Rogers noted that America was the first country "to go to the poor house in an automobile."

Both style and technology made great strides. Ford issued the first V-8 engine in a low-cost car. Plymouth became a major player. Cadillac and Marmon launched magnificent V-16 models. Cars became lower, streamlined (like the latest locomotives), and easier to handle. Graham introduced a supercharger. Auburn submitted its sumptuous Speedsters, while Cord debuted its timeless "coffin-nosed" 810/812.

Gearshifts became synchronized. Seats broadened to hold three. Built-in trunks were adopted. Independent front suspensions helped smooth the bumps. Even Henry Ford finally gave in to hydraulic brakes. By 1940, sealed-beam headlights led the way, gearshifts rode the steering column, and running boards were rapidly becoming extinct.

Not every innovation lasted long. Freewheeling faded after a few years—in part because some states made such "coasting" illegal. Startix units enjoyed a brief fling. Overdrive boosted the economy of 1934 Chrysler Airflows and spread to other makes, but never quite captured the imagination.

As for automatic shifting, Reo's "Self-Shifter" of 1933-34 drew modest attention. GM's Safety Automatic Transmission made a smaller splash. When Oldsmobile introduced Hydra-Matic for 1940, the public was interested, but widespread adoption wouldn't come until after the war.

The number of significant makes slimmed from about 60 in 1929 to 18 in 1941. A brief stab at minicars started with the American Austin and its Bantam successor; later came the Crosley.

Paved roads more than doubled in a decade, as the automobile culture grew. Drive-ins lured moviegoers. Tourist courts dotted the landscape.

At the New York World's Fair of 1939, GM's Futurama predicted the world of the Sixties, including 100-mph superhighways. The modern age was imminent, but Americans had to face another world war before enjoying all its fruits.

---

**1930**

As the Great Depression sets in, industry volume skids to 2,910,187 passenger cars and 599,991 trucks

Ford tops Chevrolet in production—1,140,710 cars to 640,980—but Chevy's "Stovebolt Six" is gaining favor

General Motors cars sport tilted windshields

Cadillac offers V-12 and V-16 engines, plus power brakes

Oakland abandons its six-cylinder engine, turns to an unreliable V-8

Studebaker pioneers free-wheeling, starting a trend that will last several years

The American Austin Car Company is formed to build a variant of the British Austin Seven; the minicar's production begins in May 1930

▲ The American Austin—based on its British counterpart—was built in Pennsylvania. The $465 coupe seated two and rode a short 75-inch wheelbase.

▲ With top and side curtains up, a $445 1930 American Austin roadster looked cozy. Its frugal 46-cid, L-head four made just 14 horsepower.

▲ Americans weren't ready for minicars when Austin arrived. Annual output reached 8558, then skidded. This roadster weighed in at 1100 pounds.

▲ A beltline molding and lower stance minimized Buick's "pregnant" look, as on this 1930 Series 40 phaeton. Its 257.7-cid six developed 81 bhp. At $1310, only 1100 were sold.

▲ Launched in 1929 as a '30 model, Buick's Marquette lasted only one season despite a production run of 35,007 units. Smaller than a Buick, it had a 67.5-bhp L-head six.

▲ Chevrolet offered one 1930 series: AD Universal. Shown is the $615 Sport Coupe; 45,311 were sold. The rear window lowered for ventilation or communication with people in the rumble seat. The 194-cid six had 50 bhp.

◄ To trounce such rivals as Packard and Peerless, Cadillac launched a V-16 for 1930. The 452-cid engine made 165 horsepower—second only to Duesenberg. Some 33 V-16 variants were listed, starting at a pricey $5350.

---

The Buick-built Marquette arrives with an L-head six in June 1929 as a '30 model; it lasts just one season

A front-drive Gardner is announced (to join the rear-drive models), but only a few prototypes are built

Cadillac, Chrysler, Dodge, LaSalle, Marmon, and Roosevelt cars are wired for radio installation

A revised Model A Ford debuts in January with taller hood-to-body lines, smaller balloon tires

Chrysler's new "Steelweld" bodies use few wooden elements

Cadillac engines have automatic hydraulic tappet clearance adjustment to reduce maintenance

Hupmobile claims to be the first American car with an oil cooler

Studebaker develops a carburetor-intake silencer, installs helical gears in its transmissions

▲ Launched in 1929 by E.L. Cord, the Classic Cord L-29 featured a 125-bhp, 299-cid straight-eight driving the front wheels. Long and low, it rode a stately 137.5-inch chassis. This 1930 dual-cowl phaeton wears custom coachwork by Murphy.

▲ Celebrities loved the L-29 Cord. An appetizing array of custom bodies included this coupe by Sakhnoffsky, sporting a unique roof/window style.

▲ Four basic bodies were offered for L-29 Cords: brougham, cabriolet, phaeton, and a $3095 four-door sedan. Total 1929-32 L-29 output was 5010.

▲ Popular crooner Rudy Vallee serenades an avid group, gathered around a '30 DeSoto Eight. The 208-cid Silver Dome straight-eight claimed 70 horses.

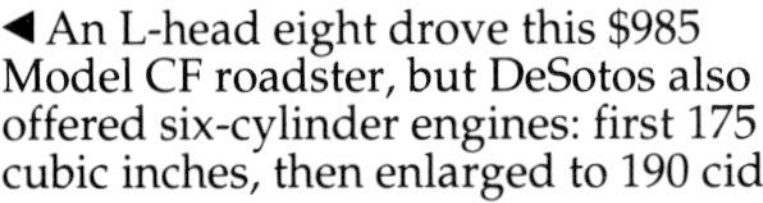

◄ An L-head eight drove this $985 Model CF roadster, but DeSotos also offered six-cylinder engines: first 175 cubic inches, then enlarged to 190 cid.

► Immodestly heralded as the "World's Finest Motor Car," the Duesenberg Model J merited the title. Under this roadster's hood sits a 420-cid, 265-bhp inline eight. Wheelbases spanned at least 142.5 inches.

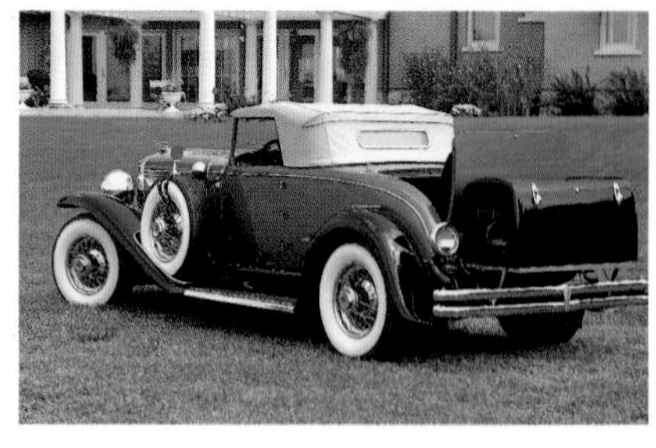

Graham-Paige uses rubber-cushioned springs and drops the "-Paige" suffix from car badges

The National Automobile Chamber of Commerce launches a plan to scrap 360,000 obsolete vehicles to help combat the "used car problem"

Industry pioneers Harry C. Stutz, Andrew Riker, and Lionel M. Woolson die

Cadillac launches the magnificent 165-bhp Sixteen in January

Chrysler debuts its "CJ" six, the "lowest-priced six ever to bear the Chrysler name"

DeSoto's K-Series starts the season, but is replaced in May by the CK Finer Six

A Speedster is DuPont's most notable model; it features cut-down doors, narrow headlights, and a $5000+ price tag

▼ Murphy did the coachwork for this elegant 1930 Duesenberg Model J Torpedo Berline. A bare chassis cost $8500.

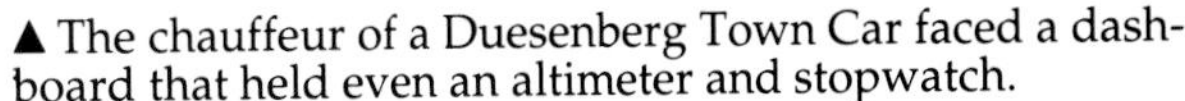

▲ The chauffeur of a Duesenberg Town Car faced a dashboard that held even an altimeter and stopwatch.

▲ No sound quite matches the sonorous blast from a Duesenberg's exhaust. The technically advanced dual-overhead-cam engine measured four feet, with a 32-valve head. Fittings were nickel, chrome, stainless steel.

◀ Duesenbergs were smooth, powerful, sophisticated, rugged—and beautiful. Exposed exhaust pipes enhanced the allure of this dual-cowl phaeton. A Model J Duesenberg could reach 116 mph—nearly 90 in second gear. Ads needed say no more than: "He [or she] drives a Duesenberg." Bodies used the very finest woods and fabrics.

---

Essex and Hudson boast a new "Sun Sedan" (two-door convertible sedan) body style

Franklins sport new styling and a reworked supercharged engine

The "Great Eight" Hudsons debut as the sixes depart

A Twin-Ignition Nash Eight is new this year

Willys adds a new straight-eight; Whippet expires early in 1931

Ford V-8 engine experiments are begun in secret

**1930 Model Year Production**

| | |
|---|---|
| 1. Ford | 1,140,710 |
| 2. Chevrolet | 640,980 |
| 3. Buick | 181,743 |
| 4. Studebaker | 123,216 |
| 5. Hudson/Essex | 113,898 |
| 6. Plymouth (1929/30 Model U) | 108,350 |
| 7. Dodge | 90,755 |
| 8. Chrysler | 77,881 |

*Some figures are estimated or calender-year*

▲ Ford's Model A earned a bit of touch-up work in 1930. Fenders were lower and wider, the hood taller, wheels smaller. DeLuxe roadsters sported cowl lights and twin taillights.

▲ The 1930 model year brought production of 24,125 Grahams, including this four-door. Graham prices ranged from $845 to a sobering $4505.

▲ Eight-cylinder Hupmobiles, like this $1695 1930 Model C coupe, were built in Detroit, sixes in Cleveland. Riding a 121-inch wheelbase, the C boasted 268.6 cid, 100 bhp.

▲ The era of station wagons had not yet arrived when Hudson created this experimental Essex Special Depot car. Not intended for public view, it was captured at Hudson's Detroit plant.

▲ Hudson's new class of convertible brought the 1930 Essex Challenger Six "Sun Sedan," with hinged pillars between disappearing windows. Underhood was a six: 58-bhp, 160-cid.

▲ Longer and costlier, 1930 LaSalles rode a 134-inch wheelbase; 14,986 were produced. Six Fleetwood bodies were offered, plus Fisher coachwork, as on this $2590 Model 340 soft-top.

▲ Packard listed the Sport Phaeton in Standard, Custom, or DeLuxe Eight form for 1930. All models had straight-eight engines: 320- or 384.8-cid. A few Speedster Eights were built on a 134-inch chassis.

◀ A Twin-Ignition Six powered this $1365 rumble-seat roadster, but Nash also added a Twin-Ignition Eight for 1930. Eights rode a longer wheelbase and had a dashboard starter button.

**1931**

Industry output plummets to 2,038,183 cars and 434,176 trucks

Automakers, in coping with the deepening Depression, are unsure whether to risk creating new models or to cut prices on existing ones

Chevrolet barely tops Ford's model-year production, as both sink below 620,000 units; Buick is a distant third

Plymouth moves up from seventh to fourth place in production

The 50-millionth American motor vehicle is built

The National Automobile Chamber of Commerce recommends grouping all new-model announcements in November-December, to stimulate fall/winter buying and even out the springtime rush

▲ With side curtains in place, this $895 Oakland roadster was bundled up for winter in 1930. The 85-bhp, 250-cid V-8, with a 180-degree crankshaft, tended to vibrate badly at high rpm.

▲ Stutz designed a 32-valve head for its Vertical Eight in 1931, begetting the DV32, here a phaeton. The 322-cid dual-cam motor made 156 bhp, compared to 113 for the SV16 (16-valve).

▲ Weymann crafted the leatherette-over-wood body for this $3495 '30 Stutz Versailles Sport Sedan, with slanted windshield and closed quarters. Tall doors hid the chassis aprons.

▲ Close-coupled coachwork by Weymann, featuring an intriguingly low roofline, made the $4495 Monte Carlo sedan for 1930 one of the most famous Stutz custom creations. Note the fancy wire wheels. Frederick Moskovics had left Stutz in 1929, but the '30 models reflected his desire to produce "an American thoroughbred." In addition to Model MA/MB Eights on a 134.5- or 145-inch wheelbase, available with a variety of custom bodies, Stutz marketed the lower-priced six-cylinder Blackhawk (a separate make) for one more year.

▲ An upscale mate to Oldsmobile, the Viking Eight saw life only in 1929-30. Three body styles included this DeLuxe convertible with an 81-bhp, 259-cid V-8. Total 1930 output: 1390.

▲ Again in 1930, sleeve-valve engines powered the Willys-Knight. A 178-cid six made 53 bhp, for cars on 112.5- or 115-inch wheelbases. This bigger Great Six sedan had 87-bhp, 255-cid.

---

Chrysler launches its first eight-cylinder engines; they're L-head straight-eights

Marmon launches an impressive new Sixteen with styling by Walter Dorwin Teague

Oakland appears for the last time but companion Pontiac continues

Free-wheeling is offered on Auburn, Chrysler, DeSoto, DeVaux, Dodge, Essex, Graham, Hudson, Hupmobile, Lincoln, Marmon, Peerless, Pierce-Arrow, Plymouth, and Willys, in addition to Studebaker

Startix is available in several makes—it recranks the engine if it stalls

Oldsmobile adopts "Synchro-Mesh" transmission for smoother, clash-free shifting—it will soon be standard on most makes

◀ Cadillac offered more than 30 Fleetwood bodies for its 1931 V-16, priced from $5350 to $15,000. Note the wind wings and wire wheels on this rumble-seat roadster. A limited-run Madam X series featured slim, sloped windshield pillars. A lower-cost V-12 line arrived nine months after the Sixteen, delivering 135 bhp from 370-cid. Best-seller: the Eight, with 353 cid, 95 bhp.

▲ At $575, a '31 Chevrolet DeLuxe Sport Coupe with rumble seat cost only $30 more than a business coupe. Wheelbase of the "Bigger and Better" Independence series was 109 inches.

▲ With 228,316 built, Chevrolet's $545 coach proved twice as popular as the $650 Special four-door sedan. Wire wheels replaced discs for 1931. The 194-cid ohv six still claimed 50 bhp.

▲ Chryslers for '31 featured "Floating Power" (rubber engine mounts) and free-wheeling. In addition to six-cylinder models, Chrysler offered new straight-eights in four sizes.

◀ Though later recognized as a certified Classic, the stunning L-29 Cord proved a failure when new. Prices were cut $800 to spark sales in 1931, yet even this handsome $2595 convertible sedan had trouble finding buyers. An L-29 took 30 seconds to reach 60 mph, and could barely hit 75 mph flat-out. An unorthodox gearshift pattern didn't help Cord's popularity, either.

---

Packard and several other makes offer shock-absorber adjustments from the dashboard

Chrysler's "Floating Power" engine mounts debut in mid-season, initially on Plymouth, which claims its four has the smoothness of a six

The National Automobile Chamber of Commerce recommends a 90-day/4000-mile warranty for new cars

The final Model A Ford is built on November 1, to be replaced by the first low-priced V-8

Restyled Auburns show greater Cord and Duesenberg influence

Buicks get new engines, all straight-eights; a Buick-powered racer qualifies for the Indianapolis 500 Memorial Day Race

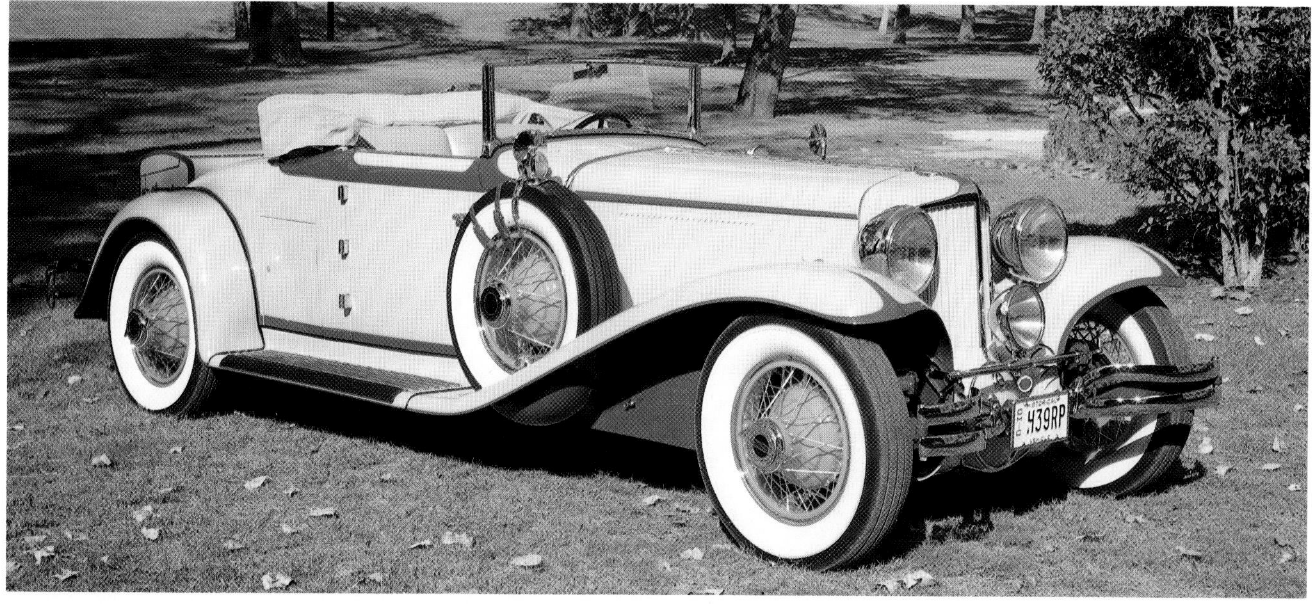


▲ Traction could be troublesome when driving an L-29 Cord, shown here in $2495 cabriolet form. Front-wheel drive was unproven technology, thus hard to sell.

▲ The Durant line shrank to two body styles for '31, priced from $675 to $775, with a four or six. After 7270 sales in '31, the firm folded early in '32.

▲ An accessory trunk added dash to a $525 '31 Ford Model A DeLuxe five-window coupe. A standard coupe (with built-in trunk) ran $35 less.

▲ Ford added a Town Sedan during 1931, featuring a slanted windshield and cowl lamps. Priced at $630, it found favor with 65,447 customers.

▲ Despite the romantic aura of boattail bodies, Hudson's Greater Eight sport roadster—with an 87-bhp, 234-cid six—was built for only six months.

▲ Murphy created this special slim-fendered, tall-hood convertible sedan for Hudson president William McAneeny. Note the headlamps.

▲ Famed race driver Barney Oldfield leans on an Essex Challenger Six coupe, one of 10 models for '31. Calendar year sales totaled 40,338.

---

A Town Sedan and Victoria coupe join Ford's Model A line, followed by a two-door convertible sedan

Graham adds a lower-cost "Prosperity Six" to its lineup, but not too many customers are feeling prosperous

Lincoln is one of the few automakers to raise prices, defying a trend; the Model K rides a longer wheelbase than the old Model L

Twin-Ignition Nash Eights adopt Bijur automatic chassis lubrication

Carryover Plymouths are replaced in May by an all-new PA-Series

Two new straight-eight engines join the Reo list—the bigger one goes into the impressive streamlined Royale

Stutz experiments with a supercharged engine, but turns instead to a 32-valve twincam head for its DV32 model

▲ Lincoln launched the massive Model K for '31, among them this $4600 dual-cowl Sport Phaeton on a 145-inch chassis. A 385-cid V-12 gave 120 bhp.

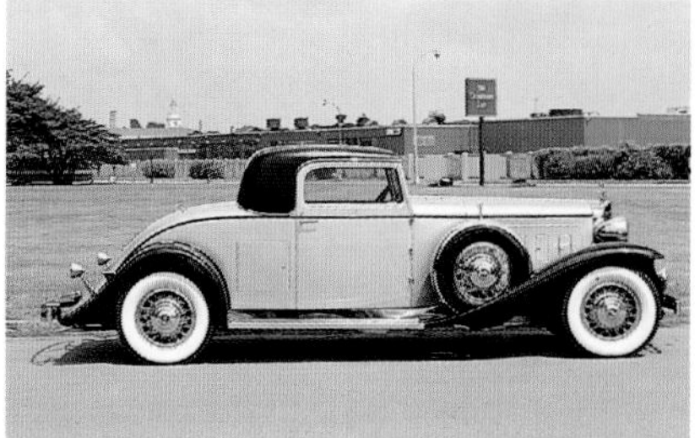

▲ After five years of research, Marmon debuted the Sixteen. Guaranteed to do 100 mph, this coupe cost $5220. About 390 Sixteens were built from 1931-33.

▲ Billed as "The World's Most Advanced Motor Car," this Marmon's Sixteen Victoria had a 490.8-cid aluminum engine making 200 horses.

▲ Boattail speedsters were the rage in 1931, exemplified by this richly hued Packard. Three model lines used two engines, rated at 100 or 120 horsepower.

◀ Pierce-Arrows for 1931 came in three series, four wheelbases, and three straight-eights (115-132 bhp). Here, a $3450 Model 42 Sports Roadster.

▶ Prices were cut for '31, but sales of Pierce-Arrow's luxury motorcars sank sharply (4522 registrations for the year). Running boards were slimmer.

Willys-Knight continues in production, but Willys now pushes conventional engines

A retractable hardtop convertible is patented by B.B. Ellerbeck

**1931 Model Year Production**

|  |  |  |
|---|---|---|
| 1. | Chevrolet | 619,554 |
| 2. | Ford | 615,455 |
| 3. | Buick | 138,965 |
| 4. | Studebaker | 96,173 |
| 5. | Pontiac | 84,708 |
| 6. | Plymouth (1930/31 30-U) | 75,510 |
| 7. | Willys | 65,800 |
| 8. | Chrysler | 65,500 |

*Some figures are estimated or calendar-year*

**1932**

As the Depression deepens, vehicle production drops to the lowest level since 1918: 1,186,185 cars and 245,284 trucks

An astounding 12 million would-be workers are unemployed

## Chrysler Motors Engineers' Greatest Contribution to Modern Motoring

The new Plymouth with Floating Power is the challenge of Chrysler Motors engineers to the whole world of lowest-priced cars.

With the discovery and development of Floating Power, they finally attain the goal which a discouraged industry had abandoned as hopeless.

For more than a quarter of a century, engineers had endeavored to wipe out the "interrupted torque" that sent tremors up through the frame to passengers and driver—but always without complete success.

One by one they admitted defeat, begging the question by adopting additional cylinders, sacrificing economy for greater smoothness.

Chrysler Motors engineers, while designing fine sixes and eights for Dodge, De Soto and Chrysler, have labored unceasingly for the perfected Four, which they have steadfastly maintained to be the ideal car for the lowest-price field.

Floating Power, new and exclusive in Plymouth, is an engineering discovery that actually achieves the smoothness of an Eight with the simplicity of design and the economy of operation that are the birthright of the Four.

The Floating Power principle allows the engine to rock on its natural axis. The Plymouth engine mountings—and there are only two—are so placed that the engine, if it were free to rotate, would do so in perfect balance. At each mounting, live rubber, nearly an inch thick, allows the engine to rock or oscillate on this natural axis, thus dissipating the power impulses.

Floating Power is so new, so startlingly revolutionary that you must experience it to understand just how sensational is this greatest contribution by Chrysler Motors engineers to modern motoring.

Get behind the wheel of a new Plymouth.

Step on the accelerator. Feel how quickly and smoothly the 56-h.p. engine whisks you to stop-watch speeds of 65 to 70 miles an hour. Then suddenly take your foot off the accelerator. Make a mental comparison of its quiet deceleration with the noise of other fours, and even of inferior sixes, when put to the same test.

The new Plymouth also includes Free Wheeling which permits quick and noiseless shifting of gears in all forward speeds without declutching.

Plymouth also gives you a new Easy-Shift transmission. You can shift quickly from second to high and back again at speeds of 35 and 45 miles an hour without clashing or grinding of gears, even with Free Wheeling locked out.

On its sturdy double-drop frame, Plymouth carries full-size Safety-Steel bodies. Plymouth is the only car in its price group with internal hydraulic brakes, unexcelled for safety.

And Plymouth has an entirely new styling, comparable in beauty with far costlier cars.

Throughout the country 10,000 dealers—Dodge, De Soto and Chrysler—stand ready today to demonstrate the phenomenal performance that wipes out all earlier conceptions of fine motoring among lowest-priced cars.

*New Plymouth Body Styles—Roadster $535, Sport Roadster $595, Sport Phaeton $595, Coupe $565, Coupe (with rumble seat) $610, Convertible Coupe $645, Sedan (2-door) $575, Sedan (4-door 3-window) $635, f. o. b. factory. Wire wheels standard at no extra cost. Low delivered prices. Convenient time-payments. Non-shatterable plate glass is available on all models at small extra cost.*

NEW PLYMOUTH IS SOLD BY ALL DODGE, DE SOTO AND CHRYSLER DEALERS

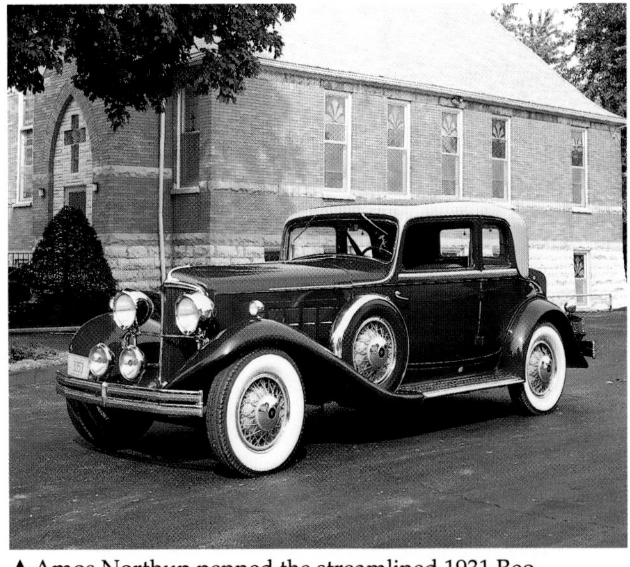

▲ Amos Northup penned the streamlined 1931 Reo Royale—the first production car with skirted fenders. Elegant straight-eight Royales wore Murray bodies on a 131- or 135-inch wheelbase, here a $2745 Victoria coupe.

◀ The reworked '31 Plymouth featured free-wheeling and "Floating Power," claiming "The Smoothness of an Eight * The Economy of a Four." A new PA series, with this $645 convertible and 10 other models, debuted during the year.

▲ Note the graceful roof contours of this Reo Royale Eight. Reo augmented the stunning 8-35 with several variants, but sales remained sluggish—only 3418 total Royales for '31.

◀ New versions of Reo's mid-price Flying Cloud, the 6-25 six and 8-30 eight, borrowed elements of Royale styling but stuck to flat radiators. An 80-bhp version of the six drove this $1705 Model 20 Sport Sedan.

Franklin D. Roosevelt is elected President in November

Ford's eagerly awaited 221-cid, 65-horsepower flathead V-8 arrives; production of upgraded four-cylinder Fords continues

Chevrolet ends the model year in the Number One spot; despite building only 313,404 cars, it's well ahead of rival Ford's 210,824

Plymouth reaches Number Three for the first time, ahead of Buick and Pontiac

Five manufacturers offer V-12 engines

Auburn issues a V-12 series and installs a "Dual-Ratio" Columbia rear axle in upper-level models; a boattail Speedster is a stunner

▲ A mere $975 in 1932 bought Auburn's 8-100A Custom Eight Speedster ($845 without two-ratio axle; V-12 higher).

▲ All Buicks had straight-eights in 1932, including this Series 60 sedan. "Wizard Control" and "Silent Second SynchroMesh" were new features.

▲ Cadillac's 353-cid V-8 was boosted to 115 bhp for 1932, as bodies grew more rounded. Eights sold far better than Twelves; V-16s were very rare.

▲ Long rear-quarter windows gave this '32 Chevrolet Confederate DeLuxe five-passenger coupe a roomy look. This body saw 7656 copies built. Synchromesh was new.

▲ Many consider the 1932 Confederate models, including the Sport Coupe, one of the sharpest Chevys of all time. This DeLuxe version with sidemount tires cost $505.

▲ Gracefully curved fenders and a rakish grille helped make the 1932 Imperial one of the loveliest Chryslers ever—more luscious yet in long, low Speedster form. Its 384.8-cid straight-eight engine cranked out 125 horsepower.

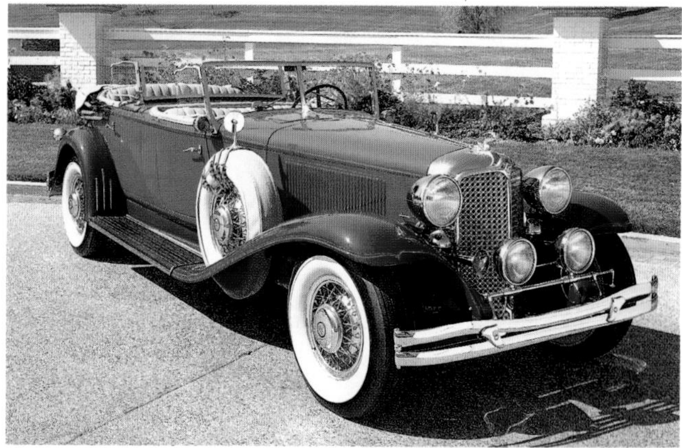

▲ Large, luxurious, and graceful, the 1932 Chrysler Series CH Imperial dual-cowl phaeton ranks with the finest Classics. Imperials rode long 135- or 146-inch wheelbases, with custom bodies from Derham, LeBaron, and Murphy.

---

Pierce-Arrow drops Eights, launches two new V-12 engines boasting hydraulically operated valve lifters

Studebaker introduces the low-priced companion Rockne ($585-$695); Hudson launches the Essex Terraplane ($425-$610)

Chrysler focuses on silent running with quieter fans, air-intakes, and exhaust systems

Vacuum-actuated clutches appear on Buick, Cadillac, Chrysler, DeSoto, Dodge, LaSalle; most makes again offer free-wheeling

Inside sun visors gain popularity, replacing outside visors

Oldsmobile and Packard engines have automatic chokes

Fred Duesenberg, Alexander Winton, Ray A. Graham, and Hugh Chalmers die this year

▲ DeSoto launched an "All New Six" SC series in 1932, here the Custom roadster with a 75-bhp, 211.5-cid engine. A 77-bhp straight-eight was also sold, but would be gone after '32.

▶ Exposed exhaust pipes suggest that this open Duesenberg has the supercharger introduced in 1932, but some unblown Duesies gained pipes in later life. With blower, it could top 125 mph, reaching 100 in 17 seconds.

▲ Like other '32 Fords, the $600 Victoria coupe came with either a 50-bhp four-cylinder engine or the new 65-bhp V-8. The fuel tank moved to the rear.

▲ Styling for the streamlined 1932 Ford was based on the big Lincoln. A V-8 roadster cost $460 ($485 with rumble seat, or $500 in DeLuxe trim).

▲ The $545 DeLuxe V-8 phaeton had cowl lights and pinstripes; a Standard phaeton cost $50 less. Production of both versions totaled only 2705 units.

▲ A Ford Sport Coupe (*shown*) had a rumble seat; regular three-window coupes didn't. Four-cylinder cars cost $50 less than V-8s. Early V-8s had overheating and oil-burning ills. Chevrolet ended '32 far ahead in sales.

▲ This Dietrich-bodied Sports Speedster runs with a 100-bhp six, but Franklin also launched a supercharged V-12 series in '32. The 398-cid V-12 made 150 bhp. Both were air-cooled. Total Franklin output was 1900 units.

▲ Graham issued a variety of six- and eight-cylinder models for 1932, including this $1225 Special Eight coupe—plus a new Blue Streak Eight styled by Amos Northup. It sported skirted fenders and a jaunty windshield tilt.

---

Unemployed workers hold a "hunger march" at Ford's Rouge plant after layoffs; four are killed

Buick's "Wizard Control" combines an automatic clutch with free-wheeling; other makes offer similar setups

Cadillac adopts more rounded styling, boosts its V-8 to 115 bhp

The last L-29 Cords appear—the marque will disappear until '36

Three Essex series are listed: Standard, Pacemaker, and Terraplane; the last is destined to help save Hudson

A supercharged, air-cooled V-12 with 150 bhp is available in Franklins, initially in the new Airman series

Hupmobile Eights are styled by Raymond Loewy; the dramatic shape doesn't translate to impressive sales

▲ "Cannon Ball" Baker, well known for transcontinental runs, drove this 1932 Hudson Standard sedan in record time between two Ohio cities. Some models could hit 90 mph; Hudson often flaunted the prowess of its cars.

◀ A $1195 Hudson Special Coupe, part of the '32 Greater Eight Standard line, cost $100 more than a regular coupe, and sported deluxe fittings. Bored to 254-cid, Hudson's straight-eight now cranked out 101 horses.

▲ Raymond Loewy styled Hupmobile's 1932 F-222 (*shown*) and I-226 Eights, featuring tire-hugging fenders, vee'd grille, and sloping windshields. Total Hupp output: 10,476.

▲ Hupmobile started 1932 with a carryover line, then issued a Second Series (*shown*)—a common practice. Buyers could choose from a six, or one of three straight-eights.

▲ Hupmobile touted the modernized F-222 (*shown*) and its mates as "A New Car for a New Age." They ranked among the best-looking cars of '32.

▲ One of seven 1932 models, this 130-inch-wheelbase LaSalle convertible coupe sold for $2545. All 3386 '32 LaSalles built used a 353-cid V-8.

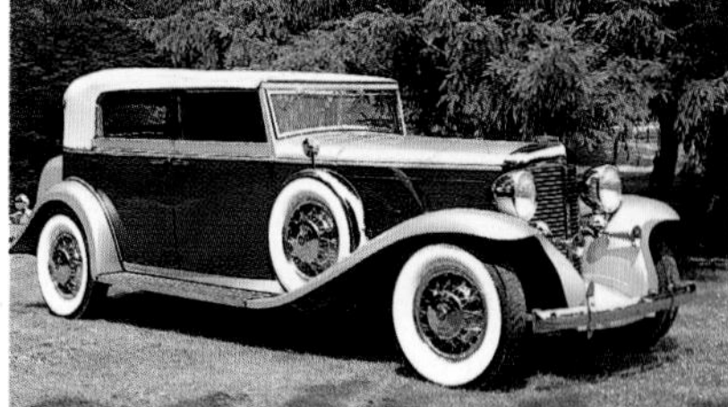

▲ Marmon narrowed its line to three choices for 1932: Model 70 and 125 Eights, plus the big Sixteen. Shown here is a V-16 convertible sedan.

---

Lincoln adds a V-12 KB Series

Nash introduces the Ambassador Eight on a 142-inch wheelbase

Oldsmobile adopts an 87-bhp straight-eight engine

The new Twin Six Packard boasts a 160-bhp V-12, while the Light Eight gives Packard a lower-priced model

Ab Jenkins drives a well-used Pierce-Arrow V-12 prototype 2710 miles in 24 hours at the Bonneville Salt Flats in Utah

Plymouth's final four-cylinder models arrive, bolstered by a convertible sedan and seven-passenger sedan

Pontiac sales sag; William S. "Big Bill" Knudsen is named general manager

▲ "Syncro-Safety Shift," with a dash-mounted lever, was new on the '32 Nash, with a choice of seven engines and wheelbases. This is a $1785 Advanced Eight Victoria coupe.

▲ Packard lowered its bodies in 1932 and launched a Twin Six (V-12). This $1940 Series 900 Coupe-Roadster, part of the new mid-priced Light Eight line, sold 1060 copies.

▲ This Pierce-Arrow Eight coupe, on a 137-inch wheelbase, cost $2985 in 1932, with a 125-bhp, 366-cid engine. Biggest news was the debut of two V-12s: 398/429 cid, 140/150 horsepower.

▲ Despite the impressive qualities of cars like this $2985 Model 54 Eight sedan, Pierce-Arrow lost $3 million in 1932. Only 2234 cars were built in the model year—far behind Packard.

▲► Created as a showpiece, the Pierce Silver Arrow claimed to offer "in 1933 the car of 1940." Five were built; one paced the Indy 500 race. Designed by Philip Wright, the tapered-tail four-door had smooth front fenders and no running boards.

---

A smaller Reo Flying Cloud emerges

Jaeger debuts with a unique twin-coil suspension; only five are built

**1932 Model Year Production**

|  |  |  |
|---|---|---|
| 1. | Chevrolet | 313,404 |
| 2. | Ford | 210,824 |
| 3. | Plymouth | 186,106 |
| 4. | Hudson/Essex | 57,550 |
| 5. | Buick | 56,790 |
| 6. | Pontiac | 45,340 |
| 7. | Nash | 30,834 |
| 8. | Willys | 27,800 |

*Some figures are estimated or calendar-year*

**1933**

Franklin D. Roosevelt is inaugurated—he declares a bank holiday and ushers in his "New Deal"

Industry output rises to 1,627,361 cars, plus 358,548 trucks

▲ Nash offered a rumble-seat coupe in each of its many model lines for 1932, except for the long-wheelbase Ambassador Eight. Ads touted the Second Series' "slipstream body" and "beavertail" sloped back panel.

▲ Jazzy striping and a low windshield must have made this 1932 Plymouth PB "Collegiate Special" Sport Roadster a hot number on campus. Boosted to 65 horsepower, the L-head engine was Plymouth's final four until the Seventies.

▲ A new 135-inch platform carried this '32 Studebaker President Eight convertible roadster, in $1750 basic or $1855 "State" trim. Its 337-cid engine made 122 bhp. Stude also listed Dictator and Commander Eights, and a Six.

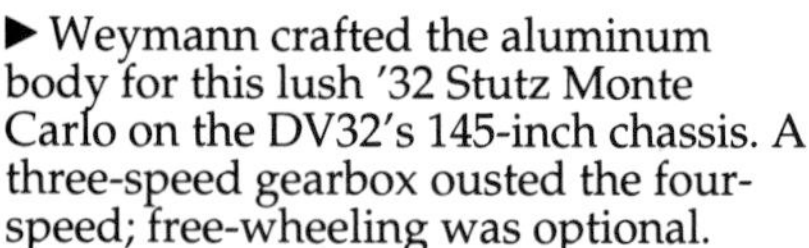

► Weymann crafted the aluminum body for this lush '32 Stutz Monte Carlo on the DV32's 145-inch chassis. A three-speed gearbox ousted the four-speed; free-wheeling was optional.

▲ Stutz revived the old Bearcat name, topped by this stubby $5895 Super Bearcat on a special 116-inch wheelbase—guaranteed to hit 100 mph.

---

Chevrolet tops Ford in production by a sizable margin; Plymouth ranks a solid third; Dodge moves up to fourth, passing Pontiac and Buick in the process

Continental debuts as the only major new make; descended from DeVaux, it lasts only into 1934

Aerodynamic streamlining is the craze at the 33rd National Automobile Show

In May, Reo introduces its "Self-Shifter," a semi-automatic transmission that's controlled by an under-dash T-handle

Power-assisted brakes are offered on various makes

GM's Fisher bodies offer "No-Draft Ventilation," with pivoting front ventwings to control airflow

Several makes adopt the gas-pedal starter arrangement

▲ The sparkling lines of a 1933 Auburn Salon Twelve Dual-Ratio Phaeton Sedan failed to translate into strong sales. Only 7939 Auburns were built this year, and the total would sink further. Eight-cylinder engines provided 100 horsepower, versus 160 bhp for the big 392-cid V-12.

▲ American Austin prices were cut in 1933, down to $275 for the business coupe and $315 for a roadster. Just 4726 were built, and fewer yet in '34. Additional body styles had been added in 1931. Prized by some as a reverse status symbol, the American Austin expired in 1935.

▲ Fresh styling by Harley Earl gave this 1933 Cadillac V-16 Victoria skirted fenders and a unique vee'd grille, on a long 149-inch wheelbase. Note the elegant four-bar bumper.

▲ Kinship with the legendary Auburn-Cord-Duesenberg empire seems bizarre, but E.L. Cord bought Checker Taxi in 1933. A 98-bhp Lycoming straight-eight powered the '33 cabs.

▲ Chevrolet's two-seat roadster was gone in 1933, and its rumble-seat mate fading, as buyers turned to cabriolets. Two Chevy series were sold: a Mercury and upmarket Eagle (*shown*).

▲ GM's 1933 models featured "No-Draft Ventilation" (pivoting wind wings), developed by Fisher Body.

◀ This 1916 Chevrolet was driven to Chicago's Century of Progress, where the 1933 Chevy coach was built in a plant at the fair's GM building.

---

New technical innovations include valve-seat inserts, independent front suspension, and reflex glass taillights

Competition forces Ford to give in to annual model changes

Cadillac limits the sale of V-16 models to 400 per year—but sells only 125

The nation's first drive-in theater opens in Camden, New Jersey

Roy Chapin returns as president of Hudson after a stint in the Hoover Administration

GM president Alfred Sloan combines Chevy and Pontiac manufacturing to cut costs, then merges Buick, Olds, and Pontiac sales divisions, so dealers must sell all three

As Studebaker falls into receivership and skids to 14th in production, chairman Albert R. Erskine resigns

▲ Walter P. Chrysler poses with his company's famed trio of engineers (*left to right*): Carl Breer, Mr. Chrysler, Fred Zeder, and Owen Skelton. Known as the "Three Musketeers," they dominated '30s engineering policy at Chrysler.

▲ The cheapest DeSoto for 1933 was the $665 business coupe. Prices were cut as production hit an all-time low: 24,896 units. The straight-eight was gone, but the 217.8-cid six made 82 bhp—five more than the '32 eight.

▲ Gracefully restyled, the '33 Ford got a more potent 75-bhp V-8 and rode a longer 112-inch wheelbase. The $510 DeLuxe roadster had a rumble seat.

▲ Graham's Blue Streak was renamed Custom Eight for 1933, topping the line at $1095. Ads called Graham "The Most Imitated Car on the Road."

▲ Al and Chet Miller drove "Marr Special" Hudson racers in the 1933 Indianapolis 500, between record-setting stints in Essex Terraplanes.

◀ Skirted fenders and a vee'd grille were new to LaSalle for 1933. So was GM's No-Draft Ventilation. This Series 345C RS coupe, with rumble seat, sold for $2245. LaSalle also offered a five-seat Town Coupe, a sedan, and convertible—plus a trio of sedans on a six-inch-longer 136-inch wheelbase. As before, the 353-cid V-8 engine developed 115 horsepower. Dashboards featured wood trim. A total of 3482 cars were built for the model year, giving LaSalle a so-so 21st place in industry output.

---

Stutz, whose days are numbered, loses a half-million dollars

Willys-Overland, reorganized after bankruptcy, pins its future on the small 100-inch-wheelbase Model 77; production is initially under court supervision

C.L. McCuen becomes president of Oldsmobile; Harlow H. Curtice is president of Buick

The National Automobile Dealers Association (NADA) publishes its first *Official Used Car Guide*

Streamlined Cadillacs sport skirted fenders, vee'd radiators

Chrysler abandons its unpopular four-speed gearbox

Essex offers the Terraplane only, now with an optional straight-eight engine that sets more than 100 stock-car records

▲ Only Marmon Sixteens were produced in 1933, their prices cut by nearly $1000. All assets were taken over by the American Automotive Corporation in January 1934. An attempt at revival failed, and the inevitable liquidation came in 1937.

▲ Marmon's V-16 again boasted 200 bhp—35 more than Cadillac's V-16. Only 86 Marmons, like this $4825 sedan, were registered for '33.

▲ Dietrich supplied bodies for Packard V-12s, including the $6070 Victoria. Standard and Super Eights were also sold. Total '33 Packard output: 4803.

▲ Only three Dietrich-bodied Packard Sport Phaetons were built in 1933, on a 147-inch wheelbase, for auto shows. The rear windshield/windows folded.

▲ A 175-bhp, 462-cid V-12 went into this '33 Pierce-Arrow 1247 convertible sedan. Other models had a 160-bhp V-12 or 135-bhp eight. Total output this year was only 2298 cars.

▲ Pierce-Arrow's smaller 429-cid V-12 powered the 1933 Model 1236 Club Brougham, whose spare tire rode far back. In August, a syndicate of bankers took over the ailing firm.

---

Low-slung Fords adopt "suicide" (rear-hinged) doors; the V-8 is boosted to 75 horsepower

Hudson's Pacemaker series gets a new Super Six engine borrowed from the Terraplane

A smaller V-12 engine (381.7-cid) powers Lincoln's KA-Series

Plymouth switches to a six-cylinder engine, sales zoom

The rakishly futuristic Pierce-Arrow Silver Arrow appears, but only five are built

A modified Pierce-Arrow V-12 sets 79 world speed records, reaches 128 mph

**1933 Model Year Production**

| | |
|---|---|
| 1. Chevrolet | 486,261 |
| 2. Ford | 334,969 |
| 3. Plymouth | 298,557 |
| 4. Dodge | 106,103 |
| 5. Pontiac | 90,198 |
| 6. Buick | 46,924 |
| 7. Studebaker/Rockne | 43,024 |
| 8. Hudson/Essex | 40,982 |

*Some figures are estimated or calendar-year*

▲ Reo trimmed its '33 line, which saw only 4112 sales. The Flying Cloud Eight was gone, so this S-2 convertible got a 268-cid six. To raise cash, Reo sold bodies to Franklin.

▲ Stutz offered its 1933 models with either a 133-bhp SV16 straight-eight or dual-cam DV32 (*shown*) with 161 bhp. Output dwindled to a trickle, less than 50 cars in 1932-33.

◀ Hudson's Essex Terraplane debuted in mid-1932 on a new 106-inch wheelbase, with a 70-bhp, 193-cid six. An eight joined in '33. Capable of 80 mph and 25 mpg, Terraplanes earned a deserved "Hill-Buster" nickname.

▲ Following bankruptcy, Willys debuted the little Model 77 in 1933, with a 100-inch chassis and 48-bhp four.



▶ Willys promoted the 25-30 mpg economy of the 77, plus its 70-mph top speed. Though snug, sedans held four, and both two-passenger and two/four-seat coupes were built— all in regular or Custom trim. All-steel bodies weighed around 2100 pounds. Later, the lightweight coupes would be popular with racers.

▲ The Willys 77 came in coupe and sedan form for $395-$475. Canted headlamps and "starfish" wheels made the 77 "audacious." This year saw the last Overlands and Knights.

---

**1934**

Labor disputes hit the auto industry with increasing intensity

Industry production rises to 2,270,566 cars and 599,397 trucks

Chevrolet beats Ford's calendar-year volume by close to 10 percent

Chrysler launches its daring Airflow, but excellence in engineering fails to tempt customers, who don't fancy the avant-garde look

Graham issues the Supercharged Custom Eight, the first moderately priced blown engine

LaFayette debuts as the "junior" series from Nash; prices start at a modest $585

The Brewster nameplate returns after nearly a decade; unique bodies go mainly on Ford V-8 and Buick chassis from 1934-36

▲ Like other GM makes, Buick adopted "Knee-Action" in '34. A 100-bhp, 278-cid eight powered this $1495 Series 60 convertible; 263 were sold.

▲ Cadillac's 1934 restyling featured pontoon fenders, a slanted grille, and torpedo headlamps. Shown is a $3045 355-D Eight convertible sedan.

▲ Knee-Action front suspension went into Chevrolet's Master series, but not Standard versions. Only 1974 Sport Roadsters were built in '34.

▲ The engineers who developed the Chrysler Airflow failed to predict public response to the radical design—especially its curvy front end. This $1345 CU sedan was the most popular '34 Airflow, but only 7226 were called for.

► A skeleton view of the Chrysler Imperial Airflow unit chassis/frame reveals its innovative cage structure, with the engine placed over the front axle. A 122-bhp, 299-cid straight-eight powered basic Airflows. Imperials got 130 bhp via 323.5-cid, Custom Imperials 150-bhp with 385-cid. Borg-Warner overdrive was made available during 1934.

---

The "Hupp Aerodynamic" features a three-piece windshield; Archie Andrews captures control of Hupmobile

Although the restyled Pierce-Arrow line includes a less-radical Silver Arrow, the company is forced to file for bankruptcy

American Austin builds its last cars this year

General Motors cars come with "Knee-Action" (independent) front suspension—optional in some models, standard in many

Various makes have radio controls built into the instrument panel

Cadillac introduces a controlled-current generator

Terraplane officially becomes a separate make, and accounts for the dominant portion of parent Hudson's sales through 1937

◀ Joe Frazer, serving as Chrysler's vice-president of sales, asked shoppers "to compare" the Airflow. Cars were scarce at first, so by the time Airflows arrived at dealerships the public was skeptical. Only 10,839 Chrysler Airflows were built in 1934, versus 25,252 conventional CA/CB models.

▶ Baseball great Babe Ruth (*left*), division manager Byron C. Foy, and Walter P. Chrysler (*right*) attended a bash to celebrate the DeSoto Airflow. Whereas Chrysler also offered an ordinary model, DeSoto sold only the Airflow, with a 100-bhp, 241.5-cid six, on a 115.5-inch wheelbase. Each of four body styles sold for $995.

▲ Dodge dropped straight-eight engines for 1934, and never produced an Airflow. This $765 DeLuxe convertible, of which 1239 were built, carried Dodge's new 87-bhp, 217.8-cid L-head six, destined for a long life.

▶ Actor/singer Dick Powell sits at the wheel of a '34 DeSoto Airflow sedan, its twin windshields open to the breeze. Priced well below Chrysler's version, the DeSoto Airflow sold a bit better, as 13,940 were produced.

---

Auburn displays new "Aero-Streamlined" styling; six-cylinder power returns

Ford receives a modest facelift, while the V-8 gains another 10 horsepower

Hudson abandons its six-cylinder engine this year

All Lincolns adopt a new 414-cid V-12, with a high 6.3:1 compression ratio

The last of Nash's big 322-cid straight-eights go into Ambassador models this year; all Nash engines have Twin-Ignition

Plymouth strokes its engine to 201.3 cid; independent front suspension is new; Westchester Suburban wagon bodies are created by an Indiana builder

Newly streamlined Pontiacs get a horsepower boost, "trunkback" sedans are featured

▲ A 95-bhp straight-eight drove this 1934 Model 67 convertible, but the big news at Graham was a Supercharged Custom Eight, blasting out 135 bhp—the first blower on a mid-price car.

◀ The brazen and sporty four-pipe outside exhausts of the supercharged Duesenberg SJ later became optional on the "ordinary" Model J. A handful of final SJs contained a ram's horn manifold, which boosted output to a whopping 400 horsepower.

▲ Wooden station wagons still looked a trifle crude in '34. Ford (*shown*) built its own bodies, but other automakers used outside suppliers.

▲ "Suicide" doors and laid-back lines gave this $615 '34 Ford DeLuxe Fordor a jaunty stance. The V-8 now had 85 bhp. This model saw 102,268 sales.

▲ Not enough bucks for a Packard Super Eight or Twelve? Then try this $2580 Model 1101 Coupe-Roadster, with its smaller 120-bhp, 320-cid eight.

▲ Custom coachwork sent Packard prices skyward. Dietrich fashioned this 1934 Victoria Twelve, with a towering $6080 tag. Only 960 Twelves were built with the 160-bhp engine.

▲ Convertible sedans were offered in each Packard series: Eight, Super Eight, and Twelve. Dealers brought '34 Packards to customers' homes for demo rides, and sales jumped to 8000.

▲ Shapely describes 1934 LeBaron-built Packard Twelve Sport Phaetons, priced at $7065. Coachbuilders also put their talents to Super Eights, which sold twice as well as the Twelve.

---

Carryover Reos are displaced by freshened models in April, led by the S-4 Flying Cloud

Ford V-8s earn high praise from "folk hero" criminals John Dillinger and Clyde Barrow

**1934 Model Year Production**

|  |  |
|---|---|
| 1. Ford | 563,921 |
| 2. Chevrolet | 551,191 |
| 3. Plymouth | 321,171 |
| 4. Dodge | 95,011 |
| 5. Hudson/Terraplane | 85,835 |
| 6. Oldsmobile | 79,814 |
| 7. Pontiac | 78,859 |
| 8. Buick | 71,009 |

*Some figures are estimated or calendar-year*

**1935**

Industry output jumps to 3,387,806 cars and 732,005 trucks

Chevrolet produces 820,253 cars during the model year, versus 548,215 for Ford

▲ For 1934, Pierce-Arrow borrowed the name of its Silver Arrow show car for a less radical fastback coupe, sold as a DeLuxe Eight or Salon Twelve. Bankruptcy came in August.

▲ Plymouth looked more streamlined in '34; here, a $660 PE DeLuxe sedan with a Gabriel form-fit trunk. It found 108,407 buyers. A coil-spring front suspension was new.

▲ As in '33, Pontiac sold only eights for 1934. Despite sharing many body panels with Chevy, this $705 two-door maintained a distinct look on a new 117.5-inch chassis.

▲ Rumble seats still had their fans, but plenty of potential passengers would rather ride inside. The 1934 Pontiac Sport Coupe sold for $725 and featured GM's new Knee-Action independent front suspension, plus a boost to 84 bhp. This model, which listed at $725, weighed in at 3260 pounds.

▲ On June 4, 1934, major auto executives met with President Franklin D. Roosevelt for a Labor Conference in Washington. Pictured (*left to right*): Roy D. Chapin, Hudson; Alfred P. Sloan, Jr., General Motors; Walter P. Chrysler; Alvan Macauley, Packard; and Donaldson Brown, GM.

▲ Produced by Hudson, Terraplane lost its "Essex" prefix for 1934, and was listed as a separate make. Most examples didn't look quite as curious as this custom-bodied tourer from Australia. Straight-eights were gone, but a new 212-cid six boasted 80/85 bhp. Terraplane output: 51,084.

---

The Automobile Manufacturers Association waits until November 1935 to sponsor the 36th National Automobile Show; meanwhile, the 35th Show is sponsored by the Automobile Merchants Association of New York

Fords appear at the 1935 National Automobile Show—for the first time in 25 years

Lower-priced cars are a trend this year; models with fewer features or less power are announced by Chrysler, DeSoto, Graham, Hudson, Hupmobile, Packard, Pontiac, and Reo

A conventionally styled "Airstream" series joins Chrysler's (and DeSoto's) slow-selling Airflow lines, helping keep the company afloat

General Motors cars begin the switch to Fisher all-steel "Turret-Top" roofs, eliminating the customary fabric inserts

▲ Seeking a cheaper heir to the Duesenberg, Gordon Buehrig and August Duesenberg wound up creating a revived Auburn Speedster for 1935—one of the most striking '30s machines, complete with supercharger. And only $2245!

► The Auburn Speedster's boattail body had little luggage space, but gobs of personality—highlighted by big exterior exhaust pipes. A dashboard plate certified that the 127-inch-wheelbase, 3706-pound car had been driven at 100 mph.

▲ Auburn's stylish 851 series comprised a full choice of bodies, including this Phaeton Sedan. The 280-cid straight-eight came plain or supercharged—115 or 150 horses.

▲ Buick called its open Series 60 four-door a Convertible Phaeton in 1935. It sold for $1675, and its 278-cid eight made 100 bhp. All four series had a different size engine.

---

Sedan bodies, particularly "trunk-back" versions, gain in popularity; open cars decline

Chevrolet introduces the Suburban Carryall, the first all-steel station wagon body, on its panel-delivery light-truck chassis

Nash offers a new "sealed-in" engine with the manifold cast inside the block

The failed American Austin firm is taken over by Roy S. Evans, who later will announce the American Bantam

Pierce-Arrow is reorganized and resumes auto operations, but fewer than 1000 cars are built

Paul G. Hoffman becomes president of Studebaker

Walter P. Chrysler turns the presidency over to K.T. Keller; F.M. Zeder is vice-chairman

▲ Chevy's upscale Master roadster was gone, and this $465 Standard Sports Roadster saw only 1176 sales in 1935. Closed Master DeLuxe models adopted an all-steel "Turret Top."

▲ Movie stars didn't limit their affection to Duesenbergs and Packards. Here, James Stewart and Wendy Barrie enjoy a more modest $895 '36 DeSoto Custom Airstream ragtop.

▲ At a dealership, a '35 Dodge DU four-door sedan would have sold for $760 ($735 as a trunkless fastback). This year's Airstream look sported a waterfall grille and skirted fenders.

▲ Dodge named its 1935 line the "New Value Six," again with the 217.8-cid L-head as sole engine. Coupes came with or without a rumble seat, and 22,299 of both types were produced.

▲ Engine designer Harry Miller teamed with Preston Tucker to enter a set of Miller-Fords in the 1935 Indy 500—the first front-drive Indycars with all-independent suspension.

◀▲ Ford greeted 1935 with a new longer, wider, sleeker look, plus front-hinged doors. This was the final year for wire wheels and outside horns. Woody wagon bodies were built in Ford's Iron Mountain, Michigan, plant. The wagon listed at $670, the DeLuxe five-window coupe for $560.

---

The stunning Auburn Speedster, destined to spawn replicars decades later, has the 150-bhp Super-Charged engine

A $925 convertible coupe joins Buick's low-priced Series 40 line

Chevrolets wear sleek new bodies with vee'd windshields

Dodge's New Value Six, displaying the "Airstream" look, enjoys a sales surge

Duesenberg offers the Rollston-bodied, 153.5-inch-wheelbase JN; only 10 are built

Ford sports an all-new look and front-hinged front doors; the convertible sedan is revived

"Second Series" Graham sedans veer from the prior Blue Streak styling; the company is suffering financially

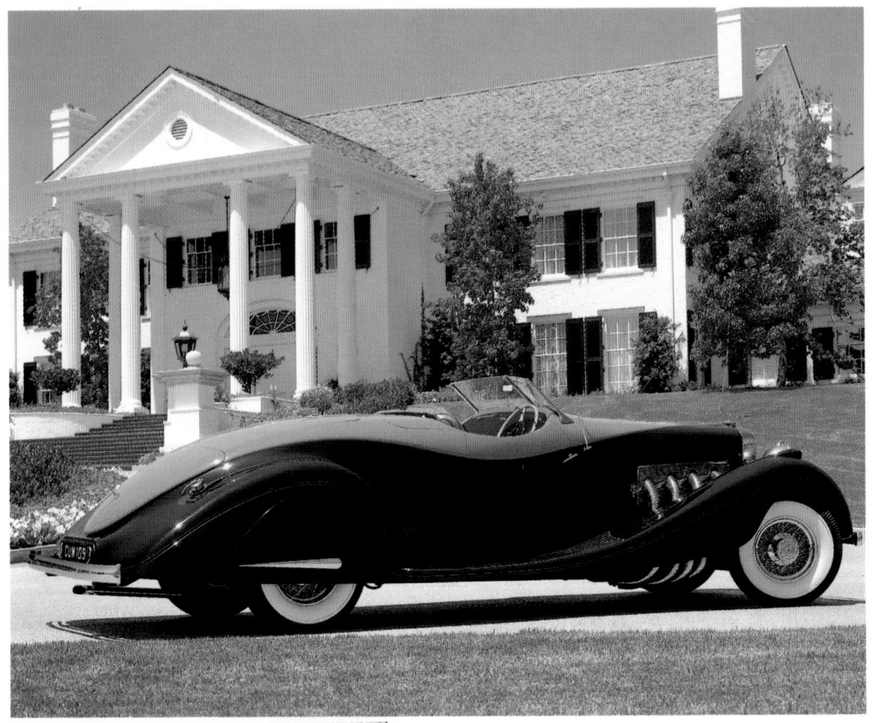

▲ Red and blue running lights were to signal whether the Maharajah or his wife was driving the Duesenberg. Celebrities from Mae West to Howard Hughes eagerly purchased Duesies.

◄ Built for the Maharajah of Indore, India, this right-drive '35 Duesenberg SJ Speedster-Roadster wore a body by J. Gurney Nutting of England, and was styled by A.F. McNeil.

▲ A smaller Graham Standard Six (sedans only) debuted in 1935, with a 60-bhp, 170-cid engine and 111-inch chassis. With prices ranging from $595 to $685, 11,470 examples were built.

▲ Graham's 1935 Special Six, including coupes and a convertible as well as this Touring Sedan, rode a 116-inch wheelbase and had an 85-bhp, 224-cid engine. Despite an overall sales increase to 15,965, output of Eights fell sharply.

---

Hudsons get a new six-cylinder engine, but still lose market share—most customers buy the cheaper Terraplanes

A new 105-bhp, 248-cid straight-eight is available in some LaSalles

Nashes gain "Aeroform Design" and hydraulic brakes

Packard launches its lower-priced One-Twenty models, which start at $980

A more streamlined Plymouth features new "Chair-Height" seats and an optional "economy" engine

Six-cylinder engines return to Pontiac after a two-year absence

Reo fields only six-cylinder models: Flying Cloud and Royale

Studebaker Dictators can have conventional or Planar independent front suspension—this unwisely named series hangs on through 1937

▲ Big Model K Lincolns, riding 136/145-inch wheelbases, gained a smoother look for 1935. Priced ranged from $4200 to $6800; output fell to 1434.

▲ Not all sidemounted spares looked natural. Restyled for '35, Plymouths now could take "trunkback" form.

▲ Studebaker fielded three series in 1935: Dictator Six, Commander Eight (*shown*), and President Eight—on 114-, 120-, and 124-inch wheelbases.

► Only a $475 basic coupe (*shown*) and sedan made up the '35 Willys Model 77 line, hyped as "The New Era Car." Note the neatly recessed spare tire.

The experimental Stout Scarab—a rear-engined forerunner of the minivan—debuts; only about five will be sold

A Ford convertible sedan paces the Indy 500 race

Oklahoma City installs the first parking meters

**1935 Model Year Production**

|  |  |
|---|---|
| 1. Ford | 820,253 |
| 2. Chevrolet | 548,215 |
| 3. Plymouth | 350,884 |
| 4. Pontiac | 178,770 |
| 5. Dodge | 158,999 |
| 6. Oldsmobile | 126,768 |
| 7. Hudson/Terraplane | 101,080 |
| 8. Buick | 53,249 |

*Some figures are estimated or calendar-year*

**1936**

Industry output totals 3,669,528 cars and 784,587 trucks for the best year since 1929

Ford tops Chevrolet in model-year output with a gracefully facelifted line, but lags in calendar-year production 975,238 to 791,812

▲ Auburn Eights, including this Supercharged cabriolet, got an 852 label for 1936, but changed little. Sixes were called Model 654. Only 1848 cars were built in Auburn's final year.

▲ Buicks adopted new model names for 1936: Special (Series 40), Century (60), Roadmaster (80), and Limited (90). Fresh styling included an all-steel "Turret Top" (a year later than other GM cars). A 120-bhp, 320-cid eight replaced three former engines.

◄ Tucking its big 320-cid engine into a light Special body, Buick created the swift-moving Century—perhaps the first "factory hot rod." Note the enclosed spare on this $1090 Touring Sedan. Specials stuck with a 233-cid, 93-bhp eight. Hydraulic brakes were new; sedans had integrated trunks.

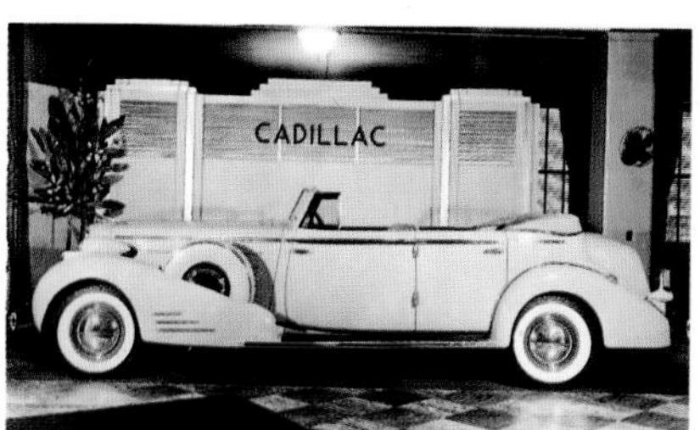


▲ Only 52 huge Series 90 Cadillacs were built in 1936—and just six Fleetwood V-16 convertible sedans. All except Sixteens had hydraulic brakes.

▲ The most popular Standard '36 Chevy was the $605 Town Sedan, which saw sales of 220,884 units. It had new hydraulic brakes and a steel roof.

▲ Even Checker taxis had "suicide" doors in 1936. Morris Markin regained control of the Checker firm following three years of E.L. Cord ownership.

---

Plymouth breaks the half-million production mark for the first time, while Oldsmobile rises to fifth place, behind Dodge

A masterpiece—the front-drive "coffin-nose" Cord 810—debuts three years after the last L-29. Many consider it one of the most beautiful designs of all time

The $1275 Lincoln-Zephyr, with a V-12 derived from the Ford V-8, is Lincoln's first medium-priced car

The final DeSoto Airflows are built; Chrysler's version will last one more season

After building 3206 cars in 1936, Reo abandons the car business to concentrate exclusively on trucks

Stutz offers its last automobiles, including a Bearcat speedster

▲ Chrysler built 59,258 cars for 1936, but only 6285 were Airflows, including this $1475 Imperial C10. Conventionally styled Airstreams fronted teardrop headlamps.

▲ Chrysler Airflow Imperials rode a 128-inch wheelbase, but Custom Imperials (*shown*) spanned 137 or 146.5 inches. Their 323.5-cid inline eight made 130 horsepower.

▼ With a "coffin" nose and crank-up headlights, this dazzling new 1936 Cord 810 could never be mistaken for any lesser auto. A fingertip pre-selector activated its four-speed gearbox.

▲ The final DeSoto Airflows came in 1936, as a sedan or this $1095 coupe, which saw only 250 built. Chrysler's version lasted a year longer.

▲ Dodge dubbed its '36s "Beauty Winner," an apt title for this $795 rag-top coupe; 1525 were sold. A convertible sedan was revived at $995.

▲ Apex of the Duesenberg legend was the supercharged, short-wheelbase SSJ Speedster. Only two were built—one each for Clark Gable and Gary Cooper.

---

The American Bantam minicar tries to take up where the American Austin left off; prices start at $295

Graham, abandoning eight-cylinder engines, introduces the first supercharged six; bodies are shared with Reo's Flying Cloud

E.L. Cord returns from England to face government inquiries; plans for a '37 Auburn fade away

Cord 810s have disappearing headlights, Lycoming V-8, and Bendix "Electric Hand" shifting (with a supercharger optional in 1937)

Many new models have the handbrake to the driver's left to allow for a roomier front seat

Many cars have sloping side windows and built-in defrosters

Nash displays a car with twin travel beds

▲ A facelift made the '36 model a prime choice of Ford fans. This $560 DeLuxe roadster sold only 3862 copies; the cabriolets were far more popular.

▲ Add-on skirts added flash to a '36 Ford DeLuxe Touring Sedan. With trunk, a Tudor cost $590. Horns were hidden; steel wheels replaced wires.

▲ Early '36 Ford convertible sedans were fastbacks. "Trunkback" styling arrived at mid-year, attracting buyers who wanted more cargo space.

▲ Graham dropped eights, but added a supercharged six. This Cavalier shared bodies with a Reo model.

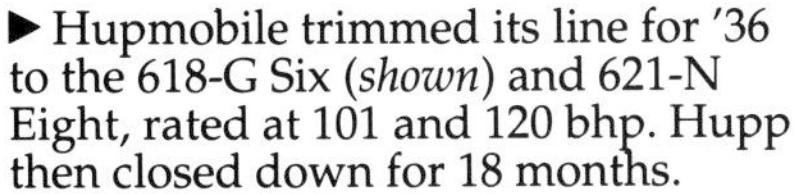

▶ Hupmobile trimmed its line for '36 to the 618-G Six (*shown*) and 621-N Eight, rated at 101 and 120 bhp. Hupp then closed down for 18 months.

▲ Produced by GM Truck and Coach and borrowing Chevrolet components, the General Taxi was similar—but not identical—to the regular 1936 General Motors cars.

▲ Fresh "art deco" styling with a tall grille gave 1936 Hudsons a slick look. DeLuxe and Custom Eights (*shown*) were sold, plus a Custom Six. Terraplanes sold far better.

---

U.S. Dept. of Commerce finds that 54 percent of families own cars

Nash Motor Company merges with Kelvinator Corporation to form Nash-Kelvinator Corporation, with George W. Mason as president and Charles W. Nash as chairman

Willys-Overland Motors is reorganized and moves out of receivership in February; 30,826 Model 77 cars are built

Buick models now have names as well as numbers and a streamlined steel-roof design courtesy of Harley Earl's Art & Colour Section

The Century mixes Buick's lighterweight body with the Roadmaster's big engine, creating a "banker's hot rod"

A cheaper Series Sixty joins the Cadillac line; all except the V-16 adopt hydraulic brakes

▲ Lincoln added the lower-priced, unibody Zephyr for '36, styled by John Tjaarda along aircraft principles. This $1320 four-door had a 110-bhp, 267-cid V-12; 13,180 were built.

▲ Babe Ruth shows off a $945 '37 Nash Ambassador Eight, with a 261-cid Twin-Ignition engine. The '37 line also included LaFayette (replacing 400) and the Ambassador Six.

◀ Many of its hoity-toity devotees were horrified when Packard assaulted the upper mid-priced market with the One-Twenty in 1935. Aimed at folks who couldn't afford a Packard before, it held an L-head eight, stroked to 282-cid and 120-bhp for 1936. A '36 convertible like this paced Indy.

▼ Touted as "World's Safest Motor Car," Pierce-Arrow promised more than 30 improvements for 1936—like the industry's biggest brakes, now power-boosted. Redesign brought a rounded shape and improved ride/handling. Twelves, as in this $4795 Model 1603 sedan, now had 185 horses.

▲ Packard continued to issue posh models, such as this massive Super Eight dual-cowl phaeton with hang-on trunk, but the cheaper One-Twenty stole the 1936 sales show. Super Eights rode 132- to 144-inch wheelbases.

Chevrolets have new hydraulic brakes, but the roadster and phaeton are gone

The "Beauty Winner" Dodge line includes a revived convertible sedan and long-wheelbase sedans/limos

Hudsons feature all-new, all-steel bodies

Hupmobile shuts its plant down early in the year, and it remains closed for 18 months

A single 105-bhp straight-eight powers all LaSalles

Nash debuts low-cost, six-cylinder "400" models; prices start at $675

The Packard One-Twenty's engine is stroked to 282-cid and a convertible sedan is added—series output doubles to 55,042 units

▲ Pierce-Arrow prices started at $3115 in 1936. Eight-cylinder models rose to 150 bhp. With overdrive, this $3795 Model 1602 Club Berline Twelve might nudge 100 mph.

▲ Even if ad claims of "America's Finest Six" were true, Reo neared extinction, building only trucks after 3206 cars for 1936. The final Flying Clouds came basic or DeLuxe.

▶ No other 1936 automobile could be mistaken for the radical Stout Scarab, created by William B. Stout. Only Buckminster Fuller's earlier Dymaxion came close. Stout's teardrop-shaped future machine, sporting flush glass, was rear-wheel drive, using an 85-bhp Ford V-8 mounted out back. Stout announced output of 100 cars, starting at $5000, but no more than nine were built. Seats could be moved all over the flat floor.

▲ Only the Dictator Six and President Eight (*shown*) made Studebaker's 1936 lineup. Most Studes had "Planar" independent front suspension.

▲ Still frisky with its 88-bhp engine, the $640 '36 Terraplane DeLuxe Six coupe rode a longer 115-inch wheelbase and wore a narrow grille.

▲ In the Thirties, one year could make a big difference. This '35 Terraplane DeLuxe Six looks a lot less "modern" than its '36 successor to the left.

---

Pierce-Arrow is redesigned and billed as the "World's Safest Car," but sales continue to slip

Reo abandons the Self-Shifter, offers overdrive instead

Studebaker temporarily drops the Commander

"Hill Holder" is introduced by Studebaker; with the clutch depressed, the car will not roll backward on a hill

A supercharged Graham wins the Gilmore-Yosemite Economy Sweepstakes, recording 26.66 mpg

**1936 Model Year Production**

| | |
|---|---|
| 1. Ford | 930,778 |
| 2. Chevrolet | 918,278 |
| 3. Plymouth | 520,025 |
| 4. Dodge | 263,647 |
| 5. Oldsmobile | 200,546 |
| 6. Pontiac | 176,270 |
| 7. Buick | 168,596 |
| 8. Hudson/Terraplane | 123,266 |

*Some figures are estimated or calendar-year*

▲ Chevrolet enlarged its "Stovebolt Six" engine to 216.5 cid and 85 horsepower for 1937 and bragged about its *"Knee-Action Gliding Ride!"*

▲ Buick offered a Convertible Phaeton in its 1937 Special and Century series, as well as a more costly $1856 Roadmaster (*shown*), which had debuted a year earlier. Longer fenders had blunt trailing edges. Specials earned a bigger straight-eight, while the upper-level 320-cid engine gained 10 bhp, to 130. Buick promoted a new steering-wheel horn ring as well as front/rear anti-roll bars.

▲ Supercharging pushed the output of a 1937 Cord 812 to 170 or 190 bhp. Unblown, the 288.6-cid V-8 rated 125 horses.

▲ Styled by a crew under Gordon Buehrig, the 810/812 Cord was one of the top industrial designs, yet only 2320 were built in 1936-37. Shown is a '37 Beverly sedan.

◄ Rearward visibility wasn't a strong point of the '37 Cord 812 Custom Beverly sedan, but who cared with a body this luscious to gaze upon? Note the bustle trunk. Long 132-inch-wheelbase sedans joined the lineup in Cord's last year.

**1937**

Industry volume totals 3,915,889 cars and 893,085 trucks

Ford beats Chevrolet in model-year output, 942,005 cars to 815,375, but trails for the calendar year

Oldsmobile introduces the Safety Automatic Transmission (a semi-automatic) late in the year

Cadillac builds its final V-12 and ohv V-16, but a new L-head V-16 will appear for '38; the 346-cid V-8 is by far Cadillac's most popular engine

Chrysler products adopt all-steel roofs and standard safety glass

In the Cord's final season, supercharging and long-wheelbase sedans are available

LaFayette, mounted on the chassis of the prior 400 series, becomes the lowest-priced Nash

▲ Airflows were gone for 1937, when DeSoto built this $880 S3 sedan. It attracted 51,889 buyers. The L-head six shrank to 228 cid and 93 bhp, while the wheelbase lost two inches.

▶ DeSoto produced 426 S3 convertible sedans in 1937, selling for $1300. Nine other models ranged in price from $770 for a business coupe to $1220 for a limousine. Wheelbases spanned 116 inches, except for the 133-inch seven-passenger models (733 were built).

▲ Ford's $775 Standard V-8 woody wagon in 1937 could have roll-down front windows and sliding glass panels, or rear side curtains for $20 less.

▲ A $611 Standard Ford Tudor could be formidable on police duty with the 85-bhp V-8, but economy-minded folks in 1937 could choose a milder V8/60.

▲ Both the Hudson Custom Six and this smaller Terraplane (still a separate make) used a 212-cid six in 1937. As usual, Terraplane sold a lot better.

◀ After three seasons with an Oldsmobile straight-eight, LaSalle turned to a 125-bhp, 322-cid V-8 in 1937, borrowed from the prior year's Cadillac Series 60. In fact, the latest LaSalle aped that popular Cadillac in a number of ways. Wheelbase grew to a 124-inch size, while output rose to a record 32,000 units. Prices began at a moderate $1155, but this Model 5067 convertible coupe went for $1350, with a rumble seat optional.

---

With 77,000 cars built, Nash enjoys its best year of the decade

Pierce-Arrow sales plunge, production is halted; the company files for bankruptcy in December, with but a handful of final '38 models built

Willys, offering slightly enlarged cars with a full restyle and a bulging nose, increases production to 63,467 units

Chrysler shows off a safety-padded adjustable seat that moves up-and-down as well as back-and-forth

Studebaker offers windshield washers

Hudsons break 40 official performance records; one of them was for 24 hours, covering 2104.22 miles at 87.67 mph

Autoworkers win their first major labor contracts

▲ Not many cars in 1937—or any other year—had a rear deck as long and shapely as the new $1295 Lincoln Zephyr three-passenger coupe, accentuated by rear fender skirts.

▲ Though slow sellers, convertible sedans came in three Packard series: One-Twenty, Super Eight, and Twelve. The old Standard Eight engine now drove Super Eights. Packard touted "the most famous radiator contour in the world."

◀ Packard output doubled in 1937, topping 122,000 for the model year. Top seller wasn't the One-Twenty (*shown*), but the new budget-priced, smaller One-Ten, with a 100-bhp L-head six. This two/four-passenger convertible cost $1060.

▲ Safety glass was standard on all Chrysler products in 1937, including the modestly restyled Plymouth P4 DeLuxe coupe. A right-hand wiper remained optional, and this was the final year for crank-open windshields. This coupe, which cost only $650, attracted 67,144 new-car buyers.

▲ Upright formal models with open driver's compartments— like this Brunn-bodied Pierce-Arrow Metropolitan Town Car with V-12 engine and 147-inch wheelbase—looked old-fashioned in 1937. Production ground to a halt in Buffalo; reorganization couldn't bring Pierce back to life.

---

Striking union leaders are beaten by Ford thugs in the famed "Battle of the Overpass" on May 26

Chrysler spends $22 million on plant improvements

Buick builds great-looking models and enlarges the Special's engine to 248 cid and 100 bhp

Buick claims its steering-wheel horn ring is a "first" in the auto industry

Chevrolet's six-cylinder engine is redesigned; Master and Master DeLuxe series are offered

Streamlined Fords get steel roofs, choice of 60- or 85-horsepower V-8

Big Lincolns sport integrated headlamps and a vee'd windshield; the V-12 adds hydraulic lifters

A three-passenger coupe and Town Limousine join the Lincoln-Zephyr line

▲ Restyled on longer wheelbases, the 1937 Pontiac gained bigger engines for its DeLuxe Six and Eight series.

▲ Only in 1937-38 did Pontiac offer a convertible sedan. Shown here is a '37 DeLuxe Eight, which at $1235 was costly at the time ($1197 for the DeLuxe Six). Both series rode a longer chassis: 117 inches for the Six, 122 for the Eight.

▲ Hoping to spark sales, Studebaker melded a car with a pickup truck, creating the '37 J-5 Coupe-Express.

▲ At $595, the DeLuxe business coupe was Terraplane's cheapest '37 model—shown here with slide-in cargo box. The Super had slightly more power.

▲ Fully restyled for '37, with a longer rounded body and pontoon fenders, the little Willys kept the same 48-bhp engine and 100-inch wheelbase as before. The bulged front end hinted at the forthcoming "Sharknose" Graham. Standard and DeLuxe coupes and sedans cost $499-$589. Willys output doubled to 63,467 cars.

---

All Packards have independent front suspension and hydraulic brakes; a wagon and long-wheelbase sedan/limo join the One-Twenty line; a six-cylinder series is added

Plymouth model-year output hits 566,128; the crank-open windshield makes its last appearance

Experiments begin with a Studebaker-powered Waterman Arrowbile, one of the early flying cars. Studebaker is interested in distribution, but the plan never materializes

A Ford V-8 wins the prestigious Monte Carlo Rally

**1937 Model Year Production**

| | |
|---|---|
| 1. Ford | 942,005 |
| 2. Chevrolet | 815,375 |
| 3. Plymouth | 566,128 |
| 4. Dodge | 295,047 |
| 5. Pontiac | 236,189 |
| 6. Buick | 220,346 |
| 7. Oldsmobile | 200,886 |
| 8. Packard | 122,593 |

*Some figures are estimated or calendar-year*

▲ Buick's major 1938 changes were all-coil suspension and more powerful 248- and 320-cid engines. This is the $1297 Century sedan; 12,673 were sold. A Century coupe held National Hot Rod Association class honors for 25 years.

▲▼ Series 60 Cadillacs, like this $1730 four-door sedan, kept their former shape for '38, adding a column gearshift. Meanwhile, the Series 90 (*below*) switched to a smaller 431-cid V-16, now an L-head, but still rated at 185 bhp.

"Oh, Dad, let's take the Chevrolet!"
"Right, my dear, it's the car for people who want to *go places!*"

"You'll be AHEAD with a CHEVROLET!"
THE CAR THAT IS COMPLETE

▶ Optional fender skirts and spotlights added intrigue to a 1938 DeSoto S5 coupe. Total DeSoto output dropped to 38,831, for a 13th-place model-year ranking. Long-wheelbase sedans and limos were available, too.

◀ Most ads promoted the 1938 Chevrolet's virtues as a family vehicle. Mildly facelifted, it came as a Master or Master DeLuxe.

**1938**

After a modest mid-decade recovery, a sharp recession sinks the still-fragile economy

Auto industry output plunges 40 percent, to 2,000,985 cars and 488,100 trucks—one of the worst slumps ever

Chevrolet is again Number One, as Ford production tumbles by more than half. With only occasional exceptions, Chevrolet is destined to hang onto the lead well into the Eighties

Graham turns to radically shaped "Spirit of Motion" styling, featuring a "sharknose" front end—supercharged and unblown sedans are listed

After four years as a separate make, Terraplane officially becomes a Hudson model; a new low-cost Hudson "112" undercuts Terraplane prices

Hupmobile is back in business, with six- and eight-cylinder models, but only 2001 are built

▲ The sharply undercut front end of the new "Spirit of Motion" Grahams soon led to the nickname "Sharknose." Only a four-door sedan was built in 1938, this being the $1320 Supercharger Custom. Some loved the styling, many others didn't.

▲ Hupmobile's return to action for 1938 brought two sedan series: 822-E Six (*shown*), and the less-popular Eight.

▲ Terraplane became part of the Hudson line in 1938. Four-door sedans listed from $864-$915.

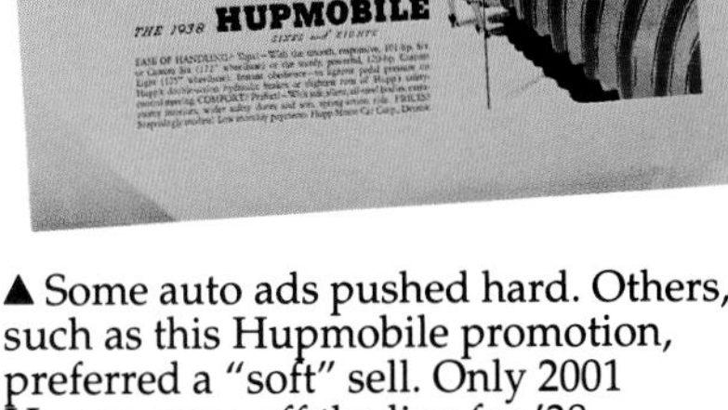


▲ Some auto ads pushed hard. Others, such as this Hupmobile promotion, preferred a "soft" sell. Only 2001 Hupps came off the line for '38.

▲ Wheelbase grew to 125 inches as part of Lincoln Zephyr's '38 restyle. An expanded lineup added a convertible coupe and sedan. Note the oval wind wings on this suave $1295 coupe.

◄ Hudson's four models covered a broad chunk of the market, as this company billboard shows. New for 1938, the economy-oriented "112" series had a 190.8-cid, 86-bhp six.

---

William L. Mitchell, protegé of Harley Earl, designs Cadillac's elegant new Sixty Special sedan with concealed running boards

Several automakers offer steering-column gearshift levers

Nash develops Weather-Eye, a "conditioned air" heating/ventilation system that heats and filters fresh outside air

Several automakers, led by Buick, turn to coil-spring rear suspensions

The new 185-bhp Cadillac V-16 is an L-head, unlike the earlier overhead-valve unit

Ford spends $40 million on plant expansion

◀ Grille differences marked a '38 Oldsmobile as a Six or an Eight. An "Automatic Safety Transmission," only available on Eights in 1937, now was optional on any Olds; the clutch was needed only when standing still.

▶ Folded back, the auxiliary seats in a 1938 Oldsmobile club coupe, here a Six, gave space for baggage. Sixes had a 95-bhp, 230-cid engine; Eights were 257-cid, good for 110 horses.

▲ Packard's One-Twenty was simply called the "Eight" for 1938; this handsome convertible coupe sold for $1365. The former One-Ten became the "Six," its engine enlarged to 245 cid. Six-cylinder Packard sales continued strong.

▲ Packard offered a convertible Victoria in both the Super Eight and Twelve series (*shown*) for 1938, priced at $3670 and a lofty $5230. Brunn and Rollston crafted other custom bodies, including cabriolets and town cars.

▲ Rust Heinz created the nothing-else-like-it 1938 Phantom Corsair. Production was planned, but Heinz died suddenly. Bodywork came from Bohman & Schwartz. A hopped-up, 190-bhp Lycoming (Cord) V-8 provided the power.

▲ Only a handful of Pierce-Arrows went on sale in 1938, including this V-12 limousine. Liquidation followed bankruptcy in December 1937. Pierce was best known for its fender-mounted headlights, initiated in the Teens.

---

Buicks gain modified "Dynaflash" engines with up to 141 bhp; the division ranks as GM's second-best-seller from 1938-47

Chrysler issues the $1378 New York Special Touring Sedan on a new 119-inch wheelbase

Dodge produces its last convertible sedans—only 132 are sold

Ford adopts two-tier styling: DeLuxe models are restyled, Standards keep the '37 DeLuxe body; slantback models are gone

LaSalle adds a four-door sedan with a sliding steel sunroof, but only 72 are ordered

Oldsmobile offers side-mounted spare tires for the last time; Safety Automatic Transmission, a semi-automatic, is available on all models

▲ The 1938 Plymouth coupe didn't win many styling kudos, but America's Number Three automaker went on to produce 45,451 examples of this body style, priced from $645 to $770. A hardy 82-bhp L-head six promised reliable service.

▲ Famed industrial designer Raymond Loewy took pen in hand to restyle Studebaker for 1938, placing semi-integrated headlamps on the "prow" front end, a year ahead of most rivals. This Commander helped keep the populace in line.

◄ A three-inch-shorter 122-inch wheelbase marked this $1130 '38 Studebaker State President three-passenger coupe, a rare model adorned here with a side-mount spare. A 250-cid straight-eight made 110 horsepower. Offered in four body styles, including a convertible sedan, the President line found only 5474 customers. A revived Commander Six (with 90 horses) succeeded the Dictator, deleting a name with unfortunate references to events unfolding in Europe.

▲ Terraplane gave up marque status to become a Hudson series for '38, slotted just above the new "112" line. Six, DeLuxe Six, and Super Six models got a 96/101-bhp motor.

▲ A seven-model '38 Willys line included new two-door sedans, plus coupes (here a $574 DeLuxe) and four-door sedans. Total Willys output fell from 63,476 units to 26,691.

---

Packard calls the One-Twenty the "Eight" this year and stretches the wheelbase seven inches to 127

Plymouth's station wagon rides the passenger-car chassis; bodies come from the U.S. Body and Forging Company in Indiana

Studebakers are restyled by Raymond Loewy, the first of many such projects for the famed industrial designer; the Dictator series is replaced by the Commander

GM builds the industry's first experimental "dream car," the Y-Job, on a '37 Buick chassis

**1938 Model Year Production**

| | |
|---|---|
| 1. Chevrolet | 465,158 |
| 2. Ford | 410,263 |
| 3. Plymouth | 285,704 |
| 4. Buick | 168,689 |
| 5. Dodge | 114,529 |
| 6. Oldsmobile | 99,951 |
| 7. Pontiac | 97,139 |
| 8. Packard | 55,718 |

*Some figures are estimated or calendar-year*

▲ Buick received a mild but pleasing facelift for 1939, with optional hidden running boards. A rumble seat was no longer offered for this $1077 Special convertible coupe; 4809 were built.

▲ An all-time styling great, the Sixty Special was a separate Cadillac series riding a 127-inch wheelbase. This $2090 example, of which 5135 were built, sports special two-tone paint.

▲ Cadillac Sixteens, among them this $5440 Fleetwood opera coupe, strutted wholly different front-end styling than the Eights. Only 11 of these two- and five-passenger coupes were sold.

▲ This top-line Master DeLuxe Town Sedan with trunk was Chevrolet's top 1939 seller: 220,181 units. Only 180 trunkless models were sold. A new wagon joined the line.

▲ Though not a standard model, this 1939 Chrysler Imperial shows that station wagons could be shapely. The flagship Imperial had a powerful 130-bhp, 323.5-cid straight-eight.

▲ Fender-mounted headlights led Chrysler's 1939 redesign. The New Yorker bowed this year (following two New York Special models in 1938), and is now the longest-running series nameplate in the auto industry. This sedan listed at $1298.

▲ Radio/refrigerator tycoon Powel Crosley, Jr., developed a minicar bearing his name. The '39 Crosley had an 80-inch wheelbase and an air-cooled two-cylinder engine. Early convertible coupes and sedans were sold in hardware/appliance stores—the cheapest cars in America. Here, the $325 ragtop.

---

**1939**

The New York World's Fair opens; thousands marvel at the technology to come, including television and futuristic highways

Chevrolet leads Ford in sales by nearly 100,000 units; Plymouth isn't far behind

The Bantam-size two-cylinder Crosley debuts, created by Powel Crosley, Jr.

The mid-priced Mercury is launched; though similar to Ford, it boasts a longer wheelbase and bigger V-8—and quickly gains a reputation for performance

Studebaker has spent $3.5 million in tooling for the new low-cost, lightweight Champion series

▲ DeSoto's 1939 restyle gave the front end an eager look, with a new V-split windshield. This $1145 Hayes-bodied S6 Custom Club Coupe—of which only 264 were built—stood above the pack with its stylish thin pillars.

▲ The Hayes company built bodies for this glamorous limited-edition, thin-pillared Dodge Town Coupe, well-equipped for $1055. Only 363 were produced. Fully redesigned, '39 Dodge "Luxury Liners" came in nine models.

▲ Ford finally adopted hydraulic brakes for 1939. DeLuxe models wore a vertical-bar grille; Standards looked like the '38 DeLuxes. This $742 Tudor sold best: 144,333 units.

▲ As since 1937, Ford offered two V-8s: "Thrifty Sixty" with 136 cid/60 bhp, or 221 cid/85 bhp. Only three '39 Series 92As with the "old" styling got the small V-8: coupe, Tudor, and Fordor.

▲ A "Combination" coupe (*shown*) and two-door sedan—both $940, $1070 Supercharged—joined the "Sharknose" Graham line for '39. But sales continued to languish: just 5392 units.

▲ Fully reworked, with a tall, newly slimmed grille and a shorter 120-inch wheelbase, 1939 LaSalles looked smart—and sales rose 50 percent to 21,127 units. This Model 5027 opera coupe featured a 125-bhp, 322-cid L-head V-8.

▲ A 118-inch-wheelbase Pacemaker and 122-inch Country Club joined the 30th Anniversary '39 Hudson lineup, both using the departed Terraplane's 212-cid six. Also offered: Country Club Eights and two 119-inch "Big Boy" sedans.

---

Packard builds its last V-12 models this year

Lincoln-Zephyr is one of several models that lack running boards, or hide them under doors

Most cars (except Fords) now have a column-mounted shift lever

At long last, Ford adopts hydraulic brakes, as do Mercury and the Lincoln-Zephyr

Chevrolet introduces a vacuum-operated gearshift

Chrysler brands are restyled by Ray Dietrich—headlamps move into the fenders

Chrysler introduces a fluid-coupling powertrain, Fluid Drive, for Imperial

Pontiac adopts "Duflex" rear springs, featuring smaller auxiliary leaf springs

▲ Why are these folks so fascinated? They're watching a demonstration of Airfoam latex rubber seat cushions, introduced on the six-model 1939 Hudson Country Club series, which now had its headlights faired into the fenders.

▲ Overshadowed by the Zephyr, the '39 Lincoln lineup still included a long list of massive Model Ks. This LeBaron convertible sedan is one of only nine built. Custom coachwork also came from Willoughby, Brunn, and Judkins.

◀ This Lincoln-Zephyr convertible coupe was new for '39; 640 were sold at $1747 apiece. Zephyrs adopted hydraulic brakes, while the big Model Ks stuck with mechanical binders. Gearshift levers remained on the floor for one last year. Zephyrs could have any of six bodies: coupe-sedan, three-passenger coupe, four-door sedan, Town Limousine, convertible coupe—even a convertible sedan (a style soon to disappear entirely from American cars). Vestigial running boards were now covered by skirts. Total Lincoln output for the '39 model year rose slightly to 21,134 units.

▲ Mercury debuted in 1939, filling the gap between the Ford DeLuxe and Lincoln-Zephyr. Lushly curved, it rode a 116-inch chassis (Ford, 112; Zephyr, 125) and had a 95-bhp V-8.

▲ Mercury's 239-cid V-8 (good for about 95 mph) was slightly larger than Ford's. Four body styles were issued, but this $957 four-door Town Sedan sold best. First year output: 70,835.

▲ Both the big Nash and the cheaper LaFayette (*shown*) earned a total restyling for '39, with flush headlamps and a prow-like hood. LaFayettes sold for $770 to $950.

---

Chrysler develops the "Superfinish" method of mirror-finishing engine/chassis parts with no scratches deeper than one-millionth of an inch, which helps cut friction

Under-seat heaters and pushbutton radios appear in several models this year

The 75-millionth American-built motor vehicle is produced

Chrysler launches Windsor, New Yorker, and Saratoga series

DeSotos come in DeLuxe and Custom series; open cars are gone, and an announced sliding sunroof never makes production

A Silver Anniversary brings fully redesigned Dodges, but long-wheelbase sedans depart

Ford's convertible sedan is in its final year; the phaeton is already gone

◀▲ From the beginning, Mercury had hydraulic brakes—plus a look very similar to Ford's, although no body panels were shared.

▶ Hydra-Matic could be ordered for $57 on any 1940 Olds model. The fully automatic four-speed had a fluid coupling—no clutch.

▲ Ray Dietrich penned the neat '39 Plymouth restyle, which featured rectangular headlights. This $775 Touring Sedan has the new column shift.

▲ Pontiacs wore wider "pontoon" fenders in 1939, sharing some body panels with Chevrolet. This is the $1046 DeLuxe Eight ragtop.

▲ Studebaker's '39 Commander Six and President Eight featured a fresh face and column shift. This milestone Stude was built on April 21, 1939.

▲ Clean styling, miserly mileage, and sprightly performance marked the new '39 Studebaker Champion, here a $720 DeLuxe coupe. Priced to rival the Big Three, it had a 78-bhp six.

▲ Light-truck buyers could enjoy the benefits of Studebaker passenger-car styling for 1939. How? By choosing the dual-purpose Coupe-Express, powered by the 90-bhp Commander six.

▲ Willys kept its Model 38 for '39, but added a revived Overland, coupe or sedan (*shown*). Slightly larger, Overlands had a peppier 62-bhp four and hydraulic brakes; 15,214 were built.

---

A two-door sedan and "Combination Club Coupe" join Graham's "Sharknose" series, but sales remain sluggish

Terraplane leaves the Hudson lineup, but 101-bhp Pacemaker and Country Club sixes debut, as do "Big Boy" sedans

Hupmobile output dwindles to just 1000 cars

Packard designs and builds marine engines for U.S. Navy PT boats; White builds Army scout cars

Poland is invaded by Germany on September 1

**1939 Model Year Production**

|  |  |
|---|---|
| 1. Chevrolet | 577,278 |
| 2. Ford | 487,031 |
| 3. Plymouth | 423,850 |
| 4. Buick | 208,259 |
| 5. Dodge | 186,474 |
| 6. Pontiac | 144,340 |
| 7. Oldsmobile | 137,249 |
| 8. Studebaker | 85,834 |

*Some figures are estimated or calendar-year*

▲ Buicks came in six series for 1940: Special, Super, Century, Roadmaster, Limited 80, Limited 90. Only 550 copies of this $1343 Century convertible coupe were built. This was the last year for the sidemounted spare tire.

▲ Cadillac's 1940 facelift wasn't the finest ever, but Caddy's usual virtues lay beneath the skin. This is the $2090 Sixty Special; 4472 were sold. A Series Seventy-Two debuted, slotted between the Sixty-Two and Seventy-Five.

▲ No ordinary 1940 Cadillac, this dazzling convertible wears a custom body, with neatly dipped-down doors, by Bohman & Schwartz. Built on a Series Sixty-Two chassis with the stock 135-bhp, 346-cid V-8, this car even sports bucket seats.

◀ Freshly modern profiles on longer wheelbases marked the 1940 Chrysler line, like this $960 six-cylinder Royal coupe. Fluid Drive was a $38 option on New Yorker/Saratoga eights.

▶ Running boards cost an extra $10 on this Dodge DeLuxe sedan; 84,976 were built at $905 apiece. The cheaper Specials and upmarket DeLuxes shared an 87-bhp, 217.8-cid L-head six.

**1940**

A war buildup is underway in the U.S.; automakers' European branches turn to military output

GM president William S. Knudsen is tapped by FDR to direct production for national defense

Industry production totals 3,692,328 cars and 777,026 trucks

Chevrolet builds nearly 765,000 cars in the model year, beating Ford by more than 220,000 units

Hydra-Matic Drive—the first true automatic transmission—is offered by Oldsmobile

The Lincoln Continental debuts with the Zephyr's enlarged V-12 engine; it's regarded as one of the most striking designs of all time

The last of the huge K-series Lincolns are built; model-year production is only 133

◀ The racy-looking DeLuxe convertible coupe, priced at $849, was Ford's only open car in 1940, and 23,704 were produced. This year's facelift was styled by "Bob" Gregorie, working under Edsel Ford. A total of 22 important improvements were claimed, including "finger-tip" column shift and sealed-beam headlights (installed on most 1940 cars). This was the final year for the small V-8/60 engine, which was never popular.

▼ LaSalle was in its final year when this 1940 Series 52 Special sedan was assembled. Featuring Harley Earl's "torpedo" look, it became the top-selling model: 10,250 units. A lower-priced Series 50, with the same 130-bhp V-8, stuck closer to 1939 looks.

▲ Taking a last stab at the market, Graham issued the $1250 Cord-based Hollywood (*shown*). Only 1597 were built for 1940-41. A similar-looking Hupmobile Skylark also surfaced. Unlike Cord, both used rear-drive and sixes. Output ceased in late 1940.

▶ "Bob" Gregorie had designed a custom Lincoln-Zephyr convertible for Edsel Ford in 1939, "continental style" with a rear spare. A year later, it was produced as the Continental—one of the Classic Lincolns, sold as a $2783 coupe (530 built) or $2916 soft-top (54 built). Mechanical details hailed from the far-cheaper Zephyr.

---

The Graham Hollywood and Hupp Skylark share a Cord-based body, but are rear-drive; Grahams are supercharged

LaSalle's final cars come in two series, one featuring GM's new "Torpedo" style

Cadillac's V-16 makes its last appearance, but only 61 are sold

Nash LaFayettes are produced for the last time

Nearly all makes, now including Ford, have a column gearshift and enclosed running boards

Sealed-beam headlights become the industry standard this year

Chrysler develops Safety-Rim wheels that keep the tire on the rim after a blowout

Many models have a standard heater/defroster

▲ Fun-in-the-sun folks could buy this sharp '40 Mercury convertible coupe with vacuum-powered top for $1079, and 9741 did. They could also move up to a $1212 convertible sedan; only 1083 did. Overall, Mercury sold well: 86,062.

▲ Bigger and a bit roomier than a Ford, the $987 '40 Mercury Town Sedan aimed at buyers who might otherwise choose, say, a Dodge or Pontiac. Sealed-beam headlamps, column shift, and vent wings were new.

◀ Mercury's $987 "Coupe-Sedan," chosen by 16,819 customers in 1940, sported a distinctive thin-pillar (almost hardtop-like) look. Ford lacked an equivalent model. Mercury was promoted for both the impressive performance and frugality of its 95-bhp V-8.

▲ Packard V-12s were gone by 1940, but a new 160-bhp, 356-cid straight-eight went into Super Eight One-Sixty and One-Eighty models. This, however, is a 120-bhp, $1166 One-Twenty.

▶ Glamour in Packard's 1940 lineup came from custom-built Darrins, styled by Howard "Dutch" Darrin. Note the cut-down doors on this $4593 Super Eight One-Eighty Victoria.

---

A demonstration of what will become the "Jeep" is held by Colonel Arthur W.S. Herrington; it's to be built by Willys

Walter P. Chrysler dies in August

A larger 50.1-cid, 22-bhp engine goes into the little American Bantam

The final Buick Century convertible sedans are built (203 of them); the Super series debuts

Cadillac's Series Seventy-Two lasts just one season, but the new Series Sixty-Two will become the top seller

Chevrolet's new "Royal Clipper" styling imparts a fresh look; three series are offered, as is Chevy's first true convertible coupe

Crosley cuts prices to as low as $199; a convertible, woody wagon, and "covered wagon" are added

▲ Not much similarity is evident between a 1920 Oldsmobile and its 1940 successor. During the two decades, price was more than halved, from $1995 to $899.

**R.I.P.**
**Makes That Expired 1930-41**

| | |
|---|---|
| American Austin | Kissel |
| American Bantam | LaFayette |
| Auburn | LaSalle |
| Blackhawk | Marmon |
| Brewster | Marquette |
| Continental | Oakland |
| Cord | Peerless |
| Cunningham | Pierce-Arrow |
| Detroit Electric | Reo |
| De Vaux | Roamer |
| Doble | Rolls-Royce of America |
| Duesenberg | Rockne |
| du Pont | Roosevelt |
| Durant | Ruxton |
| Elcar | Stearns-Knight |
| Erskine | Stutz |
| Essex | Terraplane |
| Franklin | Whippet |
| Gardner | Viking |
| Graham | Willys-Knight |
| Hupmobile | Windsor |
| Jordan | |

◀ Replacing Oldsmobile's Series 80 for 1940 was a new top-of-the-line Series 90, on a 124-inch chassis with a 110-bhp straight-eight. This is the $1131 sedan (33,075 sold), and there was even a convertible sedan (50 built).

▲ Oldsmobile's Series 90 models, like this $1069 Custom Cruiser club coupe, was notable for its smoother tail and rear rooflines. Hydra-Matic quickly gained converts.

▲ Studebaker offered a Coupe-Delivery in 1940, with a short pickup bed stuffed into the trunk. Except for styling touch-ups, Champion, Commander, and President changed little.

---

Running boards cost $10 extra on Dodges, but soon will be history

Ford offers the last V-8/60 engines; it was never popular

Hudson adopts front coil springs

Mercury lists a $1212 convertible sedan for this year only

Oldsmobile offers its first convertible sedan; only 50 are built

Four striking custom-built Darrin models, led by a low-slung Convertible Victoria, capture the attention of Packard fanciers

**1940 Model Year Production**

| | |
|---|---|
| 1. Chevrolet | 764,616 |
| 2. Ford | 541,896 |
| 3. Plymouth | 430,208 |
| 4. Buick | 278,784 |
| 5. Dodge | 225,595 |
| 6. Pontiac | 217,001 |
| 7. Oldsmobile | 192,692 |
| 8. Studebaker | 107,185 |

*Some figures are estimated or calendar-year*

▲ The fastback Sedanet was new to Buick for '41; here, a $1241 Century. "Compound Carburetion" (dual carbs) entered most engines.

▲ Convertible Phaetons still existed in Buick's 1941 Super and Roadmaster series. At $1555 and $1775, sales reached only 508 and 326 units.

▲ Cadillac's $2195 '41 Sixty Special sported a touch of GM's "torpedo" look. Some of the 3878 sedans built had the now-available Hydra-Matic.

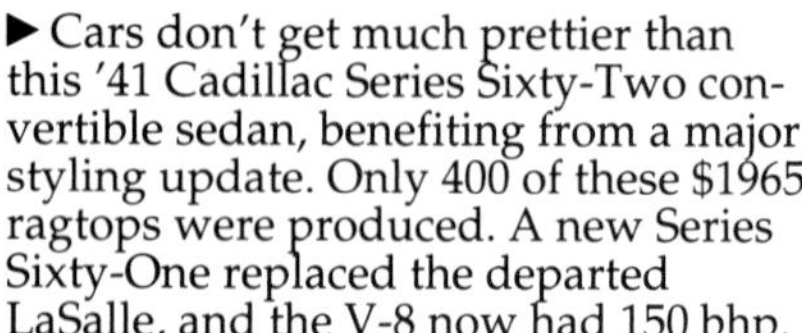

► Cars don't get much prettier than this '41 Cadillac Series Sixty-Two convertible sedan, benefiting from a major styling update. Only 400 of these $1965 ragtops were produced. A new Series Sixty-One replaced the departed LaSalle, and the V-8 now had 150 bhp.

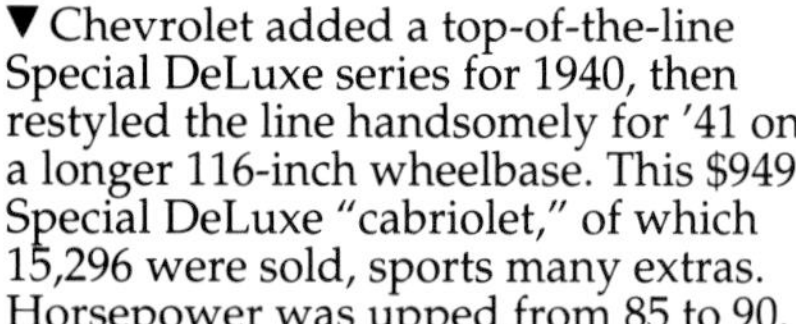

▼ Chevrolet added a top-of-the-line Special DeLuxe series for 1940, then restyled the line handsomely for '41 on a longer 116-inch wheelbase. This $949 Special DeLuxe "cabriolet," of which 15,296 were sold, sports many extras. Horsepower was upped from 85 to 90.

▲ Chevrolet got into the car-or-truck act in 1936, continuing into 1941 with this $754 Master DeLuxe Coupe Pickup—a business coupe with a tiny cargo box fitted onto the rear. It could be replaced by a normal trunklid. Running boards were gone, and flared door bottoms hid the sill plates.

---

**1941**

War buildup helps bring about the end of the Great Depression

Pearl Harbor is bombed on December 7; Congress declares war a day later

Following a violent wildcat strike, Henry Ford allows a union vote and the first closed shop in the industry

Total industry production comes to 3,744,300 cars and 1,094,261 trucks

Just over a million Chevrolets are built in the '41 model year, far ahead of Ford's 691,455

Packard becomes the first make to offer air conditioning, but at $1080 it's a *very* expensive option

▲ The new $1245 Chrysler Saratoga business coupe had a frightfully long decklid. Including the $1325 New Yorker, only 771 '41 Chrysler eight-cylinder business coupes were built.

◀ Only 2045 Chevrolet Special DeLuxe station wagons were built in 1941—a price topper at $995. Lots of extras could be ordered, from vacuum shift to turn signals to bumper guards.

▲ Blanked rear quarters marked the $1760 Chrysler Crown Imperial Town Sedan; 984 were sold. "Vacamatic" semi-automatic changed gears without use of the clutch.

▲ This '41 DeSoto Custom convertible struts a load of extras to complement its new "toothy" grille. Priced at $1240, it found 2037 buyers. DeSoto was in tenth place this year.

▲ Aided by a clean 1941 facelift, Dodge's blanked-quarter Custom Town Sedan sold quite well: 16,074 units. Fluid Drive was optional, and the 217.8-cid six edged up to 91 horses.

▲ Like other '41 Dodge Customs, this $995 club coupe (18,024 built) had extra trim and Airfoam cushions. Long-wheelbase sedans and limos remained, but only 654 were ordered.

▲ Running boards were minimal, but still there, on the 1941 Ford Super DeLuxe convertible, which came with a power top. Price was $946 with V-8, $931 with the new 90-bhp L-head six.

---

Nash's new "600," which replaces the LaFayette, features unitized construction; Nash sales expand to 84,007 units

Buick offers "Compound Carburetion" for the Fireball straight-eight—a second carb kicks in when the gas pedal is pressed to the floor

Hydra-Matic becomes available for $110 in Cadillacs; 30 percent of buyers choose it

Chrysler and DeSoto offer a four-speed semi-automatic transmission that delivers a low-to-high shift in either a Low or High Range when the driver lets up on the gas

Hudson earns nearly $4 million, mostly from defense contracts

Willys-Overland names all its cars Americar, begins deliveries of Jeeps to the U.S. Army

Buick's last Super and Roadmaster convertible sedans—834 of them—are produced

▲ Graham halted production of the Cord-based Custom Hollywood sedan in September 1940, but remaining cars were sold as '41s. The 218-cid six made 95 bhp (124 with supercharger).

▲ Like the similar Graham Hollywood, the handful of '41 Hupmobile Skylarks were leftovers. Only 319 Skylarks had been built, each with a 101-bhp "Hornet Six." Wheelbase was 115 inches.

▲ In addition to sleek three- and five-passenger three-window coupes, Lincoln produced this five-passenger, five-window club coupe. Retailing at $1541, it attracted 3750 customers.

▲ Pushbutton door handles gave the 1941 Lincoln Continentals a high-tech touch. Only 850 $2812 coupes and 400 $2865 cabriolets (*shown*) were produced this year. Performance from the 120-bhp V-12 didn't quite match the luscious shape.

▲ Nash turned to unit construction for 1941 for the new, smaller "600" series, but not for the big Ambassador, here a fastback sedan. The Ambassador six delivered 105 bhp; the eight, 115 bhp. Nash calendar-year output was 80,428 units.

▲ Inboard headlamps made Oldsmobiles easy to spot in '41. This $1089 Model 68 "Special 8" convertible coupe rode a new 119-inch wheelbase, with a 110-bhp, 257-cid straight-eight. Nearly all bodies could have either a six or an eight.

---

Fastback sedans join the Buick line; the two Limited lines meld into a single 90-Series Limited

Cadillac's revived, lower-priced Series Sixty-One takes the place of the departed LaSalle

All redesigned Chevrolets now have an independent front suspension; a formal-look Fleetline sedan appears at mid-year

Town and Country is Chrysler's first station wagon

Crosley modifications include the addition of U-joints and an engine smaller than the 1939-40 version, and they are now sold and serviced by car dealers

DeSoto's facelift includes its first prominent grille "teeth," and a 10th-place sales ranking is the make's best showing ever

◀ Packard headlights finally moved fully into the fenders for 1941. The top-priced series was the One-Eighty, including this $4695 Custom Super Eight All-Weather Cabriolet by Rollston, with a 160-bhp, 356-cid straight-eight. At mid-year, Packard launched the Clipper sedan, positioned between the One-Twenty and One-Sixty, displaying an all-new, nearly flush-sided look.

▲ Unlike most '41s, Plymouth clung to running boards. This $1007 Special DeLuxe convertible showed off the facelift; 10,545 were sold. Powermatic vacuum shift was optional.

▲ Most convertibles still lacked rear side windows in '41. Pontiac's $1048 DeLuxe Torpedo Eight was no exception. Pontiacs came in three series for both sixes and eights.

▲ All Studebakers, like this President Skyway sedan, gained a handsome Raymond Loewy restyling for '41. Commander sixes and President eights added horsepower, to 94 and 117. Presidents cost from $1140 to $1260.

▲ Studebaker bored the Champion six to 169.6-cid and 80 bhp for 1941. Note the novel two-toning on this top-line $860 Champion DeLux-Tone Cruising Sedan. With 84,910 built, the Champ became Stude's best-selling line ever.

▲ Willys called its slightly enlarged 1941 models "Americar." In Speedway, DeLuxe, and Plainsman trim, each had a 63-bhp, 134-cid four. This DeLuxe coupe cost $685. Joseph Frazer had left Chrysler to run Willys in 1939.

---

Ford replaces the V-8/60 with an inline L-head six developing 90 horsepower

Convertible sedans are still available in the Hudson line, and there's now a station wagon and a "Big Boy" car-pickup

Oldsmobile adds fastback sedans, and reaches sixth place in industry rankings

Packard's Clipper four-door sedan debuts at mid-year, predicting postwar styling; an "Electromatic" clutch is available

**1941 Model Year Production**

|  |  |
|---|---|
| 1. Chevrolet | 1,008,976 |
| 2. Ford | 691,455 |
| 3. Plymouth | 522,080 |
| 4. Buick | 374,196 |
| 5. Pontiac | 330,061 |
| 6. Oldsmobile | 270,040 |
| 7. Dodge | 215,575 |
| 8. Chrysler | 161,704 |

*Some figures are estimated or calendar-year*

CHAPTER FIVE

# 1942-1945

# DETROIT GOES TO WAR

The winds of war aimed toward America as the '42 models debuted in the autumn of 1941. Across the Atlantic, combat had been raging for two full years, and Hitler controlled nearly all of Western Europe. Despite its biggest peacetime military buildup ever, the U.S. had steered clear of the conflict—while shipping war materiel to beleaguered Britain. Isolationist sentiment was strong, and the initiation of the military draft in 1940 had drawn considerable criticism. People were wary, if not quite worried, so the news of the Japanese bombing of Pearl Harbor, on December 7, 1941, came as a profound shock.

President Roosevelt placed the nation on an immediate wartime footing, and Detroit quickly followed. By early February 1942, production of civilian automobiles screeched to a halt. In fact, those few cars built after the first of the year, billed as "blackout" models, lacked their customary brightwork. Quite a few '42s were impounded by the government, earmarked for use by officials. Car registrations fell by about 1.6 million in 1942, as departing GIs put their cars up on blocks for the duration.

Packard had obtained a contract to produce aircraft engines in 1940, so conversion to war work came easily. Ford dedicated its huge government-financed Willow Run plant to the production of B-24 Liberator bombers. Dodge's new Chicago factory, also paid for by the government, built B-29 engines. Chrysler issued Sherman tanks and anti-aircraft guns.

All told, automakers turned out $29 billion worth of armaments and related products for the war effort—everything from trucks and planes to lifeboats and sandbags. General Motors became the biggest producer. Second was Curtiss-Wright, followed by Ford. "Cost-plus" contracts provided the incentive to get the work done in a hurry—and earn ample profits.

Best-known of the wartime products was the four-wheel-drive Jeep, initially designed by American Bantam. Bantam produced fewer than 3000, but Willys and Ford were responsible for some 650,000.

On the "home front," gasoline rationing began in the Northeast during 1942, spreading nationwide in December of that year. Accompanied by a 35-mph national speed limit, rationing's major purpose was to conserve rubber. A motorist with the basic "A" sticker was entitled to four gallons of gas per week (later, three). "B" stickers went to priority workers, "C" to doctors and officials—or people with "connections."

Not every citizen cooperated eagerly. A black market in fraudulent and stolen ration coupons grew rampant as the war dragged into 1944-45. Used-car dealers were supposed to stick to government pricing limits, but more than a few vehicles sold for more than they'd cost when new.

Young men went off to war, but their bobby-soxer girlfriends—and exempted fellows—jitterbugged and jalopied in search of a good time. Jobs were easy to find, wages high—in stark contrast to the recently departed Depression. Women were applauded for their "Rosie the Riveter" roles, though their efforts would quickly be forgotten when returning veterans reclaimed those factory jobs.

By V-J Day in 1945, some $49 billion in War Bonds had been bought. Urban dwellers planted Victory Gardens to grow vegetables, and participated in scrap drives. Air-raid wardens enforced blackouts and scanned American skies for enemy planes—none of which were ever spotted.

The end of hostilities found many Americans with stuffed wallets from war-time work, and hungry for the civilian products—especially automobiles—they'd been deprived of. Postwar would be a new world.

---

**1942**

As America enters the war early in the '42 model year, customers clamoring for cars are worried that production will be halted rather than simply curtailed

Under government mandate, automakers quickly convert from civilian to full wartime production, turning out shells, aircraft engines, anti-aircraft guns, combat cars, Jeeps, and more

"Blackout" '42 automobiles—those produced after January 1—get government-ordered painted parts instead of chrome trim; most cars look lower, longer, more massive

Fleetline Chevrolets include a Torpedo two-door Aerosedan and a four-door Sportmaster

▲ Stylists pondered GM's "Y-Job" show car when reworking '42 Buicks. Full-length "Airfoil" fenders went on most models, including Roadmaster.

▲ Cadillac got a new look for '42 with big bullet-shaped fenders, plus a fastback roofline for Series Sixty-One (*shown*) and Sixty-Two sedanets.

▲ Only 1750 Series Sixty-Three Cadillacs were built on a 126-inch wheelbase, including this Town Car with open chauffeur's compartment.

▲ Preparation for war had helped bring an end to the Great Depression and sparked car sales, but American two-lane highways would feel less carefree when the government placed strict limits on pleasure driving.

▲ Chevrolet fenders extended into doors, as on other GM makes. This January 1942 ad focused on economy.

◀ Chevrolet claimed the title "America's Most Popular Car." A new Fleetline sub-series included a "torpedo-style" Aerosedan and conventional Sportmaster four-door.

▶ Two-tone paint looked fine on a 1942 Chevrolet Fleetline Aerosedan. This body style had been popular in other GM divisions in 1941, and sold well in the short '42 season.

---

Chrysler's "alligator-style" hood opens from the front; running boards are hidden beneath flared door bottoms

After a price rise, Crosley prices start at $413; the "covered wagon" model is dropped

While Dodge strokes its engine to 230.2 cid, the body gets a heavy facelift with a massive grille

Ford gets a "big car" look via a new grille and bulkier fenders

Hudson can be ordered with Drive-Master semi-automatic shift

Nash produces its final straight-eight engines; only sixes will return after the war

Officially, Oldsmobile is now a division of GM—the Olds Motor Works name is history

▲ Introduced a year earlier, Chrysler's steel-roofed 1942 Town & Country was unlike any other "woody" wagon—and was the first such model offered by the company.

▲ A sloping rear roof and "clamshell" doors gave the original Chrysler Town & Country a unique spot in wagon history. For '42, running boards were hidden.

▲ The final prewar Chrysler rolls off the assembly line on January 29, 1942, less than two months after Pearl Harbor, with 36,586 assembled. After facelifting its lineup for 1942, with grillework that reached around front fenders, Chrysler joined industry colleagues in the war effort. Cars built in January had painted metal trim, per government edict.

CAR OF THE TIMES
YOUR DE SOTO
NEW AIRFOIL
INTERIORS
FLUID DRIVE
TOMORROW'S STYLE TODAY

▲ Only DeSoto presented a dramatically different face for 1942, in the form of hidden "airfoil" headlights, billed as "out of sight except at night." A larger six made 115 bhp.

◀ DeSoto convertible coupes came in DeLuxe and Custom trim in 1942, with a $67 price difference. A plush Custom Town Sedan, dubbed Fifth Avenue, featured leather and Bedford cloth upholstery trim.

---

Turbo-matic Drive, a semi-automatic gearbox, is optional on the Studebaker Commander and President

Civilian car production is halted on February 9; civilian truck output ceases on March 3

Strict rationing of new automobiles begins on March 2

A national 40-mph speed limit is imposed to conserve fuel and rubber; later, it's reduced to 35 mph

Gas rationing is ordered effective December 1, 1942

Graham-Paige undertakes production of amphibious tanks

Pontiac is the first automaker to win the U.S. Navy's "E" Award, while Chrysler earns the first Army-Navy "E" distinction

▲ Extensive facelifting with a broad eggcrate grille gave the '42 Dodge a fresh look, if less noticeable than DeSoto's new look. This Custom four-door sedan cost $1048.

▲ Just 1185 Dodge Custom convertibles were built in the brief model year, with a larger (230-cid) 105-bhp six. Moldings on optional skirts matched fender trim.

▲ A reduced-height frame gave 1942 Fords a lower stance, while softer springs improved the ride. Both the V-8 and the six made 90 bhp. Shown: a DeLuxe Fordor.

▲ Mahogany paneling decorated Ford's 1942 Super DeLuxe station wagon, while maple or birch went on DeLuxe versions. Rear doors gained roll-up glass.

▲ Could this 1942 Hudson Commodore Eight sedan be aspiring to official duty with that red spotlight? Running boards now were hidden, bodies a tad chubbier.

▲ That final Hudson had better last, because there would be no more civilian autos for more than three years. Hudson turned out 40,661 cars for the model year.

By mid-year, output of war materiel by auto manufacturers exceeds the peacetime production rate

The Automotive Council for War Production reports $4.665 billion in arms production for the year

**1942 Model Year Production**

|  |  |
|---|---|
| 1. Chevrolet | 254,885 |
| 2. Ford | 160,432 |
| 3. Plymouth | 152,427 |
| 4. Buick | 92,573 |
| 5. Pontiac | 83,555 |
| 6. Dodge | 68,522 |
| 7. Oldsmobile | 67,783 |
| 8. Studebaker | 50,678 |

*Some figures are estimated or calendar-year*

**1943**

In January, the Office of Price Administration (OPA) bans nonessential driving in 17 eastern states; 25 million gasoline ration books have been issued to motorists nationwide

▲ The Lincoln Continental's V-12 engine earned a 1942 enlargement to 305 cid, for 10 extra horsepower. Only 200 club coupes were produced, with a $3000 price tag.

▲ Facelifting of the 1942 Lincoln Continental roughly foretold its postwar look, especially at the front end. Fenders were taller and longer, with headlamps flanked by dual parking lights. Weight was up by 200 pounds. Output totaled 136 convertibles.

◄ Still sitting in the shadow of the classic Continental, Lincoln's Zephyr earned a similar restyling for the abbreviated 1942 season, with taller, squared-up fenders. Note the pushbutton-operated doors on this flashy $2150 convertible, like those on the Continental. A three-passenger coupe, club coupe, and four-door sedan also made the 1942 lineup. The last prewar Lincoln left the factory on February 10, 1942, after a run of just 6547 cars.

▲ Mercury's flathead V-8 engine got a boost from 95 to 100 bhp for 1942. A semi-automatic "Liquamatic" transmission could be ordered—but soon proved troublesome.

▲ Parking lights moved inboard on Mercury, above a two-section horizontal-bar grille. This eight-passenger station wagon sold for $1260—the most costly '42 model.

▲ A spotlight wasn't standard fare on a 1942 Mercury convertible coupe. Like other makes, "blackout" Mercurys produced after December 1941 had painted, not chromed, trim.

---

Income-tax withholding is introduced in 1943, as the war rages on

With 1.25 million workers going strong, annual war production from 1000 automobile plants is twice the rate of the top prewar (peacetime) year

The Automotive Council for War Production reports 1038 auto plants cooperating voluntarily in the war effort; this year, the value of materiel produced totals $13 billion

Cadillac's wartime output includes tanks, aircraft engines, munitions

Chrysler's contributions include anti-aircraft guns, Wright Cyclone aircraft engines, land-mine detectors, radar units, marine engines, tanks, "Sea Mule" harbor tugs

Crosley develops an overhead-cam, four-cylinder "CoBra" engine for the U.S. Navy; its block is made of brazed copper and sheet steel

▲ For the last time, a Nash Ambassador could have either a six- or eight-cylinder engine on a 121-inch wheelbase. Fastback and trunkback sedans were available.

▲ Just 31,780 Nashes were made before government-ordered closing in February 1942. The last of the line were "blackout" models with painted (instead of chrome) trim.

▲ Besides the Ambassador, Nash again offered the smaller 600, shown here as a trunkback sedan with a 75-bhp, 172.6-cid six-cylinder engine.

▲ All Packards took the Clipper name for '42; nearly all had Clipper styling. One-Eighty sedans came on three wheelbases: 127/138/148-inch.

▲ Packard's own designers penned this upright 1942 One-Eighty limousine, far removed from the forthcoming "Clipper" shape. Window moldings wound up on production models.

◀ Packard unveiled the trendsetting Clipper in mid-1941, positioned between the One-Twenty and One-Sixty. Both "Dutch" Darrin and Packard's stylists contributed to the modern design, which featured a slim grille and a nearly flush-sided "envelope" body, wider than it was tall. Front fenders "swept-through" into the doors. Except for convertibles and custom bodies, all Packards—including sixes and this two-toned Custom One-Twenty sedan—adopted the "Clipper" look for 1942. The only traditional bodies that remained were convertibles and very rare wagons.

Ford also turns out gliders and gun carriers—plus the vital bombers from Willow Run, led by the B-24 "Liberator"

Studebaker's varied contributions mainly include trucks and aircraft engines, plus "Weasel" personnel carriers

Hudson issues Invader landing-craft engines and body sections for Curtiss Helldiver aircraft, Martin B-26 bombers, Boeing B-29 super bombers, and Bell Aircobra helicopters—plus a selection of naval munitions, such as Oerlikon anti-aircraft guns

During the war years, Oldsmobile turns out some 350,000 precision aircraft engine components, 175 million pounds of gun forgings, 140,000 machine guns, and vast quantities of ammunition

Packard is kept busy producing Rolls-Royce Merlin aircraft engines, PT boats, and power units

▲ "Fuselage fenders" edged into doors on 1942 Oldsmobiles, including this Special Series Sixty "torpedo" styled club sedan. Series Sixty and Seventy could have a six or an eight; the Ninety was straight-eight only.

▲ This 1942 Plymouth ad explained that the company was building, "under allotment," a limited number of civilian cars. Door sheetmetal now hid the running boards.

▲ More than 152,000 Plymouths went to buyers in the brief 1942 season, keeping the company in third place.

7 BEAUTIFUL VERSIONS OF ONE GREAT STORY!

Buy Wisely—BUY PLYMOUTH

▲ Special DeLuxe '42 Plymouths came in seven body styles; the cheaper DeLuxe in five. Plymouth's 217.8-cid six-cylinder engine rose from 87 to 95 horsepower.

◀ A new model joined the Plymouth lineup for 1942: the $980 Special DeLuxe Town Sedan, with enclosed rear quarters. Standard-trim models were history.

---

Joseph Frazer leaves the Willys-Overland firm in 1943 to take over Graham-Paige

With $20 million in defense contracts for the war effort, Graham-Paige finally prospers

Henry Kaiser announces a plan for a postwar automobile

Edsel Ford dies on May 26; Henry Ford is re-elected company president on June 1, 1943

Henry Ford II is released from the U.S. Navy on July 26, and elected vice president of Ford Motor Company on December 15

**1944**

Franklin D. Roosevelt is elected to an unprecedented fourth term as President of the United States

Even more U.S. auto plants are converted to war production by 1944, as most automotive items are rationed

▲ Final prewar Plymouths, like other Detroit cars, had "blackout" trim to save on materials for the war effort.

▲ Even the boost to 95 horsepower didn't quite transform Plymouths into speedsters, but Michigan State Police put this '42 two-door into service anyway. Four-door sedans outsold two-doors by a wide margin.

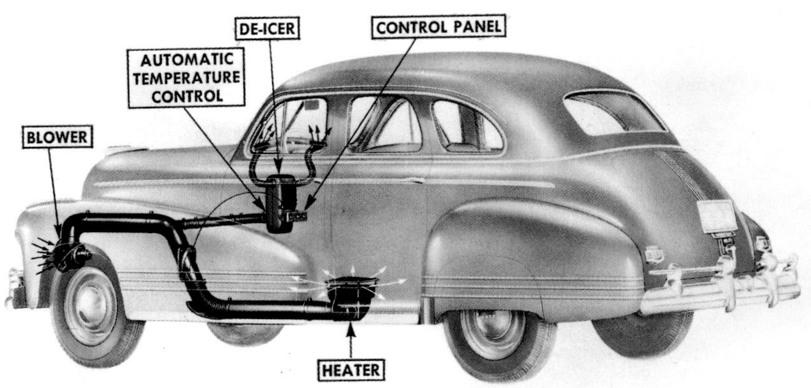


▲ Phantom view of this 1942 Pontiac reveals its new heat/vent system, claimed to eliminate steaming and fogging of windshield and windows. The heater used outside fresh air only, with a thermostat to control temperature.

▲ Pontiac explained that the '42 model looked much wider, despite modest growth overall. Reasons: a broader grille, hood, and bumpers, with headlamps spaced farther apart.

▲ Pontiac trimmed its '42 line to four series: Streamliner and Torpedo (shown), each with a six or eight.

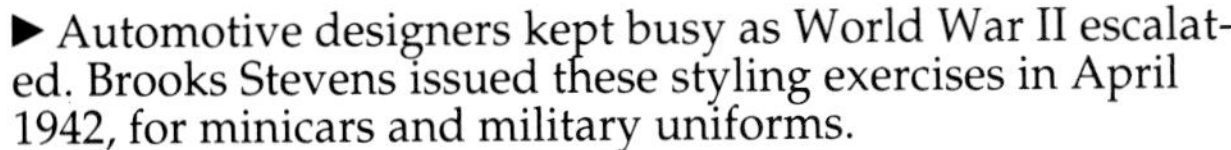

► Automotive designers kept busy as World War II escalated. Brooks Stevens issued these styling exercises in April 1942, for minicars and military uniforms.

---

The War Production Board authorizes Detroit to build one million trucks for military and civilian use

In November, the Board approves the manufacture of light civilian trucks for the first time since 1942

More than 13 percent of Allied war materiel comes from Detroit

The automotive industry produces $9 billion worth of armaments during 1944

Automakers build 57 percent of the tanks that go to U.S. and Allied forces

The basic civilian gasoline ration is cut to two gallons per week

According to the Office of War Information, 4000 passenger cars are being scrapped every day

The G.I. Bill of Rights is signed in 1944 to provide benefits to veterans; millions of returning vets will attend college in the late Forties and eagerly buy new homes and automobiles in the Fifties

▲ Wartime ads helped bolster morale, emphasizing the expertise of auto plants that now served the military.

▲ Rather than deal with gasoline rationing, or because car owners served overseas, thousands of motorists put their cars in storage for the duration. Here, two relax under tarps in Redding, California, in 1942.

◀ Conversion to all-out military production began right after war was declared. Eight million artillery shells came out of Chevrolet plants. Here, ordnance inspection takes place at the St. Louis Shell Division.

---

Synthetic rubber is invented during the war years

The War Production Board forms the Automobile Industry Advisory Committee to consider basic problems involved with the eventual resumption of passenger-car production

Willys-Overland announces its plan to manufacture a civilian Jeep after the war ends

Joseph W. Frazer, now chairman of Graham-Paige, announces his intent to produce automobiles when peace arrives

**1945**

FDR dies on April 12; Vice President Harry S Truman is sworn in as President

The War Production Board announces a program for the transition to civilian vehicle production, to begin on July 1

## U.S. Automakers' Contributions to the War Effort

### American Bantam
Fire pumper trailers
Jeeps
Jeep trailers (amphibious)

### Chrysler Corporation
Aircraft engines
Airplane components/body sections
Ammunition of various types
Bofors anti-aircraft guns
Chrysler-Bell air-raid sirens
Duraluminum forgings and castings
Explosive rockets
Fire pumper units
Fuselage sections for Martin B-26 Marauder bombers
General Grant M3 tanks (also M4/M26)
Gun barrels/shells
Landing-gear assemblies
Land mine detectors
Magnesium and bronze parts
Marine engines
Medium tank major assemblies
Personnel boats
Pontoons
Radar units
Refrigerating and heating equipment
Sea Mule marine/harbor tugs
Searchlight reflectors
Sherman tanks
Sperry Gyro-Compasses
Submarine nets
Tank engines
Trucks (Dodge)
Wright Cyclone aircraft engines (Dodge)

### Crosley
CoBra four-cylinder engines

### Ford Motor Company
Aircraft generators
All-terrain trucks
Amphibian Jeeps
Anti-aircraft detectors
Armored personnel carriers
B-24 Liberator bombers
GAA four-valve, dohc V-8s for Sherman tanks
General Electric Turbosuperchargers
Gliders
GPW Jeeps
Gun carriers
Jettison gas tanks
M-4 Sherman tanks
M-10 tank destroyers
M-20 Utility Commando Cars
Magnesium castings
Moto Tugs
Pratt & Whitney R-2800 radial engines
Rate-of-climb indicators
Tires
Trucks

### General Motors
Aircraft engine components
Aircraft engines
Airplanes
Ammunition (Olds)
Amphibious Ducks
Anti-aircraft torpedoes
Artillery shells (Chevrolet)
B-26 bomber landing gear
Bofors automatic field guns
Cannons, 20-mm/37-mm
Car/truck parts (Chevrolet)
Crankshafts (Olds)
Forgings
GMC buses for the civilian market (Pontiac)
Grumann Avengers
Gun forgings (Olds)
Hellcat M-18 tank destroyers
High-explosive shells
Hydra-Matic for tanks
Machine guns (Olds)
Military cannons (Olds)
Munitions (Cadillac)
Oerlikon anti-aircraft cannons
Pratt & Whitney aircraft engines (Buick)
Precision parts for aircraft engines
Staghound T-17 armored cars, 4-wheel (Chevrolet)
T-19 armored cars, 6-wheel
Tanks/motor gun carriages: M-5/M-8/M-19/M-24 (Cadillac)
Trucks (Chevrolet/GMC)
V-8s for tanks (Cadillac)

### Graham-Paige
Amphibious tanks

### Hudson
Ailerons for pursuit planes
Aluminum aircraft pistons
Ammunition boxes
Auxiliary fuel tanks
B-29 bomber parts
Body sections for aircraft
Bomb fuse adapters
Fire control apparatus
Gun mounts
Invader landing-craft engines
Marine mine anchors
Oerlikon anti-aircraft guns
Torpedo tubes

### Nash
Pratt & Whitney aircraft engines

### Packard
Marine engines
P-T boats
Rolls-Royce Merlin aircraft engines
Shells, 37-40-mm

### Studebaker
Military trucks, mainly 6x6s and 6x4s
Pratt & Whitney R-2800 radial aircraft engines
Weasel personnel carriers
Wright Cyclone R-1820 radial aircraft engines

### Willys
Jeeps

Note: This list is not comprehensive; rather, it is intended to provide a general idea of how involved the auto industry was in the war effort. Much work was subcontracted, even among the automakers themselves.

▲ Just weeks after Pearl Harbor, Chrysler president K. T. Keller (*left*) helped celebrate production of the company's 60,000th gun barrel.

▲ Ford produced components for the four-engine Boeing B-24 "Liberator." A new plant at Willow Run, Michigan, turned out 8685 bombers.

▲ Henry Ford (*left*) and wife Clara pose with grandson Henry Ford II, who was released from the U.S. Navy in 1943 to assist with war production.

---

Germany surrenders on V-E Day, May 8, 1945

Restrictions on production of replacement automotive parts are lifted on May 22

Ford closes the huge Willow Run, Michigan, aircraft plant on June 23 after producing a total of 8685 bombers

Kaiser-Frazer Corporation is formed on July 26; production will begin in a leased aircraft plant at Willow Run, where the first cars will roll off the line in June 1946

Atomic bombs are dropped over Hiroshima and Nagasaki on August 6 and 9; Japan surrenders on V-J Day, August 14, 1945

Gasoline rationing ends on August 15; restrictions on truck production end five days later

A gradually failing Henry Ford finally resigns; Henry II becomes company president on September 21, 1945, and soon hires a team of "Whiz Kids" to revitalize the weakened company

▲ Millions of women entered the work force during World War II, including this 1943 group that helped produce Hudson-built aluminum aircraft pistons.

▲ Independent automakers—Crosley, Hudson, Packard, Studebaker, Willys—turned to war work with gusto. Shown is Hudson's B-29 bomber production facility.

▲ Some top executives did more than contribute to the war effort from home. William S. Knudsen (*shown*) served as a lieutenant general.

▲ Developed by the GMC Truck & Coach Division, the amphibious "Duck" saw duty worldwide during World War II, carrying troops on land or water. All five GM passenger-car divisions also turned their facilities over to the war effort. Plenty of M-24 light tanks used Cadillac V-8s and Hydra-Matic.

◀ General Motors produced a total of 854,000 trucks for wartime use, including these light-duty models. Cadillac, among others, earned an Army-Navy "E" Award for its military production efforts.

▶ Two-thirds of the heavy trucks employed during World War II came from GM plants, along with one-fourth of aircraft engines. GM also produced 13,000 finished airplanes.

---

The Automotive Council for War Production is officially dissolved on October 15

The new 1946 Fords are shown to the public on October 26, 1945

A wave of strikes (authorized and "wildcat"), absenteeism, and general labor unrest mark the early postwar recovery period, beginning in late 1945

Many materials, such as sheet steel, are scarce—and will remain so for several years

O.P.A. price ceilings try to curb inflation, but unwittingly help to curtail production and earnings in the early postwar period

Crosley announces its intent to manufacture more small cars, but with four-cylinder engines (instead of the prewar two-bangers)

▲ The Fisher Body plant in Trenton, New Jersey, issued Grumman Avengers for the U.S. Navy. Forty percent of GM's $12.25 billion in war materiel was aviation-related. Other automakers served with similar distinction.

▲ GM built 206,000 engines for the U.S. Air Force. Two of them powered this Lockheed P-38 "Lightning."

◀ Khaki coloring and a star on the door mark this 1942 Packard sedan as a military staff car. In addition to such adaptations of prewar passenger autos, Packard turned out power units, including supercharged engines for PT boats, under the slogan: "Precision-built Power."

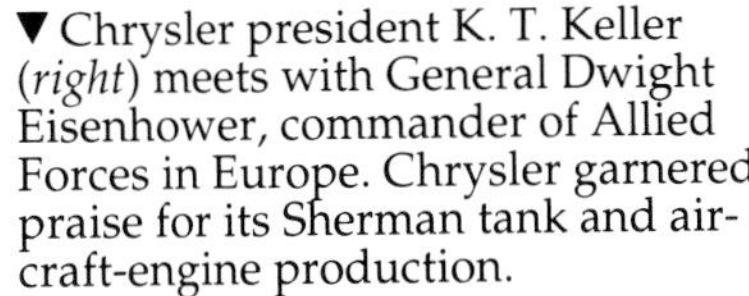

▼ Chrysler president K. T. Keller (*right*) meets with General Dwight Eisenhower, commander of Allied Forces in Europe. Chrysler garnered praise for its Sherman tank and aircraft-engine production.

▲ Henry Ford (*left*) and grandson Henry Ford II sign the 5000th "Liberator" aircraft built by the Ford company. Edsel Ford died in 1943, and Henry II soon became a vice-president.

▲ Henry Ford II drives the first civilian postwar Ford off the assembly line, on July 3, 1945. Production resumed just after V-J (Victory in Japan) Day. Consumers were ready to buy.

---

The '46 models generally are lightly facelifted '42s, but this does nothing to dampen the vast pent-up demand for new cars

In an effort to get production underway quickly, some makers at first offer a severely limited selection of models and options

Although most auto companies are in production by October, Chrysler Corporation and Studebaker don't get rolling until December

Clayton Moore—who portrays *The Lone Ranger* on radio—buys the first '46 Pontiac

As sales of conventional cars boom after the war, executives begin to doubt the feasibility (or profitability) of small cars in the postwar marketplace

CHAPTER SIX

# 1946-1948

# THE POSTWAR "SELLER'S MARKET"

Even before World War II ended, automakers began promising cars for discharged troops. One Buick ad featured a '42 model accompanied by the headline, "So nice to come home to!"

Because automakers had trouble rebuilding their assembly lines after the war ended in August 1945, and because materials were in short supply, just over 83,000 cars were built that fall. Labor unrest didn't help, highlighted by a 119-day strike against General Motors in 1945-46. Production soared during 1946, even if the cars themselves differed little from the final '42 models.

Ford ushered in a new postwar regime, after Henry Ford II took over the helm from his illustrious grandfather. He soon brought in a team of "Whiz Kids" to help transform the company's antiquated management—and financial fortunes.

Automakers expected a massive "seller's market" to develop, and they were correct. After 15 years of economic hardship and wartime limits, shoppers were eager to buy just about anything Detroit could supply. In fact, many were willing to pay jacked-up prices for new cars in those heady postwar days, snapping them up as soon as they hit the dealerships—if not before. Bargaining? Not a chance.

At first, the Office of Price Administration limited prices to 1942 levels, but the scarcity of new cars created long waiting lists. Still, shoppers who wanted a car badly enough could usually find a way to obtain one. Dealers were known to accept—or solicit—bribes, and customers might have to accept high-priced (and unwanted) extras tacked onto the list price. A "gray market" sent new models onto used-car lots, priced hundreds of dollars higher than their official new-car price. Some buyers even turned around and resold their cars and pocketed the profit.

Studebaker was the first among the existing automakers to offer a totally restyled model. Though some derided Stude's "which-way-is-it-going?" shape, eager crowds marveled at the Starlight coupe with its wraparound back window. A year later, Hudson's dramatic "Step-down" design was ready, wearing a startlingly low roofline.

Willys left the passenger-car market, except for a civilian version of the Jeep and some offshoots, but Americans had two brand-new makes from which to choose: Kaiser and Frazer. Introduced before the '47 Studebaker, but in actual production slightly later, both sold well at first, as did the other independents.

Preston Tucker's sensational new Torpedo drew even more attention. Packed with ahead-of-its-time safety features and technological advances, the rear-engined "Car of Tomorrow" attracted eager crowds—until the Securities and Exchange Commission charged Tucker with fraud. Though exonerated by a jury, Tucker's dream was dead on arrival.

Visionaries proposed three-wheeled cars, flying cars, cars that turned into boats. Few progressed beyond the prototype stage (if that). None went past minimal production. Americans weren't quite ready for a minicar, either, as the eventual failure of the improved Crosley demonstrated.

No less acute than the automobile shortage was the housing shortage. Returning veterans often had to move into Quonset-hut developments, and some looked closely at the new prefabricated homes. Many vets returned to school, earning benefits under the G.I. Bill of Rights. Christian Dior penned the "New Look" for women's fashions. Television was entering a handful of American homes. What Americans appeared to want most, however, was a new car, and Detroit scurried to fulfill those aspirations.

---

**1946**

The average car is now nine years old

With pockets stuffed with money from war-time work, car-starved Americans eagerly snap up the warmed-over '42s as they slowly begin to trickle off Detroit's assembly lines

Price increases over 1942 are sizeable; Chevy's most popular '46 model, the Stylemaster Sport Sedan, is up a whopping 43 percent—from $760 to $1205

Auto price and wage controls are lifted in November 1946

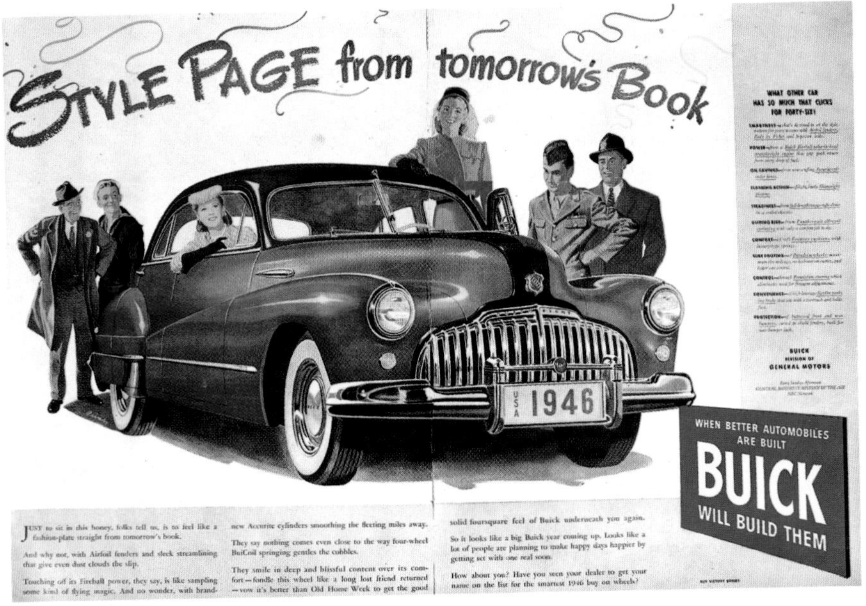

▲ The top 1946 Buick seller was the Super (Series 50) four-door, with full "airflow" fenders. Roadmasters sold well; Specials did not. Century and Limited did not return from '42.

◀ Despite a promise that its owner might become a "fashion-plate," the '46 Buick didn't look much different from '42s. Shoppers were invited not to buy, but to join a waiting list.

▲ Like other 1946 makes, Cadillac earned only a mild facelift. This $2284 Series Sixty-Two sedanet had longer rear windows than its Sixty-One mate.

▲ With the war over, Cadillac buyers could place orders—choosing from fewer models than in '42. Series Sixty-Two proved the most popular.

◀ Cadillac's Sixty Special Touring Sedan returned for 1946, at $3095, but the division-window version did not. All Cadillacs added a crest and "V" on the hood and deck.

---

More than 28 million vehicles are registered, 2,155,924 of them having been built in the 1946 model year

Due to an early production start-up, Ford leads in model-year production: 468,022 cars

Chevrolet builds 398,028 cars; Plymouth and Dodge come in third and fourth

Despite impressive volume, Ford Motor Company posts an $8.1-million loss

Chevrolet's reduced total is attributed to strikes and shortages; GM's 1946 output is just 45 percent of its '41 figure

A January steel strike closes assembly lines; in addition, the industry faces critical shortages of copper, brass, lead

▲ Chevrolet and its rivals sold all the cars they could build in 1946. Ads lost their somber wartime tone.

▲ New names went on Chevrolet series: Master DeLuxe became Stylemaster, Special DeLuxe was now Fleetmaster. Fleetlines ranked top-of-the-line, led by the 1946 Aerosedan—the third most popular model, selling for $1249.

▲ Chevrolet specifications were virtually identical to '42 models. The 216.5-cid six again put out 90 bhp.

▲ Comedian Bob Hope appears to approve of this 1946 Chrysler Town & Country convertible, priced at $2743.

▶ Because the wood-trimmed Town & Country was Chrysler's glamour car, celebrities promoted its stylistic virtues. Here, actress Marie "The Body" McDonald shows off a convertible. No more Town & Country wagons were built, but Chrysler offered the 135-bhp eight-cylinder ragtop and a seldom-seen six-cylinder sedan. The grille pattern was new, but differences between Chrysler products built from 1946 to early '49 are difficult to discern.

---

An April coal strike causes layoffs in the auto industry; rail strikes also hurt

The Ford Light Car Division is formed to develop a lightweight economy car, with a rumored five-cylinder engine, but the project is quickly axed, as is Chevrolet's similar program

Studebaker's '46 Skyway Champion has only a brief production run (19,275 units) before the all-new '47 models are introduced in May 1946

Kaiser-Frazer begins production in June 1946; its cars go on sale as '47 models, and along with Studebaker are the first totally new postwar cars

◀ Two of these 1946 Chrysler "Continental" coupes were specially built by Derham. Both went to the same man, who liked the look of the Lincoln Continental. Priced at $17,000 apiece, the cars had squared-off, top-opening trunks with exposed spare tires, and padded leatherette tops. The coupes rode on Saratoga chassis and carried 135-bhp eights. From B-posts forward, they looked all-Chrysler.

▲ Crosley returned for 1946 and took a serious stab at styling with a sedan that measured 28 inches longer than prewar models. A station wagon joined in '47.

▲ Despite a longer look, Crosley's wheelbase again spanned 80 inches. The new 44-cid four made 26.5 bhp—double the prewar rating—but the "CoBra" copper-brazed engine block proved troublesome. Prices doubled, too.

▲ Crosley's all-metal station wagon won more than 80 percent of total company sales by 1948. Far fewer examples of the roll-down-roof convertible came off the line.

---

Crosley announces a four-cylinder engine, instead of the two-cylinder that powered prewar models; production also begins in June

William Stout develops a fiberglass prototype with a rear-mounted engine

Detroit's Automotive Golden Jubilee celebrates the 50th Anniversary of the auto industry in America

Disabled veterans can get cars with special equipment developed by the Society of Automotive Engineers

Chevrolet is one of first automakers to advertise on network television: Others will soon follow

Automakers announce plans for the construction and/or purchase of 25 assembly plants

Tucker Corp. announces its plan to issue $20 million in common stock

▲ Headlights no longer were hidden on the postwar DeSotos, as front fenders flowed into doors. This 1946 Custom convertible went for $1761. The 236.6-cid six yielded 109 bhp.

▲ Just $1511 bought a 1946 DeSoto Custom sedan—but all prices were sharply higher than in '42. DeSoto also offered a new Suburban with fold-down rear seat and a roof rack.

▲ Except for a new crosshatch grille, the 1946 Dodge Custom convertible was similar to its prewar counterpart. Its 102-bhp, 230-cid six now started with a dashboard pushbutton.

▲ Only one Ford model was new for '46: the wood-trimmed Super DeLuxe Sportsman. Topping the line at $1982, it rivaled Chrysler's Town & Country.

▲ The 1946 Ford "coupe sedan" came only in top Super DeLuxe trim ($1307 with a V-8). That V-8 was now the same as Mercury's, at 239.4-cid.

▲ Fords could have a 226-cid six or the enlarged V-8. Fastback styling looked a bit more graceful on the 1946 Super DeLuxe Tudor—the most popular body—than on the Fordors.

▲◄ Americans craved cars and had money, so dealers had no trouble moving Fords. Nearly four out of five were Super DeLuxe. Coupes with a back seat still had takers, but few people wanted one-seat business coupes. Chassis revisions improved the ride.

**1946 Model Year Production**

1. Ford 468,022
2. Chevrolet 398,028
3. Plymouth 264,660[1]
4. Dodge 163,490[1]
5. Buick 153,627
6. Pontiac 137,640
7. Oldsmobile 117,623
8. Nash 94,000[1]
9. Hudson 91,039
10. Mercury 86,608
11. Chrysler 83,310[1]
12. DeSoto 66,900[1]
13. Packard 30,793
14. Cadillac 29,214
15. Studebaker 19,275
16. Lincoln 16,645
17. Crosley 4,999

[1]*Calculated or estimated*

▲ This 1946 Hudson Super Six convertible Brougham could also come as a Commodore Eight, for $171 more.

◀ In September 1945, workmen at the Detroit plant prepare the first batch of mildly facelifted '46 Hudsons for rail shipment. Note how cars were stacked two high.

◀ Looks like this 1946 Mercury sedan, revealing a modest postwar facelift, is nearing the end of the line. Fords now had the same engine as Mercury: 239.4-cid and 100 bhp. This year only, Mercury issued a wood-trimmed Sportsman convertible.

▶ A boost to 82 bhp gave the 1946 Nash 600 a little extra oomph. Nash Ambassador sixes also added horsepower, but the Eight was history. Like other '46 models, Nashes were basically warmed-over '42s, but displayed a reasonably fresh look anyway. About 94,000 cars were built, putting Nash in eighth place for the model year.

▲ Nash pushed the roominess and economy of its "600," promising 25-30 mpg and space for "six big people."

---

Dodge's former Chicago war plant, intended for lease to Tucker, is awarded instead to Lustron Corp. for building prefabricated homes

Some 82 million tires are produced in 1946—an all-time high

The Century series and dual carburetors are missing from Buick's postwar lineup; a novel "gun-sight" hood ornament is widely copied by accessory manufacturers

Nicholas Dreystadt, formerly at Cadillac, becomes Chevrolet's general manager

Chevrolets face the postwar world with a new grille; Fleetlines sport triple chrome speedlines on all four fenders

◀ Oldsmobiles for '46 wore a clean, updated grille but lacked parking lights. The big shove went to Hydra-Matic. As the ads said, "all you do is step on the gas and steer." Olds touted the fact that the fully-automatic four-speed transmission had served in tanks during the war. Ads also promised a stable ride from "Quadri-Coil Springs."

▼ Topping the Oldsmobile lineup was the 98 Custom Cruiser convertible, on a 127-inch wheelbase. Its 257-cid straight-eight, which unleashed 110 horsepower, also went into the Dynamic Cruiser 78 series. Note the shapely factory fender skirts.

▲ Oldsmobile fielded a pair of convertibles for 1946, the Special Series 66 at $1681 (*shown*), plus a bigger 98 at $2040. Neither was produced in large quantity: 1409 and 874, respectively. The 238-cid six-cylinder L-head engine developed 100 horsepower. Oldsmobile's Dynamic Cruiser 76, also six-cylinder, rode a six-inch-longer wheelbase than the Special 66.

► One or two rivals might have challenged Packard's claim of top glamour car, but in 1946 the Clipper still looked impressive. Eights came in 282- and 356-cid versions; Clipper was also available with a 105-bhp six.

Chrysler's elegant Town and Country is now a wood-trimmed convertible and sedan; a glitzy new "harmonica" grille rides up front and the front fenders blend smoothly into the bodysides

An enlarged Crosley starts with a sedan, then adds a convertible; a cast-iron engine block soon displaces the troublesome copper-steel "CoBra" unit

DeSoto fields a new long-wheelbase Suburban sedan with a fold-down rear seat; headlamps are again exposed

Dodge receives faired-in front fenders and a bold eggcrate grille

Ford borrows Mercury's 239.4-cid V-8, adding 10 horsepower; a handsome wood-trimmed Sportsman convertible debuts

▲ Plymouths took DeLuxe or Special DeLuxe form for '46, with the same 95-bhp, 217.8-cid six as in 1942. Utility models were deleted from the line.

◀ Pontiacs sold in two flavors for 1946: notchback Torpedo or fastback Streamliner (shown), each with a 239-cid six or 249-cid straight-eight.

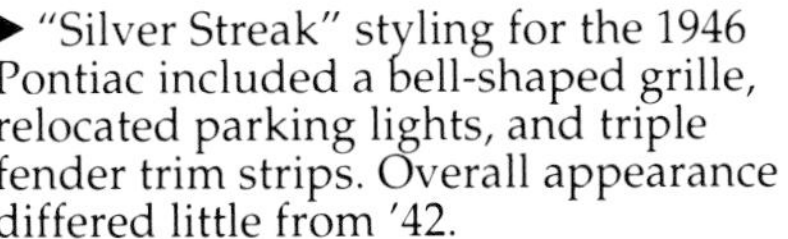

▶ "Silver Streak" styling for the 1946 Pontiac included a bell-shaped grille, relocated parking lights, and triple fender trim strips. Overall appearance differed little from '42.

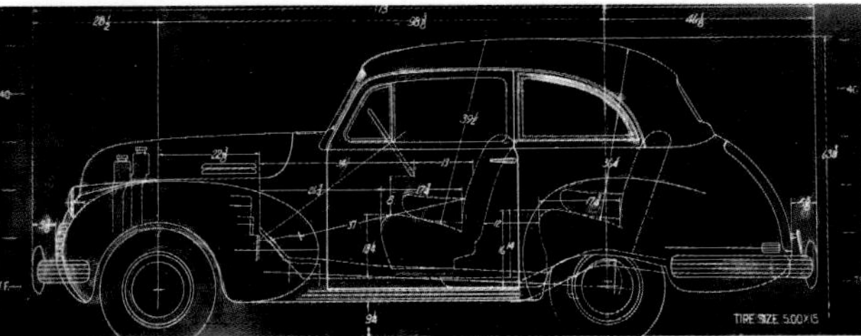

▲ Willys-Overland planned a postwar passenger car, code-named 6/66, to replace the abandoned Americar. Industrial designer Brooks Stevens penned the compact two-door on a 98¾-inch wheelbase (173 inches overall), with separate fenders and a "coffin-nose" hood, slightly reminiscent of the 1936-37 Cords.

▲ Just one 6/66 was built, with production aimed at 1947. After an accident destroyed the prototype, the project fizzled and Willys issued only a Jeep-based wagon.

---

Unlike most makes, Hudson keeps its '42 Drive-Master semi-automatic transmission option; a grille with a recessed center section is the styling keynote

Lincoln gains a two-layer cross-hatch grille and loses both its Zephyr name and three-passenger coupe

Mercury trades its '42 three-passenger coupe for a '46 Sportsman woody convertible; only 205 will be built

Nash drops the Ambassador Eight to concentrate on six-cylinder engines: an L-head for the 600 series, and an overhead-valve for the Ambassador

Self-shift Hydra-Matic gains popularity in Oldsmobiles, which feature a new four-bar grille that tapers downward at the outer ends

Willys introduces an all-steel Station Wagon with Jeep-like styling

▲ One of several roadsters planned for postwar America, the Bobbi-Kar rode an 80-inch wheelbase, with a 25-bhp four. Production never began.

► Except for a revised grille that gave a lower look, Buick's '47 Roadmaster hadn't changed much. Postwar inflation kept prices zooming upward, sending the convertible to $2651.

◄ Cadillac convertibles came only in Series Sixty-Two in 1947, priced at a princely $2902. Hydro-Lectric window lifts were standard—an uncommon extra. Sixty-Two was Caddy's most popular series, with 6755 ragtops finding buyers.

▼ Even Cadillac's Series Sixty-Two sedanet (also called a club coupe) was no lightweight at 4145 pounds. Full wheel covers replaced hubcaps in 1947, and stainless steel stone guards protected rear fenders.

▲ The big Series Seventy-Five Cadillacs stuck to old-time styling. This seven-passenger sedan, weighing 4895 pounds and priced at $4686, appeared in *The Godfather*.

Kaiser-Frazer negotiates with Fiat to build a lightweight car, but nothing comes of it

Bobbi Motor Car Corp. acquires an option for a factory to produce the "Bobbi-Kar" roadster

The Cushman motor scooter company offers shopping cars

Airphibian is one of first postwar flying cars; the Convaircar, meanwhile, uses a Crosley engine on the road, a 190-bhp Lycoming in the air

The buckboard-style King Midget, sold as a kit (later assembled), is advertised in *Popular Mechanics* and similar magazines

Two three-wheeler, rear-engined cars debut—the plastic-bodied, 4½-bhp Comet and the 10-bhp Brogan—but production is minuscule

Californian Frank Kurtis also develops a three-wheeler; it will evolve into the '47 Davis

▲ Only a prototype of the three-wheeled Californian was built, by former racer Frank Curtis. With a 58-bhp engine, it promised 100 mph top speed and 40 mpg. A successor, the Davis, actually went into production.

▲ If Ford could offer a woody-look convertible, why not Chevy? This 1947 Fleetmaster wears a dress-up "Country Club" kit, offered by Engineering Enterprises for $148.50. Chevrolet built a record 28,443 ragtops.

▲ Chevrolet's 1947 Fleetmaster station wagon was the most expensive model ($1893) as well as the slowest seller (4912 built). Grilles changed slightly this year.

▲ Idaho troopers didn't have to endure spartan patrol duty, while driving this Fleetline Aerosedan—the most costly two-door Chevrolet sedan, and also the most popular.

▲ More than 750 dealers attended this parade in Flint, Michigan, to mark the opening of a new Chevrolet plant. Demand still exceeded supply of cars, so automakers scrambled to turn out more.

▲ General manager Nicholas Dreystadt (*left*), sales manager T.H. Keating, and manufacturing boss Hugh Dean show the 20-millionth Chevy.

**1947**

With the seller's market still the dominant factor, demand for autos continues to outstrip production

Automobile list prices reach an all-time high; inflation is a serious problem throughout the entire economy

Auto production reaches 3,555,792 units in calendar 1947

Chevrolet returns to Number One with 671,546 cars built; Ford is second with 429,674, followed by Plymouth, Buick, and Dodge

Studebaker has already introduced its all-new postwar design, with a similar front and rear shape—wags joke that the Champion and Commander look the same coming or going

▲ Only straight-eight engines went into the 1947 Chrysler Town & Country convertible; the car was based on the New Yorker chassis with 127.5-inch wheelbase. With 135 horsepower and Fluid Drive, Chrysler Eights weren't terribly quick at startup, but delivered smooth takeoffs and a luxurious ride.

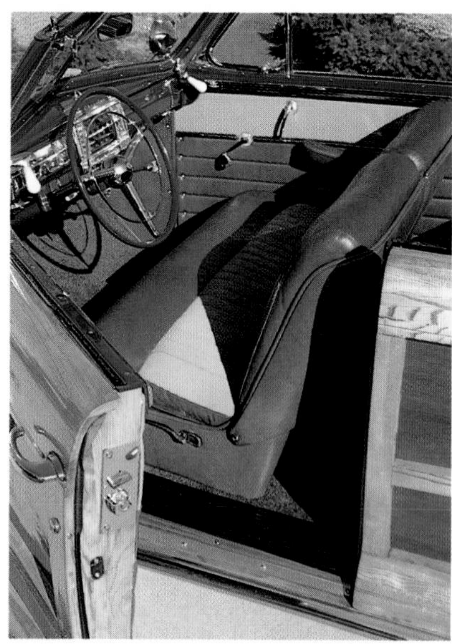

▲ Elegance was evident in the two-tone interior of a Chrysler Town & Country convertible, as well as on its handsome wood-and-metal body.

▲ The $2998 open Town & Country was expensive, but lured plenty of customers into dealerships.

▲ Almost forgotten amid the flurry of attention given to convertibles was the similarly wood/steel Chrysler Town & Country sedan. Only a six-cylinder engine was installed, making 114 bhp. Some sedans had a roof rack.

▶ Body components for Chrysler's Town & Country were assembled in this fixture, claimed to deliver the same accuracy as an all-steel body.

The most striking Studebaker, the five-passenger "Starlight" coupe, boasts a huge four-piece wraparound rear window

Two all-new makes, Kaiser and Frazer, have already gone on sale; on February 1, Kaiser-Frazer purchases the assets of the prewar Graham-Paige Motor Corp.

Kaiser-Frazer achieves the highest calendar-year production of any of the independent automakers: 139,249

Most makes differ little from '46, except for trim and detail revisions; in fact, the '47s receive even fewer changes than did the '46s

A total of 164,492 convertibles and 82,665 station wagons are built this year

After declining in the Thirties, outside sun visors regain favor as an accessory

▲ Top-dollar Crosley for 1947 was the convertible coupe, with innovative "roll-top" roof, at $949. A two-door sedan cost $888; the new station wagon, $929. Crosley did well for a time, but good fortune wouldn't last.

▲ A total of 4005 Crosley convertibles were produced in 1947, along with a brace of mini-trucks. Though easy to repair, the initial "CoBra" four-cylinder engine became notorious for internal leakage.

► Fluid Drive eased clutch operation in the 1947 Dodge, sold in DeLuxe or Custom trim. A fluid coupling between the engine and three-speed transmission gave smooth startups, but gears had to be shifted manually.

▲ Early '47 Fords showed little change, but a modest restyle came in the spring, led by round parking lights.

► This 1947 Ford Sportsman wears the facelifted front end introduced at mid-season; three wood patterns were used. Production rose to 2250—but that was barely one-tenth the output of the all-steel convertible.

---

Packard offers hydraulic power seats and windows in some top-line models

In January, the government agrees to let Tucker Corp. lease the former Dodge war plant after all; the Tucker Torpedo is unveiled in Chicago, but only 51 will be built before the demise of this ill-fated company

The auto industry and millions of Americans mourn the death of Henry Ford I on April 7, 1947, at the age of 83

Lincoln marks its 25th Anniversary

▲ Kaiser and the similarly shaped Frazer were the first all-new cars of the postwar era. People lined up to get a look at the first '47s.

▲ Top-of-the-line at Kaiser-Frazer was the 1947 Frazer Manhattan. Introduced in mid-1946, Kaisers and Frazers featured slab-sided styling and unadorned hoods. Frazer produced only four-door Frazer sedans, priced at a hefty $2712 for the Manhattan, or $2295 for the less-posh "standard" model.

▲ A 123.5-inch wheelbase helped give the Frazer Manhattan a smooth ride. Power came from a 226-cid Continental L-head six, rated at 100 horsepower (112-bhp optional later). The sedan's 64-inch front seat was the widest in the industry. Overdrive was optional for the three-speed gearbox. Early examples had a tiny "Darrin-styled" logo on the trunklid and "Graham-Paige" plate on the firewall. Joseph Frazer headed what was left of the Graham-Paige company when he joined Henry J. Kaiser in this new venture.

▲ Hudson retained its prewar look for one more season, with only detail changes. The 3-millionth car (a Commodore Eight) was built in 1947. Hudson president A. E. Barit is seated in the Commodore; other execs in Number One, a 1910 roadster. Hudson ended the season in 11th place.

---

Ford and the United Auto Workers reach a tentative labor agreement in June; foremen have been on strike

Chrysler and GM sign new autoworkers' union contracts

The Taft-Hartley Labor Act brings a halt to strikes

A new synthetic rubber is developed by Phillips Petroleum Company

The Automobile Manufacturers Association approves an SAE recommendation to standardize bumper heights

Cadillac prices rise $150-$200; most sales are for the Series Sixty-Two models

Chryslers ride Goodyear low-pressure "Super Cushion" tires

▲ Ray Russell designed the 1100-pound three-seat Gadabout, on a short (80-inch) wheelbase, during the war. The prototype had a duraluminum body on an MG chassis.

▲ Hudson Eight sedans came in two levels: $1862 Super and $1972 Commodore, both with a 128-horsepower, 254-cid engine. Six-cylinder Hudsons, rated at 102 bhp, rode the same 121-inch wheelbase but sold much more vigorously.

▲ This 1947 Kaiser Special sedan seems to have every accessory on the list, including twin spotlights and a sun visor. No doubt it cost a lot more than the $2104 list price. The Continental L-head six gave 100 bhp.

▲ A more costly Custom sedan joined the Kaiser Special (*shown*) later in 1947. Howard Darrin penned the flush-fendered Kaiser-Frazer bodies, built in a former Ford plant in Michigan. Note the single backup light.

▲ At this point on the Kaiser assembly line, metal finishers ground and polished bodies, adding doors and trunklids. Kaisers cost less than Frazers.

▲ Only one of these 1947 Kaiser Pinconning Special sedans was produced—the sole two-door Kaiser prior to 1951. Because of its U-shaped davenport rear seat, it was called a "conference car." A 112-bhp version of the Kaiser-Frazer engine became available during 1947.

---

Crosley adds a station wagon to its two-door sedan and convertible lineup; production nearly triples to 19,344 units

Fluid Drive semi-automatic transmission is made standard on Dodges

Ford announces lightly facelifted "Spring Models" for all three of its car lines in April; many consider these to be the "true" '47s

Although the first few Frazers are built at the Graham-Paige plant in Detroit, production quickly shifts to Kaiser's sprawling Willow Run facility

Kaiser and Frazer wear slab-sided sedan bodies styled mainly by Howard "Dutch" Darrin; Frazer is the more costly of the duo

Lincoln adopts pull-type door handles, replacing pushbuttons

▲ Postwar Lincoln Continentals sported a fresh grille, decried by some purists. Output for 1947 totaled 831 coupes and 738 convertibles.

▲ Non-Continental Lincolns lost their pushbutton doors for 1947. The Zephyr name no longer was used for the sedan, club coupe, or convertible. Lincoln's L-head V-12 shrunk to its 1941 size: 292 cid and 125 bhp.

▲ Lincoln-Mercury became a separate division in 1947, as this company station wagon demonstrates. For public sale, a wagon went for $2202. Cars used more formerly scarce materials, including chrome and aluminum.

▲ Nash turned to wood trim for its fastback 1947 Ambassador Sedan Suburban, which sold for $2227. Only 595 were built this year, up from 272 in '46. The 234.8-cid six-cylinder engine developed 112 horsepower.

▲ A wider upper grille and raised-center hubcaps were the most evident changes for Nash in 1947, including this "600" Brougham with an 82-bhp engine. At $1415, it cost more than a comparable Ford or Chevy.

### 1947 Model Year Production

1. Chevrolet....................671,546
2. Ford....................429,674
3. Plymouth....................382,290[1]
4. Buick....................272,827
5. Dodge....................243,160[1]
6. Pontiac....................230,600
7. Oldsmobile....................193,895
8. Studebaker....................161,496
9. Chrysler....................119,260
10. Nash....................101,000[1]
11. Hudson....................92,038
12. DeSoto....................87,000[1]
13. Mercury....................85,383
14. Kaiser....................70,474
15. Frazer....................68,775
16. Cadillac....................61,926
17. Packard....................51,086
18. Lincoln....................21,460
19. Crosley....................19,344

[1] *Calculated or estimated*

▲ Notchback versions of the 1947 Nash Ambassador four-door sedan (*shown*) went for $1464; "slip stream" fastbacks cost $44 less. Note the spotlight and sun visor—two popular add-ons. Two-toning highlighted the rooflines of many late '40s models. An Ambassador sedan paced the 1947 Indianapolis 500.

▲ General Motors chairman Alfred P. Sloan, Jr. (*right*) congratulates Ransom E. Olds at a dinner to mark the auto pioneer's 80th birthday in 1947. Olds had left the company that bore his name—and that later became part of GM—decades earlier, to begin production of the Reo.

▲ Many 1947 drivers would hesitate to dispute Oldsmobile's claim that Hydra-Matic was "the greatest advancement since the self starter."

◀ Virtually identical to the 1946 models, this 1947 Packard Custom Super Clipper four-door sedan sold for $3449. Packard produced 51,086 cars this year, ranking 17th (down from 13th). Note the elegant Vanderbilt Gray metallic roof and spotlights. Only serial numbers distinguish '46s from '47s.

---

The Lincoln-Mercury Division, formed in October 1945, now has its own separate dealer network

Packard unveils a major restyling on the '48 convertible in March, to be followed in the fall by the rest of the '48 line

Eight-cylinder Pontiacs outsell the sixes for the first time, a sign that customers are willing to spend the extra money for upgraded models

The Davis Motor Car Co. is organized to build a three-wheeler; the first car is completed in October, but only about 17 will be built through 1949

The War Assets Administration accepts a bid from Playboy Motor Car Corp. for a former Chevrolet plant; the three-seater convertible features a novel folding steel top, but only about 90 will be produced by 1951

▲ Like big GM makes, Packard fielded a line of fastback two-doors, many two-toned and visored, including this 1947 Custom Super Clipper club sedan. Beneath the hood sat Packard's biggest engine: 356 cid and 165 bhp.

▲ A total of 5690 two- and four-door sedans were produced in Packard's Custom Super Clipper series, on the 127-inch wheelbase—plus 1790 of the 148-inchers. Interiors featured broadcloth or leather upholstery.

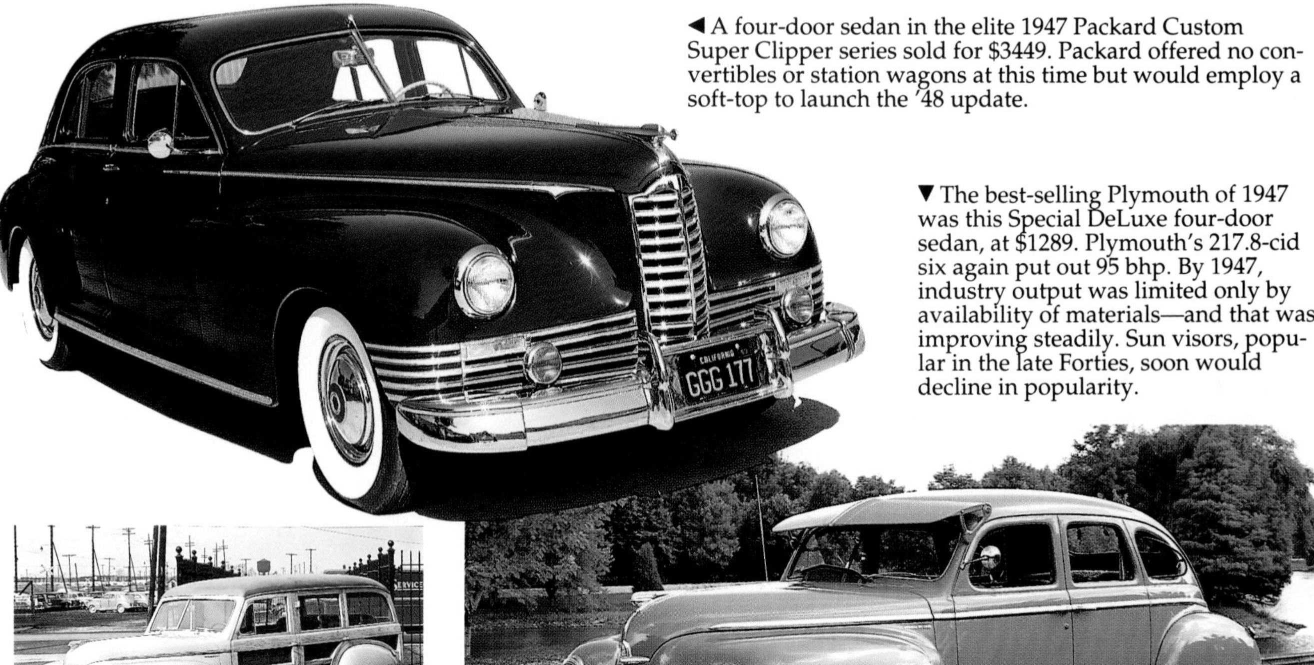


◀ A four-door sedan in the elite 1947 Packard Custom Super Clipper series sold for $3449. Packard offered no convertibles or station wagons at this time but would employ a soft-top to launch the '48 update.

▼ The best-selling Plymouth of 1947 was this Special DeLuxe four-door sedan, at $1289. Plymouth's 217.8-cid six again put out 95 bhp. By 1947, industry output was limited only by availability of materials—and that was improving steadily. Sun visors, popular in the late Forties, soon would decline in popularity.

▲ Plymouths looked virtually identical from 1946 to early '49, when the all-new models arrived. The 1947 woody station wagon came in Special DeLuxe trim only, priced at $1765.

---

Although a fold-up Airscoot three-wheeler is developed, production never begins

North American Motors reveals a plan to build the Cortez Six

Kaiser-Frazer buys the rights to the Scarab rear-engined car

The Bobbi company changes its name to Keller Motors Corp. and moves from California to Alabama

▲ Pontiacs wore a simplified grille for 1947, when a six-cylinder Torpedo convertible sold for $1811 ($1853 in DeLuxe trim). Eights cost a bit more. The 239-cid six made 90 bhp; the eight, 103 bhp. Note the factory skirts.

▲ Streamliner Pontiacs, including this 1947 Eight DeLuxe woody station wagon, rode a 122-inch wheelbase. Slightly cheaper Torpedo models measured 119 inches.

▲ "Dramatic" barely describes the 1947 Studebaker, styled by Virgil Exner and Robert Bourke. This $1902 Champion Regal DeLuxe has an 80-bhp, 169.6-cid six.

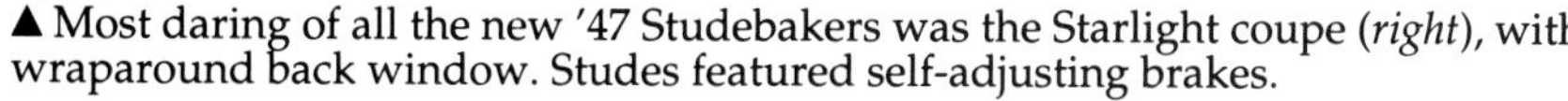

▲ Most daring of all the new '47 Studebakers was the Starlight coupe (*right*), with wraparound back window. Studes featured self-adjusting brakes.

▲ Willys launched its all-steel Jeep wagon in 1946, with "Planadyne" semi-independent front suspension.

▲ The Beech Aircraft Co. of Wichita, Kansas, developed this Beechcraft Plainsman sedan, but built only a prototype. An air-cooled, four-cylinder Franklin engine drove an electric generator, powering separate electric motors at each wheel that also served as braking backups.

▲ Spacious enough for six, the fastback Beechcraft Plainsman featured fully independent air suspension, with air-filled shocks at each corner. If Beech's aircraft contracts had not been fattened by the onset of the Cold War, the Plainsman might have seen production.

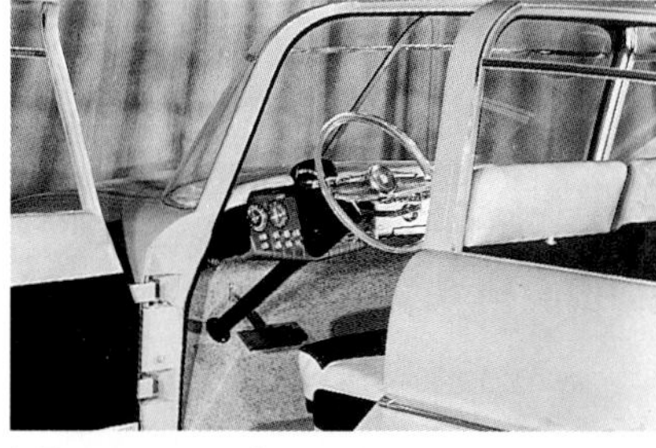

▲ Doors curved into the roof of the Beechcraft Plainsman's aluminum body/frame, which featured a "glassy" cockpit. A $4000-$5000 price was proposed, but a production sedan probably would have cost more.

▲ Dynaflow—the first passenger-car torque converter—joined Buick's option list in 1948, available for $244 on Roadmasters. This Estate Wagon weighed a whopping 4460 pounds and cost $3433 ($1015 more than a sedan). Only 350 were built.

◀ Buick offered a convertible in the Super and Roadmaster series for 1948, priced at $2518 or $2837. Sluggish, droning takeoffs prompted some critics to nickname the new automatic transmission "Dyna-slush."

---

**1948**

Critical material shortages and labor strife continue all year; sheet steel remains in tight supply

Wage disputes close many auto plants in the spring; suppliers are struck, too

Calendar-year production rises to 3,910,213 cars despite all the problems

With 696,449 built, Chevrolet is again tops in model-year production; Ford is second with 430,198, followed by Plymouth and Dodge

Chrysler Corp. ranks second in total car production, behind GM

Independent automakers earn a 22-percent market share, versus 9.3 percent in 1941

Many 1948 models differ little—if at all—from 1947

▲ Leather upholstery and Hydro-Lectric windows were standard in the 1948 Cadillac Sixty-Two convertible. The masterful, aircraft-inspired redesign featured curvaceous roof and fender lines, plus a shapely hood.

► Modestly sized when they first appeared on the 1948 Cadillac, tailfins would grow enormous over the next decade. Fins gave the rear end as much "importance" as the front. This Series Sixty-One sedanet, at $2728, was Cadillac's cheapest model.

▲ Yes, a Chevrolet convertible paced the Indianapolis 500 in 1948. The Fleetmaster Cabriolet cost $1750; 20,471 were produced.

▲ Chevrolet's Fleetline Sportmaster looked a lot like senior GM four-doors in 1948. Nicely fitted inside, it cost $1492, with 64,217 built.

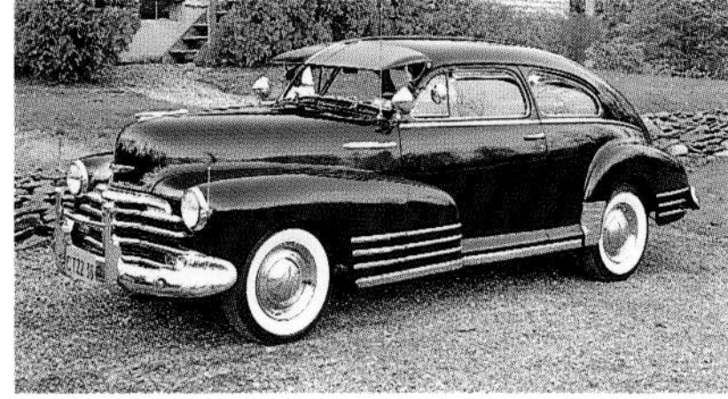

▲ Even at $1434, Chevy's Fleetline Aerosedan was the most popular 1948 model, with 211,861 produced. Fifteen-inch tires were now optional.

---

After a short '48 model year, Lincoln and Mercury introduce their all-new '49s in April, followed by Ford in June

Chrysler Corp. continues to sell its '48 models into early 1949 (as "First Series" '49s), waiting until the modern postwar replacements are ready

Ford Motor Company is in financial chaos, but orders for the '49 model pass two million by July, an all-time industry record; many of the orders will go unfilled

Hudson introduces an all-new, revolutionary "Step-down" series for '48: safe, stylish, and with a surprisingly low center of gravity

The all-new Cadillac introduces tailfins, inspired by the Lockheed P-38 fighter plane

▲ M. E. Coyle, GM's executive vice president, contrasted a 1948 Chevrolet to a 1929 Buick to demonstrate to a congressional committee how cars had risen in value. GM's slogan: "More and Better Things for More People."

▲ Whatever wouldn't fit inside a leather-upholstered 1948 Chrysler Traveler four-door sedan could be loaded onto the wood/chrome roof rack. Part of the 114-horsepower Windsor six series, Travelers sold for $2163.

▲ The lowest-priced 1948 Chrysler New Yorker was the three-passenger business coupe, sporting a super-long trunk. From 1946 to early '49, only 701 of these strictly business, compact-cockpit coupes were produced.

▲ "Beautiful Chryslers" of '48 included the six-cylinder Royal and Windsor, plus straight-eight Saratogas, New Yorkers, and Crown Imperials.

▲ Deluxe versions (*shown*) of DeSoto's '48 four-door cost $1825; Customs ran $1892. Both rode a 121.5-inch wheelbase (seven-seaters, 139.5-inch).

◀ "Tip-toe" shift cost $121 extra on DeSotos. Shown is a 1948 Custom convertible, priced at $2296. DeSoto also issued a line of taxis.

---

Cadillac Series Seventy-Five long-wheelbase sedans and limos keep the old prewar design

Buick introduces its Dynaflow torque-converter automatic transmission, which is available on Roadmasters

Pontiac offers Hydra-Matic, which goes into half the sixes and four-fifths of the eights

The unique Willys Jeepster "phaeton convertible" is launched; 10,326 are sold

Dodge announces a protective oil coating on the cylinder walls of its latest engines to prevent scoring during the break-in period

Ford develops a thermostatically controlled fan

▲ Dodge, like other Chrysler products, continued into 1948 with virtually no change—and would linger even longer as "First Series" '49 models. This spacious Custom seven-passenger sedan carried a $2179 price tag.

▲ The familiar 230-cid L-head six-cylinder engine still put out 102 horsepower in 1948 Dodges, hooked to Fluid Drive. Offered only in Custom trim, this club coupe cost $1774. The seductive convertible went for $2189.

▲ Only 28 Ford Sportsman convertibles were built for 1948, the model's final season. Total Ford output was scant, as shoppers awaited the early debut of all-new models for '49.

▲ San Diego scofflaws faced a tight fit in the back of this close-coupled Ford coupe-sedan, supposedly able to carry six. Civilian versions cost $1409 with the 100-bhp V-8.

▲ Despite the growth of suburbia, the era of wood-bodied wagons was ending. This 1948 Super DeLuxe Ford seated eight, and 8912 were built. Ads pushed Ford's "Rest-ride" springs.

◄ Kaiser-Frazer touted 35 improvements in style and mechanical details for 1948. In reality, this $2746 Frazer Manhattan didn't look much different from the '47, though its price rose moderately. Posh interiors helped the Manhattan attract customers, but a standard Frazer cost $263 less than the Manhattan. Only Manhattans, though, could get the optional engine, with dual manifolds for an extra dozen horsepower. Overdrive was optional with either the 100- or 112-bhp six. Kaisers were selling reasonably well, but the similarly contoured—and more expensive—Frazers had a tougher time moving through dealerships.

---

Borg-Warner announces that it can supply automatic transmissions to automakers—and it will do so before long

Green is the year's most popular color; black is considered by many to be a "Depression" hue

Tucker operations are halted in July so that the Securities and Exchange Commission can examine the firm's books

The U.S. auto industry builds its 100-millionth vehicle (cars and trucks)

B.F. Goodrich develops the tubeless tire, which in the mid-Fifties will dominate the industry

Henry J. Kaiser announces his plan to build an inexpensive car "at some future date"

▲ Hudson had a radically new design in 1948: the stunning "Step-down," named for its dropped floorpan. Note the heavy upper windshield molding on this Commodore Eight Brougham, a feature of 1948-54 Hudson convertibles.

▲ "Step-down" Hudson occupants rode within the unitized body's girders. Hudsons soon gained a reputation for great handling. A Commodore sedan might have the new 121-bhp, 262-cid Super Six engine or a 128-bhp eight.

▲ Final examples of the classic Lincoln Continental came off the line in 1948, and Henry Ford II drove one to pace the Indy 500. Only 452 of the $4746 cabriolet convertibles were built this year, versus 847 coupes.

▲ Neither Kaiser nor the upscale Frazer changed notably in 1948, their second year. Only 1263 Kaiser Customs were built; but Special's production was a splendid 90,588.

◀ The last American-built V-12 engines went to customers in 1948, powering both the Continental and regular Lincoln line. A reputation for overheating and other troubles hadn't helped the V-12. In addition to this sharp $3142 convertible, Lincoln offered final sedans and club coupes.

**1948 Model Year Production**

|  |  |  |
|---|---|---|
| 1. | Chevrolet | 696,449 |
| 2. | Ford | 430,198 |
| 3. | Plymouth | 412,540 |
| 4. | Dodge | 243,340[1] |
| 5. | Pontiac | 235,419 |
| 6. | Buick | 213,599 |
| 7. | Studebaker | 184,993 |
| 8. | Oldsmobile | 172,852 |
| 9. | Chrysler | 130,110[1] |
| 10. | Hudson | 117,200 |
| 11. | Nash | 110,000[1] |
| 12. | DeSoto | 98,890[1] |
| 13. | Packard | 92,251 |
| 14. | Kaiser | 91,851 |
| 15. | Cadillac | 52,706 |
| 16. | Mercury | 50,268 |
| 17. | Frazer | 48,071 |
| 18. | Crosley | 26,239 |
| 19. | Lincoln | 7,769 |

[1]*Calculated or estimated*

▲ Like other automakers, Nash clung to the past in 1948, planning a major move for '49. Two-toning looked tidy on the Ambassador brougham coupe.

◀ An even thousand Ambassador Custom cabriolets went to buyers in '48—the first open Nash model since the war. Deletion of side moldings helped give the cars a taller profile.

▶ Tourist cabins make a fitting site for this 1948 Nash DeLuxe 600 business coupe. Though that model came stripped for $1478, this example is loaded with add-on accessories.

◀ Oldsmobile's 238-cid L-head six made 100 horsepower. The 257-cid straight-eight yielded 110 bhp (115 bhp in the new "Futuramic" 98).

▲ GM fastbacks, two- and four-door, continued to lure a fair share of buyers. This Oldsmobile Series 76 club sedan, at $1726, changed only in detail for '48.

---

Studebaker begins production at its new Hamilton, Ontario, plant—destined to be the final source of Studes in 1965-66

Ford's six-cylinder engine is boosted to 95 bhp

George Mason becomes chairman of Nash in June, succeeding the deceased Charles W. Nash

Oldsmobile sees only detail changes for "Dynamic" 1948 models, but the "Futuramic" 98 bows in February as one of GM's first all-new postwar models

Packard adds extra sheetmetal to create "flow-through" fenders, quickly derided as the "pregnant elephant" shape; a convertible and Station Sedan join the model lineup

▲ How "scientific" it was may be debatable, but the 1948 Oldsmobile "Futuramic" 98, from Harley Earl's Art & Colour studio, was one of GM's first totally new postwar designs.

► Modern shaping—especially in the rear—gave the new Oldsmobile 98 a longer, lower look. Actually, its wheelbase was now a tad shorter. More than 65,000 "Futuramic" 98s (12,914 of them convertibles) were built in '48.

▲ Even in four-door form, the fresh lines of Oldsmobile's Futuramic 98 are evident. This two-toned DeLuxe sedan was the top 1948 seller.

▲ Packard's 1948 revamp evolved from a "Phantom" car built for styling vice-president Ed Macauley. Convertibles arrived first, in March 1947, including this $3250 Super Eight on a 120-inch wheelbase.

---

Production of the rear-engine/front-drive Gregory is set to begin in June, but only one is actually built

The Playboy convertible is ready for pilot production in April; an announced three per day will soon be constructed

Keller enters minimal production, evolved from the earlier Bobbi-Kar; about 18 will be produced through 1950

The Kurtis sports car is made up of stock components, including a supercharged Studebaker Champion engine; it will evolve into the Muntz

Development of the Aerocar begins; the first one is to go on sale in 1954

The Airway prototype has a fast-back body and 10-bhp air-cooled aluminum engine; top speed is 45-50 mph

▲ Roof, decklid, and inner panels remained from the prior Clipper, but Packard stylists packed on metal to give a modern "flow-through-fender" effect. This seven-passenger Custom Eight limo rode a 148-inch wheelbase.

▲ Bulged bodysides and excess weight prompted critics to dub the 1948 models "pregnant elephants." Not everyone appreciated the squat grille, either, but this $3750 Custom Eight sedan displays a dignified demeanor.

◀ Custom Eight Packards rode a 127-inch wheelbase, versus 120-inch for the Super, and had a 356-cid straight-eight. Supers used a new 145-bhp 327-cid engine, while the standard eight was 288 cid. Convertibles came in Super and Custom trim.

▼ In DeLuxe trim, a 1948 Plymouth four-door sedan sold for $1441. Moving up to Special DeLuxe meant paying an extra $88. That sum bought fancier upholstery, a bright windshield frame, and hoodside lettering.

▲ Its price sticker jumped from $1289 in 1947 to $1529 in '48, but otherwise the 1948 Plymouth Special DeLuxe four-door sedan hadn't changed a bit.

---

The six-passenger Beechcraft Plainsman uses a Franklin air-cooled four to drive electric motors; only one or two prototypes are ever built

▲ Twin spotlights weren't included in the $1857 base price of a 1948 Plymouth Special DeLuxe convertible, which had no rear side windows. Fifteen-inch tires (replacing 16-inchers) gave Plymouths a slightly lower stance.

▲ Except for highline two-tone upholstery, the interior of a Plymouth looks typical of 1948 cars—packed with protruding knobs that would horrify today's safety advocates. Plymouth's 217.8-cid six yielded 95 bhp.

▲ Pontiacs carried "Silver Streak" nameplates for the first time in 1948, also adding a "floating" bar to the grille and round taillights in back. Four-door sedans came in fastback (Streamliner) or semi-notchback (Torpedo) style. Eights sold far better than sixes.

▲ Paramount Pontiac news for 1948 was Hydra-Matic, available for an extra $185. This DeLuxe Streamliner woody wagon cost $2490 with a 104-bhp straight-eight, or $2442 with a 90-bhp six. The new DeLuxe trim option included chrome fender moldings and gravel guards.

▲ Studebakers wore a new hood medallion for '48, but otherwise looked the same. Carrying a 94-bhp, 226-cid six, the Studebaker Commander Regal DeLuxe convertible cost $2431.

▶ Americans clamoring for a "car of the future" thought they had one in the Tucker. Hailed as the "First Completely New Car" in half a century, the four-door fastback looked like nothing on the road in 1948. Styled by Alex Tremulis on a 128-inch wheelbase, the sedan stood only 60 inches tall.

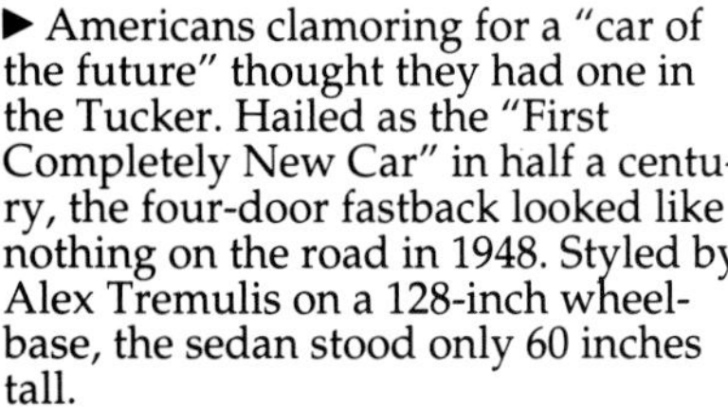

▲ Preston Tucker (*left*) gathers with radio personality Art Baker (*holding microphone*), son Preston Jr., and press agent Charles Pearson. By the time 51 cars were built, Tucker was being charged with securities fraud.

▲ Though exonerated, Tucker's dream of a radical—and safe—auto was dashed. Innovations had included fully independent suspension, a moving "Cyclops-eye" headlight, pop-out windshield, and recessed controls.

▲ Slipping into a Tucker wasn't typical of '48. Doors cut into the roof and controls clustered around the steering wheel. Audrey Moore Hodges served as color/fabric coordinator. The Chicago plant closed in August.

▲ Tuckers were roomy, quick, powerful, and aerodynamic. The rear-mounted 335-cid flat-six engine delivered 166 horsepower and a walloping 372 pounds/feet of torque. A recipe for success, it would seem; but failure came quickly.

▲ Willys launched the jaunty Jeepster in 1948, a touring mate to the wagon on the same 104-inch wheelbase. Brooks Stevens styled both cars.

▲ Beneath the $1765 Jeepster's hood sat the same basic engine that had powered prewar Americars: a 134-cid four, rated at 63 bhp. Clip-in side curtains were reminiscent of 1930s roadsters. First-year output topped 10,000.

◄ Mechanical details of the 1948 Willys station wagon were similar to the new Jeepster. All early models were painted maroon, with a wood-like trim pattern. The tailgate folded down, and the rear window swung upward.

CHAPTER SEVEN

# 1949

# A NEW ERA BEGINS

Never had more American automobiles changed more in a single year than the 1949 models. Of course, Cadillac, Hudson, Oldsmobile Ninety-Eight, Packard, and Studebaker had been redesigned for 1947-48—which hindsight suggests was a bit ahead of necessity—and Kaiser-Frazer had been an astounding success since opening for business in mid-1946. Now everyone else made the much-anticipated "big switch" from warmed-over prewar products to all-new postwar styling, and many nameplates offered new or improved engines to go with it. The result was a record industry year (eclipsing 1929) as Americans eagerly gobbled up over six million cars.

"New" was the biggest factor in this banner sales performance, hyped to the heavens in most every showroom. But new didn't mean the same thing to every automaker. Chrysler, for instance, stayed on the conservative path it had started down after the mid-Thirties Airflow disaster, issuing high and boxy new models that were long on practicality but short on pizzazz. Such cautiousness would cost Chrysler dearly—but not this year.

At the opposite end of the Big Three styling spectrum was General Motors, whose sleek new '49 Chevys, Pontiacs, Buicks, and junior Oldsmobiles continued the aircraft-inspired themes favored by corporate design domo Harley Earl. These cars confirmed GM as the industry's design leader, a role it would play for most of the next 40 years. A further jewel in GM's '49 styling crown was a new concept that would soon sweep the nation. This, of course, was the glamorous "hardtop convertible."

Between GM's stylishness and Chrysler's stuffiness stood Ford Motor Company, whose biggest attraction by far was the most changed Ford in a generation. A trim and tasteful design, the all-new '49 Ford was an instant hit—a good thing, too, as Dearborn was still teetering on the brink of financial ruin. Had it not sold well, Ford might not have lived to celebrate its 50th birthday. But fortunately, the '49 Ford did sell.

"Bathtub" styling, a legacy of sporadic wartime design work at Ford and elsewhere, was fairly popular in '49. Its best expressions were a burly new Lincoln and Mercury and Hudson's year-old "Step-down"; the worst was arguably Nash's advanced but awkward new Airflyte. Packard offered bathtubs for a second season in '49, though the later "pregnant elephant" sobriquet still seems more appropriate.

Other '49 developments were more predictive. Compression ratios began sneaking up in preparation for an industry-wide "horsepower race," with GM looming as the odds-on favorite thanks to the introduction of America's first modern, short-stroke overhead-valve V-8s at Oldsmobile and Cadillac. What's more, Olds chief Jerrod Skinner had the foresight to drop his lively "Rocket" engine into a smaller, lighter platform to create the granddaddy of all "muscle cars," the speedy new Olds 88. Automatic transmissions were still a high-cost feature, but GM offered one in more models for '49—and where GM led in those days, others were bound to follow. The year also saw the death of structural-wood models and the birth of all-steel wagons at GM and Chrysler.

Upstart Kaiser-Frazer could manage only facelifts for '49, and president Joe Frazer advised that wasn't nearly enough against so much new competition. But chairman Henry Kaiser wouldn't retrench, and ordered tooling up for 200,000 cars. He should have listened. With 1949 sales of only half that, K-F began a long downward spiral.

---

**1949**

Industry production hits a record high: 6,253,651 vehicles roll off American assembly lines

All Big Three makes display modern postwar styling, two years after Studebaker's "radical" totally new redesign

Ford's model-year production beats Chevrolet by more than 100,000, topping 1.1 million; Plymouth ranks third, followed by Buick and Pontiac

Calendar-year production totals put Chevrolet in the Number One spot, well ahead of Ford

New-car prices continue their postwar upward spiral

With so much new to see, regular auto shows finally return to the American scene

▲ The cover of Buick's '49 brochure pretty much said it all. New styling was the big news for all models, save the low-priced Specials.

▲ Besides all-new styling, Buick's top-line Roadmasters, like the $3150 ragtop, sported four "VentiPorts" on the front fenders.

► Buick's Super Estate Wagon lost a lot of wood with the new '49 styling, though the timber remained structural. List price was $3178, and 1847 were produced for the model year.

▼ Buick—along with Cadillac and Olds—pioneered the hardtop-convertible with the '49 Roadmaster Riviera. At $3203, it cost $53 more than the soft-top; 4343 were built.

Chevrolet and Pontiac adopt curvaceous modern bodies, like other GM makes, while Ford and Chrysler turn to boxier profiles

Buick, Cadillac, and Oldsmobile offer the first true pillarless "hardtop convertible" coupes, blending the coziness of a closed car with the airiness of a ragtop

Hardtop coupes give GM a lead on this glamorous body style that will dominate the Fifties

The emergence of all-steel station wagons from Chevrolet, Olds, Plymouth, and Pontiac establishes a new trend for burgeoning suburbia; "woody" wagons will soon become extinct

Cadillac and Oldsmobile tout high-compression, overhead-valve V-8 engines—Cadillac's 331-cid version cranks out 160 horses, the 303-cid Olds Rocket boasts 135

Cadillac and Olds V-8s can zip from 0-60 mph in only 13 seconds—especially when tucked into the lightweight Olds 88 body

## 1949

▲ Cadillac's 331-cid overhead-valve V-8 was a '49 breakthrough (shared with Olds). It boasted short-stroke design and 160 bhp, and was more economical as well.

▲ A gem of a car: The Sixty Special in an ad typical of Cadillac's early postwar magazine campaigns.

▲ The Series Sixty-Two Coupe de Ville "hardtop convertible" was Cadillac's new glamour leader for '49.

▲ Cadillac's new postwar styling saw only minor changes for '49, when the Series Sixty-Two convertible sold for $3442. It appealed to 8000 customers.

▲ With 39,977 sales, the Series Sixty-Two four-door sedan was Cadillac's best-seller in 1949. It was priced at $3050.

---

GM's new ohv V-8s allow higher compression ratios with available (and future) fuels; they're lighter in weight and "breathe" more easily, while the shorter strokes cut friction and reduce wear

Nash displays new "inverted bathtub" Airflyte styling; aerodynamics are excellent and sales are fairly impressive, but the shape draws scornful comments

Studebaker thwarts Ford's attempt to purchase rights to Borg-Warner's automatic transmission

The first two Volkswagens arrive in America—few suspect the import invasion that's destined to follow in the Fifties

The Renault 4CV and other mini-size European cars are available, especially in the Northeastern states; sales are slow

▲ Fleetline fastbacks looked better than ever with Chevy's all-new '49 styling. A DeLuxe four-door cost $1539; 130,323 were built.

▲ Chevy replaced its woody wagon with a look-alike all-steel model in mid-1949, still a Styleline DeLuxe listing at $2267. This is one of the 3342 "true" woodies built.

▲ This fleet of '49 Chevys was bound for Cleveland aboard the freighter *T.J. McCarthy*.

▲ A '49 from each of GM's U.S. car divisions poses on the banked high-speed oval at the firm's Milford, Michigan, proving grounds.

▲ Non-fastback '49 Chevys, like this $1508 DeLuxe Sport Coupe, were "Stylelines," and were also offered in cheaper Special trim. Sport Coupe sales totaled 106,282.

---

A sleekly restyled Buick lineup includes the pillarless two-door Riviera hardtop

Buicks feature front-fender VentiPorts, commonly called "port-holes," plus an aircraft-inspired appearance

Buick finishes the model-year production race in fourth place, behind third-ranked Plymouth; Pontiac is fifth

Cadillac retains its '48 tailfins, but launches a Coupe de Ville pillarless hardtop as a Series Sixty-Two model late in the model year

Chevrolet adopts a modern streamlined body with a curved, two-piece windshield; the model lineup gets new names, but the overhead-valve six harks back to the Thirties

▲ A convertible was the only wood-bodied Town and Country in Chrysler's new '49 lineup. The price was a stiff $3970, so production only reached 1000 units.

► Chrysler dashboards, as on the rag-top T&C, still dazzled for '49, and they were padded, too. The pistol grip to the left controls a spotlight.

▲ The eight-cylinder New Yorker again topped Chrysler's standard line. The $2726 four-door was the series' best-seller: 18,779 were built.

▲ Windsor stood a step above Royal among six-cylinder Chryslers. Again, the four-door was the series' mainstay: 55,879 found buyers.

▲ For Chrysler, the "good life" in 1949 meant genteel hunts in the country with a T&C convertible.

---

Fleetline fastbacks and all-steel station wagons are part of the Chevrolet lineup for '49; vacuum shift is gone

Chrysler starts the new season with carryover '48 models; an all-new, boxy-but-modern Silver Anniversary series debuts at mid-year, with familiar six- and eight-cylinder L-head engines

The similarly restyled "Second-Series" DeSoto, Dodge, and Plymouth models also arrive in the spring—all powered by the old, reliable L-head sixes

◀ Still pitching small-car virtues, Crosley built only 7431 cars for '49. This ad depicts the full line with interim "1948½" frontal styling.

▲ Crosley took a shot at a sports car with the new doorless $849 Hotshot, which surprised many people with its stamina. Only 752 '49s were built.

▲ The "Cubster" roadster was one of many short-lived kit-car ventures that sprang up after World War II.

▲ Gary Davis sought dealers for his novel three-wheeler, but built only 17 of a planned 100 cars.

▲ The four-cylinder, 30-mpg Del Mar from San Diego was a no-hope '49 newcomer. Fewer than 10 were built.

▲ Like Chrysler's other "Second-Series" '49s, DeSoto was shiny but upright and boxy. The $2156 Custom Club Coupe found 18,431 buyers.

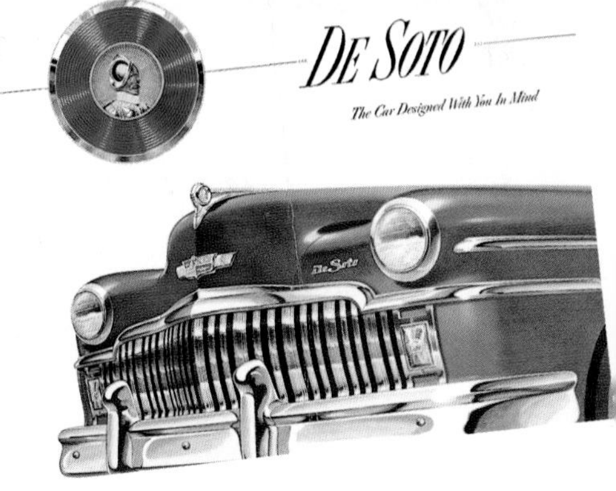


▲ With all its chrome dental work, DeSoto's '49 "face" was dazzling.

---

Chrysler and DeSoto employ semi-automatic "Tip-Toe" Fluid Drive, so no gear shifting is needed when moving forward; GM cars offer true automatic transmissions

DeSoto offers an all-steel Carry-All "sedan-wagon" with a fold-down back seat, along with a "woody" wagon and nine-passenger Suburban sedan

Dodge issues a single-seat, three-passenger Wayfarer roadster; it lacks roll-up windows—a throwback to the '30s

A restyled Crosley with integral front fenders sags sharply in sales, despite adding a sporty new Hotshot roadster

The handsome, slab-sided Ford restyle earns credit for helping to save the company, evidence that the youthful team under Henry Ford II is now in charge

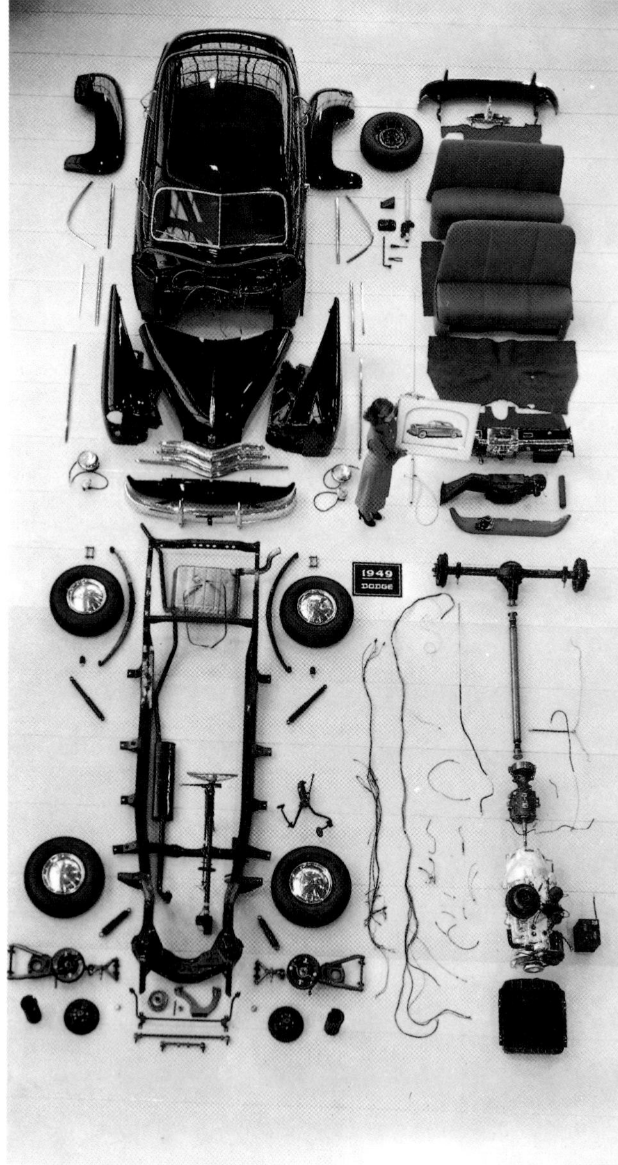


▲ A '49 Dodge was "broken down" to show all its new components. The engine is missing because it was basically a carryover of the division's dull but sturdy L-head six. Prices this year ranged from $1611 to $2865.

▲ Dodge's most affordable '49 was this trim, three-seat Wayfarer business coupe priced at $1611. Even so, only 9342 were sold. The car's weight was 3065 pounds.

▲ Like Chrysler's other '49s, the Dodge Wayfarer business coupe offered chair-height seating with room to wear a hat. The 103-bhp six provided average performance.

▲ Dodge stepped up the price and luxury ladder this year with four lush new Coronet models on a longer 123.5-inch chassis. The four-door listed at $1927. Total output of the "real" '49 Dodges came to 256,857 units.

Fords are quick and nimble with a 100-bhp L-head V-8; Mercurys are too, with 110 horses on tap; overdrive is optional for both

Hot rodders continue to clamor for aftermarket add-ons to hop-up the legendary Ford/Mercury flathead V-8 engines

Coil-spring front and semi-elliptic-leaf rear suspension replaces Ford's antiquated front-and-rear transverse-leaf setup

Kaisers and Frazers receive a facelift amid a serious corporate shakeup; sales of both makes falter

The Frazer lineup includes an awkward-but-unique four-door Manhattan convertible sedan

Notable Kaiser models include Traveler and Vagabond utility sedans, plus both a Virginian hardtop and a convertible sedan

▲ Ford spared no expense when it introduced the press to its all-new '49 models in June 1948.

▲ A '49 Ford Custom Tudor body meets its chassis on the Dearborn, Michigan, production line.

▲ Ford's wagon still used structural wood, but changed from a four-door Super DeLuxe to a two-door Custom.

▲ The '49s, like the $1511 Custom V-8 Club Coupe (150,254 built), were the most changed Fords in many years.

▲ Ford built 433,316 '49 Custom Tudor sedans. This $1590 V-8 model shows off its neat, all-new lines.

▲ Ford's only '49 convertible was predictably reserved for the upper Custom V-8 line. It cost $1886.

▲ President Henry Ford II drives the one-millionth '49 Ford built with brothers Benson and William Clay.

▲ The '49 Ford was a fast seller—1,118,308 were built. The reasons for its success were trumpeted with ads like this.

---

Hudson continues its stylish Step-down body, as introduced in mid-1948, without noticeable change

Recessed headlights mark the '49 Lincolns, which wear heavy-looking, slab-sided bodies; a 337-cid L-head V-8 is new

The beautifully curved Mercury attracts hot rodders and customizers; small Lincolns share the Merc bodyshell, and get attention, too

A mildly customized '49 Mercury club coupe will later be immortalized as the car that actor James Dean drives in the 1955 movie, *Rebel Without a Cause*

The aerodynamic Nash Airflytes are packed with innovations, including a "Uniscope" gauge pod atop the steering column and traditional reclining front seatbacks that form a bed

▲ A heavy and glittery facelift marked the '49 Frazer, here the new Manhattan convertible sedan, which cost $3295—just $147 less than a Cadillac ragtop. Production for 1949-50 totaled only about 70 units.

▲ Leather adorned the Manhattan's interior. Note the glass-filled B-posts and fixed window frames.

▲ Joe Frazer (here circa 1945) protested when Henry Kaiser tooled up for 200,000 '49s. The reality: half that.

▲ Sedans remained Frazer's sales mainstay, but the upmarket $2595 Manhattan attracted only 9950 buyers.

▲ Looking rather Studebaker-like, the small four-cylinder, rear-engine, front-drive Gregory saw only a prototype.

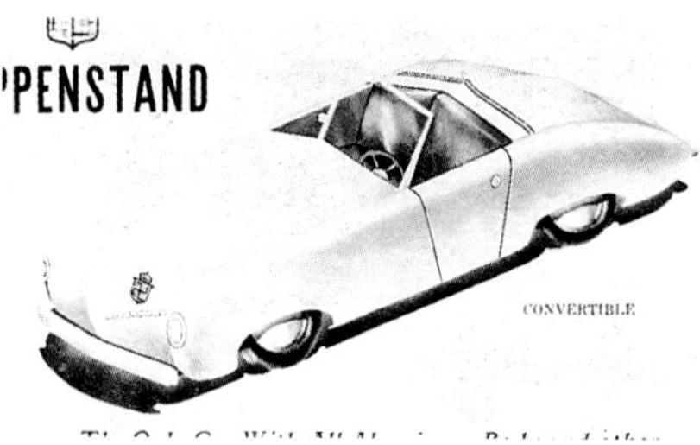


▲ Another late-'40s dead end was the aluminum-bodied, two-cylinder, two-seater Hoppenstand convertible.

▲ Toy-like describes the aptly named Imp, a rear-engined prototype that would never see volume production.

---

The sharpest Futuramic 98 Oldsmobile is the Holiday pillar-less hardtop coupe, which debuts late in the model run

Packards are carryovers until mid-season, when mildly facelifted 50th Anniversary "Twenty-Third Series" models bow

Plymouth offers a new all-steel station wagon to rival those issued at mid-season by Chevrolet, Oldsmobile, and Pontiac

Restyled Silver-Streak Pontiacs wear notchback or fastback bodies, again carry six- or eight-cylinder L-head engines

Despite little change, Studebaker remains one of the most advanced designs on the road

Willys launches a mid-year Jeepster, with a new F-head six-cylinder engine replacing the original L-head configuration

▲ Hudson's bold "Step-down" returned little-changed for '49; output rose to 159,100. This is the $3041 Commodore Eight Brougham convertible.

▲ A '49 Hudson Super Six sedan sports rare two-toning and "cadet" windshield visor. Power came from a 121-bhp six.

▲ Derham Body Company, of Rosemont, Pennsylvania, turned three '49 Hudsons into formal "division" sedans.

◀ Kaiser added the Special Traveler "hatchback" sedan for '49, a wagon substitute conceived by chairman Henry Kaiser. About 22,000 were built through 1950 at a price of $2088.

▶ For an extra $200, Kaiser offered the $2088 Traveler as this DeLuxe Vagabond. Output was only 4500 units through model-year 1950. Note the metal cargo skids and spare tire location. The left rear door didn't open.

## 1949 Model Year Production

|  |  |  |
|---|---|---|
| 1. | Ford | 1,118,308 |
| 2. | Chevrolet | 1,010,013 |
| 3. | Plymouth | 520,385 |
| 4. | Buick | 409,138 |
| 5. | Pontiac | 304,819 |
| 6. | Mercury | 301,319 |
| 7. | Oldsmobile | 288,310 |
| 8. | Dodge | 256,857 |
| 9. | Hudson | 159,100 |
| 10. | Nash | 130,000 |
| 11. | Studebaker | 129,301 |
| 12. | Chrysler | 124,218 |
| 13. | Packard | 116,955 |
| 14. | DeSoto | 95,051 |
| 15. | Cadillac | 92,554 |
| 16. | Kaiser | 79,947[1] |
| 17. | Lincoln | 73,507 |
| 18. | Frazer | 21,223[1] |
| 19. | Crosley | 7,431 |

[1]*Calculated or estimated*

▲ GM pioneered true hardtops for '49, but Kaiser offered a clever semi-hardtop in its new $2995 DeLuxe Virginian. An estimated 946 were produced for 1949-50.

▲ Virginians sported leather-look tops. They rode on a specially reinforced frame, had a curb weight of 3541 pounds, and the 112-bhp six had its work cut out.

▲ Like Frazer, Kaiser was able to field only a modest '49 facelift against all-new Big Three models; here, the $2195 DeLuxe sedan.

▲ Kaiser's '49 advertising tried hard to make its cars seem new, but they had really seen little change since debuting in 1947. The restyled horizontal-bar grille, however, was less fussy.

◀ Famed race-car designer Frank Kurtis sold his sleek Kurtis Sport both as a kit and fully built. Only 35-36 were completed in 1948-49. The design was later modified to become the Muntz Jet.

---

All-steel Jeep two-door Station Wagon models continue mainly unchanged in the Willys lineup

Crosley introduces Goodyear-Hawley four-wheel disc brakes at mid-year; all-disc brakes also go on the limited-production Chrysler Crown Imperial

The ignition key operates the starter on Chrysler products; key-actuated starting will soon become nearly universal, but most cars still use a dashboard button

The separate foot-operated starter pedal is gone from all GM cars, but some models keep gas-pedal starter control

Earl "Madman" Muntz buys out the Kurtis operation and begins production of the Muntz Jet, one of the most-noticed sports-type cars of the early Fifties

Del Mar prototypes are subcompact in size, with Continental engines and styling similar to the British Hillman

▲ Lincoln adopted "bathtub" styling for its first all-postwar line, as on this $3186 Cosmopolitan coupe.

▲ A standard Sport Sedan sails by a fastback Cosmopolitan Town Sedan in an introductory '49 Lincoln ad.

▲ Lincoln dropped the bulbous Cosmo Town Sedan after '49 due to slow sales. It sold for $3238.

▲ Lincoln offered junior and senior ragtops for '49. This standard model shared a basic bodyshell with Mercury and listed at $3116.

▲ This ad put Lincoln's $3948 Cosmo ragtop in a rather sporty setting.

▼ The standard Sport Sedan was Lincoln's best-seller. Total Lincoln output was 73,507 units.

The $500, 475-pound Imp mini-convertible has a 7.5-bhp air-cooled engine and a no-door fiberglass body; it will be produced in minimal quantity as late as 1951

A race-oriented Fitch sports car never progresses beyond the prototype stage

The Davis Motor Company collapses after 17 three-wheelers are built (1947-49); Gary Davis is convicted of fraud

▲ This fastback two-door was mocked up as one of Mercury's all-new '49 models, but never made production. Styling stemmed from wartime work.

▲ Still with one nameless series but a bigger flathead V-8, Mercury offered a $2410 convertible for 1949; 16,765 were produced.

▲ The '49 Sport Sedan body style sold very well for Mercury: 155,882 were built. Base-priced at $2031, it weighed 3386 pounds for the model year.

▲ Mercury's '49 price-leader was this $1979 coupe. Low, sleek lines would make it a favorite among "Kustom Kar" fanatics in the '50s.

▲ Mercury's '49 wagon retained the wood-look metal dash trim used in previous years, but the dash itself was somewhat cleaner and better organized. Leather covered the seats.

◀ Like Ford, Mercury switched from four-door to two-door wagons for '49, though with less structural wood. Base price for this eight-seater, of which 8044 were built, was $2716. The bodies were built in Ford's Iron Mountain, Michigan, plant.

▲ Meet another Mustang, a wild rear-engine experiment evidently inspired by Dick Stout's Scarab and Bucky Fuller's Dymaxion. A prototype was shown in 1949, but production of this six-seater never materialized.

▲ A quartet of radical new '49 Airflytes, of which 130,000 were sold, departs Nash's California plant. Styling was aerodynamic.

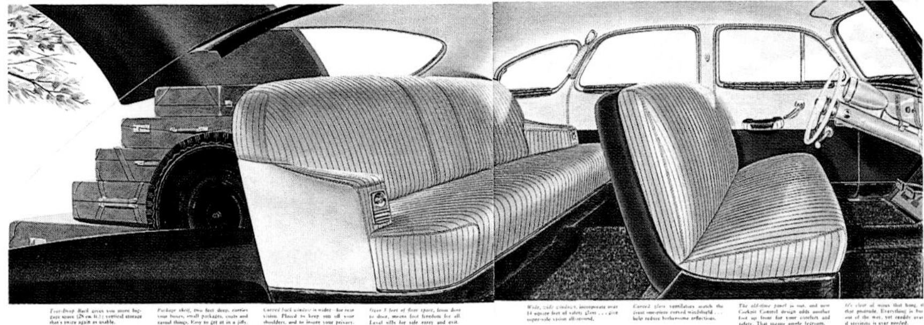


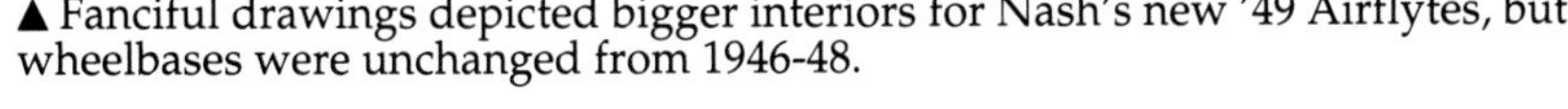

▲ Fanciful drawings depicted bigger interiors for Nash's new '49 Airflytes, but wheelbases were unchanged from 1946-48.

▲ Nash's '49 advertisements touted bigger *exteriors*, too.

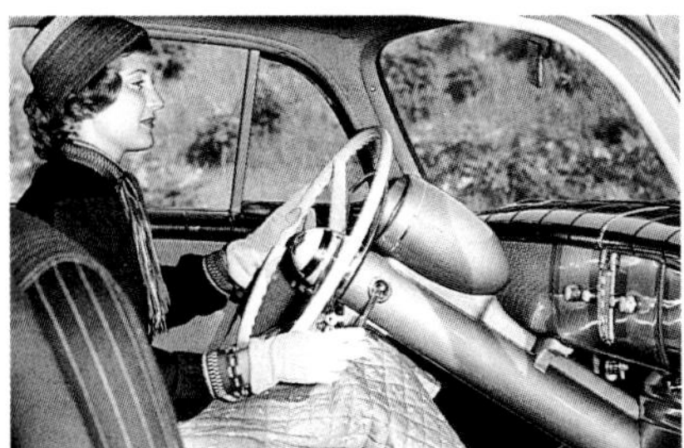

▲ "Hello, Buck Rogers!" Nash's new Airflyte dash with bullet-shaped "Uniscope" instrument pod was definitely futuristic for '49.

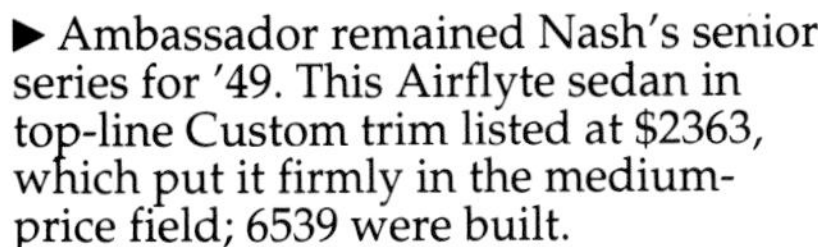

▶ Ambassador remained Nash's senior series for '49. This Airflyte sedan in top-line Custom trim listed at $2363, which put it firmly in the medium-price field; 6539 were built.

▲ The Olds Ninety-Eight, here a $2594 DeLuxe four-door, retained its '48 "Futuramic" styling. Output of this model was 49,001 units.

▲ Lansing's big news for '49 was the modern "Rocket" V-8. In new Series 88 models like this ragtop, it made Olds a hot performer.

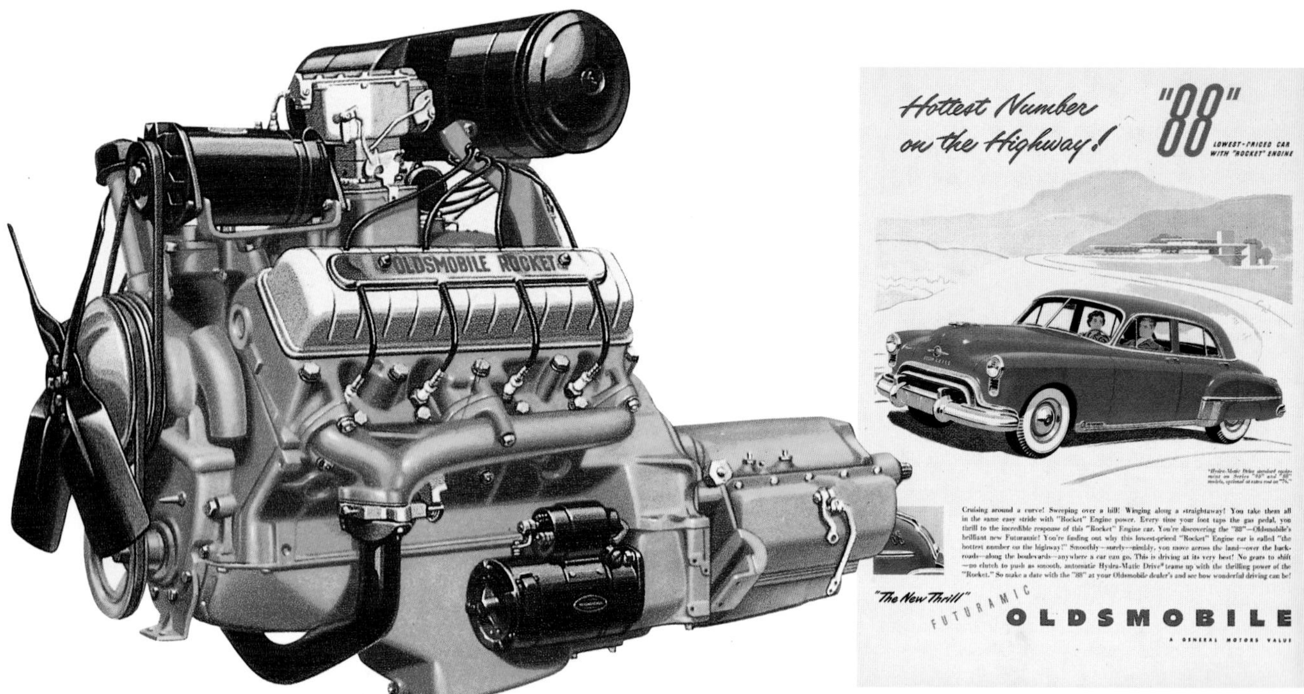


▲ Arriving with 303.7 cubic inches, Oldsmobile's "Rocket" pioneered the modern short-stroke, high-compression, overhead-valve V-8 that would soon sweep Detroit. Horsepower for '49 was a lively 135.

▲ The "Rocket's" go-power figured prominently from the first in ads for the Olds 88, even when the subject was an everyday four-door.

▲ Along with Buick and Cadillac, Olds debuted a hardtop for '49, the lush Ninety-Eight DeLuxe Holiday. At $2973, it was snapped up by 3006 eager new-car buyers.

▲ Olds 88s quickly began setting stock-car racing records. Symbolizing this performance, an 88 soft-top served as the Official Pace Car for the '49 Indy 500 Memorial Day Race.

▲ From Buffalo, New York, the four-cylinder Playboy boasted a manual folding steel top for just $985, but tiny size and only two seats held total production to about 90 cars.

▲ Packard had restyled for '48, so its '49s offered little new except the mid-year debut of self-shift Ultramatic Drive. This 50th Anniversary '49 Eight DeLuxe sedan (Twenty-Third Series) was priced at $2383. This model rode Packard's shortest wheelbase: 120 inches.

**Packard owners get a break in hot weather**

***—once every minute!***

In this great new Packard, summer weather is what *you* make it—thanks to the most efficient all-season ventilation system ever built into a motor car.

On a hot, sultry day, you create your own summer breeze, *just by pushing a button!*

Even with the car standing still, with all windows closed, stale air is completely replaced by a flow of crisp, fresh, *circulating* air . . . at the rate of *once every minute!*

On the open road, too, you ride refreshed with windows closed. The nerve-tensing roar of outside air is silenced forever. And gone are the days of the wind-blown hair-do!

Amazing? Wait . . .

When the scene changes to winter, *you keep right on* making your own weather. You simply set the dial at the *temperature* you want—the rest is automatic.

Drop in soon—let your Packard dealer give you a demonstration of how it's done. From that minute on, you'll want to drive a Packard and be your own weatherman, the whole year 'round!

PACKARD

ASK THE MAN WHO OWNS ONE

120-HP EIGHT 145-HP SUPER EIGHT 160-HP CUSTOM EIGHT

▲ As ever, Packard's advertising aimed to convey a certain genteel elegance. Junior models, the Eight and DeLuxe Eight, rode a 120-inch wheelbase, as did the Super Eight. Custom Eights got a 127-inch stretch.

▲ This view of a Twenty-Second Series '49 Super Eight Club Sedan shows why Packards of this period came to be called "pregnant elephants." No matter—the cars sold well. Total 1949 production came to 116,955 cars.

Designed for a Roamin' Holiday!

Golden Anniversary PACKARD

◀ This '49 Packard ad stresses the cars' long-distance travel comfort. Alas, ads also tended to stress the lower-priced models—good for short-term sales and profits, but bad for Packard's luxury image over the long term. Right now, the 135-bhp Club Sedan cost just $2224 before options, but prices ranged upward to $4295 for a Custom Eight convertible.

▲ Despite boxy lines, the $1982 '49 Plymouth Special DeLuxe ragtop found 15,240 buyers.

▲ Plymouth's $1629 four-door Special DeLuxe was the year's best-seller: 252,878 units.

▲ Despite the new all-steel Suburban, Plymouth persisted with woody wagons for '49 with this $2372 Special DeLuxe four-door. Production: 3443.

▲ Plymouth also looked to the future with its new all-steel Suburban two-door wagon (here in prototype form). It sold for $1840; 19,220 were sold.

▲ Like sister Chrysler makes, the '49 Plymouths were compact outside but roomy inside. The Special DeLuxe dash featured woodgraining.

▲ This full-page ad shows but a sampling of Pontiac's broad 36-model lineup for '49.

▲ Notchback '49 Pontiacs, like this $1779 DeLuxe Coupe Sedan, were named Chieftain.

▲ Pontiac's famous "Silver Streak" hood trim was bolder than ever for '49. This DeLuxe Chieftain Eight four-door listed at $1924.

▲ Fastbacks fast faded from public favor after '49, when Pontiac offered this four-door Streamliner DeLuxe Eight for $1903. Total model year output came to 304,819 units, good for fifth place.

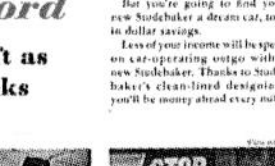

▲ Studebaker's '49 ads talked value—and 129,301 buyers responded. The Champion four-door sedan shown here was the firm's best-seller.

▲ Studebaker's '49 Commanders had a 100-bhp six (Champions 80 bhp). The Starlight coupe cost $2135 in top-line Regal DeLuxe trim.

▲ Still casting its fate with Jeep-inspired vehicles, Willys again offered Station Wagons for '49, here with handsome wood-look trim.

▲ This odd little thing is the wood-bodied Pup, one of many here-today gone-tomorrow autos that sprouted in the early postwar period.

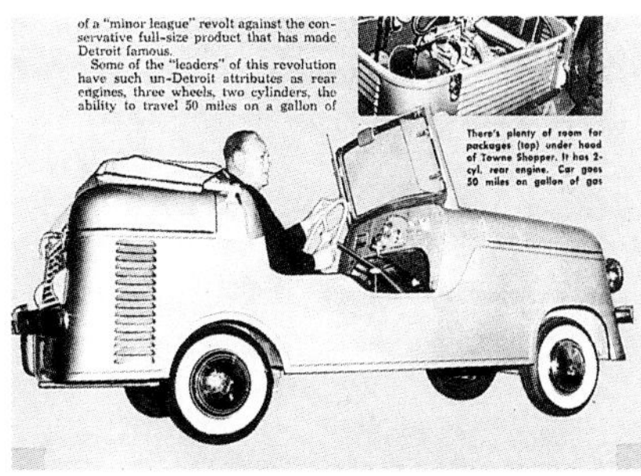

of a "minor league" revolt against the conservative full-size product that has made Detroit famous.

Some of the "leaders" of this revolution have such un-Detroit attributes as rear engines, three wheels, two cylinders, the ability to travel 50 miles on a gallon of

There's plenty of room for packages (top) under hood of Towne Shopper. It has 2-cyl. rear engine. Car goes 50 miles on gallon of gas

▲ Another would-be hit was the Towne Shopper, a two-seat runabout with a small two-cylinder engine in back. Up to 50 mpg was claimed.

▲ The two-cylinder, three-wheel Thrif-T was a short-lived economy-car venture circa 1949. It was likely intended more for factories than freeways.

CHAPTER EIGHT

1950-1952

# THE "BUYER'S MARKET" RETURNS

The American auto industry might have been expected to pause after its frantic product pace of 1948-49, and it did. Yet there was still plenty to keep buyers interested in 1950-52.

In fact, 1950 saw record calendar-year production of nearly 6.7 million cars, up more than 1.5 million from banner '49, though this wasn't entirely Detroit's doing. In June, President Truman committed U.S. troops to support the United Nations "holding action" against an incursion by Communist insurgents into South Korea. It looked like the start of a new world war, and Americans rushed to buy, fearing another drought of consumer goods *a la* World War II. That fear proved exaggerated, but the government did curb civilian production for a time and diverted strategic materials to military production while awarding fat contracts to car companies. With that, the booming postwar seller's market was over.

Predictably, 1950 was a quiet model year. The all-new 1948-49 designs were still fresh, so changes were evolutionary, not revolutionary, though Studebaker's bizarre "bullet-nose" facelift was a notable exception. A more predictive one was Nash's new Rambler, which quickly became America's best-selling compact car based on a combination of sturdy, unitized construction and thrifty, reliable engines. The "hardtop convertible"—that '49 General Motors innovation—spread to encompass Chevrolet and Pontiac models, as well as belated entries from Hudson and most divisions at Chrysler Corporation, which had blown a chance to pioneer this fast-selling style back in '47.

The pace of change literally accelerated for 1951. Chrysler Division introduced a milestone in a 331-cubic-inch "Firepower" V-8 with efficient hemispherical combustion chambers. It delivered performance without peer. No less significant was Studebaker's 1951 small-block V-8, a lively new 232.6 cubic-incher as standard power for the senior Commander line. Though less illustrious than the Hemi, it was the first modern overhead-valve V-8 from an independent automaker, and would serve Studebaker well for 15 years.

But the performance surprise of 1951 turned out to be a six: a 308-cid wonder in a new Hudson line called Hornet. With the factory providing thinly disguised racing parts, and tuners like Marshall Teague knowing how to use them, Hornets rewrote the record books in stock-car racing while trouncing V-8 Oldsmobile 88s.

Elsewhere on the '51 scene, the ungainly "pregnant elephants" gave way to the first fully fresh Packards since the elegant Clipper of a decade earlier. Designer John Reinhart called them "high pockets" because of a high beltline, but they were clean, modishly square, yet dignified. Alas, they were but a temporary help. Like Hudson, Packard would be stuck with a platform it could not afford to change very much, to the detriment of sales.

More stunning was a new second-generation Kaiser shaped by the redoubtable "Dutch" Darrin. Sleek, ground-hugging, and low-waisted, it offered superb visibility, a fine ride, a predictive safety-styled interior—and the same staid old Kaiser six. It really should have had a V-8, but most of the money for that had gone into a new 1951 compact. Egotistically named for the company chairman, the Henry J was sturdy but little more, and though it sold well at first, it didn't have the staying power of the Rambler.

While most automakers offered light touch-ups for 1952, Ford Motor Company overhauled its entire fleet. Like the newest Packards, these were square and slab-sided but neat—perhaps too neat for a public gone gaga for glitz. But they sold well enough to restore Dearborn to the number-two spot in industry volume, helped by true hardtops at Lincoln-Mercury—and continued bungling at Chrysler. Also, Lincoln gained a fine new ohv V-8 destined to sire a whole slew of such engines throughout the Ford family.

Nash also redesigned along similar lines, but its new Airflytes were arguably less pleasing despite aesthetic assistance from Italy's renowned Pinin Farina. After a decade's pause, Willys reentered the auto business with its compact Aero line, which included two- and four-door sedans and a neat Eagle hardtop.

Out on the fringes were more small-time sports cars, minicars, and even electrics; most were poorly planned, under-financed ventures that were present one day and gone the next. The low-volume Nash-Healey roadster was an interesting exception. So was a Kurtis Sport puffed up from two to four seats to become the Muntz Jet, launched by California radio and used-car baron Earl "Madman" Muntz, also with visions of vast fortune. But the car game was fast becoming one for major-league players only, as events would soon prove.

▲ Like all 1950 Buicks, the Roadmaster Riviera hardtop wore more fulsome styling—and higher prices. This new Deluxe-trim version cost $2854; 8432 were produced.

◀"Dynaflow" script on the rear fenders of this $1983 Deluxe-trim Special Touring Sedan identified an increasingly popular Buick option in 1950. This model garnered 144,396 sales.

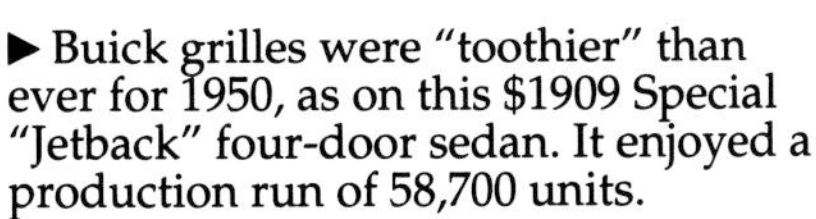

▶ Buick grilles were "toothier" than ever for 1950, as on this $1909 Special "Jetback" four-door sedan. It enjoyed a production run of 58,700 units.

▲ Cadillac also adopted a bolder look for 1950. The posh Sixty Special sedan, which cost $3797, rode on its own new 130-inch chassis and attracted 13,755 customers.

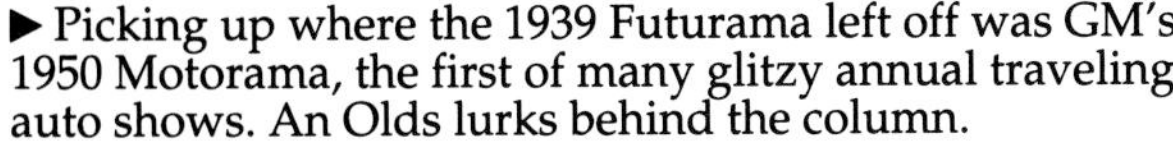

▶ Picking up where the 1939 Futurama left off was GM's 1950 Motorama, the first of many glitzy annual traveling auto shows. An Olds lurks behind the column.

---

**1950**

On June 25, President Truman orders U.S. troops to Korea in a "police action," which officials will call the Korean "conflict"—but which will be known to the American public as the "Korean War."

Fear of wartime shortages triggers a car-buying frenzy

The National Production Authority orders conservation of raw materials; a "state of emergency" is proclaimed in December

Defense work rises: Cadillac wins a $110 million contract to produce tanks; Ford inks an agreement to build Pratt and Whitney aircraft engines

Chrysler endures a 104-day strike starting January 25

▲ A $1529 Styleline DeLuxe Sport Sedan rolls off the assembly line. This model was easily Chevy's best-seller in 1950—316,412 were built.

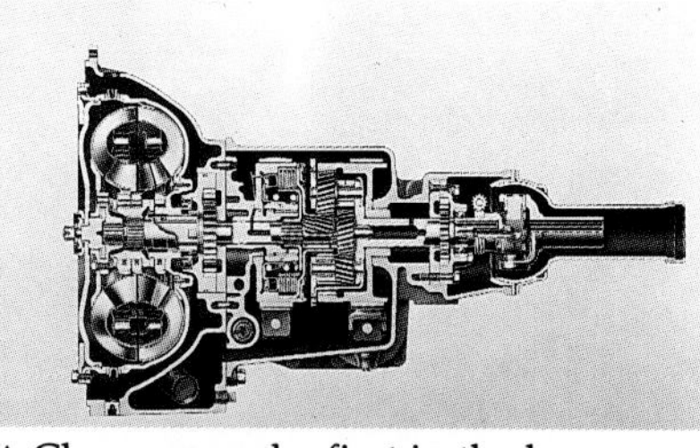

▲ Chevy scored a first in the low-priced field with fully automatic two-speed Powerglide transmission, a $159 option for DeLuxe models. This cutaway drawing shows the original 1949-50 design.

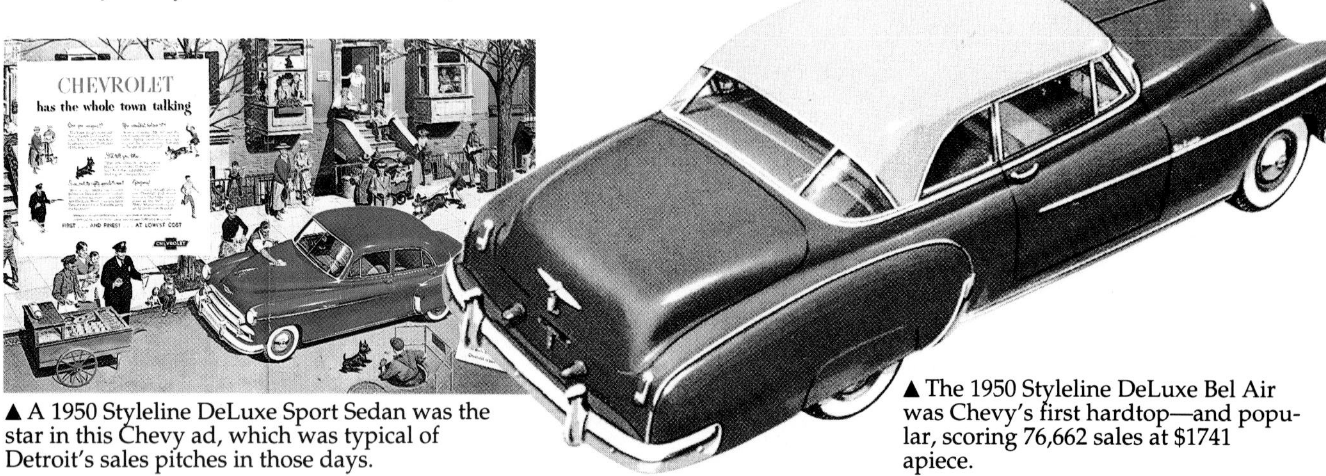

▲ The 1950 Styleline DeLuxe Bel Air was Chevy's first hardtop—and popular, scoring 76,662 sales at $1741 apiece.

▲ A 1950 Styleline DeLuxe Sport Sedan was the star in this Chevy ad, which was typical of Detroit's sales pitches in those days.

▲ Chrysler kept its boxy year-old styling, but simplified the grille for 1950. At $3232, the New Yorker convertible attracted only 899 buyers.

▲ GM beat Chrysler to hardtops, but Highland Park got one for 1950 and called it Newport. This is a $3133 New Yorker, of which 2800 were built.

▲ Chrysler moved Imperial from semi-custom to spiffier New Yorker for 1950 and built 10,650 of these sedans. A wrapped rear window set them apart.

---

A coal strike early in the year leads to steel shortages

The Federal Reserve Board places stricter limits on automobile credit

Auto sales smash early predictions and set an industry record at more than 6.3 million units

Ford slips to second place with 1.2 million cars built; Chevrolet turns out nearly 290,000 more for the model year

Chevrolet prices start at $1329, while a Crosley can be bought for just $872; average full-time workers earn $2992 yearly

Some 39.6 million passenger cars travel on American roads—40 percent more than in 1941

▲ DeSoto was also new to hardtops in 1950. Its sole entry was this top-of-the-line Custom model called Sportsman. At $2489, it found 4600 takers.

◀ Briggs Cunningham built the first of his great sports cars, the C-1, in late 1950. It's shown here with the derivative 1952 C-2R racer.

▲ Dodge, like Chrysler, stood mostly pat for 1950, but a cleaner new "face" was notable. This four-door sedan, whose base price was $1927, wears top-line Coronet trim.

▲ Like other MoPar makes, Dodge got into hardtops for 1950 by building 3600 Coronet Diplomats. At $2233, they were priced just $96 less than their soft-top counterparts.

▲ Ford was still a year away from hardtops in 1950, so it offered a jazzed-up Custom Tudor called Crestliner, with wild two-toning, padded roof, and deluxe interior.

▲ A minor restyle and major engineering changes made the 1950 Fords "50 Ways Better." This $1472 six-cylinder DeLuxe Fordor saw fairly low sales of 77,888 units.

---

About 60 percent of American families own a car, whose average age is 7.8 years

Briggs Cunningham's Cadillacs come in 10th and 11th at the Le Mans road race in France

The new Chevrolet Bel Air is a true pillarless hardtop coupe; a hardtop body style is also offered by Pontiac, Chrysler, Dodge, and DeSoto

GM's fastback body styles are rapidly losing popularity

Chevrolet's DeLuxe models can now be ordered with a two-speed Powerglide automatic transmission, a $159 option

Chrysler products receive a mild facelift of the three-box shape introduced in 1949

▲ Diagonal grille bars and detail changes marked the 1950 Hudsons, here the top-line Commodore Eight Custom Brougham convertible. At $2893, only 425 were built.

▲ Hudson reached down to the lower medium-priced field for 1950 with a five-model Pacemaker line that included this $1933 four-door. DeLuxe versions bowed at mid-year.

◀ This restored 1950 Hudson Commodore Six Club Coupe is nicely accessorized. Base price was $2257.

▲ The aptly named Imp was little all right, but it would have no future. Microcars just didn't sell in 1950, and this Glendale, California, effort vanished quickly.

► Many early Fifties Detroit sales brochures had only "faces" on their covers; witness these artful "mugshots" of the 1950 Lincoln (inset) and Kaiser.

---

Chrysler's Town and Country employs disc brakes

Crosley introduces the Super Sports roadster, a Hot Shot with doors, and returns to drum brakes after a brief flirtation with discs

The Wayfarer roadster continues in the Dodge lineup, with roll-down windows phased in late in the 1949 model run

Lacking a pillarless "hardtop convertible" body style, Ford offers a two-tone Crestliner two-door sedan with a padded vinyl top and deluxe interior; Mercury's Monterey coupe has a similar theme

▲ Mercury's 1950 wagon sales plunged from 8044 in 1949 to 1746 in 1950 despite a price cut from $2716 to $2561.

▲ Mercury made minor changes for 1950—and raised the price of its ragtop only $2 to $2412; 8341 were built.

▲ The Sports Sedan, which started at $2032, repeated as Mercury's second-best-seller for 1950: 132,082 units.

▲ Like Ford's Crestliner, Mercury's new padded-top Monterey two-door was a hardtop stand-in. It cost $2146 (canvas) or $2157 (vinyl).

▲ Nash celebrated a production milestone in 1950 with its two-millionth car, an aerodynamic Airflyte sedan.

◄▲ Despite few changes, Nash enjoyed higher volume for 1950—160,354 units. Among the year's 49,056 Ambassadors was this $2064 Super four-door sedan.

A shorter Pacemaker series joins the Hudson lineup, accounting for half of model-year production

Kaiser-Frazer fields leftover, reserialed '49s until the completely restyled '51s arrive in the spring

Lincolns may be ordered with Hydra-Matic, purchased from GM

Lincoln finishes ninth in the first grueling *Carrera Panamericana* (Mexican Road Race), which is won by an Oldsmobile 88

In March, Nash launches the Rambler on a 100-inch wheelbase—the first volume-built U.S. "compact"

The Rambler debuts as a unique convertible, followed in June by a two-door station wagon

▲ Nash's Rambler bowed as a convertible in March 1950, followed by a two-door wagon in June. It would quickly prove to be America's most successful postwar compact.

▲ Another debut-year publicity shot highlighted Nash's new Rambler Custom Landau Convertible, priced at $1808. Production of this "Bridge-Beam" ragtop, which had an 82-bhp L-head six, reached 9708 units in the short model year.

▲ Rambler's other new model bowed on June 23. This nifty 100-inch-wheelbase Custom two-door wagon also listed at $1808; 1713 were sold.

▲ UAW president Walter Reuther (*second from left*) negotiated an historic five-year "peace accord" with GM in May 1950. The handshakes took place on the 23rd.

### 1950 Model Year Production

|  |  |  |  |  |  |
|---|---|---|---|---|---|
| 1. Chevrolet | 1,498,590 | 8. Studebaker | 320,884 | 14. Cadillac | 103,857 |
| 2. Ford | 1,208,912 | 9. Mercury | 293,658 | 15. Packard | 42,627 |
| 3. Plymouth | 610,954 | 10. Chrysler | 179,299 | 16. Lincoln | 28,190 |
| 4. Buick | 588,439 | 11. Nash | 171,782 | 17. Kaiser | 15,228[1] |
| 5. Pontiac | 446,429 | 12. DeSoto | 136,203 | 18. Crosley | 6,792 |
| 6. Oldsmobile | 408,060 | 13. Hudson | 121,408 | 19. Frazer | 3,700[1] |
| 7. Dodge | 341,797 | | | | |

[1] *Calculated or estimated*

▲ A one-piece curved windshield replaced two-piece glass on some late-1950 junior Oldsmobiles, like this 88.

▲ The Olds Rocket V-8 continued burning up race tracks in 1950, as noted in its brochures. Horsepower remained at 135 at 3600 rpm; torque was 263 lbs/ft at 1800 rpm.

▶ Olds's little-changed 88 convertible remained fast, flashy, and highly desirable in 1950—and 9127 were sold. The base price was $2294.

▼ Like Buick, Olds added junior-series hardtops for 1950. This DeLuxe 88 Holiday also came in standard trim; output of both totaled 12,612. There were six-cylinder Series 76 versions, too.

Hydra-Matic transmission is available on Nash Ambassador models; the engine is started by lifting the gearshift lever

Oldsmobile issues its final six-cylinder Series 76 models

A Rocket 88 Oldsmobile breaks a class speed record at Daytona, averaging 100.28 mph

Oldsmobiles win 10 of 19 major stock-car races

Packard's "pregnant elephant" bathtub shape is in its final season

Many Packards are ordered with Ultramatic (introduced in mid-1949)—the only automatic transmission developed by an independent automaker

▲ Olds fastbacks like this 98 Club Sedan would not return after 1950 due to fast-falling sales—down to 11,989 units.

▲ Olds 98s, such as this $2641 Holiday hardtop, looked more "important" for 1950; 8263 were built.

▲ The 1950 Packards were identical to the "Second-Series" '49s—sales plunged from 116,955 to 42,640 for the year.

TRAVEL DIRECTIONS!

Packed with value and ready to prove it! NEW PLYMOUTH

▲ A 1950 Plymouth ad stressed spacious travel comfort in a $1982 Special DeLuxe convertible; 12,697 were sold.

◀ Like sister MoPar makes, Plymouth cleaned its face for 1950—and looked better for it. The convertible, which weighed 3295 pounds, was again sold only in top Special DeLuxe trim.

---

The last Plymouth wood-bodied station wagon rolls off the line; an automatic choke is new

Plymouth displays the Ghia-styled XX-500, the first of Chrysler's "idea cars"

Studebaker front ends display a "bullet nose," and sales soar to a record of 320,884 units

Late in the season, Studebaker introduces "Automatic Drive," designed in cooperation with Borg-Warner's Detroit Gear Division

▲ Prominent new grille dentistry marked the 1950 Pontiacs, like this $1908 Chieftain Eight DeLuxe sedan.

▲ Aside from station wagons, the $2190 Chieftain Eight DeLuxe convertible was the priciest Pontiac for 1950.

▲ Pontiac added four new Chieftain Catalina hardtops for 1950. This is the $2069 DeLuxe Eight version.

▲ Pontiac's 1950 wagons were Six and Eight Streamliners—standard or DeLuxe. This standard model looked a bit plain without Di-Noc wood-look trim. Price range: $2264 to $2411.

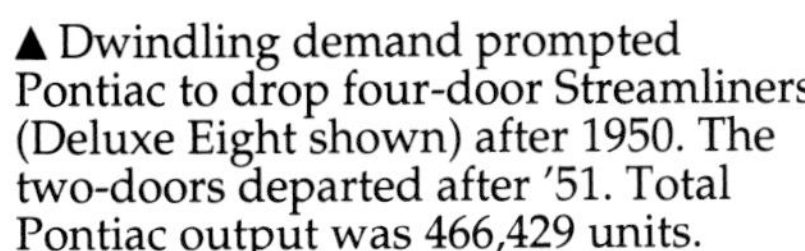

▲ Dwindling demand prompted Pontiac to drop four-door Streamliners (Deluxe Eight shown) after 1950. The two-doors departed after '51. Total Pontiac output was 466,429 units.

► The word "bizarre" has long been used to describe the new "bullet-nose" grille on the 1950 Studebakers. It's worn here by a $1644 Champion Regal DeLuxe two-door sedan, of which 21,976 were sold. Wheelbase was 113 inches, horsepower 85.

---

Willys Jeepsters get an F-head four-cylinder engine and a bigger six (also F-head) at mid-year

Crosley announces the "Quicksilver" engine with 10.0:1 compression, running on gasoline plus water-alcohol injection

Goodyear develops a puncture-sealing tubeless tire

The Glasspar roadster is developed to be sold mainly in kit form for about $650, but a few will be fully assembled

Nash-Kelvinator exhibits the NXI two-seater on a Fiat chassis; it will evolve into the Metropolitan minicar of 1954

▲ A one-inch-longer wheelbase improved 1950 Studebaker profiles, but Starlight coupes retained their wildly wrapped four-piece rear window. This uplevel $2018 Commander Regal DeLuxe rode a 120-inch wheelbase and had 102 bhp.

**Sleek new Studebaker styling saves gasoline for you!**

GAS economy is written all over the trim, clean dream lines of this low, long, alluring, excitingly new 1950 Studebaker.

Its very look tells you it's a car with the right build for thrift. You don't see a trace of bulging excess bulk that would squander power needlessly.

You see instead a beautifully flight-streamed car—with the sleek, going-somewhere distinction of a jet plane—Studebaker's "next look"!

What's more, a new perfection of balance in this Studebaker's rugged structure gives you a ride that's like a skyway glide for smoothness.

Stop in now at your nearest Studebaker dealer's showroom and try out that ride—the 1950 "miracle ride" of motoring.

Watch how quickly and completely this Studebaker convinces you that it's the tops-in-value 1950 car—tops in everything you've wanted!

*New 1950 Studebaker*

*Out ahead in style... in thrift... in value!*

**Plenty of "stretch-out" room** gives you relaxed comfort in all the 1950 Studebakers—even the low-price Studebaker Champion two-door sedan that you see pictured here is richly appointed and upholstered.

**Gasoline really delivers mileage** in a Studebaker. No burdensome excess bulk hitch-hikes a ride at your expense. Studebaker's automatic overdrive is available too at extra cost—assures extra economy.

**Brakes automatically adjust themselves!** This exclusive Studebaker advancement gives you the swift, sure stopping power of a brand-new car right down to the last layer of lining! New safety and new savings!

**This Studebaker father-and-son team** is one of many. They're famous for painstaking craftsmanship that puts a plus of enduring value into every Studebaker car.

▲ A 1950 Studebaker ad tried selling the bullet-nose look by parking it next to a USAF F-86 Sabre jet fighter. Copy extolled the gas-saving virtues of allegedly superior aerodynamics. Studebaker output was a record 320,884 cars.

▲ The aluminum-bodied Yank two-seater, built in San Diego, was one of many short-lived early '50s sports cars. It used a Willys four-cylinder engine in a 100-inch-wheelbase chassis. Even at a list price of $1000, few were built.

▲ Willys's jaunty Jeepster phaeton sold well in debut 1948-49, but demand dropped sharply for 1950 (from 12,623 to 4066 units) despite a nice new eggcrate grille and more modern F-head engines. Jeepster vanished after '51.

▲ Buick again listed long-chassis Super and Roadmaster Riviera sedans for '51, here the $3044 Roadmaster; 48,758 were produced.

▲ At $3780, the '51 Roadmaster Estate Wagon remained the costliest Buick—and the rarest, as only 679 were sold. Buicks retained structural wood through 1953.

▲ Buick chief engineer Charles Chayne towers over the 1951 XP-300 show car. In the cockpit are GM president Charles Wilson and his wife.

▲ The Super Sedanet was Buick's sole surviving "Jetback" for '51; with only 1500 sales, it would not return for '52.

▲ Bullet-like front bumper guards were among minor changes for the '51 Cadillacs. Even with a base price of $3987, the Series Sixty-Two ragtop attracted 6117 buyers.

▲ Cadillac's $3843 Series Sixty-Two Coupe de Ville hardtop more than doubled its sales for model-year '51, soaring from 4507 to 10,241—and it would soon triple that.

**1951**

As the Korean War intensifies, production cutbacks are ordered by Washington, via the National Production Authority

The auto industry faces government-ordered ceiling prices and rising labor costs

A rail strike in February temporarily cuts off supplies of critical raw materials

Industry output of 5.3 million cars is second only to 1950

The 100-millionth U.S. car is built in December

▲ The $2030 Chevy Styleline DeLuxe convertible wore a broader "smile" for '51, captivating 20,172 customers.

▲ This ad's headline inspired the theme song for TV's *Chevy Show.*

▲ Chrysler's new "Firepower" 180-bhp V-8 won Indy Official Pace Car honors for the New Yorker ragtop.

▲ Bolder grille aside, Chryslers were still dull and boxy for '51—but 25,000 New Yorker sedan buyers disagreed.

▲ This cross-section drawing appeared in 1951 Chrysler brochures to help explain the superior power and efficiency of the division's new expensive-to-build Hemi V-8.

Chrysler introduces its 331-cid, 180-bhp "Hemi" Firepower V-8 engine in the Saratoga, New Yorker, and Imperial

The "hemispherical-head" V-8 offers technical advantages, but is costly to produce

Hardtop pillarless coupes join Ford and Plymouth lineups, as well as Hudson's and Packard's

Hardtops gain in popularity while convertibles decline; 480,597 hardtops are built (nine percent of total), versus 140,205 ragtops

More than three-fourths of all cars are considered "deluxe" models, as postwar prosperity and public optimism continue

The Town and Country nameplate now applies only to Chrysler's all-steel station wagon

▲ Briggs Cunningham's Chrysler Hemi-powered C-2R, evolved from his C-1, competed in 1951 with no real success. Only three were built. Top speed: 152 mph.

▲ Like all '51 DeSotos, the $2438 Custom four-door sedan wore a lower, wider, but still toothy grille. Total DeSoto production reached approximately 106,000 units.

▲ The misnamed Comet two-seat roadster had just six horses and a 40-mph top speed, but yielded 60 mpg. A period "California kit car," made in Sacramento, it was also sold fully assembled, but only in 1951-55.

◀ Meet the Electrobile, which was promoted in '51, but likely didn't go beyond this sketch. An unknown company planned the three-wheeler for a fiberglass body atop an aluminum inner structure and a high-speed direct-current motor with a range of 25-35 miles via a built-in charger. Projected price was $350.

▶ A trio of '51 Ford Customs about to face the future: the $1949 convertible (*top left*), new $1925 Victoria hardtop coupe, and $1505 Tudor sedan (*on road*). Note the new twin-spinner grille, the year's main styling change.

---

Hydraguide power steering, an industry first, becomes available on Chryslers

Briggs Cunningham builds a prototype C-1 racing car, which evolves into the C-2R that fails at Le Mans

Bill Sterling places third in the *Carrera Panamericana* (Mexican Road Race) driving a Chrysler Saratoga

Dodge continues the all-steel Sierra station wagon introduced during 1950; the Wayfarer Sportabout roadster returns for its final season

Ford's Custom Victoria is the only low-priced hardtop with a V-8

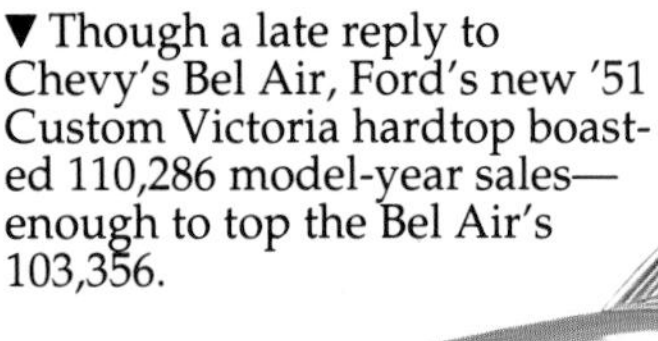

▼ Though a late reply to Chevy's Bel Air, Ford's new '51 Custom Victoria hardtop boasted 110,286 model-year sales—enough to top the Bel Air's 103,356.

▲ Ford's Crestliner returned for '51 at $1595 (a $116 price cut!), but after only 8073 were built it was dropped.

▲ Forget the ugly setting. This photo of Ford's $1465 DeLuxe Fordor was turned into brochure artwork.

▲ Another '51 brochure-art photo shows off the newly named Country Squire wagon; 29,017 were built.

▲ The '51 Frazers, like the $3075 Manhattan "hardtop sedan," were actually leftover 1950 Kaisers with a heavy front and rear facelift. After 10,183 '51s, Frazer was gone.

▲ Included in the final Frazer Standard line was this novel Vagabond utility sedan. Kaiser had pioneered this early hatchback idea in 1950. About 3000 were sold at $2399 each.

---

Three-speed Ford-O-Matic and Merc-O-Matic transmissions, built in cooperation with Warner Gear, become available

This is Frazer's final year; it sports a rather radical restyling front and rear

The Kaiser-built Henry J economy car debuts, lacking both a glovebox and trunklid

Hudson's hot new Hornet—which debuts with a 145-bhp, 308-cid six—begins to earn a long list of stock-car racing victories

▲ Kaiser's new 1951 Henry J compact, a two-door fastback starting at $1333, was thoroughly tested. Ads stressed ruggedness that owners quickly confirmed.

▶ When in doubt, use "star" power. That's what K-F did to introduce its 100-inch-wheelbase Henry J for '51, enlisting George Burns and Gracie Allen of film and radio comedy fame.

▲ The Henry J was styled by an outside company; 81,900 '51s were built.

▲ A Henry J of a different color, but another '51 DeLuxe. The car was sold with Willys engines.

▲ Hudson debuted the potent new six-cylinder Hornet for '51, and it quickly began setting stock-car racing records, as this ad proudly proclaims.

▶ "Twin H-Power" in 1951 meant a new Hornet with optional dual carbs and manifolds—the first twin manifolds on any production six. With 308 cubic inches, it cranked out 145 horses.

---

Hudson ads promise "Miracle H-Power" from the H-145 engine, the most powerful and largest six built in the U.S.

The factory soon offers "severe usage" parts for the Hudson Hornet, to boost its already-swift performance for racing

Top-line Hudsons may be ordered with Hydra-Matic, soon making the Drive-Master/Super-Matic semi-automatic transmissions redundant

The restyled "Anatomic" Kaiser, penned by Howard "Dutch" Darrin, debuts in May 1950 as a '51 model

Kaiser promotes safety with a padded dash, pop-out windshield, and recessed instruments

▲ Like Ford and Plymouth, Hudson introduced hardtops for 1951; here, the $2869 Hornet Hollywood.

▲ Besides a Hollywood, Hudson's debut Hornet line included this $3099 Brougham Convertible; about 550 were built.

▲ The $795 Imp still struggled for life in 1951 as a 7½-bhp, 63-inch-wheelbase microcar, but the Glendale, California, squirt vanished by year's end.

▲ Low and sleek, the all-new '51 Kaiser was a styling sensation and a good handler. This $2296 Club Coupe (6000 built) was in the DeLuxe series.

▲ The '51 Kaiser was the original work of famed designer "Dutch" Darrin. With about 70,000 sold, the DeLuxe four-door was the most popular model.

▲ Kaiser persisted with utility sedans in its new second-generation '51 line. All were called Traveler, and included this $2433 four-door DeLuxe.

▲ Kaiser's '51 Special Traveler featured a safety-inspired padded dash.

### 1951 Model Year Production

| | | |
|---|---|---|
| 1. Chevrolet ........ 1,229,986 | 8. Oldsmobile ........ 285,615 | 15. DeSoto ........ 106,000[1] |
| 2. Ford ........ 1,013,381 | 9. Studebaker ........ 246,195 | 16. Packard ........ 100,713 |
| 3. Plymouth ........ 611,000[1] | 10. Nash ........ 205,307 | 17. Henry J ........ 81,942 |
| 4. Buick ........ 404,657 | 11. Chrysler ........ 163,613 | 18. Lincoln ........ 32,574 |
| 5. Pontiac ........ 370,159 | 12. Kaiser ........ 139,452[1] | 19. Frazer ........ 10,214 |
| 6. Mercury ........ 310,387 | 13. Hudson ........ 131,915 | 20. Crosley ........ 6,614 |
| 7. Dodge ........ 290,000[1] | 14. Cadillac ........ 110,340 | [1] *Calculated or estimated* |

▲ Lincoln still lacked hardtops for '51, so the stand-in Cosmopolitan Capri coupe returned at $3350 with a wider "mouth" and reshuffled trim.

▲ Lido, which remained Lincoln's standard-series pseudo-hardtop for '51, measured 214.8 inches overall. Few were sold at $2702.

◀ Unlike the '51 Mercurys and standard Lincolns, which wore newly extended rear fenders, Lincoln Cosmopolitans retained a rounded look—plus top-shelf trim and equipment, of course. The Cosmo convertible weighed in at a hefty 4614 pounds, and with only 857 built was Lincoln's rarest regular-production '51 model. List price was $3891, a lofty sum at the time.

▲ Still a nameless model in one nameless series, Mercury's 1951 two-door wagon more than doubled its volume from 1950, going from 1746 to 3812 units. Base price was $2530.

▲ Probably even rarer than Mercury's '51 wagon was the Monterey coupe, back for a second and final year. Price: $2116 with canvas top, $2127 with vinyl top.

---

The first Muntz Jets are produced in Evanston, Illinois, courtesy of Earl "Madman" Muntz

Nash Rambler adds a Country Club hardtop coupe to the lineup, but the wagon is far more popular

The "bathtub" Nashes make their final appearance, adding prominent rear fenders for a "racing teardrop tail"

The new two-seat Nash-Healey sports car places bodywork by Donald Healey atop a Nash chassis

Restyled Oldsmobiles win 20 of 41 stock-car starts

The Super 88 series joins the Oldsmobile lineup; station wagons depart

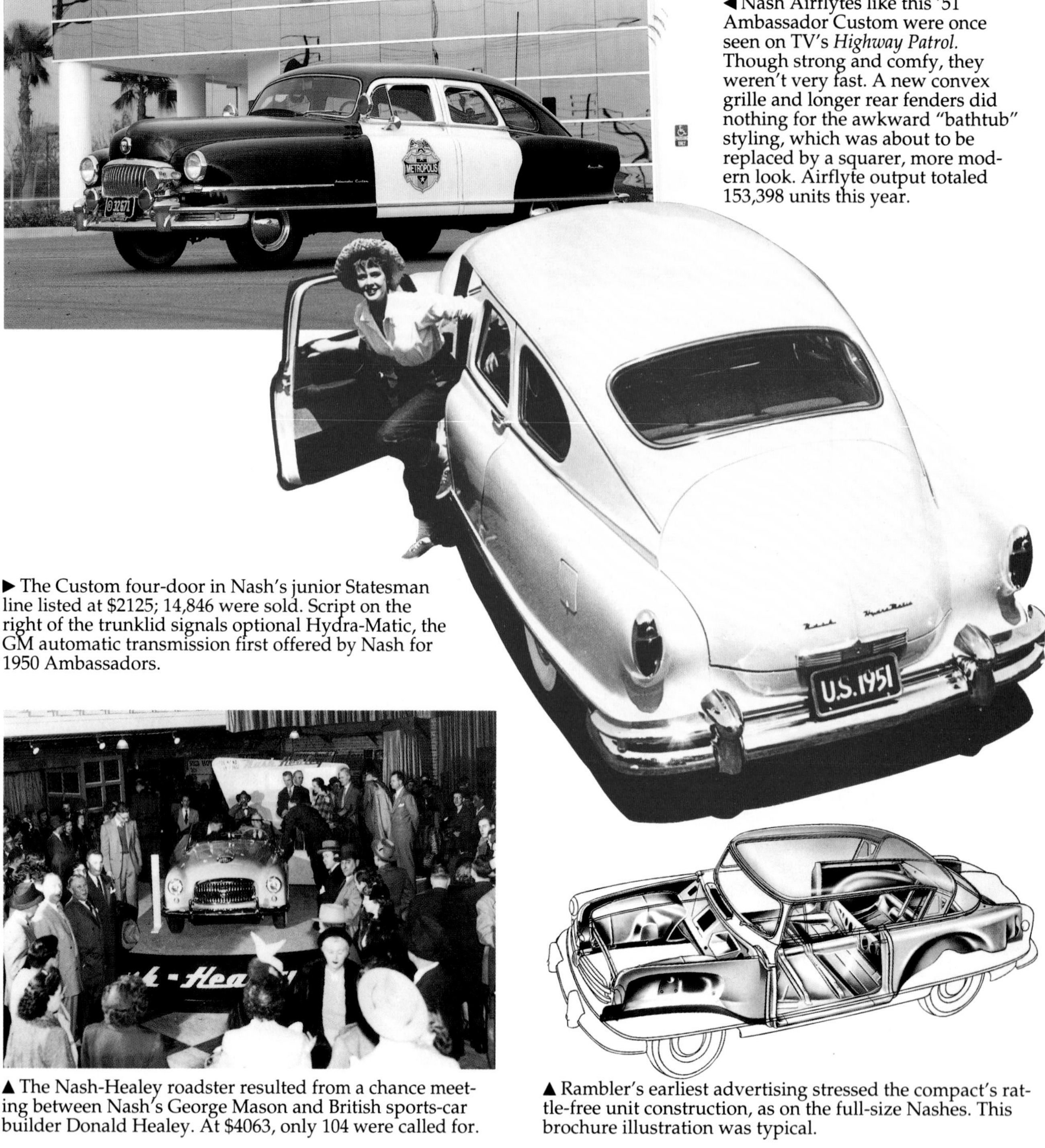


◀ Nash Airflytes like this '51 Ambassador Custom were once seen on TV's *Highway Patrol.* Though strong and comfy, they weren't very fast. A new convex grille and longer rear fenders did nothing for the awkward "bathtub" styling, which was about to be replaced by a squarer, more modern look. Airflyte output totaled 153,398 units this year.

▶ The Custom four-door in Nash's junior Statesman line listed at $2125; 14,846 were sold. Script on the right of the trunklid signals optional Hydra-Matic, the GM automatic transmission first offered by Nash for 1950 Ambassadors.

▲ The Nash-Healey roadster resulted from a chance meeting between Nash's George Mason and British sports-car builder Donald Healey. At $4063, only 104 were called for.

▲ Rambler's earliest advertising stressed the compact's rattle-free unit construction, as on the full-size Nashes. This brochure illustration was typical.

---

Packard gains a modern squared-off profile, adds a lower-priced 200 series

Packard is named "the most beautiful car of the year" by the Society of Motion Picture Art Directors

The top Packard engine is a 327-cid, 155-bhp straight eight, still an L-head

Plymouth offers a Belvedere hardtop coupe, which will receive distinctive two-toning for '52

Oriflow shock absorbers improve Plymouth's ride/handling

Pontiac production is the second-best ever: 370,159 units

▲ Rambler remained its trim self into '51, but added a third model in June, a neat Custom-trim hardtop coupe dubbed Country Club that attracted 19,317 customers.

▲ Semi-enclosed front wheels gave early Nash Ramblers, like the $1968 Custom Country Club hardtop, an overly large turning circle. This model weighed 2420 pounds.

◀ As if to remind everyone how much cars had changed since horseless carriage days, Olds issued this publicity photo of a new '51 Super 88 Holiday hardtop posed with the little Curved-Dash Oldsmobile of 1900-04. Olds dropped its six for '51, made 88 the base series, and added the new mid-range Super 88. It became Lansing's best-selling line—150,456 units for '51.

▲ Oldsmobile's senior 98s retained their basic 1950 styling for '51. The "cadet" sun visor on this $2882 DeLuxe Holiday hardtop was a popular period accessory.

▲ With "Contour Styling," the '51s were the first fully redesigned Packards since the original Clipper of a decade before. Perhaps Richard Nixon saw this brochure cover!

---

The Pontiac Streamliners are dropped during the model year; fastback bodies are quickly becoming extinct

Studebaker Commanders are now available with V-8 power: 232.6 cid, 120 bhp

Studebaker is the first to install Orlon convertible tops

A Comet two-seat roadster is offered in kit or assembled form; it reportedly can do 40 mph and gets 60 mpg

The Paxton Phoenix, styled by Brooks Stevens, is to be offered with a steam engine (but ultimately isn't)

▲ At $3662, the luxurious Patrician 400 sedan was the priciest of Packard's '51 models. Just 9001 of the 4115-pound sedans were produced.

▲ The '51 Patrician interior seems simple now, but the quality of materials was, as always for Packard, first class.

▲ Packard still relied heavily on medium-priced 200 Series two- and four-door sedans for '51, but also hopped on the hardtop bandwagon with the Mayfair, a 250 Series model tagged at $3234.

▲ Cranbrook replaced Special DeLuxe as Plymouth's best for '51. Like other models, this $1826 four-door wore a new face but had no major changes. Total Plymouth output was about 611,000 units.

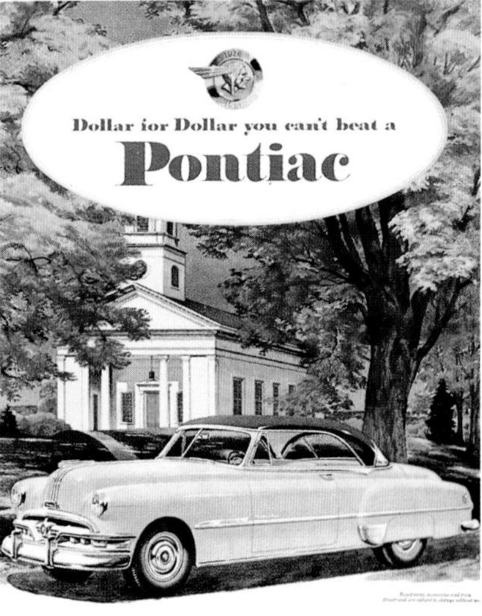


▶ Chieftain hardtops, like this Super Catalina, again featured in Pontiac advertising. This model listed for $2320; grille and side trim were revised for '51.

---

Chrysler's experimental K-310 show car, designed in Detroit but built in Italy, demonstrates some of Virgil Exner's early ideas

The experimental Buick LeSabre and XP-300 feature a supercharged aluminum V-8; the former struts "Dagmar" front bumpers (named for a buxom TV performer)

The King Midget continues, now more car-like in appearance and with room to seat two people

▲ Another look at Pontiac's Chieftain Eight Super Catalina, this time in the metal. Total Pontiac production reached 370,159 units for the model year.

▲ Studebaker muted its "bullet-nose" for '51 by painting the chrome ring around it, as on this Champion two-door sedan. Total output this year came to 246,195 cars.

▲ San Francisco import-car baron Kjell Qvale poses in the fiberglass-bodied, Singer-engined roadster he hoped to sell for $3000 as the B.M.C.

▲ Buick styling stood mostly pat for '52, but Roadmasters like this $3306 Riviera hardtop were upped to 170 bhp. This model found 11,387 buyers.

▲ Still structured with genuine wood, Buick's $3296 Super Estate Wagon saw production of only 1641 units. A leather interior was standard.

▲ Though the '52 Golden Anniversary Cadillacs looked much the same, horsepower was up 30 (to 190) via a four-barrel Quada-Jet carb. The posh $4323 Sixty Special sedan saw 16,110 examples built.

◀ Buick's '52 Special line again used Chevy/Pontiac tooling. Exclusive to the series was this $2115 "Tourback" two-door sedan; only 2206 were built.

**1952**

The Korean conflict limits auto production: the National Production Authority sets a total of 4,342,000 cars (actual calendar-year output is 4,337,481)

Ford Motor Company is the only Big Three automaker to fully restyle its cars this year; Chrysler and GM field lightly facelifted '51s

Automotive gadgets proliferate as general prosperity continues

More than two million automatic transmissions are installed during this model year

V-8 engines go into one-third of all 1952 automobiles

▲ Despite a $100 higher price tag, Chevy's DeLuxes still handily outsold Specials in 1952. This $1761 four-door sedan topped the entire line with 319,736 sales.

◀ Chevy bared its grille teeth for '52, but otherwise looked much the same as in 1951. The popular $1707 Styleline DeLuxe two-door captured 215,417 customers.

▲ The '52 Chryslers were all but identical to the '51s, but this $3969 New Yorker Newport hardtop is really a '52.

▲ Chrysler's 180-bhp Hemi V-8 gave its most potent performance in its lighter '52 models, like this $3215 Saratoga.

► Making its premier at the 1952 Paris Salon, the Chrysler Special show car was built by coachbuilder Ghia of Italy, but designed by Highland Park's Virgil Exner. One of several "idea cars" used to jazz up Chrysler's image during a period of dull production styling, the Special rode a cut-down New Yorker chassis and was powered by a Hemi V-8.

---

Chevrolet output drops to 818,142 cars, but Ford builds only 671,733; Plymouth clings to its traditional number three position, followed by Buick and Pontiac

Sears, Roebuck markets a new compact Allstate, a Henry J with a different grille and badging

Power steering becomes available on Buick Roadmasters for $199

Cadillac installs dual exhaust outlet tips in the rear bumper

With a four-barrel carburetor, Cadillac's V-8 has the highest horsepower in the industry: 190

▲ The Cunningham C-3 bowed in 1952 with pretty Vignale bodywork and a Chrysler Hemi V-8 modified to 220 bhp. Fewer than 30 were built.

▲ Except for the hubcaps, the '52 Dodges were virtual '51 reruns. The Coronet four-door sedan, $2256 in 1952, was by far the best-seller in both years.

▲ Ford was all-new for '52, thus more competitive against holdover Chevy and Plymouth—but the Korean War forced production cutbacks.

▲ Predictably, Ford trumpeted its new '52 styling in splashy magazine ads.

◀ Ford offered four-door wagons for '52, its first since 1948, but with new all-steel bodies. The $2060 Country Sedan in the mid-range Customline series saw 11,927 sales, but the cheaper two-door Ranch Wagon did better: 32,566.

▶ Glamour leader of Ford's '52 line was the newly named Sunliner convertible, priced at $2027; 22,534 were built.

---

Crosley production ceases in July as the company merges with General Tire and Rubber

Three hemi-powered C-4R Cunninghams compete at Le Mans; Briggs Cunningham drives to a fourth-place finish

A 160-bhp Firedome "Hemi" V-8 is made available in DeSotos

Ford gets an overhead-valve, six-cylinder engine; the long-lived flathead V-8 soldiers on

All-steel Ford station wagons debut, including a woody-look Country Squire

Ford's all-new cars get new "Power-Pivot" suspended brake and clutch pedals

▲ Hudson's Step-down design, now in its fifth year, was looking dated when this Hornet Club Coupe was built.

▲ Kaiser's Henry J was nicely facelifted for '52, but sales plummeted to 30,585.

▲ Hudson scored 27 NASCAR wins in 1952, but that didn't help sales of this Hornet sedan. Overall, output fell from 131,915 units in 1951 to 70,000 in 1952.

◀ With a body made from three aircraft fuel tanks, the Jetmobile was a three-wheeler with a rear-mounted Ford V-8/60. It came and went in 1952 despite top-speed claims of 110 mph.

▶ A part-plywood body made the teensy rear-engine Korff three-wheeler very stingy with gas, but this was another hopeful automotive venture that failed even before it began.

The Henry J "Vagabond" wears a "continental" spare tire in the rear

Hudson launches the 119-inch-wheelbase Wasp series and drops the Super Six; Hydra-Matic is now available in all models

Marshall Teague wins 12 of 13 stock-car events at the wheel of a Hudson Hornet; Hudsons also claim 27 NASCAR victories

Mildly facelifted Kaiser sedans arrive late in the season

Lincoln adds ball-joint front suspension, a 317.5-cid overhead-valve V-8, and hardtops for the completely redesigned Cosmopolitan and Capri

Power steering and a four-way power seat are Lincoln options

▶ Kaiser adopted a heavier-looking face during model-year '52, but it did nothing for sales, which began a long downward spiral (only 32,131 this year). Shown is the $2654 Manhattan four-door sedan.

▼ Like Ford and Mercury, Lincoln was all-new for '52. Cosmopolitan was now the base-line series, and came as a Sport hardtop coupe or this $3198 four-door sedan. Hampered by Korean War restrictions, total Lincoln output fell to 27,271.

▲ The '52 Lincoln also boasted a modern overhead-valve V-8 and its first hardtops; here, the $3518 uplevel Capri. With 12,916 built, it was the year's most popular model.

▲ A Maverick but not a Ford, this $3850 roadster appeared in 1952 with a fiberglass body atop a contemporary Cadillac V-8 chassis. Only seven were built through '55.

---

Lincolns take the top five spots in the 2000-mile *Carrera Panamericana* (Mexican Road Race)

Mercury's flathead V-8 is boosted to 125 horsepower via a higher 7.2:1 compression ratio

Mercury dashboards feature aircraft-type sliding levers

Italian stylist Pinin Farina helps redesign the Nash line, replacing the "bathtub" look with a squared-off shape

Nash-Healey is also restyled by Pinin Farina

Nash-Healey wins a first in class, third overall at Le Mans

Packards get power brakes for the first time

▲ New in 1951, the four-place Muntz Jet was a literal extension of Frank Kurtis's 1949-50 Sport two-seater.

▲ The Muntz Jet, priced at $4450, was arguably America's first "personal-luxury" car. Nearly 400 were built 1951-55.

▲ Mercury shared in Ford Motor Company's linewide overhaul for '52. This $2370 convertible, one of three new Monterey models, had a production run of 5261 units.

▲ Wagons remained the costliest '52 Mercs, but were now four-doors with fake-wood trim on all-steel bodies; only 2487 were built.

► The dawning "jet age" was the evident inspiration for Mercury's 1952 dashboard with its big push-pull lever controls astride a semicircular speedometer. This Monterey convertible sports power windows and seat, rare and costly options at the time, plus Merc-O-Matic automatic transmission.

---

James Nance takes the helm at Packard, promising a new focus on luxury cars

Overdrive transmission is available in Plymouths and DeSotos

Dual-Range Hydra-Matic is installed in Pontiac, Oldsmobile, and Cadillac cars

Studebaker celebrates its 100th Anniversary

Studebaker joins the "hardtop" ranks with its Starliner coupe; the bullet-nose front end is replaced by a "clam-digger" grille

Unibodied Willys Aero sedans arrive with L-head or F-head six-cylinder engines

▲ Nash was all-new for '52, entering the hardtop race at last with this $2829 Ambassador Custom Country Club; 1228 were built. A shorter $2433 Statesman version saw 869 built.

▲ Like all '52 Nashes, this $2716 Ambassador Custom sedan wore the badge of Italy's Pinin Farina, but the actual styling work was by Nash's chief designer, Ed Anderson.

▲ This modified Nash-Healey won its class and finished third overall (91.5 mph) in the 1952 Le Mans 24-Hour Race.

▲ Pinin Farina definitely figured in the Nash-Healey's attractive '52 restyle. A stiff $5868 price held output to 150.

▲ Oldsmobile's base series for '52 was tagged 88 DeLuxe and included this $2262 two-door sedan, plus a four-door. The more potent Super 88s outsold the 88s six-to-one.

▲ Plymouth's first hardtop bowed for '51 as the $2114 Cranbrook Belvedere. This nearly identical '52 model added distinctive "saddleback" two-toning.

## 1952 Model Year Production

| | | |
|---|---|---|
| 1. Chevrolet ........ 818,142 | 8. Mercury ........ 172,087 | 15. Packard ........ 62,921 |
| 2. Ford ........ 671,733 | 9. Studebaker ........ 167,662 | 16. Kaiser ........ 32,131 |
| 3. Plymouth ........ 396,000[1] | 10. Nash ........ 154,291 | 17. Willys ........ 31,363 |
| 4. Buick ........ 303,745 | 11. Cadillac ........ 90,259 | 18. Henry J ........ 30,585 |
| 5. Pontiac ........ 271,373 | 12. DeSoto ........ 88,000[1] | 19. Lincoln ........ 27,271 |
| 6. Oldsmobile ........ 213,490 | 13. Chrysler ........ 87,470[1] | 20. Crosley ........ 2,075 |
| 7. Dodge ........ 206,000[1] | 14. Hudson ........ 70,000 | [1]*Calculated or estimated* |

◀ Pontiac offered a sedan delivery in the early '50s, but sales were slim—only 984 units for '52. The famous "Silver Streak" trim is evident on this example.

▲ This '52 Chieftain Eight DeLuxe drop-top shows how little Pontiac styling changed from the '49 redesign to the major facelift due for 1953. This model was priced at $2518, but the new Dual-Range Hydra-Matic cost an extra $178.

▲ Skorpion was a $645 fiberglass kit built for a Crosley chassis/engine—good for 80 mph. With Crosley gone, the body was altered to fit a shortened Ford Chassis.

◀ Studebaker used its old '47 design one last time for '52, but with a new "clam-digger" face. Commanders had the firm's fine 232-cid V-8; 32,035 four-door sedans were built.

▶ The all-new Studebaker planned for the firm's 1952 centennial was delayed, so this Champion Starlight coupe and other models were changed only at the front. Output this year: 167,662 cars.

---

Ford's Continental 195X show car features phone, dictaphone, and automatic jacks

The experimental Packard Pan-American will evolve into the '53 Caribbean

A three-wheel electric shopping car, the Autoette, is produced from 1952-57; it's little more than a golf cart

Skorpion two-passenger roadsters, made of fiberglass in Anaheim, California, from 1952-54, come as a kit or assembled

The 1952-56 Woodill Wildfire sports car with a Glasspar fiber-glass body is sold as a kit, although about 15 will be sold fully assembled

▲ Willys returned to passenger cars for '52 with the unit-body Aero-Willys, styled by Phil Wright and engineered by ex-Packard hand Clyde Paton. Among three two-door sedans offered was this $1989 Aero-Wing; 12,819 were sold.

▲ A look inside the '52 Aero-Willys shows uncommon roominess for a compact, and simple trim.

▼ Willys claimed 24 cubic feet of trunk capacity for its '52 Aero—good even today. Note the rear fender kick-up.

▲ The Willys six fitted with an F-head configuration improved from 75 to 90 horsepower. Though no fireball, it gave the 2500-pound '52 Aero-Willys lively go-power.

▶ Willys boasted that the Aero's 61-inch-wide front and rear seats could hold up to six passengers, but despite the appearances here, four were far more comfortable.

CHAPTER NINE

# 1953-1959

# THE DESIGNER IS KING

Americans were still seeking their promised postwar peace and prosperity when they elected a new President in 1952. With the Korean War dragging on, the specter of the atomic bomb hovering over the new "Cold War" with Communist powers, and increasingly thorny domestic challenges like inflation, McCarthyism, and civil rights, it was perhaps no great surprise when General Dwight David Eisenhower of D-Day fame swept into office on the Republican ticket ahead of "egghead" Democrat Adlai Stevenson. Ike went to Korea to help end the fighting, then returned home to usher in eight years of self-absorbed prosperity. In many ways, the Eisenhower years were a triumph of style over both substance and science. How else to explain a time when Cinerama made as much news as the first polio vaccine?

Detroit reflected the national bent for good times and free spending by spewing forth a dazzling array of cars. Each yearly crop was seemingly more colorful, complex, and contrived than the last—as well as longer, lower, wider, heavier, and more powerful.

Year-to-year changes were often far more dramatic than young people could now imagine. Between 1954 and '55, for example, Chevrolet, Dodge, Plymouth, and Pontiac were all transformed from relatively simple, low-suds family haulers to hot V-8 performers with acres of new "dream car" sheetmetal, miles of chrome, and gallons of multi-color paint.

Designers were the true kings of Detroit in 1953-59, and the public paid homage by buying cars like crazy, peaking with 1955's record seven-million-plus. Many of those buyers were newly better-off middle-class types still fast forsaking cities for suburbia, where the station wagon was the family's new vehicle of choice. Yet, hardtops kept increasing even faster in popularity, and if two-door models were good, why not four-doors? General Motors again led the way, and by 1956 you could find hardtop sedans in most every showroom—and two cars in many driveways.

Alas, there were fewer makes to choose from by decade's end. One factor was the frantic 1953-54 Ford/GM price war that mortally wounded surviving independents. The second was the sharp 1958 recession that turned Americans sharply away from frivolous flash toward more sensible cars. Thus, Nash and Hudson consummated a desperate 1954 marriage to form American Motors, only to vanish in three years after AMC decided to focus on more saleable Rambler compacts. Similarly, once-proud Packard hoped for better times with its 1954 takeover of struggling Studebaker, but was sacrificed for the corporate good in 1958. Even heady 1955 couldn't save postwar upstart Kaiser-Frazer, and Willys likewise abandoned the U.S. car market to concentrate on Jeeps.

No such retrenchment for Ford, which regained its position as the industry's number-two in 1952, then set its sights on giant GM by ambitiously expanding from two divisions to five. Among the results were the elegant Continental Mark II and the spectacularly unsuccessful Edsel. Meanwhile, number-three Chrysler roared back with bold new Virgil Exner-styling for '55, then seized industry design leadership with its befinned "Forward Look" '57s.

Throughout these years, Detroit waged a "horsepower race" to rival the U.S.-Soviet arms buildup. Sadly, handling and braking were anything but ideal (ditto fuel efficiency—gas was a quarter a gallon), yet a few automakers timidly tried selling safety features like seat belts and padded dashboards.

But that's the way it was in an age when glitter, go, and gadgets were the principal keys to automotive success. The Fifties was the last decade in which America was truly innocent, and American cars, like the country itself, would never be the same again.

---

**1953**

Auto production controls are lifted in February, as Dwight D. Eisenhower takes over the presidency from Harry S Truman

The Korean War ends July 26, 1953

The postwar "seller's market" is over; automakers now focus on style as well as engineering

Calendar-year car output soars to 6,134,534 units

Ford production comes within 100,000 units of Chevrolet's 1.3 million

A selling "blitz" begins as Ford mounts an all-out challenge on Chevrolet; factories force cars on dealers

▲ The new '53 Buick Roadmaster Skylark sold just 1690 copies at $5000 each.

◀ The '53 Buick dash displays the glittery "jukebox" look typical of period American instrument panels. The selector quadrant above the wheel hub was for the optional Dynaflow automatic now ordered by most Buick buyers.

◀ The $3002 Super soft-top boasted much-improved performance with Buick's new ohv "Fireball" V-8.

▲ Save Skylark, the Roadmaster Estate Wagon was again the costliest Buick for '53 with a $4031 price tag.

▲ Though denied the new V-8, the $2197 Special four-door remained Buick's best-seller for '53: 100,312 units.

---

The blitz of 1953-54 helps kill off the independent automakers

Both Ford and Buick celebrate their 50th Anniversaries

GM's Motorama "dream car" show tours for six months, hosting 1.7 million visitors

Chevrolets start at $1524; average workers now earn $3581 annually

The average motorist drives 10,000 miles yearly

Motels now outnumber hotels by a two-to-one margin

American cars, such as Buick, begin to adopt 12-volt electrical systems

Half of all new cars have automatic transmissions; most makes offer power steering

▲ Cadillac's smooth new Eldorado was one of three limited-edition GM ragtops for '53. A lofty $7750 price held production to only 532.

▲ Small rear-fender scoops were part of Cadillac's optional air conditioning for '53, as shown here on a Sixty Special sedan.

▲ Unlike Eldorado, Cadillac's '53 Series Sixty-Two ragtop had a full-height windshield and a flexible top boot—and 8367 were built.

▲ Although the Sixty-Two convertible cost "only" $4144, it had all the amenities, such as a leather interior and stylish instrument panel.

▲ Chevy sported a heavy restyle and new series names for '53, with Bel Air topping the line. Chevy built 247,284 of these $1874 Bel Air four-door sedans.

▲ Despite new looks outside, the '53 Chevys were largely 1949-52 underneath. This sporty Bel Air convertible cost $2175. Some 24,047 sun lovers bought one.

---

Hardtop production accounts for 14.5 percent of total output

Restyled, still-boxy Chrysler products finally adopt one-piece windshields

Buick offers a limited-production Skylark convertible with a lowered beltline, rounded wheel openings, and Kelsey-Hayes wire wheels

Eldorado and Fiesta, limited-edition ragtops from Cadillac and Oldsmobile, boast "Panoramic" windshields; the $7750 Eldorado is the most costly car of the year

All Buicks except the Special have V-8 engines; most also have improved Twin-Turbine Dynaflow

▲ Chevy offered another '53 ragtop in its mid-line Two-Ten series. At $2093, it saw only 5617 sales.

▲ Resolute symmetry marked the dashboard of Chevrolet's flashy new '53 Corvette sports car.

▲ The production '53 Corvette was all but identical to the show car seen at that year's Motorama.

▲ At $3513, the '53 Corvette offered modern lines but some oddly old-timey features like side curtains.

▲ Chevy's long-lived "Blue Flame Six" gave '53 Corvettes 150 horses via triple carbs and other tweaks.

◀ Corvettes began coming off a small Flint assembly line in June '53. Early fiberglass body problems limited '53 model output to a mere 315 units. Production moved to St. Louis for '54.

---

Because of an August fire at GM's Hydra-Matic plant, many Cadillacs and Oldsmobiles come with Dynaflow this year; some Pontiacs get Powerglide

Chevrolet introduces the Corvette sports car with a tuned 150-bhp six-cylinder engine and Powerglide

Full-size Chevrolets are restyled; a new 235.5-cid six delivers up to 115 bhp

Briggs Cunningham drives a Chrysler-powered Cunningham C-5R to third at Le Mans; a C-3 grand tourer becomes available

PowerFlite two-speed fully automatic transmission is installed in Chryslers beginning in June

A Red Ram "Hemi" V-8 engine delivering 140 horsepower is available in the all-new Dodge

▲ Despite more chrome, staid styling remained a Chrysler sales drawback for '53. This New Yorker DeLuxe convertible sold for $3945; 950 were built.

▲ Mounted on a 133.5-inch wheelbase, the '53 Chrysler Custom Imperial Town Limousine offered extra-luxurious seating for six at $4762. Just 243 were sold.

▲ DeSoto again offered long sedans for '53. This $3529 FireDome with a 160-bhp V-8 found 200 buyers.

▶ The lone DeSoto convertible again came only in top-line FireDome form for '53. Just 1700 were called for at $3114 apiece. Note the squared-up rear fenders and toothier grille.

▲ A hot new "Red Ram" V-8 gave '53 Dodge Coronets extra sizzle. The $2494 ragtop saw just 4100 sales.

▲ Dodge's new '53 "Red Ram" V-8 was a small-scale Hemi with 140 horses from 241.3 cubic inches.

---

Dodge is one of the first production cars styled for Chrysler by Virgil Exner (formerly of Studebaker)

A Dodge V-8 averages 23.4 mpg in the Mobilgas Economy Run, and also breaks 196 AAA stock-car records at Bonneville

Ford's venerable flathead V-8 is in its final season

Twin H-Power for Hudson Hornets uses dual carburetors; the "7-X" race engine yields 210 bhp

Hudson's economy-priced compact Jet debuts, but sells poorly

Kaiser's posh Dragon sedan flaunts gold-plated trim, padded roof, and innovative interior

Lincolns capture the first four spots in the Mexican Road Race

▲ A Cleveland real estate mogul prompted Brooks Stevens to design the Cadillac-based Die Valkyrie. Front-end styling was radical, to say the least.

▲ Die Valkyrie starred at the '53 Paris Show. Just six were ultimately built, although 100 had been planned. The body was crafted by Spohn of Germany.

▲ Ford marked its 50th birthday in '53 by making few changes to its all-new '52 models. This woody-look Country Squire wagon sold 11,001 copies at $2203.

▲ The Ford Crestline Victoria hardtop listed at $2055 for '53; 128,302 were sold. This one wears a dealer-installed "continental kit," a popular accessory.

◄▲ *Left:* This '53 Crestline Sunliner did Official Pace Car duty at that year's Indianapolis 500 race, honoring Ford's 50th Anniversary. *Above:* Interior was stock except for special gold paint on dash and doors. All '53 Fords had special anniversary emblems on the steering wheel.

---

A Le Mans option for the Nash Ambassador includes dual carburetors and high-compression head, good for 140 horsepower

The Nash-Healey convertible is joined by a Le Mans coupe

Packard's glamorous Caribbean convertible outsells Cadillac's Eldorado

Plymouths get all-new styling and a Hy-Drive option, combining manual shift with a torque converter

Studebakers enjoy a Euro-style redesign by Robert Bourke, of the Raymond Loewy Studio

Demand for the stunning Starlight and Starliner coupes tops sedans four-to-one—to the surprise of Studebaker executives

▲ A facelifted Henry J bowed during '52, so the '53s were little-changed. All were called Corsair.

▲ Henry J again offered four- and six-cylinder models, but sales continued to slide, to 16,672 for 1953.

▲ The '53 Henry Js cost $1400-$1600—a lot for a compact—but interiors nonetheless remained quite stark.

▲ Hudson killed Commodores and Pacemakers for '53 to regroup around Hornets and new Wasp and Super Wasp models. This Super Wasp two-door sold for $2413.

▲ The original '48 Hudson "Step-down" styling was quite dated by '53, and output fell to 66,143. This Hornet Club Coupe has optional "Twin-H Power."

▲ Luxury $3924 Dragon was Kaiser's newest '53. Just 1277 were built.

▲ Kaiser priced its more basic '53 Manhattan four-door at $2650.

▲ Kaiser fielded stripped Carolina sedans, but sold only about 1800 copies.

▶ Here's another Kaiser Manhattan four-door, this one with two-toning. Kaiser's only engine for '53 was the old 226.2-cid L-head six, whose 118 horses had to lug around 3650 pounds of car.

---

The Edwards American convertible enters limited production; about a half-dozen are built from 1953-55

A Ford V-8 powers the Detroiter fiberglass-body convertible

The Fibersport roadster, based on the Crosley Hot Shot, is sold either as a kit or assembled

Fina Sport combines bodies from Vignale of Italy with Detroit V-8 power

The Maverick three-seater rides a Cadillac chassis

Studillac stuffs a large Cadillac V-8 into the light Studebaker coupe body

▲ Lincolns like this $3549 '53 Capri hardtop began winning big in the gruelling Mexican Road Races.

▲ Mercury offered its first two-series line for '53. Here, the four-door sedan in uplevel Monterey trim.

◀ This '53 Mercury Monterey convertible was part of Ford Motor Company's 50th Anniversary hoopla. Posing with it (*left to right*) are Ford brothers Henry II, Benson, and William Clay.

▼ Only detail changes marked the year-old "Farina" Nashes for 1953. Rear fender skirts grace this Statesman Custom two-door sedan, which cost $2310 basic.

▲ A new face with "floating" grille spruced up '53 Ramblers and gave a closer resemblance to senior Nashes. Here, the $2125 Custom Country Club hardtop with the optional "continental kit," an oft-purchased extra.

---

A fiberglass-bodied Buick Wildcat with wraparound windshield appears at the GM Motorama; the sporty Oldsmobile Starfire wears an aircraft-inspired oval grille

Lincoln's XL-500 show car features an all-glass roof

**1953 Model Year Production**

| | | | | | |
|---|---|---|---|---|---|
| 1. Chevrolet | 1,346,475 | 8. Mercury | 305,863 | 15. Hudson | 66,143 |
| 2. Ford | 1,247,542 | 9. Chrysler | 170,006 | 16. Willys | 42,224 |
| 3. Plymouth | 650,451 | 10. Studebaker | 151,576 | 17. Lincoln | 40,762 |
| 4. Buick | 488,755 | 11. DeSoto | 132,104 | 18. Kaiser | 27,652[1] |
| 5. Pontiac | 418,619 | 12. Nash | 121,793 | 19. Henry J | 16,672 |
| 6. Oldsmobile | 334,462 | 13. Cadillac | 109,651 | 20. Metropolitan | 743[2] |
| 7. Dodge | 320,008 | 14. Packard | 90,252 | | |

[1]*Calculated or estimated* [2]*Calendar year sales*

▲ A new long-chassis Nash-Healey Le Mans coupe bowed for '53 at a towering $6399. Styling was again the work of Italy's Pinin Farina.

◀ At $5908, the '53 Nash-Healey cost only $60 more than the '52, but that was still a bundle. No wonder total N-H production was just 162 for the model year.

▲ The Ninety-Eight Fiesta completed GM's trio of flashy, limited-edition '53 convertibles. Olds sold only 458 Fiestas at a base price of $5717.

▲ Looking clean and purposeful in profile is this 1953 Olds Super 88 two-door sedan, of which 36,824 were built. The original list price was $2410.

▲ Packard also proffered a pricey low-volume ragtop for 1953, the $5210 Caribbean. Some design cues came from Packard's recent Pan American show cars.

▲ The 1953 Packard Patrician sedan came in this $3740 standard model and as a $6531 Formal Sedan by Derham. Respective production was 7456 and just 25.

◀ Packard debuted Clipper in two new 1953 sub-series as a first step to divorce itself from a "medium-priced" image. This DeLuxe club sedan sold for $2691, and 4678 were sold.

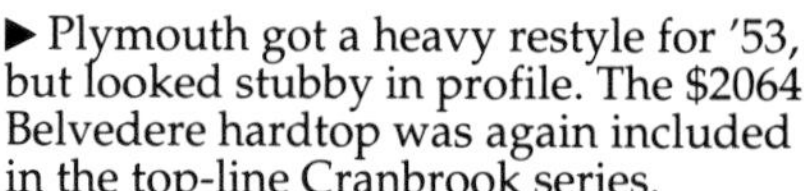

▶ Plymouth got a heavy restyle for '53, but looked stubby in profile. The $2064 Belvedere hardtop was again included in the top-line Cranbrook series.

▲ Pontiac also got a new look for '53. This Chieftain Eight Catalina hardtop sold for $2446.

▲ Ample cargo space was featured in Pontiac's 1953 Chieftain wagons. Wood-look trim remained optional.

▲ With low sales, the Pontiac Sedan Delivery was in its next-to-last year in 1953; 1324 were built.

▲ Studebaker's all-new '53 "Loewy coupes" were a design triumph.

▲ "Loewys" came as a pillared Starlight and pillarless Starliner, Champ or Commander.

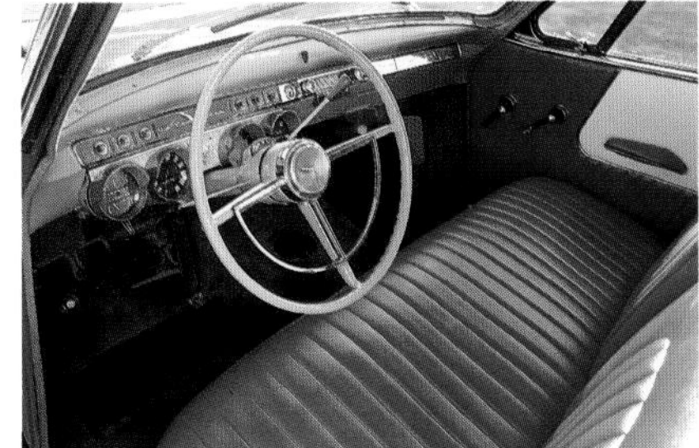

▲ All 1953 Studebakers featured a European-inspired, low-profile instrument panel design.

▲ Loewy-based lines appeared on Stude's new '53 sedans like this $2316 Commander Land Cruiser.

▲ Willys was also 50 years old in '53. Aero models, like this $2157 Eagle hardtop, changed little.

▲ Willys's Aero-Ace two-door sold in '53 for $1963—as much as some cheaper full-size cars.

▲ The 1953-54 Yankee Clipper used a Ford chassis and off-the-shelf fiberglass body. Few were built.

▲ The tiny three-wheel Autoette electric was built in 1952-57.

▲ GM show car styling showed up on the '54 Buicks. Here, the $2964 Super ragtop; 3343 were built.

▲ After a 12-year absence, Buick's Century returned in mid-'54 with four models, including a wagon.

▲ Less special than the '53, Buick's '54 Skylark saw but 836 copies.

▲ Cadillacs like the '54 Sixty Special followed Buick to wrapped windshields and blockier lines.

▶ Cadillac's '54 Eldorado was also less "custom" than the debut '53, which yielded a lower $5738 price and a healthier 2150 unit sales.

**1954**

The horsepower race is underway: 15 of 18 makes announce higher engine ratings

Nash-Kelvinator and Hudson combine to form American Motors Corporation—George Romney is named chief after the untimely death of George Mason

Studebaker and Packard meld into Studebaker-Packard Corporation

Henry Kaiser buys the Willys-Overland firm, moves all production to Toledo, Ohio

GM and Ford warn dealers about "bootleg" sales of new cars

▲ Though little-changed, Chevy's Corvette saw '54 output jump to 3640.

▲ Chevy's '54 Bel Air hardtop was officially called Sport Coupe. At $2061, it garnered 66,378 sales.

▲ The Bel Air convertible remained the most glamorous standard Chevy for '54. The price was $2185.

▲ Chevy built its 30-millionth car in 1954, shown in this publicity photo with top division managers.

▲ Still on its own chassis, the '54 Chrysler Custom Imperial sedan listed at $4260; 4324 were built.

▲ Extra chrome again marked the DeLuxe Chrysler New Yorkers for '54. Here, the $3406 four-door sedan.

---

The Detroit Public Library opens its auto history collection to the public

Ford's "Y-Block" overhead-valve V-8 replaces the long-lived flathead

Ford's model-year production of 1,165,942 beats Chevrolet by 22,381—the new ohv V-8 gets the credit

The wraparound windshield is a new trend, led by Buick, Cadillac, and Oldsmobile

The Buick Special runs with a new ohv 264-cid V-8

Buick launches its hot Century, stuffing a Roadmaster engine into the lightweight Special body

▼ Chrysler's only V-8 soft-top for '54 was the $3938 New Yorker DeLuxe, but only 724 were ordered.

▲ William Boyd of "Hopalong Cassidy" Fifties TV fame saddles up a '54 Chrysler New Yorker DeLuxe ragtop.

▲ DeSoto did more detail changes for '54, as on this FireDome sedan, which listed new for $2673.

▲ Dodge wooed buyers in mid-'54 with two-toned "spring specials" like this Coronet Sport Coupe hardtop. Base price was $2380.

▲ A hot mid-'54 Royal 500 ragtop was inspired by the Indy 500 Dodge Pace Car. Just 701 were built.

---

A revamped Buick Skylark wears tacked-on fins, lacks the radical stylishness of '53

Cadillacs are longer, lower, wider, with up to 230 bhp—and the first with standard power steering

The Dodge Royal 500 convertible sports a "continental" spare tire and wire wheels

Dodges finish in five of the top six positions in the Medium Stock class at Mexico's *Carrera Panamericana*

Chrysler and DeSoto sixes appear for the last time

DeSotos and Dodges are available with PowerFlite, but a three-speed stick is still standard

▲ San Franciscan Sterling H. Edwards built but six cars in 1953-55, including this unique hardtop.

▲ Which way is it going? Hard to tell on the rare Baltimore-built Eshelman Sportabout, a 30-mph midget sold in small numbers from 1953-60.

◀ Ford's new '54 Crestline Skyliner sported a green-tint Plexiglas front half-roof that brought the outside inside—and, according to critics, made people perspire on sunny days. At $2164, same as the convertible Sunliner, the "bubbletop" attracted respectable sales of 13,344 for the model year.

▲ With 293,375 built, the Customline Tudor remained a mainstream Ford for '54. It cost $1744 with six, but the big news was a modern ohv V-8 to replace the time-honored flathead as a new linewide option.

◀ A Ford publicity shot dramatically—and literally—highlights the airy interior of the new-for-'54 Crestline Sunliner hardtop, which came with a clip-in sunshade, too.

---

Ford is the first low-priced car with ball-joint front suspension

The Ford Skyliner and Mercury Sun Valley hardtops debut with tinted Plexiglas roof panels

Hudson's dramatic aluminum-bodied Italia, built by Carrozzeria Touring in Italy, sees minimal production: 26 units

The fiberglass Kaiser-Darrin sports car features sliding doors, landau top, Willys F-head engine

Designer "Dutch" Darrin later buys 100 leftover Kaiser-Darrins, installs Cadillac V-8s

Facelifted Kaiser Manhattan sedans boast a supercharged engine

▲ Hudson updated its "Step-down" for '54, but the effort was too late. Here, the Hornet convertible.

▲ Hudson's dumpy Jet compact bowed for '53 and promptly bombed. Here, a '54 Jet-Liner two-door.

◀ The radical 1954 Italia was eyed as the next new Hudson, but only 26 were built before funds ran out. All wore aluminum bodywork.

▲ Though nearly dead, Kaiser managed an effective '54 restyle.

◀ Kaiser also managed a sports car for '54, styled by Dutch Darrin. But the $3668 Kaiser-Darrin was no help; just 435 were built.

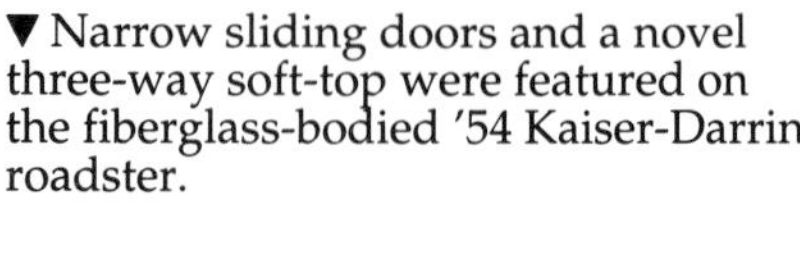

▼ Narrow sliding doors and a novel three-way soft-top were featured on the fiberglass-bodied '54 Kaiser-Darrin roadster.

---

Nash markets the bright little Metropolitan hardtop and convertible, built in Britain with an Austin A40 engine

Air conditioning becomes available in Packards for the first time since 1942 (some late '53s are equipped with it, too)

**1954 Model Year Production**

| | | | | | |
|---|---|---|---|---|---|
| 1. Ford | 1,165,942 | 8. Dodge | 154,648 | 15. Lincoln | 36,993 |
| 2. Chevrolet | 1,143,561 | 9. Chrysler | 105,030 | 16. Packard | 31,291 |
| 3. Plymouth | 463,148 | 10. Cadillac | 96,680 | 17. Metropolitan | 13,162 |
| 4. Buick | 444,609 | 11. Nash | 91,121 | 18. Willys | 11,856 |
| 5. Oldsmobile | 354,001 | 12. DeSoto | 76,580 | 19. Kaiser | 8,539 |
| 6. Pontiac | 287,744 | 13. Studebaker | 68,708 | 20. Henry J | 1,123 |
| 7. Mercury | 259,305 | 14. Hudson | 50,660 | | |

▲ The aptly named King Midget bowed in 1946 and hung on until 1970. All came with a one-cylinder engine.

▲ Lincolns wore a bolder face for '54. Price for this ragtop Capri was $4031, and 1951 were sold.

▲ Here's a replica of the Lincolns that ran 1-2 in the Stock Class of the last Mexican Road Race of 1954.

▲ Lincoln priced its '54 Capri sedan at $3711.

▶ Like Ford, Mercury got a new ohv V-8 for '54, with 256 cid and 161 horses, versus a 239 with 130.

▲ The 1954 Mercury Custom two-door sedan was priced at $2194.

▲ The singular Muntz Jet was near the end of its road in 1954.

▲ Mercury's $2582 Monterey Sun Valley was a cousin to Ford's new '54 Skyliner, but sold only 9761 units.

---

Packard adopts tubeless tires during the year; other manufacturers will follow for '55

Plymouths gain the PowerFlite automatic transmission option in March, making Hy-Drive semi-automatic redundant

An overdrive-equipped Studebaker Land Cruiser V-8 wins the Mobilgas Economy Run

Jomar blends a British TVR chassis with an aluminum body

Chrysler road-tests an experimental gas turbine engine in a Plymouth Belvedere

DeSoto's Adventurer I show coupe rides a shortened wheelbase, sports outside exhausts—and comes close to production

◀ Nash president George Mason (*center*) shakes the hand of Hudson chief A.E. Barit in April 1954, after the talks leading to Nash's takeover of Hudson and a new combined auto company called American Motors Corporation. Mason had long dreamed of a four-way merger involving Packard and Studebaker, too, but that was precluded by his untimely death in October 1954. However, Packard did buy out Studebaker that year, thus setting the stage for its ultimate demise. Taking over for Mason as AMC president was trusted lieutenant George Romney, seen here on the right. Romney would lead struggling AMC to a surprising resurgence by dumping Nash and Hudson after 1957 and pushing Rambler economy compacts, which went from strength to strength, helped by a sharp recession in 1958-59.

▲ Looking like a shrunken big Nash, the four-cylinder two-seat Metropolitan coupe and ragtop were fair sellers in the mid-Fifties at around $1450.

▲ This 1954 Nash Statesman Custom Country Club hardtop is a modern rarity (2726 were built). It sold new for $2423.

---

A Dodge Firearrow roadster, initially a mock-up show car, is made road-ready; the Firearrow coupe and convertible appear later, leading to the Dual-Ghia

Plymouth's Belmont show car is seen as a possible rival to the Corvette, but isn't produced

Experimental/show cars include a Corvette-based Nomad wagon, Buick Wildcat II, Packard Panther, GM turbine-powered Firebird, Plymouth Explorer, Ford FX-Atmos, and Mercury Monterey XM-800

1954 Ford FX Atmos show car.

▲ A trendy wrapped windshield and blockier contours marked the '54 Oldsmobiles. The Super 88 Holiday saw a healthy 42,155 sales.

▲ Olds added the name Starfire to its Ninety-Eight convertible for '54. Many were attractively two-toned. Base price was $3249. Some 6800 were built.

▲ Oldsmobile's Ninety-Eight Holiday hardtop came in standard and new DeLuxe versions for '54, priced at $2826 and $3042. The DeLuxe proved far more popular.

► A bigger bore swelled Oldsmobile's "Rocket" V-8 from 303.7 to 324.3 cubic inches for '54. Power rose from 165 to 185 on Ninety-Eights and Super 88s; 88s went from 150 to 170 bhp.

▲ This Olds Ninety-Eight DeLuxe wears Duotone paint typical of 1954.

▲ Olds emphasized airy views in its 1954 models with its new "Panoramic" wrapped windshield.

▲ Packard hoped to have an all-new car for '54, but carried on with old styling instead. That year's $3935 standard convertible saw only 863 copies.

▲ Pacific replaced Mayfair as Packard's senior-line '54 hardtop, but was much the same except for a larger straight-eight with 212 horses, versus 180—1189 were sold.

▲ Caribbean came back for '54 as Packard's glamour leader, but the price went up to a staggering $6100, one reason volume dropped to only 400 units.

▲ This $2815 Packard Clipper Super sedan attracted 6270 customers.

▲ Belvedere became Plymouth's top series for '54, and again listed a hardtop, up-priced to $2145.

▲ The '54 Plymouths were the last of the staid and stubby generation introduced for '49. This ragtop Belvedere was one of only 6900 built.

◀ Pontiac moved upmarket for '54 with four new top-line Star Chief models on a two-inch-longer wheelbase. Among them was this $2557 Custom Catalina hardtop.

▲ Like all '54 Pontiacs, the new $2630 Star Chief convertible wore a light redo of 1953's heavy facelift, which included longer, more prominent rear fenders.

▲ The 1954 Studebaker "Loewy" coupes showed few changes to their stunning year-old styling. This pillared Commander Regal Starlight sold for $2341 with standard V-8, but only 3151 were built. Starliner hardtops numbered 5040.

▲ Studebaker added wagons for '54 with two-door Conestoga models like this $2448 Commander DeLuxe.

▲ Willys fitted Kaiser's big six to new '54 Aero-Ace DeLuxe two- and four-door sedans. Only 1507 were sold.

▲ A standard "continental kit" graced the '54 Willys Aero Custom models like this Eagle hardtop, but the now-struggling firm could afford few other changes. Output skidded to 11,856 cars for '54.

▲ The Vaughn surfaced in '54 as an Italian-styled American GT. But like many other period projects, it was rendered stillborn.

▲ Once Buick's best-seller, the next-to-the-top Super line again listed three models, including this $2831 Riviera hardtop coupe—85,656 were built.

◀ A deft facelift helped Buick to record production for 1955—738,814 units. Priced at $3453, this Roadmaster Riviera hardtop coupe garnered 28,071 orders. It rode a 127-inch chassis.

▲ Buick's Century returned for '55 with an extra 36 horsepower, 236 in all. Buicks were occasionally chosen for police work, as witness this Century two-door sedan.

▲ This Estate Wagon expanded Century offerings from four to five for '55. Only 4243 were called for, likely due to a stiffish $3175 base price. This model weighed 3995 pounds.

▲ Buick introduced four-door Riviera hardtop sedans in the Century and Special lines as mid-'55 models (shared with Olds). The $2409 Special is seen here; 66,409 were produced.

▲ Italy's Pinin Farina built this grand two-seat convertible on a stock Cadillac chassis in 1955. It was strictly one-of-a-kind, which perhaps was just as well.

▶ Cadillac's own 1955 Series Sixty-Two convertible wore a tasteful facelift of its all-new '54 styling. List price was $4448, and 8150 found customers.

**1955**

The first McDonald's drive-in opens

Big boom year: auto output leaps 44 percent

American production totals 7,920,186 cars and 1,249,090 trucks—setting a new record

Ford's model-year car output is the highest since 1923, yet one quarter million below Chevrolet's 1,704,667

Buick takes over third spot, ousting Plymouth; Oldsmobile holds down fifth place

The average car retails for $2300, while the average full-time worker earns $3851 yearly

▲ The Series Sixty-Two four-door sedan remained Cadillac's single-best-selling model for banner 1955: 45,300 units. A broader eggcrate grille announced it.

▲ Distinctive "shark" fins graced Cadillac's '55 Eldorado, and would do so for several years. Price was up sharply to $6286, and so were sales, to 3950 units.

▲ Cadillac never offered a wagon, but Hess & Eisenhart built custom models in small numbers, usually converted four-door sedans, to special order for various purposes.

▲ Chevy's first V-8 since 1917 bowed for '55 with 265 cubic inches and 162 or a lively 180 horsepower.

▲ A prototype '55 Chevy with a modified '53 front end undergoes salt-bath tests at GM's proving grounds.

▲ Chevy's new '55 Bel Air Nomad pioneered the "hardtop" wagon, but attracted just 8386 buyers.

◀ Every '55 Chevy was all-new, but none was more desirable than the $2305 Bel Air V-8 convertible.

Led by Buick and Oldsmobile, the four-door hardtop ranks as the trend of the year

V-8 engines are adopted by Chevrolet, Plymouth, Pontiac, Hudson, Nash, and Packard

Seven out of 10 new cars have an automatic transmission; 78.6 percent get V-8 engines

Air conditioning is on the upswing: 184,027 installations in 1955 versus 57,469 in 1954

Installment buying is big: The National Automobile Dealers Association warns of "crazy credit terms"—some things never change

Automatic transmission shift levers poke from the dashboards of Chrysler products, which get "Forward Look" styling inspired by Virgil Exner

▲ Chevy's '55 Chevy Bel Air Sport Coupe hardtop listed at $2067 with a six. This one, though, carries a V-8 and extra trim. In all, 185,562 were sold.

▲ A desirable model in Chevy's Two-Ten series was the $1835 Delray, basically the standard $1775 two-door sedan with uptown interior trim.

▲ Even Chevy's unadorned One-Fifty series looked good in its new '55 finery. This two-door cost $1685, and 66,146 buyers drove one home.

▲ Luck of the draw made this '55 Chevy Bel Air Sport Coupe the 50-millionth car built since General Motors' founding in 1908, and thus a parade star.

▲ Chevy's Corvette retained its original styling for '55, but was nearly dropped as sales sank to just 674. All but seven of the '55s had Chevy's new V-8.

▲ Chrysler was dramatically lower, wider, and more handsome for '55, as shown in this side-by-side comparison with the '54 model (*left*).

► Chrysler Corporation spent a cool $100 million to restyle its entire 1955 line, so Chrysler Division boasted its cars had the "$100 Million Dollar Look." This New Yorker DeLuxe Newport hardtop sold 5777 copies at $3652 apiece.

---

Three-tone color schemes appear on Chrysler products, led by the DeSoto Coronado

Cadillac's Eldorado V-8 delivers 270 horsepower

The completely restyled Chevrolet offers a 265-cid V-8 engine—its first V-8 since 1917

The Corvette also adopts V-8 power

A Nomad wagon is Chevrolet's style leader; Safari is Pontiac's equivalent

Chrysler's C-300 supercar dominates NASCAR racing

Imperial is now listed as a separate make, not a Chrysler series

▲ Chrysler put an Imperial front on a New Yorker hardtop and added a new 300-bhp Hemi V-8 to create the first of its memorable high-performance 300s for 1955. List price was $4110; 1725 were sold.

▲ The Nassau was a lower-priced hardtop fielded to replace the club coupe in Chrysler's 1955 Windsor DeLuxe line. Price was $2703 versus $2818 for the standard Windsor Newport. Styling still looks good.

▲ Chrysler started offering more elaborately trimmed "spring specials" like this '55 Windsor sedan to spark mid-season sales.

◀ Chrysler's 300 quickly dominated 1955 stock-car racing. Here's one on the pole for a 100-miler at Asheville, North Carolina.

▲ DeSoto was handsomely restyled for '55, though a toothy front remained. The new top-line Fireflites included a $2939 Sportsman hardtop; 26,637 were produced.

▲ Optional wire wheels added extra sportiness to this '55 DeSoto Fireflite convertible, which sold for $3151. Only 775 examples were built for the year.

---

The C-6R, Cunningham's final stab at racing, fails to finish at Le Mans

Dodge's showcase La Femme hardtop features a pink/white exterior and interior, folding umbrella, fitted purse; for 1956 it'll be two-tone lavender

Ford's Thunderbird, a "personal car," bows—and sells 16,155 first-year copies versus Corvette's 674

The rakish Ford Crown Victoria adopts a "basket-handle" roofline, with a transparent half-roof optional

Hudsons are really Nashes in disguise; the 308-cid six continues in the Hornet, but Packard's V-8 is available

Ramblers and Metropolitans wear both Nash and Hudson badges

▲ DeSoto helped pioneer triple-tone paint jobs at mid-'55 with the Fireflite Coronado sedan. This example wears the colors most commonly used.

▲ Dodge too offered tri-color paint as part of an altogether flashier '55 lineup headed by new V-8 Custom Royal models like this $2543 Lancer hardtop; 30,499 were built.

◀ Also included among Dodge's topline '55 Custom Royals was this Lancer convertible priced at $2748. Just 3302 were built. A standard new 270 "polyhead" V-8 gave Customs 183/193 horsepower.

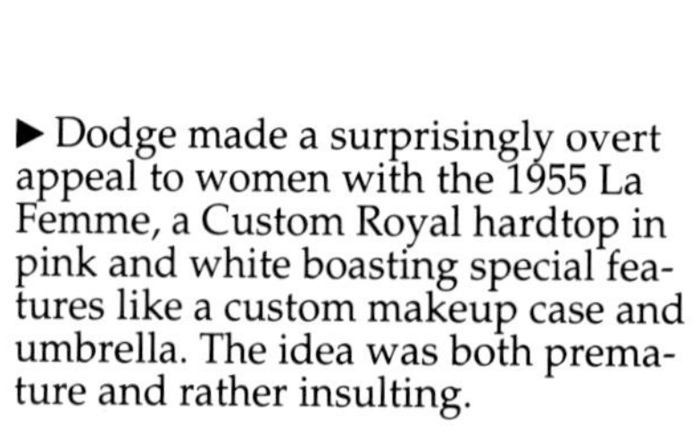

▶ Dodge made a surprisingly overt appeal to women with the 1955 La Femme, a Custom Royal hardtop in pink and white boasting special features like a custom makeup case and umbrella. The idea was both premature and rather insulting.

▲▶ *Above:* FoMoCo president Henry Ford II posed for reporters in Ford Division's new Thunderbird, a two-seat "personal" car to counter Chevy's Corvette. *Right:* The $2944 T-Bird promptly trounced the 'Vette in sales. Svelte good looks and a lift-off hardtop were two of the reasons. Buyers quickly ordered 16,155 examples.

The final few Kaiser Manhattans and Willys sedans are built; tooling for both then goes to South America

Nashes feature a wraparound windshield, inboard headlights, and an available 320-cid Packard V-8

Tech-oriented Packard offers "Torsion-Level" ride, with motor-controlled torsion bars instead of springs

Studebaker's Speedster features wild two-tone paint, quilted-vinyl interior, and tooled dashboard

Tubeless tires are now standard on almost all American cars

The American Automobile Association halts sanctioning of auto races

▲ The '55 "standard" Fords were so heavily restyled they looked all-new. The $2095 Victoria hardtop sat in a new top-line Fairlane series; 133,372 were sold.

▲ Ford's new '55 Fairlane group also embraced the glamorous Sunliner convertible, which rose $60 to $2224 with a six. Buyers snapped up 49,966 copies.

◀ Wagons became a separate Ford series for '55, but with 106,284 sold, the four-door Country Sedan remained the most popular model.

▶ Saucy dipped side trim identified Ford's new '55 Fairlanes. The line's Tudor was called Club Sedan and listed at $1914.

▲ Hudson used Nash-based bodies for 1955. The $3145 Hornet V-8 Custom Hollywood topped the new lineup.

▲ AMC restyled Ramblers for '55 and sold some with triangle logos to boost Hudson sales. Here, the $1995 Custom Cross Country wagon.

▲ "Hash" is often used to describe the 1955-57 Nash-based Hudsons, but the '55s at least looked good. Wasp models like this four-door shared Nash Statesman tooling, but ran with a 202-cubic-inch Hudson six.

**1955 Model Year Production**

| | | |
|---|---|---|
| 1. Chevrolet....1,704,667 | 8. Dodge....276,936 | 15. Hudson....45,535 |
| 2. Ford....1,451,157 | 9. Chrysler....152,777 | 16. Lincoln....27,222 |
| 3. Buick....738,814 | 10. Cadillac....140,777 | 17. Imperial....11,432 |
| 4. Plymouth....705,455 | 11. Studebaker....116,333 | 18. Willys....6,565 |
| 5. Oldsmobile....583,179 | 12. DeSoto....115,485 | 19. Metropolitan....6,096[1] |
| 6. Pontiac....554,090 | 13. Nash....96,156 | 20. Kaiser....1,291 |
| 7. Mercury....329,808 | 14. Packard....55,247 | [1]*Calendar year sales* |

▲ Chrysler made its luxury Imperial a separate make for '55. Designer Virgil Exner made it handsome. At $4483, this four-door sedan captured 7840 buyers.

▲ The '55 Imperial introduced distinctive "gunsight" taillamps that would become a make hallmark. This $4720 Newport hardtop was the other standard model.

◀ Reflecting too many management mistakes and not enough money, Kaiser abandoned the U.S. car market after 1955 and a brief run of little-changed '54 Manhattan sedans. Of the 1291 built for '55, only 270 were sold domestically. However, Dutch Darrin's winning design would have a second life in Argentina, where it was built through 1962 by a Kaiser subsidiary as the Carabela. It might have gone on even longer, but by then the tooling had worn out and was just too costly to replace.

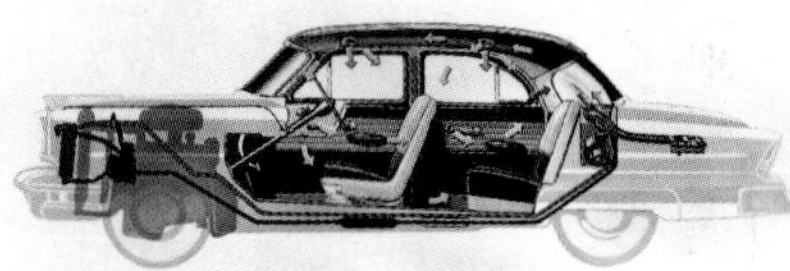

▲ Lincoln added optional factory air conditioning in early 1953. This cutaway drawing shows how air circulated in a '55 sedan.

◀ Lincoln was one of Detroit's few '55s without a wraparound windshield, settling instead for a fairly heavy facelift. This Capri hardtop sold new for $3910, and 11,462 were built.

---

Michigan is the first state to require a driver's education course before issuing a license to youths under 18

The tiny American Buckboard roadster prototype uses a two-cylinder motorcycle engine and fifth-wheel drive

Glasspar Company develops the Ascot roadster

The Gaylord luxury two-seater, styled by Brooks Stevens, features a Spohn (German) body and a Chrysler Hemi V-8; six are built

A Panda roadster debuts, with four-cylinder or flat-twin engine

The Tri-Car three-wheeler has a rear engine and plastic body

▲ Mercury's "bubbletop" Sun Valley transferred to 1955's new top-line Montclair series, but would not return after only 1787 were built. Price was $2712.

▲ All '55 Mercs shared a brighter, bolder look and a bigger new 292 V-8 with 188/198 bhp. This Montclair convertible also cost $2712; 10,668 were built.

▲ Nash gained the trendy wrapped windshield and inboard headlamps in a major '55 restyle. This Ambassador Country Club hardtop carried a $3095 price tag.

▲ Twin carbs and other 1955 changes lifted Nash's junior Statesman six from 100 to 110 horses. Nash called it "Dual Powerflyte," which must have irked Chrysler.

▲ Rambler again offered two-toning for '55, but was typically more subdued than on most other '55s. This is the Custom Country Club hardtop, base priced at $1995.

▲ A new oval grille announced the facelifted '55 Oldsmobiles like this $2894 Super 88 convertible, of which 9007 copies were built.

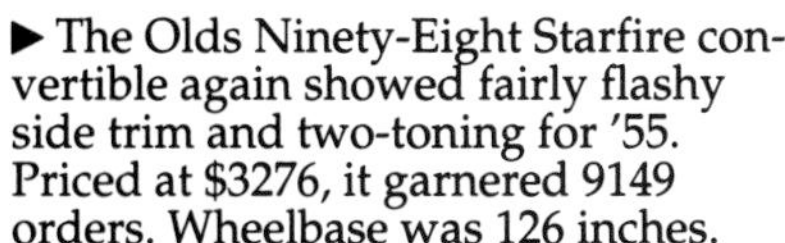

▶ The Olds Ninety-Eight Starfire convertible again showed fairly flashy side trim and two-toning for '55. Priced at $3276, it garnered 9149 orders. Wheelbase was 126 inches.

---

Show cars include the Chevrolet Biscayne, Oldsmobile Delta, Buick Wildcat III, LaSalle II, Chrysler Falcon and Flight Sweep, DeSoto Adventurer II, Ford Mystere, Lincoln Futura, and Universelle truck

1955 Chrysler Flight Sweep I show car.

1955 Ford Mystere show car.

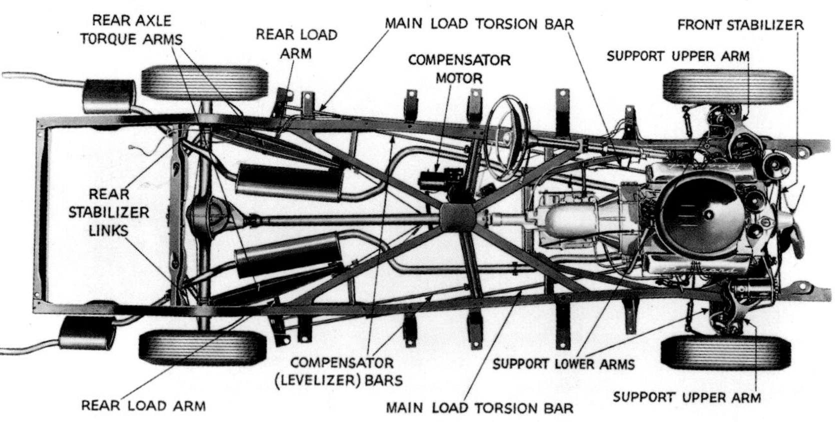


◀ Full-length torsion bars with electric ride-height control were the heart of Packard's novel new 1955 "Torsion Level" suspension, which worked impressively well.

▲ Exterior running/courtesy lamps were another '55 novelty for senior Packard models.

◀ Stylist Dick Teague conjured a remarkable '55 facelift that made Packard's '51 bodyshell look almost new. The Caribbean ragtop again topped the line at $5932.

▲ Packard's senior 1955 hardtop was named "The Four Hundred," after the social elite of bygone days. Priced at an elite $3930, it managed 7206 sales.

▲ Like Chevy, Plymouth was dramatically new for '55 in both looks and performance. The $2217 Belvedere Sport Coupe hardtop attracted 33,433 buyers.

▲ Plymouth's top '55 wagon was the $2425 Belvedere Suburban, seen here with "Sportone" trim.

◀ The Belvedere convertible was the only '55 Plymouth with a standard V-8, the division's first, an efficient new 260-cid "poly-head" design with 167 or 177 horses.

▲ Chrysler first experimented with gas-turbine power in a '54 Plymouth. A '55 Belvedere sedan was used to test an improved engine the following year.

▲ Plymouth denoted 1955 six-cylinder models by omitting "V" emblems from hood and trunklid, as on this Belvedere four-door sedan, which sold for $1979. Sales reached 69,128 units.

▲ Pontiac won approval for its own version of Chevy's new-for-'55 Nomad wagon. The result was the stylish $2962 Star Chief Custom Safari; only 3760 were sold.

▲ Silver Streak hood trim was about the only styling holdover on Pontiac's all-new '55s. This $2691 Star Chief convertible enticed 19,762 eager buyers.

▲ A modern new 287 V-8 was standard across a smaller but more focused '55 Pontiac line. Here is the Star Chief Custom Catalina hardtop, priced at $2499.

◀▲ *Left:* The lemon/lime paint scheme on this President Speedster Hardtop was a model exclusive, as was the $3000-plus price. Just 2215 of these one-year-wonders were produced. *Above:* The pillared President State coupe was offered in more conventional color combinations than the Speedster.

▲ Faltering Willys hoped for a sales miracle with a contrived facelift, but it didn't happen, so the firm quit building cars in the U.S., after only 6565 '55s. This newly named Bermuda hardtop listed at $1895 or $1997.

▲ Another look at the Willys '55 Bermuda hardtop, which replaced the Aero-Eagle but was much like it except for styling details. Exactly 2215 of these were built with either the 161- or 226-cid six.

▲ Buick facelifted its 1954 body one last time for '56. This $3256 Century Estate Wagon is one of only 8160 originally built.

▲ With a list price of $3704, the Roadmaster convertible remained Buick's costliest model for '56. Just 4354 units were produced.

▲ More popular by far was Buick's 1956 Special Riviera hardtop coupe, which attracted 113,861 buyers. The price was $2457.

▲ Cadillac was also in the last year of a three-year design cycle for 1956. Here, the popular Coupe de Ville hardtop, which carried a $4624 list price and found 33,300 buyers.

▲ An instant hit, Cadillac's new $4753 Sedan de Ville was the division's first four-door hardtop and, with 41,732 sales, its most popular 1956 model.

► Cadillac's Eldorado retained its distinctive "shark" fins for '56, but benefited from the same deft restyle applied to sister models. The convertible now carried the Biarritz name to distinguish it from the first Eldorado hardtop, a new two-door named Seville, which sold 3900 copies to the ragtop's 2150. Both models were priced at a princely $6556. For the first time since 1949, all Cadillacs had a larger V-8, a bored-out 365-cubic-inch unit with 285 horsepower. With dual four-barrel carbs, the figure rose to 305 bhp for Eldorados.

**1956**

A 41,000-mile Interstate Highway Network is approved; the federal government will pay 90 percent of costs

The 156-mile Indiana Toll Road opens, joining the Ohio Turnpike for a complete Chicago-New York superhighway

Industry output eases to 6.3 million for the model year

Ford builds 1.4 million cars, but trails Chevrolet's 1.56 million

Ford joins the Automobile Manufacturers Association; Henry II is elected president

Ford stock is sold for the first time since 1919

▲ This prototype '56 Chevy charged up Pikes Peak in October '55 in record time for an American sedan.

▲ Corvette wizard Zora Arkus-Duntov greets NASCAR officials after his record run up Pikes Peak.

▲ Chevy facelifted to good effect for '56, as shown on this Bel Air Sport Coupe hardtop. At $2176, this model sold 128,382 copies.

▲ If less "pure" than the '55 Chevy, the restyled '56 was right in tune with buyer tastes. This is the $2344 Bel Air convertible, of which 41,268 were built.

▲ Chevy joined the swing to four-door hardtops for 1956 with pillarless Sport Sedans in middle Two-Ten and top-line Bel Air trim (*shown*).

---

Four-door Chevrolet and Ford hardtops debut; they're also now offered by Plymouth, Dodge, DeSoto, Chrysler, Imperial, and Pontiac

Four-fifths of all '56s have a V-8 engine; only eight makes offer a six

A dozen makes offer leather interiors, most often at extra cost

Pushbutton automatic transmission selectors are installed on Imperial, Chrysler, DeSoto, Dodge, Plymouth, and Packard

Highway Hi-Fi record players are optional in Chrysler Corp. cars

Chrysler's 300-B engine is uprated to 355 bhp—one horsepower per cubic inch

▲ Chevy's Corvette was all-new and dramatically improved for '56. A new lift-off hardtop option shown here helped boost model-year output to 3467.

▲ Corvette prices started at $3149 for 1956. That bought more amenities and more power: 210 horses standard and 225 with an optional "Power Pack."

▲ Built for General Motors designer Bill Mitchell in mid-1956, the experimental Corvette SR-2 racer saw action at Daytona, Sebring, and Road America.

► Engineer Zora Arkus-Duntov worked handling wonders on the Corvette chassis for '56. Braking remained weak, but cornering was flatter, more stable, and more predictable.

▲ Detroiter Ruben Allender began offering "Cadillacized" Chevys during 1956 under the name El Morocco. Of the 20 built for '56, 18 were ragtops.

► The '56 El Morocco's Cadillac influence was most visible in an Eldorado-style rear end with similar "shark" fins above small round taillamps. Up front were prominent "Dagmar" front bumper guards made from '37 Dodge headlight shells. The price was $3400.

---

A limited-edition Adventurer is DeSoto's response to the high-performance Chrysler 300-B, Dodge D-500, and Plymouth Fury

Fords are offered with seat belts, padded dash, and other safety features—but they fail to take hold

Ford's Thunderbird adds a "continental" spare tire and "porthole" roof option

AMC's new 250-cid V-8 replaces Packard's V-8 in the Hudson Hornet and Nash Ambassador

The $10,000 Continental Mark II coupe debuts, separate from the Lincoln line, with a 285-bhp V-8

▲ Sheetmetal fins flew on Chrysler's facelifted '56s, including this $3995 New Yorker St. Regis hardtop.

▲ Only 921 Chrysler New Yorker convertibles were built for '56, making this restored survivor all the more interesting. Original list price came in at $4243. Weight was 4360 pounds.

▲ Chrysler's 1956 Windsors wore their own unique grille for the first—and last—time. This four-door sedan was the line's best-selling model with 53,119 orders.

▲ The 1956 Chrysler 300-B exceeded the magic "1 hp per cu. in." ideal by extracting 355 horses from 354 cubic inches. Just 1102 were built. Base price was $4419.

▲ DeSoto's most popular '56 hardtop was the $3346 two-door Fireflite Sportsman—but at 8375 units, sales weren't all that high.

◀ Topping the '56 line of nicely reworked DeSotos was a new high-performance hardtop called Adventurer with 320 horsepower from a 341 Hemi V-8. Strictly a limited edition with gold trim, it saw 996 copies, each priced at $3728.

---

Lincoln and Rambler are the only automakers with a major restyle this year

Packard's Clipper is now listed as a separate make, but it's too late and sales go nowhere

The Packard Caribbean features reversible leather/fabric seat cushions and 310 horsepower

Packard offers electrically controlled door latches and a limited-slip differential

Plymouth's fast Fury hardtop runs with a 240-bhp, 303-cid V-8

Rambler's Cross Country ranks as the first four-door hardtop station wagon, starting a mini-trend

▲ Like sister MoPar makes, Dodge sported prominent fins for '56, as on this $2513 V-8 Royal sedan.

▲ Dodge's '56 V-8 Royal Lancer hardtop coupe sold for $2583.

▲ Fender skirts grace this '56 Dodge La Femme two-tone lavender specialty model that came with compact, umbrella, etc. for milady. Sales were minuscule.

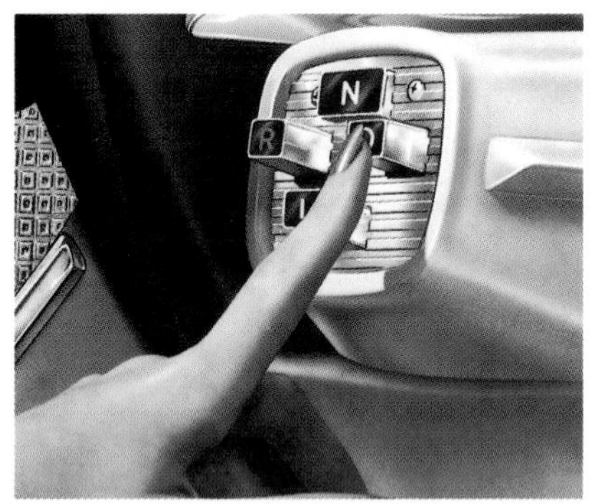


◀ Dodge and sister Chrysler makes offered a futuristic new feature for '56: pushbutton controls for the two-speed PowerFlite automatic transmission (but no Park button).

▶ This badge denotes a special 1955-56 Dodge trim package for Coronet hardtops sold in the Lone Star State. Such packages were a period sales-boosting ploy favored by Chrysler and other automakers as well.

▶ Customline remained Ford's mid-price series for '56, but added a $1985 Victoria hardtop coupe as a lower-cost alternative to the $2194 Fairlane model. Still, the fancier version outsold this Customline Victoria by better than five-to-one, with 177,735 units versus 33,130. All '56 Fords wore a minor touch-up of their '55 styling, highlighted by a new grille and side trim.

---

Studebaker launches a quartet of sporty Hawks, highlighted by the Golden Hawk with Packard's big 352-cid V-8

Plymouth's experimental gas-turbine car is driven from New York to Los Angeles

General Motors displays the XP-500 with a "free-piston" engine that burns a variety of fuels, including whale oil or peanut oil

American Motors develops an air-cooled V-4 that weighs only 200 pounds

A quad-headlamp system is announced by the Automobile Manufacturers Association, for 1958 models

The single-passenger Auto Cub runabout with tiller steering is developed

▲ Ford's "bubbletop" Skyliner became the '55 Fairlane Crown Victoria, which made a last appearance in 1956 due to plummeting sales: only 603 for '56.

▲ Like Chevy, Ford added a hardtop sedan for '56, a $2249 Town Victoria in the top-line Fairlane series, but model-year sales were modest: 32,111.

▲ Atypical for a wagon, this '56 Ford Country Squire wagon wears fender skirts; 23,221 were built.

◀ Seen here are a solid-roof '56 Ford Crown Vic and that year's Thunderbird, which was modestly updated with a "continental" spare and hardtop "portholes."

▲ Contrived "V-Line" styling and tri-tone paint made the '56 Hudsons look a lot busier than the '55s. This V-8 Hornet sedan is one of only 3490 built.

▲ The Hornet V-8 Hollywood hardtop was one of just six senior Hudson models for '56. Hudson built only 1282 V-8 hardtops that year, plus 358 with six-cylinder power.

▲ Hudson's six-cylinder '56 Hornets included this $2544 Super sedan. It looked slightly less gaudy than the V-8 models, but still showed plenty of hokiness. Total Hornet output: 10,671.

---

Dual-Ghia features a Dodge chassis/Italian body—and captures the attention of Hollywood celebrities

The El Morocco convertible and hardtop, based on the 1956-57 Chevrolet, is intended to impart the look of a Cadillac Eldorado

Oldsmobile's dramatic Golden Rocket show coupe sports an aerodynamic body; roof panels rise when the door is opened

Plymouth's Plainsman show wagon has its spare tire hidden inside the rear fender

Firebird II, a gas-turbine vehicle, appears at the '56 GM Motorama

Pontiac's wild Pontiac Club de Mer dream car stands only 38.4 inches tall

▲ Imperial grew longer and higher rear flanks for '56, but remained quite tastefully restrained. The mainstay four-door sedan listed at $4832 and pleased 6821 buyers.

▲ Lincoln was dramatically changed for '56 and scored dramatically improved sales: 50,322. A new uplevel Premiere series included this $4601 hardtop coupe.

▲ A big new 368 V-8 with 285 horses powered all '56 Lincolns, like this $4601 Premiere sedan. Lower-body styling had been previewed on recent Dearborn "dream cars."

◀ The $4747 Premiere convertible topped Lincoln's five-model '56 line-up, but garnered only 2447 sales. All Lincolns were bigger and heavier than the trim '55s.

▼ Elegant lines, superb semi-hand craftsmanship, and a startling $10,000 list price made Lincoln's reborn Continental, called the Mark II, unique among 1956 cars. The design was chosen from 13 proposals submitted during a four-year development program. The Mark II rode a generous 126-inch wheelbase.

**1956 Model Year Production**

| | | |
|---|---|---|
| 1. Chevrolet 1,567,117 | 8. Dodge 240,686 | 15. Hudson 22,588 |
| 2. Ford 1,408,478 | 9. Cadillac 154,577 | 16. Clipper 18,482 |
| 3. Buick 572,024 | 10. Chrysler 128,322 | 17. Imperial 10,684 |
| 4. Plymouth 571,634 | 11. DeSoto 109,442 | 18. Packard 10,353 |
| 5. Oldsmobile 485,458 | 12. Nash 83,420 | 19. Metropolitan 9,068[1] |
| 6. Pontiac 405,730 | 13. Studebaker 69,593 | 20. Continental 2,550 |
| 7. Mercury 327,943 | 14. Lincoln 50,322 | [1]*Calendar year sales* |

▲ The Mark II would have looked great as a convertible, but the idea went no further than this one prototype built in 1956 for Mrs. William Clay Ford.

▲ Mercury got a jazzy facelift for '56. The Custom series expanded from four to seven models. A two-door sedan cost $2351, and 16,343 were bought. This model weighed in at 3505 pounds.

▲ The '56 Customs again included Mercury's cheapest wagons: six- and eight-passenger models priced at $2722 and $2819. A bigger new 312 V-8 gave them 210/225 horses.

▲ Most '56 Mercs wore jazzy Z-line side moldings. Top-line Montclairs, like this $2765 hardtop coupe, got more go from a standard 312 V-8 with 235 horses.

▲ Mercury moved to hardtop sedans in a big way in 1956. Called Phaeton, Merc offered four, one in each series. This is the $2700 Monterey version, which found 10,726 customers.

▲ Added tinsel and tri-tone paint did nothing for Nash sales in 1956. Ambassadors, like this Custom sedan, found just 15,271 total buyers.

▲ Nash's long-famous reclining seats explain the vanity plate on this '56 Ambassador Custom sedan.

▲ The last of Nash's Series 54 Metropolitans were sold in '56.

1956 Buick Centurion show car.

1956 Pontiac Club de Mer show car.

1956 Packard Predictor show car.

▲ Oldsmobile's Rocket V-8 packed 230 horses in 88 models, such as this $2599 Holiday hardtop coupe, which topped the line in '56 sales at 74,739 units.

▲ The '56 Olds Ninety-Eight Starfire convertible shows the new bifurcated grille used on all models. At $3740, Starfire was Lansing's priciest offering—8581 were produced.

▲ Now at $5995, the Caribbean ragtop again led the Packard line for '56, which would be the last "real" Detroit-built models. Only 276 were sold.

▲ Clipper became a separate make for '56, but was still obviously a Packard. Here, the $3164 Custom Constellation hardtop coupe; 1466 found buyers.

▲ Another '56 Constellation shows the big "banana" taillamps and ship's-wheel emblems that helped set Clippers apart from Packards.

◄▲ *Left and above:* Big-Packard fronts on shorter Clipper bodies made for a new entry-level '56 senior line called Executive, a sedan and two-door hardtop priced around $3500. But no '56 Packard sold well, and Executive orders totaled just 2815.

▲ Plymouth returned for '56 with a modest facelift marked by higher fins and revised side trim. Here, the Belvedere convertible, which was newly up-priced to $2478.

▲ Even low-line '56 Plymouths like this $1883 Plaza two-door could be dressed up with optional duo-color "Sportone" trim, but rear fender skirts were non-stock.

▲ Heating up Plymouth's performance image for '56 was the new $2866 Fury hardtop with a 240-horse 303 V-8 and special gold-anodized side trim. Just 4485 were built.

▲ The '56 Pontiacs had a brighter—if still blunt—face. The line's only convertible again appeared in the top-shelf Star Chief series, priced at $2857, and 13,510 were sold.

▲ Pontiac's Safari "hardtop" wagon returned for '56 to score slightly improved sales of 4042 units. All models got a larger 316.6-cid V-8 with 192-285 bhp.

▲ Ramblers were totally redesigned on a 108-inch chassis. The $2494 Custom Cross Country was Detroit's first hardtop wagon.

▲ The '56 Rambler line also listed this Custom hardtop sedan, priced at $2224 without "continental" spare or new tri-tone paint. Weight was 2990 pounds.

▲ A deft makeover turned Studebaker coupes into 1956's new Hawk line of "family sports cars." Here, the $3061 V-8 Golden Hawk.

▲ A step below Studebaker's '56 Sky Hawk was the pillared Power Hawk, which carried a 259 V-8 instead of a 289 and sold for $2101.

▲ Studebaker's most affordable '56 family sports car was this six-cylinder, 101-bhp Flight Hawk, tagged at a modest $1986.

▲ A look at Studebaker's pillarless $2477 Sky Hawk. Renowned designer Raymond Loewy supervised its remarkably effective restyle.

▲ Pinehurst was the new '56 name for Studebaker's best wagon, trimmed and equipped to the top-line President level. List price was $2529. All wagons were two-doors.

▲ Despite fast-falling sales, non-coupe Studes were also fully restyled for '56. This lush, new long-wheelbase President Classic sedan sold for $2489.

▲ The '57 Buicks were longer, lower, and more rakish. A $4373 Riviera coupe highlighted the new top-level Roadmaster 75 series.

▲ Recent Buick styling "cues" were quite evident on the all-new '57s, such as this $3270 Century Riviera coupe; 17,029 were built.

▲ GM planned pillarless wagons like the $3706 Buick Century Caballero long before its '57 models bowed. Buyers ordered 10,186 copies.

▲ Cadillac also rebodied for 1957, and nicely blended boxy and rounded lines on the Eldorado Biarritz, whose price was up to a stiff $7286. Only 1800 were built.

▲ A more compact new ultra-luxury Cadillac bowed for '57 as the Eldorado Brougham, a show car-inspired hardtop sedan stratospherically priced at $13,074.

▲ Non-Eldorado '57 Caddys bore flat-top fins and blocky rear contours. Sales fell off—the $5256 Sedan de Ville dropped 43 percent to 23,808 units.

**1957**

The 42nd National Automobile Show—the first since 1940—is held at New York's new Coliseum in late 1956 to display the '57 models

This year's National Auto Show is the first to be televised; Vice President Nixon speaks at the banquet, gaining national exposure

The Automobile Manufacturers Association bans factory-sponsored racing, resolves to eliminate speed from auto advertising

Ford, with all-new styling, outsells Chevrolet for the model year: 1.67 million to 1.5 million

Plymouth retakes the Number Three ranking, ahead of Buick and Oldsmobile

▲ The "Classic Chevy" reached its peak in 1957 by offering Cadillac style and more go. The $2399 Bel Air V-8 Sport Coupe attracted 166,426 customers.

▲ Disappointing sales did in the $2857 Bel Air Nomad after just 6103 were built for 1957, though Chevy would continue using the name on conventional wagons.

▲ Chevy's V-8 grew to 283 cubes for '57 and offered up to 283 horses via new "Ramjet" fuel injection.

▲ A '57 Chevy Bel Air V-8 convertible like this costs a bundle now, but it sold new for just $2611 before options; 47,562 were built. Compared with Ford's canted blades and Plymouth's rear fenders, Chevy's fins were quite modest.

▲ A rapid rarity for sure was this '57 Chevy One-Fifty two-door with fuel injection, identified by the rear-fender insignia and script.

◄▲ Chevy made a mark in stock-car racing during 1957 thanks to the likes of Smokey Yunick (*left*) and Bob Welborn (*above*). But it all stopped—officially at least—when the automakers agreed with the Automobile Manufacturers Association to get out of racing in June.

---

The five-mile Mackinac Bridge opens, linking Michigan's Upper and Lower Peninsulas

An average car sells for $2749; the average worker now earns $4230 yearly

Nash and Hudson names are dropped after the '57 model year; '58 models are to be part of the Rambler line

Virgil Exner's sensational second-generation "Forward Look" styling is featured on all Chrysler products

Chrysler Corp. cars replace front coil springs with a torsion-bar suspension

Pontiac celebrates its Golden Anniversary; Oldsmobile marks its 60th

▲ Chevy crafted the lightweight Corvette Sebring Special to win the 12-hour Florida race in 1957. It was fast—but unfortunately failed to finish.

▲ The production Corvette changed little outside, but the new 283 V-8s offered from 220 to 283 horses, the latter via Chevy's new "Ramjet" fuel injection.

◀ Ruben Allender's Chevy-based El Morocco looked even more Cadillac-like for '57, but only 16 were built, spread among three body styles.

▶ The '57 El Morocco came as this convertible, as well as coupe and sedan hardtops. High prices kept sales low, killing the project.

▲ Chrysler's all-new 1957 300-C got its own front end and 375 or 390 horses. Here it leads a 1957 Speed Weeks parade at Daytona Beach.

---

Fuel injection is optional on Chevrolet and Pontiac

American cars begin the switch to quad headlamps, but they're ruled illegal (temporarily) in several states

Buicks get an ambitious restyle; Cadillac's reworking is inspired by the earlier Eldorado Brougham and Park Avenue show cars

Cadillac's $13,074 Eldorado Brougham features a brushed aluminum roof, air suspension, and quad headlights

Corvette boasts a 283-cid V-8 that develops one horsepower per cubic inch with fuel injection

▲ Soaring fins, acres of glass, and a lower "dart" profile marked all '57 Chryslers. Shown here is the $4202 New Yorker hardtop coupe.

◀ All '57 Chryslers were stunningly restyled. Here, the New Yorker convertible, which cost $4638 and saw only 1049 examples produced.

▲ Adventurer became DeSoto's top-line '57 series and added this $4272 convertible. Horses were up to 345, but only 300 of these ragtops were built.

▲ Like Chryslers, the '57 DeSotos were dramatically restyled, though "Tri-Tower" taillamps remained. This Adventurer hardtop coupe is one of 1650 built.

▲ Dodge's equally new '57 design was billed as "Swept-Wing Styling." This Coronet Lancer hardtop coupe sold for $2580 with standard V-8.

▲ The limited-edition Dual-Ghia was evolved by Detroit trucking mogul Gene Cassaroll from the 1953-54 Dodge Firearrow show cars. It bowed in 1957 as this $7646 Dodge-powered convertible. Only 103 or 104 were built through 1958.

---

Triple-turbine Turboglide automatic is available on Chevrolets

A D-500 package gives Dodge's Hemi V-8 up to 340 horsepower

Ford sports a sculptured restyle; Fairlanes are inspired by the Mystere show car

Ford's unique Skyliner retractable hardtop debuts; so does the Ranchero car-pickup

The "classic" Ford Thunderbird sports canted fins in its final two-seat season; a supercharged 312-cid V-8 thunders out 300/340 bhp

Imperial displays curved side-window glass and nearly beats Lincoln in production

The gadget-packed Mercury Turnpike Cruiser features a retractable rear window and 49-position driver's seat

▲ Model-year 1957 brought the first all-new Fords since 1952: longer, lower, wider, heavier. A new top-line Fairlane 500 series included this $2404 Victoria hardtop sedan; 68,550 were built.

▲ The '57 Ford Sunliner was another new Fairlane 500 model offering V-8 options from 272 to 312 cubic inches and 190 to 245 horses. Priced at $2505, the '57 Sunliner saw very respectable sales of 77,726.

▲ Reviving the prewar car/pickup idea was Ford's '57 Ranchero, offered in Custom trim (*shown*) and as a basic standard model.

◀ Ford scored a Detroit first with the '57 Fairlane 500 Skyliner and its novel retracting metal hardtop. This multi-exposure view shows how it worked. Priced at $2942, the '57 model won 20,766 orders.

▲ At around $2500, the popular Ford Country Sedan (186,889 built) seated six or eight passengers on its 116-inch chassis.

▲ This $1991 Tudor sedan was one of three base Custom models that fell just below the Custom 300 series.

---

Station wagons return to the Oldsmobile lineup for the first time since 1950

A J-2 Rocket triple-carb option gives Oldsmobiles 300 horsepower

Packards, now built in South Bend alongside similar Studebakers, are powered by a supercharged V-8

The Packard Clipper comes in station wagon form—Packard's first since 1950

Pontiac's fast and flashy Bonneville convertible comes with fuel injection or Tri-Power (triple carburetion)

A super-quick Rambler Rebel four-door hardtop arrives at mid-year, powered by a 327-cid V-8

▲ Thunderbird was handsomely restyled for '57, the last year for the original two-seater concept. Exactly 21,380 were built. Base price was $3408.

◄ Ford's Thunderbird offered a new instrument panel for '57, plus "Lifeguard Design" features like the dished steering wheel and padded dash seen here.

▲ Joe Weatherly's Ford leads Billy Myers' Mercury in a convertible race at Daytona in early '57. Detroit soon put all factory racing in limbo.

▲ Chuck Daigh in the modified '56 T-Bird he drove at the 1956-57 Daytona Speed Weeks. It was fast, but rival Corvettes were faster.

▲ Hudson cut back to four models for '57, all V-8 Hornets. This Custom Hollywood hardtop cost $3101 and weighed 3693 pounds.

▲ Years of declining sales sealed Hudson's fate after 1957 and just 4180 final cars. Here, the $3011 Hornet Custom four-door sedan.

▲ Hudson went out after '57 with only minor styling changes from '56. The "Continental" spare shown here was a factory option.

## 1957 Model Year Production

|  |  |  |
|---|---|---|
| 1. | Ford | 1,676,449 |
| 2. | Chevrolet | 1,505,910 |
| 3. | Plymouth | 726,009 |
| 4. | Buick | 405,086 |
| 5. | Oldsmobile | 384,390 |
| 6. | Pontiac | 334,041 |
| 7. | Dodge | 287,608 |
| 8. | Mercury | 286,163 |
| 9. | Cadillac | 146,841 |
| 10. | DeSoto | 126,514 |
| 11. | Chrysler | 122,273 |
| 12. | Rambler | 91,469 |
| 13. | Studebaker | 63,101 |
| 14. | Lincoln | 41,123 |
| 15. | Imperial | 37,593 |
| 16. | Metropolitan | 15,317[1] |
| 17. | Nash | 10,330 |
| 18. | Packard | 4,809 |
| 19. | Hudson | 4,180 |
| 20. | Continental | 462 |

[1] *Calendar year sales*

▲ Imperial was all-new for '57, and sales would prove the best in the make's history: 37,593 units. Seen here is the $5406 Crown Southampton hardtop sedan.

▲ The '57 Imperial Crown Southampton rode a 129-inch wheelbase and measured 224.2 inches long. A dummy trunklid spare tire was a dubious new styling idea.

▲ The '57 Lincolns were '56s with big canted fins and stacked quad headlights tacked on. Here, the $5381 Premiere convertible.

▲ Lincoln belatedly added hardtop sedans for '57. This uplevel Premiere Landau listed at $5294 and attracted 11,223 orders.

▲ The '57 Lincoln Premiere hardtop coupe cost $5149 and sold 15,185 copies. The new '57 fins were huge—but fairly tasteful.

▲ The ultra-luxury Continental Mark II returned for '57 with 15 more horsepower, 300 total, as the major change. Exactly 3012 1956-57 models were built before Ford abandoned its flagship as unprofitable.

---

Studebaker offers budget-priced, minimal-trim Scotsman models

The freshly finned Golden Hawk exchanges its Packard V-8 for a 275-bhp Studebaker V-8, breathing through a Paxton supercharger

Most domestic cars now ride on 14-inch wheels

Several makes offer optional six-way power seats

Luxury cars come with electric door locks

Some cars have a speedometer buzzer that sounds when a pre-set speed is reached

Several makes offer optional limited-slip differentials

▲ Mercury added a Turnpike Cruiser convertible to its line of bigger and gaudier all-new '57s to win Indy 500 pace-car honors. Regular ragtop Cruisers sold for $4103, but only 1265 of the '57s were called for.

▲ All '57 Mercurys looked like something from outer space, but none more than Turnpike Cruisers like this $3758 hardtop coupe. Only 7291 were sold.

▲ The $3849 Cruiser hardtop sedan had a drop-down rear window among many "space age" gimmicks. This model found only 8305 customers.

▲ Built from a '57 Merc Monterey, the "Mermaid" raced to 159.9 mph in its only run, at Daytona.

▲ Nash, like partner Hudson, finally succumbed to insufficient sales and was put out to pasture after '57. The final lineup shrunk to four Ambassadors, including this $2847 Custom Country Club hardtop.

▲ Before it departed, Nash pioneered quad headlamps on its '57 models, like this $2670 Country Club hardtop coupe in base Super trim. A total of 10,330 '57 Nashes were built, after which American Motors hitched its star exclusively to compact Ramblers.

---

Jack Kerouac publishes *On the Road,* the "bible" of the forthcoming Beat Generation

John Keats writes *The Insolent Chariots,* a devastating comic critique of the auto trade

Pontiac's Firebird III was introduced at the '59 Motorama.

▲ Olds was all-new for '57, but rather stodgy next to rival Chrysler products. This Starfire Ninety-Eight Holiday cost $3937, and attracted 17,791 customers.

► All '57 Olds Ninety-Eights were Starfires, not just the convertible (shown here with a non-factory "continental kit"). This ragtop listed at $4217; 8278 were produced.

◄ The first Olds wagons since 1950 bowed for '57 as a trio of four-door Fiesta models. This hardtop Golden Rocket Super 88 was also offered in the standard 88 line along with a pillared companion. This Super 88 sold for $3541 and attracted a modest 8981 sales, compared to 10,819 88s.

▲ Veteran Olds driver Lee Petty leads a '57 Chevy in a convertible race at Daytona. Petty's son Richard later became the king of NASCAR stock-car racing.

▲ Plymouth naturally shared in Highland Park's total '57 redesign, emerging bigger, bolder, and better-handling. Here, the $2419 Belvedere Sport Sedan.

▲ The limited-edition Fury hardtop returned for '57 with Plymouth's handsome new styling, a 290-horse 318 V-8, and a $2925 price. Just 7438 were built.

◀ The '57 Packards became gussied-up Studebakers in a ploy to save money. This $3212 Clipper Town Sedan was one of only two models.

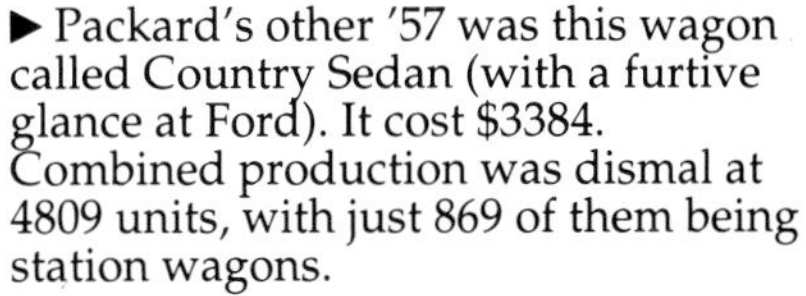

▶ Packard's other '57 was this wagon called Country Sedan (with a furtive glance at Ford). It cost $3384. Combined production was dismal at 4809 units, with just 869 of them being station wagons.

▲ Pontiac raced more actively in 1957. Here, Cotten Owens bends his new Chieftain stocker into a turn ahead of a Chevy and two other Ponchos.

▲ Pontiac's first Bonneville bowed as a 1957 convertible to bolster a more youthful divisional image. Priced at $5782, it saw 630 copies, most used for promotion purposes.

▲ Pontiac's original "hardtop" Safari wagon departed after 1957 and a final run of 1292 units.

▲ Only a bit more saleable was Pontiac's second '57 Safari, a $3636 four-door; 1894 were built.

▲ The Pontiac V-8 grew for a third time in as many years when it was punched out to 347 cubes for '57.

▲ An unexpected Rambler was the hot limited-edition '57 Rebel hardtop sedan with a 255-horse 327 V-8.

▲ The fast, flashy $2786 Rebel was hardly in Rambler's economy image, and only 1500 were built.

▲ Desperately seeking '57 sales, Studebaker added cheap Scotsman models like this $1995 wagon.

▲ Stude also offered new four-door wagons for '57. This is the lush $2666 President Broadmoor.

▲ To save money, Studebaker trimmed '57 Hawks from four to two. New was this $2263 Silver Hawk V-8.

▲ Stude's other '57 sportster was the $3182 Golden Hawk with a hot 275-bhp supercharged 289 V-8.

▲ Buick vied with Olds as 1958's "glitter king." This $5125 ragtop, one of 839 built, was one of three models in a newly revived top-of-the-line Limited series.

▲ Buick's shiny '58 Limiteds also counted two Rivieras. This coupe cost $5002; just 1026 were built.

▲ No fewer than 160 chrome squares made up the '58 grille. Here, the $2416 Special four-door sedan.

▲ No '58 Buick sold well, so this ragtop Century is a now quite a rarity—only 2588 were built.

▲ Cadillac's Eldorado Brougham was outwardly unchanged for '58, but horsepower rose by 10 to 335. Customers bought just 304 of these $13,074 cars.

**1958**

America suffers its worst recession of the postwar era—car sales plummet 31.4 percent for the model year

Only 987,945 Fords are built, compared to Chevrolet's 1.14 million; Plymouth is third again

Oldsmobile captures fourth place, ahead of rapidly falling Buick

Imports take an unprecedented 8.1 percent of total new-car sales

Unemployment hits 5,437,000 in June—the highest since 1941

▲ Regular Caddys received a facelift that was fairly restrained for 1958. This Eldorado Seville hardtop coupe cost $7500 and won over a mere 855 customers.

▲ The Eldorado Biarritz and its hardtop Seville cousin retained a rounded rump for '58. Also priced at $7500, the ragtop garnered a lowly 815 sales.

▲ All-new show car-inspired styling was featured on 1958 Chevys (*bottom*) and the Corvette (*immediately above*). Providing previews were the experimental 1955 Biscayne (*top left*) and Sebring SS (*far right*).

▲ Chevy reached upmarket with its new 1958 Bel Air Impala models. This ragtop stickered at $2734.

▲ The '58 Impalas sold well despite stiff-for-Chevy prices. This Sport Coupe started at $2586.

▲ Chevy's mid-range series for '58 was the new Biscayne. This is the $2236 two-door sedan version.

---

The long-rumored mid-price Edsel debuts with pushbutton transmission controls in the steering wheel hub

Studebaker-Packard announces a halt to Packard production, to focus on the upcoming compact Lark

Chrysler products begin to abandon Hemi V-8s in favor of the cheaper-to-produce wedge-head configuration

The Automobile Information Disclosure Act—"price label law"—is passed; window stickers must show make, model, serial number, and suggested retail price

Nearly all makes/models adopt the quad-headlamp setup

▲ Chrome trunklid strips would be exclusive to the '58 Corvette, which started at $3631 and had 230 standard horsepower.

◀ A new third-generation Corvette arrived for 1958 with a quad-lamp front, more chrome, and slightly increased weight. Available power rose to 290 with fuel injection. Production jumped to 9168 units.

▲ Chrysler facelifted its year-old "Forward Look" for '58. The New Yorker hardtop coupe listed at $4347.

▲ Chrysler's '58 New Yorker hardtop coupe, of which 3205 were built, sported new trim and taillights.

▲ DeSoto suffered more than most medium-priced makes in the 1958 recession—output skidded to 49,445. Seen here is the top-line Adventurer hardtop coupe.

▲ The 1958 DeSoto Adventurer hardtop sold for $4071 and offered 345 or 355 horsepower from a new wedge-head 361 V-8. Just 350 of these cars were built.

---

GM celebrates the 50th Anniversary of its incorporation

Ford marks the 50th Anniversary of the Model T by reassembling a 1909 model at its New Jersey plant

The chrome-laden "B-58" Buick ranks as one of most garish designs of the year; Flight-Pitch triple-turbine Dynaflow debuts

Buick dealers now sell the German-built Opel subcompact; Pontiac dealers take on the British Vauxhall

Chevrolet adds two luxury Impala models and a 348-cid V-8

DeSoto output shrinks below 50,000, the lowest since 1938; even Edsel sells more cars

Adventurer is the most costly DeSoto ever—and the fastest

▲ Like sister MoPar models, the "Swept-Wing" '57 Dodges were modestly facelifted for '58. This factory photo shows a sampling of the lineup.

▲ At $3298, the Custom Royal Lancer remained Dodge's premium ragtop for '58. Just 1139 were built.

▲ Dodge's Coronet hardtop, here in springtime trim, again offered plenty of style. Price was $2679.

▲ Dodge added this Regal Lancer hardtop coupe to the Custom Royal line at mid-1958 as a limited-edition paint-and-trim "spring special." Base price was $3245—just $53 below the convertible. Only 1163 were sold.

---

A handful of Dodges go on sale with fuel-injected 361-cid engines

Ford debuts the unibody four-passenger Thunderbird, pioneering the "personal-luxury" car; it easily outsells former two-seater

Fords get a heavy facelift and big-block V-8s

Lincoln fields the largest unibody cars ever built; the Continental Mark III is now Lincoln-based

Lincoln's 430-cid V-8 is the biggest U.S. engine

The last Packards go on sale; the Hawk is a weird luxury version of the Studebaker Golden Hawk, sporting outside "armrests"

Short-wheelbase Ramblers, called American, return alongside a new long-wheelbase Rambler Ambassador series

▲ Ford president Henry Ford II chauffeurs brothers Benson and William Clay in this publicity shot staged to launch the new 1958 Edsel. This top-line Citation ragtop cost $3801, but just 930 were called for.

▲ Edsel manager Richard Kravke stands behind Ford design chief George Walker and Benson Ford.

▲ Edsel's second '58 ragtop was this Ford-based Pacer version, priced at $3028. Just 1876 were built.

▲ A more popular '58 Edsel Pacer was the $2805 hardtop coupe, which attracted 6139 buyers.

▲ This fully restored Citation convertible shows off Edsel's 1958 "gull-wing" taillamps, finless deck, and expansive bodyside/back-panel two-toning.

▲ Edsel's top '58 wagon was the Ford-based Bermuda with woody-look side trim. Only 2235 were built, split between six- and nine-passenger models.

All GM makes offer optional air suspension; all are troublesome and soon abandoned

Other makes plan for air suspension, but give up the idea

Remote-controlled mirrors are offered on Cadillac and Lincoln/Continental

Paper air-cleaner elements are found on some of the latest engines

Some Chrysler Corp. cars display a double compound windshield that extends into the roofline

Automatic speed control is offered on Cadillac, Chrysler, and Imperial

▲ Ford's Thunderbird switched from two to four seats in a full 1958 redesign. The convertible was a late arrival at $3929, limiting output to 2134 units.

▲ Ford Division chief Robert S. McNamara (*front*) and colleagues show some of their 1958 wares. McNamara was later President Kennedy's Defense Secretary.

▲ The '58 passenger Fords borrowed styling cues from the new four-seat T-Bird, mostly up front. Here, the Fairlane 500 Victoria coupe, priced at $2435; 80,439 were built.

▲ This '58 Ford Fairlane 500 Sunliner is accessorized with fender skirts and a "continental kit." Base-priced at $2650, the model sold 35,029 copies.

▲ The $2397 two-door Ranch Wagon, Ford's cheapest '58 wagon, accounted for 34,578 deliveries. A new $2451 four-door stablemate landed another 32,854 sales.

### 1958 Model Year Production

| | | |
|---|---|---|
| 1. Chevrolet 1,142,460 | 8. Dodge 137,861 | 15. Lincoln 17,134 |
| 2. Ford 987,945 | 9. Mercury 133,271 | 16. Imperial 16,133 |
| 3. Plymouth 443,799 | 10. Cadillac 121,778 | 17. Metropolitan 13,128[1] |
| 4. Oldsmobile 294,374 | 11. Chrysler 63,681 | 18. Continental 12,550 |
| 5. Buick 241,892 | 12. Edsel 63,110 | 19. Packard 2,622 |
| 6. Pontiac 217,303 | 13. DeSoto 49,445 | [1]*Calendar year sales* |
| 7. Rambler 162,182 | 14. Studebaker 44,759 | |

▲ A light 1958 restyle preserved Imperial's good looks, as on this Crown Southampton coupe. Production, however, was well down to 1939 units.

▲ Pride of the Lincoln line for '58 was this massive new Continental Mark III convertible, priced at a stiff $6283. Sales came to 3048.

▲ Non-Mark '58 Lincolns used the same massive new unibody design and 131-inch wheelbase. This is the $4794 Capri Landau hardtop sedan; 3084 were sold.

▲ A pair of Lincoln-Mercury executives try out a Mark III convertible in this 1958 factory press photo taken at Ford's Dearborn Proving Grounds. Up on the hill are trios of the facelifted '58 Mercurys (*left*) and all-new Lincolns.

---

Studebaker President and Commander series add a hardtop body style

GM displays the experimental Firebird III with a single-stick control system (no steering wheel or pedals); it steers itself over a special road via a wire buried in the road surface

Plymouth's Cabaña hardtop show wagon has a sliding sunroof

Ford displays a model Glideair vehicle that travels on a thin cushion of air

▲ The lightly restyled '58 Mercurys sported even more gingerbread, as seen on this $3536 Montclair ragtop wearing "cruiser skirts."

▲ Mercury Turnpike Cruisers thinned to a pair of Montclair hardtops for '58. At $3498, the two-door attracted a mere 2864 customers.

▲ The woody-look, hardtop-styled Colony Park remained Mercury's top-shelf wagon for '58. Just 4474 were sold at $3775 apiece.

▲ Oldsmobile Fiesta wagons, like the $3623 Super 88, returned from 1957 with the same blunted new front and excess chrome as other '58 models. This model weighed in at 4334 pounds and sold to an audience of 5175.

▲ A pull-out "Trans-Portable" transistor radio was an innovative new Olds option. Total '58 Olds sales: 294,374.

▲ For 1958, Olds again offered a convertible in all three of its series. This mid-range Super 88 version cost $3529 and attracted 3799 customers.

▲ The Super 88 Holiday hardtop coupe shows why '58 Oldsmobiles are now remembered as "Chromesmobiles." Base-priced at $3262, this model got 18,653 sales.

---

The Bocar XP-4 sports car goes into production with Chevy or Pontiac V-8 power

A two-seater economy car, the Colt, uses a one-cylinder engine

The Corvette-powered Devin SS sports car is marketed in kit or assembled form

The German-built Ford Taunus enters the U.S. market; the first few Toyotas—called Toyopets—and Datsuns arrive from Japan

▲ After a year's absence, Packard's hardtop coupe returned for '58 as this Studebaker-based model with clumsy styling add-ons. Customers didn't approve—only 675 were built.

▲ The hardtop was one of four '58 "Packardbakers" that ended the once-great Packard marque after just 2622 total sales. The hardtop listed at $3262.

▲ The first and last Packard Hawk was a Studebaker Hawk with a "fish-mouth" front and 275-horse Stude supercharged V-8. Only 588 were sold.

▲ Like the '57 Packards, the '58s were built in the Studebaker plant in South Bend, Indiana. Rarest of all is this wagon—a mere 159 had been assembled when management abandoned Packard as no longer profitable. The price tag for this model read $3384.

▲ Quad headlights and a horizontal-bar lower grille were among the trim changes identifying the '58 Plymouths. The Belvedere Sport Sedan hardtop stickered at $2528; 18,194 were sold.

▲ Plymouth's mid-range Savoy series again included a Sport Coupe two-door hardtop for '58. Base price was $2329, and 19,500 were built.

▲ A simple full-length side molding identified Plymouth's mid-range Savoys for '58. Bodyside two-toning, called Sportone, was optional. The year's best-seller was this $2305 six-cylinder, four-door Savoy, which found favor with 67,993 new car buyers, many of whom paid $100 extra for a V-8.

▲ Bonneville remained Pontiac's best for '58 and added this $3481 hardtop coupe. Fender script here identifies optional fuel injection with 310 horses. Production reached 9144.

▲ Like all '58 Pontiacs, the $3586 Bonneville ragtop boasted fully changed "New Direction" styling and more zip from six 370-cid V-8s with 240 to 310 bhp. Output: 3096.

▲ Special dummy side scoops identified '58 Pontiac Star Chiefs like this Catalina hardtop coupe, which sold for $3122. Buyers bought 13,888 examples.

▲ Like Chevrolet, the '58 Pontiac would be a one-year-only design. This Star Chief Safari wagon was one of just 2905 built. It sold new for $3350.

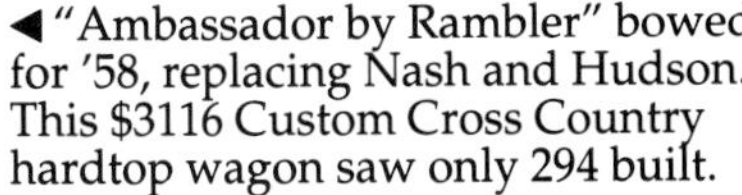

▲ Regular '58 Ramblers were divided into V-8 Rebels and six-cylinder models. The latter included this $2327 Custom four-door sedan.

◄ "Ambassador by Rambler" bowed for '58, replacing Nash and Hudson. This $3116 Custom Cross Country hardtop wagon saw only 294 built.

▲ Studebakers wore ugly fins and other tacked-on touches for '58. This $2378 Commander four-door sedan found only 6771 takers.

▲ Three bare-bones Scotsman models were Stude's best-sellers—20,872 units—but this $1795 two-door sedan recorded just 5538 sales.

▲ Studebaker's President Starlight hardtop coupe was a '58 newcomer at $2695, but only 1171 were built in that dismal sales year.

▲ The Argonaut was hyped in 1959 as an aluminum-bodied super-luxury car in seven models—like this two-seat "Smoke" coupe, with an air-cooled, overhead-cam V-12 and $25,000-$36,000 prices. Plans went no further than sketches.

◀ The '59 Buicks were a happy change from the '58s. Here, the $3129 convertible and $2925 hardtop sedan in new entry-level LeSabre trim.

▲ The LeSabre four-door sedan took over from its Special predecessor as Buick's best-selling '59 model: 51,379 were built. The price started at $2804, but options often added $1000.

◀ Invicta replaced the Century as Buick's mid-range series for '59. Among its five models was this hardtop sedan priced at $3515. It proved the most popular Invicta by attracting 20,156 customers.

◀ Buick's '59 flagship was this $4192 Electra 225 convertible, one of three models in that new top-line group. Production came to only 5493 units, the second lowest total in the line.

**1959**

Model-year auto output expands by 30.7 percent to more than 5.5 million units

Studebaker-Packard launches its compact Lark; the compact-car race begins in earnest

Chevrolet and Ford race neck-and-neck in production, topping 1.4 million cars; Chevy barely edges ahead for the model year

Plymouth finishes third, followed by Pontiac and Oldsmobile

All GM cars share a basic bodyshell, but with vastly different styling

▲ Like Buick, Cadillac gained all-new styling and huge fins for '59, but the results were debatable. Here, the $5455 Series Sixty-Two ragtop. Sales rose to 11,130.

▲ Tailfins reached record heights with the '59 Cadillacs, but would go no higher. This is the $7401 Eldorado Seville hardtop coupe; just 975 were built.

▲ Cadillac's '59 hardtop sedans offered six-window styling, as on this $5080 Series Sixty-Two—or a flat-top four-window roofline for the same money.

▲ The '59 Cadillac Eldorado Brougham was a larger hardtop sedan built by Italy's Pinin Farina, but workmanship wasn't as good as on the 1957-58 original. Only 99 of the '59s were built. Base price remained $13,075.

▲ Cadillac's '59 Eldorado Biarritz ragtop (*above*) and Seville hardtop shared rear-end styling with other models, so their main visual distinction was just wider bodyside moldings. All '59 Caddys used a newly stroked 390 cubic-inch V-8 with 325 horses except on Eldos, which got 345. Still, the Eldorado had entered a period of decline that wouldn't end until 1967. At $7401, the '59 Biarritz attracted just 1320 well-heeled customers.

---

Imported cars hit record sales with a 62-percent increase over 1958

The federal gasoline tax is raised from 3 to 4 cents per gallon

The Automobile Manufacturers Association announces that a crankcase-ventilation device to cut hydrocarbon emissions will go on all cars sold in California, effective with the '61 models

Buick renames its entire model lineup; a 401-cid V-8 is standard in the three top series

Cadillacs boast a new 390-cid V-8 and flaunt massive tailfins

▲ Chevy was "all new all over again" for '59, and wilder-looking than ever. The Impala Sport Coupe shown here was part of a new full top-line series. It sold for $2599 with six, $2717 with base V-8.

▲ Like all '59 Chevys, the Impala convertible sported a "bat-fin" rear and acres more glass in a hasty reply to Chrysler Corporation's trend-setting '57 styling. The $2967 ragtop was popular—65,800 were sold.

▲ This airy Sport Sedan and a pillared four-door were added to make Impala Chevy's new full-range top-line series for '59. The hardtop sedan sold for $2664 with six, $2782 with base V-8.

▲ Chevy replied to Ford's Ranchero in '59 with the El Camino, a two-door wagon with a pickup box instead of a rear cargo bay. An abbreviated roofline mimicked that of the hardtop sedans. Wheelbase was 119 inches.

▲ Because its all-new '59s were quite a bit lower than the '58s, Chevy issued these "how-to" photos with recommended body English for maintaining a semblance of modesty when entering the car.

---

Chevrolet offers an optional fully synchronized four-speed manual gearbox; Corvette already has one

Most Chryslers are powered by a 383-cid wedge V-8; Hemis are gone

Chrysler's 300-E gets 380 horsepower from a 413-cid V-8

Swivel semi-bucket seats are available on Chrysler products

This is the final year for the hoary Dodge/Plymouth L-head six

DeSotos receive a heavy facelift, but sales continue to be glum

A Galaxie luxury series sporting a Thunderbird roofline joins the Ford line

Ford Thunderbirds can have a huge 430-cid Lincoln V-8

▲ Chevy's Corvette sports car lost some needless tinsel for '59, and gained rear radius rods that improved handling. Horsepower was unchanged, but output rose about 500 to a healthier 9670 units. Curb weight was 2840 pounds.

▲ Indented bodyside "coves" remained a Corvette hallmark for '59, and were often two-toned to match the color of the soft-top, as shown here. Base sticker price rose $244 from 1958 to $3875. As since 1953, wheelbase was 102 inches.

◀ GM's new design chief Bill Mitchell built his experimental Stingray on the "mule" chassis rescued from the abortive '57 Sebring SS project. The basic shape would appear on post-1962 showroom Corvettes.

▲ Chrysler Division chief engineer Bob Rodger fathered the original 300. Here he shows off the new 380-horse wedge-head engine of the '59 300-E.

◀ Mitchell's Stingray (#111) was designed specifically for racing, and he campaigned it privately with good success starting in 1959.

Lincoln's Continental Mark IV line includes a limited-production Town Car and limousine

AMC's Metropolitan adds a trunk-lid and vent windows

Pontiac introduces a split grille design and "Wide-Track" stance

AMC earns a $60 million profit while building a record 374,000 Ramblers

Studebaker drops the Golden Hawk and issues a non-super-charged Silver Hawk; the new Lark comes with an L-head six or 259-cid V-8

The Checker Superba passenger car, an upgraded taxicab, goes on display in May

A caravan of 16 vehicles drives 4239 miles, from Detroit to Alaska's Susitan Valley, to move into homesteads in the new 49th state

▲ A rather uninspired facelift marked 1959's "Lion-Hearted" Chryslers. Windsors like this $3289 hardtop coupe used a new 305-horse 383 V-8; 6675 were built.

▲ The '59 Chryslers gained more than 6000 sales over the '58s, but the $4890 New Yorker convertible dropped from 666 to a mere 286.

▲ Chrysler's '59 300-E kept the big trapezoid grille from 1957-58 and looked better for it. The $5319 hardtop weighed 4290 pounds.

▲ The '59 300-E convertible stickered at $5749, but garnered a mere 140 orders versus the hardtop's 550, a record Letter-Series low.

▲ Police in Hialeah, Florida, chose Dodge Coronets with the hot D-500 package for patrol duty in 1959, which meant a 383 wedge-head V-8 with 320 or 345 horsepower.

◀ Optional swivel front seats were a new Chrysler gimmick for 1959, demonstrated here on a Dodge Custom Royal hardtop sedan.

---

Curtiss-Wright Corp. and NSU Werke of West Germany announce a "rotary" internal combustion engine with few moving parts

Willys announces a deluxe Jeep Station Wagon known as the Maverick Special

Buicks adopt a seat lock to prevent the passenger's front seatback from moving forward suddenly

Chrysler offers an electronic control that changes the rear-view mirror to non-glare when a headlamp beam hits its surface

Oldsmobiles have flanged brake drums for quicker cooling

The luxury hand-built aluminum Argonaut debuts—but production never happens

▲ Like its MoPar sisters, Dodge's '59 facelift was heavy but not that successful. This $3422 Custom Royal ragtop was one of only 974 built.

▲ Special fin badges signal the hot D-500 engine option on this $3201 Custom Royal Lancer hardtop coupe, which enticed 6278 buyers.

▲ DeSoto's Adventurer was still hot for '59, but overall make output cooled to 45,734 units. Just 590 of these hardtops were built.

▲ This '59 DeSoto Fireflite four-door sedan wears a simple monotone finish. The base price was $3763, and 4480 were produced for the model run.

◀ Dearborn's top managers in 1959, with new president Robert McNamara in the center, pose with that year's "Ford Family of Fine Cars" in a company publicity photo. Above (*from left*) are the $3425 Edsel Corsair hardtop sedan, $6845 Lincoln Continental Mark IV Landau hardtop sedan, and the $4031 Mercury Park Lane hardtop sedan. Below are the $3979 Ford Thunderbird convertible (*left*) and the $2537 Ford Fairlane 500 Victoria hardtop coupe.

## 1959 Model Year Production

| | | | | | |
|---|---|---|---|---|---|
| 1. Chevrolet | 1,462,140 | 7. Buick | 285,089 | 13. DeSoto | 45,734 |
| 2. Ford | 1,450,953 | 8. Dodge | 156,385 | 14. Edsel | 44,891 |
| 3. Plymouth | 458,261 | 9. Mercury | 150,000 | 15. Lincoln/Continental | 26,906 |
| 4. Pontiac | 383,320 | 10. Cadillac | 142,272 | 16. Metropolitan | 22,209[1] |
| 5. Oldsmobile | 382,865 | 11. Studebaker | 126,156 | 17. Imperial | 17,269 |
| 6. Rambler | 374,240 | 12. Chrysler | 69,970 | | |

[1] *Calendar year sales*

◀▲ Reflecting poor first-year sales, Edsel returned for '59 with only Ford-based models, lower prices, fewer gimmicks, and somewhat more conservative styling. The top-line Corsair convertible (*left*) cost $3072 and saw only 1343 copies. The bottom-line $2629 Ranger two-door sedan (*above*) sold a bit better: 7778 units. Total Edsel production for the year totaled 44,891.

▲ This $3346 Skyliner "retrac" shows the extensive but tasteful restyle that helped Ford outsell Chevy for the 1959 calendar year. Ford's total: 1,450,953.

▲ A part of 1959's new Fairlane 500 Galaxie sub-series, the Skyliner managed 12,915 sales—too few for Ford to continue the model.

▲ Ford's Thunderbird scored higher '59 sales despite few changes. The $3696 hardtop coupe was again the mainstay with 57,195 orders.

▲ Pretty in pink or burgundy, Ford's '59 Thunderbird convertible, which weighed 3903 pounds, attracted 10,261 orders. The "Continental kit" cost extra.

▲ Although overshadowed by the $61-more-expensive Victoria hardtop coupe, the $2528 Ford Galaxie Club Sedan nonetheless attracted 52,848 buyers in 1959.

1959 Cadillac Cyclone show car.

▲ The rarest of post-1954 Imperials are the special Ghia-built Crown Imperial limousines. This is one of only seven built to 1959 specs. Cost: $15,075.

▲ Mainstream Imperials got a toothy grille for '59, plus a big new 413-cid, 350-bhp wedge-head V-8. The $5403 Crown Southampton coupe saw 1728 produced.

▲ Continental went from separate make to Lincoln series for '59. The little-changed Mark IV Landau hardtop sedan attracted 6146 buyers.

◀ Few changes also attended Lincoln's non-Mark 1959 models. This base-series (*nee* Capri) four-door Landau listed at $5090, and 4417 were purchased.

▲ Mercury's '59s were fairly tasteful despite newly added bulk. At $4206, this Park Lane convertible was the priciest model. Only 1257 were built.

◀ The "Big M" grew bigger with Mercury's all-new '59 design. Here, the Montclair Cruiser hardtop sedan.

---

The Asardo fiberglass-bodied sport coupe carries an Alfa Romeo engine, but dies aborning

Experimental vehicles include the DeSoto Cella, which converts liquid fuel into electrical energy; Cadillac Cyclone, with a radar object-warning system; plus the Ford Levacar and Curtiss-Wright, which float on a cushion of air

▲ Oldsmobile touted "The Linear Look" for its bigger all-new '59s like this $3036 Dynamic 88 Holiday hardtop sedan, of which 48,707 were sold.

▲ An airy, thin-pillar roofline prompted the name "SceniCoupe" for '59 Olds two-door hardtops. This top-line Ninety-Eight was base priced at $4086 and 13,669 were sold.

▲ Olds continued offering three ragtops for '59, with the Dynamic 88 the most affordable at $3286. Here is one of 8491 examples built during the model run.

▲ Oldsmobile four-door sedans were called Celebrity for '59. The $3890 Ninety-Eight found 23,106 buyers and ran with a new 315-bhp, 394-cid Rocket V-8.

▲ The heavily restyled '59 Plymouths were basically 1957-58 underneath. A new Sport Fury line included this $3125 convertible, of which 5990 were sold.

▲ Chrysler's terrific new-for-'57 TorqueFlite automatic retained push-button control for '59. This is the panel Plymouth used.

◀ Sport Fury was Plymouth's performance offering for '59. The $2927 hardtop coupe enjoyed a production run of 17,867 units.

▲ Pontiac soared to fourth in industry sales with its handsome all-new "Wide-Track" '59 models. This top-line $3478 Bonneville convertible attracted 11,426 sun worshippers.

▲ Pontiac's '59 instrument panel could literally dazzle drivers, and individual—and colorful—"buckety" front seats arrived as a new option to further Pontiac's burgeoning performance image. Tri-Power boasted 310 bhp.

◀ All '59 Pontiacs wore a handsome "split" grille motif that would become a make hallmark. Here's the Bonneville Sport Coupe hardtop. It stickered at $3257, and 27,769 buyers flocked to Pontiac dealerships to buy one. Total Pontiac output: 383,320.

▲ This '59 Pontiac Bonneville Vista hardtop sedan went to Moscow along with six other General Motors cars as part of the six-week American National Exhibition trade show in the Soviet capital.

▲ American Motors president George Romney proudly poses with his company's 1959 Rambler Ambassador Custom Country Club hardtop sedan outside AMC headquarters. Only 1447 of these cars were built.

▲ Only minimal styling changes marked the '59 Ramblers. The $2327 six-cylinder Custom four-door sedan found 35,242 buyers. Its Rebel V-8 counterpart cost $130 more, but sold only 4046. Economy was king at AMC.

▲ AMC sold the tiny British-built Metropolitan from Nash days in improved 1500-series form as introduced in 1956. Met sales peaked in 1959 at 22,209. The last cars were sold in '62. New for '59 was a trunklid.

▲ AMC scored extra '58 sales with a modified '55 Rambler two-door sedan called American. For '59, AMC added two-door wagons in Super (*shown*) and DeLuxe trim at around $2100—and sold 32,639 of them.

CHAPTER TEN

# 1960-1963

# DETROIT THINKS SMALL

Suddenly it was 1960, and the times began changing as never before. True, the Cold War was far from over, the specter of nuclear armageddon remained all too tangible, and the civil rights struggle had barely begun. Worse, a new Cuban dictator named Fidel Castro had brought the Communist threat to just 90 miles from U.S. shores. Yet America had reasons for optimism. The economy continued its slow but steady recovery from the doldrums of 1958, and the country's space program had finally—and literally—gotten off the ground.

An historic 1960 presidential election gave narrow victory to the youngest individual—and the first Roman Catholic—ever to hold the office. As a symbol of the nation's hopes for the years ahead, John F. Kennedy was perfect: compellingly dynamic and vigorous in refreshing contrast to the starchy Dwight Eisenhower. The new chief executive immediately set the tone for what were touted as the "Soaring Sixties" by committing the nation to putting a man on the moon by decade's end. Tragically, he would not live to see that goal achieved.

As if to herald the momentous times ahead, Detroit's Big Three automakers offered their smallest cars in 30 years. American Motors' Rambler had pioneered compacts in the Fifties, and Studebaker belatedly chimed in by trimming the fat from its old platform to find sales salvation in the tidy '59 Lark. For 1960, Chevrolet added the rear-engine Corvair, Ford the utterly conventional Falcon, and Chrysler the rather oddly styled Valiant. Mercury came along at mid-model year with a spiffier Falcon called Comet. Though Corvair was the most radical in engineering terms, all four of these compacts were new designs conceived to stem the growing tide of import sales. And to an extent, they did, reducing the foreigners' market share from just over 10 percent for calendar '59 to 7.6 percent in 1960.

But that only meant that most of the 6-7 million cars Americans bought each year in 1960-63 were full-size or "standard" models. Yet, even here there were changes aplenty. Though Falcon promptly ran away with the compact market, a mid-1960 Corvair offering called Monza accidentally unearthed a sizeable demand for sporty cars with bucket seats, floorshift, and other "foreign" features. An instant—if modest—hit, Monza saved Corvair from an early grave and set the stage for a far greater success, though that would be another Ford, much to Chevy's chagrin. But the industry took immediate note of Monza's popularity, and by 1962 most every nameplate was offering bucket-seat interiors and snazzy appearance touches like vinyl roof coverings.

Meanwhile, Buick, Olds, and Pontiac stoked the compact craze with clean, trim new '61 models mirroring another period trend: the swift public rejection of Fifties styling excess. With certain bizarre exceptions from Chrysler Corporation, Detroit fast abandoned fins, needless chrome, and outsized proportions for more rational and tasteful designs. This movement reached memorable culmination in Buick's striking new 1963 Riviera, which bowed to near-universal acclaim as the most elegant American car since the Continental Mark II of the mid-Fifties.

Compacts may have been on Detroit's collective mind, but performance was still closest to its heart. Indeed, the Fifties "horsepower race" had not really abated—it had merely gone underground with the June 1957 manufacturers' agreement to abandon racing and performance advertising. In 1961, however, the race came aboveground when Chevrolet unleashed its "real fine" 409 big-block V-8, along with a sporty new big car, the Impala SS. Ford replied for '62 with a burly 406, and Chrysler kept pace with a husky 413 wedge-head. At the performance pinnacle in these years were two 1963 stunners, Studebaker's singular (and unexpected) Avanti and the first all-new Corvette since 1953, the Sting Ray.

With all this, the U.S. car market was fragmenting into specialized size/price segments. Ford furthered the process for 1962 by successfully pioneering the "mid-size" car with a new Fairlane. Intriguingly, Chrysler tried the same tactic that year with "resized" standard Plymouths and Dodges, but they bombed because they were too small and looked weird.

Finally, America lost another old friend as DeSoto departed after a token '61 model run, squeezed out of a recession-decimated medium-price field. The same fate attended the once-ballyhooed Edsel, dropped in late 1959 after just three model years and far more controversy than Ford Motor Company had expected.

▲ American Motors gave 1960 Rambler Ambassadors a heavy facelift and a "Scena-Ramic" compound-curve windshield. This Custom hardtop sedan cost $2822, and 1141 were sold.

▲ The '60 AMC Ambassador Custom Cross Country hardtop wagon carried a $3116 price tag—and garnered only 435 orders. A 250-horse 327 V-8 was standard, 270 bhp optional.

▲ American remained AMC's smallest compact, and not greatly changed save for the addition of four-door sedans like this top-trim Custom. Priced at $2059, it found 2172 buyers.

▲ Buick's 1960 styling was a muted version of '59. A $3145 ragtop again headed the entry-level LeSabre line and saw slightly higher sales of 13,588 units.

▲ Like all 1960 Buick LeSabres, this $2915 hardtop coupe offered 364-cid V-8s with 250 horses, or 235 for economy-minded drivers. Production of this model: 26,521.

▲ At $2756, the LeSabre two-door sedan remained Buick's price-leader model. This is a real no-frills example, right down to plain disc hubcaps and blackwalls.

**1960**

Three new compacts debut: Chevrolet Corvair, Ford Falcon, and Plymouth Valiant (ostensibly a separate make); Mercury Comet arrives in March 1960

A new Plymouth-based Dart serves as Dodge's "junior" series

The horsepower race continues to heat up

Industry production edges past six million cars for the model year; 11.5 percent are two-door hardtops, 11 percent four-door hardtops

Ford output slips slightly to 1,439,370 cars; Chevrolet's rises to 1,653,168, strengthening its hold on the Number One spot

Plymouth retains third place, for the last time until the Seventies; Rambler grabs fourth, with the highest total production ever from an independent

▲ Cadillac's Sixty Special remained a hardtop for 1960, but wore less chrome and lowered fins. Sticker price was $6233, and 11,800 were produced.

◀ Like Buick's, Cadillac's styling was somewhat simplified for 1960, as seen on this Eldorado Biarritz convertible. At an upmarket $7401, only 1285 were built. They rolled on a long, ride-cradling 130-inch wheelbase.

▲ Newly installed GM design chief Bill Mitchell dictated Cadillac's cleaner 1960 look. This is the popular $5252 Coupe de Ville, which attracted 21,294 buyers.

▲ The Cadillac Eldorado Seville said goodbye after 1960, when sales amounted to only 1075. It was still priced at the same lofty level as the ragtop Biarritz.

▲ The standard-size 1960 Chevys weren't appreciably tamer than the '59s, but available horses went up 20 to a maximum 335. Here, the $2769 Impala Sport Sedan hardtop.

▲ The Nomad name continued to grace Chevy's best wagon for 1960, but the car was very different from the 1955-57 original. The sticker price read $2996 with the base 283-cid V-8.

▲ A more conventional face appeared on all full-size 1960 Chevrolets, including the popular Impala Sport Coupe hardtop, which sold for $2599 with the standard 135-horse six.

---

Lee Iacocca takes the helm at Ford Division, is ready for a new focus on "excitement"

More than 9100 miles of the Interstate Highway System are completed, with 4700 more under construction

Four-fifths of all families own one or more automobiles—up 30 percent since 1940

All Chrysler Corp. cars save Imperial adopt Unibody construction; so do the new Corvair and Falcon

The last Metropolitans are built in England at mid-year

Studebaker offers a $100 rebate on late '60 models

Buick's instrument panel adjusts for easy visibility; a separate rear heat control is another industry "first"

▲ Chevrolet built 65,800 Impala convertibles for 1960, priced at $2967 with the 283 V-8. Full-size Chevys kept their 119-inch wheelbase and weighed 3455-3960 pounds.

▲ A number of considered changes—and up to 315 fuel-injected horses—made Chevy's 1960 Corvette the best yet. Sales finally broke the 10,000 mark (by 261 units).

*The only American car with an airplane-type horizontal engine!*
*The only American car with independent suspension at all 4 wheels!*
*The only American car with an air-cooled aluminum engine!*

THE FLOOR IS PRACTICALLY FLAT

▲ Corvair bowed with neat four-door sedans in two trim levels. This upper 700 model, which sold for $2103, saw output reach 139,208 units. Coupes were added at mid-model year.

◀ Chevy's Corvair was by far the most "revolutionary" of the Big Three's new 1960 compacts. This early ad touted its air-cooled rear engine.

▲ Less exterior chrome and fewer frills marked Chevy's low-rung $2038 Corvair 500 sedan, which found 47,673 buyers. The costlier 700 sedan outsold it by nearly three-to-one.

▼ Corvair claimed seating space for six, as this press photo shows. Hopefully they were all friends! Total 1960 Corvair production: 250,007.

▲ Suddenly it's 1955 again! This stubby dashboard lever controlled the Corvair's Powerglide automatic transmission (*a la* Chrysler Corporation).

## 1960 Model Year Production

| | | | | | |
|---|---|---|---|---|---|
| 1. Chevrolet | 1,653,168 | 8. Mercury | 271,331 | 15. Imperial | 17,719 |
| 2. Ford | 1,439,370 | 9. Buick | 253,807 | 16. Metropolitan | 13,103[1] |
| 3. Plymouth | 483,969 | 10. Cadillac | 142,184 | 17. Edsel | 3,008 |
| 4. Rambler | 458,841 | 11. Studebaker | 120,465 | 18. Checker | 1,050[2] |
| 5. Pontiac | 396,716 | 12. Chrysler | 77,285 | | |
| 6. Dodge | 367,804 | 13. DeSoto | 26,081 | | |
| 7. Oldsmobile | 347,142 | 14. Lincoln/Continental | 24,820 | | |

[1] *Calendar year sales*

[2] *Estimate, excludes taxicabs*

▲ Fins flew higher than ever on the all-new 1960 "Unibody" Chrysler lineup. Here, the $4875 New Yorker convertible, which managed to snare only 556 buyers.

▲ Chrysler's gimmicky swivel seats returned as an option for the 1960 high-performance 300-F; 964 hardtops and 248 ragtops were sold.

▲ A full-length center console and four bucket seats were new for Chrysler's 300-F hardtop and convertible, which started at $5841. Note the "toilet seat" rear deck.

▲ The 1960 Chrysler 300-F hardtop cost $5411. Horsepower: 375 or 400.

▶ Chrysler Division chief engineer Bob Rodger shows off Chrysler's big 413 "Ram Induction" V-8, good for up to 400 horses in the 300-F. Sixty mph was but eight seconds away.

▲ Imperial's fake trunklid spare tire was an option for 1960 Chryslers, like this $4518 New Yorker hardtop sedan. This model found a home in 5625 well-heeled garages.

---

Cadillacs adopt self-adjusting brakes, plus an automatic vacuum parking-brake release

Checker's new passenger cars—Superba sedan and wagon—look similar to the familiar taxis and are powered by either an L-head or overhead-valve version of Continental's 226-cid six

Total output for the Superba Standard and slightly fancier Superba Special reaches about 1050 units (plus 5930 taxis)

Chevy's radically engineered Corvair carries an air-cooled, six-cylinder engine at the rear and is the first mass-produced U.S. car with a swing-axle rear suspension

A new "Slant Six" engine replaces the long-lived L-head under Dodge and Plymouth hoods; it will last well into the Eighties

Ram-Induction manifolding is available for the high-performance Chrysler 300-F and for the big Dodge/Plymouth V-8s

▲ The Crofton Bug, a Crosley-powered, mini-Jeep takeoff of Crosley's "Farm-O-Road," sold in 1959-61 for $1350. About 200 were produced.

▲ Dwindling sales dictated far fewer 1960 DeSotos: 25,581 total. They were much more like Chryslers; this $3663 Adventurer hardtop coupe was one of six models.

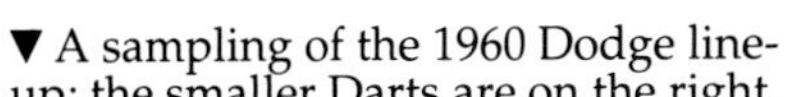

▼ A sampling of the 1960 Dodge lineup; the smaller Darts are on the right.

▲ A new two-tier '60 Dodge line included this $3506 hardtop wagon in the senior Polara series. Rare then, rarer now.

◀ Dodge and Plymouth boasted a plus in Chrysler's new, rugged ohv "Slant Six," destined to be a corporate mainstay for three decades.

▲ The Dart line was Dodge's big '60 seller. This entry-level Seneca four-door sedan cost $2330; 138,904 Seneca sedans and wagons were sold.

▲ The Plymouth-based Dart doubled Dodge's 1960 sales: 367,804, versus 156,385 in '59. This car was built on April 7 in Hamtramck, Michigan.

---

A Chrysler 300-F buyer can specify a French *Pont-a-Mousson* four-speed manual gearbox (this year only)—but only seven do

Chrysler touts an electro-luminescent dashboard; automatic swivel seats are optional

Valiant features an alternating-current alternator in place of the traditional generator; this device will soon be standard on virtually all U.S. cars

The final Edsels go on sale—production is halted in November 1959 after just 3008 cars are built for the abbreviated 1960 model run

A sliding metal sunroof (unseen on U.S. cars since prewar days) is offered on the Ford Thunderbird hardtop; 2536 are ordered

T-Bird convertibles, borrowing 1957-59 Ford Skyliner technology, stow their tops neatly in the trunk

▲ Edsel was canned in November 1959 after a brief run of 1960 models, including just 76 Ranger convertibles. Original sticker price was an even $3000. Total production for all three years, 1958-60, was 110,847.

▲ The last Edsels were very much like 1960 Fords. This $2705 Ranger hardtop coupe saw only 295 sales.

▲ This $2697 Ranger four-door sedan was the most numerous 1960 Edsel, yet only 1288 were produced.

▲ A prototype for a two-door 1960 Edsel Villager wagon that wasn't offered; 275 four-doors were built.

▲ A no-nonsense type, Robert S. McNamara (*left*) served briefly as Ford Motor Company president in late 1960, when Henry Ford II (*right*) became the firm's chairman.

▲ The all-new 1960 standard Fords were bigger in practically every way. This ad touts their new style and room.

---

Led by the slippery semi-fastback Starliner, the big Fords are noticeably longer, lower, wider

A dragstrip-ready Pontiac delivering 348 horsepower is predictive of the performance cars to come during the '60s

An overhead-valve six replaces the old L-head engine in the Rambler American at mid-year

Rambler station wagons feature an innovative side-hinged rear door

Studebaker's Lark adds a four-door station wagon and convertible to the line; Hawks come only with V-8 power

Oldsmobiles get an optional vacuum-operated remote decklid opener, while most Chrysler models offer vacuum door locks

◀ Simple in both looks and concept, Ford's Falcon was by far the most popular of the Big Three's new 1960 compacts, with 435,676 model-year sales. Priced in the $2000-$2300 range, Falcon offered this $1974 four-door sedan as well as a two-door and companion wagons. All used a 144-cubic-inch, 90-bhp six.

▼ An accessory hood ornament graces this restored 1960 Ford Galaxie Sunliner convertible, which sold 44,762 copies at a base list price of $2860. Big Ford engines that year ranged from a modest 145-bhp, 223-cid six to optional big-block 352s with up to 300 horses. Wheelbase measured 119 inches.

▲ This Galaxie Victoria hardtop sedan displays the well-formed styling common to all 1960 standard-size Fords. Priced at $2675, this model attracted 39,215 buyers.

▲ A sliding metal sunroof was a new option for the $3755 Thunderbird hardtop in 1960, the last year for the original '58 "Squarebird" design. Sales hit a record 90,843.

▲ Imperial was restyled for 1960, but arguably not for the better. This $5774 Crown convertible saw only 618 copies built. Top-line honors went to two new LeBaron models.

---

Ford Falcons employ an air-cooled torque converter

GM announces an experimental "electric fence" that would warn a driver if the vehicle nears the pavement's edge

Chevrolet displays the XP-700 Corvette show car; Plymouth exhibits its asymmetrically styled XNR sports car

Glenn Pray buys the assets of the Auburn/Cord/Duesenberg plant

The new Jeep-type Saviano Scat is powered by a 25-bhp air-cooled Kohler engine; very few are built

▲ The last of Lincoln's square-rigged giants appeared for 1960 with only minor changes from '59. That year's Continentals were dubbed Mark V and again included a convertible, still priced at $7056; 2044 were built.

▲ Lincoln's big 430 V-8 was detuned from 350 to 315 horsepower for 1960 in a faint nod to buyers' new-found concern with gas mileage. Now a Mark V, this Continental hardtop sedan again cost $6845—and 6604 were sold.

▲ The big 1960 Mercurys offered a cleaned-up, rounded-off version of '59 styling, plus engines that guzzled a bit less gas. The base-line Montereys still sold the best; this $3077 ragtop saw only 6062 copies built.

▲ At $2631, the Monterey two-door sedan remained the most affordable '60 "Big M," and 21,557 were sold. A 312 V-8 was again standard, but horses were down five to 205.

▲ Mercury ended its fling with hardtop wagons after 1960 and just 7411 examples of the woody-look Colony Park model. The original list price came in at $3837.

▲ Once intended for Edsel, the Comet bowed in mid-1960 to put Mercury into the new compact market. At $2053, this 114-inch-wheelbase four-door sedan was the most popular of the four models, with 47,416 sales.

▲ The '60 Comets were basically Ford's new Falcons in Mercury suits, and likely sold well because of that. Wagons, riding Falcon's 108.5-inch wheelbase, were offered with two or four doors, the latter priced at $2365.

▲ Olds traded 1959's "Linear Look" for cleaner "Balanced Design" on its 1960 models, shown here by a pair of Ninety-Eight hardtops. Prices: $4086 and $4162.

▲ Oldsmobile's tidier 1960 styling is evident on this $3402 Super 88 Holiday hardtop sedan; 33,285 were built.

▲ The 1960 Plymouths had a new "Unibody" platform and styling that was nothing if not different. This top-line $2967 Fury convertible managed a meager 7080 sales.

◀ Again for 1960, Super 88s carried Oldsmobile's 394 V-8 with 315 horsepower, as did Ninety-Eights. Here, the Super convertible, of which just 5830 were sold.

▲ With up to 330 available horses in a 383 V-8, the 1960 Plymouths made fast mounts for the law. The styling, meanwhile, made for easy spotting by law-breakers.

▲ Just visible in this view of Plymouth's 1960 Fury hardtop sedan is an optional squared-off (and odd) steering wheel. This $2656 model attracted only 9036 customers.

▲ Chrysler released this "teaser" shot in September 1959 to herald the arrival of its new 106.5-inch-wheelbase Valiant compact, which it described as bearing "crisp lines and completely fresh silhouette."

▲ At 184 inches long, Valiant was the biggest of the Big Three's new 1960 compacts, and it showed inside. A floor stick shifted a three-speed manual gearbox; dash-mount buttons controlled the optional TorqueFlite automatic.

▲ The Valiant arrived with a large Chrysler-style rhomboid grille, dual headlights, blade-type fenderlines, long-hood/short-deck profile—and surprisingly enough, no fins. This four-door sedan was sold in base V100 trim and, as shown here, in nicer V200 form.

▲ Valiant also offered four-door wagons for 1960 with seating for six or eight, in V100 and V200 trim. This V100 stickered at $2365. Total Valiant output for 1960: 194,292.

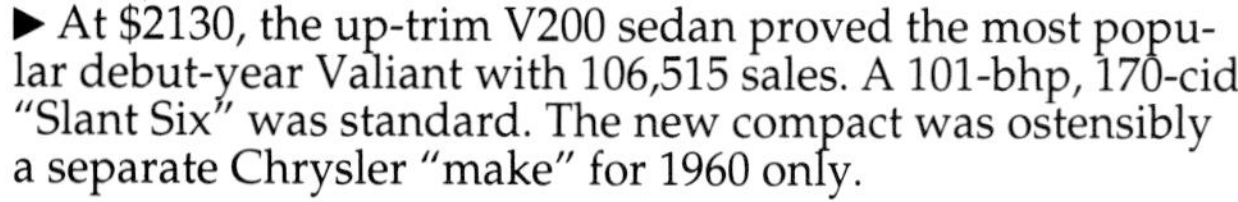

► At $2130, the up-trim V200 sedan proved the most popular debut-year Valiant with 106,515 sales. A 101-bhp, 170-cid "Slant Six" was standard. The new compact was ostensibly a separate Chrysler "make" for 1960 only.

▲ The successful 1959 "Wide Track" Pontiacs gained a slightly different look for 1960. It wasn't necessarily better, but the division did see a sales increase to 396,716 units. Here, the Bonneville convertible, which enticed 17,062 buyers. It listed at $3476.

► A full-width grille marked the 1960 Pontiacs, but the handsome "split" motif from '59 would return to become a division design hallmark. This $2842 Vista hardtop sedan, of which 32,710 were built, was again one of seven models in the low-line Catalina series, which remained Pontiac's sales leader.

▲ The $2631 Pontiac Catalina two-door Sport Sedan—in a dumpy setting typical of reference photos used to prepare brochure artwork.

◄ Wheels of fortune? Considering Pontiac's 1960 sales, the answer is yes. This PR photo shows a Catalina Safari wagon nearing the end of the assembly line, with its deluxe, deep-dished steering wheel installed.

▲ No, it's not a King Midget, but a Saviano Scat, a $1395 Jeeplet built in tiny numbers in 1960. It had a small, air-cooled, 25-horse two-banger and an 80-inch wheelbase.

▲ Fresh from saving Studebaker in '59, the '60 Lark saw few changes save for four new four-door wagons; 18,797 were sold. This is the $2591 "VI" in top Regal trim.

▲ Now just plain Hawk and looking quite dated, the 1960 edition of Studebaker's "family sports car" sold for $2360, or $2495 with V-8. Just 3939 were built.

▲ Though little changed and despite new Big Three rivals, Studebaker's compact Lark had another good year in 1960, with sales only a bit short of 1959. Here, the workaday $2040 "VI" (six-cylinder) DeLuxe four-door sedan.

▲ Lark was alone among 1960 compacts in offering a convertible, another new addition. Sold only in top-line Regal trim, it listed for $2621 with the 169.6-cid six, $2756 with 259 V-8. The latter delivered 180 horsepower, 195 optional. Ragtop output was 8571 units.

▲ A rather dubious "shovel nose" identified AMC's facelifted '61 Ambassadors. The price of this Custom four-door sedan was $2682; 9269 were built.

▲ AMC's Ambassador Custom Cross Country four-door wagon offered only pillared styling for '61, and its base price went up $85 to $3111. Only 784 were produced.

▲ A mild facelift marked American Motors' mid-size 1961 Ramblers, now called Classic. This Custom sedan sold for $2413 or $2512 (six or V-8); 28,568 were sold.

▲ New outer sheetmetal made AMC's '61 Rambler Americans blockier-looking and a tad shorter. Here, the $2165 mid-range Super two-door wagon.

▲ Only 969 examples of AMC's tiny two-seat Metropolitan coupe and convertible were sold in 1961. The ragtop shown here listed at a low $1697.

▲ Though specifications hadn't changed since '56, AMC ads touted the $1673 Met coupe in 1961 as a smart choice in modern "smaller" cars.

**1961**

The National Automobile Show, held at Detroit's new Cobo Hall in October 1960, attracts 1.4 million visitors wanting to view the '61 models; an "Auto Wonderland" exhibit demonstrates how a car is produced

President Eisenhower speaks at an industry banquet during the show, and the U.S. Post Office issues a commemorative "Wheels of Freedom" stamp

Four new upmarket compacts debut: Buick Special, Oldsmobile F-85, Pontiac Tempest, Dodge Lancer

Mid-year additions include the Buick Skylark; Dodge 770 Lancer Sport Coupe; Ford Falcon Futura; Mercury Comet S-22; Oldsmobile Starfire convertible, F-85 three-seat wagon, and Cutlass; also the Pontiac Tempest Le Mans

▲ Buick revived its familiar Special name for new 112-inch-wheelbase '61 compacts with crisp lines, small all-aluminum V-8, and standard or Deluxe trim.

▲ A pair of pillared coupes bolstered Buick's Special sedans and wagons in mid-'61. This uplevel $2621 bucket-seat model resurrected the Skylark badge; 12,683 were sold.

▲ Buick's big '61s were a bit lighter than before and much cleaner-looking. This LeSabre convertible attracted 11,951 buyers at a $3382 base sticker price.

▶ Styling-wise, the full-size '61 Buicks were light-years removed from the excesses of 1958-59. As on all full-size GM cars that year, new arc-shaped A-pillars replaced the "dogleg" knee-bangers of old. Buick's top-line '61 four-door sedan was this Electra model with "six-window" roof styling and a $3825 base price—all of which appealed to 13,818 buyers. A big 401-cid V-8 with 325 horses continued as the Electra's standard powerplant.

Due to a brief recession early in the year, industry output slips to 5.4 million cars

Ford output edges past Chevrolet as both makes top 1.3 million cars; Plymouth drops to fourth, behind Rambler

General Motors faces sporadic strikes, hampering production

New-car warranties are extended to at least 12-months/12,000-miles

AMC offers a U.S. Savings Bond as a conditional rebate

Two-ply tires become available, replacing the usual four-ply rubber in many instances

The "Special" nameplate is revived on the smallest Buick in 50 years: a compact with an aluminum V-8, plus a sporty Skylark Sport Coupe that debuts in May

▲ Save for tiny front-fender script, the $6477 '61 Cadillac Eldorado Biarritz looked the same as this $5455 Series Sixty-Two convertible.

▲ Likewise, this $4892 '61 Cadillac Sixty-Two hardtop looked much like the uplevel $5252 de Ville. Sales: 16,005 versus 20,156 de Villes.

▲ Here's another look at Cadillac's 1961 Series Sixty-Two hardtop coupe. Crisply drawn, all-new styling was dictated by GM's Bill Mitchell.

▲ Chevrolet sparked an industry-wide move toward sporty big cars with its new '61 SS (Super Sport) package for Impala hardtop coupes and ragtops. It cost just $53.80.

▲ Only 453 of the '61 Impala SS models were sold, making this restored survivor a rare find. A mid-year 409 V-8 boasted 360 horses, but only 142 were available in '61.

▲ Chevrolet fared as well as any GM make in the company's total big-car makeover for 1961, as shown here by the popular Impala Sport Sedan hardtop. It sold for $2662 with six, $2704 with base 283 V-8. The 348 V-8 remained the top power option (until the 409), but the most potent version was newly boosted from 335 to 350 horsepower.

▲ The influence of GM design chief Bill Mitchell was strikingly clear in the '61 Corvette's new "ducktail," lifted directly from his 1959-60 Stingray racer. Chevy sports-car sales reached 10,939 units; base price was $3934.

---

Checker's Superba Special becomes the Marathon; total Superba and Marathon sales equal an estimated 860 units

Chevrolet's tauter, fin-free look shows the influence of GM design chief Bill Mitchell

A Super Sport option is offered on Chevrolet Impalas at mid-year—and it's available with a lusty new 409-cubic-inch V-8

Because Chevy targets enthusiasts, the Corvair Monza can be ordered with a four-speed manual gearbox

Corvettes display a new flowing "ducktail" rear seen earlier on the XP-700 show car

Chrysler issues its last Windsors, while launching a cheaper Newport series

▲ Detail changes improved the '61 edition of Chevy's rear-engine Corvair compact. This 700 coupe sold for $1985, and 24,786 were built. Horsepower was 80 or 98 this year.

▲ Corvair added neat Lakewood wagons for 1961 in base 500 and, as shown here, spiffier 700 form. The latter, with 20,451 sales, was preferred nearly four-to-one.

▲ Chevy's sporty Corvair Monza coupe got this $2201 sedan companion for '61, but the latter managed only 33,745 sales, versus 109,945.

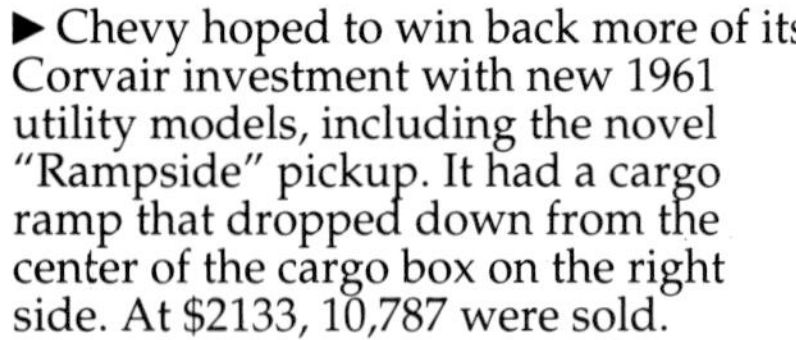

► Chevy hoped to win back more of its Corvair investment with new 1961 utility models, including the novel "Rampside" pickup. It had a cargo ramp that dropped down from the center of the cargo box on the right side. At $2133, 10,787 were sold.

▲ Who says Chrysler invented the minivan? Chevy's new Corvair Greenbrier "Sports Wagon" offered much the same thing back in 1961.

---

DeSoto makes a final short appearance—production halts in November 1960 after only 3034 '60 models are built

Dodge fields a new Valiant-based Lancer compact, but output of 74,776 units is considered so-so

A thumping 413-cid V-8 is available in Dodges and Plymouths

The third-generation Thunderbird has a new optional "Swing-Away" steering wheel

Ford offers its first four-speed manual transmission

The massively finned Imperial displays freestanding headlights in an attempt to revive the "Classic" look of the Thirties

Lincoln launches a downsized Continental, including the first U.S. convertible sedan since the '51 Frazer Manhattan

▲ Sales improved only slightly for the '61 Chryslers, mainly due to the Newport models. This New Yorker hardtop sedan snared 5862 buyers.

◀ Chrysler worked a debatable facelift for 1961, bumped Windsor to mid-line status (replacing Saratoga), and fielded a Newport line starting at $2964. Here, the $3025 Newport hardtop coupe pairs up with a $4261 New Yorker hardtop sedan, which rode a four-inch-longer 126-inch chassis.

▲ The 1961 Letter-Series Chrysler was the 300-G, with unchanged 375/400-bhp 413 V-8s. The hardtop coupe again cost $5411, but saw sales improve to 1280 units.

▲ Chrysler's $4592 ragtop New Yorker remained a marginal seller for 1961, as just 576 were built.

▲ DeSoto bowed out after '61 and only 3034 sales, of which this $3167 hardtop sedan accounted for 2123.

▲ The front end of the last DeSotos looked a tad bizarre. The car itself was basically a Chrysler Windsor.

---

Continentals carry an unprecedented 2-year/24,000-mile warranty; others will follow

Oldsmobile's "personal-luxury" Starfire convertible rides a Super 88 chassis; 7600 are built

The Pontiac Tempest offers GM's first postwar four-cylinder engine, plus a unique flexible "rope" driveshaft and rear transaxle

A rebodied Rambler American line adds a pert little convertible; 12,918 are sold

AMC offers an aluminum-silicon alloy engine for the Rambler Classic—an industry "first"

Studebaker updates the old Champion-based L-head six to overhead valves for the Lark; horsepower increases from 90 to a more competitive 112

▲ Dart remained Dodge's mainstay seller for '61, when a heavy facelift made it look more like senior models. Seen here is the top-line Phoenix hardtop coupe.

▲ The '61 Dart Phoenix hardtop coupe again. Prices started at $2737 with the 230-bhp 318 V-8. Tapered "reverse slant" fins were a dubious Dodge design exclusive this year.

► Senior '61 Dodges slimmed to a single line of Dart-look-alike Polaras with "ingrown toetail" taillights and standard 265-bhp 361 V-8. This ragtop sold for $3252.

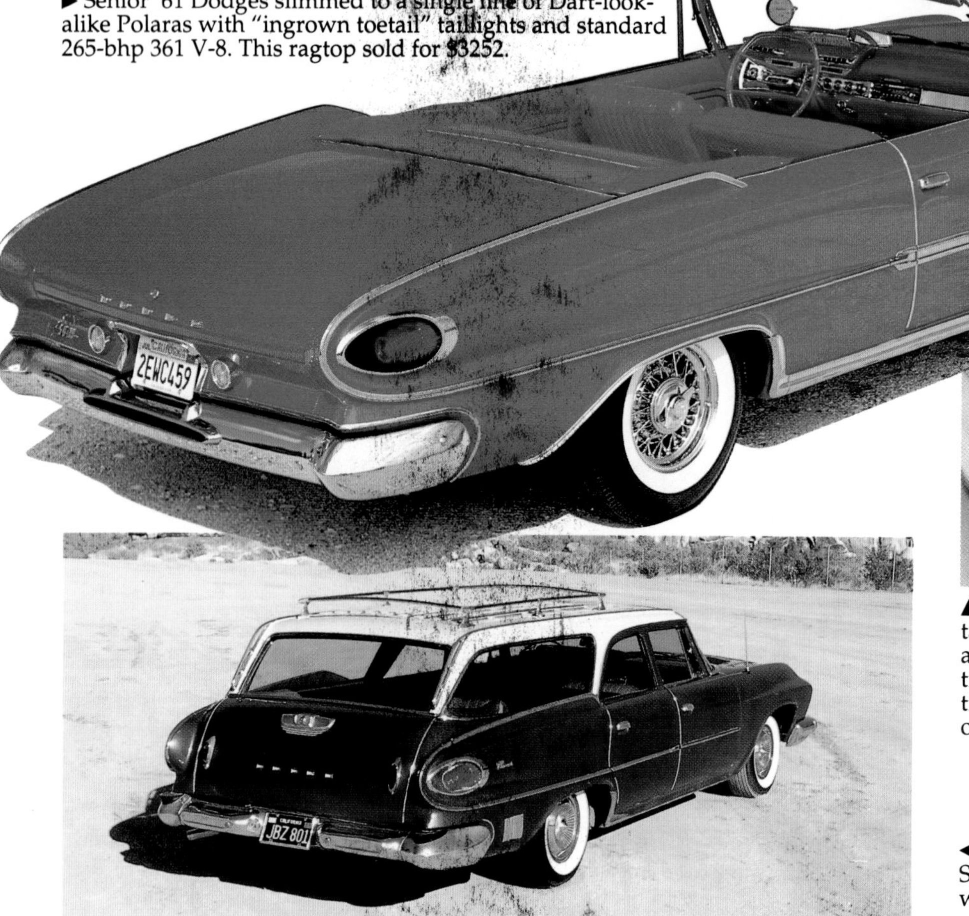


▲ Mid-'61 Dodge Darts added an extra taillamp inboard of each tapered fin, among several other "spring special" trim changes. Total '61 Dart production: 183,561. Senior Polaras managed only 14,032 units.

◄ Dart wagons in 1961 consisted of Seneca and Pioneer models, the latter with room for six or nine. Wagon prices ranged from $2695 to $3011.

## 1961 Model Year Production

| | | | | | |
|---|---|---|---|---|---|
| 1. Ford | 1,338,790 | 7. Mercury | 317,351 | 13. Lincoln | 25,164 |
| 2. Chevrolet | 1,318,014 | 8. Buick | 276,754 | 14. Imperial | 12,258 |
| 3. Rambler | 377,902 | 9. Dodge | 269,367 | 15. DeSoto | 3,034 |
| 4. Plymouth | 356,257 | 10. Cadillac | 138,379 | 16. Metropolitan | 969[1] |
| 5. Pontiac | 340,635 | 11. Chrysler | 96,454 | 17. Checker | 860[2] |
| 6. Oldsmobile | 317,548 | 12. Studebaker | 59,713 | | |

*[1]Calendar year sales [2]Estimate, excludes taxicabs*

▲ The '61 Galaxie Sunliner shows its restyled tail and tiny fins in an ad extolling Ford's hot new 390 V-8, good for 300 horsepower.

▲ Although base-priced at $2849, this '61 Galaxie Sunliner carries several accessories, including fender skirts, "continental kit," special hubcaps, and factory hood ornament. Ford built 44,614 Sunliners this year, about the same as 44,762 in 1960.

▲ The Fairlane was the volume low-priced big Ford series for '61; here, the $2317 four-door sedan. Production: 96,602.

▲ Lincoln lost many pounds, inches, and models with 1961's all-new Continental. This revived convertible sedan, of which only 2857 were built, retailed for a lofty $6713. Wheelbase was 123 inches, down eight.

◀ Mercury's compact Comet came back for '61 with modest changes, but a new bucket-seat S-22 coupe was the big news. Here, the standard two-door, which listed at an even $2000. It attracted 71,563 customers. Total Comet output soared to 197,263.

---

Studebaker Hawks gain a four-speed option, while the Lark can be ordered with a "Skytop" sliding fabric roof

Ford products are pre-lubed with 30,000-mile grease fittings; Cadillacs boast lifetime chassis lubrication

Experimental vehicles displayed during 1961 include Chrysler's Turboflite, the gyroscope-controlled Ford Gyron, and the Dodge FliteWing

The Fitch GT rides a modified Corvair chassis

▲ Big Mercurys were a bit smaller and lighter for '61, now on a 120-inch wheelbase. Montereys topped the line, and this $3128 ragtop was the choice of 7053 buyers.

▲ For the first time since 1956, full-size Mercs were "senior Fords." The top-line '61 woody-look $3191 Colony Park saw 7887 copies. A 175-bhp 292 V-8 was standard.

▲ Mercury's bottom-rung '61 big cars were the Meteor 600 and spiffier 800. At $2535, this 600 two-door sedan was the price leader. It could be ordered with a 135-bhp, 223-cid six.

▲ Olds helped start the swing to sporty big cars with the new mid-1961 Starfire, a specially trimmed Super 88 convertible priced at $4647. Just 7600 were sold.

▲ An Olds PR photo shows the '61 Starfire's upmarket interior: standard "buckety" front seats, console with floorshift and hard-to-see tach, and abundant bright trim.

▲ Unlike sister GM divisions, Oldsmobile's full-size '61s looked busier than the 1960 models. This $4159 Ninety-Eight Sport Sedan hardtop boasted a 325-bhp "Skyrocket" V-8.

▲ The '61 Olds Ninety-Eight line also embraced this more formal "six-window" Holiday hardtop sedan at $4021. Weighing in at 4269 pounds, it found 13,331 buyers.

▲ Low-line Dynamic 88s, like this $2956 Holiday coupe, remained the plainest Oldsmobiles for '61—and arguably the best-looking. Some 19,878 coupes were built.

▲ Olds persisted with Dynamic and Super 88 wagons for 1961. This eight-seat Super 88 sold for $3773, but only 2170 were sold. It boasted 4445 road-hugging pounds of heft.

▲ Sportiest of Oldsmobile's new F-85s was this mid-year, Deluxe-trim, bucket-seat pillared coupe called Cutlass. Priced at $2621, it attracted 9935 sales for 1961. There was only one engine, a 155-bhp aluminum V-8.

◀ The smallest Olds in decades, the new F-85 (*right*) was a compact companion to the full-size Super 88 Holiday (*left*), and looked much like it up front. The four-door here sold with the coupe and four-door wagons in the $2300-$2900 range. F-85 output totaled 76,394 for '61. Compared to the Super 88's 123-inch wheelbase, F-85s rode a 112-inch chassis.

▶ Full-size Plymouths went from finned to finless for '61. Here, the Fury hardtop coupe; 16,141 buyers drove one home.

▲ A truly bizarre face announced Plymouth's radical '61 big-car restyle. This mid-range Belvedere hardtop coupe cost $2461; 9591 were built.

▲ Plymouth's 1961 full-size sales tumbled down sharply, odd looks being one reason. The $2967 Fury V-8 convertible appealed to just 6948 customers.

▲ The Sport Suburban remained Plymouth's top-line wagon for '61, but only 5932 were called for. The nine-passenger model cost $3134. Total suburban production: 34,929.

▲ Now badged as a Plymouth, the '61 Valiant line added this spiffy $2137 V200 hardtop coupe, which pleased exactly 18,586 new-car shoppers. The rear-quarter windows were stationary.

▲ Valiants changed little for '61, but again sold well—143,078 units—though they couldn't offset Plymouth's big-car losses. This V200 wagon listed at $2423, but only 10,794 were produced.

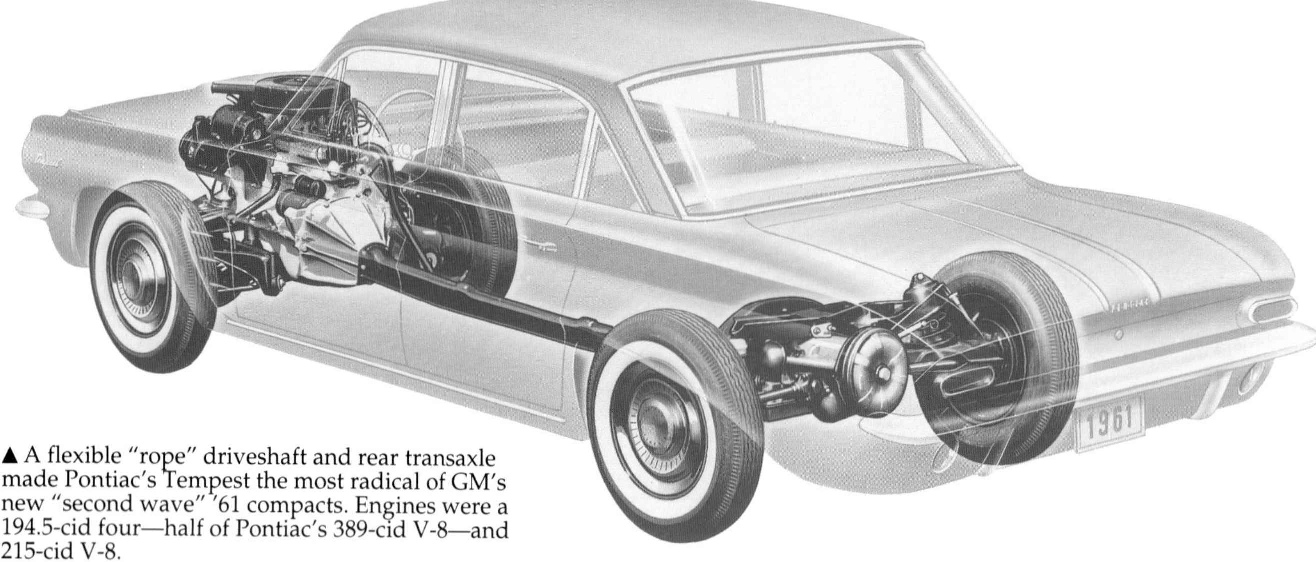

▲ A flexible "rope" driveshaft and rear transaxle made Pontiac's Tempest the most radical of GM's new "second wave" '61 compacts. Engines were a 194.5-cid four—half of Pontiac's 389-cid V-8—and 215-cid V-8.

◀ Tempest bowed with four-door sedans and wagons, adding coupes at mid-year. All offered base or Custom trim. Coupe output totaled 14,887.

▶ Tempest's first "face" evoked thoughts of '59 Pontiacs and was related to full-size '61 styling. Pontiac built 100,783 Tempests.

▲ Pontiac turned out a few '61 Catalina two-doors with big 421 V-8s as drag-race specials.

▲ Returning from 1960, the '61 Ventura was an uptrim Catalina two-door Sport Coupe costing $2971 (*shown*) or four-door Vista hardtop. This example wears the handsome extra-cost aluminum wheels Pontiac offered in this period.

◀ Big-Pontiac interiors could be among Detroit's sportiest for '61. This Ventura Sport Coupe, of which 13,297 were built, sports optional front bucket seats and manual floorshift (a rarely ordered extra). Venturas rode the Catalina's 119-inch chassis.

▼ Like all full-size '61 "Ponchos," the Bonneville Sport Coupe revived 1959's split-theme grille in a squarish new interpretation. "Bonnies" rode a 123-inch chassis.

▲ Full-size Pontiacs were arguably the cleanest and best-looking of GM's fully revamped 1961 big cars. Triple taillamps identified top-line Bonnevilles, like this $3255 Sport Coupe hardtop. It attracted 26,906 buyers.

▲ Studebaker's Lark compacts were lightly facelifted for '61, and sales slipped. Here, the top-line Regal convertible; 1981 were produced. This Lark weighed 3315 pounds.

▲ Another Regal ragtop, also an "VIII" (V-8), shows off the dual headlamps worn by upper-trim '61 Larks. This model topped the line at $2689, but a six cost $135 less.

▲ Seagrave Fire Apparatus built three prototype 1960-61 coupes (two fiberglass, one aluminum), then gave up the idea of building cars. The hardtops rode a 93-inch wheelbase, weighed 1700 pounds, had a 65-bhp four, and would have cost $3000.

▲ AMC's first Rambler American convertible returned for '62 with a new grille and 400 name. At $2369, it enticed 13,497 sun lovers.

▲ AMC demoted the '62 Ambassador to the 108-inch Classic chassis, and cut prices a bit. The new $2605 top-line 400 sedan saw 15,120 copies built.

▲ Sales of AMC's mini Metropolitan reached 412 for '62, though assembly had actually ceased in mid-1960. Mets still sold for around $1700.

▶ Buick broadened the appeal of its compact Special for 1962 with convertibles in Deluxe and, shown here, bucket-seat Skylark trim. At $3012, it attracted 8913 buyers. The $2879 Deluxe sold 8332 copies.

◀ The '62 Skylark bore an obvious Buick look, *a la* senior models. A Skylark hardtop (*nee* coupe) was also added to the line for 1962.

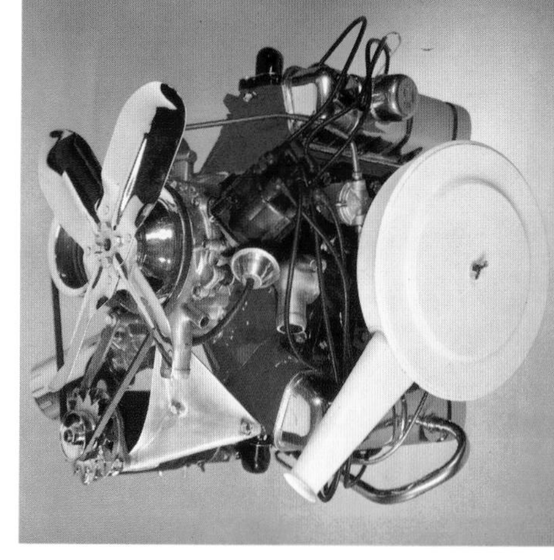

▶ This 198-cubic-inch V-6 was the Special's new base engine for '62. With 135 horses, it would be the first in a long line of Buick V-6s.

**1962**

New '62 offerings include the Chevy II, Ford Fairlane, Mercury Meteor, Pontiac Grand Prix, Studebaker Gran Turismo Hawk

Mid-year ushers in the Buick Wildcat hardtop and Skylark convertible, Corvair Monza convertible and Spyder, Dodge Custom 880, Ford Galaxie 500/XL, Mercury S-55, Oldsmobile Jetfire, Plymouth Sport Fury

Chevrolet output passes the two-million mark, but Ford builds fewer than 1.5 million cars; industry volume hits 6.7 million

Pontiac reaches Number Three in production, and holds that spot through 1970; Plymouth skids to eighth

▲ Buick joined the sporty big-car crowd for '62 with the Invicta-based Wildcat hardtop coupe. A vinyl roof and buckets-and-console interior were included for $3927, as was a 325-bhp 401 V-8. Sales totaled exactly 2000.

▲ One of only two built, this 1962 Buick Electra 225 stretch limousine was a "special project" that came to naught. It remained in use for many years at the division's Flint headquarters, but is now in the hands of a collector.

▲ Like Buick, Cadillac took on a slightly huskier, more blunted look for 1962. As in '61, all models carried the division's 390 V-8 with 325 horses. This $5588 Series Sixty-Two convertible was one of 16,800 examples built.

▲ Cadillac offered no fewer than six different hardtop sedans for '62. The "six-window" Series Sixty-Two model, which carried a $5213 price tag, attracted 16,730 buyers.

◀ Though still much like the standard Series Sixty-Two ragtop, the '62 Eldorado Biarritz cost $1022 more: $6610. Production totaled 1450, same as the '61 model run.

---

Rambler ranks fourth in output; George Romney departs, and so does the Classic V-8 (for now)

Bucket-seat installations triple, to 14.3 percent, as the sporty "personal-car" craze takes hold

Close to one-third of all cars sold are "pillarless" body styles

Big-engine power grows again: Chevrolet's 409-cid V-8 can deliver 409 bhp; Ford's 406 reaches 405 horsepower

Ford withdraws support of the 1957 AMA resolution against promoting power/speed

A Plymouth Fury hits 190.073 mph at the Bonneville Salt Flats—the fastest ever for a stock-body production car

▲ At the other end of the '62 Chevy II spectrum were base-trim 100 sedans and wagons. This two-door sold for $2003 with a four-cylinder engine, $2063 with a six. No V-8s were offered.

◀ Chevy II bowed for 1962 as a more conventional, more saleable, 110-inch-wheelbase compact to supplement the Corvair. This $2465 Nova 400 convertible, which garnered 23,741 orders, topped the line.

▲ Chevy's burly 409 V-8 made a mark in 1962 drag racing. Here, "Dyno Don" Nicholson's Bel Air runs at Pomona.

▶ Beneath the hood of that '62 Bel Air lurks the year's top big-Chevy power option, a new 409-horse 409 with big dual-quad Carter carbs. It's a legend even today.

▲ It looks stock, but this '62 Chevy Bel Air "bubbletop" Sport Coupe sports a very rare aluminum front end, part of a package offered for serious drag racers.

Dual-braking systems are standard in American Motors and Cadillac models

Studebaker drops the Packard name from the corporate title and acquires Paxton Products, a supercharger manufacturer

American Motors announces factory-installed seat belts for both front and rear seats; all cars have anchorages in floorpans for belt installation

Buick issues Skylark and Special Deluxe convertibles, plus an optional four-speed gearbox

The bucket-seat Wildcat attracts 2000 customers and boosts the Buick image

Cadillac offers optional front-fender cornering lights

▲ Unlike the Bel Air, Chevy's 1962 Impala hardtop coupe (SS shown) wore a new, more "formal" roofline with convertible-like ribbing. Wheelbase was 119 inches.

▲ Symbolic of the day's changing market, the '62 Chevrolet line comprised four distinct car types (*from left*): Corvette, full-size, Chevy II, and Corvair.

▲ Chevy's Corvair Monza line added this wagon for '62, but only 2362 were called for. Base price was $2569.

◀ The "ducktail" Corvette returned for '62 with even tidier looks (no two-toning), plus enlarged 327 V-8s with up to 360 horses. Base price was also up—to $4038—but so were sales, to a new record of 14,531 units.

◀ Shearing off the familiar tailfins vastly improved Chrysler's styling for 1962, though some company designers derisively termed this change the "plucked chicken" look. Shown here is the New Yorker hardtop sedan, which listed at $4263 and found only 6646 buyers. Most '62 Chrysler sales came from the low-priced Newport models, whose 122-inch wheelbase was four inches shorter than on New Yorkers.

---

Chevrolet's 283 V-8 grows to 327-cid, but the 283 remains through '67; Super Sport is now an Impala subseries

The Chevy II compact, Chevrolet's orthodox response to Ford's Falcon, employs single-leaf rear springs

Mid-year brings a Corvair Monza convertible, plus a turbocharged, 150-bhp Spyder

Corvettes run with new 327-cid engines rated up to 360 horsepower with fuel injection

Chrysler issues a non-letter 300 series, as well as the hot 300-H with 380 or 405 horses

Dodge and Plymouth "standard" cars shrink to near-compact size, and sales suffer; the full-size Custom 880 arrives at mid-year to boost Dodge sales

▲ At the start of '62, Highland Park's family included (*from lower left*): Plymouth Valiant and Fury, Imperial, Dodge Dart, Plymouth Fury Suburban, Chrysler 300, and (*center*) Dodge's Valiant-based Lancer.

▲ Chrysler replaced Windsors with "non-letter" 300s for '62, among them this $3883 ragtop; 1848 were sold.

▲ Chrysler delivered 362 of these 1962 "Enforcer" police pursuits to the California Highway Patrol.

▲ Dodge's downsized '62 "standard-size" cars were also popular with police, if not the car-buying public.

▲ Valiant-like lines marked Dodge's "full-size" 1962 Darts. The 440 series included one of the line's two ragtops, which sold for $2945 with standard 318 V-8; 3166 were built.

▲ New for '61, Dodge's Valiant-clone Lancer sported a new grille for '62. A 770 hardtop with bucket seats became the $2257 GT; 13,683 were produced.

---

The Ford Fairlane and similar Mercury Meteor pioneer the "intermediate-size" field; small V-8s are available

Full-size, bucket-seat Fords—the 500/XL Victoria hardtop and Sunliner convertible—arrive at mid-season as part of the "Lively Ones" promotional theme

The Thunderbird line includes a Sports Roadster with a fiberglass tonneau over the rear seat

Mercury issues the full-size S-55 hardtop and ragtop with bucket seats; 4087 are produced

The last Metropolitans, 412 of them, are sold

A hardtop coupe joins the Oldsmobile Starfire convertible

Oldsmobile's new Jetfire and the Corvair Monza Spyder are the first high-volume turbocharged models; a 215-bhp engine with unique water/alcohol injection powers the compact Olds hardtop

▲ Sportiest of Dodge's smaller '62 "standards" were the Polara 500s: ragtop, hardtop sedan, and this hardtop coupe. Priced at $3019, the coupe found 6834 buyers.

▲ All '62 Dodge Polara 500s came with bucket seats, unique styling touches, and a 305-horse 361 V-8. Sales were dismal: 3345 hardtop sedans, 2089 convertibles.

▲ At $3268, the bucket-seat Polara 500 convertible was the costliest Dodge at the beginning of model-year '62—but not after the big Custom 880 arrived at mid-year.

▲ Though it looks innocent, this light base-series '62 Dodge Dart two-door sedan could be had with a big-inch 413 V-8, making it perfect for the dragstrip. . .

▲▶ . . . As indeed this example was. Here's its 413 "Ram-Charger" engine with dual-quad carbs covered (*above*) and exposed (*right*). Horsepower? A formidable 410.

## 1962 Model Year Production

| | | |
|---|---|---|
| 1. Chevrolet 2,061,677 | 7. Mercury 341,366 | 13. Lincoln 31,061 |
| 2. Ford 1,476,031 | 8. Plymouth 339,527 | 14. Imperial 14,337 |
| 3. Pontiac 521,933 | 9. Dodge 240,484 | 15. Checker 1,230[1] |
| 4. Rambler 442,346 | 10. Cadillac 160,840 | 16. Metropolitan 420[2] |
| 5. Oldsmobile 428,853 | 11. Chrysler 128,921 | [1]*Estimate, excludes taxicabs* |
| 6. Buick 399,526 | 12. Studebaker 89,318 | [2]*Calendar year sales* |

▲ A discreet front-fender emblem is the only tip-off to the big 406 V-8 lurking within this 1962 Ford Galaxie 500 Club Victoria hardtop coupe.

▲ Full-size Fords looked more massive for '62, but weren't. Galaxie 500s, like this $2749 Town Sedan, were the line's big sellers.

▲ This $2674 Galaxie 500 Club Victoria found 87,562 buyers. It struts the big, round taillights that were a Ford hallmark in this period.

▲ Ford prototyped—but never sold—a removable, aerodynamic "Starlifter" hardtop option for the '62 Sunliner. It was intended for racing, but NASCAR said no.

▲ An "electric shaver" grille identified '62 Ford Falcons. This $2273 bucket-seat Futura sold 17,011 copies, including mid-year models with a T-Bird-style roof.

▲ This ad's headline perfectly describes Ford's brand-new in-between '62 car, the mid-size Fairlane.

▲ Though Falcon-based, the '62 Fairlane was longer and more "grown-up," and had a slick new V-8 option. Here, the base $2154 two-door; 34,264 were sold.

---

The Pontiac Grand Prix hardtop, based on the Catalina, debuts

"E-Stick" manual shift with automatic clutch is available on the Rambler American

A Rambler American wins the Mobil Economy Run, averaging 31.11 mpg

Studebaker's Gran Turismo Hawk hardtop boasts a Thunderbird-style roofline and a 289-cid V-8

Shelby-American begins production of the AC Cobra roadster

The Apollo sports car features an Italian body and Buick's aluminum V-8

▲ Ford's Thunderbird was all-new for '61, so '62 changes were modest. This standard ragtop wears a rear tonneau borrowed from the slinky new Sports Roadster model.

▲ Thunderbird's '61 "projectile-look" front end would last through '63. This '62 convertible, which enticed 7030 buyers, stickered at $4788. It weighed 4370 pounds.

▲ Imperial looked better for 1962 due to finless fenders and a new divided grille. The make's sole convertible again appeared in the mid-line Crown series. This is one of only 554 built at $5770 apiece.

▶ The LeBaron Southampton hardtop sedan remained the top-line standard Imperial for '62. Just 1449 were built. Base price was $6422. The wide rear-quarter "formal" roofline was exclusive to this model.

Chrysler announces it plans to produce 50 turbine-powered cars, which will be tested by selected motorists

Experimental cars shown in 1962 include the Ford Cougar 406, Mustang I V-4 roadster, Chevrolet CERV I, Pontiac Monte Carlo

Glenn Pray announces that he will build a scaled-down, Corvair-powered Cord 8/10

▲ As promised, Lincoln's latest Continental was little changed for 1962. At $6720, this 5370-pound, 123-inch-wheelbase convertible sedan found just 3212 buyers.

◀ Full-size Mercurys, wearing a Ford-type facelift for 1962, were regrouped into low-end Monterey and uplevel Monterey Custom lines, plus Commuter and Colony Park wagons. Colony Park continued with woody-look side trim in six- and nine-passenger versions priced at $3200-$3300; 9596 were sold. A 170-horse 292 V-8 was standard.

▲ Mercury issued a sporty bucket-seat big car in mid-1962. Called Monterey Custom S-55, it came either as a hardtop coupe or as this $3738 convertible with a standard 300-horse 390 V-8. Ragtop sales totaled just 1315; hardtops, 2772.

▲ Comet's modest 1962 facelift maintained a family resemblance to bigger Mercurys. Here, the new $2170 Custom four-door station wagon.

▲ Also new for mid-'62 was this woody-look Comet Villager wagon, sold only in four-door form for $2710. Customers ordered only 2318 copies.

▲ Priced at $2526, this four-door sedan was one of four new 1962 Comet Custom models. A two-door and two wagons were also offered.

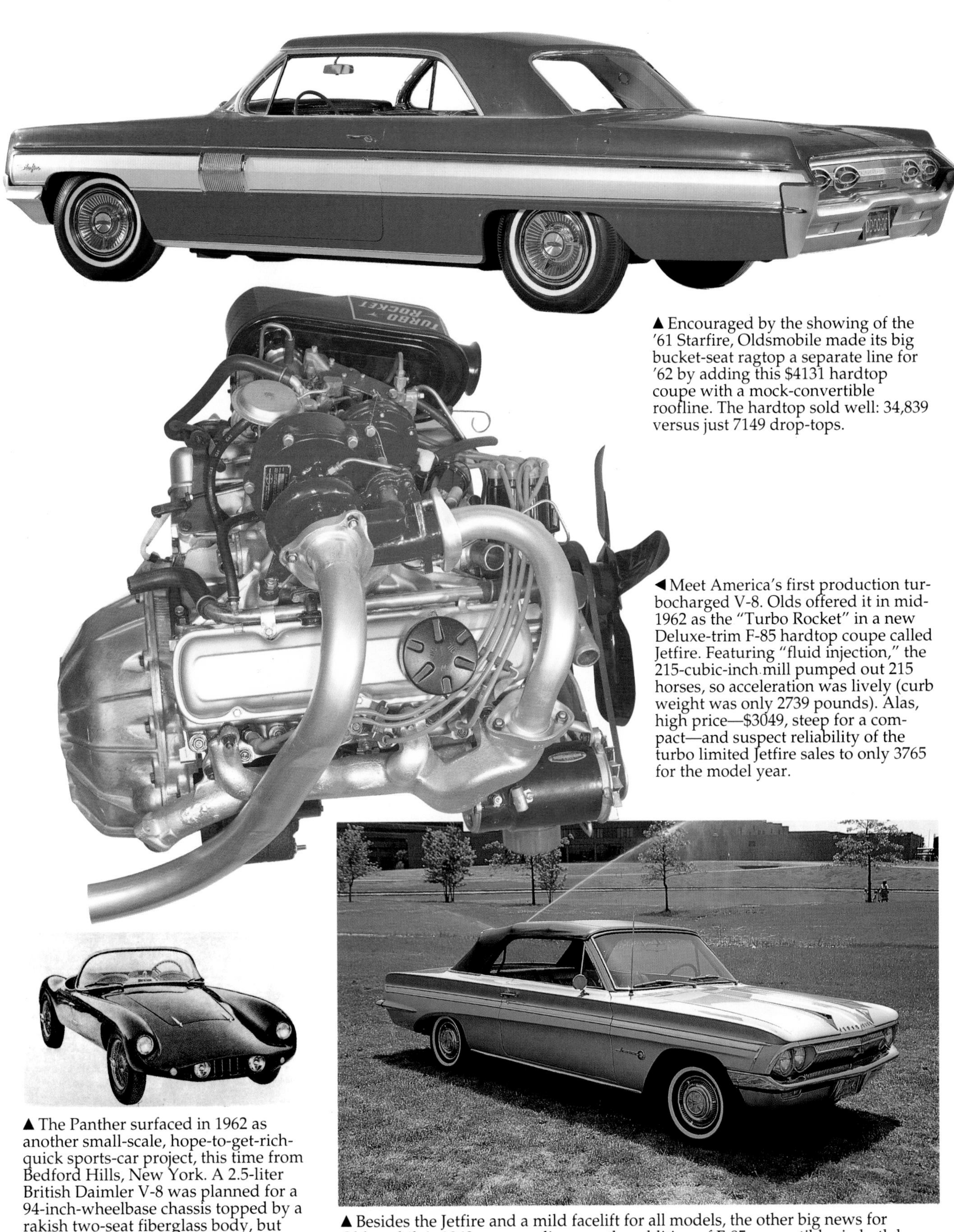


▲ Encouraged by the showing of the '61 Starfire, Oldsmobile made its big bucket-seat ragtop a separate line for '62 by adding this $4131 hardtop coupe with a mock-convertible roofline. The hardtop sold well: 34,839 versus just 7149 drop-tops.

◀ Meet America's first production turbocharged V-8. Olds offered it in mid-1962 as the "Turbo Rocket" in a new Deluxe-trim F-85 hardtop coupe called Jetfire. Featuring "fluid injection," the 215-cubic-inch mill pumped out 215 horses, so acceleration was lively (curb weight was only 2739 pounds). Alas, high price—$3049, steep for a compact—and suspect reliability of the turbo limited Jetfire sales to only 3765 for the model year.

▲ The Panther surfaced in 1962 as another small-scale, hope-to-get-rich-quick sports-car project, this time from Bedford Hills, New York. A 2.5-liter British Daimler V-8 was planned for a 94-inch-wheelbase chassis topped by a rakish two-seat fiberglass body, but the idea went no further than a prototype or two. Projected prices of $4250 and $4995 didn't help.

▲ Besides the Jetfire and a mild facelift for all models, the other big news for Oldsmobile's 1962 compact line was the addition of F-85 convertibles in both base and bucket-seat Cutlass trim. Respective output was 3660 and a healthier 9893 units. Seen here is a ragtop wearing Jetfire trim.

▲ Plymouth revived the Sport Fury name at mid-1962 for a $3082 bucket-seat convertible (1516 built) and hardtop coupe. Both had a standard 305-horse 361 V-8.

▲ The '61 Plymouth Valiant V200 hardtop gained bucket seats and modest styling changes to become the 1962 Signet. Priced at $2230, it garnered 25,586 sales. The "Slant Six" again gave 101 or 145 optional horses.

▲ Like Dodge, Plymouth shrunk its standard models to a 116-inch, intermediate-size wheelbase for '62—and watched sales plunge. This Fury hardtop coupe sold for $2585 with the Slant Six, $2693 with the 230-bhp 318 V-8.

▲ Plymouth's lightest '62s—the low-line Savoy sedans like this $2313 two-door—could be very speedy when equipped with one of the optional 413 V-8s with 365-415 bhp.

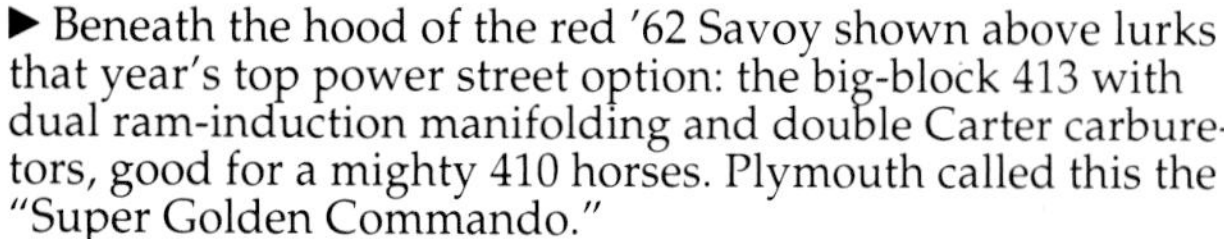

► Beneath the hood of the red '62 Savoy shown above lurks that year's top power street option: the big-block 413 with dual ram-induction manifolding and double Carter carburetors, good for a mighty 410 horses. Plymouth called this the "Super Golden Commando."

▲ Pontiac announced an expanded group of '62 Tempest compacts—now five body styles—with this splashy ad.

▲ Like the Buick Special and Olds F-85, Pontiac's Tempest added a convertible for '62, plus a spiffy bucket-seat Le Mans trim option (*shown*) that found immediate buyer acceptance. Total Tempest ragtop sales: 20,635.

▲ Pontiac replaced Ventura with the sportier Catalina-based Grand Prix hardtop in mid-1962. For $3490, bucket seats, console, 389 V-8, and unique styling touches came standard. Wheelbase measured 120 inches.

◀ Grand Prix was Detroit's most popular sporty big car for '62, attracting a healthy 30,195 orders. Grille treatment was unique, as was the standard all-vinyl interior. Side trim was minimal. The handsome aluminum wheels seen here were optional.

▲ All 1962 Pontiac hardtop coupes sported a rear roofline with pseudo-convertible ribbing. This is the big Bonneville version, priced at $3349; 31,629 were produced.

▲ Promoted in 1961-62, the stillborn Stuart electric was a fiberglass-bodied mini with eight six-volt batteries and a mere 40-mile range at a modest 35 mph. Only one was built.

▲ Designer Brooks Stevens gave '62 Studebaker Larks a mock-Mercedes grille and a $185 Skytop fabric sunroof, as on this $2190 Regal four-door sedan. Unfortunately, sales kept sliding.

▲ A sample of AMC's 1963 Rambler lineup, which won *Motor Trend* "Car of the Year" honors, led by the all-new Classic sedan and Ambassador wagon.

▲ AMC's 1963 Ambassadors offered smooth new lines on a longer 112-inch wheelbase. The top-of-the-line 990 four-door sedan listed at $2660.

▲ Save for a standard 250-bhp V-8 instead of a six, the '63 Ambassador was much like the new Classic. This 990 two-door sedan sold for $2606.

▲ The Ambassador 990 wagon shown here listed at $2956, or $3018 with eight-passenger capacity. Only 8299 were produced for the model run.

**1963**

Industry output soars to 7.3 million cars; car/truck sales top the 1955 record

Most models are facelifted, with the focus on luxury, performance, size; compacts are fading

Chrysler adopts a 5-year/50,000-mile powertrain warranty to boost sales; others increase to 2/24,000

The average full-time worker earns $5243; an average new car sells for $2310

New '63 models include the Buick Riviera; Chrysler 300-J and New Yorker Salon; Mercury Marauder and Comet Sportster semi-fastback hardtops; Studebaker Avanti, Super-Lark, and Super-Hawk

▲ AMC's boxy Rambler American changed little again for '63. The convertible was in the new top-trim 440 line and sold for $2344, but just 4750 found buyers.

▲ Buick's compact '63 Specials wore "more important" looks for the final year of their original '61 design. Here, the $2857 Skylark hardtop, of which 32,109 were sold.

▲ The Buick Riviera was reborn for '63 as a stunning $4365 hardtop coupe artfully blending American and British style. Exactly 40,000 copies were built for the model year.

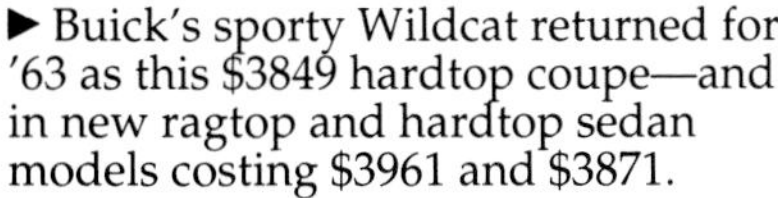

▶ Buick's sporty Wildcat returned for '63 as this $3849 hardtop coupe—and in new ragtop and hardtop sedan models costing $3961 and $3871.

Big-block V-8 engines grow again; four-on-the-floor gearshifts, bucket seats, and consoles continue to gain in popularity

Ford offers the industry's first fully-synchronized three-speed manual transmission, while three-speed automatics gain favor over two-speeds

Power front disc brakes are now optional on Studebakers (standard on Avanti)—a first for production U.S. cars

Half of all '63s are ordered with power steering, three-fourths with automatic transmission, nearly two-thirds with V-8, and one-seventh with air conditioning

Most 1963 cars have self-adjusting brakes; Studebaker was first in '47

Studebaker begins installation of seat belts in March 1963; other automakers follow for '64

Amber front turn-signal lights are adopted by the auto industry

▲ A heavy 1963 restyle gave Cadillac its lowest fins in years—and they'd go lower still. Here, the Eldorado Biarritz, which was priced at $6608; 1825 were built.

▲ Again for '63, Chevrolet offered three convertibles with seating for more than two (*from top*): the $2481 Corvair Monza, $2472 Chevy II Nova 400, and $2917 full-size Impala ($3024 with the base 283 V-8). Only the Impala sported new sheetmetal this year.

▲ Chevy's bucket-seat Corvair Monza coupe (*shown*), which sold for $2272, and convertible remained strong sellers for '63—117,917 and 36,693 units, respectively.

▲ Only detail appearance and mechanical changes were made to 1963's Chevy II models. This Nova 400 Sport Coupe hardtop sold for $2267 with standard 194-cid, 120-bhp six, and 87,415 were delivered. This one has the sporty SS trim package, which added $161 to the sticker price.

---

PCV (positive crankcase ventilation) systems are installed in all cars to reduce pollution

A tilt steering wheel is optional in full-size GM cars

Pontiac offers optional transistorized ignition—an industry "first"

GM management orders all corporate-sponsored race activity halted

Nearly nine million households have more than one automobile—up from 4.2 million in 1954

Buick's shapely Riviera "personal-luxury" hardtop runs with a 401- or 425-cid V-8

The Corvette Sting Ray adopts independent rear suspension, but passes on disc brakes

Chrysler issues a limited-edition 300 Pace Setter hardtop and convertible to mark its Official Pace Car status at the Indy 500 race; the 300-J comes as a hardtop only

▶ The first fully redesigned Chevrolet Corvette since the '53 original arrived for 1963 with the Sting Ray name. The convertible, priced at $4037, found 10,919 customers.

▲ Every bit as stunning as the new '63 Sting Ray convertible was the first Corvette coupe, a fastback tagged at $4252. Sales came in at 10,594 units.

▲ The '63 would be the only Sting Ray coupe with the unique "split" rear window, and is now more highly coveted because of that. The coupe weighed in at 2859 pounds.

▲ Chrysler touted its "crisp, clean custom look" in a major '63 restyle. The mid-year $5860 Salon hardtop sedan topped the New Yorker line, but sold only 593 copies.

▲ Non-letter Chrysler 300s paced the 1963 Indy 500, and a replica "Pace Setter" convertible (*shown*) and hardtop coupe were issued. Ragtop orders totaled 1861 units.

---

The Dodge/Plymouth big-block engine expands to 426-cid, with a super-performance "Ramcharger" delivering 425 bhp

Dodge completely restyles its compact and renames it Dart (dropping the Lancer moniker)

Ford's sporty bucket-seat Falcon Sprint hardtop and convertible are mid-year arrivals

A lightweight 289-cid V-8—with up to 271 horses—becomes available in Ford Fairlanes

Full-size Fords get a 427-cid V-8 option; semi-fastback Galaxie 500 and 500/XL "Scatback" hardtops bow at mid-year

The lightly facelifted Imperial loses its freestanding taillamps and reinstates the Crown Imperial Ghia limo (13 built)

▲ Chrysler launched a consumer test program of its latest automotive gas turbine engine in 1963. The engine was packaged in this striking hardtop coupe styled by Elwood Engel, and 50 were built by Ghia in Italy.

▲ Dodge made its 1963 "standards" longer and more orthodox, and sales improved. Here, the $2963 V-8 Polara convertible; 2089 were built.

▲ A still-odd face was the one dubious aspect of the restyled '63 standard Dodge. This $2732 Polara 500 hardtop coupe found 6823 buyers.

▲ Hastily revived during '62, the true big Dodge continued with a '63 facelift as the Custom 880. Seen here is the $3109 hardtop sedan.

▲ Lancer left as Dodge's 1963 compact, replaced by an all-new Dart. This bucket-seat GT ragtop stickered at $2512.

► Functional hood scoops identify this as one of the rare, lightweight '63 Dodge 330 "Ramcharger" two-door sedans with the big new 415/425-bhp 426 wedge-head V-8.

---

Pontiac Tempest gains a 326-cid V-8 option, launches a separate Le Mans series

A 421-cid V-8 is available in full-size Pontiacs

The all-new Rambler Classic's one-piece "Uniside" door-frame structure is a U.S. industry "first"

Studebaker's Wagonaire wagon has a rear roof panel that slides forward to accommodate tall loads

The rakish fiberglass Avanti coupe offers a selection of R-series 289-cid V-8s, with or without a supercharger

▲ The sporty bucket-seat Galaxie 500/XL ragtop (*shown*) and hardtop coupe returned from mid-'62 as two of 1963's heavily restyled "Super Torque" Fords.

▲ Most '63 500/XLs, like this "formal" hardtop, got a 390 V-8, but 406 and new 427 options were also available.

▲ Ford added Galaxie "Scatback" semi-fastback hardtop coupes at mid-'63 for more speed in stock-car racing.

▲ Convertibles in Futura and sporty new V-8 Sprint trim expanded the '63 Falcon lineup. Ford built 31,192 of the $2470 Futura ragtops (*shown*).

▲ A nice frontal redo gave the '63 mid-size Fairlanes a "big Ford" look. This 500 two-door sedan started at $2242, and 34,764 were sold.

▲ Fairlane's sportiest '63 was this new $2504 Sports Coupe hardtop; 28,268 were built. It was also sold with a bench front seat for $2324.

## 1963 Model Year Production

| | |
|---|---|
| 1. Chevrolet | 2,237,201 |
| 2. Ford | 1,525,404 |
| 3. Pontiac | 590,071 |
| 4. Plymouth | 488,448 |
| 5. Oldsmobile | 476,753 |
| 6. Rambler | 464,126 |
| 7. Buick | 457,818 |
| 8. Dodge | 446,129 |
| 9. Mercury | 301,581 |
| 10. Cadillac | 163,174 |
| 11. Chrysler | 128,937 |
| 12. Studebaker | 69,555 |
| 13. Lincoln | 31,233 |
| 14. Imperial | 14,121 |
| 15. Checker | 1,080[1] |

[1]*Estimate, excludes taxicabs*

▲ The '63s were the last "projectile-nose" Ford Thunderbirds, and again came in four models. This $4912 convertible attracted 5913 upmarket shoppers.

▲ Imperial lost its "gunsight" taillamps for '63. This is the $5243 Custom hardtop sedan; 3264 were built.

▲ Lincoln's Continental returned to a fine-checked grille for '63. This $6270 sedan weighed a hefty 4936 pounds.

▶ The '63 Lincoln Continental convertible sedan cost $6916 and was again vastly outsold by the regular sedan: 28,095 units versus 3138. Among detail refinements made to both models that year was an extra 20 horsepower—320 total—from the 430-cubic-inch V-8, the sole engine offering. This was the last year for the Continental's "compact" 123-inch wheelbase.

Experimental vehicles appearing in 1963 include the Chevrolet Monza GT and SS; Ford Allegro, Cougar II, and Mustang II; Mercury Super Cyclone and Super Marauder; Oldsmobile J-TR; Plymouth Satellite convertible; Pontiac X-400

Goodyear introduces a premium safety tire with an inner "spare" that allows driving for 100 miles after the outer carcass blows out

The consumer evaluation program for the experimental Chrysler Turbine gets underway as the first cars are delivered in November

Studebaker ends U.S. automobile and truck production in South Bend on December 20, 1963, consolidating output of a much reduced model range in its small Hamilton, Ontario, plant

▲ "Breezeway Design" came to closed full-size Mercurys via a major 1963 restyle, as touted in this ad.

▲ Mercury's S-55 had less success than many sporty big cars, but lasted longer than most. For '63 it came as a hardtop coupe (formal or fastback), ragtop, and hardtop sedan. A drop-down, reverse-slant Breezeway rear window is evident on this $3650 formal hardtop, of which 3863 were sold.

▲ Introduced as a close copy of Ford's Fairlane, Mercury's mid-size Meteor returned for '63 with more impressive looks and new hardtop coupes in $2448 Custom and $2628 bucket-seat S-33 trim; the latter is shown here.

▲ Full-size Mercurys again were grouped into Monterey and Monterey Custom lines for 1963. This Custom hardtop sedan came with a 250-bhp 390 V-8 and a $3148 base price.

▲ Like Ford's Falcon, Mercury's Comet added hardtops and convertibles for 1963: Custom and bucket-seat S-22 models. This is the $2605 Custom hardtop; 9432 were sold.

▲ Crisper sheetmetal marked the big '63 Oldsmobiles, like this sporty Starfire hardtop coupe, which attracted 21,148 customers at a starting price of $4129. It shared its concave rear window with only the Pontiac Grand Prix.

▼ The "Pocket Rocket" Olds Jetfire continued with its hardtop styling for 1963. Sales of this $3048 coupe rose a bit to 5842 units, but it would not return for '64. Its 215-bhp turbocharged 215-cid V-8 developed one bhp per cubic inch.

▲ Plymouth (like Dodge) issued a big new 426 wedge-head V-8 option for 1963 with up to 425 nominal horsepower. Most went into the lightest Savoy two-door sedans for stock-class quarter-mile competition. Here, Tom Grove's "Melrose Missile III" lights off at the NHRA Pomona Winternationals.

▲ Without changing the trim 112-inch wheelbase, Olds gave its 1963 F-85 compacts more of a big-car appearance, as buyers wanted. This Deluxe four-door sedan was the F-85's second-best-selling '63 model, after the new Cutlass Sport Coupe hardtop, snaring 29,269 buyers with an appealing base price of $2592. All F-85s ran with the 215-cid aluminum V-8 rated at 155 or 185 bhp, with 215 horses reserved for the Jetfire.

▲ One of the quickest Plymouths in NHRA Super Stock competition, Arlen Vanke's '63 Savoy two-door was one of 105 factory "drag specials" built with aluminum hood, 426 wedge-head V-8—and absolutely no frills.

▲ Plymouth styling improved greatly for '63, sales somewhat less so. The mid-range Belvedere series again included a hardtop coupe. Priced at $2431 with the Slant Six, $2538 with the 318 V-8, it snared only 9204 buyers.

▲ Just 9057 Plymouth ragtops were built for '63, of which 3836 were $3082 bucket-seat Sport Furys like this one.

▲ As in '62, Plymouth's 1963 Sport Fury convertible came with a standard V-8, albeit a 318 versus a 361, which was optional along with a 383 and the new 426.

▲ Newly stacked quad headlights gave a wider front-end look to 1963 full-size Pontiacs, like this top-line $3568 Bonneville convertible. Some 23,459 were built.

◄▲ A big-block 421 V-8 remained the top power for big '63 Pontiacs, but now delivered up to 410 horses in ultimate "High Output" tune with two four-barrel carbs. This $2859 Catalina Sport Coupe (*left*) is so equipped. A discreet front-fender badge (*above*) was the only clue.

▲ Pontiac's Grand Prix was even more handsome for 1963. The grille was again unique to the bucket-seat hardtop, which scored 72,959 sales at $3489 apiece.

▲ This '63 Pontiac Catalina two-door sedan carries a Super Duty 421—and a definite rear-end rake. It drag-raced for four years early on. Stock weight: 3685 pounds.

▲ Like its Buick and Olds sisters, Pontiac's 1963 Tempest was squared up and slightly bulked up on an unchanged wheelbase. The sporty Le Mans became a separate series that year with a $2418 hardtop coupe and this $2742 convertible, of which 15,957 were sold. Power options ran to a 260-bhp 326 V-8.

▲ Shown in '62 but not genuinely available until 1963, Studebaker's Avanti wowed everyone with its unique Raymond Loewy styling, aircraft-inspired four-seat interior, and ample V-8 power. Price: $4445. Production: 3834.

▲ Studebaker's aging Lark compacts saw tumbling 1963 sales despite more cosmetic tweaks and a bucket-seat Daytona series with wagon, hardtop coupe, and a $2679 convertible. Only 1015 ragtops were sold.

▲ An optional—and rare—"Euro-style" fabric sunroof graces this '63 Studebaker Lark Daytona hardtop, which carries that year's also rare 289 R2 V-8 option with 290 horses, which gave the Lark scorching performance.

▲ Studebaker's R2 option was also available for workaday '63 Larks like this $2315 Custom two-door sedan, which looks deceptively stock except for small front-fender R2 badges. Curb weight was only 2940 pounds.

▲ A '63 Studebaker novelty was the Wagonaire wagon with a sliding rear roof section, which was unfortunately prone to water leaks. This is the top-line Daytona version, which sold for $2835 with the base 180-bhp V-8.

CHAPTER ELEVEN

# 1964-1971

# THE MUSCLE CAR ERA

American history accelerated like some new "muscle car" in 1964-71, fueled by the power of television. Words and pictures flooded America's living rooms in a relentless electronic torrent: a man on the moon, too many men fallen in Vietnam; assassinations in Los Angeles and Memphis; riots in Watts, Detroit, and Chicago; "hippies," "hawks," and "doves"; sit-ins, "love-ins," and "Laugh-In"; the "British invasion" and the "Motown sound"; long hair and mini-skirts; thalidomide and marijuana; the rise and fall of Lyndon Johnson, the fall and rise of Richard Nixon.

If the nation seemed to be suffering the worst of times, the Big Three automakers and American Motors enjoyed some of their best. Sales shifted into overdrive, spurred by a host of flashy new models, a national economy that revved up in lockstep with America's war effort in Vietnam, and a fast-growing pool of more affluent buyers and multi-car households. Thus, in 1965 the industry built over nine million cars for the first time in a single calendar year. Ironically, Studebaker ceased production the next year after closing its 112-year-old South Bend, Indiana, plant in late 1963 to make a last, short stand in Canada with "Common Sense Cars."

The keys to Detroit's success in this period were "think young" styling and unprecedented performance. Sounding the gun for another all-out "horsepower race," Pontiac stuffed a big 389 V-8 into its newly enlarged '64 Tempest to create a "muscle car." Oldsmobile unleashed its now-famous 4-4-2 package that same year. For 1965, Chevrolet listed a big-block option for its year-old intermediate Chevelle, and Buick issued racy Gran Sport Skylarks. Chrysler continued mid-sizers with wedge-head 426 options, then upped the ante by offering its hulking Hemi, which had been cleaning up in stock-car racing, as a showroom option for 1966. By that time, Dearborn had jazzy Ford Fairlane GTs and Mercury Cyclones with similar big-inch powerplants.

Yet as popular and awe-inspiring as muscle cars were, Ford scored the decade's biggest coup with the Mustang, a stylish new "sporty compact" with more sheer youth-appeal than anything except the Corvette. Suddenly, Detroit had yet another new breed: the "ponycar." Again, competitors rushed to lasso stampeding buyers, and by 1968 there was a menagerie of Camaros, Firebirds, Cougars, Barracudas, Javelins, and AMXs.

But "bigger" still meant "better" in these years, so bread-and-butter Detroiters all grew larger, heavier, and more complex. Even ponycars soon vied with high-power intermediates for horses and cubic inches. Symbolizing this trend was Oldsmobile's big new personal-luxury Toronado of 1966, America's first production front-drive car since the late-Thirties Cord. But radical engineering alone still didn't assure success, and dwindling sales brought on by ponycars claimed Chevy's rear-engine Corvair after 1969. More saleable by far were Detroit's new lower-priced big luxury cars, the 1965 Ford LTD and Chevrolet Caprice.

Of course, the go-go good times couldn't last, and sobering new realities were evident by 1971. Demand for both ponycars and muscle cars was plummeting, and Congress was adding new requirements for safety features and exhaust-pipe emissions to the original list mandated for 1968-70. What's more, imports had made a comeback, including a new horde from Japan. The Sixties had been a weird, wild, wonderful ride, but times were a-changing, and Detroit, like all America, would never be quite the same.

---

**1964**

Specialty and sporty cars are rapidly gaining favor

New models include the Chevrolet Chevelle, Mercury Comet Caliente, Oldsmobile Jetstar 88 and Jetstar I, Studebaker Challenger

Ford Mustang is launched on April 17, 1964, as a 1965 model; Plymouth's sporty Barracuda fastback, a '64, had already bowed on April 1

Industry output leaps to 7.9 million cars

All '64 models have front seatbelts

More than one-fourth of the '64 cars are two-door hardtops; nearly 69 percent have a V-8 engine; 18.5 percent sport bucket seats

Dodge marks its 50th Anniversary and provides the Official Pace Car, a Challenger convertible, for the Indy 500 race

▲ AMC's small 1964 Rambler Americans wore attractive all-new styling on a six-inch longer wheelbase (106 inches). Here, the top-trim 440 convertible, hardtop, and wagon.

▲ A minor facelift freshened AMC's larger cars for 1964. One of four models in a slimmed-down Ambassador line, the $2985 990 wagon attracted only 4407 customers.

▲ The sporty Rambler Classic Typhoon hardtop bowed in mid-1964 to introduce a modern new inline-six of the same name (232 cid, 145 bhp). Just 2520 were sold at $2509 apiece.

▲ New competition was hurting AMC by '64, yet sales remained good. The company passed a major production milestone that year with this Classic 770 station wagon.

▲ Hardtop coupes graced AMC's '64 lineup for the first time since the last Nash/Hudson models of 1957. This bucket-seat Ambassador 990-H was the premium offering, priced at $2917. Just 2955 buyers succumbed to its charms.

---

Studebaker arranges to buy engines from General Motors for Canadian-built 1965-66 models

Automatic transmission selectors are standardized at "Park-Reverse-Neutral-Drive-Low" in some GM models; others follow for '65

A 340/360-bhp, 425-cid V-8 is available in big Buicks, standard in the Riviera

Buick's Special/Skylark models ride a new 115-inch-wheelbase, intermediate-size A-body platform

Wildcat puts the Electra's 401-cid V-8 into the Buick LeSabre chassis

An automatic heat/air conditioning system, optional on Cadillacs, holds a pre-set temperature, while Twilight Sentinel controls the headlights

Cadillac's 390-cid V-8 grows to 429 cubic inches and 340 horses

▲ Buicks looked brawnier for '64. Sporty Wildcats, like this $3267 hardtop coupe, boasted a new 425 V-8 option with either 340 or 360 horsepower.

▲ No longer compacts, Buick's 1964 Specials rode a new 115-inch wheelbase to become mid-size cars. This $2834 Skylark convertible saw output reach 10,225 units.

▲ Buick's 1964 Electra 225s wore a nice blend of rounded and razor-edge lines. One of five models in that top-of-the-line series, the $4070 hardtop coupe accounted for 7181 sales.

▲ There was no need to fiddle much with Riviera for 1964, and Buick didn't. But there was more standard power in the 340-horse 425 V-8. Output slipped slightly to 37,658.

▲ Cadillacs achieved a wider look via a restyled face. Here is the lush '64 Eldorado Biarritz convertible, which started at a lofty $6610. At that, only 1450 of the 4605-pound ragtops were produced for the model year.

◀ Giving new meaning to the term "family bus" was Buick's new 1964 Skylark Sportwagon with "Greyhound Sceni-Cruiser" roofline. Body and wheelbase (120 inches) were unique to this model, which sold for around $3100.

Checker drops its Superba sedan and wagon, but keeps Marathon

The mid-size Chevrolet Chevelle debuts; Malibus can have a Super Sport package

Chevy II adds the 283-cid V-8 and four-speed gearbox to the options list

Corvairs adopt a transverse rear camber-compensating spring to improve handling

A convertible returns to the Letter-Series Chrysler 300, now the 300-K

For the first time, a V-8 (273 cid) is available for the Dodge Dart and Plymouth Valiant

Dodge's "Ramcharger" is now a race-only 426-cid Hemi; everyday buyers get a tamer "Street Wedge" V-8 with 365 bhp

A prototype Studebaker SS roadster is shown—it will evolve into the limited-production Excalibur

▲ The full-size "Jet Smooth" Chevrolets looked a little boxier for 1964, but also less busy. Impala SS was again the sportiest of the lot, though this hardtop coupe came with a 140-horsepower 230 six for $2839, $2947 with the 195-bhp 283 V-8.

▲ Chevy's "real fine" 409 V-8 remained the top power option for full-size '64 Chevys, and could belt out up to 425 horses at the tap of the toe.

▲ As usual, spartan Biscayne sedans anchored the bottom of Chevy's full-size '64 fleet. This two-door stickered at $2363 with the standard 140-horse 230 six.

▲ Atypical for Detroit, Chevy's stunning Corvette Sting Ray returned for '64 with less "gingerbread," which on fastbacks like this also meant a one-piece instead of a split rear window. Base price was still $4252; 8304 were built.

▲ A flat-six stroked to 164 cid boosted 1964 Chevy Corvair standard horsepower to 95 or 110. Styling changes were very modest. Here, the $2335 Monza four-door sedan, which attracted 21,926 buyers, only one-fourth as many as the Monza coupe.

---

Ford's Falcon and Mercury's Comet are reskinned, bulkier-looking; the 260 V-8 is still offered

The restyled fourth-generation Thunderbird features "Silent-Flo" ventilation

Mercury adds a Cyclone hardtop; slantback Marauders deliver awesome performance with a 427-cid V-8 option

The full-size, bucket-seat Jetstar I joins the Oldsmobile line, while the mid-size Cutlass lineup adds its first muscle car, the 4-4-2, at mid-year

A more orthodox Pontiac Tempest uses an inline six as the base engine; the legendary GTO, considered the first "muscle car," arrives at mid-year

Pontiac offers a Catalina "2+2" option that includes bucket seats

▲ Chrysler's "crisp, clean custom look" was tastefully warmed over for '64. This New Yorker four-door sedan was downpriced to $3994—and sales rose modestly to 15,443.

▲ Chrysler held onto hardtop wagons longer than anyone else—witness this 1964 New Yorker Town & Country. But the body style would not be back for '65. The main reason was meager model-year sales of only 2793 units.

▼ The Letter-Series Chrysler 300 convertible was reinstated for '64 after a year's absence, but the $4522 ragtop 300-K managed a production run of only 625 units.

▲ With 3022 built, the $4056 300-K hardtop coupe easily outsold the ragtop. Alas, both Letter-Series Chryslers were even more like non-letter 300s, which cost about $600-$700 less—a significant difference in 1964.

▲ The non-letter 300 ragtop sold for $3803. Trim details and a 305-horse 383 V-8 set the 300s apart from the 300-Ks, whose standard 360-bhp 413 was nonetheless optional on 300s. All '64 Chryslers rode a 122-inch wheelbase.

### 1964 Model Year Production

| | | |
|---|---|---|
| 1. Chevrolet 2,318,619 | 7. Oldsmobile 493,991 | 12. Studebaker 36,697 |
| 2. Ford 1,594,053 | 8. Rambler 393,859 | 13. Lincoln 36,297 |
| 3. Pontiac 715,261 | 9. Mercury 298,609 | 14. Imperial 23,295 |
| 4. Plymouth 551,633 | 10. Cadillac 165,909 | 15. Checker 960[1] |
| 5. Buick 510,490 | 11. Chrysler 153,319 | |
| 6. Dodge 501,781 | | |

[1]*Estimate, excludes taxicabs*

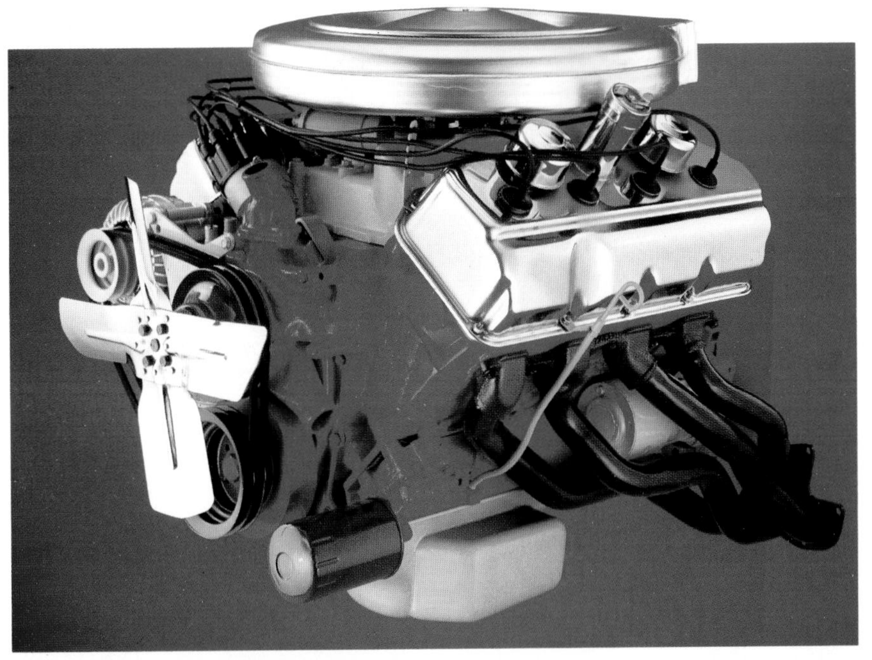

▲ Obviously ready for quarter-mile action, this two-door '64 Dodge 330 is a rare "Hemi-Charger" with the factory Maximum Performance Package. Front-end styling was new for '64.

◀ To keep pace in a burgeoning new "horsepower race," Chrysler put hemi heads on its biggest 426 wedge-head V-8 in 1964—but strictly for competition. The result, aptly nicknamed "King Kong," was rated at 425 horsepower, but MoPar experts figured actual output was closer to 570.

▲ Dodge's big 880 models wore a smoother look for '64 via tasteful restyling front and rear. Although this Custom ragtop was attractively priced at $3264, only 1058 were sold.

▲ Still based on '62 tooling, mid-size Dodges looked better still for '64. Vee'd C-pillars were new to hardtop coupes like this $2978 Polara 500, which found 15,163 buyers.

◀ Dodge's new compact Dart had sold well in '63, so the '64s were little changed. However, a new 273.5-cid small-block V-8 option with 180 horses gave sporty GTs like this hardtop coupe more satisfying go.

---

Rambler debuts the specially trimmed, yellow-and-black Typhoon hardtop to showcase its new 232-cid six; 2520 will be built

The last American-built Studebakers leave South Bend, Indiana, on December 20, 1963; the Gran Turismo Hawk, Avanti, hardtops, convertibles, and trucks are dropped

Experimental and show vehicles during 1964 include the Mercury Park Lane 400; GM Firebird IV, Runabout, and GM-X; Chevrolet Toronado and Super Nova; Buick Silver Arrow; and Ford Aurora station wagon

▲ A full lower-body reskin made Ford's compact Falcon look more "grown-up" for '64. This Futura Sprint convertible, 4278 of which were built, boasts the 260-cid small-block V-8 option with 164 lively horses.

▲ After a class win in 1963, Ford followed up by entering eight V-8 Falcon Sprint hardtop coupes in the 1964 Monte Carlo Rally. One finished second overall in a fine display of "Total Performance."

▲ Ford's mid-size Fairlane looked a tad busier for '64, but again offered 289 V-8 options with up to 271 horses. The bucket-seat 500 Sports Coupe hardtop listed at $2502, and 21,431 buyers happily drove one home.

◀▲ After years of watching MoPars go by on the strips, Ford conjured a Fairlane drag car in '64. Called Thunderbolt, it packed a "High-Riser" 427 V-8 (*above*) with 425 nominal horses, but at least 500 actual, plus lighter fiberglass body panels and many more speed-enhancing tricks. Ford built only 100 at a cost of $5300 each, but priced them just under $4000.

◀ Ford's personal-luxury Thunderbird picked up sales steam with all-new 1964 models featuring a "begadgeted" interior with a curved "cove" back seat, plus a crisp yet more conservative look outside. The convertible shown here listed at $4953. It garnered 9168 sales—compared to 60,552 hardtops and 22,715 Landau hardtops. Although the 113.2-inch wheelbase was about the same, weight was up about 250 pounds (4586 for the ragtop).

---

Vetta Ventura emerges as the successor to the Apollo sports car; the targa-roofed Warrior has a rear-mounted V-4; the Griffith sports coupe wears a modified fiberglass TVR body; the scaled-down Cord 8/10 Sportsman convertible uses a Corvair drivetrain

A 45-day strike beginning in September idles 275,000 workers at General Motors

▲ Big Fords still used a lot of 1960 tooling for '64, but it wasn't evident with that year's massive lower-body restyle. This bucket-seat Galaxie 500/XL hardtop coupe sold for $3233 with the standard 289 V-8; 58,306 were built.

▲ A *bona fide* collectible now, the Ford Galaxie 500/XL convertible sold for $3495 in 1964. Most big XLs continued to be ordered with one of the big-block 390 V-8s and self-shift Cruise-O-Matic. This ragtop attracted 15,169 buyers.

▲ The '64 Galaxie 500/XL boasted new thin-shell front bucket seats with heavy chrome moldings. Dashboard design was much as in the '63 model, and so was the wide center shift console (here with the four-speed manual). Padded dash and dished steering wheel were standard.

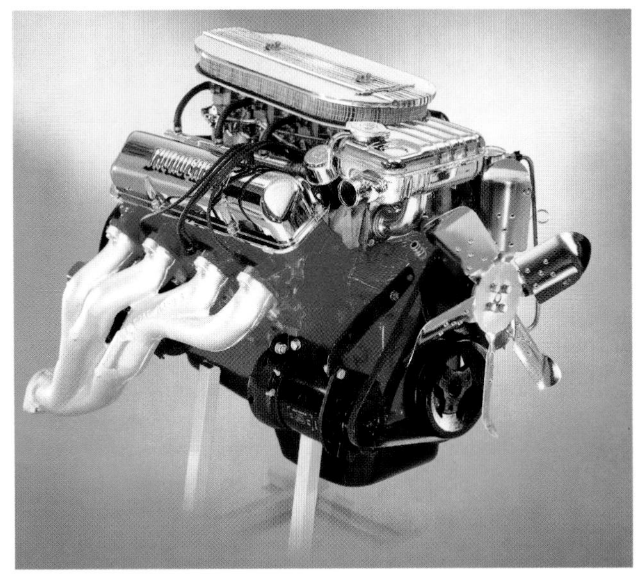

▲ Helping to cement Ford's advertising claim as the home of "Total Performance" for 1964 was this new big-block 427-cubic-inch V-8. Basically a bored-out version of the previous 406, it delivered 410 horsepower with a single four-barrel carb, and a mighty 425 with dual-quads, as seen here. Racing versions, with even more power, made the big Galaxies the '64 champ on the NASCAR stock-car racing circuit.

◀ Ford opened up a big new market with the Falcon-based Mustang. Introduced on April 17, 1964, at the New York World's Fair, the new sporty compact sent people scurrying to Ford showrooms like nothing in years, touching off "Mustang Mania" and Detroit's greatest sales success of the Sixties. This ragtop, one of three debut 1965 models, cost $2614 with the 101-bhp six, and scored an amazing (for a ragtop) 101,945 sales.

▲ This $5739 Imperial Crown took on a Lincolnesque look for '64 in a tasteful makeover by Chrysler design chief Elwood Engel (principal designer of the '61 Lincoln).

▲ Lincoln grew three inches in wheelbase for 1964 (to 126), but retained the classically simple lines of 1961-63. This convertible sedan sold for $6720, but only 3328 were called for.

▲ Mercury marked its Silver Anniversary in 1964 with an adroitly facelifted full-size line led by performance-oriented Marauder semi-fastback hardtops like this mid-range Montclair two-door. Priced at $3127, 6459 were sold.

▲ Mercury's Marauder hardtops had bowed in mid-1963 along with Ford's big "slantback" Galaxies. The '64 line listed a coupe and sedan in all three series, starting as low as $2884 for the two-door Monterey, which rung up 8760 sales.

▲ Mercury bulked up its '64 Comet compact to fill in for the mid-size Meteor, which was dropped due to slow sales. Here, the low-line 202 two-door sedan; 32,425 were sold at $2154.

▲ Like Buick, Oldsmobile debuted a "split-level" wagon in mid-'64. Called Vista Cruiser, this F-85 model cost around $3000, and 3394 were built (plus 10,606 pricier Cutlass versions).

▲ Lansing's big bucket-seat Starfire twosome received crisper styling and new features. But that didn't help—demand for the $4138 hardtop dropped one-third to 13,573 units.

◀ Oldsmobile's F-85 went from compact to mid-size for '64 by adopting a handsome new "A-body" platform shared with Buick's Special/Skylark, Pontiac's Tempest/Le Mans, and Chevy's new Chevelle. The sporty Cutlass became a separate five-model series, of which this $2784 Holiday hardtop coupe was the best-seller: 36,153 units. Cutlasses came with a new cast-iron 330 V-8 making 290 horses.

▲ Regarded as the first modern "muscle car," Pontiac's GTO blew in for 1964 as a Tempest-based convertible, hardtop coupe, and this $3200 pillared Sport Coupe with a standard 325-horse 389 V-8. Total GTO production was 32,450 units.

▲ Full-size '64 Pontiacs wore a more rounded rendition of '63 styling. The Catalina ragtop, as well as this $2869 Sport Coupe (74,793 built), offered a new $291 "2+2" option. With buckets-and-console interior and up to 370 horses, 7998 were ordered.

▲ Plymouth continued clawing its way back up the sales charts with prettier '64 styling on its still mid-size "standards." This Sport Fury hardtop coupe more than doubled output to 23,695 units. Major stock-car racing wins helped.

▲ Sport Furys remained the sportiest big Plymouths for '64, but were still smaller than Ford and Chevy rivals. The ragtop sold for $3095, this hardtop for $2864 with the standard 230-horse 318 V-8 (361, 383, and 426 V-8s optional).

▲ Like Dodge's Darts, '64 Plymouth Valiants, like this $2256 Signet hardtop, could have a new 180-bhp V-8.

▲ Studebaker Larks, like this $2451 Daytona hardtop, wore a neat new look for '64—but sales still tumbled.

▲ The 1964 Studebakers, here the $2805 Daytona ragtop, would be the last to be built in South Bend, Indiana.

◀ Studebaker's singular Avanti coupe returned for '64 with the same $4445 price tag and square headlamp bezels as one of the few changes from debut '63. A 240-horse 289 V-8 remained standard, and options ran to a 290-horse "R2" version—or a 335-bhp, 304.5-cid "R3." Unfortunately, sales dropped from 3834 to just 809, which helped force Studebaker's exit from South Bend. Happily, the Avanti would have a new—and long—life afterward, though not as a Studebaker.

▲ American Motors tried to one-up Ford's Mustang 2+2 fastback with its mid-1965 Marlin, a Classic-based "3+3." Priced at $3100 with the 232 six, it offered a wide range of options and attracted 10,327 customers.

▲ A fleet of Ramblers heads out of Kenosha to American Motors dealerships in 1965. AMC's total production for the model year was 391,366, but bleaker days were ahead.

▲ The '65 Rambler Americans showed only detail changes. AMC built 3882 of its $2418 440 ragtops that year.

▲ Ambassadors, like this $2656 990 four-door sedan, wore straight-edged lines and stacked headlamps.

▶ AMC's mid-size Rambler Classic added a convertible for '65, a first for the line. Sold only in top-trim 770 guise, it stickered at $2696 with the 145-bhp, 232-cid six. Sales were modest, as only 4953 were built.

**1965**

New models include the Chrysler 300-L, Dodge Coronet and Monaco, Ford LTD, and Gran Sport (GS) editions of the Buick Skylark and Riviera

American car production sets a record: 8.8 million for the '65 model year

Front disc brakes are installed on many '65 models

The Automotive Products Trade Act of 1965 eliminates tariffs on new North American motor vehicles crossing U.S. or Canadian borders from either direction

Ralph Nader publishes *Unsafe at Any Speed,* a critique on auto safety that springboards into a potent consumer movement

▲ The 1965 Buick catalog listed no fewer than five basic convertibles (*from left*): Special, Skylark, LeSabre, Wildcat, and Electra 225 Custom. Prices ranged from $2605 to $4440. With 10,456 orders, the Skylark GS was the most popular.

▲ This Electra 225 Custom hardtop sedan shows off the flowing new lines worn by all big Buicks for 1965. It stickered at $4389, and 29,932 were purchased. A standard-trim companion cost $4206, but it found only 12,842 buyers.

▲ A good-looker then and now, Buick's '65 Wildcat convertible came as a $3502 Deluxe or as this spiffier $3727 Custom. Combined sales: 9014. Wildcats now rode Electra's 126-inch wheelbase, rather than LeSabre's 123-inch chassis.

▲ With a standard 155-horse, 225-cid V-6, Buick's Skylark Thin Pillar Coupe was a fairly rare commodity for 1965, as just 4195 were built. The less deluxe Special Standard Coupe, priced at $2343 (versus $2537), sold better, attracting 12,945 buyers. A 300-cid V-8 was optional.

▲ For 1965, Buick hid the headlights on the Riviera, which now stickered at $4385. Production slipped to 34,586 units, but Buick wasn't too concerned because it had an all-new model in the wings for 1966. The Gran Sport option as seen on this car was installed on 3355 Rivs.

A nationwide "HELP" communications network is announced; it will use CB radios

GM's full-size models adopt perimeter frames

Chrysler products abandon the automatic transmission pushbutton controls used since 1956

FM stereo radios become available in Chevrolets

AMC introduces its fastback "3+3" Marlin on February 10, 1965; it's based on the Rambler Classic

The Avanti II enters production; it's much like the original Studebaker version, but is powered by a potent Corvette V-8

The Gran Sport option for Buick Riviera and Skylark includes the Wildcat 401-cid V-8

▲ Having introduced a big new 429 V-8 for '64, Cadillac completed its product renewal with trim new '65 styling. The standard convertible, now a de Ville priced at $5639, sold 19,200 copies. Calais was the new bottom-rung series.

▲ Checker Motors of Kalamazoo began selling civilian versions of its famous taxis in 1959. This $3140 Marathon wagon was one of three '65 models.Total sales: 930 units.

▲ Chevy's mid-size '65 Chevelle received only minor style tweaks that also appeared on the Chevelle-based El Camino pickup. Prices started at $2380; sales improved to 34,724.

▲ The sassy Chevelle Malibu SS got a big performance boost at mid-'65 with a big-block 396 V-8 option with 375 horses. Just 201 cars got one, but '66 would see many more.

▲ Early Chevelles like this '65 Malibu SS ragtop were ideally sized—much like the "classic" mid-Fifties Chevys. This model sold for $2750 with base six, $2858 with the 283 V-8.

---

A tilt/telescope steering column is optional on Cadillacs, as is an automatic leveling suspension

Checker turns to Chevrolet for engines, six or V-8

Caprice Custom Sedan joins the Chevrolet line at mid-year as the top Impala and LTD-fighter

Chevrolet's Chevy II Nova gains a 327-cid V-8 option; Dodge Dart and Plymouth Barracuda can have a 273-cid, 235-bhp Commando V-8

The Corvair sports all-new hardtop styling and a redesigned all-independent suspension; Corsa replaces the Monza Spyder

Corvette gains optional four-wheel disc brakes, plus its first big-block V-8 engine

Chrysler's 300-L is destined to be the final Letter-Series model; 2405 hardtops and 440 ragtops are built

▲ Chevy's big '65 news was a totally revamped full-size line with curvy new contours and a full-perimeter frame. The sporty Impala SS continued as a hardtop coupe and as this convertible, which listed for $3104 with base six; most buyers opted for a V-8.

◀ Helping to open up a new market for lower-priced, full-size luxury cars was the mid-1965 "Caprice Custom Sedan by Chevrolet," a $200 package option for the Impala hardtop sedan—a quick response to Ford's lush new Galaxie LTD. A beefed-up frame was included with the posher trim.

▲▶ Chevy further cleaned up the Corvette Sting Ray's looks for '65 and added leather seats, AM/FM radio, and four-wheel power-disc brakes to the options list. The convertible seen above wears the extra-cost factory hardtop. Corvette sales reached another new high: 23,562 units. So did power, with the mid-year 396 V-8 option with up to 425 horses.

---

Dodge output starts a rapid rise; the Coronet name returns on revamped mid-size models

Dodge's Coronet Hemi-Charger aims at the dragstrips, while the Monaco is a full-size sport/luxury hardtop

Resembling the prewar Mercedes SSK, the neoclassic Excalibur SSK roadster enters limited production priced at $7250

Ford Falcons now can have the 289-cid V-8 with 200 bhp

Ford's posh new Galaxie 500 LTD is claimed to ride as "Quiet as a Rolls-Royce"

A 2+2 fastback joins the initial Mustang coupe and soft-top; 680,989 Mustangs are sold from April '64 through August '65

▲ The compact Chevy II line got a mild 1965 freshening that included a new grille and, for sedans, a more formal roofline. Shown here is the low-line 100 two-door sedan, which carried a base price of $2011.

▲ The Corvair Greenbrier wagon was in its final year for '65, when its commercial brothers gave way to more conventional new front-engine "ChevyVan" models. Just 1528 were sold this year at $2609 apiece.

▲ Regular Corvairs got a new lease on life for '65 with pretty new all-hardtop styling. This $2519 Corsa coupe, of which 20,291 were built, has the 180-horse "Turbo Air" flat-six, which added only $158 to the price.

▲ The last of the Letter-Series Chryslers were the '65 300-L hardtop and $4618 convertible, which shared a bigger, brand-new design with linemates—but were even less special. Production was 2405 hardtops and just 440 ragtops.

▲ Crisp but not altogether boxy describes Chrysler's 1965 styling, the work of corporate design chief Elwood Engel. Top-line New Yorkers like this $4161 hardtop coupe wore unique translucent taillamps. This model sold 9357 copies.

▲ Dodge revived the Coronet name for 1965 "mid-size" cars descended from its 1962-64 "standards." This sporty 500 hardtop coupe stickered at $2674.

### 1965 Model Year Production

| | | |
|---|---|---|
| 1. Chevrolet 2,375,118 | 7. Dodge 489,065 | 13. Studebaker 19,435 |
| 2. Ford 2,170,795 | 8. Rambler 391,366 | 14. Imperial 18,409 |
| 3. Pontiac 802,000 | 9. Mercury 346,751 | 15. Checker 930[1] |
| 4. Plymouth 728,228 | 10. Chrysler 206,089 | 16. Excalibur 56 |
| 5. Buick 600,145 | 11. Cadillac 182,435 | 17. Avanti II 21 |
| 6. Oldsmobile 591,701 | 12. Lincoln 40,180 | |

[1] *Estimate, excludes taxicabs*

▲ A 180-horse, 273-cid V-8 was standard for '65 Coronet 500s, like this $2894 convertible, but optional wedge-head 383s and big 426s were still available. Coronet 500 sales—hardtop and ragtop—totaled 32,745 units.

▲ Dodge built only a few '65 Hemi-Coronet "altereds" for drag racing. Like "Dandy" Dick Landy's mount here, they were banned by NHRA and thus ran in AHRA. Landy's car could turn in quarter-mile times of 10.2 seconds.

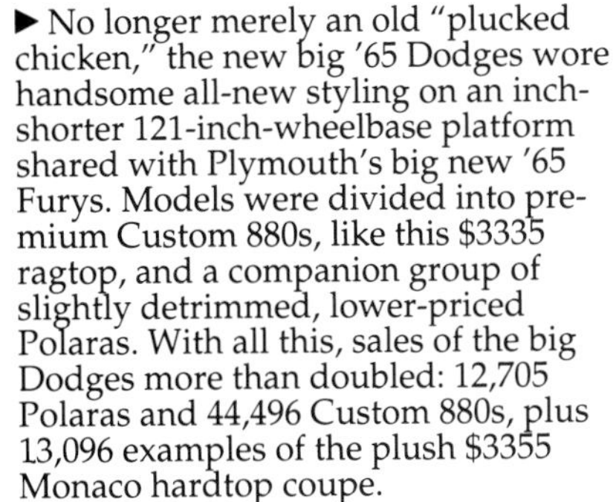

▶ No longer merely an old "plucked chicken," the new big '65 Dodges wore handsome all-new styling on an inch-shorter 121-inch-wheelbase platform shared with Plymouth's big new '65 Furys. Models were divided into premium Custom 880s, like this $3335 ragtop, and a companion group of slightly detrimmed, lower-priced Polaras. With all this, sales of the big Dodges more than doubled: 12,705 Polaras and 44,496 Custom 880s, plus 13,096 examples of the plush $3355 Monaco hardtop coupe.

▲ Dodge's compact Dart wasn't vastly changed for 1965, but a new checked grille made for easy identification. At $2628, the sporty GT ragtop remained the priciest model; many were ordered with the V-8 option.

▲ The '65 Dodge Dart GT hardtop listed at $2404 with the standard Slant Six, but two small-block 273 V-8 options boosted horsepower to 180 or 235. A low 2715-pound curb weight helped performance.

▲ Dart's liveliest engine option was this four-barrel 273-cubic-inch V-8 with a wilder cam, which boosted horsepower to 235. An optional four-speed manual transmission was also new to the Dart for the '65 season.

---

Mustangs can be optioned with a 271-bhp "Hi-Po" 289 V-8

Thunderbirds boast sequential turn signals, standard front disc brakes, reversible keys, and a keyless locking system

Oldsmobile adopts a 400-cid V-8 for its 4-4-2 option package

Full-size Plymouths return; the Fury models are the biggest Plymouths ever

Mid-size Belvederes and bucket-seat Satellites join the Plymouth stable; 11 models are offered

The Mustang-based Shelby GT-350 fastback features a modified 289 V-8 with 306 bhp

Studebaker drops the Lark name, and offers Canadian-built sedans and wagons only

▲ Widely advertised as being "Quieter Than a Rolls-Royce," the Galaxie 500 LTD was the costliest and cushiest of the all-new 1965 full-size Fords. This hardtop sedan stickered at $3313, and scored an impressive 68,038 model-year sales.

▲ Ford's new '65 Galaxie 500 LTD was also offered as this $2685 hardtop coupe, but it didn't sell as well: 37,691 units. LTDs came with a V-8 as standard, the 200-bhp 289.

▲ As the first fully revised big Fords since 1960, the chiseled '65s were quieter, stiffer, and handled better. Production of the $3498 Galaxie 500/XL ragtop reached 9849 units.

▲ Ford's wildly popular Mustang got a revised engine slate with up to 271 horses for the formal '65 model year, and sales kept galloping. The hardtop's price crept up to $2416.

▲ Whitewalls, wire wheel covers, and a decklid luggage rack were just three of a myriad of options for 1965 Mustangs like this convertible, which was now base priced at $2653.

▲ This racy "2+2" fastback expanded the Ford Mustang stable for the formal 1965 model year, and galloped off with 77,079 buyers. It sold for $2589 with the base 120-horse 200 six.

---

Experimental vehicles displayed during 1965 include AMC's St. Maritz and Tahiti; Dodge Charger II; Plymouth XP-VIP; Mercury Astron; Comet Escapade and Cyclone Sportster; Lincoln Continental Coronation Coupe; Ford Bordinet Cobra, Mercer Cobra, and Black Pearl; Chevrolet Mako Shark II and Concours

Don Yenko offers the limited-edition Yenko Stinger—a race-modified Corvair Corsa

▲ A squarer, more sculptured look marked Ford's '65 mid-size Fairlanes. At $2538, this bucket-seat 500 Sports Coupe hardtop was the sportiest offering; 15,141 were produced.

▲ The '65 Falcon finished out the original 1960 design. Changes were few, save for a revised grille. The popular $2226 Futura hardtop coupe attracted 25,754 customers.

▲ A rear-seat tonneau *a la* the '62-'63 Sports Roadster graces this $4953 Ford Thunderbird convertible, of which 6846 were built for '65—2352 fewer than its '64 predecessor.

▲ Imperial's four-model '64 lineup returned for 1965 with minor trim and equipment revisions. This Crown hardtop sedan remained the top seller, with 11,628 orders at a base price of $5772. Glass plates covered the headlights.

▲ Lincoln Continental scored higher 1965 sales despite no major changes. As before, the "pillared-hardtop" sedan greatly outsold the convertible sedan—this year, 36,824 to 3328. Prices: $6292 and $6938, respectively.

▲ Mercury's Comet received another restyle for '65, with vertically stacked headlights being the focal point. As before, Comet's lone ragtop resided in the plush Caliente series. Although affordably priced at $2664, it sold just 6035 copies.

▲ As in prior years, full-size '65 Oldsmobiles were differentiated by trim, equipment, and grille treatment. The most formal look, as usual, was reserved for top-line Ninety-Eight models, like this $4197 hardtop coupe, of which 12,166 were built.

▲ With an extra 35 horses—345 in all—Oldsmobile's hot 4-4-2 package was definitely hotter for '65. As in '64, the option package was available for F-85/Cutlass pillared coupes, hardtop coupes, and this ragtop—and 25,003 people ordered it.

▼ Like its full-size GM sisters, the big 1965 Oldsmobiles had a more flowing look. This sporty $4778 Starfire ragtop got only 2236 orders.

▲ Headlining Plymouth's lineup of "Roaring '65s" was the first genuine full-size Fury since 1961, with four trim levels and a complete range of body styles. At $2863, 21,367 customers chose this upper-level Fury III hardtop sedan.

▲ Plymouth's Barracuda bowed on April 1, 1964, as a Valiant-based "glassback" coupe—but not a direct reply to Ford's Mustang. Sales were good for the little-changed '65 model: 64,596 units, compared to 23,443 for '64.

◀ The "standard" 1962-64 Plymouth was restyled into the mid-size '65 Belvedere. Sporty Satellites topped the line: a hardtop and this rare $2910 ragtop (1860 built).

▶ Like Dodge, Plymouth built a relative handful of Hemi-powered mid-size "altereds" for drag racing in 1965. Note the abbreviated wheelbase.

◀ Big Pontiacs became even bigger for 1965, with fulsome new lines and longer wheelbases (121 and 124 inches) on an even wider "Wide Track" chassis. As usual, the line's glamour queen was the Bonneville convertible, which carried a base sticker price of $3594 with standard 389 V-8, Turbo Hydra-Matic, and skirted rear wheels. Sales for this model were respectable, all things considered: 21,050. Total '65 Bonneville production increased 17 percent to 134,020 units.

▲ Stacked headlights continued on Pontiac's all-new big '65s, as did the performance-oriented "2+2" package option for the Catalina convertible and this semi-fastback Sport Coupe hardtop, which sold for $3287 so equipped. The 2+2 came with a 338-horsepower 421 V-8 as standard.

▲ Tempests adopted a crisper look for '65, announced by newly stacked quad headlamps as on full-size Pontiacs. The drop-top GTO shown here stickered at $3057 and boasted 335 standard horses, 10 up on the debut '64 "Goats," with 360 bhp optional. This model attracted 11,311 buyers.

▲ Rogue replaced the 440-H as the sporty hardtop in American Motors' '66 Rambler American line. Despite a low $2370 price, only 8718 were sold.

▲ The $2601 Marlin fastback was not a Rambler for '66, but a new AMC "marque." Otherwise, changes were modest. Sales withered to a mere 4547.

▲ Ambassador also became a separate AMC "make" for '66, and offered a swank new top-line hardtop: DPL. It cost $2756, and 10,458 were built.

▲ Mid-size '66 Buicks got a "mid-life" makeover. Big-inch bucket-seat Gran Sports were now a separate line distinct from Skylarks, which included a new hardtop sedan, shown here with the $3019 GS hardtop coupe, of which 9934 were built.

▲ Buick's personal-luxury Riviera was all-new for '66, and somewhat bigger and heavier, too—but still quite elegant. Base price rose to $4408, production to 45,348 units. The GS option was again offered, and 5718 buyers chose it.

▲ After record sales in '65, Cadillac stood basically pat for '66, yet fared nearly as well. Only minor appearance changes were seen on all models, including this $5555 de Ville convertible, whose sales held steady at 19,200.

**1966**

Chevrolet output trails Ford's for the second time in the '60s; both top 2.2 million cars for the model year, as industry volume eases to 8.6 million

Dodge reaches fifth place in the production race, with a record 632,658 cars built

Oldsmobile launches the Toronado—the first production American front-wheel-drive car since the '37 Cord

Other new models include the AMC Ambassador DPL, Rambler Rebel, and American Rogue; Chevrolet Caprice Custom Coupe; Dodge Charger fastback; Ford Fairlane 500/XL and GT; Mercury Comet Capri; and the luxurious Plymouth Fury VIP

▲ Chevrolet had a hot new number for 1966 full-size cars: "427," an even bigger big-block V-8 with 390 or 425 horses. A new grille and taillights updated the styling. Seen here is the $2947 Impala SS Sport Coupe hardtop.

▲ Police-equipped cars were nothing new to Chevy in 1966. This bottom-line Biscayne six-cylinder sedan carries the exact decals and lights used on Chicago police cars in 1966.

▲ Chevy followed up on the success of the '65 Caprice hardtop sedan by adding wagons and this two-door with its own greenhouse for '66. Total Caprice output: 181,000 units.

◀ A standard big-block 396 V-8 and smooth new styling gave Chevy salesmen plenty to talk about in the mid-size 1966 Chevelle Malibu Super Sport, or SS 396. A three-speed manual was standard, but four-on-the-floor and "Turbo-Hydro" automatic were available. Incredibly, the hardtop coupe shown here started at $2776, the convertible at $2984—huge performance bargains, to say the least. The two models accounted for 72,300 sales.

---

It's the "last hurrah" for 114-year-old Studebaker. Canadian production ceases in March 1966 after a two-season trial; output for '66 is just 8947 units

Pontiac's Tempest adopts an overhead-camshaft six—ohc motors won't arrive in force in American cars until the late '80s

Rear seatbelts are made standard on all 1966 models

The average full-time American worker earns $5967 yearly; the cheapest full-size Chevrolet starts at $2379

Ford's 428-cid V-8 powers the 7-Litre hardtop and convertible models; boasting 345 bhp, it's optional on other big Fords

The National Traffic and Motor Vehicle Safety Act and the Highway Safety Act are enacted; the Department of Transportation is established

▲ With GM mandating no further development after '65, Chevy's Corvair changed little from then on. Yet it remained a desirable semi-sports car, and looked terrific. The Monza Sport Coupe cost $2350; 37,605 were built.

▲ As in 1965, Corvair offered this pillarless four-door sedan body style in base "500" trim and, shown here, sportier Monza trim, and produced 12,497 of the latter priced at $2424. The 95-horse flat six was unchanged.

▲ Chevy dropped "fuelie" small-blocks for 1966, leaving a big new 427 with up to 425 horses as Corvette's ultimate 1966 power option. It came with a domed hood. The $4295 coupe sold 9958 copies this year.

◀ Dart was part of "The Dodge Rebellion" for 1966, but changes were evolutionary, not revolutionary. A landau-type vinyl roof was a new extra for that year's GT hardtop, which stickered at $2417.

---

AMC—now a distinct make—replaces Rambler badging on the Marlin and Ambassador, and will do so soon on the Rebel

The second-generation Buick Riviera is kin to the Oldsmobile Toronado, but keeps its rear-wheel-drive setup

Variable-ratio power steering is available on Cadillacs

Chevelle's Super Sport becomes the SS 396, courtesy of a 396-cid engine; big Chevrolets add a 427-cid V-8 option

A 440-cid V-8 is now standard in the Chrysler New Yorker, and available in the big Dodge and Plymouth models

Dodge Charger is a fastback Coronet with hidden headlamps

▲ A mid-1966 surprise was Dodge's Coronet-based Charger fastback, which had originally been slated for a mid-'65 introduction to preview the Coronet's all-new '66 styling. No matter, the sleek Charger managed a healthy 37,344 sales in its abbreviated debut season.

▲ Hidden headlamps and wall-to-wall taillamps marked the '66 Dodge Charger fastback, which also came with four bucket seats and a full-length center console. A mild 230-bhp 318 V-8 was included in the $3122 base sticker price, but more power was available—even the 425-bhp Hemi.

◄◄ Chrysler muscled up its '66 mid-sizers in a big way with really impressive Hemi V-8s. One was the soon-to-be-famous 426-cubic-inch "Street Hemi" (*far left*). With dual-quad carbs, it was rated at a nominal 425 horsepower, though some estimates put the actual output at up to 575 horses. Another was the racing Hemi (*left*), which ran with a single four-barrel carb because that's all that NASCAR rules allowed on its high-speed ovals.

◄▲ Built on a new B-body platform shared with the Plymouth Belvedere/Satellite, the '66 Dodge Coronets wore crisp, fairly conservative lines on a 117-inch wheelbase. The lineup again included a full range of body types spread among base, Deluxe, 440, and bucket-seat 500 trim levels. Here, the 500 convertible (*left*) and hardtop coupe (*above*), which sold for $2600-$2900. Including the four-door sedan, 55,683 Coronet 500s were produced.

---

A 425-bhp "Street Hemi" is now available in mid-size Dodges and Plymouths

Ford's Falcon now ranks as a shorter version of the Fairlane; the rebodied Fairlane line is topped by the bucket-seat 500/XL (Mercury Comet is similar)

Ford Fairlanes can get an optional 410/425 bhp, 427-cid V-8

Ford station wagons feature a convenient two-way tailgate

Lincoln revives the two-door hardtop body style (its first since 1960) and adopts a 340-horse, 462-cid V-8—the largest on the market

The new Mercury Comet Cyclone GT paces the Indianapolis 500 race

Hertz rents out 936 Shelby GT-350H fastbacks ($17 a day/17¢ a mile); many are surreptitiously raced on weekends

▲ This '66 Dodge Coronet 440 hardtop coupe looks a tad plain, but could be a super-stormer with that year's new 440 wedge or Street Hemi options. Base price with V-8 was $2551.

▲ Dodge's full-size sporty car for '66 was this $3604 Monaco 500 hardtop coupe. It was a big car—121-inch wheelbase, 3895 pounds—that found modest success as 10,840 were sold.

▲ Though little-changed save for a new grille, the '66 Imperial adopted Chrysler's big new 440 V-8 with 350 horses, up 10. Here, the $5887 Crown hardtop coupe; 2373 were built.

▼ Mid-Sixties Imperials were far more tasteful than early decade models, one reason that overall sales improved. This, however, is one of just 514 Crown convertibles built for '66.

▲ What better setting for America's favorite mid-Sixties car? A '66 Ford Mustang hardtop, of which 499,751 were built, visits Washington D.C.

◀ Ford's '66 Mustang saw only minor grille and trim changes—no need to mess with a winner. This $2653 convertible wears styled steel wheels, a new option. Ragtop sales: 72,119.

▶ Seeking to sell more sporty big cars, Ford unleashed a new '66 Galaxie 500/XL "7-Litre" hardtop (*shown*) and convertible, both boasting a big new 345-horse 428 V-8. Sales were low: 8705 hardtops, 2368 ragtops.

**1966 Model Year Production**

| | | |
|---|---|---|
| 1. Ford 2,212,415 | 8. Mercury 343,149 | 15. Shelby 2,378 |
| 2. Chevrolet 2,206,639 | 9. Rambler/AMC 295,897 | 16. Checker 1,056[1] |
| 3. Pontiac 831,331 | 10. Chrysler 264,848 | 17. Avanti II 98 |
| 4. Plymouth 687,514 | 11. Cadillac 196,685 | 18. Excalibur 90 |
| 5. Dodge 632,658 | 12. Lincoln 54,755 | |
| 6. Oldsmobile 578,385 | 13. Imperial 13,742 | |
| 7. Buick 553,870 | 14. Studebaker 8,947 | |

[1] *Estimate, excludes taxicabs*

▲ The mid-size Ford Fairlane was all-new for 1966, wearing swoopier GM-type styling on slightly larger dimensions, though weight was about the same. Like most Fairlanes, this $2378 Fairlane 500 hardtop coupe came with a standard 200 six, with a 200-horse 289 as the base V-8 option. This model sold 75,947 copies.

▲ Ford left plenty of room for big-block 427 V-8s in '66 Fairlanes—mainly for drag racing. Here's one lighting off at the Miami Speedway Park.

▲ The Ford Thunderbird completed another three-year styling cycle for 1966 with a new pointy nose and eggcrate grille, plus wall-to-wall taillights. The soft-top, shown here, stickered at $4879, but sales were down to just 5049 units.

▲ Because T-Bird ragtop sales continued to fall, the body style would not return for '67. All '66s got a new power option: Ford's high-torque 428 big-block V-8 with 345 horses. The 390 V-8, upped to 315 bhp, was still standard.

▲ This little-known limousine conversion on the '66 Ford LTD hardtop sedan was done with Ford's blessing by Hollowell Engineering and Dearborn Steel Tubing. Only 85 were produced, some of them as Mercurys.

◀ The T-Bird dash was very "Buck Rogers" in 1964-66; the Swing-Away steering wheel dated to '61. Newly optional front disc brakes on this '66 are announced on the brake pedal.

---

GM demonstrates two electric vehicles: Electrovan and Electrovair II

Ford announces development of a sealed sodium-sulphur battery

Experimental cars seen this year include the AMC Cavalier, Vixen, and AMX; Corvair Monza SS roadster and GT twin-canopy coupe; and Pontiac Banshee

The Mars II electric car, from Electric Fuel Propulsion Inc., uses a Renault 10 body; its lead-cobalt batteries can be recharged up to 200 times for a claimed 50,000-mile life, but this sounds optimistic

▲ First seen in 1964, the mid-engine Ford GT40 endurance racer won the gruelling Le Mans 24 Hours in 1966 in this Ferrari-eater "Mark II" guise. In addition, a few roadgoing cars were later built as "Mark III" models.

▲ With help from Lotus of England, Ford started the mid-engine revolution that changed the shape of Indy-car racing in the early Sixties. Seen here is a trio of Ford-powered '66 contenders at "The Brickyard" in Indianapolis.

▼ Crisper lines marked the 1966 Lincoln Continentals. This $6383 convertible sedan captured just 3180 sales.

▲ Lincoln's '66 redo added five inches to length, plus a 430 V-8 enlarged to a massive 462 cubic inches, upping horsepower to 340. A reborn hardtop coupe, priced at $5485, helped boost total Lincoln production to 54,755.

▲ Oldsmobile's "4-4-2" legend meant 400 cubes, four-barrel carb, and dual exhausts, and there was sharp new styling to go with the 400 standard horses. Here, the $2923 4-4-2 Holiday hardtop. Total 4-4-2 sales for 1966: 21,997.

---

Excalibur Series I models, now including a $7950 phaeton, are powered by Chevy's 327-cid Corvette V-8; production reaches 90 cars this year

Glassic's fiberglass-bodied Model A replica rides an International Scout four-cylinder chassis; this $3800 roadster will be available into 1975, when it will cost $8900

Fritz Duesenberg displays a Virgil Exner-designed, Ghia-built prototype neoclassic sedan bearing the legendary nameplate; production never happens

▲ A design and engineering *tour de force,* Oldsmobile's new 1966 Toronado was the largest front-drive car ever attempted—119-inch wheelbase, 4366 pounds—and America's first such production car since the late-Thirties Cord. Base priced at $4617, the Toro won a healthy 40,963 sales.

► Hurst Performance Products gave this '66 Olds 4-4-2 a *pair* of supercharged 425-cid Toronado V-8s and all-wheel drive. The result was billed as "drag racing's wildest exhibition vehicle." Required fuel was a nitro-alcohol blend.

◄ The 1966 Plymouth Barracuda showed off an unchanged "glassback" profile and squared-off nose. Priced at $2556 basic, it scored 38,029 sales—still way behind Ford's galloping Mustang. Carried over from 1965 was a "Formula S" option comprising a high-output 235-horse, 273-cid V-8—plus firm suspension, special wheels and tires, tachometer, and unique identification.

▲ Plymouth's revived full-size Fury returned for '66 with minor styling tweaks, including vertically stacked headlights, and Chrysler's new 440 big-block V-8 as an option. This $3251 Sport Fury convertible saw a mere 3418 sales.

▲ Accepting the challenge of the Ford LTD and Chevy Caprice was Plymouth's lush new '66 Fury VIP, a $3069 hardtop coupe (*shown*) or $3133 hardtop sedan. The 230-bhp 318 V-8 was standard, 325-bhp 383 or 365-bhp 440 optional.

▲ As did Dodge, mid-size Plymouths offered a very muscular new Street Hemi option for 1966, here on a top-of-the-line, bucket-seat Satellite hardtop coupe. The Hemi added a hefty $907.60 to the model's $2695 base price.

▲ Pontiac's hot GTO looked better than ever for '66, thanks to a deft outer-body reskin. Standard horses numbered 333, with 360 optional. This pillared Sport Coupe had a base price of $2783, weighed 3445 pounds, and saw 10,363 sales.

► Though still posh and potent, Pontiac's personal-luxury Grand Prix ran into sales trouble starting in '66, when production dropped from 57,881 to just 36,757. This happened despite the fact that the base price was actually $5 less than in '65: $3492.

▼ As usual, Catalina was Pontiac's most popular full-size line for '66. This sleek $2893 hardtop coupe was the series' second-best-seller (nosed out by the four-door sedan), attracting a sizeable 79,013 customers.

▲ The last Studebakers were 1966 models, basically warmed-over 1964-65s with Chevy six or V-8 power and a revised grille. This Cruiser sedan was among the 8947 Canadian-built cars that ended the historic nameplate.

◄ Ford asked Carroll Shelby, creator of the awesome early Sixties Cobra sports cars, to turn Mustangs into race-winners. His answer, the '65 GT-350, saw few changes for '66. At $4557, 2380 enthusiasts figured it was a huge bargain.

▲ AMC's fastback Marlin looked miles better for 1967, thanks to curvy new lower-body lines and a switch from the Classic chassis to Ambassador's longer 118-inch wheelbase. But the public remained unmoved, so the 3+3 coupe was dropped after a run of just 2545 units.

► The '67 AMC Marlin shared front sheetmetal with the Ambassador, so proportions were better balanced, but the fastback roof with its sweeping elliptical side-window shape was unchanged. Price was $2963 with the base 232 six, but power options ran to brand-new 290 and 343 "thin-wall" V-8s with up to 280 horsepower.

▲ Trendy new "coke bottle" fenderlines and a more up-to-date chassis made the '67 Ambassador AMC's best big car yet. The top-line DPL hardtop coupe cost $2958, and 12,552 were sold. A new companion ragtop got just 1260 sales. AMC had far more success with family sedans.

▲ AMC's '67 mid-size cars were still called Rambler, but their surname changed from Classic to Rebel. Styling and engineering were all-new too, and performance improved via modern new 290 and 343 V-8 options. This top-line 770 wagon listed at $2710; 18,552 were built.

**1967**

President Johnson's deficit spending for the Vietnam War is destined to lead to serious inflation—but for now prosperity continues and jobs are plentiful

Production of '67 models slips to near 7.6 million; Chevrolet tops Ford, 2.2 million to 1.7 million

The year's biggest high-performance engine is Chrysler's 440 Magnum V-8

The Mercury Cougar and Chevrolet Camaro ponycars make their debut, followed at mid-year by Pontiac's Firebird

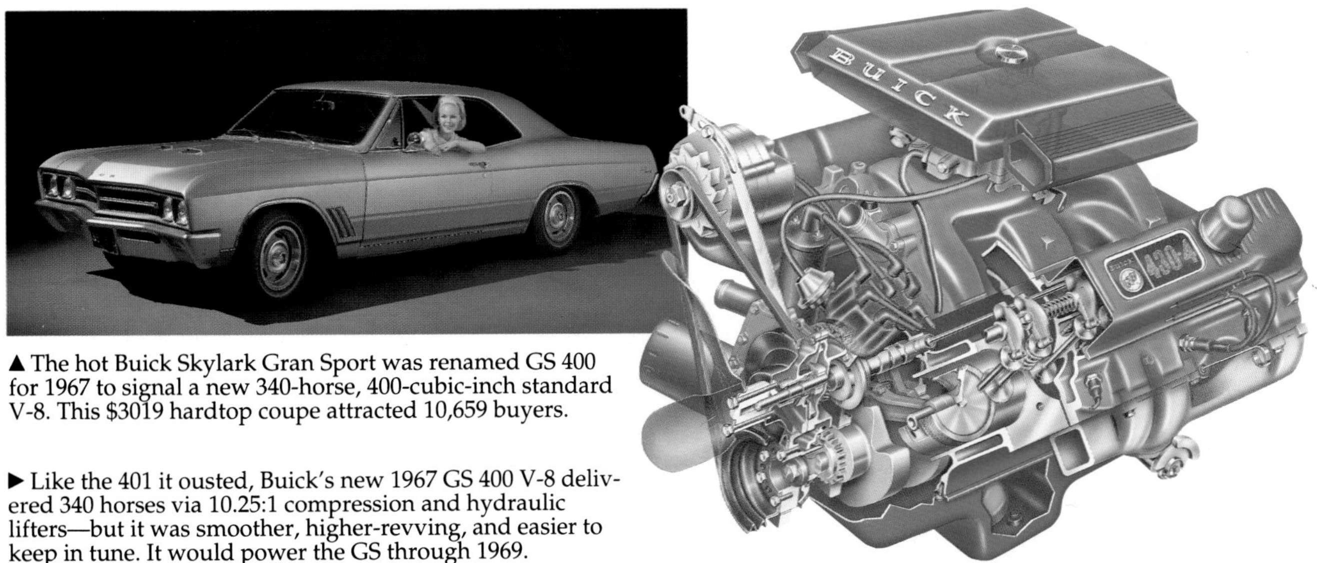


▲ The hot Buick Skylark Gran Sport was renamed GS 400 for 1967 to signal a new 340-horse, 400-cubic-inch standard V-8. This $3019 hardtop coupe attracted 10,659 buyers.

▶ Like the 401 it ousted, Buick's new 1967 GS 400 V-8 delivered 340 horses via 10.25:1 compression and hydraulic lifters—but it was smoother, higher-revving, and easier to keep in tune. It would power the GS through 1969.

▲ Though Buick built some of the most potent muscle cars of the Sixties, some models were surprisingly rare—like this '67 GS 400 convertible, one of only 2140 produced.

▲ Bright accents adorn the bodysides and wheel openings of this '67 Buick Skylark Custom Sportwagon, which rode a 120-inch chassis. Total output for this body style was 19,083.

▲ A sweeping new full-fastback roofline and curvy bodysides marked Buick's '67 Wildcat hardtop coupe. Offered in both base and Custom form, it attracted 22,456 buyers.

▲ Buick's 1967 Riviera had its own Gran Sport handling option and a new 360-horse 430 V-8. Sales: 42,799.

---

Other new models include the Chevrolet Chevelle Concours; Dodge Coronet R/T; Mercury Marquis and Brougham; front-drive Cadillac Eldorado; and Shelby GT-500

Most 1967 cars have underbodies of corrosion-resistant galvanized steel; 38 percent come with the increasingly popular air conditioning

Safety issues grow: A dual braking system is installed in all cars; collapsible steering columns emerge

Firebirds have a deflated mini-spare tire; Pontiac boasts the first concealed wipers

GM cars get buzzers that sound when the driver leaves the key in the ignition switch

▲ The huge success of Ford's Mustang inspired Chevy's new-for-'67 Camaro. This $2466 hardtop coupe has the SS and RS packages, two of many extra-cost items offered to entice buyers. Camaro also came as a convertible, but not a fastback like Mustang. Total Camaro sales: 220,917.

► Created for the recently formed Trans-Am racing series, the Camaro Z/28 option package included numerous performance goodies, including a special 302 V-8 with a nominal 290 horses, plus disc brakes and distinctive badging. Only 602 were built for '67, all hardtops.

◄ The '67 Camaro convertible listed at $2704 with the 140-bhp 230 six, $2809 with the base 210-horse 327 V-8. Some 25,141 customers drove one home. As with Mustang, liberal use of a long options list could boost delivered price to near $5000. Despite being over two years behind Ford's ponycar, Camaro quickly established itself as Chevy's true contender in the sporty compact field, ousting fast-fading Corvair.

---

GM, Ford, and American Motors adopt a 5-year/50,000-mile powertrain warranty

In just over a decade, 57 percent of the Interstate Highway System is completed and open

AMC's Marlin switches to the longer Ambassador platform, but only 2545 are called for

A smoother 430-cid V-8 replaces the 425 in big Buicks

A GS 400 option for the Buick Skylark includes a 340-bhp, 400-cid V-8

A new 350-cid V-8 is phased in on the Chevrolet Camaro; the Impala SS 427 gets a 385-bhp 427 V-8

Like the Mustang, Chevy's new Camaro hardtop and convertible sport a long-hood/short-deck profile and a long options list

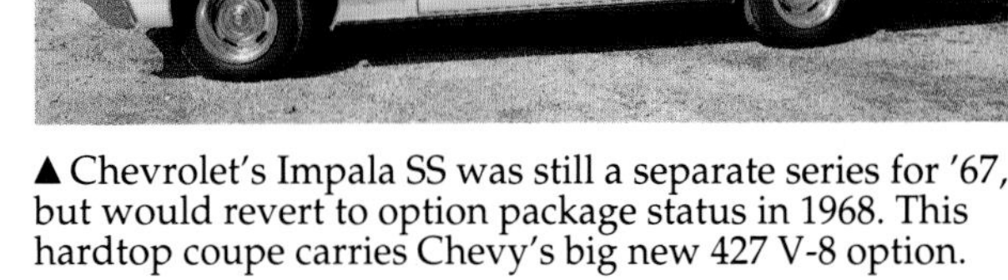

▲ Chevrolet's Impala SS was still a separate series for '67, but would revert to option package status in 1968. This hardtop coupe carries Chevy's big new 427 V-8 option.

◀ "Body drop" assembly line photos were a longtime staple of Chevrolet's Public Relations staff. Here, a '67 Impala body mates up with its chassis. Note the gas tank location.

▲ A mild facelift marked '67 Chevy Chevelles, like this SS 396 convertible, of which only 2286 were built. This model started at $3102, $239 more than the Malibu V-8 ragtop.

▲ Slotted "Rally" wheels teamed with power front-disc brakes as a new option for the '67 Chevelle SS 396. The big-block V-8 cranked out 325 standard horses, 350 optional.

▲▶ An all-new Chevy Corvette was planned for '67, but development problems delayed it a year. The Sting Ray thus put in one more appearance—and looked cleaner than ever. This $4141 convertible added the $437 top-line power option, the triple-carb big-block 427 L71 V-8 pumping out 435 horses. Aluminum heads added another $368. Total 'Vette sales eased to 22,940, 14,436 of them "roadsters."

---

Camaro's Z/28 competition package includes a hot 302-cid V-8; only 602 are built

The Corvair line is trimmed to just five models—and the turbocharger is gone for good

Dodge Dart gets a completely restyled unibody; about 38,000 sporty GT hardtops and ragtops are produced, 43 percent of them equipped with a V-8

The full-size Dodge Polara and Monaco are extensively redesigned and larger, now riding a 122-inch wheelbase

The Coronet R/T with a tuned 440 Magnum engine gives Dodge a rival to Pontiac's GTO; Plymouth's Belvedere GTX is comparable

Hemi engines are still available in mid-size Dodges and Plymouths

▲ Only some 8200 Chevy II Nova Super Sports were ordered with the optional 327 V-8s for 1967. In place of the 275-bhp engine, a few got the 350-horse version, even though it was no longer officially available.

▲ A lower-body restyle made '66 Chevy IIs a little more grown-up, so the '67s saw only minor changes. The Nova wagon cost $2566 with the 120-horse six, $2671 with the V-8. Chevy II wagon output totaled 12,900.

▲ It was hard to spot any changes in Chevy's 1967 Corvairs—like this Monza convertible—mainly because there were none. Priced at $2540, the ragtop landed only 2109 sales, out of 27,253 total Corvairs.

▲ Another '67 Cadillac Eldorado shows off its elegant, semiformal lines in a contemporary photo using the Chicago skyline as a backdrop.

◀ Cadillac's Eldorado was rejuvenated for 1967 as a posh close-coupled hardtop coupe based on the front-drive Olds Toronado, but on a 120-inch wheelbase. Though costly at $6277, it scored a healthy 17,930 sales.

▲ Full-size Caddys weren't neglected for '67, gaining a brand-new GM C-body with more rakish lines. Despite a $5608 tariff, 18,202 customers bought a new de Ville ragtop.

---

A four-door Landau with rear-hinged "suicide" back doors joins the all-new Thunderbird line

Imperial adopts Chrysler's lighter-weight unibody construction, but on a longer 127-inch wheelbase; output increases to 17,614 (plus six long-wheelbase limos)

Lincoln offers its final four-door convertible, but only 2276 are sold

Mercury's Cyclone GT can have an optional 427-cid V-8

The Mercury Cougar hardtop, posher and slightly larger than Ford's Mustang, sports hidden headlights—but no convertible or fastback models are offered

Oldsmobile's lightly retouched Toronado can have front disc brakes and radial tires

▲ Chrysler took on a sharpened look for 1967. Wide lower-body trim identified a popular new line of Newport Customs priced above entry-level Newports. Among them was this $3407 hardtop coupe, which enjoyed 14,193 sales.

▲ Padded vinyl C-pillar trim was a unique touch for '67 Chrysler New Yorker hardtop sedans, which again came with a 350-horse 440 V-8. Priced at $4339, it was the year's most popular New Yorker—21,665 were sold.

▲ Eclipsing Coronet 500 as Dodge's raciest '67 mid-size model was the new R/T (for "road and track"), offered as a $3613 convertible and this $3379 hardtop.

▲ A 375-horse "Magnum" 440 V-8 (with four-barrel carb and dual exhausts) was standard for '67 Coronet R/Ts, along with a beefed-up chassis, red-line tires, and bucket seats. The optional Hemi was still underrated at 425 bhp.

▲ Although Dodge's fastback Charger looked little different in its second year, the '67 could now be had in R/T trim *a la* Coronet, as shown here. Unfortunately for Dodge, sales plummeted by more than half to just 15,788 for the year.

---

Valiant is restyled, but wagons, hardtop, and convertible are gone; the likewise restyled Barracuda takes up the slack with a new convertible and notchback hardtop

Pontiac's Firebird, a Camaro clone, accepts V-8s up to 400-cid; the base motor is an overhead-cam six

A Grand Prix convertible is marketed this year only—5856 are sold

A restyled, curvier Rebel replaces the Classic as AMC's mid-size series; 1686 Rebel convertibles find customers

Rambler American gets a 200- or 225-bhp V-8 option and a Rogue convertible, of which only 921 are built for the model year

An Auburn 866 Speedster replicar enters production; priced at a towering $8450, it's powered by a 428 Ford V-8

▲ Full-size '67 Fords followed the industry trend to more billowy lines with a handsome restyle. This $3493 Galaxie 500/XL ragtop, which came with the 289 V-8, is one of 5161 built.

▲ "Faster" rooflines were featured on Ford's big '67 hardtop coupes. This bucket-seat Galaxie 500/XL version stickered at $3243 (plus $75 for the vinyl roof), and found 18,174 buyers.

▲ Big-block 427 power was still on tap for '67 Fairlanes, but most GTs, like this hardtop (18,670 built), ran with 270- or 320-bhp 390s (the 289 was standard). Wheels here are non-stock.

▲ Ford's Mustang took on a beefier look for 1967 via new lower-body sheetmetal, and offered a big-block 390 V-8 option with 320 horses for the first time. Base price for convertibles like this was up to $2698; 44,808 were produced.

▲ This '67 Mustang hardtop is nicely optioned with styled-steel wheels, whitewalls, vinyl roof, GT package (note rocker-panel racing stripes), and Cruise-O-Matic—which made it a "GTA." Hardtop sales totaled 356,271 units.

► Paul Harvey Ford campaigned this modified '67 Ford Fairlane 427 hardtop coupe on National Hot Rod Association dragstrips, typically touring the quarter-mile in the low 10.9s at 127 mph. That was good, but not good enough against the rival Hemi-powered MoPars, so Ford failed to win any major NHRA contests in the '67 season (also partly because the Fairlane was put in the same class as the sohc Mustang and other experimentals). On the other hand, Fairlane 427s began appearing on NASCAR high-speed ovals—and winning, at the Riverside 500, Daytona 500, and Atlanta 500, for example.

**1967 Model Year Production**

| | | |
|---|---|---|
| 1. Chevrolet 1,948,410 | 7. Dodge 465,732 | 13. Imperial 17,620 |
| 2. Ford 1,730,224 | 8. Mercury 354,923 | 14. Shelby 3,225 |
| 3. Pontiac 782,734 | 9. Rambler/AMC 235,293 | 15. Checker 950[1] |
| 4. Plymouth 638,075 | 10. Chrysler 218,742 | 16. Excalibur 71 |
| 5. Buick 562,507 | 11. Cadillac 200,000 | 17. Avanti II 60 |
| 6. Oldsmobile 548,390 | 12. Lincoln 45,667 | [1]*Estimate, excludes taxicabs* |

▲ With sales sliding in 1965-66, Imperial lost its unique platform for '67 to become a Chrysler New Yorker in disguise. Although based on a shorter 127-inch wheelbase, the result was pleasing. This convertible listed at $6244.

▲ Chrysler's penchant for producing rare models certainly held with the '67 Imperial convertible (no longer in the Crown series)—just 577 were built. Pristine survivors like this example are extremely rare nowadays.

▲ Lincoln's Continental kept on evolving with no great change needed, but convertible sedan output hit a new low for 1967: only 2276. That's why it wouldn't return for '68. Sedan and hardtop coupe volume was 33,331 and 11,060.

▲ Having grown from compact to mid-size for 1966, Mercury's Comet carried on for '67 as a kissing cousin to Ford's Fairlane. Hottest in the line was the Cyclone GT, here in $3034 hardtop coupe form, but only 3419 were called for.

▲ The big Oldsmobiles were facelifted for '67 to achieve a faint similarity to the singular Toronado. This $4498 Ninety-Eight, one of two convertibles in that year's full-size line, appealed to 3769 buyers.

▲ The '67 Olds 4-4-2 again offered 350 standard horses and a hot W-30 option with close to 375, but the 360-horse tri-carb setup was dropped. Base price for this Holiday hardtop coupe, which saw about 16,500 sales, was $3015.

---

Mohs Ostentatienne Opera coupe costs $19,600 or $25,600 and measures 246 inches long; a modified truck chassis accommodates International Harvester V-8s

Omega, evolved from the Griffith GT, sports an Italian body and runs with a Ford 289 V-8

The fiberglass-bodied Valkyrie packs a 450-bhp Chevrolet V-8, good for 0-60 mph in 3.8 seconds

The U.S. Department of Commerce holds a seminar on electric vehicles—Ford announces Comuta electric, GM exhibits Electrovair II, Westinghouse displays the two-seater Markette

Dynamic braking helps generate power for the Rowan electric

GM begins a navigation study that does without maps or road signs; a driver dials in the destination and uses codes from roadside landmarks for guidance

Ford suffers a 65-day strike in the fall; 159,000 workers are idle

▲ Mid-size Plymouths sported numerous refinements for 1967. This bucket-seat Satellite hardtop coupe, which appealed to 30,328 buyers, stickered at $2747 with the standard 273 V-8.

▲ Plymouth was "Out to Win You Over" in '67. One way they did was the new Belvedere GTX, a hardtop coupe (*shown*) and convertible packing a standard 375-horsepower Super Commando 440 V-8, plus beefed-up chassis and racy cosmetics. Sticker prices read $3178 and $3418, respectively.

▲ This is one of only 75 special-order Belvedere drag-race cars that Plymouth built in '67. Designed to run in the NHRA A/Stock class, they carried blueprinted, high-tune Street Hemis. Wheels here are latter-day high-tech items.

▲ Valiant was completely restyled for 1967, looking bigger (on a two-inch-longer 108-inch wheelbase) and more blocky. Gone were the hardtop, convertible, and wagons, but this top-line Signet four-door sedan nonetheless looked rather dapper. Price: $2308. Production: 26,395 units.

◀ Again for '67, Plymouth offered Chrysler's veteran 383 V-8 in high-compression four-barrel form with 325 horses as a Fury/Belvedere option. A similar 280-horsepower version was reserved for the completely redesigned '67 Barracuda—that sporty car's first big-inch V-8.

▲ Plymouth's handsome '67 Barracuda added convertible and hardtop coupe models (transferred from the Valiant line) to the familiar fastback. Standard engine was the 145-bhp Slant Six. This $2779 ragtop scored just 4228 sales.

▲ The new '67 Barracuda notchback hardtop, now riding a 108-inch wheelbase, sported an abbreviated roofline with a concave backlight, and trailed the fastback in sales, 28,196 to 30,110. Still, total 'Cuda sales nearly doubled from 1966.

▲ More, and tougher, competition hurt '67 Pontiac GTO sales, which slipped to 81,722, including 9517 ragtops.

▼ Pontiac's Firebird bowed at mid-'67 as a Camaro cousin. The Sprint hardtop boasted a 215-bhp ohc 230 six.

▲ GTO's standard V-8 for '67 was a new four-barrel 335-horse 400. Here, the $2935 hardtop; 65,176 were built.

◄ To lift Grand Prix sales, Pontiac issued this $3813 convertible as a new '67 companion to the hardtop coupe. Both had unique hidden-headlamp front ends on a facelifted full-size "Poncho" body. Alas, with only 5856 orders, the ragtop Grand Prix ended up being a one-year-only model.

▲ Carroll Shelby one-upped the restyled '67 Mustang fastback with even more aggressive-looking GT models with standard grille-centered driving lights. Note the hood scoop.

▲ The '67 Shelby GT-350 retained a high-winding, 290-horse 289 V-8, but offered new "luxury" options like air conditioning. The GT-350, which cost $3995, saw 1175 model-year sales.

▲ A new big-block 428 Shelby-Mustang, the GT-500, bowed for '67 with 355 advertised horses, but those in the know said it was surely more. Just 2050 were sold at $4195 apiece.

▲ Unveiled in 1965, the Anglo-U.S. Shelby-Cobra 427 was the most brutish muscle car ever. Evolved from the early-Sixties AC Ace-based small-block Cobra 260/289, the 2600-pound 427 packed 345-425 horses in various guises through 1967, when production ceased at a mere 348 numbered chassis. The Cobra has seen many replicas.

► Spicing up the '67 scene was a new Jeepster *a la* the 1948-51 original, but based on the Jeep CJ. This Sport Convertible was offered along with the Commando roadster, pickup, and wagon with I-4 or V-6 power. With changes, including a restyling and AMC sixes and V-8 for '72, the line continued through '73. Production totaled 77,573.

▲ AMC's Marlin was shot down for 1968 by Javelin, a hardtop coupe "ponycar" in base (*shown*) and ritizer SST trim. A 232 six was standard, but 343 and new 390 V-8s with up to 315 bhp were optional. Demand was strong at 56,444 units.

▲ AMC shortened the Javelin 12 inches to create the two-seat show car-inspired AMX coupe for mid-'68. Craig Breedlove drove one to several speed records in Texas prior to launch. Price was $3245, but sales reached only 6725.

▲ Designed under AMC's Dick Teague, the 109-inch-wheelbase Javelin was one of the few ponycars that looked good with an optional vinyl top. This SST version cost $2587, the base model $2482. The styling still looks good.

▲ Besides setting records with the AMX, land-speed-record driver Craig Breedlove ran this Javelin at the Bonneville Salt Flats in Utah in August 1968 as a promotional ploy.

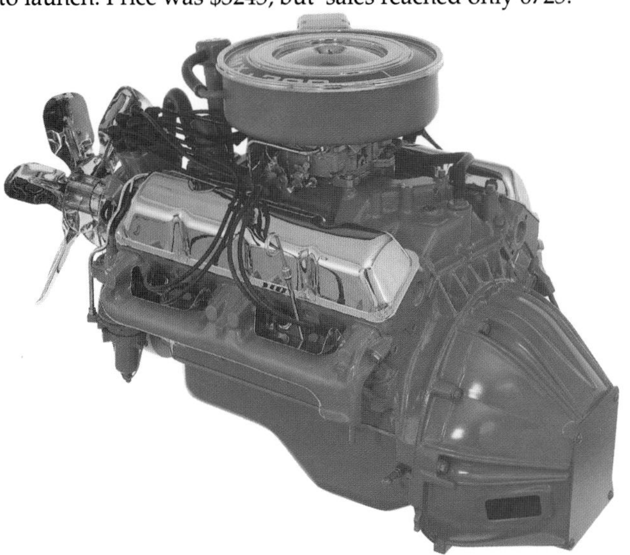

◀ AMC's biggest '68 V-8 was this new 315-horsepower 390. It was optional for AMX, Javelin, Rebel, and Ambassador.

---

**1968**

Big Three automakers extensively rework their mid-size models

New federal pollution regulations take effect—all makes have an exhaust-emission control system

Despite a long strike, Ford's model-year output reaches 1.75 million cars; Chevrolet remains first, with 2.1 million

A total of 9,403,862 new cars are registered this year, topping the 1965 record; model-year output hits 8.4 million

An average full-time worker earns $6657; the average new-car buyer pays $2936 (plus trade-in)

New models include the AMC Javelin, Ford Torino, and Mercury Montego; mid-season brings the AMX and Lincoln Continental Mark III luxury coupe

▲ Though no longer a Rambler in name, the mid-size '68 AMC Rebel was little-changed save for the big 315-horse 390 V-8 option. This $2775 SST was the sportiest of three available hardtop coupes; 11,516 were produced.

▲ After one year with a convertible companion, AMC's sporty Rambler American Rogue hardtop coupe soldiered on alone for 1968 with few changes. Base price was still attractively low: $2244. Sales were *un*attractively low: 4765.

▲ The big '68 Buicks still wore a Fifties-style bodyside "sweepspear." Wildcats, like the $3416 four-door sedan, went like a scalded cat due to the standard 360-horsepower 430 V-8. This model attracted 15,201 paying customers.

▲ The top-line '68 Electra 225 retained a more formal look—right down to the four "VentiPorts" on each front fender—to stand apart from lesser full-size Buicks. This hardtop coupe sold for $4221 in standard trim, $4400 in ritzier Custom dress. Together, they appealed to 27,531 buyers.

▲ The 1968 Buick Riviera, now weighing 4222 pounds, hid its headlamps within a restyled "face." Changes were few—and mostly dictated by government safety and clean-air mavens. Sales rose to 49,284 units, the base price to $4615.

▲ Government-mandated side-marker lights were a subtle visual change for Cadillac's '68 Eldorado, but a big new 375-horse 472 V-8 lurked beneath the hood. Base price rose $328 to $6605; output jumped 37 percent to 24,528. Despite the svelte looks, the Eldo weighed in at 4580 pounds.

---

Front shoulder harnesses are required on cars sold after January 1; other mandated safety features include rear lap belts, side marker lights, non-reflective windshields, padded interiors

Nearly one million imported cars are sold, triggering a call for more American-built compacts and subcompacts

A 12-cent postage stamp commemorating Henry Ford is issued

Fords employ "controlled-crush" front ends and recessed squeeze-type inside door handles

Hidden windshield wipers are seen on more GM cars; some adopt no-vent side windows

An optional buzzer in AMC cars sounds when the lights are left on

▲ Chevy's fully restyled '68 Corvette wasn't called Sting Ray, but it was built on the same chassis. This $4663 T-top coupe replaced the beloved fastback; 9936 were sold.

▲ With some under-the-counter help from Chevy, "privateers" had raced Corvettes successfully for years, and 1968 was no exception. Here, driver Tony DeLorenzo poses in one of the Owens-Corning team cars that first contested SCCA that year, and then went on to dominate 1969.

▲ As in 1966-67, a prominent hood bulge signaled 427 big-block power in the new '68 Corvettes. With 18,630 orders, the $4320 convertible still easily outsold the coupe. As since 1963, the 'Vette rode a 98-inch wheelbase, but weight had gradually crept up to 3055/3065 pounds.

▲ Full-size Chevys wore a huskier look for 1968, and the Impala Super Sport was demoted from separate model to option status. This ragtop wears the so-called "party hat" wheels included with the optional power front-disc brakes. Only 2455 SS 427s were built—big-car buyers were shifting to luxury models.

▲ A new GM A-body with a shorter 112-inch wheelbase for two-doors highlighted the '68 Chevy Chevelles. With 325 horses (375 optional), the SS 396 remained the line's top performer. Priced at $2899, this hardtop coupe captured 60,499 youthful buyers.

---

Pontiac GTOs flaunt "Endura," an energy-absorbing, steel-reinforced, body-color rubber bumper

Pontiac introduces an engine-driven emergency air pump; Chrysler Corp. station wagons can have a washer/wiper to clean the tailgate window

The AMC badge now appears on Ramblers; AMC introduces the Javelin ponycar and stubby two-seat AMX sport coupe

Rebel offers AMC's only convertible, and only 1200 are built—it will be the last true AMC ragtop

Buick's restyled mid-size Skylark enjoys record sales; an inline six replaces the V-6, which has been sold to Kaiser-Jeep Corp.

Cadillac's new 472-cid, 375-bhp V-8 is designed specifically to meet tougher emissions regulations

▲ Chevy's Camaro wore minor style changes for '68, including federally required side-marker lights. Ventpanes vanished with newly standard "Astro Ventilation." This hardtop was one of 27,844 SS-equipped cars built for the model year out of a grand total 235,147 Camaros.

▲ The Chevy Corvair was nearing the end of its road in '68, losing four-door models and the 140-horsepower option, but gaining government-mandated side-marker lights. Base-priced at $2507, this Monza coupe found 6807 buyers. Total Corvair sales skidded to 15,399 units.

◀▲ For its second year without a Letter-Series sister, Chrysler's 300 shared a mild facelift with other '68 models, as well as a unique hidden-headlamp front end. At $4337, the ragtop (*left*) enjoyed 2161 sales, up about 500 from '67, but the series' mainstay was still the hardtop coupe (*above*), which attracted 16,953 customers at $4010 apiece.

▲ Dodge's '68 Coronet Super Bee was a budget muscle-car like Plymouth's new Road Runner. This 3395-pound member of Dodge's "Scat Pack" came only as a $3027 pillared coupe. A 335-bhp 383 V-8 was standard.

▲ The bucket-seat R/T convertible (*shown*) and hardtop coupe remained the sportiest and costliest of Dodge's '68 Coronets, respectively priced at $3613 and $3379. All Coronets got a new B-body platform that year, with handsome new styling. Powerteams, however, remained about the same. With its stock 375-horse 440 V-8, an R/T could do 0-60 in well under seven seconds.

---

Checker makes Chevy's 307-cid V-8 available for all models

Chevy II Nova is now near mid-size (111-inch wheelbase); the hardtop coupe, convertible, and wagon are gone

The all-new Chevelle two-doors ride a shorter 112-inch wheelbase, and come with a choice of three 396-cid V-8s

The restyled Corvette stretches an extra seven inches; it sports vacuum-operated flip-up headlights

Dodge reworks the intermediate-size Coronet and Charger, while the compact Dart adds a hot GTS hardtop and convertible with a 340- or 383-cid V-8

A no-frills Super Bee coupe with a 335-bhp 383 V-8 joins the Coronet lineup; it starts at $3027

▲ Dodge surprised everyone with a curvy, all-new Charger for '68, offered in three flavors of "tunnelback" hardtop coupe. The most potent was naturally this $3506 R/T version, with standard 440 Magnum V-8. This one has the optional 425-horse Hemi.

► "Bumblebee" stripes marked the tails of Dodge's '68 performance models. The Charger R/T sported rounded "fuselage" styling, which quickly proved a big asset in stock-car racing—and in the showroom: 96,108 Chargers were produced for 1968.

◄▲ Dodge shoehorned a 383 V-8 into its unassuming compact Dart to create a hot new '68 GTS hardtop coupe and convertible, but Hurst-Campbell went the factory one better by stuffing in 440s and even a few Hemis to create a lightweight dragstrip terror. "Mr. Norm's" Grand Spaulding Dodge in Chicago was where you went to buy one. Here (*left and above*) are two of these very rapid rarities.

---

A plush Torino series joins the Ford stable as the Fairlane is restyled again

The final Crown Imperial convertibles go on sale, but at $6497 only 474 are produced

Late in the season, the "personal-luxury" Continental Mark III joins the Continental sedan and hardtop; all Lincolns come with a new 460-cid, 365-bhp V-8

The big Oldsmobiles have a new 455-cid V-8, so Hurst/Olds stuffs a Force-Air 455 V-8 into a limited-edition 4-4-2

Road Runner is Plymouth's new budget muscle car; with prices starting at $2896, it attracts 44,599 eager buyers

Pontiac launches the revised A-body Tempest on two wheelbases: 112 inches for two-doors, 116 for four-doors

▲ Side-marker lamps and a revised grille were the main visual changes to 1968 Mustangs. With its many options, this hardtop cost far more than the base $2602. Sales this year: 249,447 hardtops, 42,581 fastbacks, 25,376 ragtops.

▲ This is one of 50 special lightweight Mustangs built to showcase the Cobra Jet 428 V-8 that replaced the high-winding 427 option in mid-1968. The cars dominated the S/S class at the '68 NHRA Winternationals.

▲ Mid-size Fords were fully revised for '68, and lush new Torino models were added above Fairlanes. Both lines offered racy new fastback hardtop coupes. This is the top-line $2747 Torino GT version; 74,135 were built.

▲ This Torino GT ragtop paced the '68 Indianapolis 500. Ford also offered a notchback GT hardtop (23,939 sold), but the new slippery fastbacks were favored for stock-car racing. Total GT ragtop demand topped out at 5310 units.

▲ Ford kept pushing sporty big cars for 1968, but with diminishing success despite a mild but adroit facelift. Side-by-side "peek-a-boo" headlamps were featured on the Galaxie 500/XL convertible and hardtop coupe (*shown*), with the latter picking up the name "SportsRoof" to denote its sweeping fastback lines. XL output totaled 50,048 fastbacks and 6066 convertibles.

▲ The first-ever four-door T-Bird had bowed for '67 as part of a full redo for Ford's personal-luxury flagship. The '68s sported a new grille and offered a new high-torque, 360-horse 429 V-8 option instead of a 428. Standard power remained the 315-bhp 390. Convertibles were gone. At 21,925 units, the longer new Landau sedan wasn't as popular as the base and Landau hardtop coupes, whose sales totaled 43,006.

**1968 Model Year Production**

| | | |
|---|---|---|
| 1. Chevrolet 2,139,290 | 7. Oldsmobile 562,459 | 13. Imperial 15,367 |
| 2. Ford 1,753,334 | 8. Mercury 360,467 | 14. Shelby 4,451 |
| 3. Pontiac 910,977 | 9. AMC/Rambler 272,726 | 15. Checker 992[1] |
| 4. Plymouth 790,239 | 10. Chrysler 264,853 | 16. Avanti II 89 |
| 5. Buick 651,823 | 11. Cadillac 230,003 | 17. Excalibur 57 |
| 6. Dodge 627,533 | 12. Lincoln 46,904 | [1]*Estimate, excludes taxicabs* |

▲ Lincoln's '68 Continentals kept the basic square look of debut '61, but ran with a new 365-horse 460 V-8. The convertible sedan was gone, leaving a $5970 pillared sedan and this $5736 hardtop coupe, which saw sales slip to 9415. A new mid-season Mark III coupe was the reason.

▲ The modestly restyled '68 Imperial offered two 440 V-8s: a standard 350-horse unit and a new dual-exhuast 360-bhp option. With 8492 orders, this $6115 Crown hardtop sedan was the most popular model for the year. Total Imperial sales slipped from 17,620 to 15,367 units.

▲ Unwrapped for '67 as "Mercury's Mustang," the elegant Cougar returned for '68 with this new GT-E edition of the hardtop coupe—a $1311 package with a stout 390-horse 427 V-8 with Select-Shift and numerous "go-fast" styling cues.

▲ Cougar styling was unchanged for 1968 save for side-marker lights added at Washington's insistence. Here, the posh $3232 XR-7, which again offered a woody-look, Euro-style interior. Some 32,712 were produced for the year.

▲ Chrysler and Mercury offered pseudo-wood bodyside trim as a new '68 option. Merc confined it to the top-line Park Lane hardtop and convertible. Only 1112 ragtops were built—how many got the "yacht planking" is unknown.

---

GTO has new styling and a standard 400-cid V-8—production increases to 87,684 units

Shelby adds the GT-500KR "King of the Road" with a new 428 Cobra-Jet engine; Shelbys are now built by Ford

The Autolite "Lead Wedge" travels at 138.862 mph, setting the first U.S. Auto Club speed record for electrics

A new Lincoln Continental presidential limousine constructed by Lehmann-Peterson enters service; it wears '69 cosmetics

GM and Chrysler experiment with air-activated accessories; Lincoln-Mercury and Plymouth try periscope-like devices to improve visibility; engineers experiment with inflatable gas bags to cushion occupants in the event of a serious head-on collision

▲ The first Hurst/Olds bowed in 1968 as a limited-production coupe, pillared or hardtop, based on the 4-4-2. The 515 built featured a special 390-horse 455 V-8, Turbo Hydra-Matic, Hurst Dual Gate shifter, heavy-duty everything, H/O emblems, and a special black-and-silver paint job.

▲ Plymouth got back to muscle-car basics with its new '68 Road Runner, a no-frills Belvedere (except for a "Beep! Beep!" horn) with all the needed go-faster mods, including a hot 335-horse 383 V-8 and fortified chassis. This $3034 hardtop, added at mid-year, sold 15,359 copies.

▲ Plymouth first offered the Road Runner only as this lightweight pillared coupe at a bargain $2896. Options were plentiful, though, and even included the mighty Street Hemi. Demand for this model was strong: 29,240 units.

▲ The Sox & Martin team won drag-racing fame and fortune for Plymouth throughout the Sixties. The new '68 Road Runner looked a natural, and the team quickly modified some for quarter-mile action at dragstrips around the U.S.

▲ This '68 Barracuda hardtop coupe wears one of that year's new options: the so-called "Mod Top," a vinyl roof covering with a "flower power" motif. Plymouth sold it as a package with seat and door-panel inserts done in the same pattern. How many of the 19,997 coupes sold got this wild option package isn't known.

▲ A look inside the Mod Top '68 shows the fairly roomy front seat passenger space common to all second-generation Plymouth Barracudas, though the back seat was no fit place for adults in any Detroit ponycar. Seatbelts are missing here, but were standard per Federal edict.

---

The Amitron electric compact, powered by lithium-nickel fluoride batteries, is developed by AMC and Gulton Industries

Mid-engine Chevrolet Astra II and Ford Mach II prototypes appear; Lincoln shows off a Mark III Dual Cowl Phaeton; Ford displays a "clean air" experimental vehicle

Spook Electric operates with rear chain-drive

Under new ownership, the Cord replicar switches to rear-drive and V-8 power—and leaves the headlights exposed

▲ A husky new look was featured on mid-size '68 Pontiac two-doors, which moved to a tighter 112-inch wheelbase. This $2786 Le Mans hardtop coupe, of which 110,036 were built, wears optional Rally wheels and redline tires.

▲ Pontiac's GTO lost its pillared coupe model for '68, but the new hardtop (*shown*) and convertible looked great. Total GTO sales rose to 87,684; 77,704 of them hardtops.

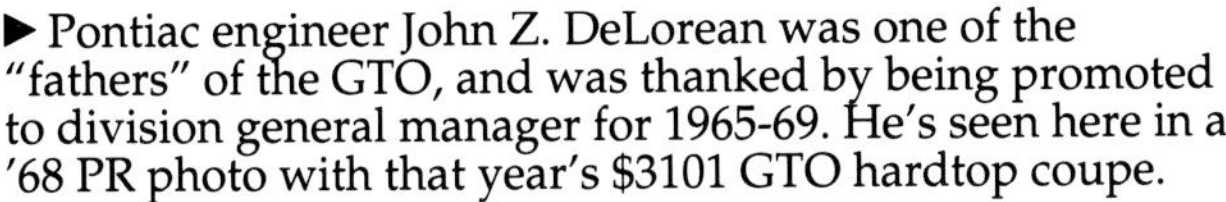

► Pontiac engineer John Z. DeLorean was one of the "fathers" of the GTO, and was thanked by being promoted to division general manager for 1965-69. He's seen here in a '68 PR photo with that year's $3101 GTO hardtop coupe.

◄ Shades of Edsel—or so said some regarding Pontiac's new '68 big-car "face." Here, the $3089 Catalina hardtop coupe chosen by 92,217 buyers.

► Skirted rear wheels and a heavier look marked Pontiac's 1968 Grand Prix. Sales of the $3697 coupe declined 26 percent to a new low of 31,711.

▲ Pontiac's Firebird was visually little-changed for '68, but V-8 choices were shuffled to include new, more emissions-friendly 350 and 400 engines. Still available was the high-output "Sprint" ohc-six with 215 horses, which this convertible has. Ragtop sales totaled 16,960 units.

▲ Shelby-Mustangs became a bit plusher for 1968—now built by Ford, not Shelby. GT-350 and GT-500 fastbacks and ragtops returned, with 400-horse GT-500KR "King of the Road" substitutes at mid-year. Here, an early 500 soft-top; 402 were built (plus 318 KRs and 404 GT-350s).

▲ A revised nose and tail carried American Motors' big Ambassadors through 1969, when this SST hardtop coupe stickered at $3622, and 8998 were sold. The series also listed a $3605 four-door sedan and $3998 four-door station wagon.

▲ AMC's mid-size Rebel was lightly retouched for '69, but also deemphasized with fewer models: sedan, wagon, and hardtop coupe in base and jazzy SST trim. This SST hardtop, which captured just 5405 buyers, started at $2598.

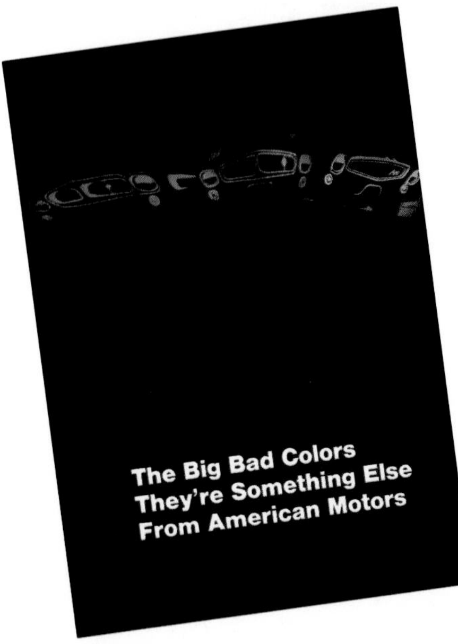


▲ Shuffled trim, equipment, and colors were the main changes for AMC's 1969 Javelin, but sales dropped sharply to 40,675, with the base model suffering most of the loss. Here, the jazzy $2633 SST (23,286 were built) in early year trim with the popular vinyl top and white-letter-tire options.

◀ Rather surrealistic artwork adorned the cover of the catalog announcing AMC's bright new 1969 "Big Bad" color options for the Javelin and AMX.

▲ Javelin changed its optional tape stripes in January 1969 to a "C-shape" motif, as on this SST. Dummy side pipes and a wispy roof spoiler were other new extra-cost goodies.

▲ The light AMX was a minor drag-racing success with big-block power. AMC didn't run its own cars, but did support private entries like this modified '69, "Pete's Patriot."

▲ This production '69 AMX is done up in "Big Bad Orange" with black dorsal racing stripes. Total sales of the $3297 AMX rose 1558 units to 8293. Base engine was the 225-bhp 290 V-8.

**1969**

New models include the Mercury Marauder and the mid-size Pontiac Grand Prix

New at mid-year are several muscle cars: AMC's SC/Rambler, Pontiac Firebird Trans Am, Dodge Charger Daytona, Mercury Cyclone Spoiler

On the economy front, Ford introduces the mid-year Maverick coupe as an early '70 model

The last Rambler American goes on sale as simply the Rambler; this will be AMC's last use of the famous nameplate that dates all the way back to 1902

Chevrolet releases its final Corvairs; only 6000 are called for

▲ The last Ramblers and Americans appeared for 1969, headed by this outrageous SC/Rambler-Hurst performance hardtop packing AMC's 315-horse 390 V-8 and wild patriotic paint. Only 1512 were sold at a bargain-priced $2998.

▲ The '69 "Scrambler," as it was aptly nicknamed, was a joint AMC/Hurst effort and of course came with a Hurst four-speed shifter. One road test clocked 0-60 at just over six seconds, the quarter-mile in about 14 at 100+ mph.

NOW SOME OF THE GOODIES CAN'T BE SEEN.

Take that 10½" heavy-duty clutch, for example. Or the Twin-Grip differential with 3.54 to 1 cogs. There are even heavy-duty U-joint spiders and special rear-axle torque links.

Then there are heavy-duty springs and shocks . . . a larger-diameter front sway bar . . . heavy-duty cooling system . . . power disc brakes (in front) . . . and special 20:1 ratio AMX-type manual steering.

Of course you'll also find all of the regular Rogue safety and comfort equipment including the Weather-Eye Heating and Ventilating system, plus electric windshield wipers.

That's it. The SC/RAMBLER from Hurst and American Motors.

There is one more thing, however.

It lists for exactly $2998!*

We think that makes the SC/RAMBLER unbeatable on every count.

1969 SC/RAMBLER SPECIFICATIONS
(See regular sales catalog for basic Rambler Rogue specs)

- 390 Cubic-inch AMX V-8 Engine (315 HP).
- 4-speed all-synchromesh close-ratio transmission.
- Special Hurst 4-speed shift linkage with T-handle.
- Sun tach mounted on steering column.
- Dual exhaust system with special-tone mufflers and chrome extensions.
- Functional hood scoop for cold-air induction.
- "Twin-Grip" differential.
- 3.54:1 (11-39) axle ratio.
- 10½" diameter clutch.
- Power disc brakes (front).
- Rear axle torque links.
- Handling package (larger-diameter front sway bar plus heavy-duty springs and shocks).
- Heavy-duty cooling system (heavy-duty radiator, "Power-Flex" fan and fan shroud).
- A 20:1 AMX manual steering ratio.
- Special application of new Red, White and Blue exterior colors.
- Two hood "tie-downs" with locking safety pins and cables.
- Custom "teardrop" racing mirrors (one each side).
- Custom-finished grille.
- Custom SC/RAMBLER-Hurst emblem on front fenders/rear panel.
- Mag-styled steel wheels, 14" x 6" specially painted blue to compliment exterior color scheme.
- Five E70x14 Goodyear Polyglas™ wide-tread, red-line tires.
- Sports steering wheel.
- Custom-upholstered head restraints in red, white and blue vinyl.
- All-vinyl charcoal seat upholstery with full carpeting.
- Individually-adjustable reclining seats.

SC/RAMBLER H

*Manufacturer's suggested retail price, federal taxes included, state and local taxes, if any, destination charges excluded. All items of equipment mentioned included.

American Motors, whose policy is one of continuous improvement, reserves the right to discontinue or change specifications, models, equipment or prices at any time without incurring obligation.

▲ No mere engine swap, AMC's '69 "Scrambler" had all sorts of performance upgrades compared to the stock Rambler hardtop, as neatly listed on this original sales folder.

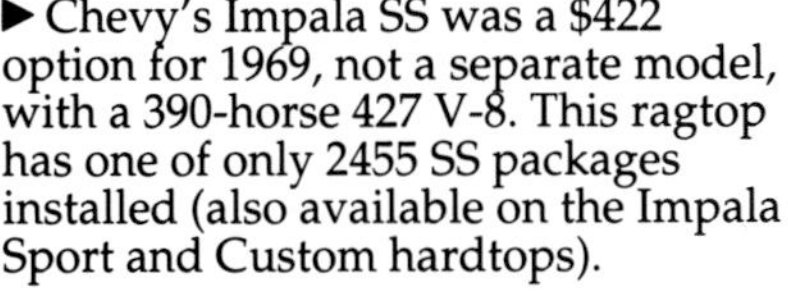

▶ Chevy's Impala SS was a $422 option for 1969, not a separate model, with a 390-horse 427 V-8. This ragtop has one of only 2455 SS packages installed (also available on the Impala Sport and Custom hardtops).

▲ Studebaker was long gone by '69, but its sporting Avanti lived on. South Bend dealers Leo Newman and Nate Altman acquired manufacturing rights in 1965 and began building the "Avanti II" as a limited-edition luxury GT with Corvette running gear and detail styling changes. Base price was $7145 in 1969, when 103 cars were produced. Production would continue through the 1980s.

▲ "Second thoughts" changes marked Chevy's '69 Corvettes, including a return to the "Stingray" name (now one word) and 350 small-block V-8s.

An average full-time American worker earns $7095; a Chevelle retails for as little as $2458

Chevrolet beats Ford again in model-year output, 2.1 million cars to 1.8 million; the industry total reaches 8.4 million units

Cars must now have front headrests, as per government edict

Warranties on '69 models are set at 1-year/12,000-miles for the entire car, 5/50,000 for the drivetrain

GM's "tell-tale" odometers provide visual evidence of tampering

The federal Truth-in-Lending Law requires auto dealers to state costs, terms, and conditions in a uniform manner

Mobil Oil discontinues its long-standing annual Economy Run

▲ The Chevelle Malibu continued on for '69 as one of America's most popular cars—367,100 were sold. Shown here is the $2690 V-8 Sport Coupe.

▲ For '69, the Chevelle SS 396 (with 325, 350, or 375 bhp) was demoted to option status (86,307 sold). Here, a 300 DeLuxe SS 396 two-door sedan.

▲ A heavy lower-body restyle marked Chevy's Camaro "ponycars" for '69. Now more readily available, the Z/28 hardtop saw sales shoot up to 19,014.

▲ Camaro paced the Indianapolis 500 in 1967 and again in '69, when 3675 replica hardtops and convertibles were built with white paint and "Hugger Orange" stripes and interiors. About 100 had the hot 396 V-8s, the others 350s. Total Camaro production for the year dropped to 143,095 units.

▲ Pennsylvania performance whiz Don Yenko built 201 of these 427-powered Yenko/SC Camaros for 1969. Chevy, meanwhile, built a mere 69 drag-ready ZL-1 models with aluminum-block 430-horsepower engines and sold them at a whopping $7300 through a few selected dealers.

► Fulsome "fuselage styling" came to Chrysler Corporation's full-size '69s. Sporty Chrysler 300s like this $4450 ragtop retained "peek-a-boo" headlights. All models added inches in length and width, but weight was up less than 100 pounds, even if it looked like more. This would be the next to last year for the open 300, of which just 1933 were ordered in '69. As before, a 350-horse 440 V-8 remained standard 300 fare, with a 375-bhp "TNT" version returning at extra cost. Today, big Highland Park cars of this era, convertibles especially, have sparked new interest among collectors.

---

The U.S. government proposes a rule that would require installation of inflatable airbags

A recreational vehicle (RV) boom is underway; 540,000 camper-pickups are on the road

Optional on Thunderbird and Continental is a rear-wheel skid-control braking system, which is activated by a miniature computer

Chrysler and Ford follow GM's lead and adopt concealed wipers

Safety door beams are installed on most GM cars

Energy-absorbing S-frames on full-size Ford and Mercury models are designated to keep front-end collision impact away from the passenger compartment

A grille-mounted Super-Lite gives Dodges better visibility for high-speed freeway driving

▲ Styling mods highlighted the hot mid-size '69 Dodges like this Coronet R/T hardtop coupe, base priced at $3442. Powerteams were unchanged, but new "delta-theme" nose and tail treatments were notable. Just 7328 of the '69 R/Ts were built, including the convertible.

▲ Dodge's Coronet Super Bee added a hardtop companion to the fixed-pillar coupe for 1969; at $3138, it was priced a mere $62 higher. This restored beauty shows off that year's restyled rear and "Scat Pack" striping. Super Bee sales for both models totaled a strong 27,846 units.

▲ Added to Super Bee's engine chart at mid-'69 was the tri-carb "Six Pak" 440 V-8 with 390 horses and a big hood scoop. Only some 1907 cars, like this hardtop, got the $463 option.

▲ Dodge added a Charger 500 for 1969 with low-drag styling (note the rear window) for stock-car supertracks, but it couldn't quite keep up with its slicker Dearborn rivals.

▲ A flush backlight and Coronet grille identified the '69 Charger 500s, of which just 52 were built for the street with Hemi power, plus another 340 with the 375-horse 440 V-8.

▲ Mainstream '69 Chargers saw little appearance change—not that any was needed. The R/T remained the sportiest of this lot, again with standard 375-horse Super Magnum 440 V-8. Base price was up to $3592, and 20,057 were built. Total Charger sales fell by 6404 units to 89,704.

▲ Dodge's "mini muscle" Dart GTS with its 275-bhp 340 V-8 (or 330-bhp 383) still seemed quite incongruous in 1969, one reason sales ended after a final 6702 units, again split between a $3419 ragtop and this $3226 hardtop. Many compact buyers wanted economy rather than blistering "go."

---

Pontiac Grand Prix's radio antenna is imbedded in the windshield

Cadillacs get a sealed cooling system with an overflow tank

Chevrolet offers Liquid Tire Chain—a device to spray blended resins on tires to boost traction

Corvettes come with headlight washers, a European-inspired idea

Chrysler wagons have roof-mounted air spoilers to help keep the rear window clean

Chevrolet's 350-cid V-8 is now available in both Avanti II and Checker

The Chevrolet Impala SS appears for the last time; 2455 SS 427s are built with 330/390 bhp

New Chryslers with "fuselage" styling are bigger than ever

▲ Ford went chasing Plymouth's Road Runner for '69 with its new Torino Cobra, a budget muscle car with a 335-horse 428 Cobra Jet V-8. This seldom-seen notchback hardtop version started at a low $3164. Most Cobras were fastbacks.

▲ For $3189, a buyer could opt for this racy '69 Torino Cobra SportsRoof fastback. Fat F70x14 tires on six-inch-wide rims were standard issue, as was a beefed-up suspension.

▲ Early '69 Cobras wore cartoon "snake" decals on the front fenders. Metal emblems were substituted during the model year. The "Ram Air" hood scoop seen here was optional.

▲ The long-nose, flush-front Torino Talladega fastback was Ford's new stock-car racing weapon in 1969. Only 754 were built. It captured 26 wins and the NASCAR Manufacturer's Cup.

▲ Ford's Mustang bulked up in a 1969 redesign featuring exaggerated styling. The base hardtop coupe now started at $2635, but this lush new $2866 Grandé delivered extra luxury touches, among them vinyl roof, color-keyed mirrors, wire wheel covers, and extra bright trim.

▲ The Mustang 2+2 became a "SportsRoof" fastback for '69. New models were Mach 1, Boss 302, and Boss 429. And there was a GT package (*shown*), with lower-body racing stripes, hood scoop, styled steel wheels, and heavy-duty suspension. This car has the 335-bhp 428 Cobra Jet V-8.

---

The Dodge Dart Swinger replaces the GTS, while the "Winged Warrior" Charger Daytona aims at winning NASCAR racing events

A 440 Six-Pak (triple-carb) engine is available in the Dodge Super Bee and Plymouth Road Runner

Full-size Fords and Mercurys are restyled on longer wheelbases: 121.0 inches for Ford, 124.0 for most Mercurys

High-performance Torino Cobras are launched by Ford; Mercury issues the Cyclone CJ

Mustangs grow longer, wider, lower—the Mach 1 fastback debuts, followed by the Boss 302 and Boss 429

Thunderbirds again offer an optional electric sunroof

▲ As Chrysler adopted "fuselage" styling for '69, so did Imperial, ending up even more Chrysler-like. But the result was pleasing—except in sales, which dropped to 22,077. Here, the $6131 LeBaron hardtop sedan, which found 14,821 buyers.

▲ Introduced in mid-1968, the Continental Mark III personal-luxury coupe returned for '69 virtually unchanged. An under-the-skin twin to Ford's Thunderbird, it listed at $6758, with many goodies standard. After a run of 7770 in 1968, another 23,088 were built for '69.

▲ Henry Ford II personally named Lincoln's latest personal-luxury car Mark III as the direct successor to the 1956-57 Mark II. Ford stylists under Eugene Bordinat took pains to preserve a formal look, with "classic" cues like a humped rear deck and Rolls-Royce-style grille.

▲ Still pushing sporty big cars, Mercury revived the Marauder name for a pair of hardtop coupes based on the '69 Ford's new 121-inch chassis. This uplevel X-100 version was priced at $4091; 5635 were produced.

▲ Both '69 Marauders wore Ford's sloped "tunnelback" rooflines and a hidden-headlamp front borrowed from the uplevel Marquis. The X-100 packed a 360-horsepower 429 V-8, versus the base model's 265-horse 390.

▲ Mercury's hottest mid-size street car for '69 was this new Cyclone CJ 428 fastback hardtop coupe. A 335-horse Cobra Jet 428 V-8 was included at the reasonable price of $3224, but only 3261 muscle-car buyers purchased one.

## 1969 Model Year Production

| | | |
|---|---|---|
| 1. Chevrolet 2,092,947 | 7. Dodge 611,645 | 13. Imperial 22,103 |
| 2. Ford 1,826,777 | 8. Mercury 398,262 | 14. Shelby 3,150 |
| 3. Pontiac 870,081 | 9. AMC/Rambler 282,809 | 15. Checker 760[1] |
| 4. Plymouth 751,134 | 10. Chrysler 260,773 | 16. Avanti II 103 |
| 5. Buick 665,422 | 11. Cadillac 223,237 | 17. Excalibur 91 |
| 6. Oldsmobile 635,241 | 12. Lincoln 61,378 | [1]*Estimate, excludes taxicabs* |

▲ Mercury's '69 Cougars featured rounder styling, new convertibles, and new muscle in an Eliminator package. The last, introduced May 8, carried a standard four-barrel 351 and 12-hole wheels. The 335-bhp CJ 428 was optional.

▲ Continuing their muscle-car collaboration, Hurst/Olds again offered a Cutlass-based hardtop coupe—the only body style this year—which ran with the huge 455 V-8 and gold-and-white paint. Horses numbered 380; cars built, 906.

▲ Oldsmobile's Toronado wore a longer tail for '69 to help visually balance its new eggcrate face. Also back from '68 was a premium-fuel-gulping 455 V-8, now rated at 400 bhp. Base models started at $4835, Customs at $5030, and combined sales increased modestly to 28,494.

▲ Plymouth built only 1442 ragtop Barracudas for 1969, so this Formula S with its high-winding, 275-horse 340 small-block is a rarity. Introduced in 1968, this was the engine of choice for those seeking the best balanced Barracuda overall. Total sales sank to 31,987 units.

▲ Although it wore a revised grille for '69, Plymouth's famous "Beep! Beep!" Road Runner shifted gears by emphasizing luxury options, such as bucket seats, console, and power windows. The matte-black "performance" hood on this hardtop remained optional.

▲ Plymouth added a ragtop Road Runner for '69, but sold only 2128 copies. No matter, total RR volume nearly doubled to 84,420—the series' high-water mark. The convertible was priced at $3313, and like the $2945 coupe and $3083 hardtop, it ran with the high-output, 335-horsepower 383 V-8. A new mid-year "440+6" with triple two-barrel carbs boasted 390 horses.

---

Smoother-looking Imperials share much of Chrysler's sheetmetal; prices start at $5592

Mercury's full-size Marauder coupe can be ordered with X-100 trim and a 429-cid V-8

As the Cougar grows bigger, so does the lineup, which adds its first convertible and a hot Eliminator hardtop

A convertible joins the Plymouth Road Runner series (2128 are sold), and the last GTX ragtops are built (700 of them)

Pontiac turns out "The Judge," a hairy, wild-looking GTO option package

On March 8, 1969, a $724.60 Trans Am option with a Ram Air III engine debuts for the Firebird; 697 are produced

▲ Road Runner was named *Motor Trend*'s 1969 "Car of the Year." Here, *MT* publisher Ray Brock (*right*) hands the trophy to Chrysler-Plymouth division chief Glenn White. The big cartoon Road Runner on the door wasn't stock.

▲ Big Plymouths got Chrysler Corporation's rounded "fuselage" look for 1969. The Sport Fury came in this standard hardtop coupe, a new formal-roof model, and convertible, but total sales dropped sharply to 17,868.

▲ Like Chevy's Camaro, Pontiac's Firebird got a lower-body restyle for '69, but demand slumped to 76,059 hardtop coupes and 11,649 ragtops, like this Carousel Red example.

▲ Grand Prix was reborn for 1969 as a smaller 118-inch-wheelbase, personal-luxury Pontiac, which was lighter and quicker. Power options ran up to a burly 428 V-8, sales to 112,486.

▲ "Here come da Judge," a new $332 option package for Pontiac's '69 GTO with a 366-horse "Ram Air III" 400 V-8 and loud "The Judge" decals. A 370-bhp RA/IV engine added $390.

▲ Like the GTO, lesser mid-size Pontiacs wore only modest styling changes for 1969. This Le Mans convertible is equipped with the division's novel hood-mounted tachometer, as well as extra-cost wire wheel covers. Overall, this model won a surprisingly low 5676 orders, even at its modest $3064 base price.

▲ The 1969 Shelby-Mustangs were the biggest and brightest of the breed, with stripes and scoops galore, plus a prominent "loop" bumper/grille. GT-350s gained a modest 290-horse 351 V-8; GT-500s kept the big-block 428, but with only 375 advertised bhp. After 3150 units, plus 636 reserialed "1970" leftovers, Carroll Shelby got out of car-making, though he would return to it in the Eighties.

---

The AMC-Hurst SC/Rambler, a Rogue hardtop with a new 390 V-8, costs only $2998 and does about 100 mph in the quarter-mile

A U.S. Senate report urges the development of steam cars to cut pollution

GM's "Progress of Power" show features five experimental vehicles

The Aerocar III flying car is shown

Stutz Motor Car Co. of America announces a jaunty Bearcat replica with an International Scout chassis and engine; priced at $4950, only a very few are built

Don Yenko issues ultra-hot Corvette-engined Camaro 450s for only one year; about 50 are built

▲ AMC fielded an "import-fighter" in mid-1970, the Gremlin—a chopped-tail, two-door spin-off of that year's brand-new compact Hornet. Priced at a base $1879, Gremlin sold fairly well, and was a half year ahead of the new Ford and Chevy subcompacts that would bow for '71.

▲ Gremlin was identical to the bigger Hornet from the doors forward and came with the same 128-horse, 199-cid six-cylinder engine, but rode a shorter 96-inch wheelbase. Trim was spartan, but options helped, including the roof rack, striping, wheel covers, and whitewalls shown here.

▲ The 1970 AMX shared its new front end with the '70 Javelin, but falling hot-car demand held sales to only 4116, meaning that the sporty coupe would not return. A new 290-horsepower 360 V-8 was standard.

▲ The 1970 AMC Javelin sported a more aggressive face and a new base 360 V-8. Returning options again included 390 engines with up to 340 horses and the colorful "Go Package," as shown here with scoops and stripes.

▲ AMC built a few 1970 Javelins with this wild tri-color paint job, the same used by the Penske Javelins that were winning SCCA's Trans-Am racing series. Javelin sales totaled 28,210 in a rapidly disappearing ponycar market.

▲ Racing ace Mark Donohue poses with a Javelin in Trans-Am livery outside AMC's Plymouth, Michigan, headquarters (factory still in Kenosha, of course). As chief driver for the Roger Penske team, Donohue won the 1970 T-A crown, though AMC had the only official "factory" effort in 1970.

▲ Hoping to claim the 1970 Trans-Am crown and boost Javelin sales, AMC lured the Penske/Donohue team away from Chevy, which had won the 1967 and '68 series with Camaro Z/28s. This is one of the Penske/Sunoco cars that helped win the 1970 manufacturer's trophy.

**1970**

A recession curtails new-car sales; model-year volume slips below 7.6 million cars

Ford hits Number One, turning out 2.1 million cars; Chevrolet, meanwhile, sinks to 1.46 million

Japanese automakers offer a rising challenge as imports take a record 14.6 percent of sales

Chrysler, lacking subcompacts, begins importing the low-priced Japanese-built Dodge Colt and British-made Plymouth Cricket

Three-fifths of all new cars are now air conditioned

Anti-theft steering-column/ignition locks and front/rear side marker lights are required

GM issues 402-, 454-, and 500-cid V-8 engines, all designed with low emissions in mind

▲ Like the '69 "Scrambler," AMC's 1970 "The Rebel Machine" was a gaudy muscle car from an unexpected source. Only 2326 were built before AMC gave up on the idea. All were $3475 hardtop coupes with a 340-horse 390 V-8, hood scoops, fat tires, and Hurst four-speed gearbox.

▲ Styled by AMC's Dick Teague, the AMX/3 bowed at an early 1970 Rome preview as a new low-volume exotic car with a mid-mounted 390 V-8 and a chassis engineered by Italy's Giotto Bizzarrini. Only a half-dozen were built, all effectively pre-production prototypes.

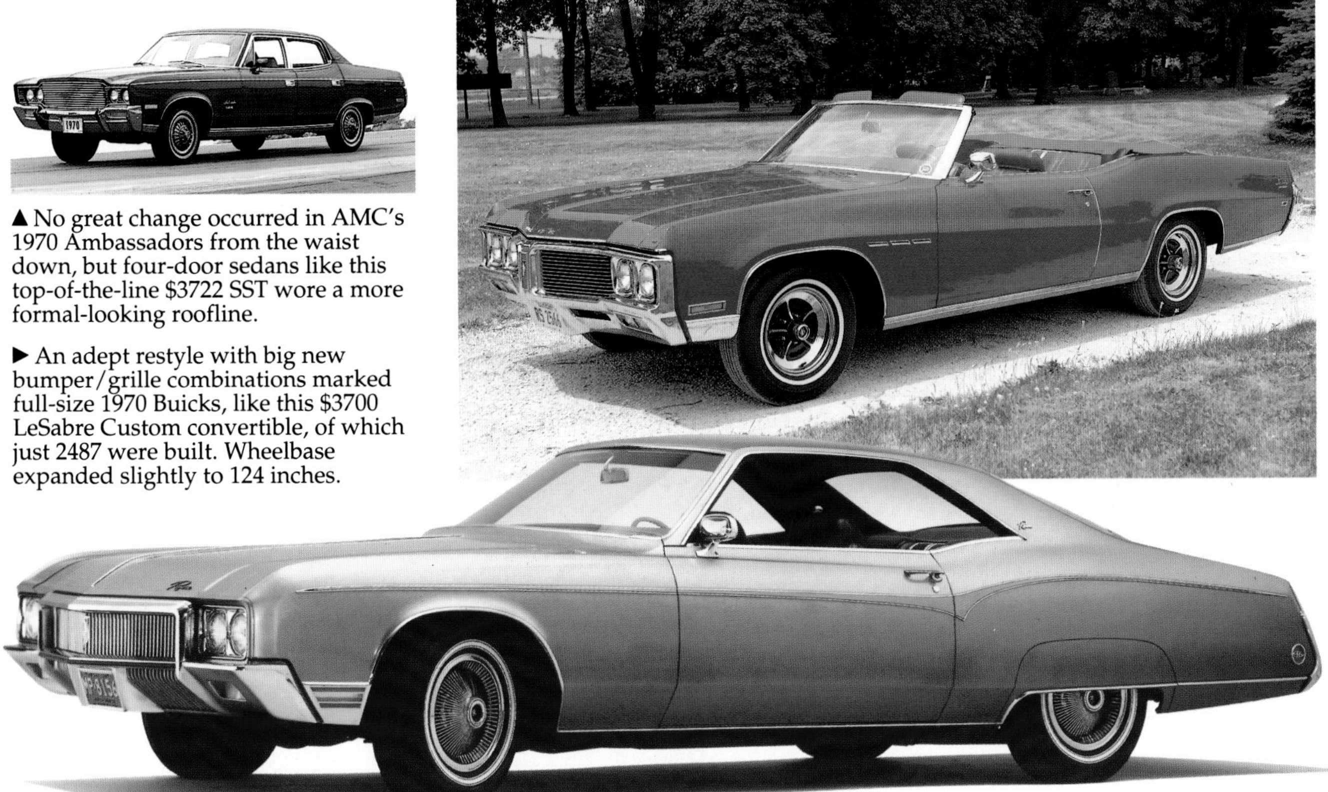

▲ No great change occurred in AMC's 1970 Ambassadors from the waist down, but four-door sedans like this top-of-the-line $3722 SST wore a more formal-looking roofline.

► An adept restyle with big new bumper/grille combinations marked full-size 1970 Buicks, like this $3700 LeSabre Custom convertible, of which just 2487 were built. Wheelbase expanded slightly to 124 inches.

▲ A starchier face and retro-look rear fender skirts did nothing for the looks of the 1970 Riviera, or so some said. Nonetheless, it adopted Buick's new 455-cubic-inch V-8 with 370 horses. Sales slid to 37,336; base price rose $153, to $4854.

---

AMC introduces the compact Hornet, replacing the Rambler American

Gremlin debuts in April as the first American subcompact; prices start at a low $1879

The new Monte Carlo personal-luxury coupe displays the longest hood in Chevrolet's history—six feet: 130,657 are sold

All-new 1970½ Camaro and Firebird coupes arrive in February; convertibles are history

Other 1970 debuts: Buick GSX muscle car, Chrysler 300-H "Hurst" hardtop, and Dodge Challenger ponycar

Late in 1970, Ford abandons most racing efforts

▲ Chevy's 1970 Chevelle SS package included a 350-horse 396 V-8 in its $445 retail price. A new 350-bhp 402 replaced it at mid-year, but badges still read "396." Total SS sales fell to 53,559; only 3733 had the 360-bhp 454 V-8.

▲ GM dropped its displacement limits on mid-size muscle engines for 1970, so Chevy stroked its 427 to 454 cubes. SS Chevelles were rated at 360 bhp, and there was an LS-6 450-horse version.

▲ Corvette also offered Chevy's new 454 big-block option for 1970. A strike limited model-year output to 10,668 convertibles like this and 6648 T-top coupes. Styling changed little, though weight edged upward to 3196 pounds.

▲ Chevy unwrapped a handsome new Camaro coupe for mid-1970. Ragtops were gone, but the Z28 was again on hand as the performance star. This is one of three Z28 "Sunshine Special" prototypes proposed by Hurst.

▼ A 300-horse 350 repeated as Corvette's base 1970 V-8, with 350- and new 370-bhp options. Big-blocks were 390- and 460-bhp 454s, but the latter didn't materialize.

Trends include plastic grilles, front seatbacks that unlatch when the door is opened, tamper-proof odometers, electrically heated rear defrosters

Electronic skid-control braking goes into GM's Eldorado, Riviera, and Toronado

Ford switches to a 12-month warranty with no mileage limitation

AMC Javelin and AMX windshields have a chemically treated inner pane to reduce the possibility of facial lacerations upon impact

The federal government awards contracts to develop a safety vehicle in which passengers could survive a 50-mph crash

GM signs a $50-million license agreement with Curtiss-Wright Corp. for the rights to develop a Wankel rotary engine

▲ Chevy's new 1970 Monte Carlo coupe was a cousin to Pontiac's year-old Grand Prix. Most of the 130,657 sold had mild 350 or 400 V-8s, but 3823 got a hot SS package with the 360-horsepower 454. Still, the Monte Carlo was mostly about luxury. Prices started at a reasonable $3123.

▲ The "fuselage" Chryslers evidenced only "second thoughts" changes for 1970. This 300 convertible, which sold for $4580, is one of only 1077 built that model year. Engines were again 350- or optional 375-horse 440 V-8s. This unabashedly large car weighed in at 4175 pounds.

▲ Hurst converted 501 hardtops and two convertibles into white/gold 1970 Chrysler "300-H" models with a rear spoiler and fiberglass power-bulge hood.

▲ With hot-car insurance premiums soaring by 1970, Dodge sold only half as many Charger R/Ts as in '69—just 10,377. This example is equipped with 1970's new SE option package, which featured leather seat facings.

▲ Dodge belatedly entered the ponycar corral with the 1970 Challenger, a close kin to that year's new-design Barracuda. Convertibles and hardtops were offered in base, luxury SE, and sporty R/T trim (*shown*). This R/T cost $3226.

---

AMC acquires Kaiser-Jeep Corp., suddenly becoming the leading four-wheel-drive vehicle producer

AMC's Rebel "The Machine" runs a potent 390-cid, 340-bhp V-8 and displays wild muscle-car striping

Chevrolet's 350-cid, 300-bhp V-8 is now standard in Avanti II, whose styling remains unchanged

A 455-cid V-8 with 350-370 bhp is standard or available in most Buicks; the new GSX offers a hot "Stage 1" version that'll top 100 mph in the quarter-mile

Cadillac's Eldorado V-8 displaces 500 cubic inches—it's the world's biggest production passenger-car engine (and good for 400 bhp)

Cadillac offers a power sunroof and signal-seeking radio

▲ This "Panther Pink" Challenger T/A was one of 2539 built to qualify the new Dodge ponycar for Trans-Am racing. Street versions boasted a "Six Pak" (triple-carb) 340 small-block V-8, as the fender logo says. It developed 290 horses, double the 145 on base Slant Six models.

▲ SE and R/T trim could be combined on 1970 Dodge Challengers, as on this $3498 hardtop finished in "Plum Crazy," one of five optional "High-Impact" colors. Total Challenger sales were 83,032, nearly 11,000 higher than Mercury's Cougar, which Dodge had aimed to beat.

◀ "Bumblebee" stripes adorned the tails of 1970 Challenger R/Ts, continuing Dodge's "Scat Pack" motif of 1968-69. Hardtops like this way outsold convertibles, and base V-8s far outnumbered the big-block V-8s, indicating that Challenger had arrived just as ponycar demand was beginning to free-fall.

▼ The '70 Ford XL "SportsRoof" retained "tunnelback" hardtop styling, but falling demand for all sporty cars would prompt Ford to put its bucket-seat biggies out to pasture after 1970. The $3293 SportsRoof came with a standard 250-horse 351 V-8; 27,251 were built.

▲ Ford's big XLs were separate models for 1970, not Galaxies. This convertible styling model wears incorrect wheel covers. Only 6348 of these $3501 ragtops were built. Big Fords rode the 121-inch wheelbase introduced in '69.

Chevy II changes its name to Nova, while the facelifted Chevelle more closely resembles the full-size Chevrolet

A big-block 454 V-8 is available for big Chevys and Corvettes; the personal-luxury Monte Carlo gets an SS 454 option

Chrysler offers an optional headlight-delay system, releases its last big Newport/300 convertibles (2201 built), and adds the limited-edition Cordoba hardtop coupe and sedan (1868 and 1873 built)

The Hurst-modified Chrysler 300-H reminds fans of the old Letter-Series models; 501 are produced

Dodge finally responds to Camaro/Mustang with the new Challenger hardtop and ragtop; the redesigned Plymouth Barracuda is similar

In this final year for the high-performance Dodge Coronet R/T series, it is rare: 2319 hardtops and 296 convertibles

▲ Ford scored big with a smaller, 103-inch-wheelbase new compact called Maverick, arriving in spring 1969 as an early 1970 model with a low $1995 starting price. Ford built 578,914 copies, all two-door fastback sedans with standard 170- or optional 200-cubic-inch sixes.

▲ Mustang sales fell 50 percent for 1970, when minor styling changes brought a return to single headlamps. This convertible was one of only 7673 built for the model year, with a starting price of $3025. Rising insurance rates helped depress ponycar sales industry-wide.

▲ The Mach 1 fastback coupe remained the hottest "volume" Mustang for 1970, with a standard 250-horse 351 V-8 and an optional 428 big-block with 335 bhp via Ram Air induction. Base price was $3271, and 40,970 were produced for the model year.

▲ Ford unleashed the potent Boss 302 Mustang to win the 1969 Trans-Am series—which it did. Just 1934 were built, followed by 6319 of the similar 1970 models like this. Alas for Ford, AMC captured the 1970 Trans-Am crown with its Javelin.

▲ Kansas City Ford dealers sold 100 "Twister Special" 1970 Mustang Mach 1s, half of which got 428 Super Cobra Jet power, as shown here. All were done in "Twister Orange" and wore cute rear-fender cartoon decals and the obligatory paint striping.

▲ Another 1970 Ford rarity was this King Cobra, a long-nose, aerodynamic offshoot of that year's restyled Torino designed to succeed the famed Talladega on NASCAR's supertracks. But it wasn't enough to best Chrysler's winged wonders, and only a few were built.

▲ Ford's Ranchero car/pickup went through a Falcon-based design before becoming a Fairlane/Torino derivative for 1967. By 1970, it looked like this. Hidden headlamps were included on the sporty GT version and this Squire model with wood-look trim from the station wagon.

### 1970 Model Year Production

| | | | | | |
|---|---|---|---|---|---|
| 1. Ford | 2,096,184 | 7. Oldsmobile | 633,981 | 13. Lincoln | 59,127 |
| 2. Chevrolet | 1,451,305 | 8. Dodge | 543,019 | 14. Imperial | 11,822 |
| 3. Plymouth | 747,508 | 9. Mercury | 324,716 | 15. Checker | 397[1] |
| 4. Pontiac | 690,953 | 10. AMC | 242,664 | 16. Avanti II | 111 |
| 5. Plymouth | 684,975 | 11. Cadillac | 238,744 | 17. Excalibur | 37 |
| 6. Buick | 666,501 | 12. Chrysler | 180,777 | | |

[1] *Estimated, excludes taxicabs*

◀ Lincoln's 1970 Continental Mark III hadn't changed much from the '68 original, but base price was now up to $7281. Perhaps as a result, demand dropped slightly to 21,432 units. As before, a 365-horsepower 460 V-8 sat beneath the mile-long hood.

▲ "Fast Eddie" Schartman ran this 1970 Mercury Cougar with the hot 429 V-8 in stock-class quarter-mile competition. Street models wore the same prominent new vertical "nose."

▲ Mercury's Cougar Eliminator returned as a package option for 1970, still with the four-barrel version of the 351 V-8 standard. The rear spoiler was more form than function.

▲ Mercury's Cougar Boss 302 Eliminator was something like Ford's Mustang Boss 302, with 290 horses. This one sports one of the "Competition Colors" new for 1970.

▲ New outer tinware and a "gunsight" grille marked the 1970 version of Mercury's hottest mid-size model, the Cyclone Spoiler. Only this notchback was offered at $3759.

▲ Mercury built a mere 1631 Cyclone Spoilers for 1970, reflecting fast-falling muscle-car demand. A burly 370-horse 429 big-block was standard, with or without Ram-Air.

---

Excalibur evolves into the Series II roadster and phaeton, featuring a 111-inch wheelbase and Chevy's 300-bhp, 350-cid V-8

The final Ford Falcons are offered as a basically unchanged 1969 model (15,694 sold) and as a "1970½" stripped Fairlane 500/Torino (67,053 sold)

At a $1995 base price, the import-fighting Ford Maverick sells very strongly: 578,914 are produced in a long model year

Imperial drops its Crown series after 1587 '70 models are built; the LeBaron series will continue

The all-new Lincoln Continental sedan and hardtop adopt body-on-frame construction and conventional front-hinged rear doors

Lincoln-Mercury dealers now sell the German-built Capri, a "mini-ponycar" destined to top 113,000 units in its best year (1973)

▲ This 1970 Olds 4-4-2 hardtop, of which 14,709 were sold, carries the max-performance W-30 option with a 370-horse 455 V-8, which fed through functional twin hood scoops and used an aluminum intake manifold and special long-duration cam. "Cooking" 4-4-2s had "only" 365 bhp.

▲ Olds pulled a fast one for 1970 by switching its muscular 4-4-2s to a huskier new Cutlass Supreme platform. This convertible, which was base priced at $3567, is one of only 2933 built for the model year. All intermediate-size Oldsmobiles wore detail style changes.

▲ A '70 Olds 4-4-2 racer breaks free at the 1971 Winternationals. Showroom versions with the top V-8 generated 370 bhp.

---

Plymouth adds the popular Valiant-based Duster coupe (217,192 sold) and the startling winged Road Runner Superbird (1920 built)

Overall output tumbles nearly 180,000 units at Pontiac as buyers turn to more economical cars; California-bound station wagons receive plastic gas tanks

General Motors endures a 67-day strike as the '71 model year begins

▲ Evolved from Dodge's 1969-only Charger Daytona, the 1970 Plymouth Superbird carried Chrysler's colors in NASCAR racing. Exactly 1920 were built, versus 505 Chargers. Together, they dominated the 1970 NASCAR racing season.

▲ Superbird's drooped "nose cone" (which added 17.2 inches to overall length) resembled the '69 Charger Daytona's, yet was subtly different and not interchangeable. Both models came with a four-barrel 440, with Hemi or 440 "Six Pak" optional. The Superbird's price was $4298.

▲ Plymouth's 1970 mid-sizers wore a nice restyle. The hot but luxurious GTX was down to this lone $3535 hardtop coupe; 7748 were built. Part of Plymouth's "Rapid Transit System," this car carries the hulking "440+6" option (triple two-barrel carbs), rated at 390 horses.

▲ Plymouth Barracuda convertibles were never high-volume sellers, and they became even rarer for 1970. Just 635 'Cuda versions were built, this one to hot 'Cuda 340 specs.

▲ A cousin to the Dodge Challenger T/A, Plymouth's 1970 'Cuda AAR was a special street version of Dan Gurney's All-American Racers' Trans-Am race car. Just 1500 were produced.

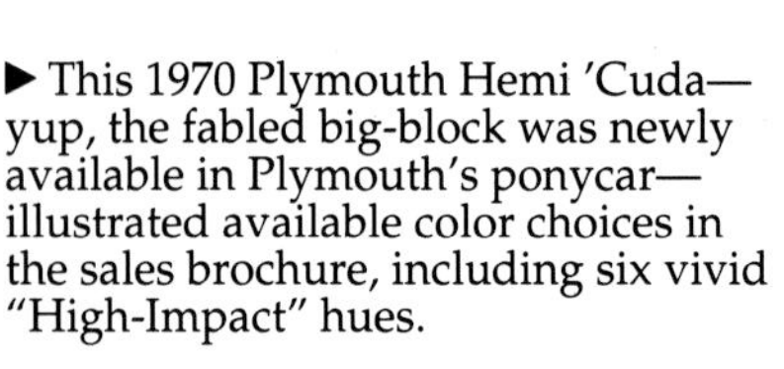

► This 1970 Plymouth Hemi 'Cuda—yup, the fabled big-block was newly available in Plymouth's ponycar—illustrated available color choices in the sales brochure, including six vivid "High-Impact" hues.

▲ Pontiac strove for a "classical" look at the front end of its 1970 full-size models like this plush Bonneville hardtop coupe, of which 23,418 were sold. It was priced at $3832. A 360-horse 455 became "Bonnie's" standard engine.

▲ Pontiac brochures of the '60s and '70s were among the industry's most artistic. Here's the cover of the 1970 full-line catalog. Note the ad slogan.

▲ Pontiac altered the GTO's styling for 1970, giving it a new Endura nose with exposed headlamps, bodyside creases, and a revised rump. Newly optional for regular GTOs, such as the ragtop pictured here, was a 360-bhp 455-cid V-8. That engine wasn't initially offered in the Judge (*left*), most of which used the 366-bhp 400-cid Ram Air III V-8. Total 1970 GTO output came to 36,366 hardtops and 3783 convertibles.

◀ A variety of factors was conspiring against convertible sales by 1970. This Catalina was Pontiac's lowest priced full-size soft-top offering that year. Starting at $3604, it offered new 455 V-8 options with up to 370 horses; a 330-horsepower 400 came standard. Only 3686 of these open Catalinas were ordered, compared to 3537 of the $4040 Bonnevilles.

▲ AMC's 1971 performance special was the Hornet SC/360, a bestriped $2663 compact two-door with a 360 V-8 giving 245 standard horses, 285 optional, and a handling suspension. Curb weight was 3057 pounds. Only 784 copies were built.

▲ American Motors chairman Roy D. Chapin, Jr., poses with the '71 Gremlin outside company headquarters. This model started at $1999. Gremlin sales totaled 53,480.

▲ AMC Javelins wore new humped-fender styling for '71. The $3432 AMX, shown here, was now the high-performance Javelin. Top power choice was a new 401 V-8 with 330 horses; it cost $137 extra in the AMX.

◀ The mid-size AMC Rebel became a Matador for '71 and acquired a bolder look front and rear, plus a new hardtop roofline. Sedans, wagons, and hardtop coupes (*shown here*) were priced in the $2800-$3500 range.

**1971**

As the consumer movement gains strength, the auto industry faces rising criticism

President Nixon announces a 90-day wage/price freeze on August 16 and the end of the excise tax on automobiles

Horsepower ratings continue to fall as a result of tightening emission-control standards; hydrocarbon emissions are now 80 percent lower than in pre-1963 automobiles, and will fall even further

"Closed" fuel systems on all cars control evaporation from the fuel tank and carburetor

General Motors lowers compression ratios; other automakers wait until 1972

GM engines run on regular or no-lead fuel, as do some from Chrysler and AMC

▲ Buick made big changes for '71, starting with a bigger, all-new Riviera wearing controversial "boattail" fastback styling. At 33,810 units, sales of the $5253 hardtop coupe were down nearly 10 percent from 1970.

◀ Despite a three-inch-longer 122-inch wheelbase, plus added length and width, the 4325-pound '71 Riv was little heavier than the 1966-70 models. The standard engine was a 315-horse 455 V-8; a 330-bhp version was optional, as was a Gran Sport handling package, which 3175 buyers chose.

◀ Big Buicks were redesigned to be even bigger for '71. The Centurion, shown as a $4678 hardtop coupe, ousted Wildcat as the middle series.

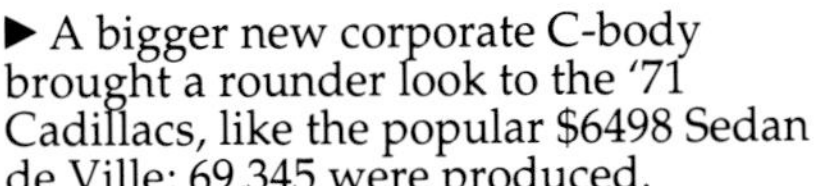

▶ A bigger new corporate C-body brought a rounder look to the '71 Cadillacs, like the popular $6498 Sedan de Ville; 69,345 were produced.

▶ The 1971 full-size Chevrolets got a wholly new GM B-body with a fuller, more rounded look as on senior C-body sisters at Olds, Buick, and Cadillac. Caprice again topped the line for luxury and price, with two- and four-door hardtops returning at $4081 and $4134. Combined production was 110,497. Most were ordered with 350 and 400 V-8s.

---

The "muscle car" era is nosediving into oblivion—the victim of federal safety/emissions rules, rising insurance rates, and the trend toward less costly cars

GM's big cars are reworked, as are the Mustang/Cougar and Chrysler's mid-size models

Once again, Ford beats Chevrolet in car production, with 2,054,351 built

Plymouth grabs third place in output, largely on the strength of its compacts; Pontiac drops to fourth

The Ford Pinto and Chevrolet Vega are launched—the subcompact race is on in earnest

Mid-year additions include two compacts: Dodge Demon, a Plymouth Duster clone; Pontiac Ventura II, a Chevy Nova clone

▲ Single headlamps helped identify Chevrolet's 1971 mid-sizers, like this mainstay Malibu hardtop coupe, which enjoyed 186,337 sales. Fender badges on this example signal an extra-cost 245- or 270-bhp 350 V-8.

▲ New low-compression engines gave '71 SS Chevelles slightly tamer performance, but cleaner exhaust pipes. Some 79,992 Super Sports were built, of which 19,292 had the big-block 454 option. An extra $485 bought 375 horses, with 425 also available.

◀ Chevrolet's svelte Monte Carlo coupe was little changed for '71, but again offered an SS 454 package with the same 425-horse engine available in SS Chevelles. This is one of only 1919 such cars built out of 128,600 total MCs. Buyers preferred luxury; the SS was canceled after 1971.

THE LITTLE CAR THAT GROWS ON YOU.

There are two ways of looking at the Vega
Hatchback Coupe.
One, you can look at it as a sporty little
2-seater which, unlike most sporty little 2-seaters,
has a back seat you can flip up on those rare occa-
sions when you have three or four people aboard.
Or you can look at it as a sporty little 4-
seater which, unlike a lot of sporty little 4-seaters,
has a back seat you can flip down when you
have a lot of stuff to haul, like on Saturday.
The Vega Hatchback was designed from
the outset to be a Hatchback.

It isn't an afterthought.
It is a beautifully balanced, beautifully
engineered car with a lot more than just a lot of
loadspace to entice you.
There's Vega's surprisingly responsive
overhead cam engine, for example. And standard
front disc brakes. A double-panel steel roof, side-
guard beams in the doors, a 50,000-mile air
cleaner, even an electric fuel pump that cuts out
to stop the car if the oil pressure ever drops too low.
Vega. It grows on you.
And it's growing on America

GM

VEGA
CHEVROLET

▲ Chevy hoped to stem a rising new tide of import sales with the innovative '71 Vega 2300. This $2196 hatchback coupe was one of three models (wagon: $2328). Total sales were good: 269,905.

▲ At $2090, this two-door notchback was the most affordable '71 Chevy Vega, but didn't come with many frills. All Vegas carried a new advanced all-aluminum four-cylinder engine rated at either 90 or 110 horses.

◀ The headline on this announcement ad for Chevy's 1971 Vega hatchback coupe would prove predictive, but in a negative sense. Engine troubles and heavy rusting tendencies surfaced early, leading to many unhappy owners and badly tarnishing Chevy's reputation for high quality.

---

The FTC insists that claims in auto ads be documented

Chrysler buys a share of Mitsubishi Motors Corp., GM purchases a portion of Isuzu—the "captive-import" business (which includes small trucks) involves Japanese as well as European companies

Lincoln-Mercury dealers market the sleek Italian-built, Ford-powered mid-engine DeTomaso Pantera; this mid-engined exotic coupe lists at $9000 and 6091 will be sold from 1971-74

The Federal Highway Administration approves standard color combinations and symbols for warning signs

Imperial employs the first four-wheel anti-skid braking system

◄▲ The Dodge Charger got a wild new shape for '71 on a two-inch shorter wheelbase. This $3777 R/T was one of six models (all hardtops) and still packed a big wallop with its 370-horse 440 Magnum or optional 425-bhp 426 Hemi. R/T sales plunged to only 3118, a sign of changing times.

▲ "Pocket" muscle cars seemed just the thing to combat soaring insurance rates, so Dodge added two Demons for '71, based on Plymouth's Valiant Duster coupe. For just $2721, this hot 275-horse Demon 340 pleased 10,098 buyers.

▲ Full-size '71 Dodges stayed with the "fuselage look" adopted for '69, but sales continued to slide. This $3992 Polara Custom wagon, for instance, is one of just 9682 sold (plus 5449 uplevel Monaco wagons).

▲ Ford's Maverick again sold strongly for 1971, aided by a new 109.9-inch, long-wheelbase four-door, a 302 V-8 option, and a jazzier two-door called Grabber. The last, shown as a styling model, featured side stripes, black hood and back panel, and a modest $2354 sticker price.

▲ Countering 1971's all-new big Chevys was a fully redesigned crop of full-size Fords headed by a posh new LTD Brougham sedan and hardtops ($4094-$4140). All save the cheap Custom models came with a 240-horse 351 V-8—needed to handle the nearly 300 pounds of added heft.

---

Ford station wagons feature a tailgate wiper-washer; full-size GM wagons boast a "disappearing" clamshell-type tailgate

Automatic temperature-control air conditioning is available on some Ford products

The Rebel "The Machine" and the two-seater AMX are gone from the AMC lineup; AMX is now a topline Javelin model

Hornet adds an attractive Sportabout wagon and the SC/360, a hot Hornet coupe that finds only 784 buyers

The redesigned full-size Buicks are the biggest ever: up to 228.3 inches long overall

Buick introduces a radically restyled Riviera that will become known as the "boattail" Riv; it offers "Max-Trac," a computerized anti-wheelspin system

▲ The Ford Mustang grew to Clydesdale size in a full 1971 redesign. Topping Mach 1 as the top street performer was this new Boss 351, a fastback with a hot 330-horse 351 V-8. Priced at $4124, only 1806 were called for.

▲ Ford's '71 Torinos kept "shaped by the wind" 1970 styling and were still capable of sizzling go with up to 370 bhp. The fastback Cobra hardtop was back at $3295, but only 3054 were sold in a fast-fading performance market.

▲ Eschewing change just for the sake of it, the 1968-vintage Lincoln Continental Mark III put in a final appearance for 1971 and scored higher sales of 27,091 units. Base price was up to $8813; the vinyl roof and body pinstriping remained standard.

► Oldsmobile's 4-4-2 was slightly detuned for '71, but still packed a wallop with the W-30 option, as on this $3552 hardtop; 6285 were produced.

## 1971 Model Year Production

| | | |
|---|---|---|
| 1. Ford 2,054,351 | 7. Buick 551,188 | 12. Lincoln 62,642 |
| 2. Chevrolet 1,830,319 | 8. Mercury 365,310 | 13. Imperial 11,558 |
| 3. Plymouth 702,113 | 9. AMC 244,758 | 14. Checker 500[1] |
| 4. Pontiac 586,856 | 10. Cadillac 188,537 | 15. Avanti II 107 |
| 5. Oldsmobile 567,891 | 11. Chrysler 175,118 | |
| 6. Dodge 551,386 | | |

[1]*Estimated, excludes taxicabs*

▲ The 4-4-2 ragtop listed at $3743 for '71, when Olds switched to *net* power ratings that put the base 455 V-8 at 260 horses and the W-30 mill at 300. But hot-car demand was falling fast, so the ragtop netted only 1304 sales. After '71, 4-4-2 would again be an option package.

▲ Full-size Oldsmobiles shared in GM's new 1971 big-car platforms, with Ninety-Eights like this $4790 hardtop coupe using the senior C-body. Other Ninety-Eights included a standard hardtop sedan and new Luxury versions of both body types. Total Ninety-Eight output was 83,291.

▲ Because Mustang bulked up again for '71, Mercury's Cougar did too—and strove mightily to look like a luxury car, though hot 429 big-block options were still listed. Here, the $3877 XR-7 hardtop coupe, which found favor with 25,416 customers.

► Cougar kept convertibles for 1971, but sinking demand for ragtops has since made these some of the era's rarest Detroit cars. This $3877 upper-level XR-7 was one of just 1717 built that year. Its $3681 base-trim sister attracted only 1723 buyers.

Cadillac restyles the Eldorado and issues its first front-drive Eldo convertible; prices start at $7383

Chevrolet's 97-inch-wheelbase Vega holds much promise, but soon suffers due to a troublesome alloy-block engine that overheats and a rust-prone body

Dodge releases its last convertible, a Challenger (2165 built); Challenger and Charger R/T models are also in their last year

Ford's 94.2-inch-wheelbase Pinto, which lists at $1919, gets off to a good start: 352,402 are built for the model run

A sporty-looking Maverick Grabber appearance package joins Ford's compact line, as does a seven-inch-longer four-door sedan

The much-changed Mustang is bigger, heavier; a new Boss 351 lasts just one year

▲ Mercury's Cyclone Spoiler saw few changes for '71, so high-compression 429 CJ and Super CJ power still reigned. With a sticker price of $3801, sales came to a piddling 353.

▲ Plymouth purged mid-size convertibles from its all-new '71 lineup. GTX remained the posh performer, a $3733 hardtop coupe. Only 2942 were sold, so it disappeared after '71.

► Similarly, Plymouth's Road Runner was down to a single hardtop for '71, priced at $3147 with base 383 V-8, which dropped 30 horses to 300. The Hemi and 440s were still optional, but so was the Road Runner's first 340 small-block V-8. Still, sales plunged by two-thirds, from 41,484 units to 14,218.

▲ Plymouth's popular Valiant-based Duster fastback returned from debut 1970 with a minor facelift. The 340, shown here in "Curious Yellow," remained the top '71 performer, and attracted 12,886 buyers. A new Twister package, here in "Sassy Grass Green," offered 340 show, but not its go—and cost less to insure.

---

Oldsmobile issues its last true 4-4-2 models—6285 hardtops and 1304 ragtops are built

In its last outing, the muscular Plymouth GTX snares 2942 buyers

Pontiac builds its 15,000,000th car on July 16

Maintenance-free batteries are installed in some GM cars

Automakers test 1600 units in an attempt to develop a catalytic converter that will meet projected emissions standards

In Los Angeles, more than 5000 fleet vehicles are converted to burn propane and natural gas

The Silver Eagle electric car sets a speed record of 146 mph

◀ Though big muscle cars were all but gone by '71, Plymouth tried one last time with its Sport Fury GT (*foreground*), a $4111 hardtop coupe with a standard 335-horse 440 V-8. Just 375 were sold, far fewer than this lesser Sport Fury Formal Hardtop (*background*), which cost $3710.

▼ Though their faces were vaguely familiar, Pontiac's full-size '71s were all-new—and as big as American big cars would ever get. The pride of the line was a new top-line Grand Ville series that included this grandly priced $4706 convertible, which sold just 1789 units. A 325-horse 455 V-8 was the standard—and only—engine offered.

▲ Formula remained a step down from Trans Am among performance Firebirds for 1971, but Pontiac added new 350 and 455 models to join the carryover Formula 400. Despite a $3445 base price, only 7802 Formulas were built.

▲ An aggressive new nose marked Pontiac's 1971 GTOs, including "The Judge" hardtop coupe, but this would be GTO's last year as a distinct series. Judge's 455 V-8 was down from 360 to 335 horses, while the base GTO's 400 V-8 dropped to 300. This $3840 Judge found only 357 takers.

▲ This base '71 GTO convertible is one of only 661 built; Judge ragtops, meanwhile, numbered a mere 17. Even base hardtop sales were little better at 9497 units. Tightening emissions regulations and soaring insurance rates had rung the death knell for all muscle cars.

---

Consumer advocate Ralph Nader publishes a new book titled, *What To Do With Your Bad Car: An Action Manual For Lemon Owners*

CHAPTER TWELVE

1972-1979

# THE GOVERNMENT STEPS IN

Many Americans recall the Seventies as a dour decade of defeat and disappointment, from the ignominious end of the Vietnam War to the Watergate fiasco that forced a president to resign. They were certainly years of diminished expectations—an age of disillusionment rather than the promised Age of Aquarius.

The decline was, perhaps, inevitable. After more than a decade of turmoil, the country needed to stop and take stock of what it had endured. Trouble was, we were too often disturbed by what we found. Drug abuse and urban poverty in particular loomed as growing national problems with serious long-term consequences.

So, too, the unprecedented embargo on oil shipments to the U.S., decreed in the winter of 1973-74 by a then little-known cartel called the Organization of Petroleum Exporting Countries. Suddenly, Americans who had never had to give a thought about a tank of gas were forced to wait in long lines for fuel that more than doubled in price overnight. This "energy crisis" wasn't confined to keeping cars chugging along (home heating oil was also scarce in many places that winter), but it dramatically underscored the nation's over-dependence on oil sources it could not control. Sadly, the situation would only grow worse, highlighted by a second crisis in 1979 that sparked a new economic recession to open the Eighties.

Congress had long since decided to make automakers answer for the social responsibility of their products, and the legislative hand became increasingly heavier in these years. The Clean Air Act of 1970 mandated ever-tighter limits on exhaust emissions that sapped horsepower; combined with soaring insurance premiums, they all but eliminated performance cars by 1973. That same year brought more required safety features, including bumpers able to endure five-mph impacts without damage, plus the diabolical ignition interlock that prevented starting up unless front-seat occupants were buckled up. The latter proved so irksome that the public got it repealed after a single year.

Of course, the first energy crisis was not forgotten. In 1978, Congress served up the Corporate Average Fuel Economy (CAFE) rule, which required smaller, thriftier engines and smaller, lighter cars to match. Actually, Detroit had already moved in that direction with "subcompacts" like the Ford Pinto and Chevy Vega, but those were meant to stem another rising import tide, including some compelling new cars from Japan. Not until GM "downsized" its biggest cars for 1977 was CAFE's full implication apparent to the car-buying public—or to GM's rivals.

Detroit convertibles went into limbo after 1976, thanks to a proposed but ultimately stillborn standard for rollover protection that would have made them illegal. To its discredit, Detroit used the threat to justify killing off ragtops, which of late had not been profitable anyway. But as we know, convertibles have a timeless appeal, and they would return.

So would performance and something like the quality workmanship we knew in the early Fifties, not to mention tasteful, rational styling. But Detroit's Seventies landscape was a mostly bleak vista of fuelish, poor-running dinosaurs with starchy stand-up grilles, "opera windows," and overstuffed velour interiors festooned with fake wood and fussy filigrees—all style passing for substance. Yet there were bright spots. The Chevrolet Corvette remained exciting, if muted from earlier days, and Pontiac's Firebird Trans Am maintained the ponycar spirit unbroken. Still, it was left to imports like the Volkswagen Rabbit and Honda Accord to point the way to Detroit's future, even as they pointed up the follies of its past.

---

**1972**

Industry output rises to 8.6 million cars for the model year

Chevrolet builds 2,420,564 cars for the model run, compared to Ford's 2,246,563; Oldsmobile ranks third, Plymouth fourth, Pontiac fifth

Congress revokes the price "freeze" and auto excise tax

The latest models focus on safety, engineering, and emissions-control; most don't change much, but buyers snap them up anyway

Ford offers the year's only all-new lines: Torino/Montego, Thunderbird, Continental Mark IV

GM cars get energy-absorbing bumpers—a year ahead of government requirements

Buzzers and warning lights remind occupants to fasten their seatbelts

▲ American Motors' Ambassador was little-changed for 1972, but models were down to SST and fancier Brougham wagon, sedan, and hardtop coupe. This $4018 Brougham hardtop has the optional 225-bhp, 401-cid V-8.

▲ AMC's Matador was also little-changed for '72. As elsewhere in the industry, engine outputs were now quoted in SAE *net* instead of gross. Hardtop coupe prices started at $2818; a 100-bhp, 232-cid six was standard.

▲ You had to look twice to tell a '72 Hornet from a 1970-71. All models were now tagged SST. This four-door sold for $2265 with the 232-cid six and $2403 with the base 150-bhp 304 V-8. AMC built 71,056 Hornets for '72.

▲ AMC's sporty Javelin countered declining "go" with new "show," as on this AMX version specially ordered with the Pierre Cardin package, usually an option only for SST models. Overall Javelin sales eased about 1000 units to 26,184.

▲ Because they were new for '71, full-size Buicks got only detail updates for '72. This $4291 Custom convertible topped the entry-level LeSabre line, which also included pillared and hardtop coupes and sedans. Just 2037 of these ragtops were built, each weighing a hefty 4235 pounds.

▲ Buick's 1972 Electra 225s retained more formal rooflines than LeSabres and Centurions. Models again comprised this hardtop sedan and a hardtop coupe in base and Custom trim. This Custom has the even fancier Limited package and sold for $5059. A 225-bhp, 455-cid V-8 was standard.

---

Horsepower and torque ratings are now given as "net" instead of "gross" (with accessories disconnected)—the revised method, which is more realistic, causes published figures to drop sharply

Nearly all engines run on low-lead regular gasoline

The Pontiac Firebird, like Chevrolet's Camaro, almost expires in the early '70s as GM worries about the future of performance-oriented machines

Chrysler and Pontiac offer solid-state ignition systems

Most automakers offer a powered or manually operated sunroof; convertibles sales continue to decline

The Detroit-based Automobile Manufacturers Association (AMA) changes its name to the Motor Vehicle Manufacturers Association (MVMA)

▲ The Buick GS remained pretty hot for '72, with an unchanged 270-horse (net) Stage 1 455 V-8. But this was its swan-song season. Production ended after 7723 of these hardtops and 852 ragtops. Note the hood-mounted tach.

▲ Like other '71 newcomers, Buick's big boattail Riviera got only minor tweaks for '72, including a new power-sunroof option. Base price eased to $5149, and sales held steady at 33,728 of these controversially styled coupes.

► De Ville remained the best-selling Cadillac line by far for 1972, even though its convertible had become an Eldorado for '71. SAE net figures pushed rated power for the 472-cid V-8 down from 375 bhp to 345, but actual performance was little-changed. Sales of the $6168 Coupe de Ville hardtop rose 44 percent to 95,000, while its $6390 Sedan de Ville stablemate jumped 43 percent, to 99,531.

▲ Updated details were also the order of 1972 for full-size Chevrolets like this top-line Kingswood Estate Wagon, which again offered Caprice-level luxury and woody-look side trim for around $4400. A third-row seat gave it nine-passenger capacity.

▲ Once oh-so sporty, the Impala had been reduced to just a big, heavy boulevard cruiser by 1972, though it still was Chevy's only full-size convertible, as shown here. Base price actually dropped $42, to $3979, and production jumped from 4576 to 6456.

▲ Chevy's most popular '72 full-size model was this Impala Custom hardtop coupe. With 183,493 built, it nipped the usual top-selling four-door sedan by only 132 units. Base price was $3787, versus $3708 for the sedan. Big Chevys rode a 122-inch chassis.

---

An electronic digital clock is standard on Imperials, optional on other Chryslers

Some 200 Mercurys with air bags go to Allstate Insurance as part of a pilot project; Eaton Corp. tests air bags with human passengers

Buick's Skylark hardtop can be ordered with a sliding fabric sunroof; the GS 455 returns, but the GSX is reduced to an appearance package

The big 454 V-8 is still available in Chevelle and Monte Carlo, but the Monte Carlo SS departs

A 400-cid V-8 replaces the 383 in Chryslers; a plush New Yorker Brougham is added

The 426-cid V-8 leaves Dodge/Plymouth, as do the Charger R/T and Super Bee models; a 400-cid V-8 is added, while the big 440 carries on

▲ The V-8 Malibu hardtop coupe was again the best-seller among mid-size '72 Chevys, the last of the 1968-generation models. Of 390,000 built, 207,000 were V-8 Malibu hardtops.

▲ Chevelle's SS package saw few changes for 1972, but sales dropped to just under 25,000. A 307 V-8 was the base SS engine. Only 5333 cars got big-block 454s, including this hardtop.

▲ Despite few changes for its third year, Chevrolet's personal-luxury Monte Carlo was more popular than ever, scoring 180,819 sales. Base price was $3362 with the 350-cid V-8.

◄▲ The "shark" Corvette was five years old in 1972, but still looked tough. Making it tougher to steal was a newly standard factory alarm system. The top 425-bhp 454 option departed, leaving a 365-bhp (270 net) version as the brawniest available. Total 'Vette sales remained depressed at 26,994.

▲ It was Chevy II for 1968-69, simply Nova after that. But concrete changes to Chevy's compact were few. For '72, power choices were down to a standard 110-horse 250 six, and optional 130-bhp 307 or 165-bhp 350 V-8s. This two-door started around $2400. Sales remained healthy at 349,733, despite a surge in the popularity of the subcompact Vega, which reached 390,478 units.

▲ The 1972 Chryslers made do with basic '69 tooling, but hid it fairly well with revised rooflines and lower-body sheetmetal. Seeking higher sales in an inflationary market, the division had added Newport Royal models for '71, and these continued in the $4000-$4200 range: a sedan, four-door hardtop, and this two-door hardtop. All sold better than their costlier Newport Custom siblings. A 360 V-8 with 175 bhp was standard; Customs got a 400 with 190 horses.

---

An era ends as the fabled Dodge/Plymouth Street Hemi fades away—it's too costly to certify for emissions

A three-door Ford Pinto wagon debuts, including a woody-look Squire option; sales reach 197,290 units

Ford's all-new and larger Torino gets body-on-frame construction; the Cobra muscle car is extinct

Mustang loses its big-block V-8s and Boss 351

A larger Ford Thunderbird shares its structure with the new Continental Mark IV; the sedan fades away, but production nonetheless increases 60 percent to 57,814 units

Four-wheel disc brakes are available on the T-Bird, along with "Sure-Track" anti-lock braking

▼ Polara remained Dodge's volume big-car line for '72, but sales began withering. This $3898 Custom hardtop sedan attracted 22,205 customers.

▲ Imperial was still a separate marque in 1972 and sported revised front and rear ends. Bendix anti-skid brakes returned as a worthy but seldom-ordered option. This $6550 LeBaron hardtop coupe was one of 2322 built. Its four-door sister managed 13,472 sales.

▲ Dodge's low-priced Dart Swinger hardtop coupes had found success in 1971, so they continued for '72 with minor improvements—and 238,828 deliveries. This standard model sold for $2528, the downmarket Special for $2373.

▲ Big "loop" bumper/grilles were a Chrysler hallmark in the early Seventies, as on Dodge's '72 mid-size Coronet Custom four-door sedan. It listed at a reasonable $2998 with the standard 225-cid Slant Six, with V-8s optional.

▲ Ford's Thunderbird was all-new for '72, with a wheelbase stretched 5.4 inches, to 120.4. A $5293 hardtop coupe was now the sole model, here with the popular Landau roof.

◀ Hidden headlamps continued to set Dodge's luxury Monacos apart from the similarly sized Polaras. This hardtop coupe stickered at $4153 with the 175-bhp 360 V-8.

### 1972 Model Year Production

| | | | | | |
|---|---|---|---|---|---|
| 1. Chevrolet | 2,420,564 | 7. Dodge | 577,870 | 12. Lincoln | 94,560 |
| 2. Ford | 2,246,563 | 8. Mercury | 441,964 | 13. Imperial | 15,804 |
| 3. Oldsmobile | 762,199 | 9. Cadillac | 267,787 | 14. Checker | 850[1] |
| 4. Plymouth | 756,605 | 10. AMC | 258,134 | 15. Avanti II | 127 |
| 5. Pontiac | 706,978 | 11. Chrysler | 204,704 | 16. Excalibur | 65 |
| 6. Buick | 679,921 | | | | |

[1] *Estimated, excludes taxicabs*

▲ Full-size, formal-look 1972 Fords were much like the redesigned '71s. Here, the $3925 LTD hardtop sedan, which attracted 104,167 buyers. The fancier $4074 LTD Brougham found 23,364 homes. A 208-bhp 429 V-8 was the top engine.

▲ Ford's all-new '72 mid-size Torinos were as big as recent full-size models. Sedans, hardtops, fastbacks, and wagons returned, convertibles didn't. Gran Torinos, like this $2878 "formal" hardtop coupe, stressed luxury.

▲ Ford's Boss Mustang retired for '72, leaving the 351-cid Mach 1 as the hottest offering. Other models, except the Grandé hardtop, could be ordered with a colorful new Sprint Decor Option, as on this convertible.

▶ After being completely redesigned for 1970, Lincoln's Continental received mostly minor yearly changes. Even so, sales for '72 rebounded to 45,969. Only 10,408 were hardtop coupes (up from 8205), like this 4906-pound, $7068 vinyl-topped chariot.

---

Oldsmobile's Cutlass convertible attracts 11,571 buyers in its last year, while the 4-4-2 is now just an appearance/handling option package

Plymouth convertibles are history, as are the GTX and big-block Barracuda; the Road Runner survives with the 240-bhp 340 V-8 (7628 are built)

Pontiac's legendary GTO reverts to a Le Mans option package

A new armor-plated Lincoln Continental with a 34-inch stretch goes to the White House

Prestolite introduces a maintenance-free battery

Fiberglass radial-ply tires go on sale—and prove popular

▲ Because Ford's Thunderbird was all-new for '72, so was the personal-luxury Lincoln. Dubbed Mark IV, it outsold both Continental models by 2622 units—48,591 in all—despite a premium $8640 base price. Its standard 460 V-8 had 212 bhp, 12 fewer than Continental's. New oval "opera windows" were soon to be much-imitated.

▲ Mercury's '72 Cougar line again consisted of base and XR-7 hardtop coupes and convertibles; lower power ratings were among the few notable changes. This closed $3323 XR-7 was the line's best-seller: 26,802 units.

▲ As at Ford, Mercury reprised its full-size '72 Marquis and Monterey lines with few alterations. The Marquis editions again outsold entry-level Montereys like this $4035 Custom hardtop coupe, which found just 5910 buyers.

▲ Mercury's hot Cyclone was gone with the wind for '72, but mid-size Montegos were all-new—and obviously similar to that year's fresh Ford Torinos. This top-line $3438 MX Villager wagon sold 9237 copies.

◀ Like most rivals, Oldsmobile's full-size '72s were mildly facelifted '71 reruns. Topping the line was this Ninety-Eight Luxury hardtop sedan. It started at $5009, $201 more than the standard-trim model.

---

Two Corvette show cars—the GT 2-Rotor and the Aero-Vette 4-Rotor—carry experimental Wankel rotary engines

GM tests an on-board diagnostic system—an item that will become common later

Ford signs an agreement to develop a Stirling external-combustion engine; it goes nowhere

GM announces a plan to install Wankel rotary engines in the Chevrolet Vega for 1975, but it never materializes

▲ The mid-size Olds Cutlass was quickly becoming America's most popular car line in 1972. This Supreme Holiday hardtop was its top-seller.

▲ After two years, the Hurst/Olds returned for '72 with a still-potent 455 V-8 at 300 net bhp. Just 499 hardtops and 130 ragtops were built.

▲ The biggest engine for Plymouth's '72 Road Runner was a 255-horse 400, though a 280-bhp 440 was offered with the "GTX" option. Sales fell to 7628.

► Trendy "strobe stripes" remained a '72 Road Runner option. They could adorn the hood or roof pillars—but not both. Road Runners still came with heavy-duty suspension and brakes. But base power was a 240-horse (net) 340, a far cry from the old 383, let alone the now-departed Hemi. But at least the trademark "Beep-Beep!" horn was still included in the $3095 base sticker price.

▲ Plymouth's Barracuda fell on hard times for '72; down to base and 'Cuda hardtops, with the latter's 340 small-block option the hottest available. Sales fell hard, too; down to 18,450, including just 7828 'Cudas. Optional stripes and a "scooped" hood dressed up base models like this one, but real muscle cars didn't wear whitewalls.

▲ Pontiac first offered its own version of Chevy's popular Nova compact as the '71 Ventura II, which continued for '72 with just a few changes. One of them was a rare optional sliding fabric sunroof as worn by this $2426 two-door, which also sports extra-cost Rally wheels and uprated tires. A $2454 four-door sedan was also available.

▲ "Grand" aptly described Pontiac's little-changed big Grand Ville models for '72. This hardtop sedan, for example, weighed well over two tons and, as a range-topper, sold for a hefty $4507. Engines were again low-tune, understressed 455-cid V-8s.

▲ The 455 HO Trans Am remained Pontiac's performance Firebird for '72—with a new four-speed manual as standard. Power fell from 335 gross to 300 net, but the car was timed at just 5.4 seconds 0-60 mph. Only 1286 T/As were built this year.

▲ Like the Olds 4-4-2, Pontiac's GTO reverted to option status for '72. A 300-horse (net) 455 was the best power listed; a base 400 and regular 455 both made 250 bhp. Only hardtop coupes were built, and only 5807 at that. Note the body-color Endura nose.

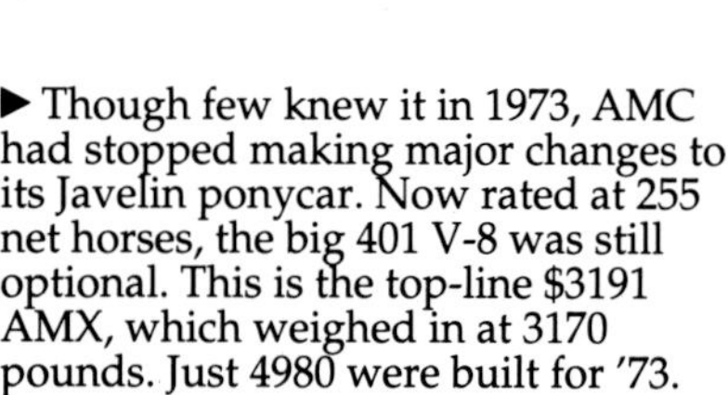

▲ American Motors stylists under Dick Teague designed this sporty hatchback coupe to expand the Hornet compact line for 1973. Priced at $2449 with the 232-cid six (304 V-8 available), it could be dressed up with tape stripes, sport wheels, and fat tires, as shown here.

▶ Though few knew it in 1973, AMC had stopped making major changes to its Javelin ponycar. Now rated at 255 net horses, the big 401 V-8 was still optional. This is the top-line $3191 AMX, which weighed in at 3170 pounds. Just 4980 were built for '73.

▲ Pillared "Colonnade" rooflines marked an all-new fleet of 1973 GM intermediates. Among them were curvy Buicks, which revived the Century name. This coupe has the $175 Gran Sport appearance/handling package; an additional $235 bought the big 455 V-8.

▲ Buick's personal-luxury Riviera again flaunted a "boat-tail," slightly blunted for 1973—a response to the controversial '71 design. The front end was also blunted to accommodate newly required five-mph "crash" bumpers. Sales held steady at 34,080 for these big $5221 coupes.

---

**1973**

The OPEC (Organization of Petroleum Exporting Countries) oil embargo on October 19 leads to severe fuel shortages, long lines, large price hikes, even the threat of rationing; it will be lifted on March 18, 1974

Chevrolet builds 2,579,509 cars for the model year, compared to Ford's 2,349,815; Oldsmobile retains third spot, followed by Pontiac, then Plymouth

The average new car sells for $3930, while the average full-time worker takes home $9298 yearly

Horsepower, torque, and compression ratios continue their downward trend

Exhaust gas recirculation (EGR) valves are installed in this year's engines to cut down on emissions of nitrogen oxide

▲ Cadillac met 1973 crash rules with bigger bumpers and a "push-back" grille that retreated a few inches to resist damage. Here, the $7765 Fleetwood Sixty Special Brougham, still the premium standard Caddy. It retained a 220-horse 472 V-8. Sales were a healthy 24,800 units.

▲ Chevrolet's Monte Carlo kept its 116-inch wheelbase for 1973, but sported GM's new Colonnade pillared coupe design—and rather florid curves. Trim levels swelled to base, S, and this $3806 vinyl-roofed Landau, all with a base 175-bhp, 350 V-8. Total sales soared to 290,723.

▲ A sportier roofline and blockier lower body marked the revamped '73 Chevelles, which included this new $3179 Laguna coupe, plus a wagon and sedan, all with tidy body-color bumper/grille treatment. Chevy built 390,000 Chevelles for the year.

▲ Chevy's Corvette sported a revised profile for 1973, thanks to a restyled body-color front end that looked elegant, yet met the Feds' new five-mph bumper rule. This coupe listed at $5635, the ragtop for $236 less. Corvette sales started upward again, hitting 30,465, four-fifths of them coupes.

▲ Chevy's '68-vintage Nova compacts got their first major facelift for '73, most of it involving bigger bumpers dictated by new federal rules. Also new that year was this three-door Hatchback version of the mainstay two-door sedan. Note its half-vinyl roof. Nova prices started at $2377

▲ Like many '73 cars, big Chevys—here the $4082 Caprice hardtop coupe—got new five-mph bumpers in front, leaving rear-end looks little changed. All '73 Caprices added "Classic" to the name; low-suds 454 V-8s were still listed. Some 77,134 of these coupes were produced.

▲ Lincoln perhaps inspired the frontal redo on '73 Chryslers. Round headlamps in square bezels were a period Detroit design fad. The Royal label was gone, so the base model was now simply Newport (there was still a plusher Custom). This $4316 hardtop sedan found 20,175 customers.

All '73 models must have five-mph front "crash" bumpers and 2½-mph rear bumpers; those built after January 1 must incorporate side beams in the doors

Subcompact and compact models enjoy record sales; big cars sink in 1973-74—a result of the oil crisis—but they'll be back

Oldsmobile launches its Nova-based Omega compact, and mid-year brings the related Buick Apollo; combined they sell less than 100,000 units

Hatchback versions of GM's Nova, Ventura, Omega, and Apollo appear

GM's rebodied mid-size lines feature "Colonnade" hardtops with fixed center pillars; safety concerns (threatened roll-over standards) help kill off pillarless hardtop coupes, which will be phased out in bigger cars over the next few years

◄▲ Dodge's once-unique Charger had become just a two-door Coronet with 1971's "fuselage" redesign, then went baroque with 1972's new SE model and its blind-spot-inducing wide rear-quarter roofline. For '73, Dodge cut in little windows to improve SE visibility (*left*). The only pillarless Charger left was the $2810 standard-trim model (*above*).

▲ Because some objected to the Demon name, Dodge's fastback compact coupes were retitled Dart Sport for '73. A $2853 "340" model (*pictured*) with that V-8 remained the sportiest offering; 11,315 were called for.

▲ Square "formal" fronts were the rage in '73, so full-size Dodges were right in style. This $4001 Polara Custom hardtop sedan, which saw 29,341 sales, came with a 150-horse 318 V-8, with options up to a 220-bhp 440.

▲ Dodge anticipated five-mph *rear* bumpers by fitting this chrome-plated protection on its '72 Dart, and carried it over for '73. It's shown on the popular $2617 Swinger hardtop, which sold strongly: 107,619 units.

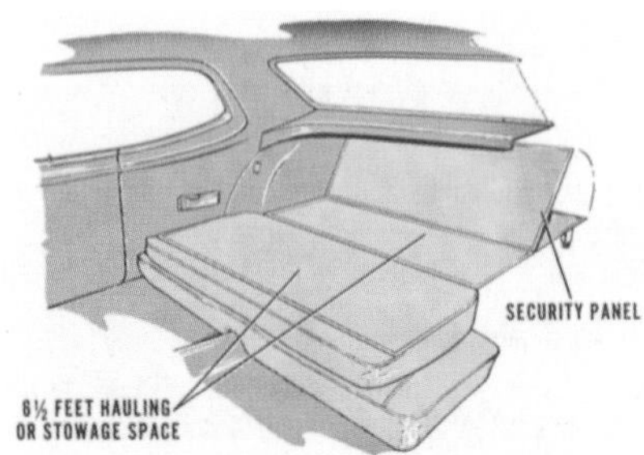


▲ A hand-cranked steel sunroof was a new $435 option for '73 Dart coupes. Of the 68,113 Sport models built, some were ordered with one, plus an optional fold-down rear seat, thus becoming a "Convertriple": a five-seat coupe combining the open air appeal of a ragtop with a wagon's versatility.

▲ Bowing in 1970, the Series II Excalibur was a hand-built "neoclassic" evolved from Brooks Stevens' original Studebaker-based 1965-69 design. Prices were $12,000-$17,000. All had GM chassis and 350 and, later, big-block 454 Corvette V-8s. Just 72 two-seat Roadsters and 270 four-seat Phaetons were built through 1974.

---

Extra-cost front vent windows appear, after fading away in the late Sixties

More than 72 percent of this year's cars are air conditioned

Electronic ignition is standard on all Chrysler engines

Swing-out bucket seats become available in Chevelle/Monte Carlo coupes

Federal law bans odometer "rollback," requiring dealers to disclose mileage before selling a used car

GM releases 1000 Chevrolet Impalas equipped with air bags.

AMC's Gremlin offers a "Levi's" option wherein the interior fabric resembles that of the famed blue jeans, replete with red piping

Hornet adds a handsome fastback/hatchback coupe

▲ Some of '73's least-elegant bumpers appeared on big Fords, here the $4001 LTD hardtop sedan. Curb weights were rising—4148 pounds on this LTD—so base power was now a 351 V-8.

▲ Except for beefier bumpers for '73, Ford's subcompact Pinto looked like it did in 1971. This $2021 two-door sedan came with a 54-bhp four. Total Pinto output: 484,512 units.

▲ Mid-size Fords wore a more formal face for '73. Luxury was emphasized via new Gran Torino Broughams, here a $3071 hardtop coupe. Base and Brougham coupes totaled 138,962.

▲ Mustang saw few changes for '73, but rumors that ragtops would be discontinued caused convertible sales to rebound from 6121 to 11,853. Alas, the rumors were true. Base-priced at $3102, this example carries an optional body-color nose and twin-scoop hood taken from the Mach 1 fastback. Top mill was a 260-bhp 351 V-8.

▲ Ford's 1973 Thunderbird sported the required front crash bumper, plus a new eggcrate grille. The trendy opera windows shown here were a new option, but required the $137 vinyl roof. A 429 V-8 remained standard, a 460 optional. Despite a higher $6437 base price, buyers liked this look and T-Bird sales winged past 87,000.

▼ Lincoln Continental's massive front end accepted 1973 crash bumpers with dignity. Shown here is the Town Car luxury package that added $467 to the $7230 price tag. Four-door production was 45,288.

▶ The '73 Mercury Cougars would be the last with any pretense of sportiness until 1983. The $3679 XR-7 hardtop seen here remained the sales leader at 35,110 units. Ragtops were again rare, with just 3165 XR-7s and 1284 base-trim models built.

## 1973 Model Year Production

| | | |
|---|---|---|
| 1. Chevrolet ........ 2,579,509 | 7. Dodge ........ 665,536 | 12. Lincoln ........ 128,073 |
| 2. Ford ........ 2,349,815 | 8. Mercury ........ 486,470 | 13. Imperial ........ 16,729 |
| 3. Oldsmobile ........ 922,771 | 9. AMC ........ 392,105 | 14. Checker ........ 900[1] |
| 4. Pontiac ........ 919,870 | 10. Cadillac ........ 304,839 | 15. Excalibur ........ 122 |
| 5. Plymouth ........ 882,196 | 11. Chrysler ........ 234,223 | 16. Avanti II ........ 106 |
| 6. Buick ........ 821,165 | | |

[1] *Estimated, excludes taxicabs*

▲ Olds had done good business with gussied-up Royale versions of its entry-level, full-size Delta 88s in 1972. The '73s continued the trend, but this $4442 convertible managed a scant 7088 sales. It weighed a hefty 4298 pounds.

▲ Against all odds, another Hurst/Olds bowed for '73, based on the new Cutlass Supreme coupe. Some 1097 were built, all with a 455 V-8 of about 250 net bhp, Turbo Hydra-Matic, padded top, and swivel front buckets.

▲ A trend toward more balanced, European-style "sport sedans" was evident in new 1973 models like the Pontiac Grand Am. Sales of the $4353 four-door sedan were just 8691, but the $4264 coupe (*right*) did much better: 34,443.

▲ Grand Ams got a squeezeable plastic nose, uprated handling chassis, and sports-luxury interior. With the standard 230-bhp, 400-cid V-8, it was a decent road car. A 455 was available, as was a four-speed stick—a rare option.

▲ Minor trim changes and beefier front bumpers marked 1973 full-size Pontiacs. This Grand Ville convertible, of which 4447 were built, remained the grandest of the lot: $4766 price tag, 4339-pound curb weight, 215-horse 455 V-8.

---

Buick revives the Century badge for its new mid-size models; a Gran Sport option is available for $175, the 455 V-8 for $235

This year marks the final appearance of Chevelle's 454 V-8; the SS option is gone

The SS designation and big-block engines depart from Camaros, but the Type LT (Luxury Touring) coupe remains

Dodge's Dart Demon is renamed Sport; some religious groups had objected to the original name and devil-with-a-pitchfork logo

After a run of 479,775 Pintos in 1972, the Ford subcompact carries on with stronger bumpers, and finds another 484,512 buyers

The '73 Mercury Cougar is the last of its ponycar-based models; the final 4449 convertibles are built

▲ A new $176 Sprint option added a dash of sportiness to Pontiac's '73 Ventura coupe. Strictly for show, it included wider 14×6 wheels and tires. The three-door hatchback listed at $2603. Total Ventura output topped out at 96,500.

▲ Pontiac's '73 Firebirds showed no evidence of crash bumpers, a tribute to the skill of GM designers. This $3276 Formula (10,166 were sold) listed two optional 455 V-8s: a 250-horse HO and 310-horse Ram Air.

▲ Plymouth tried to cash in on growing import demand in 1971 with the British-built Cricket, a small sedan and wagon. Though priced around $2000 with power front disc brakes, shoddy workmanship drove them from U.S. shores after '73.

▲ California's stricter emissions limits began demanding special engines in '73. One was this new Plymouth 360 V-8 with air injection and electronic ignition. It made 175 bhp.

▲ Electric rear-window defrosters with wires embedded into the glass began appearing as an option for several 1973 Detroit cars, even Plymouth's low-priced Duster model. The defroster required a higher-output 60-amp alternator.

▲ Still around and still pretty potent in 1973 was Plymouth's 240-bhp Duster 340 fastback, pictured here with optional tape stripes and wider Rallye wheels. Base price was attractively low at $2822, and 15,731 were built.

▲ Mid-size Plymouths met 1973 bumper rules with a new, more orthodox front end. Road Runner still hung in at $3115, but strictly as a thin-pillar coupe with V-8s of 318, 400, or 440 cid. Amazingly, sales picked up to 19,056.

---

Plymouth's "Space Duster" is similar to Dodge's "Convertriple," which blends a fold-down rear seat with a sliding steel sunroof; various Duster permutations include Gold, Twister, Special Coupe, and 340

The new Le Mans-based Pontiac Grand Am mixes Grand Prix luxury with Trans Am performance; Grand Prix is now on the same 116-inch wheelbase as Chevrolet's Monte Carlo

Pontiac's Firebird Trans Am keeps its 455-cid V-8 and flaunts a wild hood-mounted bird decal sometimes called the "Chicken"

GM experiments with a device that requires the driver to pass a sobriety test before the car will start

▲ As if to answer its "What's a Matador" TV spots, AMC unwrapped this swollen coupe to replace pillarless hardtops for '74. Despite a shorter 114-inch wheelbase, it was styled partly for high-speed aerodynamics in stock-car racing, but did little there or for Matador sales. This $3699 coupe is the sporty "X." Top engine: a 255-bhp 401.

▲ AMC's slow-selling Ambassador was down to just this $4559 Brougham sedan and a $4960 wagon for '74, which was to be its last season. Sales that year were disheartening: 24,971.

▲ An amalgam of styling cues, the AMC Javelin was also in its last year for '74, but retained as much ponycar spirit as the feds allowed. Sales: 29,536, 4980 of them hot AMXs.

▲ You could still buy a mid-size Buick Gran Sport option in 1974, but it was just a workaday Century 350 coupe with slightly sportier looks, bigger tires, and firmed-up suspension. Still, the optional 245-bhp 455 gave it some punch. Base price was $3904.

▲ Evolutionary styling changes and new five-mph rear bumpers were Cadillac's '74 news, but ultra-posh "d'Elegance" and "Talisman" options arrived for the Fleetwood Sixty Special Brougham, now priced at $9537. All Caddys (except Eldorado) got a 205-bhp, 472-cid V-8.

**1974**

Early in the year, President Nixon requests voluntary gas station closings to curtail Sunday driving, but as it turns out the OPEC oil embargo will be lifted in March

Traffic fatalities decline, with credit going to the national 55-mph speed limit

Industry output eases to 8.1 million cars for the model year

Dodge introduces rebates on the Monaco; full-size cars are not selling during the oil embargo

Chevrolet builds 2,333,839 cars for the model year, compared to Ford's 2,179,791; Plymouth rises to third on the strength of its compacts, followed by Oldsmobile and Pontiac

All cars now must have energy-absorbing bumpers front and rear

▲ Looking to Bicentennial '76, Chevy offered a "Spirit of America" trim option for several '74s, including the facelifted Vega coupe. Vega output for '74: 456,085.

▲ Some '74 Chevy Nova two-doors, like this Hatchback, also wore Spirit of America dress. A few got a $140 Super Sport package—just for show—and a 185-bhp 350 V-8.

▲ Threatened federal rollover standards began killing off hardtops in 1974, but this $4162 Chevy Impala Sport Coupe—which sold 50,036 copies—was still a true hardtop. A new $4429 pillared Custom Coupe was twice as popular.

▲ Here's Chevy's new-for-'74 full-size pillared coupe in top-line Caprice Classic Custom trim. Replacing the pillarless model, it cost $4483 and 59,484 were built. Only Caprices could get the optional 235-bhp, 454-cid V-8.

▲ Chevy's only big convertible for '74 was once again the top-line Caprice Classic, which rose $400 in price to $4745. Only 4670 were sold, a sign of the more serious mid-Seventies.

◀▲ The 1974 Chevy Corvettes were the last with optional 454 big-block power—down to 270 bhp net—and the first with a restyled body-color rear end that neatly matched the previous year's new nose. Both met federal bumper standards beautifully. Convertible 'Vette sales were falling: just 5474 against 32,028 coupes. Base prices were $5846 for the ragtop, $6082 for the coupe.

---

A federally mandated interlock prevents the engine from being started until the seatbelts are fastened; this system raises a nationwide hue and cry and is soon canceled, replaced by a warning light and buzzer

Emissions controls are more exhaustive than ever; fuel mileage ratings drop

The trim and thrifty Ford Mustang II is the first subcompact specialty car, a kin to Pinto; Mercury's Cougar forsakes sportiness in favor of a luxury image

A new overhead-cam 2.3-liter four in the Mustang II is America's first mass-produced engine built to metric measurements

The Pontiac Firebird and a handful of other models adopt fiberglass-reinforced plastic noses

▲ Bowing just in time for the first energy crisis were new-design '74 Chryslers that were shorter but wider, and much heavier. This $4752 entry-level Newport hardtop coupe appealed to 13,784 customers.

▲ Topping Chrysler's '74 lineup were the New Yorker Brougham sedan, plus a hardtop coupe and hardtop sedan. Prices were $5931-$6063. As elsewhere in Detroit, engines were detuned to run on regular gas (unleaded).

▲ Chrysler marked its Fiftieth Anniversary with this "Crown Coupe" trim option for the Imperial LeBaron hardtop coupe, with opera windows and padded canopy roof. V-8s of 400 and 440 cid were offered.

▲ Full-size '74 Dodges—13 models strong—shared Chrysler's new platform and were all Monacos; Polaras departed. With 10,585 sales, this $4539 Custom hardtop sedan beat all but one of its linemates.

▲ Dodge's mid-size '74 Coronets got a last-minute facelift (as hinted in this retouched factory photo), mainly to meet bumper rules. The $3374 Custom four-door shown was the line's best-seller: 36,021 units.

▲ A revised tail with a five-mph bumper helped add 300 pounds to the '74 Thunderbird, now 4825 pounds. A torquier 220-bhp 460 V-8 replaced the standard 429. Price rose to $7330; output skidded to 58,443.

▲ Coincidentally timed to face the energy crisis, the all-new '74 Mustang II was 14.5-inches shorter and 300 pounds lighter than the old ponycar—and scored a resounding 385,993 sales. This posh $3480 Ghia notchback came with an 88-bhp four, or optional 105-bhp V-6. A 122-bhp V-8 followed in '75.

---

Four-wheel disc brakes are standard on Imperials, which are completely restyled on a shorter 124-inch chassis; output drops to 14,426 units

While four-cylinder engines go into 12.8 percent of cars (up from 8.8 percent in '73), V-8 installations slip from 81 to 68 percent

Chevrolet's Vega plant at Lordstown, Ohio, endures a two-month strike

Buick buys back the old tooling it sold AMC in 1968 so it can again build the 231-cid V-6

The final AMC Ambassadors and Javelins are built; Matador is completely reworked into a new fastback coupe, but sales are disappointing, even for the four-door

Checker builds its last station wagon; Ed Cole retires from the GM presidency, then joins the Checker company

◀ Mustang II also came as this "fasthatch" coupe in standard trim (*shown*), priced at $3328, and in sporty Mach 1 form for $3674. The latter's standard 2.8-liter V-6 was optional for other models in lieu of the 2.3-liter four.

▼ Billed as "America's Consummate Luxury Car," the '74 Lincoln Mark IV gained a five-mph rear bumper and a new $473 Gold Luxury Group trim option, but was otherwise little-changed. Sales came in at 57,316.

▲ Ford began referring to four-door sedans as "pillared hardtops" for 1974, perhaps preparing buyers for the end of pillarless models. The title applied to this $4717 full-size LTD Brougham, which saw 11,371 copies built.

▲ Mercury's '74 mid-size Montegos lost sporty models but gained five-mph rear bumpers and wider tracks (to go with rising weight). Shown here is the $3680 MX Brougham sedan.

◀ This Mercury public-relations photo proclaimed what really was a fat new two-ton cat built strictly for luxury. All Cougars were XR-7 hardtop coupes. Sales totaled 91,670.

Chevy's sporty Laguna Type S-3 coupe, offered in 1974-76 as a replacement for the Chevelle SS, wears a "rubberized" nose

Camaro Z28 is temporarily dropped at the end of the year, replaced by the Rally Sport option

The last big-block and LT-1 engines are installed in the Corvette, which sees production jump 23 percent to 37,502 units

The final 16,437 Dodge Challengers are produced; introduced in the waning days of the ponycar craze, the model never really caught on

Dodge drops the Polara series, consolidating all full-size models under the Monaco badge

A Gran Torino Elite hardtop coupe joins the Ford line at mid-year to battle Chevrolet's high-flying Monte Carlo, and immediately scores 96,604 sales

▲ Montereys still anchored the big-Mercury line for '74, but they were pretty undistinguished, so sales fell way off—this $4523 Custom hardtop coupe got only 4510.

▲ Full-size Mercs were little changed for '74 save bigger back bumpers and more engine retuning. Top of the line was this $5519 Marquis Brougham "pillared hardtop."

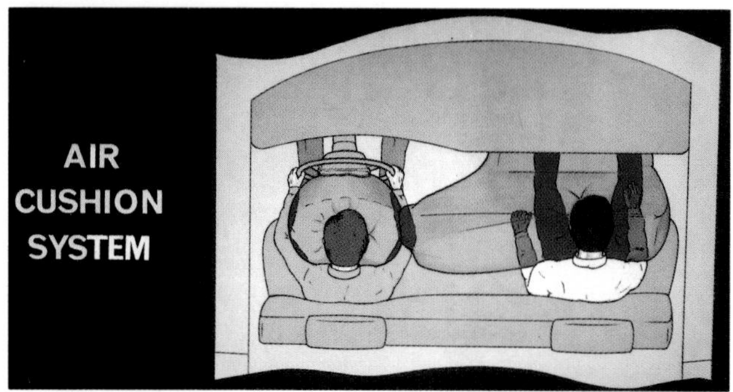


▲ Oldsmobile (and Mercury too) tested public reaction to air bags long before the government mandated passive restraints. This "air cushion system" for driver and front passenger was a '74 option for the 88 Royale, Ninety-Eight, and Toronado. But price was high, orders few.

▲ A Cutlass paced the 1974 Indianapolis 500 and led to another Hurst/Olds coupe, again in trademark white-and-gold and packing a 275-horse 455 V-8. Though just 380 were built—the lowest H/O total yet—many were actually used at the Brickyard for various duties.

◀ Like AMC's Javelin and the Dodge Challenger, the Plymouth Barracuda would vanish after '74, thanks to an all-but-dead ponycar market. The 'Cuda, shown here, still had a twin-scoop hood feeding a 245-horse 360-cid V-8, but found only 4989 buyers at $3252 apiece. The $3067 standard hardtop again came with a mild 318 V-8 but managed just 6745 sales. Holdouts from the muscle-car era were few as fuel prices, insurance costs, and safety concerns conspired against performance.

### 1974 Model Year Production

| | | |
|---|---|---|
| 1. Chevrolet 2,333,839 | 7. Dodge 477,728 | 12. Lincoln 93,983 |
| 2. Ford 2,179,791 | 8. AMC 431,798 | 13. Imperial 14,426 |
| 3. Plymouth 739,894 | 9. Mercury 403,977 | 14. Checker 900[1] |
| 4. Oldsmobile 581,195 | 10. Cadillac 242,330 | 15. Avanti II 123 |
| 5. Pontiac 580,045 | 11. Chrysler 117,373 | 16. Excalibur 118 |
| 6. Buick 495,063 | | |

[1]*Estimated, excludes taxicabs*

▲ Plymouth's '74 Duster fastback (*shown*) and its Valiant two- and four-door sedans were much like the '73s inside and out. Duster sales, 277,409; Valiant, 181,674.

▲ Road Runner remained a part of Plymouth's mid-size Satellite line for '74. Though it was more "show" than "go," the 275-bhp, 440-cid V-8 was still an option. Sales fell to 11,555.

▲ Pontiac's Firebird finally showed the effects of new federal bumper rules in a handsome '74 facelift. Trans Am (*shown*) still topped the line, and more than doubled sales to 10,255.

▲ Like other makes in '74, Pontiac began de-emphasizing hardtops. Still, this new full-size two-door coupe body style had disappearing B-posts via wind-down rear side windows. At $4278, this Catalina version sold 40,654 copies.

▲ Sometimes called the "Notch Back Hardtop," Pontiac's new '74 coupe was also available as a mid-line Bonneville for $4572. Note the fixed "C-posts" and rearmost side glass. Pinstripes here highlight the subtle upper-bodyside curves. Top mill was the 255-bhp 455 V-8.

▲ It says GTO, but this '74 was just Pontiac's compact Ventura two-door with a $195 cosmetic and handling package. A 165-horse 350 V-8 was included along with floorshift and dummy hood scoop. After 7058 of these pretenders, the "Goat" was gone, leaving Trans Am as top gun.

Mustang II comes only as a notchback coupe or fastback hatch with a four-cylinder or V-6 engine; prices start at $3134

Mercury's Cougar XR-7, now riding the mid-size Montego platform, adopts the Thunderbird "personal-luxury" formula; output tops 90,000

The Valiant Duster enjoys another production increase, to 277,409 units; meanwhile, Barracuda output is halted forever after only 11,734 '74s are produced

A hulky new Plymouth Fury debuts at $1.00 per pound: minimum weight, 4125 pounds; minimum price, $4101

The Cycolac-bodied, two-passenger CitiCar—marketed by a Florida firm—becomes one of the best-selling electric vehicles despite a range of only 50 miles per charge; 1801 are built in 1974 and '75

▲ A segmented grille and optional overdrive were new for AMC's 1975 Hornet compact, which remained the company's best-seller. This is the Sportabout wagon; 7239 were sold.

▲ Hornet hatchback coupes featured a big load opening and lots of carrying space. This '75 has the sporty "X" option package. Top engine option was the 150-bhp 304 V-8.

▲ AMC unveiled the egg-like Pacer for '75. The two-door hatch cost $3299 with standard 232 six. It had been designed for a Wankel rotary engine. Sales were 72,158 for the year.

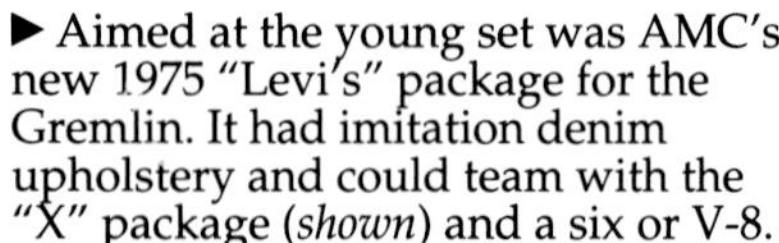

► Aimed at the young set was AMC's new 1975 "Levi's" package for the Gremlin. It had imitation denim upholstery and could team with the "X" package (*shown*) and a six or V-8.

▼ The front-engine, rear-drive Bricklin SV-1 bowed in 1974 with gullwing doors and a price around $9800. Promoter Malcolm Bricklin billed it as a "Safety Vehicle," but most considered it a sports car. Early models used an AMC 360 V-8, later ones a Ford 351. But production, in New Brunswick, Canada, never got going in earnest, and only 2889 were built through 1976.

---

**1975**

Model-year output shrinks to 6.5 million cars

Chevrolet volume skids to 1,755,773 cars, but tops Ford's 1,569,608; Oldsmobile is third, followed by Pontiac and Buick; Plymouth slips to sixth

Massive layoffs and plant closings are the norm early in the year

A bonanza of new (or revived) nameplates emerges: Astre, Bobcat, Charger SE, Cordoba, Elite (without the Gran Torino prefix), Granada, Monarch, Monza, Pacer, Seville, Skyhawk, Starfire

All four major automakers install catalytic converters to reduce emissions—but the Environmental Protection Agency (EPA) quickly charges that the devices may emit harmful sulphates

▲ Convertibles looked to be an endangered species in 1975, when this big and brassy LeSabre Custom became Buick's last factory-built ragtop. Priced at $5133, it garnered 5300 sales, which was actually 1673 more than the '74 model.

▲ Having graduated from option status to become a full-fledged subseries for '74, the Electra Limited was restyled for '75 and continued as Buick's biggest and best full-size car. This pillared two-door listed for $6352, and 17,750 were sold. Its pillarless four-door sister cost $6516.

▲ The Sedan de Ville badge still identified a four-door hardtop in the '75 Cadillac line, but rectangular headlamps and C-pillar windows were new. Base price was $8801. A lesser Calais version went for $8377.

▲ Cadillac's first "small" car was the 1975 Seville, a luxury special version of the GM X-body compact Chevy Nova. It had a 180-bhp, fuel-injected 350-cid V-8. Price was a lofty $12,479, and sales were good: 16,355 units.

► Cadillac's '75 Eldorado retained its basic '71 design, but got a wider grille with rectangular headlamps. As Caddy's only ragtop, this model found 8950 buyers.

Automakers pay sizable rebates ($200-$500) to push car sales—especially subcompacts, which are selling slowly now that the gas is flowing again

The Chrysler Cordoba and Dodge Charger SE are built in Canada; so are the new Chevrolet Monza, Oldsmobile Starfire, and Buick Skyhawk 2+2s

The subcompact Buick Skyhawk and Olds Starfire carry V-6s; Chevrolet's Monza has a Vega four or small V-8

Seville, hyped for its quality and "international" size, is the smallest Cadillac in more than half a century; it's meant to attract Mercedes-Benz buyers

A huge 500-cid V-8 with 190 horsepower is now standard in all Cadillacs except Seville, which employs a 350-cid V-8 with Bendix fuel injection

▲ The '75 would be the last Chevy Corvette convertible for 12 years, though back then some thought it might never return. At $6537, just 4629 were built.

▲ With big-blocks killed off by emissions and economy concerns, Corvette power for '75 was handled by two 350 V-8s. Total sales rose again, this time to 38,465 units.

▲ Chevy offered swivel front seats as a new option for its facelifted '75 Monte Carlo. This Landau model tallied 110,380 sales, compared to the base Monte's 148,529.

▲ Full-size Chevrolets continued moving toward Cadillac style in 1975, as on this $4891 Caprice Classic hardtop sedan. Some 40,482 customers approved.

► After years of resisting a smaller model, Chrysler tried selling a mid-size for '75. It was a cousin to Dodge's redesigned Charger, called Cordoba. "The New Small Chrysler" wasn't all that small, but at $5072 it attracted a sizeable 150,105 sales. Ricardo Montalban earned a spot in TV's Hall of Fame with commercials in which he extolled Cordoba's optional "fine Corinthian leather" and other luxury features. A 318 V-8 was standard, with 360 and 400 engines optional. Buyers were also treated to "formal" styling and "opera windows."

---

AMC's egg-shaped Pacer hatchback enters the market on March 1, and snares 72,158 buyers in the short model year

Chevrolet's limited-edition Cosworth Vega arrives in April, but at $5916 it attracts only 2061 customers

The "precision-size" Granada features a mock-Mercedes look and soon becomes a top Ford seller (302,658 in 1975); Mercury's Monarch is similar

Ford begins production of more economical "MPG" cars with catalysts: Pinto, Mustang, Bobcat

GM's domestic market share tops 53 percent; Ford takes 28, while Chrysler captures only 14 percent

Borg-Warner releases its first U.S.-built five-speed gearbox, while AMC introduces an overdrive transmission imported from England

▲ Dodge changed names like a Russian spy for 1975. What had been Chargers were once again Coronet hardtops. This is the top-trim $4154 Brougham version.

▲ The only real Dodge Charger for 1975 was this formal-looking coupe dubbed SE for "Special Edition." But special it wasn't, being nearly identical to that year's new Chrysler Cordoba. Though the Charger listed for less ($4903), it sold only a fourth as well, attracting 30,812 customers. Was Ricardo the difference?

◀ Tiny Excalibur Motors in Milwaukee unveiled new Series III models in '75. They looked much like the classically styled Series II roadster and phaeton, but boasted shock-absorbing bumpers and a 454 Chevy V-8 mildly tuned for 270 net horses, plus fuller "clamshell"-type fenders and standard leather trim. Still mostly handbuilt, the SIIIs were initially priced at $18,900, but were up to $28,600 by 1979, when production ended at 1141 units. The vast majority were phaetons (*pictured*).

▲ Though conceived to replace the Maverick, Ford's new 1975 Granada emerged as a separate upscale compact with styling cribbed from Mercedes-Benz. This coupe and a four-door sedan sold in base and posh Ghia trim for $3800-$4300. It was a hit—first-year sales topped 302,000.

▲ Expanding Ford's mid-size roster for 1975 was the Gran Torino Elite, a posh "baby T-Bird" and Monte Carlo-fighter, with all the expected styling cues, from "stand-up" grille to opera windows. Though not cheap at $4767, it proved very popular: 123,372 were bought.

The Energy Policy and Conservation Act becomes law—it will set fuel-economy standards starting with the '78 models

Experimental air bags are installed in some 1974-75 Buicks, Cadillacs, and Oldsmobiles—many owners never even know they're in the steering wheel

Ford pleads for an extension of current emissions standards through 1981

AMC's subcompact Pacer is billed as the "first wide small car," but the plan to use a Wankel rotary engine never materializes

The "final" American convertibles are built (except for Cadillac); automakers fear a federal rule on rollover protection (which never arrives)—but slow sales are the major cause for their demise

The sporty Vega-based Chevrolet Monza 2+2 fastback/hatchback arrives

▲ Ford's overweight mid-sizers benefited more than most rivals from 1975's new fuel-saving catalytic converters. This Gran Torino Brougham sedan weighed 4157 pounds!

▲ Thunderbird's base price rose $500 for 1975, to $7701. Color-keyed Silver and Copper Luxury Group trim packages were new, along with optional "anti-skid" rear brakes.

▲ Ford axed full-size hardtops for '75, but pillared two-doors appeared with gimmicky B-post opera windows. This is the $5133 LTD Brougham. A 460 V-8 was the top engine.

▲ Lincoln Continentals took on Cadillac-style "colonnade" rooflines for 1975, when this four-door sedan jumped in price by some $1400, to $9656. But total sales rose, too, by 18,000, to 54,698.

▲ Mercury put a Canadian model name on a clone of Ford's Granada to create the 1975 Monarch, a luxury compact sized and priced above Comet. This uplevel Ghia four-door found 22,723 buyers.

▲ Top dog among 1975 full-size Mercurys was Grand Marquis, formerly a Brougham trim option. Unique vinyl-insert lower-body moldings were featured. This $6469 four-door sedan found 12,307 buyers.

▲ Though muscle cars were allegedly dead, 1975 brought yet another Hurst/Olds, a $1095 conversion of that year's $4035 Cutlass Supreme coupe. V-8s of 350 and 455-cid were offered. Exactly 2535 were produced.

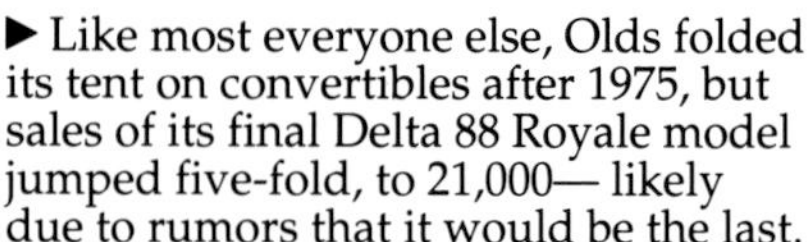

► Like most everyone else, Olds folded its tent on convertibles after 1975, but sales of its final Delta 88 Royale model jumped five-fold, to 21,000— likely due to rumors that it would be the last.

### 1975 Model Year Production

|  |  |  |
|---|---|---|
| 1. | Chevrolet | 1,755,773 |
| 2. | Ford | 1,569,608 |
| 3. | Oldsmobile | 631,795 |
| 4. | Pontiac | 531,922 |
| 5. | Buick | 481,768 |
| 6. | Plymouth | 454,105 |
| 7. | Mercury | 404,650 |
| 8. | Dodge | 377,462 |
| 9. | Cadillac | 264,732 |
| 10. | Chrysler | 251,549 |
| 11. | AMC | 241,501 |
| 12. | Lincoln | 101,843 |
| 13. | Imperial | 8,830 |
| 14. | Checker | 450[1] |
| 15. | Avanti II | 125 |
| 16. | Excalibur | 90 |

[1] *Estimated, excludes taxicabs*

▲ Satellites were renamed Furys for '75, but Plymouth's restyled mid-size line still offered a Road Runner at $3973. It sold only 7183 copies despite available 440 V-8 power.

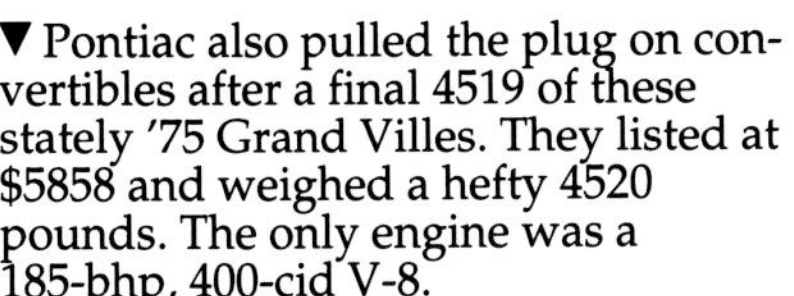

▼ Pontiac also pulled the plug on convertibles after a final 4519 of these stately '75 Grand Villes. They listed at $5858 and weighed a hefty 4520 pounds. The only engine was a 185-bhp, 400-cid V-8.

▲ Bowing in Canada for '73 and in the U.S. for '75, Pontiac's Astre was a Chevy Vega clone, with the troublesome 78/87-bhp aluminum four-banger. Here, the $3610 SJ hatchback.

▲ Astre had the same body styles as Vega, starting with this two-door S sedan at $2841, but didn't sell nearly as well. The debut '75 total was 64,480, versus 206,239 Vegas.

Chrysler's new $5072 Cordoba personal-luxury coupe is an instant hit: 150,105 are produced in its first model year

Dodge's Cordoba clone is the $4903 Charger SE, but only one-fourth as many are sold

Due to popular demand, a 302-cid V-8 becomes available in the Mustang II

Mercury pastes a stand-up grille on the Pinto hatchback and wagon, creating the $3189 Bobcat; 34,234 find buyers

The full-size Plymouth is now called Gran Fury; mid-size models adopt the Fury nameplate

The Series III Excalibur debuts, carrying a big Chevy 454-cid V-8 and $18,900 window sticker; 90 roadsters and phaetons are built this year

▲ Matador became AMC's largest car in 1975 after the Ambassador departed. A dubious '75 facelift carried over to the '76 sedans and wagons, whose sales fell to 41,513. This four-door sedan offered six or V-8 power ($3627/$3731), with a 140/180-bhp 360 V-8 optional.

▲ AMC's Gremlin sported minor styling changes and a new Custom trim level for '76. Base prices ranged from $2889 to $3160. With the public still mileage-minded, sales improved by almost 14,000 units to 59,582. Most had the 232 six; only 826 got the optional 304 V-8.

▲ Pacer, now in its first full year, was AMC's best-selling '76 model: 117,244. Changes were minimal, but a new two-barrel carb for the optional 258 six gave 120 horses to motivate this hefty 3144-pound, $3499 subcompact. The wheels and roof rack seen here were options.

▲ The '76 AMC Hornets (the $3199 six-cylinder hatchback coupe shown) got only trim shuffles and mechanical enhancements, most of the latter aimed at improved drivability of the increasingly emissions-strangled engines. Hornet sales rose by 8000 units to 71,577.

▲ Buick's Riviera, which had lost its '71 "boattail" look in a major '74 restyle, carried on with few changes for '76. Output increased modestly to 20,082. A 205-bhp 455 V-8 powered the $6798 luxury coupe.

▲ Along with the big LeSabre, the mid-size Century line remained a Buick sales mainstay for 1976, when all models shifted to a 110-bhp 231 V-6 as standard; the engine had been introduced the previous year.

▲ Big Buicks would change big-time after '76, when hardtop coupes like this $5144 LeSabre Custom would vanish—odd, as it was the second-most-popular '76 LeSabre. Buick built 45,669 of the coupes.

---

**1976**

Sales leap upward after a pair of bad years: Big and mid-size cars are faring best, but American Motors is sinking

The U.S. industry produces 8,114,376 cars for the model year; domestic sales climb 22 percent

Some 2,103,862 Chevrolets are built, compared to Ford's 1,861,537; Oldsmobile is third

Inflation continues, but no longer in double-digit figures

A sagging small-car market prompts rebates

An average new car sells for $5470, while the average full-time worker earns $11,620 annually

General Motors reports that the average monthly payment on a car loan is now $160

New nameplates include Aspen, Chevette, Sunbird, Volaré

▲ Buick had gotten back to true compacts in 1973 with a Chevy Nova clone, the Apollo. For '76, the name changed to Skylark, but coupes and this $3609 four-door sedan continued.

▲ Cadillac got a publicity windfall with its '76 open Eldorado, the so-called last convertible—though it wasn't. It cost $11,049 and 14,000 were sold, 5050 more than in '75.

▲ True hardtop coupes were a thing of Cadillac's past in 1976, but this $9067 Coupe de Ville outsold every other model in the line: 114,482 units. A 500-cid V-8 gave 190/215 bhp.

▲ Chevy's Cosworth-Vega bowed for '75 with a 111-horse, 2.0-liter, twin-cam four. It was sporty—but pricey at $5916, $6066 for '76. Only 3508 were built for the two model years.

▲ After a major '75 redo, Chevy's compact Nova coasted for '76, although luxury LN models became Concours. This $3830 four-door sedan, six and V-8, attracted 30,511 buyers.

▲ Chevy's new '75 Vega-based Monza fastback got a notchback "Towne Coupe" companion at mid-year. This '76 Towne Coupe—one of 46,735—wears the new Cabriolet option.

▲ Chevy pruned Chevelle Lagunas after 1974 to a single S-3 coupe. It had a unique color-matched "shovel nose," louvered rear side windows, GR78 tires, and appearance options like the lower-body striping and vinyl "Sport Roof" on this '76, which was much like the '75 model. A 175-bhp 400 V-8 was optional, but 9100 sales were disappointing, so the S-3 was canceled after '76.

▲ Washington okayed rectangular headlamps after 1974, and Chevy used them, along with a fine-mesh grille insert, to set Malibu Classic models apart from lesser '76 Chevelles. Malibu Classic was a '74 idea that generated high sales in coupe, sedan, and wagon body styles—over 190,000 for 1976 alone. Most were sold with a V-8, which for '76 meant a new small 140-bhp 305 as base power or optional 350 and 400s as before.

---

Oldsmobile's Cutlass is the top-selling model (and is during much of the '70s), beating out the full-size Chevrolet

Several GM divisions offer a five-speed manual gearbox

Front disc brakes are now standard on U.S. cars, due to federal regulation

One-third of domestic cars have an engine other than a V-8; 10 percent are fours

No-lead gasoline averages 61 cents per gallon

The lease/rental share of the U.S. market is 18 percent—up from just eight percent a decade earlier

A Department of Transportation study finds that 10-year ownership of a standard-size car costs $17,879, or about 17 cents per mile

▲ With the demise of the last Bel Air sedan and wagons, Impala became Chevy's entry-level full-size line for '76. This $4763 Custom coupe appealed to 43,219 buyers.

▲ A maintenance-free battery was one of the detail changes to Chevy's '76 Corvette. No ragtop was offered. Few cared—volume hit a new model-year record at 46,558 units.

▲ Rectangular quad headlamps graced Chevy's '76 Monte Carlo. The 454 died as a Monte option, but the 175-bhp 400 V-8 could replace Chevy's new 305 V-8. Sales this year totaled 353,272.

▲ Looking very similar to the debut '75, the '76 Chrysler Cordoba, now $5392, again had a base 318 V-8, but also a new fuel-saving "lean burn" system for its optional 360 and 400 engines. Production fell to 120,462.

▲ The '76 Cordoba, though handsome for its day, was hardly original. The extra-cost vinyl half-roof and "opera lights" were strictly copycat, as was the lush "boudoir" interior. Wheelbase: 115 inches. Curb weight: 4120 pounds.

▲ Dodge resurrected the Daytona name for this two-tone '76 Charger trim package, and a $3736 base-trim model joined the $4763 SE to cover more market territory. The result: Charger sales more than doubled to 65,900.

▲ Judging from the front lights, Chrysler stylists looked long and hard at the Jaguar XJ6 when styling the Cordoba and its Dodge cousin. Here, the '76 Charger SE, which sold 42,168 units in a recovered big-car market.

---

GM warns that the auto industry may have to cancel 1978 production totally, unless emissions standards are eased

Chrysler announces an agreement to purchase engines and transaxles from Volkswagen for installation in its upcoming front-drive subcompact models

GM claims a fuel economy improvement of 38 percent between 1974 and 1976, but insists that major redesign would be needed to meet the proposed 1985 standard

This is the last year for the 455-cid V-8 from Buick, Oldsmobile, and Pontiac, and for Chevy's 454

The final Cadillac Eldorado convertibles, 14,000 of them, leave the assembly line—they'll be the last factory-built American ragtops until the 1980s revival

In an obvious move to boost economy, Chevy makes the 305-cid V-8 standard in full-size models

▲ Dodge's new Aspen was a slightly bigger and plusher compact than the Dart it was supposed to replace for 1976. Big-car styling cues abounded, as seen on this top-line $4413 SE coupe.

▲ Aspen came as a coupe, sedan, and wagon in base, Custom, and Special Edition trim. A Slant Six was standard, a 318 V-8 optional. Prices were $3400 to $4400. In its first year, Aspen outsold Dart, 219,500 to 68,650.

◀ After reviving a 302 V-8 option for 1975, Ford's Mustang II carried on into 1976 with several new optional features, such as the T-roof seen on this hatchback coupe.

▲ Cast in the image of the great Shelby-Mustangs of the Sixties was a new $325 "Cobra II" option for 1976 Mustang II fastbacks. Included were nostalgic blue/white paint, louvered rear side windows, spoilers, snake insignia, and white-letter tires.

◀ New optional black-and-silver "Stallion" trim added visual spice to Ford's 1976 Pinto hatchback (*bottom*), Mustang II fastback (*center*), and two-door Maverick (*top*). Special snorting-horse decals and sport mirrors were also included. Most Stallions rolled on the styled wheels shown here, a separate extra.

---

The economical subcompact Chevette debuts; derived from the Opel Kadett "T-car" program, it's GM's first "world car"

Chrysler's new compacts, the Dodge Aspen and Plymouth Volaré, sell well, but unfortunately will soon become the most-recalled cars to date

Stallion trim is offered for the basically unchanged Ford Pintos, Mavericks, and Mustang IIs—an anemic stab at the youth market

"Designer Series" packages debut on Lincolns—they're by Bill Blass, Givenchy, Pucci, Cartier

Pinto introduces the Cruising Wagon, a tricked-up wagon sporting blanked-in rear side windows with portholes and multi-hued striping; Mustang II adds a boy-racer "Cobra II" trim package

► Ford designated its Gran Torino-based Elite luxury hardtop coupe a separate series for '76. It changed little, though its price rose to $4879. A standard 154-bhp 351 V-8 and 180-bhp 400 and 202-bhp 460 options returned. The two larger engines were really needed to move the 4169-pound coupe with any verve. Sales moved up to 146,475, yet Elite would die after this year. This example has the $550 power moonroof and $226 turbine-spoke aluminum wheel options.

▲ Lincoln's Continental Mark IV took its final bow for '76 with new "designer" trim/color options: Bill Blass, Pucci, Givenchy, and Cartier. Price was up to $11,060, sales to 56,110. A 202-bhp 460 V-8 provided power.

▲ Mercury entered the growing market for small sporty coupes by importing Ford of Europe's Capri in 1970. At mid-'75, this updated Capri II appeared with a rear hatch and more trim options. This is the posh Ghia model.

▲ Like sister GM divisions, Oldsmobile held on to pillarless four-doors through '76, then dropped them. The '76 Delta 88s sported a new face with rectangular quad headlamps. This $4918 standard-trim hardtop sedan sold 17,115 copies.

▲ At $5869, the Olds Ninety-Eight Regency hardtop sedan remained Oldsmobile's full-size flagship for '76. All Ninety-Eights wore their own new version of the division's hallmark split grille, again with rectangular headlamps. A 455 V-8 was standard.

▲ Bowing at mid-'75, the Oldsmobile Starfire was a clone of Chevy's Monza fastback, but it ran with a Buick V-6 and had no V-8. A new $391 GT option featuring tape stripes and handling upgrades was added for 1976. Total output dipped to 29,159.

### 1976 Model Year Production

|  |  |  |
|---|---|---|
| 1. | Chevrolet | 2,103,862 |
| 2. | Ford | 1,861,537 |
| 3. | Oldsmobile | 891,368 |
| 4. | Pontiac | 746,430 |
| 5. | Buick | 737,466 |
| 6. | Plymouth | 519,962 |
| 7. | Mercury | 480,361 |
| 8. | Dodge | 430,641 |
| 9. | Cadillac | 309,139 |
| 10. | AMC | 283,577 |
| 11. | Chrysler | 222,153 |
| 12. | Lincoln | 124,756 |
| 13. | Excalibur | 184 |
| 14. | Avanti II | 156 |

▲ Predictably, Plymouth got a version of Dodge's new 1976 Aspen compact, which it sold with minor styling differences as the Volaré. However, there was also a sporty trim package called Road Runner, ousting the familiar mid-size car. Here, a trio of top-tim SE models. A total of about 298,000 '76 Volarés were built.

▲ Also adopting rectangular headlamps was the '76 Pontiac Grand Prix, which inexplicably almost tripled sales to 228,091. Included were 4807 of these "Golden Anniversary" models marking Pontiac's fiftieth birthday.

▲ One of Detroit's few genuine performance cars in 1976, Pontiac's Firebird Trans Am was up to $4987 without extras but enjoyed a sales surge to 46,701. This one wears the "screaming chicken" hood decal, a popular T/A option. A 200-bhp 455 V-8 was the top mill.

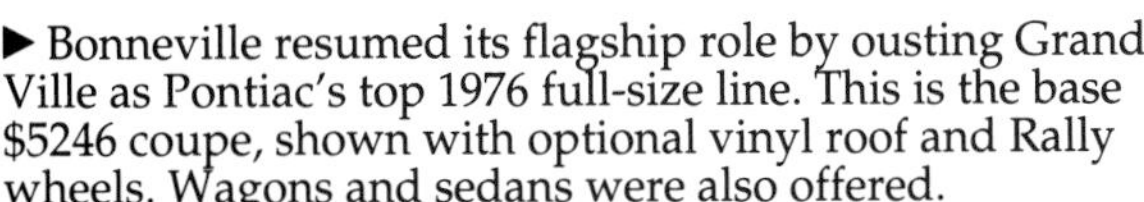

▶ Bonneville resumed its flagship role by ousting Grand Ville as Pontiac's top 1976 full-size line. This is the base $5246 coupe, shown with optional vinyl roof and Rally wheels. Wagons and sedans were also offered.

---

An economy-tuned "Feather Duster" is Plymouth's reply to Ford's MPG models—187 pounds are saved with special aluminum components

Pontiac's Sunbird is a clone of the Chevy Monza, but comes only as a notchback coupe for '76; a "Sport Hatch Back" coupe won't be added until 1977½

Eltra Corp. gets a grant for advanced study of batteries; some optimistically predict that five percent of cars could be electric-powered by the late 1980s

Ford workers strike in September, halting production for 28 days

▲ AMC Gremlins for 1977 got an eggcrate grille and their first four-cylinder base engine: an Audi-designed, 80-bhp 2.0-liter built in Indiana. It was ordered in 20 percent of Gremlins. Prices began at $3248.

▲ AMC's not-so-subcompact Pacer broadened its appeal for '77 with three-door wagon models. This upper-level D/L wears optional woody-look trim. But the bloom had worn off, and Pacer sales plunged by half, to 58,264.

▲ The little-changed '77 Hornet reflected AMC's tightening cash-flow, though the "AMX" tag was dredged up and applied to a sporty-trim hatchback coupe. Notchback two-doors like this one started at $3399.

◀ GM rocked the industry for 1977 with smaller, lighter full-size cars that were no less roomy inside than the outsize gas-guzzlers of 1971-76. Buick offered the "downsized" coupes and sedans under its LeSabre and Electra banners, with Estate Wagons a separate line as before. Engines shrank to match the cars, with a standard 350 V-8 and a new 403 at extra cost. This four-door Limited was one of four Electras in the $6700-$7200 range. The public responded and big-Buick sales picked up, Electras to 161,627.

▲ Doing fair business for Buick since 1975 was the hatchback Skyhawk coupe, yet another version of Chevy's Monza, but with Buick 231 V-6 power. The '77 wore a new cross-hatch front in a quest for greater Buick identity, but sales kept dropping—to just 12,345.

▲ Buick brought back its Regal with a new grille for 1977. The four-door sedan, which came standard with a V-8, was again outsold ten-to-one by the coupe, which had the 231 V-6 standard and the 350 V-8 as an option. Overall Regal sales jumped by 51,000, to a healthy 192,506 for '77.

**1977**

Model-year output tops 9.1 million cars

Imported-car sales hit the two-million mark for the first time

Chevrolet builds 2,543,153 cars for the model year, easily topping Ford's 1,840,427; Oldsmobile again is third, then Pontiac, Buick, and Plymouth

American workers' real earnings start to decline after 1976, following a long, nearly constant rise

GM's first downsizing wave hits the full-size cars, which lose up to 900 pounds and a foot of length—but are just as spacious as before

Ford and Chrysler, meanwhile, are forced to cling to their large cars for the time being

▲ Billed as "The Next Generation of the Luxury Car," the 1977 C-body Cadillacs shared a new downsized platform with Buick Electras and Olds Ninety-Eights. The $10,020 de Ville sedan (*shown*) and $9810 coupe were now the least costly models, and together enjoyed a sales surge to 234,171 units.

▲ Clinging to its huge '71 design, Cadillac's '76 Eldorado coupe strutted a new "Custom Biarritz" option with padded vinyl half-roof, "frenched" rear-quarter windows, "coach lamps," and other gee-gaws. A 425-cid V-8 replaced the 500-cid unit.

▲ Full-size '77 Chevrolets looked clean and trim on their newly downsized 116-inch B-body platform. Models were pared to Impala and Caprice Classic coupes, sedans, and wagons. This Caprice Classic four-door cost $5237 with the 250-cid six, $5357 with the 305-cid V-8.

▲ As usual, Chevy Impalas like this one were cheaper and simpler than Caprices, but coupes of both series for 1977 gained an exclusive wrapped rear window made by the new "bent hot wire" method. Prices started at $4876; total coupe production hit 130,365 units.

▲ After a two-and-a-half-year furlough, Chevy recalled the Camaro Z28 as a mid-1977 option package that now emphasized handling over brute acceleration. A 170-horse 350 V-8 and colorful graphics were included in the $5170 base price. Sales were strong: 14,349.

▲ Chevy's 1977 Corvette sported black A-posts, front sidelights, and column-mounted dimmer and wiper controls among several minor changes. Price rose $1050 to $8648, but sales set a record for the second straight year: 49,213 units. Top mill was again a 210-bhp 350.

---

A smaller Ford Thunderbird shares its platform with the mid-size LTD II; it's lighter, thriftier, cheaper, and a better seller than ever (318,140 units)

The Ford Elite is gone, effectively replaced by the new T-Bird

President Carter appoints Joan Claybrook—colleague of Ralph Nader—as head of the National Highway Traffic Safety Administration

Chevrolet adds the compact Concours as an upmarket Nova; prices start at $3991

Chrysler issues the "mid-size" LeBaron and Dodge Diplomat, which are based on the "compact" Aspen/Volaré

Lincoln launches the $11,500 Versailles, but to many eyes it's a thinly disguised, well-trimmed $5000 Ford Granada/Mercury Monarch sedan

▲ Mid-size Chevys lost their 400-cid V-8 option for '77; a 170-bhp 350 was now the top choice. This was the last of the '73 "Colonnade" generation. This Malibu Classic Landau coupe with standard half-vinyl top started at $4353 with a 110-bhp six, $4473 with a 145-bhp 305.

▲ Chevy's Monte Carlo was also in its last year as a Colonnade model for '77. Little was changed from '76, save trim and minor standard feature and option adjustments. The Landau model (*shown*) was up to $5298, the lesser S model to $4968, but total sales spurted to 411,038.

▲ Chrysler's $5368 Cordoba received subtle design changes for '77, when a manual sunroof and glass T-tops appeared as options. This example wears the standard half-vinyl top with slim new "coach lights" ahead of the rear opera windows. Demand rose again, by about 55,000, hitting 183,146 units.

▲ T-tops were also newly optional for Dodge's '77 Charger. The SE was again the only model, but the Daytona trim option returned. At $5098 base, Charger sales slid to 42,542. Hottest engine: the 170-bhp 360 V-8.

▲ Dodge's mid-size line dropped the Coronet name for 1977 to become the "downsized" Monaco, while the former full-size Monaco was now "Royal Monaco." This top-line Brougham four-door sedan sold for $4217, and 17,224 found buyers.

▲ Dodge Aspen's optional 360-cid V-8 switched to fuel-saving lean-burn technology for '77, ending up with 155 horses. Coupes could again get an R/T option, as shown here, but it was mainly cosmetic. Surprisingly, wagons were the top sellers.

▲ Dodge tried to recapture some of the aura of the muscle-car age with a new "Super Pak" option for '77 Aspens with the R/T package. Included were a rear spoiler, louvered side windows, heavy-duty suspension, and a performance axle ratio.

---

The U.S. Department of Transportation orders air bag installation for new cars, to be phased in starting with the 1982 model year

This year's new cars average 18.6 miles per gallon—34 percent better than in 1974

AMC adds a Pacer station wagon, but total output nosedives from 117,244 in 1976 to 58,264

Gremlin gets an 80-bhp, four-cylinder Volkswagen engine option and a restyled front and rear end

A new 403-cid V-8 rated at 185 bhp is optional in big Buicks

A more efficient 425-cid V-8 (180 or 195 bhp) goes into Cadillacs; sales rise again, to 358,488 units

▲ A hidden-headlamp front marked Ford's full-size '77 Landau, which had bowed for 1976 as a super-luxury version of the LTD. At $5717, this coupe commanded a $614 premium over the base LTD—still, 65,030 were sold.

▲ Ford hoped to cash in on big LTD popularity by restyling its mid-size Torino to become the "new" 1977 LTD II. It worked. Sales rose by 40,000, to 233,324. Four-door sedans, wagons, and this two-door coupe were offered.

▲ In another '77 "name game," Ford's Thunderbird was downsized by becoming what was really a plusher LTD II coupe. Prices started at $5063 (down $2727!) and ran to $7990 for this new Town Landau coupe. Sales rocketed to 318,140.

▲ For 1977, Ford Mustang II's Cobra II option offered new red/white and black/gold color schemes as well as blue/white. A $607 Sports Performance Package included a 139-bhp 302 V-8, four-speed, and heavy-duty chassis. The lacy-spoke wheels seen here were a separate option.

▲ Ford cruised the youth market for '77 with a new Cruising option for the Pinto wagon, which had bowed for '73. Colorful graphics and porthole windows in blanked-out side panels were included for $415. Base wagon price, $3548; Squire, $3891. Total wagon sales: 79,441.

---

After peaking at 456,085 units for '74, Vega's poor reputation catches up, cutting demand to 78,402 for '77; Chevy pulls the plug, but will offer the closely related Monza through 1980

The revived mid-year Camaro Z28 is welcomed, but it's less potent than early '70s predecessors; even so, 14,349 are sold

Dodge renames its mid-size models Monaco; prior Monaco full-size models are now Royal Monacos

Ford trots out the "new" mid-size LTD II, but it's really only a facelifted Torino—and never catches on in the marketplace

Lincoln debuts the Continental Mark V, which weighs 400 pounds less than the Mark IV; output jumps from 56,110 to 80,321 units

▲ Lincoln's new 1977 Versailles was a hasty Ford Granada-derived reply to Cadillac's popular 1975-76 Seville "compact" sedan. Dressed to the nines, the four-door sold only 15,434 copies at $11,500 each.

▲ Like Ford with its LTD II, Mercury switched all mid-sizers to a more popular name for '77: Cougar. But the ploy was less successful—though total line sales were a strong 194,823, the top-line XR-7 two-door hardtop alone accounted for 124,799. This $5230 Brougham four-door saw only 16,946 copies built.

▲ Like sister GM divisions, Olds downsized its 1977 big cars on a new B-body platform, and scored slightly improved sales. Among the Delta 88s, this $5433 Royale Town Sedan sold best: 117,571 units.

▲ Looking as much the dinosaur as its Cadillac Eldorado cousin, the front-wheel-drive Olds Toronado scored higher 1977 sales of 34,085, with the vast majority accounted for by this $8134 Brougham coupe.

▲ An electric "Astroroof" and radical hot-wire-bent wrapped backlight distinguished the new '77 Toronado XS. It also wore special striping. But at a lofty $11,132, it impressed just 2714 buyers.

▲ Oldsmobile's mid-size Cutlass had become one of America's best-selling lines by 1977, the last year for '73-vintage Colonnade styling. By itself, this handsome $4670 Supreme coupe garnered 242,874 sales, the posher $4949 Supreme Brougham another 124,712. A 110-bhp 260 V-8 was standard, with a 170-bhp 350 and 185-bhp 403 optional.

▲ Ordering a 1977 Volaré coupe and combining the Road Runner option with the new "Super Pak" option got you what Plymouth called a "Front Runner." A Dodge Aspen could be similarly equipped. The top power option was a 175-horse 360 V-8, which made this 3500-pound car sprightly, though not muscular.

## 1977 Model Year Production

| | | |
|---|---|---|
| 1. Chevrolet ......2,543,153 | 6. Plymouth ......546,132 | 11. Lincoln ......191,355 |
| 2. Ford ......1,840,427 | 7. Dodge ......526,254 | 12. AMC ......182,005 |
| 3. Oldsmobile ......1,135,803 | 8. Mercury ......521,909 | 13. Excalibur ......237 |
| 4. Pontiac ......850,620 | 9. Chrysler ......399,297 | 14. Avanti II ......146 |
| 5. Buick ......845,234 | 10. Cadillac ......358,488 | |

▲ After a confusing series of name changes, mid-size Pontiacs by 1977 had settled into standard Le Mans and Grand Le Mans models. Grands wore rear fender skirts, as on this $4614 coupe. During this era, Le Mans was consistently outsold by its divisional GM siblings.

▲ Faintly recalling GTO days was Pontiac's new '77 GT option for Le Mans Sport Coupes, which added $463 to a $4507 base price. It included special paint, "radial-tuned suspension," Rally wheels, and full gauges. A 180-bhp, 400-cid V-8 was offered. Few such cars were sold.

▲ Esprit had been the "luxury" Firebird since 1970, and remained so for '77, when Pontiac's ponycars took on a handsome new "droop-snoot" nose. Both the $4551 Esprit (*shown*) and the $4270 base Firebird got a new standard engine, too: a 231-cid Buick V-6 rated at 105 bhp.

▲ Here's another '77 Firebird Esprit, but in somewhat sportier dress, with optional Rally wheels and white-letter tires. The high-performance Trans Am with its 400-cid V-8 continued to lead line sales at 68,745, a new high. Overall Firebird sales also hit a record: 155,736.

▲ Full-size '77 Pontiacs shared a trim new body with big Chevys, yet kept a distinct design identity. They were 600-800 pounds lighter than '76 models. This $5992 Bonneville Brougham was the ritziest Pontiac sedan.

▲ Pontiac's '77 Astre subcompacts moved away from the Chevy Vega's troublesome aluminum four with the new 87-bhp, 2.5-liter "Iron Duke" four. But the damage was done—only 32,788 Astres were sold. Here, the $3741 Safari wagon.

---

Versailles is Lincoln's reply to Cadillac's Seville—just 15,434 are sold

The Cougar badge replaces Montego for all Mercury mid-sizers, including sedans and wagons

Oldsmobile's 455-cid V-8 is gone, replaced by a 185/200-bhp 403

At mid-season, Pontiac wheels out the compact Phoenix, a restyled version of the Ventura that has been around since 1971; prices start at $4075

Pontiac's new "Iron Duke" four-cylinder engine goes into the Astre, Sunbird, Phoenix, Ventura—and other GM models

Appearing at mid-year is the limited-production Pontiac Cam Am: a Cameo White Le Mans Sport Coupe with T/A 6.6 (403-cid) V-8, Rally handling package, special trim, and all the bells and whistles

▲ American Motors' aging Gremlin was little-changed for 1978—except in sales, which plunged 50 percent to 22,104 under increased competition. Sticker prices started at $3539.

▲ With a formal-look facelift, AMC turned its compact Hornet into 1978's Concord line. This D/L four-door was one of 115,513 sold, up 33 percent from '77 Hornet sales.

▲ With overall sales dwindling, AMC decided to drop its Matador line after 1978—a good thing, as the line's sales fell 66 percent to 10,576. Here, the Brougham four-door sedan.

◀ AMC offered a swank new Barcelona luxury option for '77 Matador coupes, and repeated it for '78 as Barcelona II. Though exact production is unknown, it was certainly under 1000 units. For Matador's last season, power steering and front-disc brakes, both formerly extra-cost items, were made standard. Base prices ranged from $4799 to $5299.

▲ A formal "Landau" roof and five-spoke road wheels dressed up this '78 Buick Skylark Custom coupe, which stickered at $4367. The 105-bhp 231 V-6 remained the standard engine.

◀ Jazzy two-toning and big hawk decals announced the sportiest Buick Century for 1978, the hot fastback Turbo Coupe with a turbocharged, 165-horse 231 V-6. Handling suspension and upgraded rolling stock were also included in the $5051 base price.

▲ General Motors downsized its intermediates for 1978, but Buick kept a semblance of big-car power with a new 165-bhp turbocharged 231 V-6 option for its Century and Regal. This $5958 turbo Sport Coupe was one of three notchback Regal models.

**1978**

Industry output eases to just below nine million cars

Domestic car sales defy pessimistic predictions: The year ranks as the third-best ever

The Chevrolet Impala/Caprice is the year's top seller: 612,397 units, proof positive that Americans still want big cars

After the debut of a four-door hatchback model, Chevette becomes the best-selling U.S. subcompact: 298,973 units, more than half of them four-doors

Chevrolet builds 2,375,436 cars for the model year, ahead of Ford's 1,923,655; Oldsmobile's 1,015,805 units places it in third again, and over one million for the second straight year

Subcompacts account for 10.6 percent of domestic sales; compacts, nearly 28 percent

▲ After being downsized to share 1977's new Electra platform, Buick's personal-luxury Riviera saw little change for '78, but sales declined from 26,138 to 20,535. A base-price increase of $1839, to $9224, didn't help matters.

▲ Buick's full-size Estate Wagons lost their eight-passenger model for '78, leaving this six-seater at $6934. Sales stayed about the same at 25,000-plus. The standard 350 V-8 dropped 15 horses, now making 155.

▲ Standard Cadillacs saw little change after 1977's overhaul. This Fleetwood Brougham sedan (with the d'Elegance package) still headed the line at $12,223. Total Caddy sales jumped 67,000, to 349,684 units.

▲ A big hit since its mid-'75 debut, Cadillac's compact '78 Seville offered a new 120-bhp, 350-cid diesel V-8 for the economy-minded luxury-car buyer. Also new was the ritzy "Elegante" trim package, shown here.

▲ Though still wearing its familiar florid curves, Chevy's Monte Carlo was all-new for 1978. Downsized to GM's new A-body, it lost eight inches in wheelbase, to 108.1, and 700 pounds. Despite a wider $4785-$5828 price span, sales fell about 53,000 units, to 358,191.

▲ Chevelle was gone entirely from Chevrolet's all-new line of '78 Malibus, which, like that year's Monte Carlo, were built on GM's new A-body platform. The top-line coupe was this Classic Landau, which cost $4684 with a 95-bhp, 3.3-liter V-6, Malibu's new base engine.

---

Chrysler launches the first domestically built front-drive subcompacts, the Dodge Omni and Plymouth Horizon; early models come with an enlarged Volkswagen engine

GM's mid-size cars are downsized, but the new "Aeroback" (fastback) models fail to sell as expected

The compact Ford Fairmont and Mercury Zephyr debut; their "Fox" platform will serve as the basis for many future Fords

Models dropped for 1978 include AMC's Hornet, Ford Maverick and Mercury Comet, Chevrolet Vega and Pontiac Astre, Dodge Royal Monaco, Plymouth Gran Fury

It is the final season for the AMC Gremlin and Matador, Dodge Monaco, Plymouth Fury

Lee Iacocca is fired from the Ford presidency by chairman Henry Ford II, then hired to head Chrysler Corp., as that company races toward bankruptcy

▲ With Monza sales starting to flag, Chevy grafted the 2+2's nose onto the Towne Coupe to create this new 1978 Sports notchback. It was priced at $4100; sports production was 6823.

◀ Having evolved from 1964 as a Chevelle offshoot, Chevy's El Camino car/pickup was downsized for '78 on that year's new Malibu design. Priced at $4843, some 54,236 were sold.

▲ Corvette turned 25 in 1978 and celebrated by pacing that year's Indy 500. Chevy built 6502 Pace Car Replicas like this, base priced at $13,653.

▲ A new face, optional T-tops, and a revived Rally Sport (*shown*) put new life into Chevy's Camaro for 1978. The $4784 RS had a newly standard 231-cid V-6; 11,902 were built.

▲ A crisper rear roofline, fine-checked grille, and rectangular quad headlights updated Chrysler Cordoba for '78. A 360 V-8 was again standard, with an "economy" 318 as a credit option. Prices were $5600-$5900.

▲ Topping Chrysler's 1978 lineup was this $7702 New Yorker Brougham coupe and a companion $7831 hardtop sedan. Both still looked much like the '75 Imperials they replaced, but sales fell 41 percent from '77, to 44,559 units.

---

Manufacturers observe President Carter's price guidelines for new cars, hoping to ease inflation

An average new car sells for $6470; the average household has $15,064 in annual income

The Corporate Average Fuel Economy (CAFE) standard takes effect, starting at 18 mpg; it is scheduled to rise to 19 mpg in 1979, 20 mpg in 1980

A gas-guzzler tax is enacted

Because of their propensity to catch fire in rear-end collisions, 1971-76 Ford Pintos are recalled

Firestone recalls 7.5 million 500-series steel-belted radials—the biggest tire recall ever

▲ This aggressive-looking Dodge Aspen was a new '78 idea called "Super Coupe," a built-from-the-options-list street-racer package. It could have a 175-bhp 360 V-8.

► A vital new car for Chrysler Corporation was the front-drive 1978 Dodge Omni and its Plymouth Horizon twin. A small five-door hatch sedan of the Volkswagen Rabbit school, these "L-body" models even used a VW-designed 1.7-liter four-cylinder engine. Priced from $3976, Omni enjoyed fairly strong sales of 81,611. Horizon did even better. The roof rack, whitewalls, and woody-look side trim here were among numerous dress-up options available from day one.

▲ A "Cord-type" slat grille and headlamps with flip-up glass covers marked Dodge's new 1978 Magnum XE coupe, a sportier $5509 version of that year's $5368 Charger. It handily outsold the Charger at 55,341, compared to just 2800.

▲ Magnum XE's modest bodyside bulges recalled the painted-on effect of the earlier Charger Daytona. Bucket seats, automatic transmission, and a mild "lean burn" 318 V-8 were standard. Options included 360 and 400 V-8s, Grand Touring handling/appearance package, and a T-roof. Note slats in rear-quarter glass.

---

Volkswagen of America begins production of its subcompact, front-drive Rabbit in Westmoreland, Pennsylvania, making it the first foreign automaker since the early Thirties to build cars in the U.S.

Cadillac introduces "Tripmaster," a travel computer that registers elapsed time, fuel mileage, etc.

*Automotive News* magazine estimates that federal requirements have added $519.65 to the price of a car between 1968 and '78

The last AMC Matadors go on sale; only 10,576 are produced

AMC's Hornet is facelifted, becoming the Concord in the process; output increases 64 percent to 117,513 units

▲ Thunderbird sales climbed 11 percent for '78, to 352,751. This $8420 Town Landau took a back seat to a $10,105 Diamond Jubilee model marking Ford Motor Company's 75th Anniversary. V-8s of 302-, 351-, and 400-cid were on tap.

▲ Replacing Maverick, the new 1978 Fairmont was the first in what would be a long line of Fords based on its sensible, compact rear-drive "Fox" platform. Sedans, a coupe, and this five-door wagon were offered from $3624. Sales were great: nearly 461,000.

▲ Sending Ford's Mustang II out with a bang was 1978's jazzy new "King Cobra," a $1250 hatchback option with spoilers, wheel "spats," and a big snake hood decal, plus 302 V-8, four-speed, and uprated chassis. The T-top roof pictured here was a separate extra.

▲ Ford's Granada got square headlamps for '78, and a sporty but subdued new ESS (European Sport Sedan) trim option, as shown on this four-door. Total Granada sales remained strong at 249,876 units.

▲ Color-keyed trim again marked Granada's lush "Ghia" models for '78. Coupes got a vertical divider on their "opera windows" to make what Ford called "Twindows." A 97-bhp 250 inline six was standard.

▲ Exposed rear wheels and a new dash spruced up 1978 Lincoln Continentals. Sales were a bit off from '77, but still healthy at more than 88,000. The sedan (*shown*) continued outselling the coupe, three-to-one.

### 1978 Model Year Production

|  |  |  |
|---|---|---|
| 1. | Chevrolet | 2,375,436 |
| 2. | Ford | 1,923,655 |
| 3. | Oldsmobile | 1,015,805 |
| 4. | Pontiac | 900,380 |
| 5. | Buick | 803,187 |
| 6. | Mercury | 635,051 |
| 7. | Plymouth | 501,129 |
| 8. | Dodge | 467,720 |
| 9. | Chrysler | 354,029 |
| 10. | Cadillac | 349,684 |
| 11. | Lincoln | 169,620 |
| 12. | AMC | 137,860 |
| 13. | Excalibur | 263 |
| 14. | Avanti II | 165 |

▲ Besides numerous technical updates, Lincoln's 1978 Mark V honored Ford's 75th birthday with this loaded $19,000 Diamond Jubilee special; 5159 were built.

▲ Lincoln's Versailles was little-changed for '78. Like Cadillac's Seville, its base price was higher than that of larger models: that year a princely $12,529.

▲ Mercury's full-sizers dated to a 1969 design, and this was the last of that generation. The '78s were basically '77 reruns. Here, the $7399 Grand Marquis "pillared hardtop."

▲ Zephyr breezed in to oust Comet as Mercury's 1978 compact. Though a close cousin to Ford's new Fairmont, it scored far-lower, but still healthy, sales of 152,172 units.

▲ Oldsmobile's Starfire chugged into 1978 with the sturdier Pontiac-built "Iron Duke" four-cylinder engine as its new standard power. This is the $4095 base model.

▲ The '78 Olds Toronado would be the last of the oversize, overweight '71 design. Change was needed—sales were a tepid 24,715 units.

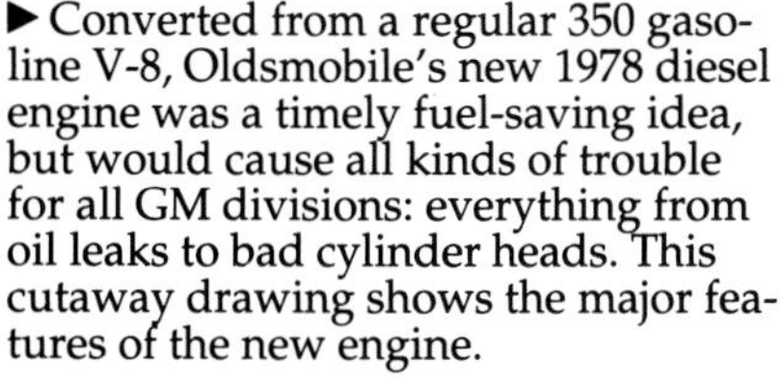

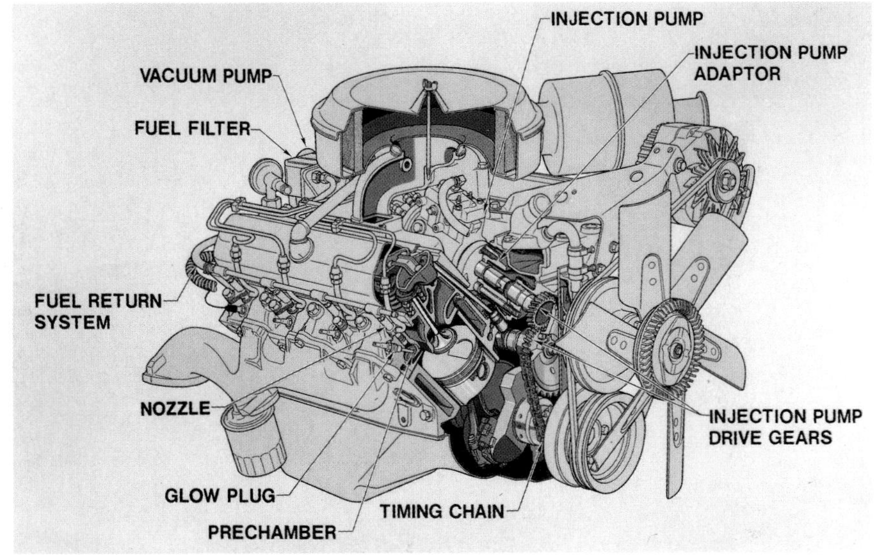


► Converted from a regular 350 gasoline V-8, Oldsmobile's new 1978 diesel engine was a timely fuel-saving idea, but would cause all kinds of trouble for all GM divisions: everything from oil leaks to bad cylinder heads. This cutaway drawing shows the major features of the new engine.

---

Buick launches the LeSabre Sport Coupe with a 150/165-bhp turbocharged V-6

Buick's mid-size lineup includes a scaled-down Century and separate Regal personal-luxury coupe; Regal sells well, Century doesn't

Corvettes display a new fastback roofline with a huge rear window; 6200 Indy 500 Pace Car Replicas and 2500 Silver Anniversary editions are produced

The 440-cid V-8 is available in Chryslers for last time; the 400 V-8 is standard except in LeBaron, which can have a Slant Six or 318/360 V-8

Magnum XE joins Dodge's Charger SE—both with the 400-cid V-8 as the top engine option

◄▲ Like Dodge with Aspen, Plymouth issued a multi-toned "Super Coupe" option on its '78 Volaré (*left*) for extroverted street racers. The Road Runner package (*above*), was still around as a cousin to the Aspen R/T. A 360 V-8 remained the top power option for all these cars, with up to 175 horses.

▲ A fraternal twin to Dodge's new Omni, the 1978 Plymouth Horizon offered economy-import virtues in an attractive domestic package. Priced from $3976, sales of the hatchback were encouraging: 106,772.

▲ Revised taillamp bezels were the only alteration to Pontiac's full-size Catalinas and Bonnevilles for '78. This Bonneville Brougham listed for $6784 with the standard 140-bhp 301 V-8.

▲ Like their GM siblings, mid-size Pontiacs were all-new, downsized cars for 1978. Back after a two-year hiatus was the sporty Grand Am as a $5634 sedan and this $5520 coupe. Output was 2841 and 7767, respectively.

◄ Switching to GM's smaller new-generation A-body made Pontiac's 1978 Grand Prix the trimmest and lightest ever. Base, sporty SJ, and luxury LJ (*shown*) models all returned with better mileage, improved handling, and similar performance, despite smaller engines. The LJ was no less costly at $5815, and the SJ started at a new high of $6088, so GP sales only held at their 1977 level—though that still meant a healthy 228,444 units.

---

Ford is still sticking to its big cars, but not for long—this is the final outing for the massive LTD

An aggressive-looking Mustang II "King Cobra" option includes the 302-cid V-8

A Diamond Jubilee Thunderbird marks Ford's 75th anniversary; 18,994 are built

This year sees the last appearance of Oldsmobile's 4-4-2 nameplate—until a 1980s rebirth

A diesel V-8 and Buick's 231-cid V-6 are available in big Olds

A fastback Pontiac Sunbird is added, along with a wagon; Le Mans is downsized to a 108-inch wheelbase

With 93,341 sold, the Trans Am is easily the most popular Firebird; the Ventura is gone, replaced by the Phoenix

▲ Again straining to look fresh, AMC's ex-Hornet Concord offered lush new Limited models for '79, including this opera-windowed two-door. Matador was dropped, and Concord saw 96,487 sales, up about 18,500 over Hornet.

▲ AMC's pudgy Pacer added Limited models of its own for '79. A 304 V-8 returned from 1978 with 125 horses as the top power option. This Limited hatchback listed at $6039. Total Pacer sales plummeted to 10,215.

▲ Officially discontinued for 1979, the AMC Gremlin lived on in spirit—as the Spirit, a restyled continuation offering this familiar chopped-tail two-door and a new hatch coupe. Series sales jumped to 52,478 units.

▲ The AMX name was hauled out once again for this 1979 "performance" version of AMC's new Spirit hatchback coupe. At $6090 with a base six cylinder or $6465 with a 125-bhp 304 V-8, it attracted just 3657 buyers.

▶ Buick's little Skyhawk hatchback was a bit more interesting with 1979's new Road Hawk option. Typical of those times, it was mainly a cosmetics package with front and rear spoilers, rear-pillar overlays, jazzy striping, and styled steel wheels. It also sported a unique front end and a firmer handling suspension. Alas, the most power available was still a standard 115-horse 231 V-6 engine. Overall Skyhawk sales fell for 1979, skidding to 23,139.

**1979**

The second energy crisis begins in the spring, abetted by a severe economic downturn

Double-digit inflation and a stagnant economy—known as "stagflation"—heralds the early '80s economic ills

Auto sales start off strong, but suffer from the oil scare and soaring prices

The slump is partly attributed to overselling in 1977-79, and to overly loose credit terms

Calendar-year industry output drops 8.8 percent (the lowest since 1975), though model-year production actually rises

Chevrolet builds 2,284,749 cars, Ford 1,835,937; Oldsmobile is third, followed by Pontiac, Buick, Mercury, Dodge, Cadillac—then Plymouth in the ninth spot

▲ Full-size Buicks moved into 1979 with no great change. The top-line Electra 225 returned with coupes and sedans in base, Limited, and new-for-'78 Park Avenue trim. This Park Avenue coupe sold for $9784.

▲ The first front-wheel-drive Buick Riviera bowed for 1979 on GM's newly downsized E-body platform. The base model listed at $10,684. A sporty new T-type with a turbo V-6 sold for $10,960. Sales leaped to 52,181 units.

▲ Cadillac's Eldorado was also redesigned on 1979's new GM E-body and was in its best shape since 1970. Engines comprised gas and diesel 350 V-8s. Sales increased a full 44 percent, to 67,436. Base price was $14,668.

▲ Cadillac's compact Seville sedan was virtually unchanged for '79, the last year for its clean, original 1975 design. Sales were off from '78, but remained healthy at 53,487. Base price was again $14,710.

▲ Berlinetta replaced the 1973-vintage Type LT as Chevrolet's "luxury" Camaro for '79. It listed for $5906 with the standard 250-cid inline six and was easily spotted via an exclusive bright-finish grille and other trimmings.

▲ Chevy hatched a true import-fighter in the 1975 Chevette three-door sedan, which got a five-door companion for '78. The '79s sported square head-lamps astride a broader grille. Sales were higher than ever at 451,161 units.

▲ Despite few changes, the base price of Chevrolet's Corvette climbed to $12,313 for '79. Styling was little-altered from that of 1978's "glassback" makeover. Still, sales were the best ever for a single Corvette year: 53,807.

---

Unleaded gasoline sells for an average 90 cents per gallon—up from 67 cents in 1978

The popularity of big-ticket power accessories begins to decline as car prices rise

Imports sell 2,327,932 cars for a record 21.7-percent market share

New models include the AMC Spirit, Dodge St. Regis, downsized Chrysler Newport/New Yorker, all-new Ford Mustang and related Mercury Capri

The Buick Riviera, Cadillac Eldorado, and Oldsmobile Toronado are downsized, all with front-wheel drive; a turbocharged V-6 is standard in the sporty Riviera S-Type

Ford finally downsizes its biggies: The LTD/Marquis weigh nearly 700 pounds less

▲ Chrysler's "new" 1979 big cars were really reskinned mid-size sedans sold as a Newport and this New Yorker, here in top Fifth Avenue trim. Wheelbase fell from 123.9 inches to 118.5, and sales to 28,574.

▲ Even in standard form, the '79 New Yorker started at a steep $10,872. "Formal" styling clichés were abundant. Power came from a choice of two 318 V-8s, but weight dropped from 4400 pounds to 3500.

▲ Highland Park stylists did a good job of hiding the mid-size origins of their full-size 1979 "R-body" cars. This Chrysler Newport had a list price of $7805 with the Slant Six, $7869 with a 318 V-8.

▲ Chrysler Corporation was fighting for survival by 1979, so most of its cars saw only evolutionary changes. That included the Chrysler Cordoba, shown here in new lower-priced $5611 "S" trim. Nonetheless, Cordoba sales dropped almost 60,000, to 124,825.

▲ A late-Seventies bright spot for Chrysler Division was the LeBaron, a new 1977 mid-size line based on the Aspen/Volaré compacts. Town & Country wagons joined the debut coupe and sedan for '78, and all models got a modest facelift for '79, as on this T&C with "wood" trim.

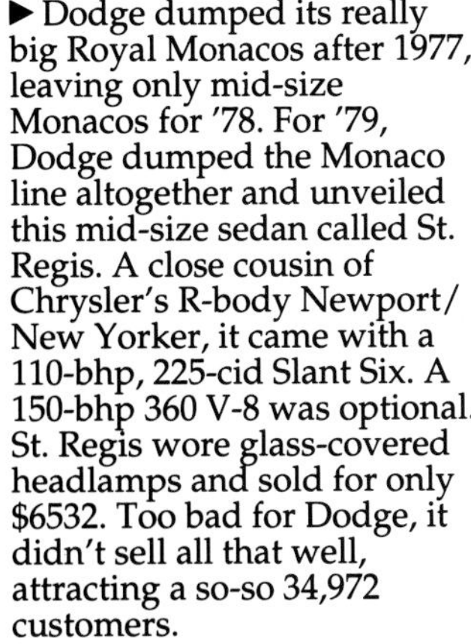

▶ Dodge dumped its really big Royal Monacos after 1977, leaving only mid-size Monacos for '78. For '79, Dodge dumped the Monaco line altogether and unveiled this mid-size sedan called St. Regis. A close cousin of Chrysler's R-body Newport/New Yorker, it came with a 110-bhp, 225-cid Slant Six. A 150-bhp 360 V-8 was optional. St. Regis wore glass-covered headlamps and sold for only $6532. Too bad for Dodge, it didn't sell all that well, attracting a so-so 34,972 customers.

The latest cars emit 90 percent fewer emissions than at the beginning of the '70s, and deliver 35-percent better fuel mileage

Chevrolet's three-point automatic lap/shoulder belt marks the first installation in a GM car

Chrysler's financial woes worsen as sales fall 17.8 percent and the corporation loses a record $1.1 billion; Lee Iacocca is elected chairman, succeeding John J. Riccardo

Henry Ford II resigns as Ford chief in August 1979, but continues as chairman

The CAFE standard rises to 19 mpg this year

Turbochargers are installed on 0.8 percent of domestic cars

More than 58 percent of the '79 cars have a V-8 engine (down from 65.8 percent in 1978); fours account for 17.6 percent

▲ A close cousin to Chrysler's LeBaron, Diplomat took over for Monaco as the mainstream mid-size Dodge for 1977, and also added wagons for '78. A new mid-price trim level was the main change for '79.

◀ Appearing for 1979 was the Omni 024, a new hatch coupe version of Dodge's L-body front-wheel-drive subcompact. Wheelbase was 96.7 inches, 2.5 shorter than on the boxy five-door, which helped handling. At $4864 to start, 024 proved popular with 57,384 new-car buyers.

▲ The all-new '79 Mustang was arguably the best Ford ponycar since the original '65 generation. Coupe (*shown*) and hatchback models were offered. Sales hit 369,936 units.

▲ Mustang came with four-cylinder engines, inline-six and V-6, and a V-8. A Cobra model offered the best balance with its 140-bhp, 2.3-liter turbocharged four.

▲ Production of Ford's Pinto remained strong at 199,018 units in '79 despite big headlines over its exploding gas tank. This hatch sedan wears the $370 Rallye trim group, a sporty returnee from 1978.

▲ Predictably, after its smash '78 debut, Ford's compact Fairmont showed little change for '79. Sales hit 395,367. This four-door sedan (shown with luxury exterior trim option) remained the top-seller.

▲ A T-bar roof was a new extra for 1979 Ford Thunderbirds like this $8866 Town Landau. A new Heritage model, outfitted much like the '78 Diamond Jubilee, cost $10,687. Total T-Bird sales eased to 284,141.

---

Cadillac offers a 350-cid, 125-bhp diesel V-8 across the board

Beleaguered AMC announces an agreement with Renault of France: AMC dealers will market two Renault models in the U.S., starting with the subcompact Renault 5 "Le Car"

Renault buys 22.5 percent of AMC in October—the deal includes an agreement to build Renault-designed cars at AMC's Kenosha, Wisconsin, facility

GM's all-new front-drive X-body cars—Chevrolet Citation, Pontiac Phoenix, Oldsmobile Omega, Buick Skylark—debut in April as early '80 models

AMC's Gremlin gets a major facelift and more conventional looks—and becomes the Spirit

▲ After years of pitching "road-hugging weight" to ever-more mileage-minded buyers, Dearborn finally followed GM with smaller big cars for 1979. Built on a new "Panther" platform, Ford's LTDs comprised two- and four-door base, Landau (*Landau coupe shown*), and standard and Country Squire wagons (*Squire in background*). Sales improved modestly to 356,535 units.

▲ Lincoln's 1979 Continental Mark V lost its 460 V-8, leaving a detuned 400 as its only engine, but designer models like this Bill Blass still abounded. A special new "Collector Series" model bowed during the year to signal the imminent end of this series.

▼ The '79 Mark V had a base price of $13,067. Designer packages like this Cartier ensemble added several hundred dollars. Sales perked up to 75,939 on word that 1979 would be the last year for a "big Mark." Changes from '78 were of the detail variety only.

► Mercury could have sold Mustang IIs, but chose to stick with its "sexy European" Capri. For 1979, however, Mercury opted for a version of that year's redesigned Mustang. The result was a new all-American Capri. It rejected Mustang's notchback coupe, but did offer base and luxury Ghia hatchbacks at $4872-$5237. A sporty RS package (*shown*) could be ordered with a turbo four, as on the Mustang Cobra.

## 1979 Model Year Production

| | | |
|---|---|---|
| 1. Chevrolet ........ 2,284,749 | 6. Mercury ........ 669,138 | 11. Lincoln ........ 189,546 |
| 2. Ford ........ 1,835,937 | 7. Dodge ........ 404,266 | 12. AMC ........ 169,439 |
| 3. Oldsmobile ........ 1,068,154 | 8. Cadillac ........ 383,138 | 13. Excalibur ........ 367 |
| 4. Pontiac ........ 907,434 | 9. Plymouth ........ 372,449 | 14. Avanti II ........ 142 |
| 5. Buick ........ 727,275 | 10. Chrysler ........ 349,450 | |

▲ Like Ford's '79 LTD, Mercury's full-size Marquis was fully redesigned to become smaller, lighter, thriftier, and more agile. Yet, it was no less roomy inside. With 32,349 produced, the line's best-seller was this $7909 Grand Marquis sedan, but total series sales dropped some 4800 units from '78, to 145,627.

▲ Where Ford offered a Fairmont Futura, Mercury had the Zephyr Z-7, a compact coupe with a distinctive "basket-handle" roofline as seen on recent T-Birds. Z-7 and Zephyr as a whole always trailed Fairmont in sales by a wide margin, even though prices were quite close: for '79, $4504 for Z-7 versus Futura's $4463.

▲ Like the 1979 Buick Riviera and Cadillac Eldorado, the Oldsmobile Toronado shed needless inches and pounds to become a more balanced personal-luxury coupe. The reward for Olds was sales that almost doubled from 1978 to just over 50,000. Toro looked much like the Eldo, but came with a 350 gasoline V-8 and offered the Olds 350 diesel V-8 at extra cost.

◀ The Hurst/Olds idea made a surprise return for 1979 as a $2054 option package coded W-30. It was available on the top-trim $5828 Cutlass Calais coupe. Underhood was a 125-horsepower 350 V-8, and 536 of the 2499 Olds sold had the optional T-bar roof. Color schemes were white body with black hood, roof, and grille, or the same colors reversed.

---

The downsized Cadillac Eldorado shrinks 20 inches, and has a new independent rear suspension

A 360-cid V-8 is now the biggest Chrysler engine offered

The Dodge Charger is gone, but the Magnum XE coupe hangs on

Omni/Horizon-based Dodge 024 and Plymouth TC3 fastback coupes debut; both are hatchbacks

Excalibur reverts to Chevy's 350-cid engine, and even at $28,600 per copy 27 roadsters and 340 phaetons are sold—a record

The fifth-generation Ford Mustang is 200 pounds lighter, but larger; a turbocharged four is optional, and during the year a 200-cubic-inch inline six replaces the German-built V-6 option

▲ The Olds 4-4-2 sputtered on after '72 with far more "show" than "go," but it was still around in 1979, offering uprated suspension and muscle-car looks. Unfortunately, the 1978-79 option was limited to the slow-selling "Aeroback" two-door sedan body style, so sales were few.

▲ Horizon TC3 was Plymouth's version of the new-for-'79 Dodge Omni 024 coupe. Note, though, the slatted versus checked grille. Base price was identical at $4864.

▲ Mid-size Pontiacs were little-changed for '79. Here, the Grand Am coupe, which, with its four-door stablemate, accounted for just 4.4 percent of total Le Mans sales.

▲ Pontiac's Firebird got yet another "facial" for '79. This is the racy Formula model, which had a base price of $6564 and could be ordered with a 220-bhp, 400-cid V-8.

◀ Trim, color, and equipment shuffles were the only changes of note for full-size '79 Pontiacs, like this top-of-the-line $7584 Bonneville Brougham four-door sedan. As before, Bonnevilles used a 301-cid Pontiac V-8, while the lower-priced Catalinas had a standard 231-cid Buick V-6. Bonneville sold better than ever for '79: 179,416 units.

---

The new Mustang sells well (369,936 units for '79), persevering with only one serious facelift through 1993; Mercury's similar Capri lasts only through 1986

Pontiac offers a new cross-flow four-cylinder engine; the last 400-cid V-8s are installed in 10th Anniversary Firebird Trans Ams

CHAPTER THIRTEEN

# 1980-1990

# FACING THE COMPETITION

Detroit entered the Eighties as a symbol of America's evident decline in an increasingly global economy. The industry had enjoyed three strong years, selling more than 11 million cars in '77 and '78, and another 10.5 million in '79. But when a second energy crisis triggered a sharp new recession, sales dropped below nine million in 1980 for record combined losses of $4.2 billion. And sales got worse: down to 8.5 million in '81, a worrisome 7.9 million in 1982.

Was Detroit suddenly falling apart? In 1980, it sure seemed so. Everyone saw Chrysler again speeding toward ruin, but so was American Motors, and Ford's cash crisis was no less acute, though much less publicized. GM went about business as usual despite suffering its first loss since 1921. All four companies were hampered by too many plants with too much overhead and too little "quality." Worse, Japanese automakers—led by Toyota, Honda, and Datsun—had come from nowhere to claim more than 20 percent of the U.S. market, and their share was growing.

Determined to not let "Japan, Inc." overrun yet another bastion of American industry, Detroit got busy. Chrysler won needed loan guarantees from Congress, then repaid the loans early with earnings from K-car compacts and a host of derivatives, including one that proved immensely popular: the minivan. Ford, too, closed unnecessary plants, won wage concessions from workers, slashed overhead elsewhere, and streamlined management, while making the smooth "aero look" its design signature. GM mainly threw money at its problems, banking on costly new automated equipment to improve vehicle quality and plant efficiency. The results were sometimes laughable, but GM did have two better ideas: a new independent subsidiary called Saturn, charged with making a competitive American small car that could also make a profit, and a bold joint-production venture with Toyota.

There was plenty of precedent for "fraternizing with the enemy." The Seventies had seen Chrysler buy into Mitsubishi, Ford into Mazda, GM into Isuzu. Though the Big Three learned from their Japanese partners even as they sold some of their cars under domestic labels, the "playing field" still wasn't "level"—or so they told the Reagan Administration, which jawboned Japan into limiting car exports to the U.S. Amid a growing U.S.-Japan trade imbalance and charges that they were "dumping" vehicles at subsidized low prices, the Japanese developed a legitimate fear of protectionist legislation. But they got around the Voluntary Restraint Agreement by setting up "transplant" factories in America.

Of course, Detroit did bounce back, thanks to the kind hand of fate. By 1983, a gasoline shortage had become a gasoline glut, the economy was rebounding, people were buying again, and the Big Three were eyeing record profits. Three years later, auto sales were back above 11 million, and Detroit was back to excitement: a new-generation Camaro/Firebird, increasingly hot Mustangs, truly sporting Thunderbirds, the first new Corvette in 15 years, even specialty two-seaters called Fiero, Reatta, Allanté . . . and Chrysler's TC by Maserati. Sadly, American Motors died with the 1987 pullout of erstwhile savior Renault, but it passed to Chrysler, then on an unwise buying binge.

Ford emerged as Detroit's big Eighties winner, with strong sellers like Taurus and the most cost-effective manufacturing operation around. Significantly, Ford became America's most profitable automaker in 1986, outearning giant GM for the first time in 42 years. That remarkable achievement only underscored how GM had delayed making the kind of wrenching, fundamental changes demanded by the new world automotive order.

---

**1980**

The recession deepens; domestic car sales suffer more than imports, in a bad year for the industry

Of 8,975,209 cars sold in the U.S., nearly 27 percent are imports

Japanese automakers agree to voluntary import restraints; "Buy American" campaigns emerge

All four major domestic automakers finish the year in the red; GM suffers its first yearly loss since 1921: $763 million

Chairman Lee Iacocca secures federal loan guarantees for endangered Chrysler Corporation

The CAFE requirement rises to 20 mpg; automakers cut weights, adopt smaller engines, improve aerodynamics, push diesels

◀ General Motors' landmark X-body family of cars appeared in mid-1979 as 1980 models. The newly downsized compacts switched from rear drive to front-wheel drive—a first for the company. They also used transversely mounted inline four-cylinder and V-6 engines. This phantom view of a Buick Skylark shows major features of the new space-saving design.

▶ Buick's 1980 Skylark offered two- and four-door notchbacks in base and luxury Limited trim. This Sport Coupe, and the Sport Sedan, boasted black exterior trim, a handling suspension, and other driving-oriented touches. Skylark base prices ranged from $5342 to $6102 with the standard 151-cid four-cylinder.

▲ Full-size 1980 Buicks emphasized economy with a slimmer "aero" nose and minor weight losses. Electras like this $10,537 Park Avenue coupe also boasted a thriftier new 4.1-liter V-6 as standard.

▲ Cadillac's '80 Eldorado got detail styling tweaks and a new 6.0-liter (368-cid) V-8 with digital electronic fuel injection. The 350 diesel V-8 remained optional. Base price rose to $16,141, and 52,685 were called for.

▲ Controversial new "bustleback" styling marked the 1980 Cadillac Seville, which shifted to the front-wheel-drive Eldorado chassis, but came standard with the 350 diesel V-8. Production was 39,344.

▶ Chevy's 1980 Corvette shed 250 pounds via greater use of lightweight materials. Integral front and rear spoilers also helped fuel economy, as did a lockup torque-converter clutch for the automatic transmission. The standard 350 V-8 was down to 170 net horses. Sales were down too, falling 13,200 units to 40,614.

---

GM's compact X-car quartet debuts to much applause, until initial models suffer a long list of factory recalls

Fewer than 30 percent of domestic new cars have V-8 engines (half the 1979 level); four-cylinder installations nearly double

Turbochargers inject extra horses into shrunken engines

Automatic transmissions lose favor as four-speed floorshifts gain popularity in small cars

On-board computers now control engine emissions

Corrosion-resistance warranties grow more common

Keyless door locks are available

Buick Century and Oldsmobile Cutlass drop "Aeroback" four-door styling, turn to notchbacks

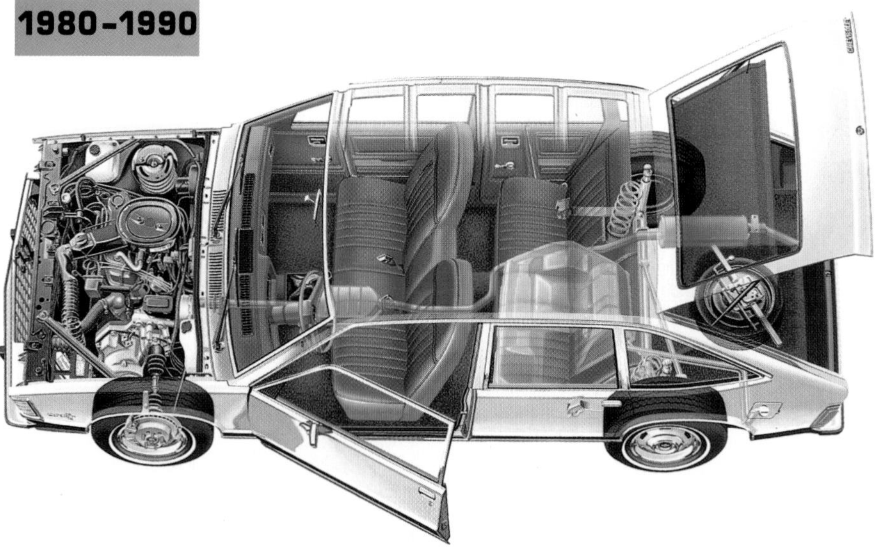

◀▲ Replacing Nova as Chevy's compact was Citation, the bowtie version of GM's new front-drive 1980 X-body cars. Citation came as two- and four-door hatchback sedans (*above and left*), plus a notchback club coupe. A sporty X-11 package (*above*) was offered for two-doors. Total '80 output: 811,540 units.

▲ Chevy's small Monza sport coupes weren't changed much for 1980, and still had a standard 151 inline four and optional 231 V-6. This is the "2+2" fastback with the $531 Spyder appearance and handling package.

▲ Checker Motors of Kalamazoo, Michigan, still sold "taxi-tough" sedans in 1980, but only a few hundred of them. This Marathon sedan started at $7800. The "blind quarter" vinyl top is a non-factory item.

▲ Chrysler's mid-size 1980 LeBarons got new "twin waterfall" grilles and other style updates. Coupes rode a 108.7-inch wheelbase. This top-line Medallion found 10,448 buyers. Price: six, $7185; eight, $7280.

▲ The 1977-79 LeBaron coupe got a major restyling to become 1980's new "downsized" Chrysler Cordoba. Base, Crown, and sporty LS models were offered in the $6800-$7500 range with the standard Slant Six engine. A 318 V-8 remained optional. Alas, sales dropped some 35,000 to 53,471.

▲ Mirada replaced Magnum as the "personal coupe" in the 1980 Dodge lineup, but retained its slat-type grille. A close cousin of that year's Chrysler Cordoba, it listed for $6600-$6900, but sold little better than Magnum at 32,746 units. This is the lower-priced "S" model.

▲ Like its Chrysler LeBaron sibling, the 1980 Dodge Diplomat coupe moved to a tighter wheelbase, and all models adopted a slightly crisper look. Base prices ranged from $6500 to $7800, but sales eased as potential buyers worried over Chrysler Corporation's future.

---

A new split-torque overdrive automatic transmission is standard in Lincolns, available in some other Ford products as well

AMC launches the four-wheel-drive Eagle; Pontiac's 151-cid four goes into Spirit and Concord

The last rear-drive Buick Skyhawk and Olds Starfire fastback coupes go on sale

"Car guy" Lloyd Reuss is named Buick's general manager

A second-generation, front-drive Seville debuts with "bustleback" tail, standard diesel V-8

Chevrolet Caprice/Impala earn a mild "aero" reskin; V-6 is standard in full-size models and Camaro

The second-generation Chrysler Cordoba debuts; a 360-cid V-8 is the biggest Chrysler choice

▲ Designer Brooks Stevens' sons, David (*left*) and "Steve," who were running Excalibur, pose with one of their last Series III cars. For 1980, they issued the bigger but slower Series IV. It sold near $40,000.

▲ Seeking higher sales and higher mileage, Ford again downsized the Thunderbird for 1980 by making it essentially a plush, rather overstyled two-door Fairmont. Sales promptly fell some 18,000 units to 156,803.

▲ Though smaller, the 1980 T-Bird wore trademark touches like wall-to-wall taillights and a big square grille. This new Silver Anniversary edition, which headed the three-model slate, started at a pricey $11,679.

▲ Ford's Granada took one last bow in original '76 form for 1980. Changes were few, but sales fell way down in a tough market from 182,000 units to just over 90,000. Pictured here is the top-line Ghia four-door.

▲ A new 4.2-liter (255-cid) V-8 replaced the familiar 302 option in 1980 Ford Mustangs. This is the hatch coupe with a turbo-four and racy Cobra package, which was restyled *a la* the '79 Mustang Indianapolis Pace Car.

◀▲ Lincoln's new 1980 Mark VI was downsized along with Continentals onto the full-size "Panther" platform. For the first time, a four-door version was offered (*left*). Opera windows were again featured on base and new Signature Series models. Mark VI coupes rode a trimmer chassis than four-doors, but again offered "designer" packages such as Bill Blass (*above*).

## 1980 Model Year Production

1. Chevrolet ....... 2,288,745
2. Ford ....... 1,162,275
3. Oldsmobile ....... 910,306
4. Buick ....... 854,011
5. Pontiac ....... 770,100
6. Mercury ....... 347,711
7. Dodge ....... 308,638
8. Plymouth ....... 290,974
9. Cadillac ....... 230,028
10. AMC ....... 199,613
11. Chrysler ....... 164,510
12. Lincoln ....... 74,908
13. Avanti II ....... 168
14. Excalibur ....... 93

▲ Downsizing cut the 1980 Continental's wheelbase to 117.3 inches, from 127.3, and its curb weight to 3900 pounds from 4650. Luxury and formal styling cues were intact, but sales plummeted to 31,233, from 92,600. The sedan (*above*) again outsold the coupe.

▲ Mercury Cougars were pared to a single $7045 XR-7 coupe for 1980. It was a near-twin to that year's new downsized Ford Thunderbird. The wide rear-quarter roof shown here came in a new $1987 Luxury Group. Production was way down in this recession year, to 58,028 units.

▲ The standard V-8's horsepower jumped by 15, to 120, but a slightly smoother profile yielded a bit more fuel economy on 1980 full-size Oldsmobiles, like this $7076 Delta 88 coupe in top Royale trim.

▲ Oldsmobile's compact Omega switched to GM's new front-drive X-body design for 1980. Like Buick's Skylark, it listed two- and four-door notchbacks. This is the uplevel $6013 Brougham four-door sedan.

▲ Compared to the '79 models it replaced, the X-body Omega was six-inches shorter in wheelbase and a full 750 pounds lighter. The SX dress-up option for standard coupes and sedans included a decklid spoiler.

▲ Pontiac's compact changed names from Ventura to Phoenix for 1977, then changed designs by adopting GM's new 1980 X-body platform with front-wheel drive. This roomy four-door hatchback sedan was sold along with a two-door notchback in base and high-luxe LJ trim (*shown*). Base prices ranged from $5470 to $6100.

▲ For the look of performance but no extra power, the '80 Phoenix offered a sporty SJ option at $502 on notchbacks like this and $460 on hatchbacks. Pontiac's firmer Rally chassis was included. Introduced on April 19, 1979, the 1980 Phoenix enjoyed a long model year, which helped push sales upward to 178,291 units.

---

Mirada replaces Magnum in the Dodge lineup, kin to the Chrysler Cordoba personal-luxury coupe (both built in Canada only)

Ford produces its last Pinto, Mercury its final Bobcat; the Crown Victoria name is revived on the top-line LTD

The Ford Thunderbird is downsized; a six-cylinder engine is available for the first time

Lincoln's Continental and Mark come closer together, both on a new downsized "Panther" platform; the last Versailles is built

The final Aspens/Volarés are built

Pontiac begins to move into the performance arena again, ready to take sales from Oldsmobile

By 1980, only Corvette and Pontiac Firebird Turbo top 190 bhp

A limited-production turbo McLaren Mustang appears

▲ After a '79 facelift, Pontiac's Firebird Trans Am paced both the Indy 500 and NASCAR races in new Turbo form, with its turbocharged 210-horsepower 301 V-8. Just 50 replicas like this one were built and later sold.

▲ Reshaped body contours and a revised engine lineup (including shelving the 350 gas V-8) helped improve fuel economy—as Washington demanded—on 1980 full-size Pontiacs. This Bonneville Brougham sedan cost $8160; 21,249 were built.

▲ The Avanti II was still around in 1981 with its singular Raymond Loewy styling from Studebaker days nearly 20 years before. It switched Chevy engines, though, from a 190-bhp 350 V-8 to a 155-bhp 305—a sign of the times.

▲ An estimated 200 Avanti IIs were built for '81, versus 100 to 170 per year in 1969-80. Inflation had swelled its price to $20,495, but you still got a mostly hand-built car trimmed and painted to your taste.

▲ New for 1980 and little-changed for '81, the AMC Eagle was America's first car with four-wheel drive—and a permanently engaged system at that. This Concord-based wagon started at $8397.

▲ The Concord itself was largely a rerun for '81. Reason: American Motors was very low on money. This top-trim Limited two-door started at $6665 with a newly standard 2.5-liter Pontiac four-cylinder motor.

▲ AMC's Spirit also offered the 2.5 (151-cid) Pontiac four as new base power for 1981, and spawned four-wheel-drive Eagle Kammback and hatchback coupe sisters. This is the $5589 Spirit D/L hatch coupe.

**1981**

Industry sales drop sharply due to continued recession and the aftermath of the energy crisis

Domestic output (including Volkswagen of America) totals 6,673,324 cars for the model year

Of 8,532,672 cars sold in the U.S., 73 percent are domestically built—nearly identical to 1980

Ford and GM offer a series of rebates to push sales; both megaliths lose market share, while Chrysler's grows a bit

Chrysler workers relinquish $622 million in salary and benefits so the company can qualify for federal loan guarantees

Ford's board of directors ponders a merger with Chrysler, but nixes any possibility

▲Maximum power in full-size 1981 Buicks was a 150-horsepower 307 gas V-8. The optional 350 diesel V-8 gave just 105. Electras, including this $11,291 Estate Wagon, also got a new four-speed overdrive automatic transmission as standard equipment.

▲A slightly lowered nose and lifted tail cut aerodynamic drag on 1981 Buick Regals. This Sport Coupe again came with a 170-bhp, 231-cid turbo V-6 and three-speed automatic, though with a new lockup converter clutch. Its base price was $8528.

▲The '81 Buick Regal Limited's "formal" styling cues included "coach lamps" and bright over-the-roof trim. Priced at $8024, it accounted for nearly half of the line's strong 240,200 model-year sales. A 110-horsepower 231 V-6 was standard.

▲As in 1980, the "civilian" 1981 Checker Marathon offered a choice of GM V-6, V-8, and diesel V-8 choices. Alas, Checker was failing, and output, including taxis, was only 2950. The opera-window roof shown here is not factory-stock.

▲Chevrolet's small rear-drive Chevette greeted 1981—and Ford's new Escort—with new electronic carburetor control and power steering as a first-time option (with air conditioning and automatic). Here, the $5395 four-door hatch sedan.

▲Computerized engine control and a lockup torque-converter clutch made news for full-size 1981 Chevys like this Caprice Classic four-door sedan. Its base price was $7667 with the standard V-6, or just $50 more with the base 4.4-liter V-8.

▲Like sister GM models, the 1981 Chevy Monte Carlo was reshaped for less gas-wasting air drag. This uplevel Landau model stickered at $8006 with the standard V-6.

◀Chevy's sporty Citation X-11 got extra fire for '81 via a high-output 2.8-liter V-6 with 135 horses (versus 110). This publicity photo displays the unique parts in that year's model, which delivered for around $6800.

---

To meet tighter emissions standards, automakers install improved catalytic converters and on-board computers

The federal CAFE requirement rises from 20 to 22 mpg

Dodge launches its Aries K-body compact; Plymouth's Reliant differs little—both aim to help "rescue" ailing Chrysler Corporation

Ford introduces the subcompact front-drive Escort "world car"

Chrysler adds a new Imperial to the list of cars built only in Canada

Cadillac makes its new V-8-6-4 variable-displacement engine standard (optional in Seville); it lasts just one season

A Buick-built 4.1-liter V-6 is optional in Cadillacs—their first six-cylinder engine ever

▲ Chevy's '81 Corvette offered but one 350 V-8, a new 190-bhp version (versus 230 bhp for '80) with electronic control. Sales held about steady at 40,614 units.

▲ The second-generation Chevy Camaro would bow out after 1981 and decent sales of 126,139. The top-performing Z28 (*shown*) grabbed 43,272 of them at $8263 apiece. Its base V-8 with a four-speed manual was now Chevy's small 305; the 350 was available only with automatic.

▲ Given a reprieve from the chopping block, Chrysler's R-body New Yorker returned for '81 as a $10,463 fully equipped four-door sedan with this carriage roof among its few options. Only 6548 were sold.

▲ There was also little new in Chrysler's 1981 Cordoba, though the 360 V-8 option died for fuel-economy reasons. A 318 was now tops. Sales sank by over 50 percent to a new Cordoba low: just 20,113 units.

▲ Change was equally hard to find on 1981 Chrysler LeBarons, a situation that reflected Highland Park's low cash reserves and that year's emphasis on the all-new K-car compacts. Here, the $7768 Medallion coupe.

▲ After a six-year absence, Chrysler revived Imperial for 1981 as a fully equipped coupe based on the LeBaron/Cordoba platform. Despite an exclusive new fuel-injected 140-bhp version of the venerable 318-cid V-8, the result was ordinary, if opulent. Base price was a lofty $18,311, one reason why sales were only 7225.

▲ Like 1980's new Cadillac Seville, the reborn '81 Imperial wore a razor-edge "bustleback" allegedly inspired by early-Fifties British custom coachwork. The similarity with Seville was pure chance, and the Imperial's treatment was arguably better-looking—but it was still uncomfortably "me-too."

---

Cadillac is the first luxury car to offer a passive restraint system

Computer Command Control is installed in all GM engines

Full-size GM cars gain automatic overdrive transmission

Roger Smith is named chairman of General Motors—and remains through the Eighties

AMC markets the Renault 18i and launches a new optional six-cylinder engine

Buick finishes the model year in fourth place (again)

Chevrolet Monte Carlo gains a handsome facelift; Chevette output hits a new peak

Corvette adopts a fiberglass rear leaf spring; production moves to a new Bowling Green, Kentucky, assembly plant

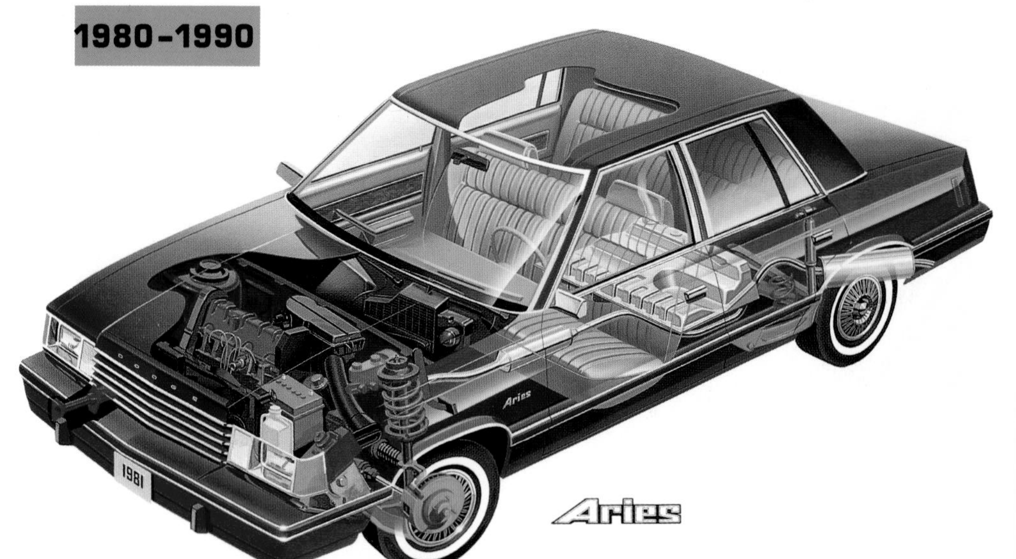


▲ The car that would save Chrysler bowed with appropriate fanfare for 1981 as the Dodge Aries (*shown*) and Plymouth Reliant "K-car" compacts. Both offered transverse four-cylinder power, front-wheel drive, and room for four passengers in coupes, sedans, and five-door wagons, priced from around $6000.

▲ Base K-car power was a new Chrysler-designed 84-bhp, 2.2-liter "Trans-4" engine. It proved to be sturdy and reliable.

▲ The '81 Dodge Aries wagon in top Special Edition trim wore woody-look appliqués. This is an early PR shot; badges were later changed to "Aries-K Front-Wheel Drive."

▲ In mid-line Custom trim, the '81 Aries coupe sold for $6315. A 100-bhp, 2.6-liter Mitsubishi four-cylinder was optional for all K-cars fitted with automatic transmission.

▲ Chrysler's small 1981 L-body models, including this $6149 Dodge Omni 024, offered the K-car's Trans-4 engine as a new option, vastly improving performance.

◀ Like Chrysler's Cordoba, the '81 Dodge Mirada lost its 360 V-8 option, but still offered two- and four-barrel 318s in lieu of the standard 225 Slant Six. Also new that year was a dressy CMX option package with wide-quarter "cabriolet" vinyl top that simulated the look of a true convertible. Mirada's base price was up to $7700, but sales were down some two-thirds from 1980, to 11,899 units.

### 1981 Model Year Production

| | | |
|---|---|---|
| 1. Chevrolet 1,673,093 | 6. Plymouth 393,633 | 11. Lincoln 69,537 |
| 2. Ford 950,301 | 7. Mercury 375,756 | 12. Chrysler 56,726 |
| 3. Oldsmobile 873,678 | 8. Dodge 340,899 | 13. Excalibur 235 |
| 4. Buick 856,996 | 9. Cadillac 240,189 | 14. Avanti II 200[1] |
| 5. Pontiac 489,436 | 10. AMC 137,125 | |

[1] *Estimated*

▲ Ford replaced Pinto for '81 with Escort, a roomier, more modern front-drive subcompact. This two-door hatchback was joined by a four-door hatch and a five-door wagon. Sales were strong, topping 320,000.

▲ Lincoln's Continental Mark VI lost its optional 351 V-8 for its sophomore '81 season, but was little-changed otherwise. Pictured is the $16,858 coupe with the Bill Blass "designer" option package.

▲ Companion to the new Ford Escort was the '81 Mercury Lynx, offered in the same range of bodystyles. This $6914 GS version topped the wagon range. As in Escort, the sole engine was a 1.6-liter four of about 70 bhp.

▲ Mercury's 1981 Zephyr compacts changed the name of their top trim option from Ghia to GS. This Z-7 coupe is so equipped. Base price that year was $6252. A 115-bhp, 255-cid V-8 was the top engine option.

▲ The 1981 Mercury Capri offered a new Black Magic paint package with contrasting gold pinstripes; it was also available in white. Also new was the T-bar roof shown here. It was available as a separate option.

▲ Revised engines and a newly standard four-speed automatic transmission marked Mercury's staid-looking full-size '81 Marquis. The new base V-8 for non-wagons was a 302 debored to 255 cubes.

◀ As for Chevy's Camaro, 1981 was the finale for Pontiac's second-generation Firebird, as well as the Turbo Trans Am (*shown*). As before, the blown 301 V-8 was optional for the Formula model. Firebird sales fell by more than 36,000 units from 1980, to just under 71,000.

▲ The 1981 Oldsmobile Toronado switched to a 125-bhp, 4.1-liter Buick V-6 as its base power; the previously standard 150-bhp 307 gas V-8 became optional. Sales slipped nearly 1000 units from 1980 to 42,604.

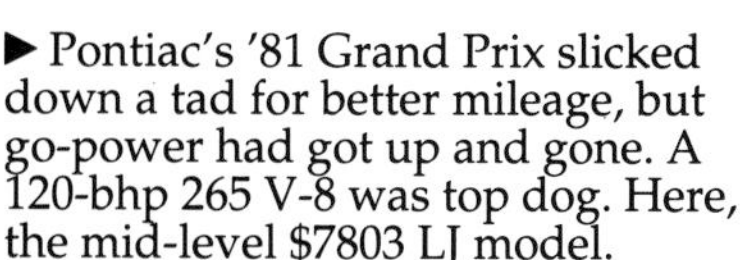

▶ Pontiac's '81 Grand Prix slicked down a tad for better mileage, but go-power had got up and gone. A 120-bhp 265 V-8 was top dog. Here, the mid-level $7803 LJ model.

Chrysler's biggest V-8 is now 318-cid; Newport/New Yorker make their last appearance

Dodge Diplomat comes only as a four-door, selling mainly to police/taxi fleets in the '80s; the last St. Regis is produced

Ford's LTD offers its final 351-cid V-8; the new Granada is Fairmont-based, lighter

Lincoln's Town Car is selling strongly—success continues through the Eighties

Lynx is Mercury's version of the Escort; the new Cougar is based on Ford's Granada

The Pontiac Catalina/Bonneville enters its last year

Pontiac issues the tiny T1000; customers fail to flock to showrooms

▲ Chrysler was so short of cash by 1981 that its new K-cars played both Dodges and Plymouths in some publicity photos; only the badges were changed. This wagon is portraying a Plymouth Reliant in SE trim.

▲ The 1981 Plymouth Reliant-K differed from Dodge's new Aries only in grille and taillamps. Even pricing was the same—$6933 in the case of this SE four-door—though for some reason Reliant sold better.

▲ Plymouth's Gran Fury came back for 1980 as a near-duplicate of Chrysler's R-body Newport sedan. Intended mainly for taxi and police duty, this '81 was the only Plymouth car available with a V-8 engine.

◀▼ American Motors began building a new small front-drive four-door during 1982, at its Kenosha, Wisconsin, plant. The aptly named Alliance was a close copy of the European Renault 9 four-door (*left*). However, AMC produced a two-door version (*below*) just for U.S. sale. Alliance bowed as an '83 and sold well at just over 142,000 units.

▲ Test drivers of this '82 Avanti II found it charming but dated, with a "tack-on" approach to meeting government requirements (note front bumperettes). But better things were ahead, as Avanti would soon be under new ownership.

▲ Still looking much like the Hornet Sportabout from which it sprang, this wagon remained the top seller among AMC's all-wheel-drive Eagle models for 1982. It tallied 20,899 units out of 37,923 total. Wagon prices started at $9566.

▲ AMC's Concord soldiered into 1982 with a five-speed manual gearbox option, but little else new. In top Limited trim, as shown, this two-door sedan started at $7213 with the standard 151-cid four and $7363 with the 258-cid inline-six.

---

John Z. DeLorean, former rising star at General Motors, markets a gullwing sports car built in North Ireland; sales are disappointing

Experimental cars include Ford's mini Shuttler, Pockar commuter car, Probe III, three-wheeled Cockpit; GM debuts Aero X

**1982**

Domestic output (including Volkswagen's) sinks to 5,157,477 cars for the model year

Of 7,978,177 cars sold in the U.S., 5,756,660 are domestically built

Falling gasoline prices affect sales of small cars and diesel engines; high interest rates scare banks away from auto loans

Automakers use downsizing, powertrain shuffles, revised gearing, and wind-tunnel testing to cut weight/emissions, boost mileage

▲ Buick boosted mid-size Century sales for '81 by replacing sloped "Aeroback" sedans with this notchback four-door. For '82, all those Centurys became Regals. Pictured here is the $9364 Limited sedan.

▲ And here's the reason for that '82 change: new front-wheel-drive Buick Century two- and four-door notchbacks were spawned from the X-body Skylark. This Limited four-door sedan topped the four-model line at $9581.

▲ Evoking muscle-car memories was Buick's mid-'82 Grand National coupe, named for the Chevy-powered Regals then cleaning up on NASCAR ovals. Just 215 were built with a 4.1 V-6 and a turbo 3.8 Buick V-6.

▲ Buick's Riviera was one of the few Detroit cars to gain sales in '81, rising to 52,007. But the '82 edition dropped back to 44,071 despite worthy technical improvements like a standard new four-speed automatic.

▲ Cadillac's Eldorado became a touch sportier with the new 1982 Touring Coupe. It featured less exterior chrome, a firmed-up chassis, blackwall tires on aluminum wheels, bucket-seat interior—and no hood ornament.

◀▲ A brand-new third-generation Chevrolet Camaro was one of 1982's biggest introductions. Though a bit smaller and lighter than the second-series design, it was more practical thanks to a lift-up glass hatch. Models were the familiar trio of base, luxury Berlinetta (*above*), and performance-oriented Z28 (*left*), with up to 165 horses available in 305 V-8s. Overall sales jumped to 182,068, including 39,744 Berlinettas and 63,563 Z28s.

---

Convertibles are back, wearing Chrysler, Dodge, and Buick nameplates

GM's J-car front-drive subcompacts debut: Buick Skyhawk, Chevrolet Cavalier, Pontiac J2000, Oldsmobile Firenza—even a Cadillac Cimarron

Wedge-shaped A-body GM compacts arrive: Chevrolet Celebrity, Buick Century, Oldsmobile Cutlass Ciera, Pontiac 6000; drivetrains are based on the X-cars

Shrunken Chevrolet Camaros and Pontiac Firebirds emerge, including Z28 and Trans Am; standard four-cylinder engines are a first

Ford issues the Escort-based EXP two-passenger sport coupe; Mercury offers the related "bubbleback" LN7—sales soon plunge

Renault acquires controlling interest in AMC, tools the Kenosha plant to produce an American version of the Renault 9

▲ Leading the way back for Detroit convertibles were Chrysler's new 1982 luxury K-car lines, the LeBaron and Dodge 400. The $12,300 Dodge attracted 5541 fun-in-the-sun buyers.

▲ The shark-generation Chevrolet Corvette would bow out after 1982. Sales that year hit 25,407, including 6759 copies of this special $22,537 Collector Edition hatchback.

▲ Chevrolet had a new Celebrity for 1982: a trimmer front-wheel-drive mid-size workhorse to supplement the rear-drive Malibu. This coupe and a sedan were offered at $8313 to $8588.

▲ Supplementing the rear-drive Chevette in Chevrolet's 1982 lineup was the new front-drive Cavalier, a slightly larger subcompact offering these four body styles and additional four-cylinder power for as little as $6278. It was just one of the "J-cars" appearing at all five GM divisions that year.

▲ Chrysler moved its strong-selling K-car upmarket for 1982 with the Dodge 400 and this new-generation Chrysler LeBaron coupe and sedan. A LeBaron ragtop bowed at mid-year in base trim starting at $11,698 and as a woody-look Town & Country for $13,998. There was also a Town & Country wagon. Buyers responded to the new LeBaron by buying twice as many as in 1981: over 90,000.

▲ Ads proclaimed "It's time for Imperial." But this little-changed '82 got fewer than half the sales of the reborn 1981 model: just 2329. A new wrinkle was this Frank Sinatra Edition, complete with a set of the crooner's hits on tape.

▲ Introduced with the redesigned 1980 Chrysler Cordoba was this LS model with a "cross-hair" grille like that of legendary Letter-Series 300s (and an abortive 1979 reprise). A "Cabriolet" roof was also included. Just 3136 of the '82s were sold.

▲ The Chrysler Cordoba again saw little change for 1982—except for sales, which withered to 14,898, a new low. This standard model started at $9197 without the pictured optional "Landau" roof treatment that covered the rear opera windows.

---

Honda now builds Accords in Marysville, Ohio

GM issues an all-new 4.3-liter diesel V-6 for mid-size models; a big diesel V-8 is now available in mid- and full-size models

GM's 2.5-liter (151-cid) four-cylinder engine switches to fuel injection; so do the Corvette V-8 and some Camaro/Firebird engines

Lincoln offers nitrogen-pressurized shock absorbers—a U.S. industry "first"

Buick rises to third in production, helped by the new front-drive Century and Skyhawk; mid-year brings the first Riviera convertible

A new aluminum-block HT4100 V-8 is standard in Cadillacs (except Cimarron and limo); a European-inspired Touring Suspension is available in the Eldorado

▲ The all-new Camaro paced the 1982 Indianapolis 500, the third such honor for Chevrolet's ponycar. Chevy built 6360 replicas—without the flags and "gumball" lights.

▲ Back for 1982 from a mid-'81 debut was Dodge's reborn Charger, a sportier Omni 024 with a standard 111-horse K-car 2.2-liter four-cylinder. Base price was $7115.

▲ Dodge didn't forget frugality for '82, again offering a no-frills, 63-bhp Miser version of its Omni sedan and 024 coupe (*shown*), as in 1981. Prices started at a miserly $5499.

◀▲ Ford's subcompact Escort reshuffled models for '82 to make room for new hatchback sedans and a somewhat oddly styled coupe called EXP (*above and rear*). The latter was Dearborn's first two-seater since the 1957 T-Bird. Like other '82 Fords, all wore newly revived blue-oval emblems. Escort sales remained strong—385,132 total—plus 98,256 copies of the $7387 EXP.

▲ Though little-changed for '82, the Mark VI was no longer badged Continental. The label was transferred to that year's new compact Lincoln sedan. But trim variations for the Mark continued without end. Witness this $23,594 Bill Blass coupe in new red/white livery with standard wire wheels.

▲ Ousting Versailles as a stronger challenger to Cadillac's Seville, the new '82 Lincoln Continental sedan wore its own "bustleback" on the humble Ford Fairmont "Fox" platform. Most every luxury amenity was included in the $21,302 sticker, but even-posher Signature Series and Givenchy models were offered.

## 1982 Model Year Production

|  |  |  |
|---|---|---|
| 1. | Chevrolet | 1,297,357 |
| 2. | Ford | 748,732 |
| 3. | Buick | 739,984 |
| 4. | Oldsmobile | 702,340 |
| 5. | Pontiac | 541,061 |
| 6. | Mercury | 328,597 |
| 7. | Plymouth | 247,936 |
| 8. | Dodge | 241,359 |
| 9. | Cadillac | 235,584 |
| 10. | Chrysler | 103,310 |
| 11. | Lincoln | 85,313 |
| 12. | AMC | 70,898 |
| 13. | Excalibur | 212 |
| 14. | Avanti | 200[1] |

[1] *Estimated*

▲ This was the last year for the squared-off Cougar design. Sedans and wagons rode a wheelbase of 105.5 inches, the coupes one of 108.4. All were basically dressed-up Zephyrs, though unlike Zephyr, could be fitted with a V-8.

► Mercury hewed to tradition with its Lynx, a Ford Escort marketed with slightly better trim and higher prices. The 1982 models weren't much changed from the debut '81s, but four-door hatchback sedans like this arrived. Lynx sales remained strong: over 119,000.

◄ Bowing in spring 1982 to replace the Starfire, Firenza was Oldsmobile's version of GM's new J-car subcompact. It was limited to this hatchback coupe and a notchback four-door. Besides Olds styling cues, it also differed from Chevy's Cavalier in having a standard overhead-cam 1.8-liter four-cylinder engine. First-year sales were modest at 30,108.

▲ Few changes attended the full-size Oldsmobiles for '82. This Regency sedan continued as one of three senior Ninety-Eight models priced in the $12,000-$13,000 range. Sales held steady at 90,967 units.

▲ Oldsmobile added the front-drive 1982 Cutlass Ciera to its line as its version of GM's new A-body family. Here, the $9599 Brougham four-door. It accompanied, rather than replaced, the rear-drive Cutlass, which outsold it 281,451 to 101,320.

▲ Still all-out for diesel power in '82, Olds introduced this 85-bhp 4.3-liter V-6 unit as an option for both front- and rear-drive versions of Cutlass.

---

The last "shark" Corvettes go on sale, carrying the next-generation drivetrain; no manual transmission is available this year

A Collector Edition Corvette features a lift-up rear window

The new front-drive Chrysler LeBaron is smaller than its predecessor; the New Yorker name is retained on a rear-drive model

Mid-year brings a woody-look Town & Country wagon to Chrysler's lineup, plus the first American-built convertible since the 1976 Eldorado

The new Dodge 400, like LeBaron, is a stretch of the K-car; a convertible bows at mid-season

Ford's Mustang GT is revived, it boasts a 157-bhp V-8

Lincoln drops the Town Coupé, offers a newly compact Continental sedan

▲ Plymouth's subcompact Horizon saw more detail enhancements for '82. Included was new top-line Custom trim, shown here with optional two-tone paint. The two-door TC3 hatch also continued.

▲ With aggressive new looks and even-better handling in a trimmer package, the 1982 debut of the third-generation Pontiac Firebird Trans Am saw an impressive sales increase to 52,960 units. Base price: $9658.

▲ J2000 was the "alphanumeric" title for Pontiac's version of the new 1982 GM J-car, offered in the same four body types as the Chevy Cavalier. The SE hatch coupe (*above*) was base-priced at $7654.

► *Right column:* Pontiac PR issued these colorful "phantom" drawings to highlight the engineering of its new '82 Trans Am (*top*), J2000 (*center*), and mid-size front-drive 6000 *(bottom).* The 6000 was similar to the Chevy Celebrity and Olds Cutlass Ciera.

---

Rear-drive Oldsmobile coupes are now called Cutlass Supreme

Plymouth downsizes the Gran Fury, a near-cousin to the Dodge Diplomat; both sell mainly to police and taxi fleets

A new medium-size Pontiac Bonneville takes the place of the former full-size model

The Avanti company is bought by Stephen Blake

DeLorean's company falls into receivership and is liquidated; the stainless-steel sports car failed to grab customers

Concept vehicles include the Ford Flair and Avant Garde, plus GM's three-wheeled Lean Machine, two-passenger TPC, and stick-controlled Aero 2000

▲ Construction magnate Steve Blake took over Avanti in late '82 and issued this Thirtieth Anniversary special in black, white, red, or silver. The production total is unknown.

▲ Bowing during the '82 model year, Buick's Skyhawk J-car was back for '83 with two new wagons and a sporty T-type coupe similar to this $7457 Limited. Total Skyhawk sales: 63,152.

▲ Base versions of Buick's 1983 Skylarks were retitled Custom, like this $7548 two-door. As with the other X-cars, mechanical problems and safety recalls were piling up.

▲ The first-ever Buick Riviera convertible bowed during 1983 with a mild 125-bhp, 4.1-liter V-6 and a wild $25,000 base price. Finished in white (*shown*) or red-toned "Firemist" paint, production was a meager 1750 units.

▲ A new four-speed automatic transmission teamed with certain V-6s as one of the few changes for Buick's 1983 rear-drive Regals. This top-trim Limited coupe stickered at $9425. Regal output continued strong at 228,239.

▲ Back for a third season, Chevy's bare-bones Chevette Scooter qualified as Detroit's least-expensive 1983 car at $5333 for this four-door hatch and just $4997 for the two-door version. Though pressed hard by Ford's more-modern Escort, Chevette still sold strongly at over 169,000 units.

▲ Chevrolet's rear-drive 1983 intermediates were '82 reruns except for some equipment and trim shuffling. Top-line models were now just Malibu, without the "Classic" surname. This four-door Malibu sedan started at $8084 with the V-6 and $8309 with the base 305 V-8.

▲ The Chevrolet Monte Carlo SS made a surprise return in 1983 as this "droop-snoot" special with a 180-horse 305 V-8. Designed both for NASCAR racing and to help renew buyer interest in performance, it carried a base price of $10,474. Production problems limited sales to just 4714.

**1983**

Excitement and performance return to showrooms; convertibles now come in six models

Domestic model-year output totals 5,683,197 cars (including foreign automakers with U.S. plants)

Of 9,181,036 cars sold in the U.S., 6,795,302 are domestically built

NHTSA eases the 5-mph bumper impact standard to 2½ mph—automakers cheer, while safety advocates and insurers jeer

Chrysler Corp. pays off its $1.2 billion in federally guaranteed loans—seven years early; the company is earning money again

J.D. Power and Associates learns that domestic new-car buyers have a median age of 49.5 years and an annual income of $34,790; import buyers are younger and earn more

▲ Chrysler kept spinning out K-car variations for 1983, including this unexpected 124-inch-wheelbase Executive Sedan and a limousine with a 131-inch chassis. Styling was similar to LeBaron's, but badges simply read "Chrysler." Stickers read $18,900 and $21,900.

▲ A future "classic"? Difficult to say for sure, but only 9891 Chrysler LeBaron convertibles were built for 1983, and there couldn't have been many of these woody-look Town & Countrys with the Mark Cross leather interior like this one. Base price was a stiff $15,595.

▲ A relic of "The Old Chrysler Corporation," the Cordoba was reduced to one model for its swan-song 1983, when changes were again minor. Interest sagged and sales were lower than ever at 13,471 units.

▲ Dodge's new 1983 600 was a stretched K-car sedan aimed at two markets. The base model (*background*) was for families, while the sportier ES quested after a new breed: import-loving "Yuppies."

▲ Unveiled during 1983, the Shelby Charger was Dodge's small front-drive coupe heated up by legendary Carroll Shelby, newly reteamed with Lee Iacocca at Chrysler. At $8290, it managed a respectable 8251 sales.

▲ Like Chrysler's Cordoba, the aging Dodge Mirada would depart after 1983 in the wake of slow sales and Chrysler Corporation's relentless march to smaller cars with front-wheel drive. This one has the CMX package with *faux*-convertible "cabriolet" top. Mirada deliveries for 1983 sagged to a mere 5597 units.

▲ Chrysler showed more budget-conscious product savvy with the 1982 Dodge Rampage and Plymouth Scamp, front-drive L-body coupes stretched into neat half-ton pickups. Both saw few changes for '83. This Rampage 2.2 was the peppiest of the Dodges, yet very affordable at $7255. Unfortunately, sales failed to reach 30,000 through 1984, so the idea had to be dropped.

---

Average new-car stickers reach $10,700, up from $9910 in 1982 and $6950 in '79

Gadgetry available includes Chrysler's "talking" dashboards (which many find annoying), digital speedometers, gas-pressurized shock absorbers

General Motors marks its 75th Anniversary

GM and Toyota agree to build small Toyota-based cars in California in a joint venture

Japan agrees to a fourth consecutive year of import restraints

"Domestic-content" legislation is enacted; it will be a significant factor in the U.S./import battle

Ford and GM fail to meet CAFE (fuel-economy) standards

▲ Ford's Thunderbird became a lot more exciting with its landmark "aero" redesign for 1983. This 142-bhp Turbo Coupe was the hottest of the three models offered. Buyers approved—sales nearly tripled, hitting close to 122,000 units.

▲ The 1983 Thunderbird dramatically signaled Ford Motor Company's turn to clean, low-drag styling. The standard model offered V-6 or V-8 power for $9000-$10,000, but the aluminum wheels shown here cost extra.

▲ After reviving a truly hot GT for '82, Ford made Mustang even more enthusiastic with an aero-look facelift, as displayed on this coupe, plus reborn ragtops. Yet for all that, sales declined some 10,000 units to 120,873.

▲ Ford restyled its Fairmont-based 1981-82 Granada into 1983's new "downsized" LTD, while the full-sizers were renamed LTD Crown Victoria. Sales rose some 35,000 units to 155,758. Here, the Brougham sedan.

▲ Heading Ford's 1983 Escort line was a stronger GT two-door hatchback sedan with 88 horses courtesy of throttle-body electronic fuel injection. Though these and other improvements helped keep Escort at the top of the sales charts, volume nonetheless declined some 70,000 units to 315,370.

▲ The Lincoln Mark VI would say goodbye after this '83 edition. Few changes had occurred since its 1980 redesign, and it remained a virtual twin to the ex-Continental Town Car. Back from '82 was a fuel-injected 302 V-8 with 145 horses, teamed with four-speed automatic transmission.

---

AMC's Renault-based Alliance sedans debut; it's the last year for Spirit and Concord, but the 4WD Eagle will carry on

Chevy's Monte Carlo SS is revived; the final Malibus are built

Convertible versions of the Chevrolet Cavalier and Pontiac 2000 Sunbird are introduced

There are no '83 Corvettes—the all-new models will be '84s

Chrysler adds a front-drive New Yorker; E Class is a stretched K-car; the last Cordobas are built

Dodge's stretched 400 sedan is called 600

The Charger name replaces 024 on subcompact Dodge coupes; Shelby Charger is the hot one

A Fairmont-based LTD joins the Ford lineup; the final Fairmonts are built

▶ Mercury's 1983 Cougar was much like that year's smoothly redesigned 1983 "aero" T-Bird, but lacked the Ford's turbo-four. Neither was there a Cougar XR-7, just base and uplevel LS coupes. Still, sales were almost 500 percent up on '82, jumping to nearly 76,000 units.

▶ The rear roofline was the biggest visual difference between the '83 Cougar and Thunderbird. The cat wore an upright backlight for the more formal look thought to be favored by Mercury buyers. This LS Cougar had a base price of $10,850; the standard model started at $9521. Both used only a new 3.8-liter V-6 with 110 horsepower teamed with a four-speed automatic transmission.

◀ Dearborn introduced new front-drive compacts for '83: Ford Tempo and *(shown here)* Mercury Topaz.

▶ Like Ford's EXP, Mercury's two-seat LN7 "bubbleback" gained a high-output engine for '83, but sales plunged from 35,000 to just 4528.

▲ Still harking back to the "muscle car" genre, 1983's new Hurst/Olds was a top-line Calais with a 180-horsepower 307 V-8, firm chassis, and triple-stick "Lightning Rod" shifter. Some 3000 were sold at $12,069 each.

▲ A fine-sounding new GM/Delco/Bose audio option was one of the few changes in the 1983 Olds Toronado, which still managed nearly 6000 more sales, reaching 39,605. Base price for the lone coupe came in at $15,252.

## 1983 Model Year Production

| | | |
|---|---|---|
| 1. Chevrolet 1,175,200 | 6. Pontiac 318,478 | 11. Chrysler 159,882 |
| 2. Oldsmobile 916,583 | 7. Dodge 304,464 | 12. Lincoln 101,068 |
| 3. Buick 808,416 | 8. Cadillac 292,814 | 13. Avanti 100[1] |
| 4. Ford 783,225 | 9. Plymouth 273,489 | |
| 5. Mercury 359,594 | 10. AMC 168,726 | |

[1]*Estimated*

▲ Plymouth revived the Scamp name from '70s Valiant hardtop days for its new 1983 twin to Dodge's Rampage pickup. But it didn't sell nearly as well, and was dropped after one year and production of only 2129 units.

▲ Pontiac's year-old J2000 line became just 2000 for 1983, and added a neat little convertible in top LE trim (*background*); 626 were built. Other models like the two-door LE (*foreground*) shared its newly standard overhead-cam, 1.8-liter four.

▲ A standard five-speed manual gearbox, new four-speed automatic option, and more engine choices highlighted Pontiac's 1983 Firebirds. Here, the mid-line $10,322 S/E. Tougher competition cut F-Bird sales more than 50 percent to 74,884.

▲ Despite few changes, Pontiac's Grand Prix registered slightly higher 1983 sales of close to 86,000. Of those, only 12 percent were garnered by the top-line Brougham model *(shown here)*; it started at $9781, $1083 over the base coupe.

▲ By 1983, the sporty SJ was a regular Pontiac Phoenix model and delivered 135 horses from an HO 2.8-liter V-6. Sales, though, were minuscule: just 853 of this $8861 coupe and only 172 $8948 four-door hatches. Neither SJ would return for '84.

▲ Pontiac brought its Canadian Chevy Chevette-clone down to the U.S. as the 1981 T1000. For '83 it was just the 1000—and a steadily declining seller: just under 26,000, split between this two-door hatchback and its four-door companion.

▲ The year-old, American Motors-built Renault Alliance returned for 1984 with few changes, but gained "bubble-back" running mates called Encore with three doors (*shown*) or five. Prices again started as low as $5800. Sales remained healthy.

---

Mustang gets its first convertible in a decade, plus a more potent V-8 and a new GT Turbo hatchback

The ninth-generation Ford Thunderbird gains an organic shape; a V-6, V-8, or four-cylinder Turbo Coupe; and the first manual transmission since 1957

Mercury Capri adopts a "bubble-back" rear window; the new Marquis is equivalent to Ford's LTD; the full-sizer is now known as Grand Marquis

A 15th Anniversary Hurst/Olds version of Oldsmobile's Cutlass Supreme goes on sale

The little Plymouth TC3 coupe is renamed Turismo; Gran Fury offers its last Slant Six

Pontiac's 6000 STE targets enthusiast drivers

Big Pontiacs, badged Parisienne, make a comeback

◀▲ Avanti updates continued for 1984 under the new Steve Blake regime. Most came from the previous year's Thirtieth Anniversary model. Evident here are newly available body-color bumpers, custom lacy-spoke wheels, and a handsome two-tone interior with multi-adjustable Recaro front seats. Sticker prices now started at $31,860. Avanti built 287 cars for the model run.

▲ Buick gave its 1984 Skyhawk J-car a turbo four-cylinder engine, but only in the sporty T-Type two-door. Wagons like this top-trim Limited sold poorly: just 5285 for the model year.

▲ A thin-bar grille was one of the few changes in Buick's Riviera for '84. The $25,832 convertible returned with a cloth headliner, but only 500 were sold that season.

▲ After a year's absence, Buick's Regal Grand National returned as this mean "Darth Vader" hot rod with 200 turbocharged horses from a 3.8 V-6. Only about 2000 of the '84s were built.

◀ Cadillac revived a drop-top Eldorado for 1984 and promptly angered those who had bought "last convertible" '76s for outrageous sums. The new Biarritz was hardly cheap at $31,286, though that partly reflected its being an outside conversion, not a "factory" job. The one and only drivetrain comprised Cadillac's year-old 4.1-liter, aluminum-block V-8 teamed with four-speed Turbo Hydra-Matic. Model-year sales were predictably limited at just 3300 units.

**1984**

Sportiness, power, and styling tempt '84 car shoppers

Domestic model-year output leaps to 8,147,849 cars (including foreign automakers with U.S. plants)

Of the 10,393,230 cars sold in the U.S., more than 76 percent are domestically built; imports actually have declined a bit

GM chairman Roger Smith begins a massive reorganization to restore each division to specific ranking in price/prestige—Buick-Oldsmobile-Cadillac form one group, Chevrolet-Pontiac-GM of Canada another

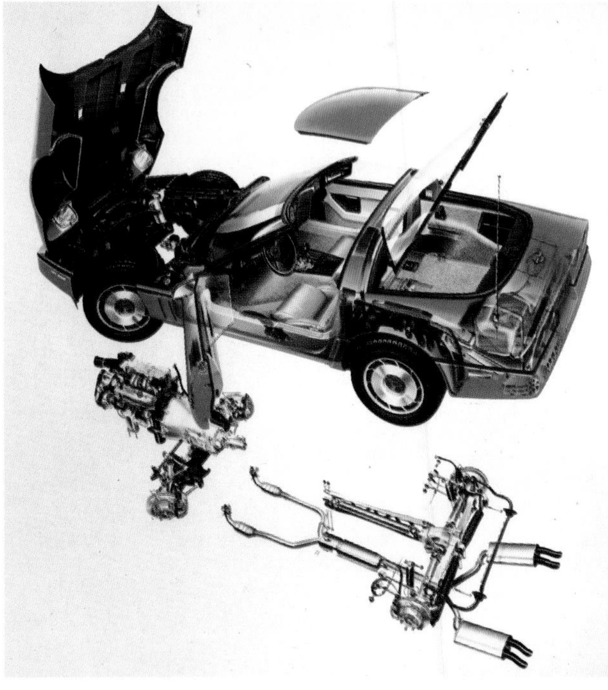

▲ The first new Chevrolet Corvette in 15 years popped up in early '83 as a *1984* model. Lighter, smaller, and much cleaner than the old "shark," it arrived at $21,800—up a cool $3510—with a 205-horse 350 V-8 and manual or automatic transmission. Sales zoomed to 51,547.

◄▲ Good ideas in the '84 Corvette (*left*) included an easy-access clamshell hood, practical lift-up "glassback," one-piece targa top, a more sophisticated all-independent suspension, and a stiff, Lotus-like backbone frame. Body panels were again made of fiberglass, but were hung on a strong new "birdcage" inner structure. Styling (*above*) was recognizably Corvette, but was less histrionic and more aerodynamically efficient. Zero-60 mph took about seven seconds.

▲ With safety and service recalls mounting, GM X-cars were little-changed for '84, though Chevy's Citation tacked on a Roman "II." This is the sporty V-6 X-11 three-door. Total output slid to 97,202 units.

▲ Chevrolet's 1984 Camaro Z28 gained a more potent four-barrel 305 V-8 with 150 horsepower, a reply to Ford's Mustang GT. Total Camaro sales boomed to more than 261,000 units, of which 100,416 were Z28s.

▲ Chrysler's 1984 convertible K-cars gained rear side windows and went from plastic to glass backlights. This Town & Country ragtop again topped Chrysler's LeBaron models, with a base price of $16,495.

---

Cadillac has a convertible again, its first since '76: Eldorado is the costliest U.S. ragtop ever, and lasts only two seasons

The sixth-generation Corvette has a lift-up hatch; a "Cross-Fire" V-8 and new "4+3 overdrive" manual gearbox may be ordered

The compact front-drive Ford Tempo replaces Fairmont; Mercury markets a Topaz cousin

Lincoln introduces the Mark VII premium coupe, derived from Ford's Thunderbird; LSC is the performance-oriented edition

The plastic-bodied, mid-engined Pontiac Fiero two-seater debuts

Chrysler launches its popular front-drive minivans: Dodge Caravan and Plymouth Voyager

The final Oldsmobile Omega and Pontiac Phoenix X-cars are built; Citation and Skylark continue

▲ Replacing Cordoba in the '84 Chrysler line was the smaller—but much-sportier—front-drive Laser, the firm's latest K-car spinoff. Sold only as a hatchback coupe, it came in base and luxury XE guises, priced from $8648.

▲ Ready to set the market afire in 1984 was Chrysler Corporation's new T-115 "minivan." Dodge sold it as the Caravan, here in top LE guise with woody-look side trim. Sales were high from day one, and a new market was born.

◀ Chrysler's charismatic chairman Lee Iacocca gave his firm's new 1984 minivans a personal sendoff at a November 1983 Detroit press preview. One exec had trouble opening the sliding right-side door on the Dodge Caravan display model, a portent of many little problems that would plague early production units. Yet even that didn't dampen demand for these practical front-drive people haulers cannily based on the compact K-car platform. Within a year of launch, Chrysler had moved no fewer than 193,000 of them.

▲ Dodge 400s became 600s for 1984, but retained the standard K-car platform with few changes. Ragtop volume rose to 10,960, including a few thousand hot Turbo ES models. The base model started at $10,595.

▲ Having "Shelbyized" the Charger coupe, Carroll Shelby pumped up Dodge's sheepish Omni sedan into a 110-horse wolf for 1984. Called GLH, for "Goes Like Hell," the underrated $7350 bargain found just 3285 buyers.

▲ The Shelby Charger itself was back for 1984 without much change. Production eased to 7552 from the previous year's 8251. Base sticker price was up to $8541. Basic colors were still contrasting blue or silver.

---

The last rear-drive Buick Electras and Oldsmobile Ninety-Eights are produced

Ford and GM again fail to meet the CAFE standard; both apply for relief, but Chrysler's cars do meet federal requirements

U.S. Secretary of Transportation Elizabeth Dole orders a phase-in of passive restraints, starting with 10 percent of '87 cars

Six Chrysler models are available with a turbocharger; GM offers four, Ford 10

Front-drive models account for 40 percent of Ford sales, half of GM's, and a whopping 87 percent for Chrysler

GM begins importation of the small, Japanese-built Sprint and Spectrum

▲ The Series IV Excalibur was still underpowered in 1984, very expensive at close to $60,000, and thus predictably exclusive: fewer than 200 built. Pictured here is the four-seat Phaeton with a bolt-on top. It weighed 4500 pounds.

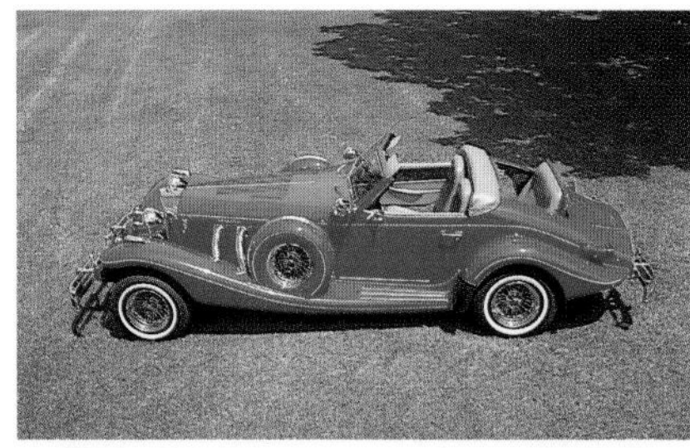

▲ Despite unhappy timing and being emissions-limited to a Chevrolet 305-cid V-8 with 155 bhp, Series IV Excaliburs were undeniably glamorous, especially when ordered as the swoopy rumble-seat Roadster. They rode a 125-inch wheelbase.

▲ Appearing in late 1984 as '85 models were new Twentieth Anniversary Signature Series Excaliburs. The run consisted of 50 Phaetons (*shown*) and 50 Roadsters with two-tone exteriors, lavish interiors, and other unique touches.

◄▲ Among 1984 Ford Mustangs was the new turbocharged, 175-horse four-cylinder SVO (*left*) and a 20th Anniversary V-8 special called GT-350 (*above*)—the latter really a paint-and-tape job whose name irked Carroll Shelby. SVO aimed at Europhiles, but didn't make many converts with just 4508 sales. One reason was a steep base price of $15,596. A GT V-8 was far cheaper.

▲ Ford's new 1984 LTD LX targeted the "Eurosedan" market as a "four-door Mustang GT" with the same chassis and 165-horse 302 V-8. Alas, only 3260 were sold before the model was axed after the 1985 season.

▲ A more-popular '84 Ford LTD was the $9980 Brougham four-door, shown with the newly optional pseudo-convertible roof. A V-8 wasn't available here, so most of these were ordered with the 3.8-liter V-6.

▲ Released in the spring of 1983, the front-wheel-drive Tempo replaced the rear-drive Fairmont as Ford's compact with the start of the formal '84 model year. This top-trim GLX coupe sold for $7621.

### 1984 Model Year Production

1. Chevrolet ........ 1,655,151
2. Ford ........ 1,180,708
3. Oldsmobile ........ 1,144,225
4. Buick ........ 987,980
5. Pontiac ........ 594,821
6. Mercury ........ 475,381
7. Dodge ........ 442,527
8. Chrysler ........ 375,853
9. Plymouth ........ 357,764
10. Cadillac ........ 300,300
11. AMC ........ 208,624
12. Lincoln ........ 157,434
13. Avanti ........ 287

▲ Reflecting Ford's newfound fondness for "aero" design was 1984's startling new Lincoln Mark VII coupe, derived from the latest Thunderbird. This $21,707 standard version was one of four models offered.

▲ First-year Mark VII sales were 33,344, up almost 3000 over the '83 Mark VI. Surprisingly popular was this new $23,706 LSC (Luxury Sport Coupe) with firmer suspension, blackwall tires, and other "more European" features.

▲ The XR-7 returned to the Mercury Cougar fold for '84 as a twin to the four-cylinder T-Bird Turbo Coupe. Shown here is the luxury-minded LS model, which started at $11,265.

▲ Mercury's 1984 Mustang clone, the Capri, kept its new-for-'83 "bubble-back" look, but reduced its models to the $7758 GS (*shown*), the $9638 RS, and the $9822 RS Turbo.

▲ Like Tempo at Ford, the front-drive Topaz was Mercury's sole compact offering at the formal start of the 1984 model year. Pictured is the uplevel LS coupe, priced at $7880.

▲ Keeping a great tradition alive, the Hurst/Olds returned from its '83 revival in much the same form for 1984. A special 180-horse 307 V-8 was again linked with the triple-stick Hurst "Lightning Rod" shifter controlling a four-speed automatic. Sales totaled 3500 at a $12,644 base price.

▲ A mild facelift with a more prominent front bumper highlighted the 1984 changes to Oldsmobile's year-old Firenza J-car line, but sales were not impressive for the class at 82,475. Also new was this sporty "Euro-style" ES, a $400 option package for both the base and LX four-door notchbacks.

---

Gadgets continue to proliferate, including video radio and climate controls, LCD displays, inflatable seat cushions

Half of '84 price hikes are attributed to federal requirements

The average transaction for a domestically built new car now comes to $11,170

Sticker prices range from $4997 for an economy Chevette to $31,286 for Cadillac's Biarritz convertible

The Corvette and Mustang SVO adopt directional Goodyear tires

Mini-spare tires are now standard, but full-size spares are generally available on special order

J. Michael Losh becomes general manager of Pontiac; William Hoglund departs to take over the new Saturn Division

▲ Plymouth dealers sold Chrysler's new 1984 front-drive T-115 minivan under the Voyager label formerly used on full-size, rear-drive vans. Apart from the name and grille, everything was the same as for corresponding Dodge Caravans—including prices.

▲ The 1984 Plymouth Reliant, like its Dodge Aries double, got a reshaped nose with a big Pentastar grille emblem, plus a more modern dash with round gauges. Reliant was now Chrysler's top-selling model, and 152,138 were built for 1984.

▲ A new nose and optional 150-horse turbo four-cylinder made news for Pontiac's 1984 J-cars, which were retitled 2000 Sunbird. This turbo SE hatch coupe was the official car for that year's Pikes Peak Hill Climb and sold for some $10,000.

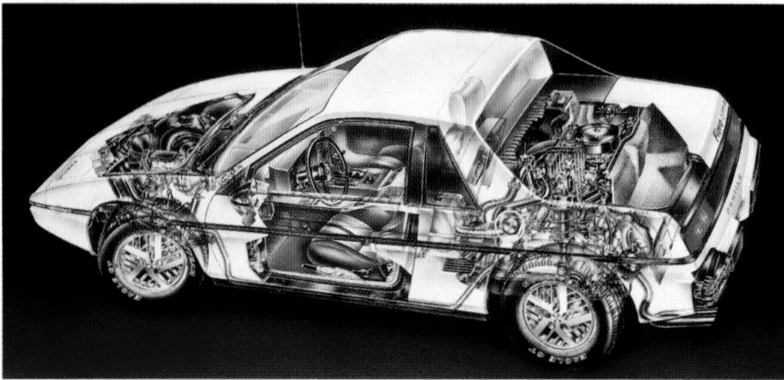

▲▶ Vying with Chevy's Corvette as 1984's most exciting new Detroit offering was the Pontiac Fiero "2M4"—a two-seat, mid-engine, four-cylinder coupe with X-car components driving the rear wheels and Chevette parts up front. Plastic outer body panels clothed a "driveable space frame." The sole engine was a 2.5-liter, 92-horse four, but this was supposed to be a thrifty "commuter" runabout, not a sports car. Still, at $8000 and up, Fiero was an instant hit, with sales approaching 137,000.

▲ Relaunched for '83 under the name Parisienne, the full-size B-body Pontiac continued into 1984 as a near duplicate of the Chevy Caprice. This uplevel $10,281 Brougham sedan attracted 25,212 big-car buyers.

▲ The first AMC-built convertible since 1968 bowed as a new Renault Alliance model for '85, when a larger 1.7-liter engine became optional. The line's mainstay, however, was this DL four-door. It started at $7250.

▲ The hatchback Renault Encore shared the 1985 Alliance's new 77-horse 1.7 engine option, plus other minor changes. This top-line LS five-door sold from $7310, a bit less than the Alliance Limited.

---

The hatchback AMC Encore debuts; only the 4WD Eagle remains as an actual AMC product, but its smaller versions are dropped due to slow sales

A turbo four is available for Chryslers; the rear-drive model is now called Fifth Avenue

Dodge puts a 600 badge on the coupe and convertible; a turbocharged four is offered for the new Daytona sport coupe, in the Turbo Z (Chrysler's Laser similar)

Mustang's new SVO features a turbo/intercooled engine and all-disc brakes

Turbocharged fours are now available in Ford EXP, Mercury Cougar XR-7, and Pontiac 2000 Sunbird

A 5.2-liter V-8 is the sole engine for the Dodge Diplomat/Plymouth Gran Fury

Pontiac's 6000 is now a best-seller; a wagon is available this year

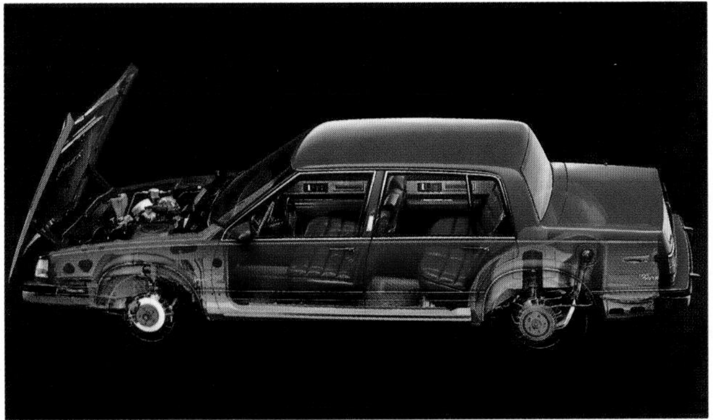

▲ The first front-drive Buick Electra bowed for 1985 as one of GM's newly downsized C-body models. A front-hinged hood was unique to the Buick, though. Power was furnished by gasoline V-6s of 3.0 and 3.8 liters, or by a 4.3-liter diesel. Interiors were quite spacious.

▲ As before, the 1985 Electra line listed coupes and sedans, but trim levels now comprised base, the ritzy Park Avenue (*shown*), and—surprisingly—a sporty T-Type with a handling package and blacked-out exterior trim. Park Avenue soon came to dominate line sales.

▲ Buick unveiled its next-generation compact for 1985 as the Somerset Regal coupe, one of three new GM N-body models. This is the lower-level Custom, priced at $8857.

▲ Estate Wagons aside, traditional big-Buick buyers had but one choice for '85: the rear-drive B-body LeSabre. The $11,751 Limited coupe is shown. It attracted 22,211 buyers.

▲ With sales falling in the wake of many publicized recalls, Buick reduced Skylark X-cars to a pair of four-doors for 1985. Pictured is the upper-level $8283 Limited model.

▲ Few changes attended the 1985 Cadillac Seville, which was about to be downsized again—and more conventionally restyled. As before, engines comprised a pair of V-8s: a 4.1-liter gas and a 5.7 Olds diesel; the former was greatly preferred for reliability. Total sales were about the same as in '84: 39,755 units.

▲ Cadillac's bread-and-butter de Villes and their ritzier Fleetwood models were again downsized for 1985, and they switched to front-wheel drive. Critics applauded, but sales dropped some 18,000, to 141,000. Higher prices hurt. This Sedan de Ville, for instance, sold for $18,571, up $950 from the '84 version.

---

**1985**

Horsepower is going up, continuing a trend that began in '83

Dealers are delighted by record sales—of both imported and domestic automobiles

Inflation is down, but sales incentives are extensive

Domestic output totals 7,817,419 cars for the model year

Of 11,045,784 cars sold in the U.S., 8,204,721 are domestically built

Chrysler launches the H-body Lancer and LeBaron GTS; GM issues the big front-drive C-body and compact N-body

The CAFE standard peaks at 27.5 mpg; in September, NHTSA approves a 1.5-mpg cutback for 1986, pleasing Detroit

▲ Still a capable compact—but with a very tarnished image—Chevy's Citation II would vanish after 1985 and a final 62,722 orders. This is the $7200 V-6 three-door with that year's sporty $941 X-11 package.

▲ After topping Detroit's 1984 sales chart, Chevy's 101.2-inch-wheelbase Cavalier offered a zesty new Z24 option for 1985. It ran with a 125-horse, port-injected V-6, as on this "fasthatch" coupe.

▲ Switching from "Cross Fire" to "Tuned Port Injection" added 25 horsepower, giving the '85 Chevy Corvettes 230 horses in all. Base price was up to $24,873, which may be why sales slipped to 39,729 units.

▲ When Camaro became the car of choice for the International Race of Champions, Chevy celebrated with this new IROC-Z for 1985. Packing up to 190 horses, it was base-priced at $11,739 and found 21,177 buyers.

▲ Chevy's mid-size Celebrity returned for 1985 with an optional 2.8-liter V-6 switched from carburetor to port fuel injection. Also back was the Eurosport option package, offering firm suspension, blackout trim, and other goodies—all for $199. The V-6 sold separately for an extra $250.

▲ Chrysler's old rear-drive LeBaron was still around for '85 as a posh Fifth Avenue, with its 318 V-8 newly bumped to 140 horses. Even at $12,865 (and despite its Plymouth Volaré heritage), sales were the best yet: 109,971.

▲ Another K-car spinoff bowed for '85, the H-body Chrysler LeBaron GTS. This roomy, faintly "Euro-style" four-door hatch started at $9024; 60,783 were built.

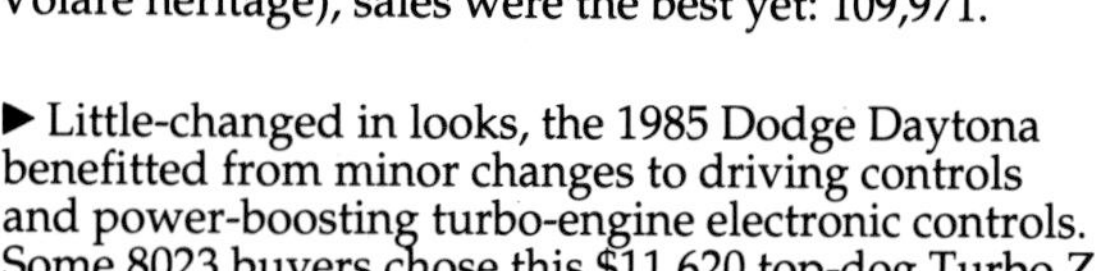

► Little-changed in looks, the 1985 Dodge Daytona benefitted from minor changes to driving controls and power-boosting turbo-engine electronic controls. Some 8023 buyers chose this $11,620 top-dog Turbo Z.

---

Ford sells 7400 special-order Tempo/Topaz models with driver-side air bags to government and insurance fleets

It's the last year for ill-fated GM X-cars and diesel engines

The Saturn company is formed as a wholly owned GM subsidiary

Volkswagen drops the Rabbit, but produces a new Golf in the U.S.

Lincoln-Mercury dealers can sell the German-built Merkur

Ford debuts its Aerostar minivan

The first Chevrolet Novas emerge from the GM/Toyota joint venture plant in California

The Big Three diversify, acquiring non-automotive subsidiaries

AMC's Alliance adds a convertible and a larger optional engine

▲ Back for '85 as Dodge's top 600 model, the ES Turbo convertible offered ample (if crude) go-power for $13,995, but was again a tough sell: just 5621 orders were taken.

▲ Dodge sold a slightly different version of the new '85 Chrysler H-body and revived the Lancer name for it. This sportier, uplevel ES model was priced at $9690.

▲ The hot-selling Dodge Caravan moved into 1985 with "convert-a-bed" rear seats and an overhead console among new optional features. Here, the mid-line SE model.

◀ Excalibur was struggling for survival by 1985—so much so that it would be forced into bankruptcy the following year. The problem was basically low performance versus high price—still around $60,000—plus a "boutique" car market besieged by fiercer competition and the cost of meeting new federal standards for things like "passive restraints." But though sales were down to a trickle, Excalibur Series IVs, like this Phaeton, remained cars of impeccable high quality—and even greater rarity.

▲ After scoring 173,489 sales for '84, Ford's big LTD Crown Victoria—one of the few big Detroit cars left—upped the ante to 185,437 for '85. This $11,627 coupe weighed 3552 pounds and rode a 114.3-inch wheelbase.

▲ Ford's 1985 Thunderbirds wore a slightly different grille, bigger "boots," and new instrumentation. Sales dipped to 151,851 units. This performance-oriented Turbo Coupe now stickered at $13,365.

▲ An air-to-air intercooler boosted Ford's 1985 Mustang SVO to 205 horses, but did nothing for sales, which dropped more than 50 percent to 1954 units—despite a base price that had been reduced to $14,251. Ponycar buyers wanted V-8s.

---

A downsized front-drive Buick Electra debuts; it's the last appearance for the Riviera ragtop

The Regal Grand National coupe is Buick's last gasp at high-performance in the old style

Cadillac de Ville is sharply downsized, adopts front-drive

A Chevrolet-built V-6 is offered in the Cadillac Cimarron to squelch criticism of its underpowered four

Full-size, rear-drive Chevrolets are selling well as Buick and Olds abandon that market

An IROC-Z package with a high-output V-8 becomes available for the Chevrolet Camaro Z28

The new LeBaron GTS serves as Chrysler's premium sedan

Dodge Lancer takes the place of the 600 ES sport sedan

▲ Production of the Lincoln Mark VII also dropped by half for '85, settling at 18,355. Anti-lock brakes were a significant new option. This sporty LSC version listed at $24,332.

▲ Like its cousin Ford LTD Crown Victoria, the big Mercury Grand Marquis still fared quite well in 1985, racking up some 161,258 sales. Here, the upper-level $12,789 LS coupe.

▲ A new dash and minor trim changes carried Mercury's Cougar through 1985, with demand reduced slightly to 117,274 units. This top-line turbocharged XR-7 sold for $13,599.

▲ Despite many 1985 enhancements, Mercury's Capri languished with just 18,657 total sales. This sporty RS hatchback included the 5.0L V-8 in its $10,223 base price.

▲ Adding spice—and perhaps a bit of confusion—to Oldsmobile's 1985 Cutlass Ciera lineup was a new "aero-skirt" GT package for both the coupe and sedan (*shown*). It was a bit more aggressive than the still-available sporty ES option.

▲ Oldsmobile's C-body Ninety-Eight was downsized again for 1985 and—like its Buick and Cadillac sisters—switched to front-wheel drive. Most were built with the 3.8-liter gas V-6. Sales soared more than 100 percent, to 169,432 units.

▲ Like Buick's LeSabre versus Electra, the rear-drive '85 Olds Delta 88 offered more metal for the money than the new front-drive Ninety-Eight. Sales remained strong at nearly 242,000 units. This is the $11,062 Royale Brougham LS sedan.

### 1985 Model Year Production

| | |
|---|---|
| 1. Chevrolet | 1,418,098 |
| 2. Oldsmobile | 1,165,649 |
| 3. Ford | 1,149,427 |
| 4. Buick | 1,002,906 |
| 5. Pontiac | 519,390 |
| 6. Dodge | 500,835 |
| 7. Chrysler | 420,780 |
| 8. Mercury | 419,869 |
| 9. Plymouth | 393,711 |
| 10. Cadillac | 384,840 |
| 11. Lincoln | 166,486 |
| 12. AMC | 150,189 |

▲ Plymouth's Voyager followed the Dodge Caravan in making minimal changes for 1985—no surprise, given the roaring demand that had buyers waiting up to six months for one of Chrysler's minivans. Here, the top-of-the-line woody-look Voyager LE.

▲ Pontiac's Grand Am would prove to be the most consistently popular GM front-drive N-body compact. Like the others, it bowed for '85 in base and uplevel coupe models, but offered extra sportiness via the proper options.

▶ Heading Pontiac's 1985 Fiero line was this new "aero-look" GT with a 130-horse 2.8 V-6 and an $11,795 sticker. Some 22,534 were called for.

▲ Pontiac's 1985 Grand Prix shed the never-loved (and troublesome) diesel V-8 option, but gained standard radial tires. Sales slipped once again, now to just under 60,000.

▶ Still fighting a horde of Japanese small cars, the AMC-built 1986 Renault Alliance sported a new face and tail-lamps, plus a 50-month/50,000-mile powertrain warranty. Sales of L and DL ragtops totaled just 2015 units.

---

Lincoln's Town Car gets an aero facelift; LSC gets Mustang GT's V-8; anti-lock braking is available

The Olds Ninety-Eight gets a new C-body, as does Buick Electra

A 4-4-2 option with a 180-bhp V-8 is revived for the Oldsmobile Cutlass Salon/Supreme

Plymouth introduces the Caravelle

The new N-body Pontiac Grand Am compact is derived from the J-car; Fiero gains a spoilered GT edition and V-6 option

The Avanti company gets another new owner—Michael Kelly

Experimental vehicles include the mid-engined Buick Wildcat, Ford T2208 (with satellite communications system) and Probe V, and Cadillac Cimarron convertible

▲ Buick's Riviera was again downsized for 1986—and plunged 70 percent in sales. The ragtop was gone, leaving a $19,831 base coupe and this sportier $21,577 T-Type edition.

▲ With "aero" styling in vogue, the 1986 Buick Century's new undercut nose looked a bit odd. Sporty V-6 T-Types were down to this four-door sedan; buyers ordered only 5126.

▲ Coil-less ignition and optional anti-lock brakes improved C-body 1986 Buicks. The Electra T-Type coupe was gone, leaving this four-door to snatch only 5816 sales.

▲ Trying hard to woo upscale import buyers, Cadillac conjured up this new 1986 de Ville Touring Sedan (and a Coupe). They featured a handling suspension and slightly less gingerbread.

▲ The return of Chevy's Corvette convertible symbolized a growing renaissance in Detroit style and performance. This 'Vette paced the 1986 Indianapolis 500 race; 7315 replicas were offered for sale. Base price was $32,032.

▲ Chevy's Camaro kept IROC-ing along with an upgraded base model, but no more power for the Z28. The IROC-Z cost $12,561 in 1986, a good bargain for the "goers-and-showers." Following a one-year sales dip, total demand for Camaros recovered to a healthy 192,128 units, 49,585 of them IROCs.

**1986**

Imported-car sales rise; after a several-year slackening, they now hold 28.3 percent of the total

Domestic model-year output tops 7.8 million cars (including foreign automakers with U.S. plants)

Of the record-setting 11,463,241 new cars sold in the U.S., 8,214,662 are domestically built

Ford earns a record $3.3 billion profit—its earnings top GM's for the first time since 1924

The average transaction for a new domestic car is $12,530

The government decrees that all '86 cars must have a high, center-mounted stoplight

Ford launches the mid-size Taurus (and similar Mercury Sable); a four-cylinder engine is available, but most get a 3.0-liter V-6

▲ Chevrolet began pursuing police business in a big way with a special 9C1 package for the big 1986 Caprice sedan. Along with a heavy-duty chassis, this model included just about everything except the "gumball" roof lights.

▲ A new LS luxury-liner capped the 1986 Chevy Monte Carlo line. Bearing a smoother new nose, it was base-priced at $10,421 with the standard 4.3 V-6. Overall Monte sales remained static at about 119,000.

▲ Chevy debuted a slicker Monte Carlo SS for 1986—the Aerocoupe. It was designed mainly for higher top speed on NASCAR supertracks. Because of this focus, only 200, priced at $14,191, were built for public sale.

▲ Washington's newly required high-mount third stoplamp is evident on this 1986 Chevrolet Cavalier Z24 hatch coupe, which again featured a sport suspension and lively 2.8-liter V-6. Base price was a low $9068.

▲ Chrysler's 1986 LeBarons got a new nose and a new engine option: a bored-out 2.5-liter version of the 2.2 "Trans-4." This top-line Town & Country ragtop in Mark Cross trim was one of just 501 examples built for the year.

▲ Recalling the legendary Letter-Series Chrysler 300s, Dodge adopted "gunsight" grilles for most of its 1986 models. This 600 convertible sold 11,678 copies at $11,695 each; a hotter ES turbo ragtop found 4759 buyers.

---

GM's all-new Riviera, Toronado, and Eldorado/Seville average 18 inches shorter; not everyone takes to the sheared-off look

Buick LeSabre and Oldsmobile Eighty-Eight follow big-brother Electra/Ninety-Eight, downsizing to a front-drive V-6

Buick and Olds have no more rear-drive models, except big wagons

The final Ford LTD and Mercury Marquis sedans go on sale

The CAFE standard drops to 26 mpg, helping Detroit meet rising demand for full-size cars, attributed to lower gasoline prices

A driver-side air bag is now optional in Ford Tempo/Mercury Topaz sedans sold to the public—11,000 are installed this year

Chrysler adds a 2.5-liter, four-cylinder engine—the first domestic motor with counter-balance shafts

▲ The hoary old Dodge Diplomat—born for 1976 as the Dodge Aspen—was still hanging around in 1986, mainly for taxi and police fleets. Orders totaled 26,953. As before, a 140-bhp 318 V-8 was standard.

▲ Chrysler's new 2.5-liter four-cylinder engine was optional in the base '86 Dodge Daytona (*shown*), but the real news was the "C/S" handling option for the Turbo Z, named in honor of Carroll Shelby.

▲ Back for a last stand in 1986, the Dodge Omni GLH (Goes Like Hell) was little-changed save sales, which fell from 6513 to 3629. One reason: that year's new and even hotter turbo-powered Shelby GLH-S.

◀▲ Widely previewed throughout 1985, the smooth, all-new '86 Ford Taurus not only replaced the dated Fairmont-based "little" LTD, but proved a much better seller at over 236,000 for its nine-month model year. Offering front drive, three trim levels, sedan (*above*) and wagon (*left*) body styles, and a host of sensible features, Taurus fast became a symbol of Detroit's new "can-do" attitude and ability to compete against even high-buck imports. Base prices were in the $10,000-$14,000 range.

---

All Ford 5.0-liter V-8s adopt sequential fuel injection

Donald Petersen is named chairman of Ford Motor Company

General Motors buys Group Lotus—not only for the British sports car, but for the company's high-tech innovations

GM ousts H. Ross Perot from its board of directors, paying him $700 million

The last AMC Encores are offered; sales of the Renault-based models have been tumbling fast

Anti-lock braking is offered for bigger Buicks; the Regal T-Type and Grand National V-6 hit 235 bhp via an air-to-air intercooler

Cadillac Fleetwood Brougham borrows a 307-cid V-8 from Olds; it is Caddy's last rear-drive model

▲ Florida was just one of many states that turned to Ford Mustangs (and Chevy Camaros) for highway patrol duty in the mid-to-late Eighties—enticed by special factory police options with extra power for catching the bad guys.

▲ After a mid-1985 redo featuring an upsized 1.9-liter engine, the Ford Escort returned for '86 with this uniquely styled GT three-door hatch at the top of the line. Boasting 108 port-injected horses, it listed at $8112.

▲ Though little-changed outside, the '86 Lincoln Mark VII offered other worthwhile improvements, including standard anti-lock brakes and a new high-compression 302 V-8 that booted LSC horses to an even 200. Unit sales improved slightly to 20,056 units. This base model carried a "Monroney" window sticker price of $22,399.

▲ Despite a sales uptick to 20,869 units, Mercury decided to can its Mustang-clone Capri after 1986, when this RS 5.0 was boosted to an even 200 horsepower via multi-port fuel injection, tuned manifolds, and roller valve lifters. Perhaps destined to be a collector car, the '86 RS was base-priced at $10,950.

◀ Sable replaced the smaller Marquis in Mercury's '86 line, but sold far better by attracting nearly 96,000 buyers. Developed with Ford's Taurus in a $2 billion program, the new front-drive middleweight Merc offered similarly smooth, low-drag styling, plus a standard 3.0 V-6 (2.5-liter I-4 on the base GS sedan) and other extras for only a few dollars more. Here, the uplevel $13,068 LS station wagon.

## 1986 Model Year Production

|  |  |  |
|---|---|---|
| 1. | Chevrolet | 1,368,837 |
| 2. | Ford | 1,253,525 |
| 3. | Oldsmobile | 1,050,832 |
| 4. | Buick | 850,103 |
| 5. | Pontiac | 799,461 |
| 6. | Dodge | 450,365 |
| 7. | Mercury | 399,240 |
| 8. | Chrysler | 367,898 |
| 9. | Plymouth | 350,573 |
| 10. | Cadillac | 281,683 |
| 11. | Lincoln | 156,839 |
| 12. | AMC | 64,873 |

▲ A distinctive "light bar" grille (that didn't actually light up until 1989) made the '86 Sable unmistakable—and launched a new Mercury design signature. This upper-level '86 LS sedan started at $12,574.

▲ Like Buick's LeSabre, the Olds Delta 88 was newly downsized for 1986, offering only coupes and sedans. Both body styles came in Royale or plusher Royale Brougham trim. This $13,461 Brougham coupe weighed 3170 pounds.

▲ Heading Pontiac's reshuffled 1986 Sunbird line were new GT models with a 150-horse turbo-four and semi-hidden headlamps. This ragtop garnered only 1268 sales.

▲ An even rarer '86 Pontiac was this NASCAR-inspired "bubbleback" Grand Prix, which revived its 2+2 name from the '60s. Just 200 were sold at $18,214, with an HO 305 V-8.

▲ Plymouth's 1986 L-body hatchback coupe retained the Turismo name used since '83, and unchanged looks from an '84 facelift. This one wears the trim option that revived the (Valiant) Duster name for '85, and included bodyside pinstriping.

▲ Renault sold AMC to Chrysler in 1987 after trying this sporty new GTA two-door coupe (and convertible) as last-ditch sales boosters for the Alliance line. Alas, AMC's final tally was just 41,500 cars, including 5203 four-wheel-drive Eagle wagons.

▲ Florida's Zimmer Motor Cars turned stretched Pontiac Fiero GTs into the Quicksilver, a $52,000 "neo-modern" exoticar of dubious aesthetic merit. It ended up being just another flash in the pan, with fewer than 1300 sales in 1986-87.

---

Mid-year adds an SS "Aerocoupe" to Chevrolet's Monte Carlo line; Cavalier Z24 debuts with a V-6

Bosch anti-lock braking is standard in Corvettes; a convertible arrives at mid-season; a resistance-coded anti-theft system is new

The final Chrysler Lasers are built; Dodge Daytona carries on with a C/S (Carroll Shelby) handling package now available

Dodge sells its last convertibles

Mercury Sable features a unique "light bar" front end

Mercury abandons the Mustang-based Capri after this year

Anti-lock braking is standard in Lincolns; LSC now has a port-injected V-8 rated at 200 bhp, plus all-disc brakes

A restyled Pontiac Fiero arrives

▲ A new marketing tack spelled the end of Buick's "modern muscle" GNX after 1987, when 547 were built. But these were the hottest of all, with 276 horses and blinding 4.7-second 0-60-mph ability. Base price was near $30,000, but high demand pushed prices much higher.

▲ Buick's turn to a "Premium American Motorcars" image left no place for the hot rod GNX after 1987, one reason for its swift demise. Still, low production and ultra high performance almost guarantee collector-car status for all 1985-87 Regal Grand Nationals.

▲ Flush "composite" headlamps and optional anti-lock brakes made big news for the 1987 Buick LeSabres. Still, this bucks-up $14,918 Limited coupe managed just 7741 sales.

▲ Buick's '87 Skyhawk offered more power and this hidden-headlamp Sport Package, but sales dropped more than 40 percent to 6,667 units. Here, the potent Turbo hatch coupe.

▲ An extra 10 horses and detail improvements couldn't keep Buick's 1987 Riviera, here a $22,181 T-Type, from skidding to record-low sales of just 15,223 units.

▲ Built by Italy's renowned Pininfarina on a shortened Eldorado chassis, the new two-seat 1987 Allanté was Cadillac's answer to the high-dollar Mercedes SL convertible. A fortified 4.1-liter V-8 sent 170 horses to the front wheels through a four-speed transaxle. Rich appointments, two tops, and power everything were included for $54,700, but sales would never really get going as Cadillac had hoped. The '87 tally, for example, was a mere 3363.

▲ Allanté wore Pininfarina badges, but was largely GM's own styling job—and quite nice, if Cadillac-style conservative. Recalling the Sixties, taillamps hid behind white lenses by day (*above left*) and glowed red by night or with the brakes applied (*above right*). The trunklid emblem doubled as a high-mount center stoplamp, per government decree—thus looking much better than the tacked-on affairs of many other 1987 cars.

---

**1987**

The finale for AMC, both cars and company—Chrysler takes over in August, lured by Jeep, which will become Jeep-Eagle division

A sleek hidden-headlamp Chrysler LeBaron coupe and convertible make their debut

Shadow is Dodge's latest small-car entry; the Plymouth Sundance differs only in detail

The Corsica sedan and Beretta coupe arrive during the year as Chevy's latest compacts; Camaro gets its first convertible in 18 years, plus a Corvette engine option

The first front-drive Pontiac Bonneville appears

Cadillac's costly Allanté two-seat convertible debuts, with a Pininfarina-built body

Model-year production from U.S. plants nears 7.4 million cars (down 6.5 percent)

▲ Chevy's Cavalier added a sporty RS convertible for 1986, then refined its powerteams for '87. The ragtop sold about 5800 units each year. This '87 model started at $13,446 with a base 2.0-liter four.

▲ Beretta bowed for 1987 as one of Chevy's exclusive new L-body models—a close relative to the Corsica sedan. In a quest to check quality control, almost all of the 8072 built for '87 went to rent-a-car companies.

▲ The first open-air Camaros since 1969 brightened the Chevy lineup in a big way in mid-1987. But at around $15,000 to $18,000 base, sales were small: just 263 base models and only 744 Z28 and IROC-Z versions.

▲ Built just for California in 1987 was a revived Chevy Camaro RS, a Z28 pretender packing (for insurance purposes) a mild V-6. Air dam, rocker skirts, and big color-keyed wheels were included for $12,411.

▲ Roller valve lifters added 10 horses to give the '87 Chevrolet Corvette 240 in all. Otherwise, few changes occurred. Ragtop sales rose to 10,625, while the coupe eased downward to 20,007 units.

▲ Chevy took its Celebrity to a new level with the boisterous 1987 Eurosport VR, a $3550 "aero" package. Some 5000 were to be built (though only 1623 were) in monotone white, red, black, or silver.

▲ The pending demise of Chevy's rear-drive Monte Carlo implied the same for sister El Camino. And so it was, only the car/pickup departed a year earlier, at the end of the '87 model run. All El Caminos sold in its last few years were built exclusively in Mexico, this to keep costs down and the model viable. Seen here is a well-optioned standard model.

▲ Though still K-cars underneath, Chrysler's new "J-body" 1987 LeBaron coupe and convertible were far more stylish, with shapely lines and neat hidden-headlamp noses. Ragtop sales were fairly scarce at 8025, but the coupe found a more-than-respectable 75,415 buyers. Prices ranged from $11,295 for the base coupe to just short of $14,000 for the soft-top.

---

Imports capture 31.1 percent of new car sales; "transplants" (foreign companies operating in the U.S) grab 5.3 percent

Buick drops to fifth place in production, behind Oldsmobile; Pontiac moves up to third, for the first time since 1970

Ford Motor Company earns $4.6 billion net profit—the highest ever for an automaker

Chrysler introduces a 7-year/70,000-mile limited warranty

The industry's average fuel economy is now 26.6 mpg—twice the '74 level

Installation of four-cylinder engines peaks at 54 percent; only 18.5 percent of American cars now come with a V-8 (down from 32.2 percent in 1983)

The average transaction price for a domestic car reaches $13,200

Chrysler buys Lamborghini

▲ Literally extending the appeal of Dodge's 1987 minivan was this new stretched-chassis Grand Caravan riding a 119.1-inch wheelbase. Also new for all models was a 3.0 V-6 option. Sales continued going nowhere but up.

▲ Designed to replace Omni, Dodge's new 1987 P-body Shadow arrived in two- and four-door hatch sedans that looked like "trunkbacks." The Shadow was very K-car in most respects, but sales were respectable at 76,056.

▲ The front-drive Dodge Daytona got its first major restyle for 1987, and expanded to base, new luxury Pacifica, and turbocharged Shelby Z (*shown*) models. For all that, sales tumbled about 11,000 units, to 33,104.

▲ Dodge waved the value flag in 1987 by reducing its aging Omni to a single model called America and giving that sedan a low $5499 base price. Options were few, but sales were quite good, all things considered: close to 67,000 for the model year.

▲ Ford finally answered the front-drive Chrysler minivans with the 1986 Aerostar, a more truck-like rear-drive design. A new 3.0 standard V-6 was the main news for '87, along with a swank Eddie Bauer trim package, which this example wears.

▲ Despite only minor equipment changes, Ford's Taurus charged up the 1987 sales chart to nearly 375,000 units—up more than 138,000 from debut '86. More than 278,000 were sedans, like this top-of-the-line LX model, base-priced at $14,613.

▲ Following its '83 facelift, Ford's Mustang was more fully restyled for 1987. GTs, like this $15,724 ragtop, were more "aero"—and controversial—than base models, thanks to new rocker skirts and "mini-blind" taillamps. Total 'Stang sales dropped 40 percent to 159,145.

▲ Mustang's 1987 engines were thinned to an anemic 90-bhp, 2.3-liter I-4 and the muscular 302 V-8, which gained 25 horses (for 225 total) via new cylinder heads. The V-8 was standard in GTs (*convertible shown*), and optional in quieter-looking LX coupes and ragtop.

**1987 Model Year Production**

|  |  |  |
|---|---|---|
| 1. | Chevrolet | 1,384,214 |
| 2. | Ford | 1,176,775 |
| 3. | Pontiac | 724,289 |
| 4. | Oldsmobile | 670,880 |
| 5. | Buick | 648,689 |
| 6. | Dodge | 501,926 |
| 7. | Plymouth | 443,806 |
| 8. | Chrysler | 360,613 |
| 9. | Mercury | 315,147 |
| 10. | Cadillac | 282,582 |
| 11. | Lincoln | 109,366 |
| 12. | AMC | 36,336 |
| 13. | Avanti | 300[1] |

[1] *Estimated*

▲ Ford spruced up its 1987 Thunderbirds with the proverbial "bold new grilles," plus all-new sheetmetal that wasn't so apparent, as well as flush side glass. New to the line was this $15,079 Sport model packing a 150-horsepower 302 V-8. Despite the restyle, overall T-Bird sales declined to 128,135.

▲ A new grille-less nose provided distinction to Ford's '87 Thunderbird Turbo Coupe, which gained the intercooled turbo-four from the late Mustang SVO. The result was 190 horses with five-speed manual, but only 150 with optional four-speed automatic. The TC was again the costliest 'Bird at $16,805.

◀ Like Ford with the T-Bird, Mercury restyled its Cougar for 1987, but the top XR-7 model (*shown*) again went its own way by losing its turbo-four in favor of a 150-horse 302 V-8—a sensible switch. The base LS again carried the 120-horse, 3.8-liter V-6. Cougar's 1987 sales were good, but not as great as the '86 tally, which fell 31,000 to 104,526. The XR-7 listed at $15,832, the LS at $13,595.

▲ The '87 XR-7 again, but in a view that emphasizes the more upright, formal rear window that deliberately separated the Mercury Cougar from the Ford Thunderbird. Lower-body two-toning lent this model a sportier, "lighter" look.

▲ Desperately seeking to lift Toronado from its '86 sales doldrums, Olds trotted out the Trofeo, a sportier 1987 edition with handling suspension, luxury cabin, and two-tone exterior. It didn't work—total production slipped slightly to 15,040 units.

▲ GM's J-cars underwent a host of evolutionary changes for 1987. The Olds Firenza was no exception, but its sales refused to budge—the '87 total was a lackluster 26,000, including a mere 783 V-6 GT hatchback coupes like this one.

---

Robert C. Stempel becomes GM president

Ford Escort/Mercury Lynx adopt motorized shoulder belts—one way to deal with the requirement for passive restraints

GM builds a Getrag-designed five-speed manual gearbox, available for high-performance models

Mazda begins car production at Flat Rock, Michigan, plans a joint-venture with Ford to build the Probe/MX-6

Chrysler pleads "no contest" to charges of disconnecting odometers from cars under test, pays a $16.4 million fine

Sixty Special nameplates return on stretched Cadillac Fleetwoods

The traditional rear-drive Cadillac is now called Brougham

▲ Pontiac's Grand Prix-based 2+2 was nominally available as an '87 model, but those sold were likely '86 leftovers. Demand was so weak, in fact, that one Pontiac expert recalled seeing a new '86 2+2 at a dealer as late as 1988.

▲ After adding four-doors like its '86 N-body sisters, Pontiac's Grand Am went sportier for '87 with a new 165-horse turbo 2.0-liter four option and an improved dash. GA sales improved to near 245,000. This is the SE coupe.

▲ Notchback '87 Pontiac Fieros like this SE got the nose of the mid-'86 fast-back-profile GT, and all models came with a standard five-speed instead of four-speed manual. Alas, rising insurance rates on two-seaters cut Fiero sales in half to 49,311.

◀ The 1987 Pontiac Firebird dropped its SE model, but still hewed to tradition with four models, two of them actually option packages. Here they are (*clockwise from top left*): base coupe, the same with Formula equipment, Trans Am, and the T/A in top-performance GTA guise, which bowed for '86. Newly standard for GTA and optional on Formula and T/A was the 5.7-liter Corvette V-8, here rated at 210 horsepower.

▲ Plymouth shadowed Dodge's new 1987 P-body compacts with Sundance models that differed mainly in grille and taillamp designs. Even prices were in the same $7800-$7900 range. Sales—75,679 in all—were good, though hardly stupendous.

▲ Like its Dodge Caravan twin, the 1987 Plymouth Voyager added new stretched-body "Grand" models and the first V-6 option for Chrysler minivans. The Grand soon vied for sales supremacy with standard Voyagers like this mid-line SE.

▲ Hard to believe just by looking at it, but the Zimmer Golden Spirit was just a post-'78 Buick Regal in gaudy neoclassic dress. It died with Zimmer Motor Cars after 1987 and dwindling sales in the $65,000-$90,000 "exoticar" field, which never did recover.

---

Dodge restyles Daytona, including a Shelby Z with Turbo II engine; Omni/Horizon drop to single "America" models

Ford Tempo/Mercury Topaz offer an all-wheel-drive option

Mustang's facelift includes flush headlamps; the V-6 is dropped, leaving only a four and a V-8

Ford Thunderbird sports new sheetmetal; the Turbo Coupe adds a turbo intercooler and automatic ride control

Mercury loses its Lynx during the year, turns to marketing a Mexican-built Tracer instead

Chevette and Pontiac 1000 are phased out; Pontiac's minicar to be a Korean-built Le Mans

The Pontiac Trans Am GTA runs with a 210-bhp, 5.7-liter V-8

▲ Conceived during Buick's sporty-car days of the early Eighties, the stylish Reatta bowed for 1988 as essentially a cut-down two-seat version of the latest front-drive Riviera with unique coupe styling. This cutaway highlights its spacious cockpit and transverse 165-horsepower "3800" V-6, the only engine offered.

▲ Buick said the Reatta name derived from a Spanish word for "lariat." Though handsome and quite roadable, the division's new image-booster didn't lasso many sales at $25,000 a copy: just 4708 for the debut 1988 model year. Buick had projected annual Reatta sales of at least 20,000. Vital statistics: 98.5-inch wheelbase and 3350-pound curb weight.

▲ You could still buy a sporty full-size Buick T-Type in 1988, but few people did. This $16,518 LeSabre coupe managed 6426 sales, the Electra T-Type four-door only 1869.

▲ One of three all-new front-drive GM10 coupes, the 1988 Buick Regal featured Custom and Limited models, but options allowed building a "Gran Sport" version like this.

▲ Buick marked 25 years of Rivieras with an improved V-6, extra-cost antilock brakes, and special identification—but sales plunged again for 1988, to just 8625 units.

▲ Called Fleetwood Brougham through 1985, then just Brougham, the basic rear-drive '77 Cadillac sedan was still around in 1988 with a 140-horse 307 Olds gas V-8. One new '88 wrinkle: a 25-gallon fuel tank (versus 20.7). Base price was a reasonable $23,846; 53,130 were built.

▲ Perhaps the least-distinguished Cadillac ever, Cimarron bowed as an upscale 1982 J-car intended to win over BMW and Mercedes buyers. But sales never met expectations, and the model disappeared after 1988 and a final 6454 units. Its best year was '82, with 25,968 sold.

▲ The front-drive Cadillac de Ville and Fleetwood gained a larger V-8 for 1988, upsized from 4.1 to 4.5 liters and 130 to 155 horses. The Coupe and Sedan de Ville remained the division's mainstay sellers, managing over 152,000 combined. Base prices were around $23,000.

---

Domestic output totals 6,973,636 cars for the model year; 6,195,090 are produced by Big Three automakers, the balance come from joint ventures and foreign automakers with U.S. plants

Of 10,595,072 cars sold in the U.S., 7,526,334 are domestically built

Market share for imports dips to 29.2 percent; costly European makes suffer most

Chrysler profits drop for fourth straight year, but Big Three earn record total profit of $11.2 billion

Chevrolet drops to Number Two in production, behind Ford

Industry fuel economy average rises to a high point: 28.7 miles per gallon

◀ After getting off to a very slow sales start, Chevy's compact Beretta coupe (*foreground*) and Corsica sedan zoomed up the '88 chart despite minimal changes. Corsica convinced over 291,000 shoppers, Beretta more than 275,000. A quality-focused approach to 1987 production partly explains these spectacular gains. As before, $1700-$2700 would option a Beretta into a GT model with extra convenience features and Z51 handling suspension, bringing maximum price with V-6 to about $13,500.

▲ Advertising Beretta's entry into 1988 IMSA Grand Touring/Under 3-Liters racing was the new GTU, a V-6 model with skirts, spoilers, and mono coloring. It won in IMSA but not in the showroom. Just 3814 were built.

▲ Still hanging in with a fairly major and quite successful 1988 restyle, Chevy's Cavalier upgraded its RS convertible to a snazzy Z24 model with a standard 125-horse 2.8 V-6. Just 8745 were sold at a $15,990 base price.

▲ Chrysler unwrapped a squarish new front-drive C-body New Yorker that would fully supplant the 1983-vintage front-drive E-body series after 1988. This base four-door and the ritzier Landau version managed nearly 71,000 debut-year sales.

▲ Despite an all-new platform, the 1988 Chrysler New Yorker Landau shared many "luxury" styling cues with the traditional old Fifth Avenue, which was still around by popular demand. List price was $19,509, compared to $17,416 for the base model.

▲ In the spirit of its old "spring specials," Chrysler added sporty GTC versions of the LeBaron coupe and convertible (*shown*) as mid-'88 sales boosters. All-white exterior, handling suspension, and turbo 2.2-liter four were all included.

---

GM launches mid-size, front-drive W-body cars: Buick Regal, Oldsmobile Cutlass Supreme, Pontiac Grand Prix

Buick introduces the two-seat Reatta coupe with a "3800" V-6

The all-new Continental sedan rides a stretched Taurus platform—it's the first front-drive Lincoln, and the first with a six-cylinder engine

Dynasty is Dodge's new front-drive family sedan

Chrysler launches another New Yorker, with a new 3.0-liter V-6

Chrysler markets departed AMC's Eagle line: Canadian-built Premier and French-made Medallion

Oldsmobile develops the "Quad-4" engine for use in Calais, Grand Am, Skylark

▲ Dodge sharpened up the looks of its 1988 Shadow ES (*foreground*) via a new face with integral foglamps and air dam, plus reshaped rear spoiler and revised body graphics. The ES came only as a three-door. Base and luxury versions continued with few changes in three- and five-door form.

▲ Chrysler's new 1988 C-body New Yorker was also offered as the Dodge Dynasty, though with fewer standard luxuries in exchange for lower list prices. This upper-rung Dynasty LE stickered at $12,226, the base model at $11,666. Sales were so-so at 55,550, with many bought by daily rent-a-car fleets.

▲ Still riding high on the sales charts, the '88 Dodge Caravan gained a new 4000-pound towing package and rear-seat air-conditioner options. Here, the long-body Grand Caravan SE. LE models could go for $20,000.

▲ This 174-bhp turbocharged Lancer Shelby was a 1988 addition to Dodge's H-body line—and very rare, with only 279 built. Evolved from the '86 Lancer Pacifica, it came only in monochrome white or red and five-speed manual.

▲ A Renault remnant from the '87 takeover of AMC, the 1988 Premier helped launch Chrysler's Eagle Division as a Canadian-built front-drive mid-size sedan with a 3.0 Renault V-6. Badges read Eagle.

▲ The 1988 Ford Mustang was a virtual '87 rerun save a larger battery and inevitably higher prices. Sales, however, made a gratifying gain to 211,225, led by LX 5.0 coupes (*hatch shown*), which started as low as $10,611.

▲ Though its basic '81 design was still apparent, the Ford Escort had become a more sophisticated small car by 1988. Better-looking too, as shown on this mid-year "third series" LX five-door wagon, which started at $8058.

▲ Despite few changes, Ford's Thunderbird scored higher 1988 sales of 147,243, up almost 20,000 from '87. However, the Turbo Coupe (*shown*), was losing ground to the cheaper yet equally speedy V-8 LX and Sport.

**1988**

This is the final year for GM's rear-drive Monte Carlo, Cutlass Supreme, and Regal coupes—plus Cadillac Cimarron, Ford EXP, AMC Eagle, Plymouth Caravelle, Dodge 600, Pontiac Fiero

The last T-Type Buick LeSabre and Riviera are offered

Cadillac adds the Seville Touring Sedan (STS), enlarges its V-8 engine to 4.5 liters, and makes anti-lock braking available

The Camaro Z28 is gone, but the IROC-Z continues as Chevrolet's high-performance machine; Cavalier gains a rounded facelift and the Z24 convertible

Chevrolet produces 2000 "anniversary" Corvette coupes

The final Dodge Aries/Plymouth Reliant station wagons are built; the new Shelby Lancer boasts a 176-bhp Turbo II engine

▲ The first Lincoln with front-wheel drive and fewer than eight cylinders arrived for 1988 in a smooth new Continental sedan. Essentially a stretched Ford Taurus with 3.8 V-6 power, it met an enthusiastic reception, more than doubling sales of its '87 predecessor, at 41,287. Base price was $26,078.

▲ The new '88 Continental boasted numerous high-tech features including computer-controlled air-spring suspension, variable-effort power steering, all-disc anti-lock brakes, and available "Insta-Clear" electric windshield defrosting. This is the uplevel Signature Series model, which listed at $27,944.

▲ Though very long in the tooth by 1988, the '81-vintage Lincoln Town Car scored its highest production ever, at over 201,000. This mid-line Signature Series sticker-priced at just under $26,000.

▲ An even-older Dearborn staple, the '79-vintage Mercury Grand Marquis gained a new face and other cosmetic touchups for 1988, when coupes were dropped. Pictured is the upmarket $16,612 LS sedan.

◀ Olds wrangled 1988 Indy Pace Car duties for this special Cutlass Supreme convertible, based on that year's new GM10 coupe platform. Working with C&C Inc., Olds ordered 55 replicas, all with the pacer's special turbocharged version of the new twin-cam Quad-4 engine, plus head-up information display (HUD). A wealth of publicity and positive public response prompted the decision to offer a similar convertible for showroom sale, though it wouldn't arrive until 1990.

## 1988 Model Year Production

| | | | | | |
|---|---|---|---|---|---|
| 1. Ford | 1,331,489 | 5. Dodge | 489,645 | 9. Lincoln | 280,659 |
| 2. Chevrolet | 1,236,316 | 6. Buick | 458,768 | 10. Chrysler | 278,287 |
| 3. Pontiac | 680,714 | 7. Plymouth | 336,070 | 11. Cadillac | 270,844 |
| 4. Oldsmobile | 535,015 | 8. Mercury | 298,859 | 12. Avanti | 150[1] |

[1] *Estimated*

◀ Like sister Buick Riviera, the '88 Olds Toronado boasted GM's revised "3800" V-6 with new vibration-damping balance shafts and improved breathing that upped horses by 15 to 165. Also, the sporty Trofeo (*shown*) was marketed more as a separate model. Unhappily for Olds, neither these nor other changes did much for Toro sales, which inched up but remained extremely sluggish at just under 17,000 units.

▲ Once a best-seller, the rear-drive mid-size Olds was down to base and Brougham coupes by 1988, when it ended a 10-year run under the appellation Cutlass Supreme Classic. Sales totaled 27,678.

▲ The Cutlass Supreme for the Nineties arrived as one of 1988's front-drive GM10 coupes. Olds listed base, SL, and this sporty International Series model—all on a 107.5-inch chassis. Sales were strong at nearly 95,000.

▲ Like Dodge's 1988 Omni America, the Plymouth Horizon America cost $200 more than the '87 ($5999) but still offered fine value. Buyers agreed, snapping up nearly 62,000 Horizons and some 60,000 Omnis.

▲ There was no reason for much change in the hot-selling Voyager minivan for 1988, but Plymouth nonetheless offered a new LX appearance package and heavier 4000-pound trailer-tow option among several refinements. Here, a base-trim standard model fronts a long-body Grand Voyager in top LE guise.

▲ Plymouth's 1988 Sundance again mimicked its P-body Dodge double by adding a sporty appearance and performance option. Dubbed RS, for Rally Sport (with a wary eye on Chevrolet), it delivered two-toning, handling suspension, foglights, uprated interior, and other goodies for around $1400.

---

Ford's Tempo is reskinned to look more like Taurus; a 3.8-liter V-6 is optional in Taurus

Lincoln's Mark VII gets a big power boost—to 225 bhp

Enthusiast editions of Oldsmobiles are called International Series; the final Firenzas are built

Pontiac's 6000 STE features an all-wheel-drive option; the top-line Bonneville SSE adds electronic variable damping

Pontiac Sunbird adopts a rounded look, along with Cavalier

The all-new Pontiac Grand Prix features all-disc brakes and all-independent suspension

Fifty Avanti Silver Anniversary coupes are built with Paxton-supercharged engines; the firm gets yet another owner, J.J. Cafaro

◀ Showing its best shape in years, the Pontiac Grand Prix was all-new for 1988. As one of the front-drive GM10 models, it boasted all-independent suspension and no less room than the old rear-drive GP, plus a specific Pontiac look to stand apart from the Buick Regal and Olds Cutlass Supreme, which had their own make identities. GM had finally learned the folly of "cookie-cutter" styling, and it paid off: Grand Prix sales rose nearly five-fold to 86,357. This is the sporty top-line SE.

▲ After spending $100 million on a superior new suspension and other 1988 improvements, GM killed the Pontiac Fiero as unprofitable. This notchback Formula was one of the final 26,402 Fieros built.

▲ The first front-drive Pontiac Bonneville returned from '87 with LE and SE sedans, plus this aggressive new 1988 SSE. The SSE offered a standard "3800" V-6 and anti-lock brakes for $21,879.

▲ Ousting a 3.3 V-6 as the top power option for Pontiac's 1988 Grand Am was Oldsmobile's new 2.3-liter twin-cam Quad-4 with 150 horses—and lots of throbby noise. This is the SE coupe, which listed at $12,869.

▲ Pontiac's 1988 Firebird engine roster was Sixties-confusing, but the venerable Trans Am (*shown*) still had fire with a choice of three V-8s and from 170 to 225 horses. Styling across the board was little-changed from a mild 1987 facelift inspired by the top-performing Trans Am GTA.

▲ When was a 1988 Firebird not a fastback? When it became a "notchback" via a new hatch, as on this prototype Trans Am GTA. Pontiac announced it as a limited-production option, but few cars got it, mainly because it reduced trunk space from meager to virtually nil.

---

Concept vehicles include Pontiac's low-snouted Banshee, Chrysler's Portofino, Cadillac Voyage, Lincoln Machete, Buick Lucerne, Plymouth Slingshot

▲ Recognizing the error of its downsizing ways, Buick added 11 inches to the tail of the '89 Riviera, plus more chrome and a cushier ride. Result? Sales more than doubled, to 21,189. Base sticker price was $22,540.

▲ Buick's Somerset Regal was renamed Skylark when four-door versions bowed for '88. The '89s boasted a more potent new "3300" V-6 option—and this retro-look dealer-installed vinyl top.

▲ Buick's 1989 LeSabre lost its separate T-Type coupe but gained a no-cost tilt steering wheel and a few other goodies. This top-of-the-line Limited sedan carried a $16,730 base price. Total LeSabre production totaled 149,572 units.

▲ Cadillac's 1989 Allanté received a new 200-horse 4.5-liter V-8, variable-rate shock absorbers, new seats, and standard anti-theft alarm. Sales rose modestly from the previous year's 2569, to 3296.

▲ Given a crisp facelift and 4.5 V-8 for 1988, the Cadillac Eldorado returned for '89 with a Touring Suspension option that gave it surprisingly good handling. Sales, which had risen sharply to 33,210, eased to 30,925. Eldo's base '89 price was $26,738.

▲ With the bigger 4.5 V-8, the Cadillac Seville jumped from some 18,600 sales to nearly 23,000 for 1988. The '89 (*shown*) wasn't greatly changed, but a new road-oriented Seville Touring Sedan (STS) proved popular. Total Seville sales fell slightly, to 20,909.

**1989**

Domestic output totals 7.1 million cars for the model year; 6,133,530 are produced by Big Three automakers, the others are from joint ventures and foreign automakers with U.S. plants.

Of 9,829,893 cars sold in the U.S., 7,072,816 are domestically built.

GM's market share bottoms at 34.7 percent; it was 44.5 percent in '81.

Honda Accord is the top-selling car, followed by Ford Taurus.

Chevrolet returns to the top spot in production, ahead of Ford.

The notchback Spirit and Acclaim arrive as Dodge/Plymouth's family sedans for the '90s.

▲ Announced in 1989 but not sold until model-year 1990, Chevy's exciting new Corvette ZR-1 (*foreground*) showed a wider tail with square lights, ultra-wide tires, and an amazing new twin-cam 350 V-8 with 375 horses. Its new six-speed manual gearbox was shared with the basic 'Vette.

▲ Corvette ZR-1's 350 (5.7-liter) "LT-5" V-8 was an all-new, all-aluminum design with port fuel injection and twin overhead cams on each cylinder bank working a total of 32 valves. A special dual induction system with electronic control featured a "valet" key that locked out ultimate power for unauthorized—or less experienced—users.

▲ Corvette's traditional lift-off hardtop returned as a new $1995 option for '89 ragtops—and 1987-88s too—complete with heated rear window and cloth headliner.

▲ Chevy shocked many by dropping the Camaro Z28 for 1989, but the IROC coupe (*shown*) and ragtop gained lower-priced RS companions with much the same style.

▲ The '89 Chevy Cavalier lineup was rearranged, and sporty Z24s gained gas-charged shock absorbers. Here, the $16,615 Z24 ragtop, of which 13,075 were built.

▲ Besides this $10,375 hatchback sedan, Chevy's '89 Corsica line added an LTZ notchback, a sort of four-door Beretta GT offering 130-horse V-6 and other, more driver-oriented features for $12,825.

▲ Originally a LeBaron, then named New Yorker, Chrysler's old M-body Fifth Avenue made a final bow for '89, still with a three-speed automatic and carbureted V-8. Even so, production was good at 43,486.

▲ Chrysler's sporty LeBaron GTC coupe (*shown*) and convertible gained 28 horses for '89—for 174 total—via an intercooler on their 2.2-liter turbo-four. Prices started at $17,435 for the coupe, $19,666 for the convertible.

---

Ford goes after family-sedan performance with the new Taurus SHO, powered by a Yamaha-engineered 220-bhp V-6; no automatic transmission is available

The Ford Probe coupe debuts; its chassis is shared with Mazda

The all-new Ford Thunderbird is shorter, but on a longer wheelbase; the V-8 and turbo four are gone, replaced by a V-6

Thunderbird Super Coupe boasts a 210-bhp supercharged V-6, as well as an all-independent handling suspension

Geo emerges as a separate GM division to market imported and joint-venture models, including the California-built Prizm (successor to Nova)

Pontiac Grand Prix, Oldsmobile Cutlass Supreme, and Buick Regal adopt a 3.1-liter V-6 engine

◀▲ Lacking no *chutzpah* for $33,000, the new 1989 Chrysler's TC by Maserati was little more than a two-seat LeBaron turbo convertible with slightly different looks, two seats, included lift-off hardtop, and some engineering and assembly work by Maserati. The public wasn't moved, so the cars didn't either, and only some 7000 would be built through 1990.

▲ New "faces" freshened up the '89 Dodge Daytonas, including this top-line Shelby model (no longer a "Z") with a 174-horse 2.2 "Turbo II" four. Overall Daytona sales improved to near 73,000.

▲ Dodge's Aries entered its last model year in '89, signaling the continued phase-out of the venerable K-cars. Sedans and coupes were offered under the single-trim level America plan, both priced at $7595.

▲ Dodge had a new Spirit for 1989, a rounded, roomier four-door sedan replacing the compact 600. Performance-minded shoppers looked at this sporty top-line ES with its 150-horse, 2.5-liter turbo-four.

▲ Adding spice to Chrysler's Eagle Premier line during 1989 was this monochromatic Limited model with standard all-disc brakes and 3.0 V-6. Relatively few were sold at the initial $19,200 base price.

▲ An AMC artifact introduced in '88 by Chrysler, the Eagle Medallion was the U.S. version of Renault's mid-size 21—and a slow seller that departed after '89. It came as a four-door sedan and this wagon.

▲ Though a virtual copy of the '89 Mitsubishi Mirage and Dodge/ Plymouth Colt, Eagle's new entry-level Summit subcompact sedan was built at the new joint-venture Chrysler-Mitsubishi plant in Illinois.

---

The average transaction price for a domestic new car is $14,920

Ford Motor Co. Vice Chairman Harold Poling warns of excess capacity worldwide, predicting that automakers will produce 20 percent more vehicles in 1990 than customers want

Buick Riviera adds 11 inches to length—sales show an upturn

Cadillac de Ville/Fleetwood are revamped, sedans stretched

A driver-side air bag and PASS-Key theft-deterrent system is optional for Cadillacs

Chevrolet Caprice drops its V-6, makes the V-8 standard

A six-speed ZF manual gearbox is available for Corvettes; it features computer-aided gear selection for forced 1st-to-4th shifts

▲ Under new owners in '87, struggling Excalibur expanded its model range in 1988-89 with this grand $73,000 Series V Touring Sedan. Only a handful were built before the company finally went under in 1992.

▲ One of Detroit's brightest '89 stars was an all-new Ford Thunderbird. It retained rear-wheel drive but gained an all-independent suspension. This 210-horse supercharged SC coupe topped the line at $19,823.

▲ Though it was a bit heavier than planned, the '89 Thunderbird SC delivered grand touring performance to rival a BMW, with an easy 7.8 seconds 0-60 mph. Alas, total T-Bird sales fell to just under 115,000.

▲ Still one of America's top sellers, the Ford Taurus returned for 1989 with a hot new 220-horse SHO sedan. Workaday models like this uplevel LX wagon no longer offered base four-cylinder power, but the standard 3.0 and optional 3.8 V-6s continued.

▲ Ford's Mustang turned 25 in 1989, but persistent rumors of a hot rod anniversary model proved false. Changes that year were minimal, but sales held steady at a still-healthy 209,769, including 42,244 ragtops. Here, the $13,272 GT hatchback coupe.

---

### 1989 Calendar Year Car Sales

1. Ford ....................1,502,878
2. Chevrolet/Geo ........1,348,265
3. Pontiac ....................678,968
4. Oldsmobile ...............600,037
5. Buick .......................542,917
6. Mercury ....................474,673
7. Dodge .......................447,688
8. Plymouth ..................306,161
9. Cadillac ....................266,899
10. Lincoln ....................200,315
11. Chrysler ..................196,125
12. Eagle .........................69,719

*Figures include cars made for the Big 3 in plants managed by Japanese companies*

▲ Cougar was bound to follow where Thunderbird led, so the Mercury employed the Ford's basic all-new design for 1989 while retaining its own distinctive styling "cues." Base LS and sporty XR-7 were again on-hand, but XR-7 returned to assisted aspiration, sharing T-Bird SC's new supercharged 210-horse V-6.

▲ Again wearing a more "formal" rear roofline, the '89 Cougar XR-7 listed for $15,832, versus $13,595 for the non-supercharged LS. A firmer suspension and uprated rubber on alloy wheels were among XR-7's many standard features. Unhappily for Mercury, Cougar production dipped from 1988's 119,162 units to 97,312.

▲ Plymouth won Acclaim for '89: a new mid-size sedan to replace its mid-decade Caravelle. Acclaim was a close cousin to the Dodge Spirit. Here, the top-line $13,195 LX.

▲ Olds dropped a new high-output Quad-4 engine with 185 horses into Cutlass Calais coupes and sedans to create the even-sportier 1989 International Series models.

▲ The Oldsmobile Toronado hit a new sales low for 1989 with just 9877 orders. Only 3734 were standard $21,995 Toros like this; the $24,995 Trofeo accounted for the balance.

▲ Marking Trans Am's twentieth year were 1500 copies of this $25,000 '89 model with a 245-horse turbo V-6 from Buick's late GNX. It came only with four-speed automatic and did 0-60 mph in just 5.4 seconds—enough to serve as that year's Indy Pace Car with no engine modifications. Former Indy winner Bobby Unser is pictured here.

▲ Pontiac built 1000 special Grand Prixs in 1988 as McLaren Turbos. They inspired the regular-production Grand Prix Turbo for '89, with a similar intercooled 205-horse 3.1 V-6 and racy body addenda. Starting at around $26,000, the '89 saw 1000 copies, followed by 4000 of the 1990 models.

---

A tire-pressure monitor and Selective Ride Control are optional in Corvettes

The Euro-American TC Maserati is marketed by Chrysler, but never catches on; the last rear-drive Fifth Avenues are built

Mercury launches a new Cougar, similar to T-Bird, including a supercharged XR-7

The 20th Anniversary Pontiac Trans Am boasts a 245-bhp turbo V-6; the 6000 STE comes only with all-wheel-drive

The Quad-4 engine, available in Oldsmobile Calais and Pontiac Grand Am, comes with 150 or 185 horsepower

Mid-year brings Pontiac's limited-edition McLaren Turbo Grand Prix, yielding 200 horsepower from its 3.1-liter V-6

▲ Buick unveiled a ragtop Reatta for 1990 after a year's delay. But at $35,000, it proved even tougher to sell than the coupe, and only 2437 would be built through 1991, when both Reattas were dropped after total production of 21,850.

▲ A mild facelift and new government-required "passive" front seatbelts were the main 1990 news for Buick's mainstay full-size LeSabre two- and four-door sedans. Base price on this Limited four-door was up to $17,400.

▲ Buick also touched up its N-body Skylarks for 1990 and added this $12,935 two-door Gran Sport with firm suspension, aluminum wheels, and upgraded interior. As before, most Skylarks were sold with the smooth 160-bhp "3300" V-6 option.

▲ After a major '89 restyle that added several inches to both length and wheelbase, Cadillac's 1990 de Ville/Fleetwood line got 25 more horses (180 total) via port fuel injection. Here, the $26,960 Coupe de Ville.

▲ After logging a slight sales dip for '89, the Cadillac de Ville/Fleetwood recovered to nearly 175,000 combined for 1990. The $25,435 Sedan de Ville (*shown*) remained the volume leader with nearly 132,000.

▲ After plugging along with the rear-drive Astro, Chevy added a more competitive front-drive minivan for 1990. Called Lumina APV (All-Purpose Vehicle), it sold respectably, but was controversially styled and no threat to Chrysler, which still dominated the market.

▲ Bowing in the spring of '89 for the 1990 chase, Chevy's mid-size Lumina coupe and sedan took over for comparable Celebrity models to complete the planned GM10 quartet. This standard four-door, riding a 107.5-inch wheelbase, took some 55 percent of the line's 295,007 debut-year sales.

▲ Ace stock-car driver Dale Earnhardt (six-time NASCAR champion) campaigned this heavily modified Chevy Lumina coupe in 1990 NASCAR events like the Daytona 500. A similar car would later vie with Tom Cruise for "star" billing in the highly touted feature film *Days of Thunder.*

---

**1990**

The industry suffers its worst year since 1983, selling only 14.1 million cars and trucks; prospects for 1991 look bleaker yet

Rebates in the neighborhood of $1000 are widespread

Automakers rely heavily on sales to rental agencies, but those nearly new "program" cars then "steal" new-car sales

Anti-lock brakes are installed in 7.6 percent of 1990 cars (double the 1989 proportion); driver-side air bags go into nearly 30 percent of North American-built cars

Domestic model-year output totals 6,276,459 cars (5,021,953 produced by Big Three automakers)

Chevrolet drops to second place in model-year car production, behind Ford

◀ Chevrolet showed prototype Beretta convertibles in 1990, with construction along the lines of Oldsmobile's drop-top Cutlass Supreme. Among them was a jazzy yellow job (*background*) to pace that year's Indy 500. Showroom sale seemed imminent, but Chevy pulled the plug in the face of production delays and escalating costs. However, the division did manage 4615 replica "Indy GT" Beretta coupes with Olds Quad-4 power. The coupes would serve as a template for the 1991 Beretta GTZ.

▲ Like all '90 Corvettes, this $37,264 drop-top got a new dash and driver's air bag. But big news for Chevy's sports car was that the ZR-1 finally went on sale—in coupe form only.

▲ The ZR-1 actually was a $31,683 option package making for a 'Vette coupe that listed for $59,000. But some rabid speculators paid double that for early examples.

▲ Chevy's first redesigned Caprice in 14 years bowed during the '90 model year. Sold as a '91, it really was the 1977-90 chassis with a swoopy new body. Sedans went on sale first.

▲ Imperial rose from the grave for a second time as one of Chrysler's new 1990 Y-body models. Though it shared a basic front-drive design with that year's revamped Fifth Avenue, its base price was $3600 higher, at $25,000. Calendar-year output was only 1370.

▲ Only a bit less posh than the reborn Imperial, Chrysler's 1990 New Yorker Fifth Avenue wore similarly square, formal lines allegedly dictated by company chairman Lee Iacocca. Calendar-year production was decent, all told, at 41,366.

---

Honda Accord beats Taurus as the sales leader for the second straight year; Cavalier and Escort run third and fourth

Driver-side air bags are standard in all American-built Chrysler products (except the Eagle Talon and Plymouth Laser)

Chevrolet releases the "King of the Hill" Corvette, the ZR-1 coupe, with a special LT1 aluminum 375-bhp engine

Lumina replaces Celebrity as Chevrolet's mid-size offering

The Lincoln Town Car is fully restyled; dual air bags are intended, but shortage of passenger bags forces Lincoln to delay usage

GM launches a sharp-nosed minivan trio: Chevrolet Lumina APV, Oldsmobile Silhouette, and Pontiac Trans Sport

▲ The 1990 Chrysler's TC by Maserati exchanged its turbo-four for a Mitsubishi V-6, provided you ordered automatic. But hardly anyone was ordering this $33,000 car in any form, the main reason it disappeared after only two years.

▲ There was a new LeBaron sedan for 1990, but it was only the A-body Dodge Spirit/Plymouth Acclaim in a more formal Chrysler suit. A 141-bhp 3.0 Mitsubishi V-6 was included in the $16,000 base price, but sales were meager at 8071.

▲ Shelving the old K-car LeBaron convertibles and wagons left the Town & Country name free for. . .a long-body 1990 Chrysler luxury minivan with woody-look trim and Chrysler's new 150-bhp, 3.3-liter V-6. Base price was a princely 25 grand.

▲ Lancer was banished for 1990, leaving this Spirit ES as Dodge's sole sports-sedan offering. A 2.5 turbo-four remained standard, a 3.0 V-6 was optional. At some 105,587 units, overall Spirit calender-year sales ran about even with the '89 tally.

▲ A blast from the past, though in name only, the 1990 Dodge Monaco was a near-copy of the ex-Renault Eagle Premier. Introduced mainly to boost sales and keep its Canadian plant busy, Monaco got off to a rather slow start.

▲ The Eagle Premier itself was treated to standard all-disc brakes for 1990, plus a floor-mounted shifter for its automatic transmission. The sporty ES Limited (*shown*) again topped the three-model line at a $20,272 base price.

▲ Unwrapped in January '89 for 1990, the Eagle Talon was a retrimmed version of Mitsubishi's new Illinois-built Eclipse sport coupe, as was Plymouth's Laser. Here, the top-line turbocharged TSi AWD (all-wheel drive).

**1990 Calendar Year Car Sales**

1. Chevrolet/Geo........1,364,096
2. Ford..........................1,321,149
3. Pontiac.........................636,390
4. Buick............................536,667
5. Oldsmobile.................511,781
6. Mercury........................390,794
7. Dodge...........................361,689
8. Cadillac........................258,168
9. Plymouth......................252,964
10. Lincoln.........................231,660
11. Chrysler......................185,535
12. Eagle.............................60,646

*Figures include cars made for the Big 3 in plants managed by Japanese companies*

▲ New for '89, the front-drive Probe was conceived to replace Mustang, which Ford continued after vocal protests from loyal Mustangers. Though based on Mazda's MX-6, Probe wore an "all-Ford" look and, for 1990, offered the 3.0 Taurus V-6 as an option for the mid-range LX model. The sporty GT here used a turbo-four with 145 very strong horses.

▲ Having given Mustang a reprieve, Ford got to work on an all-new design. Meantime, the basic '79 package got a driver's air bag as its main change for 1990. Here, the popular V-8 LX 5.0L Sport in $12,265 hatchback form. Total Mustang sales fell by almost half that year, to 128,189.

▲ Ford observed Thunderbird's thirtieth year in 1990 with a $1085 option package for the $20,390 Super Coupe. As shown, it added a unique paint scheme and interior trim. Only a few thousand were built.

▲ Fully restyled for the first time in a decade, Town Car got Lincoln's idea of the "aero look" for 1990. Sales stayed strong and were in fact up more than 19,000, to 147,160. Here, the mid-line Signature.

▲ Cross-spoke BBS alloy wheels identified the sporty LSC version of Lincoln's 1990 Mark VII. All models gained a driver-side air bag and a reshaped dashboard. Still, total Mark sales slipped to 22,313.

▲ With their fortunes falling fast, Olds dealers asked for and got their own version of GM's new 1990 front-drive minivan. Lansing called it Silhouette and offered more luxury features than Chevy or Pontiac, but the same 3.1-liter V-6.

▲ Olds again wooed import buyers in 1990 with sporty I-Series Cutlass Calais models like this four-door. Also noted was a reborn 4-4-2 (Quad-4 engine, four valves per cylinder, two overhead camshafts), a $1680 option package for the S two-door.

▲ An Olds Cutlass Supreme convertible finally arrived for a short 1990 selling season. It had a base price of $20,995, a power roof, seats for five, and a "structural top bar" not seen on the '88 Indy prototypes. It managed just 434 initial orders.

---

The industry fuel-economy average sinks to 28.1 mpg, from a high of 28.7 mpg in 1988; more powerful, fuel-consuming engines are the principal cause

Congress nixes a new CAFE standard which would require a 40-percent increase by the year 2001

Congress passes a new Clean Air Act after a decade of fumbling—emissions must be halved by 1998, starting with a '94 phase-in

NHTSA initiates a rule that will require cars to pass a new side-impact test, starting with 10 percent of 1994 models

Roger Smith retires from the GM chairmanship, Donald E. Petersen retires from Ford; Robert C. Stempel and Harold A. Poling take over the respective slots

Ford buys the famed Jaguar company for $2.5 billion

◀ The most enthusiast-oriented Plymouth since Barracuda, the 1990 Laser was one of the three "Diamond-Star" 2+2 coupes built at the new Chrysler-Mitsubishi plant in Illinois. Laser was denied an all-wheel-drive version like the Eagle Talon TSi AWD, but did offer front-drive base, RS, and RS Turbo models, as shown here (*clockwise from left*). Base prices ran in the $11,000-$14,000 range.

▲ Per government edict, a driver-side air bag was newly standard on 1990 Plymouth Acclaims. A Rallye Sport package was newly optional. Pictured is the top-line $13,805 LX sedan. Acclaim output was 120,440.

▲ Pontiac Firebirds got a driver-side air bag for '90. Trans Am GTA remained the hottest—and was even hotter because its 5.7-liter V-8 gained 10 horses, to 235.

▲ Pontiac's 1990 Grand Am sported numerous changes, including a new high-output Quad-4 engine with 180 horses as standard in SE models like this two-door. Pontiac's best-seller, Grand Am saw 197,020 cars built.

▲ Sold by Pontiac as the Trans Sport, the new 1990 "GM200" minivans featured front drive, an expansive dashtop shelf, and some exterior body panels made of ding-resistant plastic-type materials. Also evident in this cutaway view of the minivan is the shared transverse-mount 3.1 V-6. Base Trans Sports started at $14,995, uplevel SE versions at $18,125.

▲ The Pontiac Trans Sport minivan arrived for 1990 in base and SE trim, the latter two-toned via faddish lower-body "cladding," as shown here. Like the similar Chevy Lumina APV and Olds Silhouette, Trans Sport offered seating for five or optional 2+2+2 buckets, each individually moveable and *removable*. A huge, steeply raked windshield set all three apart from other minivans—and turned off some critics.

---

Traction control is available in the Cadillac Allanté—a first for a front-drive car

Corvettes get a standard driver-side air bag and ABS II braking

Dodge Daytona can have a V-6; it's the final year for Omni/Horizon

Dodge Monaco is a rebadged Eagle Premier, sold through 1991

Oldsmobile Toronado is restyled, adds a foot in length

Four-door Cutlass Supremes are now available, plus the first Oldsmobile convertible in 18 years, wearing a "structural top bar"

Diamond-Star Motors in Illinois launches the Mitsubishi Eclipse sport coupe, plus American-badged kin: Eagle Talon and Plymouth Laser

CHAPTER FOURTEEN
# 1991-2000

# MARKET SHARE BATTLE

Who could have guessed that the 1990s would turn out so well for Americans—and for the American auto industry? But who could have blamed the naysayers? After all, the 8.2 million cars Americans purchased in 1991 was the weakest total since 1982—and a full quarter of those were imports. The domestic-model tally was barely six million, the lowest since 1959.

The Big Three were clearly suffering as the decade opened, though for different reasons. Ford had made great strides, yet was struggling to break even in an economy turned sour. Chrysler was flirting with financial oblivion yet again, owing to unappealing products (its minivans being the one big exception), and costly, non-automotive acquisitions in the Eighties.

Even worse-off was General Motors, which couldn't stop hemorrhaging cash. The reasons were plain enough: stale, slow-selling designs; heavy capital spending with little tangible return; the industry's highest overhead; a bloated, inefficient organization. Loss piled upon loss, each reported in huge headlines, and by the fourth quarter of 1993 they made a towering $18 billion mountain. GM dropped a staggering $11.7 billion in 1992 alone.

Yet within two years, all Detroit was making money again—even GM. What happened? For one thing, the economy began a recovery that steamrolled to record growth. For another, the yen strengthened against the dollar, making Japanese cars more expensive than comparable domestic models, to the benefit of Detroit sales and profits. Prices for all cars still seemed steep, however, and many Americans discovered the advantages of leasing instead of buying. A lease counted as a sale, and that kept factories humming.

Several other factors were at work. After years of unfavorable comparisons, Detroit was by the mid-Nineties perceived to have closed the "quality gap." This dovetailed neatly with the desire of many import owners to give Detroit another chance, and many did so with the 1991 launch of GM's Saturn subsidiary. which featured a well-made small car, affordable "no-dicker" pricing, and exceptional customer service.

But the perhaps the real key to the decade turned out to be something quite unexpected. Americans in 1990 purchased 4.6 million light trucks, barely 30 percent of total vehicle sales. By 1998, half the vehicles sold in the U.S. were light trucks—7.4 million of them. And because the imports were slow to understand America's love of big pickups and, especially, of sport-utility vehicles, the Big 3 were the big benefactors.

Ford's smash-hit Explorer led the way, debuting in 1990 and going on to outsell the best-selling car in 1995, '96, and '98. Once buyers got a taste of midsize SUVs, they developed an appetite for even-larger 4×4s. Detroit responded, and soon, shopping mall parking lots were crawling with 5500-pound, $45,000 behemoths like the Lincoln Navigator. By the mid-Nineties, Ford and Chrysler were selling more light trucks than cars, and GM was killing off such icons as the Buick Roadmaster to devote more assembly line space to truck production. Propelled by the truck boom, 1998 ranked as the second-best year ever for U.S. car sales.

America's newfound hunger for trucks had a profound affect on automotive design. The byword as the industry raced into the new century was "hybrid." This was an altogether new category of vehicle that combined the comfort of a car with the go-anywhere attitude of an SUV. The other sea change was the consolidation of the industry itself. Small and midsize independent makes were gobbled up by giants convinced that survival in the 21st Century hinged on enormous economies of scale. Ford Motor Company acquired Jaguar, Mazda, and Volvo. GM bought out Saab. And then in 1998, Germany's Daimler-Benz AG assumed a controlling interest in Chrysler Corporation, forming a new transatlantic company, DaimlerChrysler.

The family album of the American auto had become in some ways an album of extended families. It reflected new alliances, evolving needs, unpredicted desires, shifting tastes. It was a little like any American family album might be at the dawn of the new millennium.

---

**1991**

The Persian Gulf war in January-February signals another bad year for the auto industry—the recession continues

Model-year production in U.S. plants (including transplants) totals 5,777,211 cars

Of 8,175,582 cars sold in the U.S., 6,072,255 are domestically built

Rising sales of nearly new "program" cars (used in rental fleets) harm the new-car market; Ford and GM agree to require renters to keep cars in service longer

The Big Three chairmen go to Washington in March, to seek concessions on the Clean Air Act and to oppose the prospect of tighter CAFE restrictions

Chrysler chairman Lee Iacocca warns that if Japan keeps taking market share, Chrysler could be "gone"

▲ Buick's Regal entered 1991 with minor cosmetic touch-ups and a 170-horse 3.8 V-6 as an optional alternative to the standard 140-bhp 3.1. Base price on this Limited coupe was up to $16,455.

▲ The Buick Riviera added standard anti-lock brakes, five horsepower, and a vinyl-roof option for '91, but production fell again, this time nearly 50 percent to 13,168, a record low for the model.

▲ After 33 years, the Roadmaster name returned in 1991 on Buick's redesigned B-body Estate Wagon to replace the blocky '77-vintage design. But sales were meager again: just 7466.

▲ The front-drive C-body Buicks were all Park Avenues by 1991, when this smooth new shape appeared along with GM's first electronically controlled automatic transmission. This base model was priced at $24,385.

▲ A step above the '91 Park Avenue was the new Ultra, with a supercharged 3.8-liter V-6 packing 205 horses versus 170. Prices started at $27,420.

◀ Ending a short, unhappy sales life, Buick's two-seat Reatta bowed out after 1991, when it gained an improved "3800" V-6 linked to GM's new electronic T460E automatic transaxle. Upsized wheels and tires were also included, but the Reatta had no place in Buick's future, and only 1313 of the '91s were built. Among them were just 305 convertibles, whose base price was upped nearly $1000 to $35,965. Though all Reattas stand to become collectible, the rare ragtops will surely do so before the coupes.

---

Toyota plans a second U.S. plant

Saturn debuts as the first new American make in 30 years; dealers are referred to as "retail partners," with customer satisfaction an all-important goal

GM offers a new 3.4-liter "Twin Dual Cam" (24-valve) V-6 for Lumina, Grand Prix, Cutlass Supreme; Chevrolet launches a hot Lumina Z34 with the new engine

Electronically controlled automatic transmissions are installed in a number of models

Low-cost anti-lock braking (ABS VI) is available for GM cars

The final Buick Reatta is produced

Chevrolet Caprice is restyled to a boat-like aero profile, still with rear drive and a V-8; the early '91 sedan is joined later by a wagon and sporty LTZ

▲ A 4.5-liter V-8 upped to 4.9 liters gave C-body '91 Cadillacs 200 horses versus 180. Also new were electronic automatic and Computer Command Ride shocks. Here, the $34,695 Fleetwood coupe.

▲ The '91 Seville also featured Cadillac's new 4.9 V-8 and Computer Command Ride variable-rate shocks. This sporty STS continued to find buyer favor even at a lofty base price of $37,135.

▲ The hoary Cadillac Brougham sedan switched to a standard Chevy 5.0 V-8 for 1991 and added 30 horses, for a total of 170. A Chevy 5.7 V-8 option returned with 185 bhp. Sales dropped 6510 units, to 27,231.

▲ As recognition for recent strides in quality, Cadillac received the government's coveted Malcolm Baldridge Award in 1991. Division chief John O. Grettenberger announced the honor to workers at a plant ceremony.

▲ The Z28 Camaro returned for '91 to replace the IROC-Z, as Chevy no longer sponsored the International Race of Champions. Shown here is a special new police version offered that year.

▲ The big news for Chevy's '91 Lumina was spelled Z34, an enthusiast-oriented coupe packing a new twincam 3.4-liter V-6 with 210 horses, plus uprated suspension and suitably sportier appearance. It poses here with a standard four-door and APV minivan.

▲ Chevy's redesigned full-size Caprice sedan gained a wagon running mate for the formal '91 model year, when Caprice production nearly doubled to 217,461. Here, the sedan and its 9C1 police-package partner.

---

Oldsmobile's Ninety-Eight is restyled, marking the 50th Anniversary of the nameplate

Buick offers a new front-drive Park Avenue and a big rear-drive V-8 Roadmaster Estate Wagon

Ford Escorts and Mercury Tracers are revamped

Cadillac Brougham now carries a fuel-injected 5.0-liter V-8

Chevrolet Beretta/Corsica add a standard driver-side air bag; Cavalier offers a convertible, replacing the promised Beretta ragtop that never materializes

The IROC-Z badge departs, but the Camaro Z28 is revived

Dodge Shadow now comes as a convertible; the new Spirit R/T runs with a 224-horsepower turbo-charged four-cylinder engine

Dodge offers the imported Stealth, similar to Mitsubishi's 3000GT

▲ A new tapered nose marked 1991 Chevy Corvettes, and standard models got the same rear-end look as the pricey ZR-1—to the dismay of early Z buyers. 'Vette sales kept falling, down now to 20,639.

▲ Chevy conjured up the Geo brand for several 1990 Japanese-designed import and "transplant" models. Among them was the Isuzu-built Storm hatch coupe, shown here in sporty uplevel LSi trim for '91.

▲ High above the L.A. evening smog is Chrysler's '91 LeBaron sedan, which boasted analog gauges as standard. Base price was $16,450 with standard 3.0 V-6. Anti-lock brakes were again optional.

▲ An upsized 3.8-liter version of Chrysler's ohv 3.3 V-6 was newly standard for the '91 Imperial. It gave only three more horses (150 total), but was much torquier. Imperial sales dropped to just 11,601.

▲ Except for optional anti-lock brakes, there was little '91 news for the Canadian-built Dodge Monaco, a twin to the Eagle Premier that was inherited with Chrysler's 1987 buy-out of American Motors. This is the sporty ES model.

▲ Brightening the '91 Dodge Shadow line was this new ragtop, a conversion by American Sunroof Company. Offered in "Highline" trim and, as shown here, a sporty uplevel ES, it came with manual-fold top, seating for four, and a choice of three I-4 engines, including a 152-horse 2.5 turbo.

▲ The '91 Dodge Caravan got its most sweeping changes since 1984, including mostly all-new outer panels (though appearance wasn't greatly altered), a more ergonomic dash, and optional full-time all-wheel drive. Base prices ran from $13,215 to $21,105.

### 1991 Calendar Year Car Sales

1. Chevrolet/Geo........1,161,236
2. Ford..........................1,081,290
3. Buick...........................544,325
4. Pontiac........................489,812
5. Oldsmobile.................426,306
6. Mercury.........................376,059
7. Dodge...........................324,595
8. Cadillac.........................213,288
9. Plymouth.......................192,193
10. Lincoln..........................178,701
11. Chrysler.......................126,383
12. Saturn............................74,493
13. Eagle.............................59,347

*Figures include cars made for the Big 3 in plants managed by Japanese companies*

▲ ES Limited, the priciest and sportiest Eagle Premier, got a new grille and standard anti-lock brakes for 1991. All models included air conditioning as standard, but sales still declined to 11,300.

▲ Ford's three Probe sport coupes saw few changes for '91—except sales, which dropped in a tough market, as did sales of many cars that year. The tally was just under 94,000, versus 117,000 for 1990.

▲ The big old Ford Crown Victoria was about to be updated, making 1991 the last year for the traditional "square" look that had been in force since '79. The uplevel LX sedan seen here listed for $18,863.

▲ The supercharged SC remained Ford's top T-Bird for '91, but the big news was optional 302 V-8 power for base and mid-range LX models, with 200 horses versus 210. The SC itself was up to $20,999.

▲ V-8 Ford Mustangs wore handsome new five-spoke 16-inch alloy wheels for 1991, when ragtops like this GT gained a slimmer "top stack." Total Mustang sales withered from 128,000 to a so-so 98,737.

▲ Like sister Ford Crown Victoria, the Mercury Grand Marquis would be revamped for '92, so 1991 was the last year for its old square-rigged look. Here, the $19,940 Colony Park LS wagon.

▲ Mercury unveiled a very different Capri for 1991: a new two-seat front-drive convertible based on the Mazda 323 platform but styled and built by Ford Australia. A decklid spoiler identified the sporty $15,920 XR2 with 132-horse 1.6 turbo four-cylinder.

▲ The Mercury Cougar XR7 again switched back to a conventional V-8 for 1991: a 200-horse HO version of the venerable 302, borrowed from Mustang GT and Lincoln's Mark VII. Base price was up to $20,905, versus $15,629 for the base 3.8 V-6 LS model.

---

Reworked Chrysler minivans debut with a driver-side air bag

The final Pontiac 6000 is built

Cadillacs get a new 4.9-liter V-8 and electronic transmission

All Corvettes wear a convex tail panel, as on the ZR-1

Four-cylinder Mustangs gain a needed 17 horsepower, via a new twin-plug head

A new 200-bhp, 5.0-liter V-8 is available in the Ford Thunderbird and Mercury Cougar

Lincoln's Town Car has the first mass-produced overhead-cam V-8, a 4.6-liter "modular" design; traction control is optional

Mercury dealers market the new Australian-built Capri two-seat convertible

▲ Like Dodge with Shadow, Plymouth standardized a driver's air bag for 1991 Sundance models, including new bargain-priced America versions. This is the sporty top-line RS five-door.

▲ Plymouth's 1991 Acclaim lost its turbo option but gained extra-cost anti-lock brakes. This top-line LX again came with a 141-horse 3.0 V-6 engine and four-speed "Ultradrive" automatic.

▲ Like Dodge's Caravan, the '91 Plymouth Voyager offered smoother lines, a new dash, extra seating options, and newly available all-wheel drive. Here, a standard-body with top LX trim and AWD.

▲ Belatedly following Chevy's Camaro, in January '91 Pontiac unwrapped its first Firebird convertibles since 1969, complete with a new nose inspired by the 1988 Banshee show car. The reborn ragtop came in base or T/A trim, starting at $19,159. Only about 2000 were built for that model year.

▲ Pontiac's Trans Sport minivan was only a year old in 1991, so changes were confined to details like standard 2+2+2 seating and new touring radial tires in a larger size for this uplevel SE, which base-priced at $18,889. Like its "GM200" sisters, Trans Sport sales remained steady but underwhelming.

▲ Turning 10 in '91, the Pontiac Sunbird discarded its turbo-four for a 3.1 V-6 option that was included in this sporty GT coupe selling at $12,444. Larger GT wheels and tires were new.

▲ After eight years and $8 billion in start-up costs, GM's vaunted new Saturn subcompacts debuted for 1991 in four four-cylinder models: twincam SC coupe and SL2 sedan (*foreground*), and single-cam SL and SL1 sedans (*SL1 background*). Interest was high with prices as low as $7995, but a deliberate "go-slow" policy held total production to 48,629 for the model year.

---

Plymouth Sundance "America" is the cheapest car built in the U.S.

A new GTP replaces the Pontiac Grand Prix Turbo Coupe

Pontiac Sunbird gets its first V-6; the turbo four is gone

The Pontiac Firebird convertible is finally available in mid-season

Avanti Automotive Corp. files for bankruptcy; after 29 years, no more Avantis will be built

▲ A sedan joined Buick's Chevy Caprice-based Roadmaster wagon for 1992, and both models gained a 5.7 V-8 with 180 horses. Sedan sales were quite good at 73,817; the Estate Wagon managed to move 11,715 units.

▲ GM's N-body compacts saw major changes for 1992—none more than Buick's startlingly restyled Skylark. Anti-lock brakes were newly standard on all Skylarks, including the $15,555 GS coupe seen here.

▲ Standard anti-lock brakes also appeared on 1992 Buick Regal Gran Sports, but remained optional on base Customs like this $16,865 sedan. Calendar '92 output for the line eased to 97,692.

▲ Tops in Detroit quality by 1992, Buick's full-size LeSabre was redesigned *a la* Park Avenue, with no-cost ABS—and no more coupes. This upper-level Limited sedan was base-priced at $20,775.

▲ Cadillac's Eldorado wore its own new look for '92, gaining 11 inches on an unchanged wheelbase. Its 200-horse 4.9 V-8 was unchanged. Base price was $32,470—not bad for a car of such quality.

▲ Newly optional traction control was featured on full-size front-drive '92 Cadillacs. This $36,360 Fleetwood and the Coupe de Ville again rode a wheelbase three inches shorter than that of four-door models.

▲ Cadillac's two-seat Allanté was unchanged for '92, but paced that year's Indy 500—suitably modified for the task, including the added "rollbar" shown here. Alas, such honors did nothing for Allanté sales, with model-year output easing from 2500 to just 1931 units.

▲ Cadillac also restyled its Seville for '92, again aiming for a more distinct look along the lines of Eldorado (newly revamped with the same idea). Wheelbase grew three inches, overall length more than 12. Whitewalls were no longer available, but a new "sport" interior offered a console plus analog gauges instead of digi-graphic. This base Seville started at $34,975, the sportier STS $3000 higher.

**1992**

A year of relative stability: 8,210,627 cars are sold in 1992; 6,216,488 are domestically built

Model-year production totals 5,556,364 cars

Ford Taurus edges past Honda Accord to become the top seller for '92—fleet sales help

The average domestic car sells for $17,070 (transaction price)

Following Saturn's lead, a growing number of dealerships adopt "one-price" selling

Buick LeSabre gets a handsome restyle, similar to the posh Park Avenue; Oldsmobile Eighty-Eight gets a similar treatment, as does the sportier Pontiac Bonneville (available with a supercharged V-6 and passenger air bag)

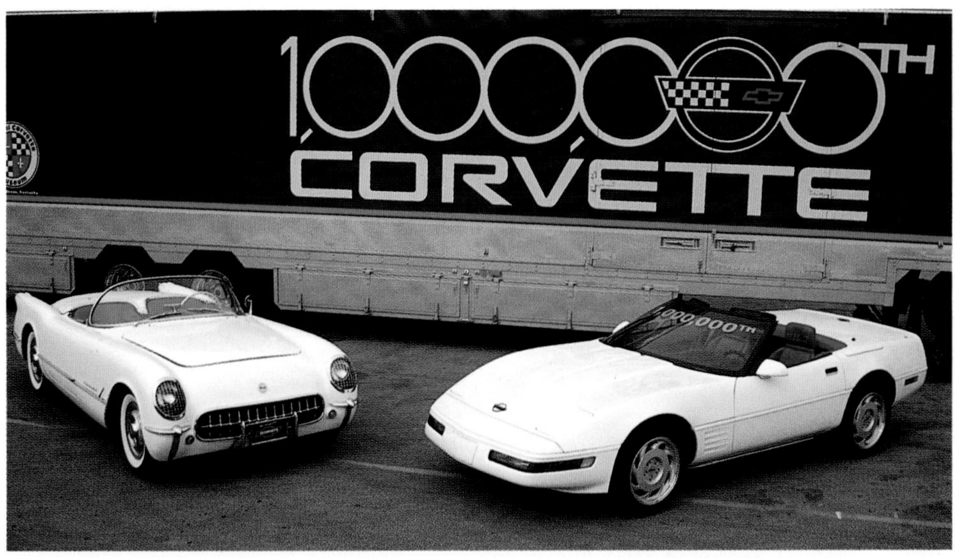


◀ Chevy passed a major milestone in 1992 by building its one-millionth Corvette, a white convertible with that year's new 5.7 LT1 V-8, which replaced the old like-size L98 as base powerplant. Also new that year: standard six-speed manual gearbox, optional ASR ("Acceleration Slip Regulation") traction control, and extra-cost "Quiet Car Package." Here, the historic millionth 'Vette poses with a 1953 original at the Bowling Green, Kentucky, Corvette plant, which hosted 'Vette owners and their cars in a week-long celebration.

▲ Planned but never built for sale was this 1992 Camaro convertible with a new "Heritage Appearance" package, marking 25 years of Chevrolet pony-cars.

▲ The Z34 coupe returned for '92 as the sportiest of Chevy's mid-size Luminas, bolstered by standard anti-lock brakes. Base price was attractive at $18,400.

▲ Chevy added this twincam Lumina Euro 3.4 sedan for '92 as a Z34 running mate, but limited it to four-speed automatic and 200 horses. Euro 3.4 sedan's base price was $15,800.

▲ The Chevy Cavalier closed out its first decade with a larger 2.2-liter four-cylinder engine as standard, plus no-cost anti-lock brakes. Seen here is the mid-level RS sedan, based-priced at $10,199.

▲ The slow-selling Chrysler Fifth Avenue got a slightly rounder face for '92, but sales remained difficult at over $28,000 base, slipping from 44,464 to just under 38,000.

▲ Though sporty ES models wore body-color bumpers, Dodge's P-body Shadow saw few changes for '92. This ragtop, with 2.5-liter turbo, ranged in base price from $14,792 to $15,349.

---

The Roadmaster badge returns on a big rear-drive Buick sedan, joining the '91 wagon; both gain a more potent 5.7-liter V-8

More models adopt anti-lock braking, including Chevrolet Cavalier and Pontiac Sunbird

The restyled Buick Skylark is closely related to the Pontiac Grand Am and Oldsmobile Achieva (replacing Calais), but with unique Buick touches and available Adjustable Ride Control

Buick Skylark has a Quad OHC four or a 3.3-liter V-6; Grand Am and Achieva have four engines

Cadillac's Seville and Eldorado are dramatically restyled, with more separate identities; body panels are not shared

Buick Park Avenue Ultra has a standard supercharged V-6; traction control is optional

▲▶ Quickly evolved from a show-stopping '89 concept—with help from Carroll Shelby—the new 1992 Dodge Viper (*above*) was America's hottest production sports car with its brutish 400-horse V-10 (*right*). Aptly termed a "modern Cobra," it came with six-speed manual gearbox, huge wheels and tires, clip-in side curtains, and skimpy "bikini" top for $55,630. Initial output was deliberately held to 200 units, all finished in red with black interior.

▲ Standard outside exhausts gave the Dodge Viper an unmistakable sound. The rear window was removable for maximum wind in your hair.

▲ Dodge's hoary front-drive Daytona got yet another facelift for '92, plus this new performance IROC R/T with 3.0 V-6 or optional 224-horse "Turbo III" four-cylinder. Prices started at $14,098.

▲ The mid-level Daytona ES came standard with a 100-horse 2.5-liter four; the optional powerplant was the IROC R/T's 3.0-liter V-6. ES retail prices ranged from $11,510 to $13,972.

▲ Like the Dodge Daytona, the Mitsubishi-designed Eagle Talon got exposed headlamps and other styling tweaks for '92. This base front-driver started at $13,631 with standard 135-horse 2.0 I-4.

---

Corvette gains a new 300-bhp LT1 base engine; traction control is made standard

Chevrolet Lumina adds a 3.4-liter Euro option

Dodge releases the eagerly awaited "retro" Viper roadster with a 400-bhp, 8.0-liter V-10 engine—it recalls the muscle cars of the distant past, but at a forbidding price. Only 200 go on sale for '92

Dodge's Daytona IROC R/T replaces the Shelby edition at mid-year

Ford restyles its full-size Crown Victoria, with dual air bags but a similar rear-drive platform; the overhead-cam 4.6-liter V-8 is new, a Touring Sedan comes later

Mercury's Grand Marquis is similar to the Crown Vic; big Ford/ Mercury wagons are history

▲ Having been redesigned for '91 to share a basic design with Mazda's Protege, the Ford Escort added this sporty LX-E four-door sedan for '92, powered by a twincam, 127-horse 1.8-liter Mazda I-4.

▲ A new Sport option with rear spoiler, alloy wheels, and upsized tires added spice to the mid-line LX version of Ford's 1992 Probe sport coupe, which continued with standard 145-horse 3.0 V-6.

▲ Ford's mid-size Taurus became America's top-selling car for 1992, helped by a restyle that, though subtle, involved mostly all-new sheetmetal. This LX sedan carried a $17,775 base price.

▲ Ford was nearing completion of a fully redesigned Mustang by 1992, so the old '79 design was altered only in detail from '91 form. Ragtops like this $19,644 V-8 LX 5.0L continued with a no-cost power top. Sales took a beating, falling almost to 79,000.

▲ A modernized 1992 Crown Victoria debuted in March '91 with smooth "aero" looks, reworked rear-drive chassis, and Ford's new single-cam 4.6 "modular" V-8 with 190 horses. This police package countered the similar 9C1 option offered on Chevy's Caprice.

▲ After a new face for 1990 and 15 extra horses for '91, Lincoln's Taurus-based Continental sedan got a standard passenger-side air bag for '92 (postponed from all but a few '91s due to lack of supply). Prices started at $32,263.

▲ With an all-new replacement just around the corner, 1992 was the end for Lincoln's Mark VII, which was down to just a Bill Blass edition and the ever-sporty LSC (*shown*). Both listed at around $32,000. Total model-year production was a mere 5732.

▲ Like fraternal twin Ford Taurus, the 1992 Mercury Sable was so subtly restyled that it almost escaped notice. A redesigned dash and optional passenger-side air bag were among other changes. Here, the entry-level GS wagon.

### 1992 Calendar Year Car Sales

| | |
|---|---|
| 1. Ford | 1,213,761 |
| 2. Chevrolet/Geo | 1,000,891 |
| 3. Buick | 523,569 |
| 4. Pontiac | 519,925 |
| 5. Mercury | 402,225 |
| 6. Oldsmobile | 389,173 |
| 7. Dodge | 290,184 |
| 8. Cadillac | 214,176 |
| 9. Saturn | 196,126 |
| 10. Plymouth | 182,176 |
| 11. Lincoln | 161,648 |
| 12. Chrysler | 148,010 |
| 13. Eagle | 59,216 |

*Figures include cars made for the Big 3 in plants managed by Japanese companies*

▲ With fortunes fallen very low, Olds overhauled its Cutlass Calais for '92 and called it Achieva. This SL sedan was one of six models offered for around $13,000. Achieva sales inched up to nearly 77,500.

▲ Arriving a bit behind the rest of the line, the SCX sport coupe was the quickest of Oldsmobile's new '92 Achieva compacts, with its own 190-horse Quad-4 engine and mandatory five-speed manual. Sales were sparse.

▲ Oldsmobile's Eighty-Eight Royale lost coupes for '92, but offered two fully redesigned sedans. Anti-lock brakes were among many standards on this upper-level LS model, which started at $21,395.

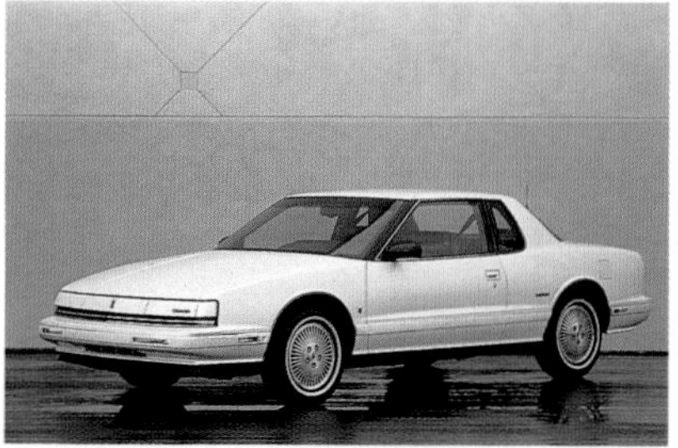

▲ The Olds Toronado (*shown*) and Trofeo bulked up for 1990 to look more "important." Sales rose to 15,022, then dropped to 8000 of the improved 170-horse '91s and just 6436 of the similar '92s.

▲ Rarity alone doesn't make a car collectible, but it may help the rear-drive Olds Custom Cruiser wagon, which was redesigned for '91 but departed after 1992, with barely 12,000 unit sales.

▲ Pontiac's sportiest Grand Prix coupe for 1991-92 was not a Turbo, but rather this new GTP. Like Chevy's Lumina Z34, it packed a 3.4-liter "Twin Dual Cam" V-6 with 200/210 horses. Anti-lock brakes and handling suspension were also included. Base price: $20,500.

▲ As with Chevrolet's Camaro, the third-generation Pontiac Firebird would say goodbye after 1992 and 11 years in production. Changes were minimal. This base coupe carried a $12,505 starting price. Not bad, but Firebird production hit a record one-year low: 27,566.

▲ Like its sister N-cars, 1992 Pontiac Grand Ams sported new—and rather controversial—styling, plus a revived 3.3 V-6 option. Trim levels thinned to just SE and the sportier GT, here in $13,799 sedan form. Sales leaped to over 119,000.

---

Ford Taurus and Mercury Sable earn a subtle restyle; twin air bags are available

Ford Tempo/Mercury Topaz get a V-6 option; the four-wheel-drive versions are gone

Lincoln Continental adds a passenger-side air bag; after nearly a decade, the final Mark VII is built

Rumors suggest that Oldsmobile's days are numbered, but GM denies it vehemently

Oldsmobile's Custom Cruiser gets a larger 5.7-liter optional V-8

A 205-bhp supercharged V-6 is an Olds Ninety-Eight Touring Sedan option

Sundance Duster is the sole Plymouth subcompact to get the 141-bhp, 3.0-liter V-6

▲ Buick's '93 Riviera, on the eve of a completely new design for '95, offered one engine, a 170-horsepower 3.8-liter V-6. The Gran Touring package seen here had an uprated suspension.

▲ The 1993 Buick LeSabre came in Custom and Limited trim, both with a 3.8-liter 170-horse V-6. Its 110.8-inch wheelbase was shared with the pricier Buick Park Avenue.

▲ Cadillac's slow-selling, two-seat Allanté gained the world-class 4.6-liter Northstar V-8 for 1993. That bit of good news was undercut by an announcement that Allanté would not return for '94.

▲ Cadillac's aluminum Northstar V-8 was an engineering triumph of which GM was justifiably proud. Displacing 4.6 liters, it was a twincam 32-valve that produced a whopping 295 horsepower.

▲ Cadillac's big rear-drive Brougham sedan was a Fleetwood again for 1993—and fully restyled *a la* Chevy Caprice and Buick Roadmaster. It even topped the Buick in sales at 31,773.

▲ Cadillac's '93 Fleetwood Brougham topped the old '77-vintage frame with a smooth new body shared with Roadmaster and Caprice. A 185-horse 5.7 V-8 was included in its $33,990 base price.

▲ Back for '93 from a '92 debut, Chevy's "boy racer" Beretta GTZ sported aero add-ons galore, plus a 180-horsepower version of the 2.3-liter Olds Quad-4 engine. A milder but more refined 140-bhp 3.1 V-6 was optional, and standard in the GT model, which started at $12,575, versus the GTZ's $15,590 base price.

▲ Hard to believe, but America's sports car turned a middle-aged 40 for 1993. Chevy celebrated with a 40th Anniversary trim option for the standard Corvette coupe and convertible, identified by special emblems, interior, and Ruby Red paint. Meantime, ZR1 output was slowed to 380 per year due to slow sales. Here, the standard $41,195 ragtop.

---

**1993**

Safety continues as a major focus: Several models offer passenger-side as well as driver-side air bags, either standard or as an option

The trend toward sportiness and performance continues, but ceaseless economic recession and unemployment hurt costly cars

Demand for used cars remains strong as people are priced out of the new-car arena

Chevrolet Camaro and Pontiac Firebird are restyled for a mid-year debut—the first full revamp in a dozen years; Z28 and Trans Am versions are still offered

Camaro/Firebird carry dual air bags, but come only in coupe form for the time being

◄▲ Chevy Camaro fans cheered at 1993's new fourth-generation coupes (ragtops would be along later): a $13,399 base model with 160-horse 3.4 ohv V-6, and a new $16,779 Z28 with a 275-bhp version of Corvette's LT1 V-8 and standard six-speed manual transmission. Also featured were modified "space frame" construction and more-ergonomic interiors.

▲ The all-new '93 Camaro paced that year's Indy 500, the fourth time this Chevy was so honored. Here, the special T-top pacer (*foreground*) and its 1967, '69, and '82 predecessors line up at the Brickyard.

▲ Chrysler wowed most everyone with its all-new 1993 Concorde, a roomy full-size sedan with front drive, V-6 power, and sleek "cab forward" styling. Prices started at $18,441. Model-year output was 56,218.

▲ The advent of Chrysler's "LH" cars spelled the end of the boxy old C-body models like this New Yorker Salon. The '93 still came with a 3.3-liter V-6. Prices started at $18,805, but production closed after a final 22,323 units.

▲ Still built on Chrysler's compact A-body platform, the 1993 LeBaron sedan again offered an LE model and this swankier Landau, the latter priced around $17,000. Sales remained steady but low: just 22,499 for the model year.

▲ Chrysler's posh Town & Country minivan no longer had pseudo-wood side trim by 1993, but did come with driver air bag and anti-lock brakes—more useful by far. All-wheel drive remained optional. Prices started at $25,613.

---

Chrysler launches "cab-forward" LH mid-size sedans: posh Chrysler Concorde, mid-range Dodge Intrepid, sporty Eagle Vision

All three LH cars have dual air bags and two V-6 engines, with traction control available

Lincoln introduces an all-new Mark VIII, again rear-drive, with a hot aluminum twin-cam 4.6-liter V-8 and dual air bags

The redesigned Ford Probe again shares its structure with the Mazda MX-6; both are built in Michigan; the turbo engine departs

Cadillac's final Allantés go on sale, now carrying a Northstar dual-cam V-8 rated at 295 bhp, plus "Road Sensing Suspension"; traction control now applies the brakes or cuts back the engine

Mercury launches the Villager minivan, produced in Ohio in a joint venture with Nissan

▲ Like Chrysler's Concorde, the 1993 Dodge Intrepid used the company's new full-size "LH" platform and boasted similarly sleek "cab forward" sedan styling. But it came with fewer standard frills and lower prices that began near $16,000 for this base model. A sportier, uplevel ES started at $17,289.

▲ Larger tires on alloy wheels marked the 1993 Intrepid ES, which also came with all-disc brakes. Anti-lock brakes were optional on both base and ES models. Power was your choice of 3.3 ohv or 3.5 twincam V-6, each pulling with a four-speed automatic. Dodge sold a healthy 81,000 Intrepids for the model year.

▲ Chrysler's new 1993 "LH" sedan was also sold (with somewhat different styling) as the Eagle Vision. It came as an ESi (*shown*) and the sportier TSi with 3.3 and 3.5 V-6, respectively. Sales totaled 30,676.

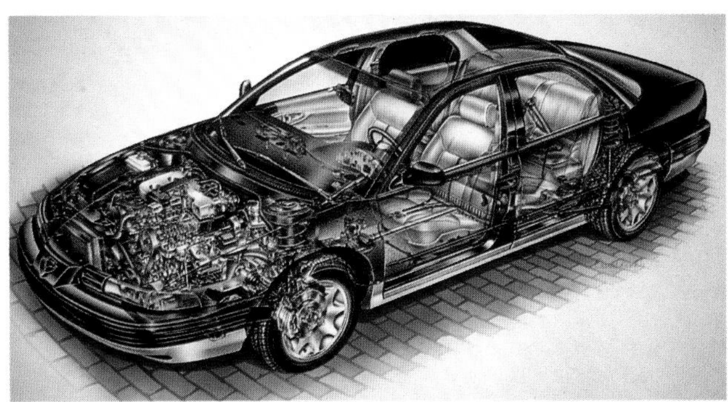

▲ A '93 Eagle Vision TSi bares all in this cutaway drawing that highlights the exceptional interior spaciousness of all the "LH" sedans, a benefit of their reproportioned "cab forward" design.

◀ The old '79-vintage Ford Mustang went out with a bang after 1993, thanks to a hot new limited-edition Cobra hatchback with tuned 235-horse 5.0-liter V-8, special upsized high-performance tires, and $20,000 base price. Meantime, regular V-8 models like this GT hatch were downrated from 225 to 205 horses, owing to a change in Ford's rating system. Mustang model-year sales leaped by 30,000 units to 114,228.

## 1993 Calendar Year Car Sales

| | | |
|---|---|---|
| 1. Ford....1,292,227 | 6. Oldsmobile....380,563 | 11. Chrysler....194,588 |
| 2. Chevrolet/Geo....1,049,618 | 7. Dodge....368,183 | 12. Lincoln....173,644 |
| 3. Pontiac....544,302 | 8. Saturn....229,356 | 13. Eagle....71,225 |
| 4. Buick....500,691 | 9. Cadillac....204,159 | |
| 5. Mercury....412,278 | 10. Plymouth....200,136 | |

*Figures include cars made for the Big 3 in plants managed by Japanese companies*

▲ Ford's sporty Taurus SHO ("Super High Output") made do with "just" a five-speed manual and 3.0 twincam V-6 on its 1989 debut. For '93 it finally got a four-speed automatic option and a 3.2 V-6 (making the same 220 horses) to go with it. Still, sales remained low.

▲ Though still an under-skin cousin to Mazda's MX-6, the 1993 Ford Probe was all-new, again with all-Ford styling and its own chassis tuning. Both the base four-cylinder hatch coupe and this sporty V-6 GT proved very popular, scoring a solid 137,422 sales.

▲ A far cry from Lincolns of old, the all-new 1993 Mark VIII boasted slick, ultra-clean lines and a silky new 4.6-liter twincam V-8, whose 280 horses could run 0-60 mph in well under 7.0 seconds.

▲ Though based on the latest Thunderbird, the '93 Mark VIII bore its own unique look. Only a single fully equipped coupe was offered, starting at $36,890. All-disc anti-lock brakes were standard.

▲ Mercury joined the minivan melee with the 1993 Villager, sharing a front-drive design with the new Ford-built Nissan Quest. A 3.0 V-6 and four-speed automatic were standard on GS and this uplevel LS at prices from $17,000. Sales were good at close to 109,000.

▲ A 1988 newcomer based on the Mazda 323, the subcompact Mercury Tracer was redesigned for '91 along with Ford's second-series Escort. The '93 lineup again included a sporty LTS four-door, with a twincam 1.8 Mazda I-4. Base price was an attractive $12,023.

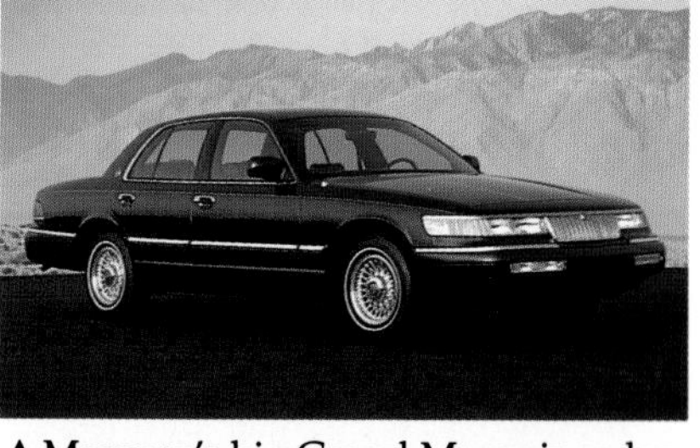

▲ Mercury's big Grand Marquis sedan was fully revamped along with Ford's Crown Victoria for 1992, losing wagons but gaining a modern new drivetrain. For 1993, the LS (*shown*) and entry-level GS got a standard passenger air bag and minor equipment changes.

---

Saturn suffers another in a series of recalls, but turns potential bad publicity into a virtual party as dealers make "fixes" easy to obtain

*Ford News* fades away after 47 years of publication

Buick Century gets a new 2.2-liter base engine; ABS is standard on all LeSabres; Park Avenue gets optional automatic ride control

The last E-body Buick Rivieras are produced, but the name is expected to return for 1995

Cadillac Seville/Eldorado hit 295 horsepower, with the new Northstar V-8 in Touring Coupe and STS; a milder Northstar comes in the Eldo Sport Coupe

Sophisticated traction control is available in the Cadillac Eldorado/Seville; passenger-side air bags are added

▲ A new Sport Handling option was among the few 1993 changes in Plymouth's Voyager minivans (and Dodge Caravans). Here, the long-body Grand Voyager with top LX trim and all-wheel drive (AWD).

▲ Plymouth's Laser listed a new Gold Decor Package option for '93 (*shown*), but would not return for '95, when a new U.S.-built design would appear only in Eagle Talon and Mitsubishi Eclipse versions.

▲ Back for 1993 from a '92 debut was the Plymouth Duster, reborn as a sub-compact three-door Sundance. A 3.0 V-6, spoiler, uprated chassis, and other extras were included for as little as $10,498 to start.

▲ Having gained mini-headlamps in a 1992 facelift, the Cutlass Supreme convertible offered a "Twin Dual Cam" 3.4-liter V-6 as a new option in Oldsmobile's 95th Anniversary year. Base price was $22,699.

▲ A fourth-generation Firebird bowed for 1993 with the same basic design as the new Camaro, but Pontiac offered two V-8 models—Formula and Trans Am—to Chevy's one, plus a V-6 base car. Here, the T/A.

▲ Formula was the bargain performance buy among 1993 Pontiac Firebirds, offering the Trans Am's 275-horse LT1 V-8 and six-speed manual gearbox for about $3400 less to start: $17,995. All the new 'Birds boasted anti-lock brakes and styling inspired by the '88 Banshee show car.

▲ With nearly 247,500 sales, the Pontiac Grand Am bowed only to the Chevy Cavalier as GM's most popular 1993 car. That year's models were much like the fully revised '92s, but gained new engine mounts and induction systems for quieter four-cylinder operation, plus a firmer "Level III" suspension for the top-line GT sedan and coupe (*shown*).

---

Cadillac's upper-rung de Ville is now called Sixty Special; the Fleetwood badge moves to a huge restyled rear-drive sedan with dual air bags

Chevrolet Caprice gets rounded rear wheel openings; a bigger 5.7-liter V-8 engine goes into the LTZ

The ZR-1 Corvette adds even more horses—now rated at 405 bhp

Optional Passive Keyless Entry System comes on Corvettes: Doors unlock as driver approaches

The final Chrysler New Yorker Fifth Avenue/Salons and Imperials are built

Dodge drops the Spirit R/T sedan, but expects to produce 800 similarly turbo-powered Daytona IROC R/T coupes

Dodge Dynasty bites the dust; anti-lock braking is available in the subcompact Shadow

▲ Buick's 1994 Park Avenues gained passenger air bags, and the uplevel Ultra (*shown*) gained 20 horses—to 225 total—via a revised supercharger. Prices this year started at $26,999.

▲ With quality vastly improved the elderly A-body Buick Century had a driver air bag and anti-lock brakes as across-the-board standards for '94. This is the top-line Custom sedan.

▲ Cadillac's sporty Seville STS saw few changes for '94, but its base-model companion was renamed SLS and given a high-torque, 270-horsepower version of its 295-bhp Northstar V-8.

▲ Cadillac was without a Coupe de Ville in '94 for the first time since the 1949 original. But the Sedan de Ville was redesigned on the Seville platform, with styling like that of the latest Fleetwood Brougham. Base-priced at $32,990, it came with Speed Sensing Suspension and a 200-horsepower 4.9 V-8.

▲ Aimed at bucks-up luxury imports, the new '94 Cadillac Concours was similar to that year's redesigned Sedan de Ville, but carried the more sophisticated Northstar V-8 in high-torque 285-horsepower form, plus variable-rate-damping Road Sensing Suspension. Prices started at $36,950.

▲ As promised, ragtop Chevy Camaros returned for 1994 in new fourth-generation guise. Like the coupes, the convertibles came in V-6 base form and (*shown here*) high-performance V-8 Z28. A power top with glass rear window was included on both. Camaro was otherwise little-changed, but traction control was a new mid-season option for Z28s with automatic.

▲ Though set to debut with the 1993 coupes, the fourth-generation Camaro convertible was delayed to '94 in the interest of defect-free quality. Beefed-up rocker panels are visible in this cutaway, but not the stout four-inch-square beam between the rear wheels.

---

Some 3000 Dodge Vipers are expected to go on sale, but production halts because of a serious hood flaw

The Touring Sedan is dropped from Ford's Crown Victoria line, which adds a grille; a passenger-side air bag is available

Ford Escort and Mercury Tracer go on sale early in the season, marketed under a special one-price, no-haggle program

The high-performance Ford Taurus SHO is finally available with automatic transmission; a passenger-side air bag is made optional in the Taurus

A limited-edition Ford Mustang Cobra debuts, with a modified 5.0-liter V-8

A supercharged V-6 is now available in the Pontiac Bonneville SSE, as well as the SSEi

◀ A new Chevy Monte Carlo bowed in early '94 as a '95 model—a redesigned replacement for the Lumina coupe. Base LS and sporty Z34 were listed, the latter with a 210-horse 3.4 twincam V-6. Part of the publicity run-up was this splashy Z34 pacer for the '94 Brickyard 400 stock-car race at Indianapolis.

▲ Renamed the Lumina Minivan, Chevy's 1994 version of the "GM200" front-drive design wore a bobbed nose that trimmed length by three inches. New options included a $295 power sliding right-rear door and $225 child safety seats.

▲ Chevy's Corvette added traction control and a passenger air bag as new standard equipment for 1994. The hot ZR-1 returned from '93 with 405 horses versus its previous 375, but remained a tough sell. Here, the dashing $42,960 ragtop.

▲ Chevy revived the nostalgic Impala SS handle for a heated-up '94 Caprice with a 260-horse version of the Corvette LT1 V-8, plus unique styling touches and police-inspired chassis tuning. Base price was just $22,495.

▲ After exposing its headlamps in a '93 facelift, the J-body Chrysler LeBaron convertible returned for a final stand with a 3.0 V-6 as its only engine—and no coupe companion. Model choices thinned to this lone GTC, base-priced at $16,999. Up for '95: an all-new replacement called Sebring, a twin of Dodge's forthcoming Avenger.

▲ Among early '94 arrivals were two stylish new top-line Chryslers: the first "cab forward" New Yorker (*top*) and bucket-seat LHS (*above*). Based on the acclaimed "LH" design, they differed in details but shared a 214-horse 3.5 twincam V-6.

**1994**

The model year begins with sharp price hikes on most models

Senator Richard Bryan prepares to try again for a 40-mpg CAFE standard by the beginning of the 21st Century; he hopes for White House backing

The emissions focus for the later '90s may be on carbon dioxide, rather than previously targeted pollutants

Various engines adopt environmentally friendly R-134A refrigerant for air conditioners

Driver-side air bags are added to the Buick Skylark; Oldsmobile Achieva, Ciera, and Cutlass Supreme; Pontiac Grand Am

▲ After adding black to its color chart for '93, the macho Dodge Viper added yellow and emerald green, with a black/tan interior for the latter (in lieu of gray/black). Also new was an electronic device designed to prevent the accidental selection of reverse gear.

▲ New for '91, the Japanese-built Dodge Stealth continued into 1994 as close kin to the Mitsubishi 3000GT. Tops again among the three hatch coupe models was this racy $37,500 R/T Turbo with a blown 3.0 V-6 sending 320 horses to all four wheels.

◀ Unwrapped in early '94, the new front-drive 1995 Neon brought Chrysler's "cab forward" look to the small-car arena—and made value news with prices starting as low as $8975. Sold in identical Dodge and Plymouth guises, it boasted a new 2.0-liter, Chrysler-designed overhead-cam four-cylinder engine with 132 horses. A twincam version followed about six months later. Trim levels comprised base, Highline (*shown*), and Sport.

▲ Though not that much sportier than other '95 Neons, the Sport version did offer anti-lock brakes (optional on lesser models) and "touring" suspension with one-inch-larger wheels and tires at a $12,215 starting price.

▲ The '94 Eagle Visions were much like the debut '93s except for power steering with variable- instead of fixed-rate assist. This TSi was base-priced at $22,773, but the entry-level ESi now looked almost the same, yet cost just $19,308.

▲ Aspire was Ford's chunky new 1994 replacment for its 1987-93 Festiva minicar. Offered in three-door form and this new five-door model, Aspire was likewise built in South Korea, due largely to its Mazda design. Prices started at $8240.

---

Passenger-side air bags are installed in the Oldsmobile Eighty-Eight and Ninety-Eight, Ford Thunderbird, Mercury Cougar, Buick LeSabre and Park Avenue, Chevrolet Caprice, and Pontiac Grand Prix/Bonneville

No Buick Rivieras are offered this year; the '95 will be all-new

Cadillac de Ville is restyled on a K-Special platform—a stretch of the Seville—with air bags that protect three front passengers

The new Cadillac de Ville Concours comes with a 270-bhp Northstar engine, like the top versions of Seville and Eldorado; a conventional V-8 is also available

Chevrolet Caprice adopts dual air bags; the sporty Impala SS debuts at mid-season; Beretta comes in standard and new Z26 form

Both the Chevrolet Camaro and Pontiac Firebird add a convertible body style

▲ Following hard on the hooves of Ford's first redesigned ponycar in 15 years was a new Mustang Cobra, launched in early 1994 with 17-inch chrome wheels, Z-rated tires, and a high-output 240-horse 5.0 V-8 among the unique features. Only some 4000 coupes like this were slated for sale.

▲ The new '94 Mustang was built on a heavily modified version of the old '79-vintage "Fox" chassis, but boasted all-new styling inside and out, plus standard all-disc brakes with optional anti-lock control. Here, the bespoilered $20,160 GT coupe.

▲ Ford's new '94 Mustang Cobra paced that year's Indy 500, and 1000 replicas were slated for sale at $23,525, versus $20,675 for the coupe and $21,970 for the normal GT ragtop. Here, the actual pacer and its 1965 forebear at the Brickyard.

◀ Recalling to mind a rare early Mustang option was this 60-pound, liftoff fiberglass hardtop for '94 convertibles.

▼ Mercury's slow-selling Capri convertible got only minor changes for 1994, its final year.

▲ Another early '94 entry was a modestly restyled Lincoln Continental sedan with new grille, taillamps, rocker trim, and standard leather cabin. Prices began at $33,750.

---

Chrysler launches a lengthened New Yorker and LHS as an early '94 model; traction control is standard on the LHS

The Chrysler LeBaron is reduced to one model, a convertible, with standard V-6; the LeBaron coupe is history, along with the Imperial and Dodge Dynasty

Chrysler's minivans meet all safety requirements through 1998

Chrysler's LH sedans—Concorde, Intrepid, Vision—can be ordered with flex-fuel V-6 engines that run on a mix of gasoline and methanol

The Dodge Shadow and Plymouth Sundance return for a final partial season, then are replaced by the all-new subcompact Neon sedans; the Shadow convertible is dropped

Ford issues an all-new Mustang after the model year begins—the first restyle since 1979. A V-6 is now the base engine

▲ The Olds Cutlass Supreme finally got a driver's air bag for '94, plus anti-lock brakes. A new Special Edition sedan and coupe offered more features at a new, lower $16,995 "value" price.

▲ Despite its 1991 redesign, the Olds Ninety-Eight still couldn't match the sales of Buick's Park Avenue. This is the top-line 1994 Regency Elite, which base-priced just shy of $28,000.

▲ There was no great change in Plymouth's Sundance for 1994. Reason: the exciting new Neon, its imminent replacement. This sporty V-6 Duster version of the three-door wore a $10,946 base sticker.

▲ Chrysler's new 1995 Neon marked some kind of first in being sold under two different nameplates—though neither the Dodge nor Plymouth versions were actually badged as such. Here, an early example of the lone four-door body style in Highline trim.

▲ After scoring a scant 9679 sales for '93, Firebird added convertibles for '94. Pontiac also marked the Trans Am's 25th birthday with a $995 white-and-blue trim package for that year's new T/A GT coupe. Only some 2000 cars were scheduled to have it.

▲ Like Chevy's Lumina Minivan, the '94 Pontiac Trans Sport wore a bobbed nose and standard driver's air bag. As in '93, an optional 170-horse "3800" V-6 gave greatly improved mid-range performance.

► GM's Saturn subsidiary had expanded models by '94 to include "SW" wagons (*foreground*) as well as a lower-priced SC1 coupe.

### 1994 Calendar Year Car Sales

1. Ford............................1,369,268
2. Chevrolet/Geo..........1,004,157
3. Pontiac..........................586,343
4. Buick.............................546,836
5. Oldsmobile..................423,847
6. Mercury..........................390,407
7. Dodge.............................354,174
8. Saturn.............................286,003
9. Cadillac..........................210,686
10. Plymouth........................197,813
11. Chrysler.......................197,342
12. Lincoln.........................179,166
13. Eagle..............................62,495

*Figures include cars made for the Big 3 in plants managed by Japanese companies*

▲ Buick's midsize mainstay returned for its 14th season with a new backlit instrument cluster and new seats among its key changes. Century's no-surprises formula wore well with its loyal audience, and sales were 93,361 for the year, second only to the LeSabre in Buick's line.

▲ Century was one of the few midsize domestic cars to still offer a station wagon body style. Engines were a 120-bhp 2.2-liter four-cylinder or a 160-bhp V-6. Prices were reasonable, ranging from $16,360 to $17,965. This is the $17,080 Special wagon. A rear-facing third seat was available.

▲ New for base versions of Buick's flagship Park Avenue was the 3800 Series II, a 3.8-liter V-6 with 205 bhp, 35 more than the Series I 3800.

▲ Like all Regals, the Gran Sport sedan gained a new dashboard with a passenger-side air bag. Two- and four-door body styles continued for 1995.

▲ Back after a one-year hiatus, Riviera returned bigger and more powerful. Buick's new coupe would find more than 41,000 buyers in 1995.

▲ Skylark's new base engine was a 150-bhp dual overhead-cam 2.3-liter four-cylinder. It replaced a 115-bhp single-cam version of that engine.

◀ Buick's biggest car was the 4600-pound Roadmaster Estate wagon. It listed for $27,070 in all its eight-seat, vista-roof, faux wood-grain glory.

**1995**

Industry sales fall short of expectations. The 14.8 million cars and light trucks sold in calendar 1995 is a 2.1-percent drop from the year-earlier period. Car sales fall 4 percent, despite a rush of year-end incentives. Truck sales grow to more than 6 million

In the last season of its original design, Ford Taurus is the best-selling car for the fourth consecutive year, despite a late charge by the Honda Accord

Ford Motor Company sells more than 2 million trucks, topping General Motors in truck sales for the first time since 1970

Honda's former top U.S. sales executive, S. James Cardiges, is sentenced to prison for accepting bribes in the ongoing Honda corruption scandal

GM embarks on a $1 billion revamp of its dealer organization. Reducing its number of "dualed" outlets is a goal

▶ A body-colored grille helps identify the Touring Coupe edition of Cadillac's Eldorado. For '95, its Northstar V-8 had 300 bhp, while base Eldorado's version made 275; both were 5-bhp increases over '94. The standard Road Sensing Suspension, which automatically adjusted firmness based on vehicle speed, body lean, and other factors, added steering angle to its parameters. The ETC listed for $41,535, the base model for $38,220. Optional chrome wheels added $1195.

▲ Headlamps that turned on automatically with the windshield wipers were among new standard features on the '95 De Ville and Concours. De Ville also gained traction control, which was already standard on Concours (*shown*).

▲ Fleetwood, Cadillac's only rear-wheel-drive car, had a 260-bhp 5.7-liter V-8 derived from the Corvette's LT1 engine and could tow 7000 pounds. New for '95 was an on/off switch for the standard traction-control system.

▲ The revamped Lumina and its Monte Carlo coupe companion were early '95 entries. Lumina was Chevy's best-selling car, at 214,595 units for '95.

▲ The 260-bhp Impala SS bowed during 1994 as the hot version of the Caprice. For '95, green-gray and Dark Cherry joined black as SS colors.

▲ The redesigned Cavalier featured two- and four-door models, plus a convertible with power top. At $17,210, it was the costliest Cavalier.

---

Former Chrysler Corporation chairman Lee Iacocca joins billionaire Las Vegas businessman and Chrysler shareholder Kirk Kerkorian in a bid to take over the automaker. Chrysler's board fends off the effort, but puts a Kerkorian ally on the board of directors, and pays Iacocca $21 million in deferred stock options

Trucks account for 41.5 percent of total U.S. vehicle sales and climb to 49 percent of combined Big 3 sales. For the first time ever, the top three selling vehicles are trucks as the Ford Explorer jumps from eighth place in 1994 to No. 3, behind perennial front runners, Ford F-Series and Chevrolet C/K

CarMax, AutoNation USA, and other "superstores" threaten to revolutionize used-car sales. They apply mass-retailing techniques, offering large inventories of used cars, computerized selection, warranties, and fixed prices. Results are mixed, but automakers and traditional new- and used-car dealers watch closely

▲ Corvette paced the Indianapolis 500 for the third time in 1995, and celebrated with 527 near-replicas of the genuine pace car shown here. With its 300-bhp LT1 V-8, the 'Vette needed no mechanical modifiactions to pace the great race.

◀ The 490 roadster was Chevy's entry-level 1919 model. It had 26 bhp and sold for $715. The '95 Camaro convertible started at $19,495 for the 160-bhp 3.4-liter V-6 model shown, while the 275-bhp V-8 Z28 ragtop listed for $23,095.

▲ The '95 Monte Carlo went on sale in the fall of '94 as this $16,770 LS model with a 160-bhp 3.1-liter V-6 or the flashier $18,970 Z34 with a 210-bhp dual-overhead-cam 3.4-liter V-6. Its NASCAR debut was in the '95 Daytona 500.

▲ Customer Montes had front-wheel drive. This is Dale Earnhardt's. Like all NASCAR Winston Cup racers, it had a 358-cid V-8 of about 700 bhp and rear-wheel drive. Jeff Gordon, also in a Monte, beat Earnhardt for the '95 title.

◀ New Yorker (*shown*) and LHS, Chrysler's versions of the corporate LH cars, now required a double push on the keyfob button to open the trunk.

▶ Sebring followed the Dodge Avenger to market as Chrysler's version of the Mitsubishi-built front-drive sports coupe.

---

Plymouth is the biggest sales loser in the U.S., declining 28.7 percent from 1994. Other big losers: Geo, down 17.6 percent, and Lincoln, suffering a 15.8-percent dip

Lincoln Continental gets a major revamp and replaces its V-6 with a dual overhead-cam V-8

A National Automobile Dealers Association survey shows the average new-car dealer spends $416 on advertising per car sold; that's up by $42 from 1994

Chrysler drops the LeBaron sedan, leaving the popular convertible as its only LeBaron model

Ford taps its European Mondeo sedan as the basis for the new Ford Contour and Mercury Mystique. They're sportier than the Tempo and Topaz they replace, but far more expensive

At 225 inches, the rear-drive Cadillac Fleetwood is the longest production car built in the U.S.

▲ Replacing the LeBaron sedan, Cirrus debuted for '95 as Chrysler's new "compact" four-door. Prices started at $17,435 for the base model and $19,365 for the plusher LXi version shown here.

▲ Cirrus and its Dodge Stratus sibling were built on Chrysler's new JA front-wheel-drive platform. They shared the corporate "cab forward" design, which furnished midsize-car interior dimensions in a car no longer overall than most rival's compact offerings.

▲ The V-10, 400-bhp Viper continued mechanically unchanged for '95, though its cabin gained a passenger assist handle and seat-cushion storage pockets. Dodge had also begun to offer alternatives to the original red exterior/gray interior colors. Emerald Green and Bright Yellow were now available, with a black-and-tan upholstery combination also available.

▲ Like its Cirrus cousin, the Dodge Stratus came standard with anti-lock brakes and dual air bags. Base prices ranged from $13,965 to $17,265.

▲ Stratus offered a four-cylinder base model and the V-6 ES. It handled well enough to serve as a training car for the Skip Barber driving school.

▲ Aggressive looks and reasonable prices were the appeal of the new-for-'95 Avenger. Dodge sold nearly 35,000 of these front-drive coupes that year.

---

Mainstream Caprices get the "dogleg" rear-roof pillar shape introduced last year on the Impala SS

Traction control is a first-time option for V-8 powered Chevrolet Camaros and Pontiac Firebirds

GM's midsize cars—the Chevrolet Lumina and Monte Carlo, Buick Regal, and Pontiac Grand Prix—add a passenger-side air bag to the already-standard driver-side air bag

Chevrolet Astro minivan loses the shorter of its two body types

GM redesigns the Chevy Blazer and GMC Jimmy with new styling inside and out and adds a driver-side air bag

Addition of a passenger air bag gives Ford Escort and Mercury Tracer dual air bags, but they retain motorized front shoulder belts and manual lap belts

▲ Targeted at import buyers was the Eagle Vision version of Chrysler's LH cars. This is '95's top-line TSi model. It had a 214-bhp overhead-cam V-6.

▲ The power driver's seat was now optional, but a CD player was newly available as Mustang cantered into '95 largely unchanged from its '94 redo.

▲ Replacing the Tempo for '95 was the far more-competent Contour. Ranging from $13,310 to $15,695, base prices were about $2400 higher, however.

▲ Starting at $9580 for the two-door hatchback and $11,040 for the four-door sedan, Escort had a winning formula. Ford sold 285,570 of the subcompacts in calendar-year '95.

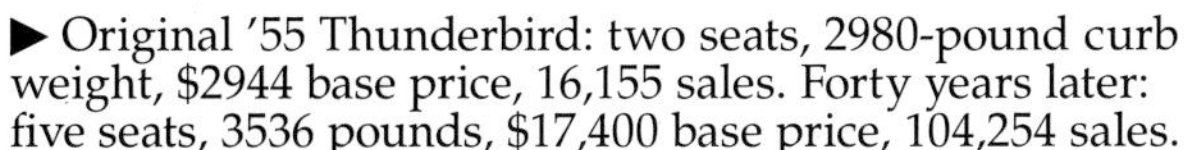

▶ Original '55 Thunderbird: two seats, 2980-pound curb weight, $2944 base price, 16,155 sales. Forty years later: five seats, 3536 pounds, $17,400 base price, 104,254 sales.

▲ Mystique was Mercury's version of the new Contour. Both had four- and six-cylinder engines. Tight rear-seat room would be an ongoing criticism.

◀ Bowing in December '95, the new Lincoln Continental retained front-wheel drive, but was longer and wider than before. Big change was underhood, where a 260-bhp dual-overhead-cam V-8 replaced the 160-bhp pushrod V-6. Starting price was $40,750.

---

Chrysler launches its import-fighting Neon as an early 1995 model. Sold in identical form under Dodge and Plymouth brands, the front-drive subcompacts debut as sedans in January 1994, and for the start of the '95 model year, gain 2-door coupe versions. Engines are single- and dual overhead-cam 4-cylinders

Chevrolet redesigns its best-selling car for the first time in 13 years, giving the Cavalier a longer wheelbase, fresh styling, and a new interior with standard dual air bags. Pontiac's version of this front-drive subcompact also is redesigned and changes its name from Sunbird to Sunfire

Dodge Spirit and Plymouth Acclaim, last of the Chrysler Corporation sedans to use original K-car platform, enter their final season. They offer a Chrysler-built 4-cylinder or a Mitsubishi-built V-6

Average new-car loan rate is 11.2 percent, highest since 1991

▲ Plain-Jane Plymouth Acclaim could be had for as little as $12,470 in '95. This was its seventh, and last, year.

▶ Aurora bowed for '95 to signal a new direction for Oldsmobile. It aimed squarely at luxury imports and was competitive, starting at $31,370.

▲ Part of Aurora's allure was its standard 250-bhp twincam 4.0-liter V-8.

▲ Supplanting Sunbird was Pontiac's new Sunfire. Coupe models were this 120-bhp, $11,074 SE or the 150-bhp, $12,834 GT.

▲ This is Bonneville's SSEi version, which kept its 225-bhp supercharged V-6 for '95, while base V-6s gained 35 bhp, to 205.

▲ Aero body trim helps ID Pontiac's Grand Prix GTP coupe. The $2256 GTP option added a 210-bhp twincam V-6. Base coupe price was $17,384.

▶ A passenger-side air bag and 15 more horsepower for the base engine were additions to the '95 Saturn line. Reasonably priced from $9995 to $13,815, these plastic-body coupes, wagons, and sedans generated strong buyer loyalty. With sales of 285,647, Saturn was GM's top-selling '95 car.

**1995 Calendar Year Car Sales**

| | | |
|---|---|---|
| 1. Ford.........................1,279,096 | 6. Oldsmobile...................371,725 | 11. Lincoln........................150,814 |
| 2. Chevrolet/Geo.......1,054,071 | 7. Mercury.........................361,315 | 12. Plymouth....................113,565 |
| 3. Pontiac........................566,826 | 8. Saturn...........................285,674 | 13. Eagle.............................53,612 |
| 4. Buick...........................471,819 | 9. Chrysler.........................215,164 | |
| 5. Dodge.........................403,839 | 10. Cadillac.........................180,504 | |

*Figures include cars made for the Big 3 in plants managed by Japanese companies*

▲ Buick still had the Century for '96, but the newer Regal finally overtook it in sales, 86,847 to 72,433. This is the Regal Custom sedan. It started at $19,740 with a 160-bhp 3.1-liter V-6.

▲ Like its Olds Eighty Eight and Pontiac Bonneville siblings, Buick's LeSabre gained the 3800 Series II V-6 for '96, but it was the 205-bhp version, not the 240-bhp supercharged unit.

▲ Buick stole a beat from its corporate cousins with the Regal GS. Its 3.8-liter V-6 was smoother and torquier than the twincam 3.4 V-6 in the Grand Prix, Lumina, and Cutlass Supreme.

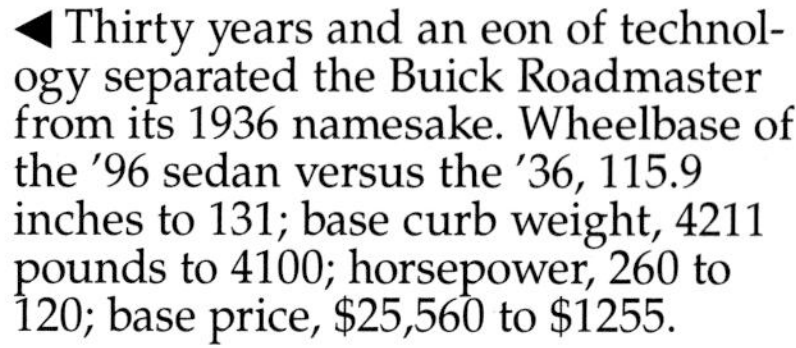

◀ Thirty years and an eon of technology separated the Buick Roadmaster from its 1936 namesake. Wheelbase of the '96 sedan versus the '36, 115.9 inches to 131; base curb weight, 4211 pounds to 4100; horsepower, 260 to 120; base price, $25,560 to $1255.

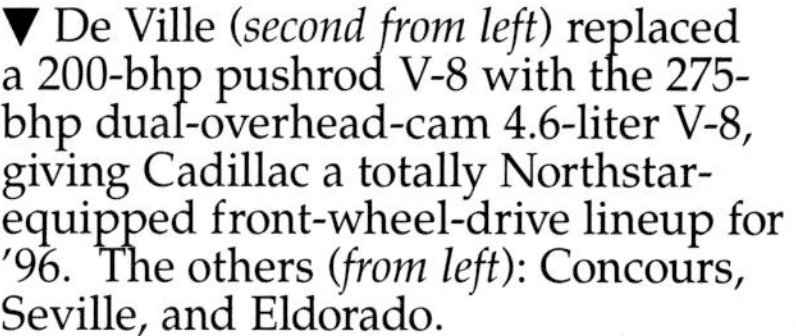

▼ De Ville (*second from left*) replaced a 200-bhp pushrod V-8 with the 275-bhp dual-overhead-cam 4.6-liter V-8, giving Cadillac a totally Northstar-equipped front-wheel-drive lineup for '96. The others (*from left*): Concours, Seville, and Eldorado.

**1996**

Nineteen ninety-six marks the centennial of the American automobile, celebrating the 100th anniversary of the first "motor wagons" built by brothers Frank and Charles Duryea in Springfield, Massachusetts

For the first time in history, the Big 3 sell more trucks than cars—5.7 million pickups, minivans, and sport-utility vehicles—versus 5.3 million cars

Cost-cutting Australian Jac Nasser appointed president of Ford Automotive Operations

Total domestic and import truck sales increase 7.8 percent to a record 6.6 million and account for 43.7 percent of all vehicle sales. Car sales fall 1.2 percent. For the year, total vehicle sales rise by 2.5 percent, to 15.1 million units. It's the best overall sales year since 1988

▲ Corvette's fourth generation went out with a flourish in '96, with silver Collector Editions and this very special Grand Sport. Just 1000 of the latter were built and they used a 330-bhp LT4 V-8. Other 'Vettes had the 300-bhp LT1.

▲ Borrowing Corvette's 5.7-liter LT1 V-8, albeit with 285 bhp for '96, was the Chevy Camaro Z28. It was hot enough to pace NASCAR's third Brickyard 400. Base Camaros, meanwhile, gained the 200-bhp 3.8-liter V-6 as standard.

▲ Out with the Quad 4, in with the twincam: Both were dual overhead-cam four-cylinder engines, but twin-cam was stronger, smoother. It was available in the '96 Chevy Cavalier.

▲ Beretta was a two-door version of the Chevy Corsica sedan. Both front-drive compacts stood pat for '96 pending Corsica's replacement by the Malibu. Beretta would not be replaced.

▲ GM shelved its big rear-drive cars after '96, including the Caprice Classic wagon. This $22,405 eight-seater came with a 5.7-liter V-8 and whitewalls. Woodgrain was a $595 option, though.

◀ Caprice's demise saddened thousands of cops, who swore by the bow-tie beasts. The final "Law Enforcement Package" was offered on sedans and wagons and included either the 200-bhp 4.3-liter V-8 or the 260-bhp Corvette-derived LT1 V-8 that also was part of the Impala SS. It also featured heavy-duty suspension, brakes, and cooling. Caprice sales to all sources totaled 46,261 for 1996.

---

Ford Taurus is redesigned for the first time since its 1986 introduction

Aided by heavy incentives, Taurus retains title of best-selling car, but 51 percent of its sales are to fleets. Runner-up Honda Accord, by contrast, tallies only 4.2 percent fleet sales

General Motors files suit against former executive J. Ignacio Lopez, charging that he stole company secrets when he and seven colleagues quit GM to join Volkswagen in 1993

Average price of a new domestic car drops to $16,998, lowest since 1991

GM's market share continues to shrink, melting to 31.1 percent during 1996. Riding the boom in truck sales, Chrysler Corporation increases its market share to 16.2 percent, its fattest slice of the U.S. car pie since 1957

▲ Fully redesigned for the first time since their debut as 1984 models, Chrysler Corporation's '96 minivans were sleeker and smarter. This is the top-line Chrysler Town & Country.

▲ Replacing the LeBaron as Chrysler's ragtop was the '96 Sebring. Sebring coupes used a Mitsubishi platform, but the attractive new convertible was built off Chrysler's own JA chassis.

▲ The New Yorker nameplate, used first in 1938 and the oldest still in use in the U.S., was retired in mid-'96. This sedan is the last to wear the badge. The related LHS continued.

◀ Dodge's Viper RT/10 roadster was joined in 1996 by the Viper GTS coupe. Both used a V-10, but the new coupe had 450 bhp to the RT/10's 415. No mechanical modification was required for the GTS to pace that year's Indy 500. Dodge also supplied Ram support trucks.

▲ For the fastest soccer mom in the league, Dodge conjured up this concept Caravan. Production models again were America's most-popular minivans, with sales of 300,117 in '96.

▲ Cloned from the Mitsubishi Eclipse, Talon ranged from this 140-bhp $14,830 ESi to the 210-bhp, $20,271 all-wheel-drive TSi. Sales of 13,842 made Talon Eagle's best-selling '96 model.

▲ Another Mitsubishi clone, the Eagle Summit Wagon offered front- or all-wheel drive and a sliding side door. It forecast later hybrid wagons. But slow sales doomed it; '96 was its last year.

---

Ford Motor Company increases its holdings in Mazda Motor Corporation to 33.4 percent, from 25 percent. The move costs Ford $500 million and effectively gives it full control over its longtime affiliate. Ford's best-selling 1996 car is the Taurus, at 401,049 units. Mazda's total U.S. car sales are 180,975 for the year

"We have bona fide car people in sales and marketing, not Pampers people."—Chrysler Corporation's outspoken president and chief operating officer Robert Lutz, commenting on a reorganization of GM's executive ranks that brought in "brand" specialists with non-automotive backgrounds

Anticipation runs high as spy photographers scramble for views of the next-generation Corvette; 1996 marks the end of the C4 generation, which debuted for 1984

Average new-car loan rate drops to 9.8 percent, from 11.2 percent in 1995

▲ Taurus defended its title as America's best-selling car with a fully redesigned model for '96. It retained front-wheel drive but was larger inside and out, and more expensive. Two V-6s and, for the SHO, a V-8, were offered.

▲ Oval styling themes on the sedan and wagon got mixed reviews. But Ford took steps to make Taurus, which started about $1500 higher than in '95, affordable. It sold 401,049 of them, and Taurus was again America's most-popular car.

▲ At 402,663 units, Explorer outsold everything in the country in '96 except the big Ford and Chevy pickups. A newly available 210-bhp 5.0-liter V-8 engine helped it lead the SUV wave.

▲ Escort's popularity helped give Ford five of 1996's top-10 selling vehicles. Escort offered hatchbacks, sedans, and wagons, including this electric-powered rig intended for fleet use.

▲ Mustang's 5.0-liter V-8 had roots in original 1965 model's. For '96, 4.6-liter overhead-cam V-8s with 215 bhp in the GT and 305 in the Cobra (*shown*) replaced the familiar pushrod 5.0.

▲ Lincoln marked its 75th anniversary in '96, and the Town Car was its best-selling model. Big, pillowy, and with base prices between $36,910 and $41,960, it defined traditional rear-wheel-drive V-8 American luxury.

▲ Mercury jumped on the sport-utility bandwagon with its Mountaineer. It was a slightly retrimmed clone of the four-door Ford Explorer and gave grateful Lincoln-Mercury dealers 26,700 sales they would have missed.

▲ Like its Ford Crown Victoria cousin, Mercury's '96 Grand Marquis came with a 4.6-liter overhead-cam V-8 of 190 bhp, or 210 with available dual exhausts. This rear-drive sedan started at $21,975. Sales were a healthy 99,770.

---

Chrysler Corporation redesigns its best-selling minivans, giving them their first complete overhall since their debut as 1984 models, when they revolutionized the auto industry. The '96 Dodge Caravan, Chrysler Town & Country, and Plymouth Voyager feature sliding doors on both sides for the first time

Dodge rolls out a coupe companion to Viper's raucous roadster; the new GTS has 450 bhp

Ford gives the Explorer an optional V-8, addressing what many viewed as the popular sport-utility vehicle's major shortfall—a lack of power

GM closes the book on its full-size, rear-wheel-drive cars, announcing assembly lines that build the Buick Roadmaster, Cadillac Fleetwood, and Chevrolet Caprice and Impala will be dedicated to truck production after the 1996 model year

▲ Sable was also redesigned for 1996 and again shared its platform and mechanicals with the Ford Taurus. Offered in sedan and wagon form, sales increased 11 percent over '95, to 114,164. It was again Mercury's top-selling 1996 model.

▲ Sable's sedan styling was slightly more conservative than that of its Taurus cousin. Like the Ford, Sable offered a 145-bhp 3.0-liter pushrod V-6 and a new 200-bhp 3.0-liter overhead-cam V-6. But Mercury had no counterpart to the SHO.

▲ Aurora got daytime running lights and a $1295 base-price increase, to $34,360, for '96. Oldsmobile also reduced the rear-window distortion that had angered some owners. Sales dipped by 2827 in the car's second season, to 23,717.

▲ Aurora's exclusive 4.0-liter dual-overhead-cam V-8 gave the 3970-pound sedan 0-60-mph in 8.2 seconds.

▲ Back for its 15th and final model year, the Cutlass Ciera offered a four-cylinder sedan starting at $14,455 and a V-6 wagon at $17,455. Belive it or not, this was Oldsmobile's best-selling 1996 car, finding 89,577 buyers.

▲ Bravada sat out 1995, but was back for '96 as an upscale take on the four-door Chevy Blazer and GMC Jimmy. Oldsmobile's version came standard with SmartTrak permanent four-wheel drive, an option on the Blazer/Jimmy.

▲ Achieva underachieved, selling just 40,344 units for Olds in '96. Even the homelier-still Buick Skylark sold 51,299. Pontiac's Grand Am, which shared their underskin design, buried them both, with sales of 222,477.

---

"Why is it that people think they have to have a 55-gallon barrel of Mountain Dew to drive to work? A long time ago, there was a horsepower race. Now there's a cupholder race." —GM designer Jerry Palmer

Average amount financed on a new car: $16,987

Tried-and-true pushrod V-8 is replaced by an overhead-cam design in the '96 Mustang

Rick Hendrick, America's biggest auto retailer, is indicted by the U.S. Justice Department, charged with paying kickbacks to Honda executives in the ongoing Honda bribery scandal

With a redesigned Wrangler due in the spring as a 1997 model, Jeep doesn't certify a '96 model, choosing instead to build out the 1995 version with no changes

The only GM product to crack the top-10 selling 1996 vehicles is the Chevrolet C/K pickup

▲ A new logo reviving its old sailboat motif wasn't the only thing fresh for Plymouth in '96. It boasted a new Breeze sedan (*third from left, above*), as well as the year's hottest show car, the retro hot-rod Prowler. Prowler would make it to production as a '97 model.

▶ Breeze contained itself to a four-cylinder engine and limited options to keep its base price a tempting $14,310.

▲ Replacing a 160-bhp 3.4-liter V-6 as the base Firebird's engine in 1996 was GM's 200-bhp 3.8-liter V-6.

▲ A new factory option for Formula (*shown*) and Trans Am, ram air kicked the 5.7-liter V-8 from 285 bhp to 305.

▲ Revised front and rear styling and 240 bhp for the supercharged V-6 (up by 15) were Bonneville's 1996 changes.

◀ For '96, Saturn's sedan and wagon got their first styling change since their debut as 1990 models. This is the $11,395 SL1 sedan.

▶ Coupes retained their original look. Here's the top-line SC2. It started at $13,295 with manual shift and delivered 124 bhp.

### 1996 Calendar Year Car Sales

| | | |
|---|---|---|
| 1. Ford............1,240,928 | 6. Mercury............354,848 | 11. Cadillac............168,703 |
| 2. Chevrolet/Geo............1,045,172 | 7. Oldsmobile............306,486 | 12. Lincoln............141,476 |
| 3. Pontiac............529,710 | 8. Saturn............278,574 | 13. Eagle............28,695 |
| 4. Buick............427,350 | 9. Chrysler............212,021 | |
| 5. Dodge............421,945 | 10. Plymouth............169,972 | |

*Figures include cars made for the Big 3 in plants managed by Japanese companies*

▲ For '97, Park Avenue moved to the strong new platform GM introduced on the Buick Riviera and Olds Aurora. Styling retained traditional Park Avenue themes, but the wheelbase grew by three inches and weight by 250 pounds.

▲ Base Parks used the 205-bhp 3.8-liter V-6 and started at $29,995. The Ultra (*shown*) included the 240-bhp supercharged 3.8, plus traction control and goodies in its $34,995 base price. Sales jumped 30 percent, to 68,777.

▲ Redesigned for '97, Buick's Century retained its conservative appeal but wrapped it in new sheetmetal. Base models started at $17,845, Limiteds (*shown*) at $19,220. Both had a V-6. Sales increased 21 percent, to 91,232.

▲ Cadillac moved to attract younger, import-oriented buyers for '97 by retrimming GM's Opel Omega and calling it Catera. The compact-sized sedan started at $29,995, but leather was part of a $3000 option package.

▲ Catera was the only rear-wheel-drive Cadillac and had a 200-bhp twincam 3.0-liter V-6 and automatic transmission. Performance was competent but not up to BMW standards. Zero-60 mph took 9.2 seconds.

▲ The rear-drive Fleetwood was dead, leaving the $36,995 De Ville as Cadillac's biggest car. It got standard side air bags and a facelift for 1997.

◀ Concours was the performance version of the De Ville. It had 300 bhp instead of 275, a more sophisticated suspension, and started at $41,995.

**1997**

Another healthy year for the U.S. auto market, with sales of 15.1 million domestic and imported cars and trucks, though there was a negligible increase in sales overall, just 0.1 percent over 1996

Of vehicle types, the big sales gainers were again light trucks. Sales of pickups, minivans, and sport-utility vehicles gained 3.9 percent, increasing their share of the overall U.S. market to 45.3 percent. Sales of cars from all manufacturers actually fell 2.8 percent in 1997

For the first time since 1991, a domestic nameplate was not the nation's best-selling car, as the Ford Taurus fell from the top spot to finish behind both the new sales champ, the Toyota Camry, and the runner-up Honda Accord

▲ Chevrolet redesigned its two-seat sports car for '97, retaining a rear-wheel-drive layout, fiberglass body panels, and V-8 power, but changing most everything else. A hatchback coupe with a removable roof panel debuted first. Wheelbase grew by 8.3 inches, to 104.5, but body length increased just 1.2 inches. A new chassis eliminated the tall frame rails of the previous generation, making it easier to get into and out of the spaciously redesigned cabin. Underhood was a new all-aluminum 5.7-liter pushrod V-8 with 345 bhp. The transmission—six-speed manual or four-speed automatic—was relocated to the rear axle, for better weight distribution and more interior room. At $37,495 to start, the fifth-generation 'Vette had Ferrari-like performance: 0-60 mph in 4.7 seconds and a 172-mph top speed.

▲ Civilian Monte Carlos gained an optional power sunroof for '97, while racing versions continued to dominate NASCAR. Here, driver Terry Labonte poses with his No. 5 Monte and the version that paced the '97 Brickyard 400.

▲ Camaro marked its 30th anniversary in 1997 with an orange-stripe package that emulated the 1969 Indy 500 pace car's. The look debuted on the Camaro Z28 that paced the 1996 Brickyard 400. Here it is with its pace-car ancestors.

---

The Japanese automakers' share of the U.S. car and light truck market in 1997 climbed to 23.5 percent, while the Europeans rose to 3.9 percent. General Motors (31.1 percent) and Ford (25.2 percent) generally held steady. Chrysler Corporation's share, however, dropped from 16.2 percent to 15.2 percent

Cadillac retained its crown as America's best-selling luxury brand, increasing sales 7.2 percent, to 182,624. But GM executives, who had earlier shelved plans for a Cadillac SUV, could not help notice that arch-rival Lincoln had a hot seller in its new Navigator 4×4 wagon

Casting a wary eye at the trend in non-traditional superstores, Ford Motor Company attempted to, in effect, buy out its dealers in Indianapolis and Salt Lake City and form a new-age retailing venture of its own. But dealers balked and refused to sell. Dealers in Tulsa would eventually sign on to the plan

▲ The left-side sliding door that proved so popular upon its 1996 introduction became standard on all 1997 Chrysler Town & Country models. This is the top-line LXi version, which listed for $31,465 and had a 166-bhp 3.8-liter V-6.

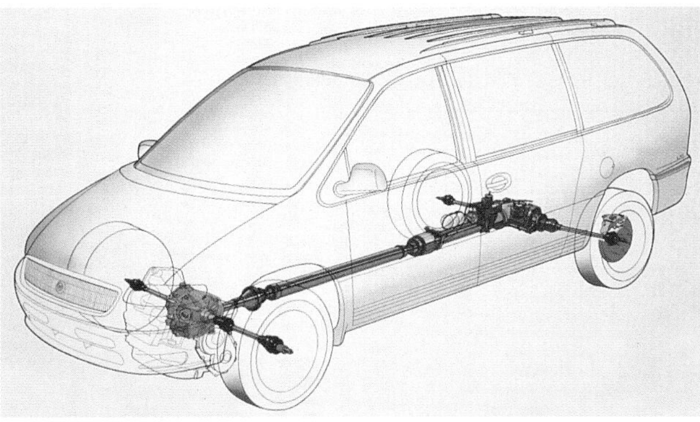

▲ The all-wheel-drive system in Chrysler Corporation's minivans used a center viscous coupling that reacted to rotational differences between front and rear axles, then transferred power to the wheels that weren't slipping.

▲ A terror on the street, Viper wasn't afraid to go racing. The GTS-R was the endurance-racing version and sported competition-ready aero addenda and suspension pieces, while boosting output of the V-10 to well over 600 bhp.

▲ Dodge's Stratus had racing in its blood, too. Its competition iteration finished first and second in the 2.0-liter class in the short-lived North American touring car series. Like production versions, the race cars were front-wheel drive.

▲ Caravan sales slipped five percent coming off its '96 redesign, but Dodge still had America's best-selling minivan in 1997, with 285,736 units. This is the Grand Caravan LE: $25,825 with front-wheel drive, $28,870 with AWD.

▲ Sharpest of Eagle's Talons was the TSi, which put the 210 bhp of its turbocharged 2.0-liter four to the pavement through an all-wheel-drive system. It did 0-60 mph in 6.5 seconds and had a base price of $20,271.

▲ Sold by Chrysler Corporation's Jeep-Eagle division, the Mitsubishi-made Talon accounted for 10,206 of Eagle's 15,352 sales in 1997. The Vision sedan made up the balance. This is the front-drive, 140-bhp, $14,830 Talon ESi.

---

Despite flat sales, Ford and GM are earning record profits. Thanks mainly to more-efficient manufacturing practices, plus the boom in truck sales, Ford's profits are up 58 percent and GM's 19 percent

Changes in the design ranks at Ford: Jack Telnack, 60, vice president of global design retires. J Mays, 43, who, as a designer at Volkswagen/Audi, was credited with the look of the New Beetle, is appointed vice president of design at Ford Automotive Operations

Drivers of cars had loathed them for years, but in the first hard evidence of an SUV backlash, *The New York Times* runs a series of articles criticizing sport-utility vehicles for fuel inefficiency and casting them as threats to smaller vehicles in collisions

▲ Thunderbird's 1990-97 generation was big and heavy, and sales fell as big coupes went out of fashion. The final 1997 model weighed 3600 pounds and came with a V-6 or V-8.

▲ Topping the Taurus line for '97 was the performance-minded SHO. It had a 235-bhp Yamaha-built 3.4-liter twin-cam V-8, but lack of a manual transmission cooled its sport-sedan appeal.

▲ Escort was redesigned for 1997. Sedans and this wagon body style carried over, but with fresh styling. A 110-bhp four-cylinder was the sole engine, and prices started at just $11,015.

▲ High-intensity discharge headlamps that cast a bright blue light were new for Mark VIII in '97, but the biggest change was to the window sticker. Declining sales prompted Lincoln to cut the base price by $2370, to $37,280.

▲ Mark VIII was freshened at the rear, too, with a full-width neon light bar. New outside mirrors tilted down when the car was shifted into reverse and incorporated LED turn-signal indicators visible to following motorists.

▲ With the demise of GM's big rear-drive cars, the 1997 Mercury Grand Marquis and its Ford Crown Victoria cousin were America's only traditional full-size V-8-powered sedans.

▲ Cougar was Mercury's more formal-looking version of the Thunderbird, and it, too, was suffering. Sales fell by 5499, to 30,516 for '97, while T-Bird's dropped by 13,387, to 66,334.

▲ Mercury's Villager was based on the design of the Nissan Quest minivan, and both were assembled at a Ford plant in Ohio. Villager outsold Quest in 1997, 55,168 to 46,858.

---

Redesigns at Buick for '97: Century gets its first complete makeover since the front-wheel-drive version was introduced in 1982, and the flagship Park Avenue moves to GM's newest big-car platform while maintaining familiar styling and carry-over powertrains

Cadillac hunts import intenders with the Catera, a retrimmed version of the Opel Omega from GM of Germany

Standard side air bags are new features for the facelifted Cadillac De Ville and Concours

Most 1997 General Motors cars, minivans, and SUVs are given standard daytime running lights

Long-awaited redesign of the Chevrolet Corvette brings new styling, a new chassis, and a new all-aluminum LS1 V-8

▲Only the second four-door sedan to pace the Indy 500, Oldsmobile's '97 Aurora could claim a kinship to the winning race car, which used a V-8 based on Aurora's production 4.0 liter.

▲ Sharing its basic structure with the new Chevy Malibu, the fresh-for-'97 Cutlass was Oldsmobile's newest mid-size entry. It came with a 160-bhp 3.1-liter V-6 and started at $17,325.

▲ Gone were the plastic body panels and "dustbuster" nose, as GM redesigned its front-drive minivans for '97. This is the Olds Silhouette. Base prices range from $21,675 to $26,235.

▲ Chrysler Corporation design chief Tom Gale (*left*) was a fan of true hot rods, and company vice chairman Robert Lutz (*right*) was a "car guy." They put their money where their hearts were by championing the transformation of the Prowler from a show car to a 1997 production Plymouth. Sticker price was $38,300, but demand for the limited-edition, rear-wheel-drive two-seater pushed some early buyers to pay double that.

◀ First-year Prowlers all were purple with a black folding top. The only powertrain was Chrysler's 214-bhp 3.2-liter overhead-cam V-6 and four-speed Autostick automatic transmission with manual-shift capability.

▶ Prowler looked retro but extensive use of aluminum, including in the body, made it pretty high tech. There was only a sliver of trunk space, so Chrysler offered this matching trailer.

Ford revamps its Escort, giving the popular subcompact and its Mercury Tracer cousin new styling inside and out

Thunderbird flies the coupe; Ford stops production of the big two-door icon, but hints strongly that the nameplate will be back before too long

Eagle Vision is dropped; Talon clings to life as Chrysler prepares to kill the Eagle brand

A redesigned Jeep Wrangler bows with classic styling cues and with a sophisticated new all-coil suspension instead of the aged leaf-spring design

GM becomes the first major car company to market an electric passenger car in modern times with the EV1, a two-seat, front-wheel-drive coupe. It's for lease only and only through Saturn dealers in Southern California and central Arizona. It's also the first vehicle marketed under the General Motors brand name

▲ Pontiac's Trans Sport was among GM's redesigned '97 minivans. It came in regular- and extended-length bodies and offered the convenience of sliding doors on both sides.

▲ Wide Track was back. Pontiac's redesigned 1997 Grand Prix had racy new styling and larger dimensions, including a front track wider by two inches and a rear wider by three.

▲ The General Motors EV1 put electric power on the street in 1997 in this aerodynamic front-drive two seater.

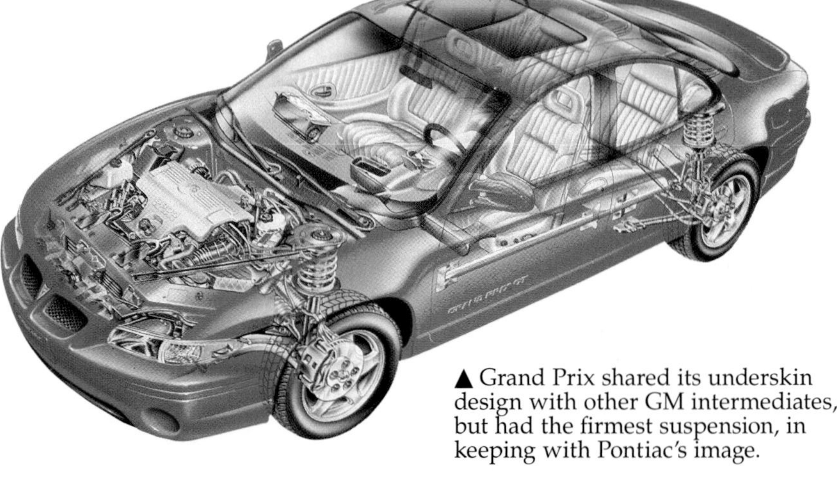

▲ Grand Prix shared its underskin design with other GM intermediates, but had the firmest suspension, in keeping with Pontiac's image.

▲ Its plastic body's aerodynamic shape gave the EV1 a 0.19 drag coefficient, lowest of any production car.

▲ Owners loved them, but the aged Saturns attracted fewer buyers for '97. Sales fell 10 percent, to 251,099.

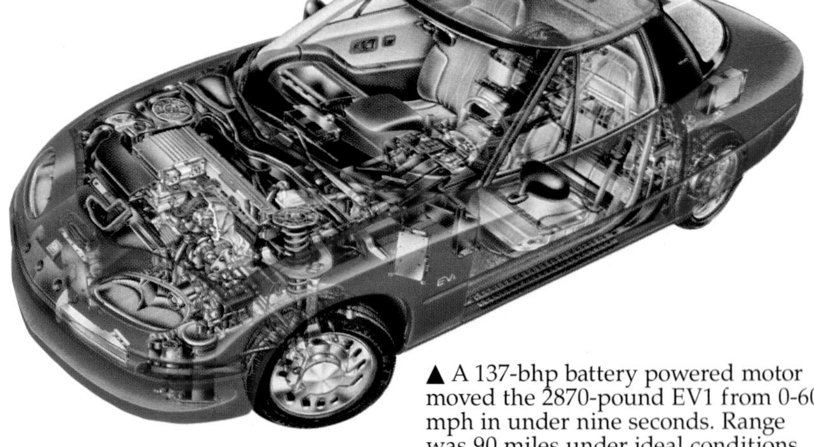

▲ A 137-bhp battery powered motor moved the 2870-pound EV1 from 0-60 mph in under nine seconds. Range was 90 miles under ideal conditions.

### 1997 Calendar Year Car Sales

1. Ford ............................1,009,297
2. Chevrolet/Geo .............980,554
3. Pontiac...........................556,662
4. Buick..............................438,064
5. Dodge............................372,832
6. Mercury...........................337,082
7. Oldsmobile......................251,663
8. Saturn..............................251,099
9. Chrysler...........................188,929
10. Plymouth.........................159,417
11. Cadillac........................157,213
12. Lincoln.........................139,540
13. Eagle..............................15,352

*Figures include cars made for the Big 3 in plants managed by Japanese companies*

▲ Buick's Park Avenue got depowered air bags and OnStar satellite communications capability, but still saw sales slip about 16 percent, to 58,187, coming off its 1997 redesign.

▲ Sales jumped 23 percent for '98 as Buick marked Regal's 25th anniversary with a special trim package. Base price was $20,945 for the 195-bhp LS, $23,690 for the 240-bhp GS.

▲ Century soldiered on as the conservative companion to Buick's other midsize, the sporty Regal. Starting at $18,415 with a 160-bhp V-6, Century trailed only LeSabre in sales for Buick.

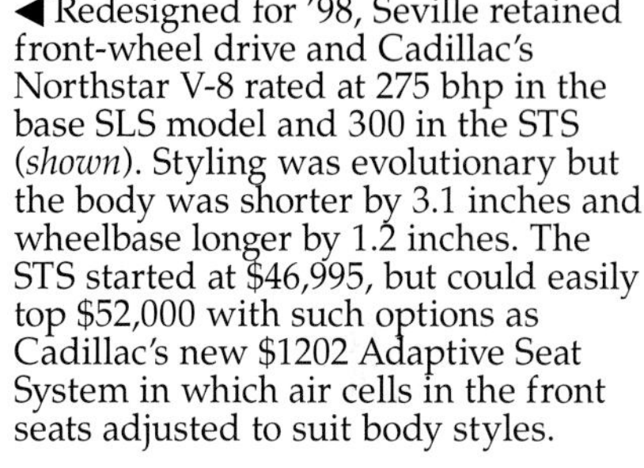

◀ Redesigned for '98, Seville retained front-wheel drive and Cadillac's Northstar V-8 rated at 275 bhp in the base SLS model and 300 in the STS (*shown*). Styling was evolutionary but the body was shorter by 3.1 inches and wheelbase longer by 1.2 inches. The STS started at $46,995, but could easily top $52,000 with such options as Cadillac's new $1202 Adaptive Seat System in which air cells in the front seats adjusted to suit body styles.

▲ Seville SLS started at $42,495, and like the STS, came standard with StabiliTrak, which aided control in evasive maneuvers by selectively applying the front brakes.

▲ Sedans in the $29,000-$40,000 range were the fastest-growing luxury-car segment and Cadillac was there with the Catera. It started at $29,995, but sales were tepid despite easy leases.

▲ Eldorado spent nearly two decades as essentially a two-door Seville, but the '98 model didn't share the new platform of the redesigned Seville. Sales fell 33 percent, to just 15,765.

---

**1998**

Propelled by the truck boom, 1998 ranks as the second-best year for U.S. car sales ever. Sales from all makes totaled 15.6 million, behind only the 16 million recorded in 1986. Trucks took 47.5 percent of the market in '98; in 1978, it was 25.3 percent

The world of business is rocked by the surprise merger of Germany's Daimler-Benz AG, maker of Mercedes-Benz, and Chrysler Corporation. The new company, DaimlerChrysler, would be controlled by Daimler, but aimed to keep Mercedes and Chrysler product lines separate and distinct

Times are good: 1998 is the first time in history Americans purchased more than 15 million cars and light trucks for the third consecutive year

Each of the Big 3 register record sales years for light trucks

▲ Chevy unveiled the sexy open-air version of its Corvette for 1998. Priced at $44,425, $6930 more than the hatchback coupe, the convertible snared about 45 percent of 29,208 sales for the year. It shared the coupe's 345-bhp LS1 V-8.

▲ The strong chassis of the fifth-generation Corvette was designed from the start to accommodate a convertible. The '98 had a manual folding top with a glass rear window and was the first 'Vette ragtop with a trunk since the '62 model.

▲ This two-wheel-drive, 5.7-liter V-8 Tahoe police package was part of Chevy's attempt to recapture some of the law-enforcement market it lost when the Caprice was dropped.

▲ Tahoe wasn't a hit with police, but Camaro's pursuit package, which could be had with the Z28's sport suspension and 305-bhp Corvette-derived 5.7-liter V-8, was just the ticket.

▲ Chevy also offered this Lumina police package. It had a heavy-duty suspension and seats. But with front-wheel drive, unibody construction, and a V-6, wasn't really cop-friendly.

▲ Lumina's two-door variant, the Monte Carlo, worked just fine as a pace car, here dressed for work at NASCAR's 400-miler in Las Vegas.

◀ Corvette's new convertible needed no mechanical modifications to pace the '98 Indy 500. It posed with the three other 'Vettes to do the honors.

---

For the 17th straight year, Ford's F-Series was the top-selling vehicle. Second and third best-sellers were also trucks: the Chevrolet C/K and Ford Explorer. Most-popular car was the Toyota Camry, for the second year in a row. Best-selling domestic nameplate among cars was the Ford Taurus, in seventh place

Although Japanese brands accounted for about 23 percent of of all U.S. car and light-truck sales in '98, and European brands about seven percent, of the 15.6 million vehicles sold here, 13.2 million were assembled in North America

General Motors loses $2.5 billion in profits and thousands of customers in a 54-day strike by the United Auto Workers

A Ford was back at the helm of Ford, as William Clay Ford Jr., 41, great-grandson of founder Henry Ford, is elected chairman of Ford Motor Company

▲ Concorde was redesigned for '98, keeping front-drive and a 113-inch wheelbase, but getting dramatic new styling and a 7.5-inch stretch in overall length. Use of aluminum in suspension, hood, and engine cut weight by 100 pounds.

▲ Concorde offered a $21,305 base model and, for an extra $3000, a plusher LXi trim level that included leather upholstery and other amenities. Even loaded, prices bettered most of the less-roomy, and less-zoomy-looking, rivals.

▲ Minivans were losing sales to SUVs, but Town & Country carved out a niche at the luxury end of the segment. This is the $33,000 LXi.

▲ Chrysler further distinguished its Cirrus from the Dodge Stratus and Plymouth Breeze for '98 by dropping the four-cylinder for a standard V-6.

▲ America's best-selling convertible was again the handsome Chrysler Sebring, though about half its 40,000 annual sales were to rental fleets.

▲ Just as distinct as the Concorde and even racier-looking than its underskin twin was the redesigned 1998 Dodge Intrepid. The Dodge version had slightly tauter suspension tuning than the Chrysler, but both had great road manners.

▲ Intrepid and Concorde shared two new V-6s, both overhead-cam designs. The base 2.7-liter had 200 bhp and the 3.2 had 225. Intrepid offered the $19,865 base model or the $22,465 ES (*shown*), which came with the 3.2-liter engine.

---

Buick Skylark and Oldsmobile Achieva, oddly styled and poorly focused, are dropped. That leaves the Pontiac Grand Am, which is clear in its mission to attract young buyers with sporty styling and affordable prices, as the sole survivor of this GM compact platform

Lincoln's Mark VIII follows its corporate relative, the Ford Thunderbird, to the grave

Moving to recapture the "Standard of the World" title it admits it lost, Cadillac unveils a redesigned Seville intended to better the quality and value of such brands as Lexus

Chevrolet drops the Geo badge, bringing the Toyota-based Prizm and Suzuki-based Metro and Tracker under the Chevy label. Chevy coined the Geo name in 1989 as a global-sounding subbrand to market Japanese-sourced or designed models

▲ Dodge's new-for-'98 Durango offered big-V-8 power and seats for eight in a compact SUV format.

▲ Both the Viper GTS coupe and RT/10 roadster now had the 450-bhp version of the 8.0-liter (488 cid) V-10.

▲ Dodge Avenger sales continued to slip, falling 25 percent, to just 24,084 for '98. This is the $17,585 ES version.

◀ Ford underestimated the popularity of dual sliding side doors when it designed its Windstar. So it had to play catchup by modifying the 1998 version with a widened driver's door designed to provide better rear-seat access from the left side. The new driver's door was six inches longer than the passenger door. Sales slipped eight percent, as Ford geared up for a fully redesigned 1999 Windstar.

▲ Ford's Special Vehicle Team did its high-performance handiwork on the Contour to create the 195-bhp SVT.

▲ Escort's two-door coupe shared little with the stodgy other versions. It was called the ZX2 and had 130 bhp.

▲ Mustang's only change for '98 was 10 more horsepower, now 225, for the GT model. This is the GT convertible.

▶ With the Thunderbird gone, Ford unveiled a NASCAR racing version of its Taurus at the 1998 Daytona 500. It was the first four-door sedan body style to compete in big-time stock-car racing in more than three decades, though it was no different under the skin from NASCAR versions of the Chevy Monte Carlo and Pontiac Grand Prix. Taurus was competitive, but a Monte Carlo won the '98 title.

---

Some auto-show concept cars don't look as advanced as the two new full-size sedans Chrysler puts into production as the Chrysler Concorde and Dodge Intrepid

Dodge dealers clamor for an SUV and get one in the Dakota pickup-based 1998 Durango

It takes less than a year on the market for the Ford Expedition to pass the Chevrolet Suburban as the best-selling full-size SUV. Success of Lincoln's dressed-up clone of the Expedition, the Navigator, shocks Cadillac into developing its own SUV

As Jeep readies a redesigned Grand Cherokee for '99, it gives the '98 a last shot of power with an available 245-bhp 5.9-liter V-8 and creates a new category: the muscle SUV

Ram pickup is Chrysler Corporation's best-selling vehicle for a third straight year

▲ Lincoln redesigned its Town Car for '98, giving it all new sheetmetal and trimming it by three inches in length and 200 pounds in heft. Sales climbed five percent, to 97,547.

▲ Base prices for the new Town Car ranged from $37,830 to $41,830, depending on trim level. All shared a rear-drive body-on-frame design and an overhead-cam 4.6-liter V-8.

▲ Gone was Oldsmobile's one-model strategy for the Intrigue. By late '98, this midsize offered three trim levels.

▲ Mystique continued for 1998 as Contour's less-popular sibling, though it didn't get Ford's SVT treatment.

▲ New front and rear styling and a revamped suspension identified the 1998 Mercury Grand Marquis.

▲ Cutlass occupied the entry-level rung of Oldsmobile's midsize ladder. It was outsold by Intrigue nearly 2-1.

▲ Olds was among the first to show a '99 model. It was this Alero, replacement for the unlamented Achieva.

▲ Alero came as a coupe or this sedan with a 150-bhp four or a 170-bhp V-8. Base price range: $16,325-$20,875.

◀ Intrigue felt more grown-up than the brash Grand Prix and more sophisticated than the Regal. It didn't share its stablemate's available supercharged V-6, keeping the regular 3.8 for '98.

▶ Bursting onto the SUV scene was the plush, $40,000 Navigator. It was Lincoln's second-best-selling '98 model and attracted relatively young buyers.

Oldsmobile continues its quest for a new image by introducing the 1998 Intrigue. It says the new midsize sedan is a "tightly focussed" car designed to take on the world's best imports. It offers just one body style, one powertrain, one seating configuration, and one suspension setup

Turning its back on the theories of its legendary brand-architect Alfred Sloan, GM in effect combines executive staffs of Chevrolet, Pontiac-GMC, Oldsmobile, Cadillac, and Buick into a single body that will serve the needs of all the divisions

Responding to new concerns about the dangers of air bags, the National Highway Traffic Safety Administration allows air-bag cutoff switches and lets automakers begin to phase in depowered air bags that explode with less force in a collision

▲ Voyager didn't offer the largest V-6 available in its Dodge and Chrysler minivan siblings, and the right-side sliding door was optional. But it was Plymouth's top-selling '98 model.

▲ Breeze followed Plymouth's basic-transportation script, but it did jazz things up a little for '98 by offering an "Expresso" trim package and a 150-bhp alternative to its 132-bhp four.

▲ Dodge or Plymouth, Neon was the same two- or four-door subcompact. Plymouth didn't field a version of the Dodge edition's sporty R/T package, though it did offer the 150-bhp engine.

▲ Grand Am was in the last year of its 1992-1998 generation, and though sales fell 13 percent for '98, it remained Pontiac's best-selling model. This is the $16,324 GT coupe.

▲ Standard instead of optional on the '98 Bonneville SSE was Pontiac's Eyecue Head-up Display, which projected speedometer readings and other information onto the windshield.

▲ The WS6 Ram Air option added $3100 to the $22,865 Firebird Formula (*shown*) or the $25,975 Trans Am coupe or $29,715 convertible for '98. It boosted the 5.7-liter V-8 from 305 bhp to 320.

▲ Saturn coupes were late to get the facelift applied to sedans and wagons. Base prices spanned $10,595 to $15,715 in this line of GM-built subcompacts.

◀ Its cars were dated, but Saturn's image was intact, nurtured by a low-pressure one-price strategy and a homey approach that included this visitor welcome center at its assembly plant in Spring Hill, Tennessee.

**1998 Calendar Year Car Sales**

| Rank | Make | Sales |
|---|---|---|
| 1. | Ford | 1,064,412 |
| 2. | Chevrolet | 876,432 |
| 3. | Pontiac | 477,421 |
| 4. | Buick | 398,156 |
| 5. | Dodge | 360,229 |
| 6. | Mercury | 324,096 |
| 7. | Oldsmobile | 261,986 |
| 8. | Chrysler | 235,860 |
| 9. | Saturn | 231,786 |
| 10. | Cadillac | 156,818 |
| 11. | Lincoln | 143,262 |
| 12. | Plymouth | 139,670 |
| 13. | Eagle | 3,458 |

*Figures include cars made for the Big 3 in plants managed by Japanese companies*

▲ Buick killed the Riviera early in the '99 model year. About 200 of the 2000 Rivs built for the year were tagged Silver Arrows, after the original 1963 Riviera concept car.

◀ LeSabre posed with its '59 namesake to mark its 40th birthday. The front-drive sedan was both Buick's best-selling model and America's most-popular full-size car again in '99.

▲Burned by the surprise success of the Lincoln Navigator SUV, Cadillac for '99 introduced the first truck in its 96-year history. Escalade moved GM's flagship division into the SUV field with a slightly restyled version of the GMC Denali, a luxury SUV based on the four-door Chevrolet Tahoe/GMC Yukon. Escalade's base price was $45,875 with standard leather and automatic four-wheel drive.

▲ Eldorado's holdover design still didn't have side air bags, as did most rivals, but for '99, the Touring Coupe version (*shown*) did get optional massaging front seatbacks.

▲ Seville met the competition with standard side air bags, but no rival offered its optional "rolling" front-seat lumbar bolsters that massaged the lower back in 10-minute cycles.

**1999**

Chrysler clips the wings of its Eagle division after closing out inventories of 1998 Talon sports coupes. The brand, launched in 1988, never caught on as a legitimate domestic alternative to import lineups

The Oldsmobile Eighty Eight celebrates its 50th—and last—birthday in 1999. General Motors retires the proud old nameplate as it revamped its large-car line. Olds had offered an Eighty Eight every year since 1949 and closed out '99 with a 50th Anniversary Edition outfitted with special leather upholstery

Slow sales prompt Buick to stop production of its Riviera after only 2000 or so 1999 models were built. About 200 of the final Rivs were Silver Arrow models with distinctive silver exterior paint and special logos. Silver Arrow was the name of the 1963 concept car that spawned the original Riviera

▶ Chevy's two-seat sports car added a hardtop body style to its convertible and hatchback choices for 1999. The Corvette hardtop (*foreground*) shared the other models' 345-bhp V-8, but not options new to them: a Head-up instrument display and a power telescoping steering column.

▼ Camaro had gotten a new-look nose for '98, and for '99, traction control, previously exclusive to V-8 models, was made available on the base V-6 versions. Here's the base coupe.

▲ Based on a Suzuki design, Chevy's Metro used a three-cylinder engine in its base two-door model and a four-cylinder on the uplevel LSi (*shown*). Curb weight was just 1895 pounds.

▲ Cavalier was Chevy's best-selling car, offering coupes, sedans, and this Z24 convertible. It included a 150-bhp twincam four cylinder and a power folding top in its $19,571 base price.

▲ Quiet and roomy, Lumina gave Chevy a high-value mainstream mid-size sedan. The LS model listed for $19,920 with standard V-6 engine, anti-lock brakes, and air conditioning.

◀ Chrysler's home-grown Sebring convertible handily outsold its Mitsubishi-sourced Sebring coupe. The JX ragtop (*shown*) listed for $23,970 and the leather-upholstered JXi for $26,285. Both came with a 168-bhp V-6, automatic transmission, ABS, and power folding top with a glass rear window and defroster.

---

Despite the explosion of auto-buying information on the Internet, auto dealers and analysts say that as of 1999, it hadn't had a significant impact on the way cars are sold

General Motors and Ford lay plans to build pickup truck beds out of plastic instead of metal

Ford acquires the auto making side of Volvo for $6.45 billion. With Jaguar and Lincoln, the move gives Ford a powerful array of luxury brands. Ford plans to capitalize on Volvo's reputation as an upscale, safety-minded, and environmentally conscious brand

Pope John Paul II greets crowds in Mexico from the elevated seat in a specially built Cadillac De Ville stretched 30 inches and shorn of its top

Nineteen ninety-nine opens with light trucks snaring 49.7 percent of U.S. vehicle sales

▲ New-for-'99 was this luxury version of the Chrysler Concorde. Called the LHS, its front and rear look was distinct from the Concorde, and it used a 253-bhp 3.5-liter version of Concorde's 225-bhp 3.2-liter V-6. Base price: $28,850.

▲ Companion to the LHS was the 300M, which cost the same and used the same V-6, but emphasized performance via tauter suspension settings and Chrysler's Autostick transmission, which helped the automatic mimic a manual.

◀ The new 300M was a spiritual descendent of Chrysler's fabled "letter-series" models of the 1950s and '60s. Unique front and rear bodywork trimmed the 300M's overall length to under 200 inches, shortest of the "LH" cars and enough to help it sell overseas.

▲ Avenger's handling was good, but its acceleration was mediocre. The Dodge's real appeal was that it looked more expensive than its base prices of $15,470 to $17,745.

▲ Optional on Dodge's version of the Neon coupe was the $2870 R/T package. Included were a 150-bhp twincam four, four-wheel discs, sport suspension, and body stripes. It did 0-60 mph in 8.5 seconds. Not bad for under $14,000.

---

DaimlerChrysler creates a "brand bible" to ensure that Mercedes-Benz products remain distinct from Chrysler, Dodge, and Plymouth models. The document is meant to preserve Mercedes prestige by prohibiting sharing of design, platforms, sales, or marketing

Former Chrysler Corporation savior-turned-nemesis Lee Iacocca resurfaces as chairman of EV Global Motors Co., a manufacturer of electric-powered bicycles

Cadillac examines creation of high-performance versions of several models

Analysis of the origin of cars and light trucks sold in America in 1999 shows that 85.6 percent were assembled in North America (including Canada and Mexico), 9 percent were imported from Japan, 3.8 percent came from Europe, and 1.6 percent were built in South Korea

▶ Ford's pony car celebrated its 35th anniversary in 1999 with new styling and more power. The base model's 3.8-liter V-6 gained 40 bhp, to 190, and the GT's overhead-cam 4.6-liter V-8 gained 35 bhp, to 260. Traction control was a first-time option on these rear-drive coupes and convertibles. A wider rear track helped handling and four-wheel discs were newly standard. This is the $24,870 GT convertible.

▲ Base-model Mustangs started at $16,470 for the coupe and $21,070 for the convertible. A lively package, they accounted for about 60 percent of Mustang sales in 1999.

▲ Windstar caught up to the competition with a 1999 redesign that included sliding doors on both sides. The doors were power operated on the top-line $30,415 SEL.

◀ Standard seat-mounted front side air bags and an increase of 15 horsepower, to 275, for its twincam 4.6-liter V-8 were the big changes to Lincoln's front-wheel-drive Continental for '99.

▶ Town Car was America's only homegrown rear-wheel-drive luxury car and the Lincoln gained standard front side air bags for '99. Base prices ranged from $38,325 to $42,825.

Responding to complaints from shorter drivers, and recognizing that women make up a healthy percentage of sport-utility-vehicle drivers, Ford gives the big Expedition and Lincoln Navigator an adjustable brake and accelerator-pedal cluster that moves forward about three inches to suit more body types

General Motors markets two generations of full-size pickups as 1999 models. As production ramps up on the new-generation Chevrolet Silverado and GMC Sierra, limited offerings of the 1988-generation Chevrolet C/K and GMC Sierra Classic continue to roll into showrooms as '99 models

Lincoln begins special training for its dealers to serve buyers of its coming LS luxury/sport sedan; dealers are coached to adjust to younger, affluent shoppers who usually consider only European or Japanese near-luxury cars

▲ Cougar debuted for 1999 as a "new-edge" styled Mercury coupe built on the Contour/Mystique platform.

▲ Four-cylinder Cougars had 125 bhp and a base price of $16,195. V-6 models had 170 bhp and started at $16,695.

◀ Skin Mercury's new cat and you'd find front-wheel drive and a four-wheel independent suspension. It had a firmer ride than the Mystique sedan upon which it was based, plus seating for four instead of five. Both engines came with manual or automatic transmission. The five-speed V-6 Cougar could do 0-60 mph in 7.8 seconds. A power sunroof was a $615 option.

▲ Mercury Villager's 1999 makeover included sliding doors on both sides.

▲ Oldsmobile's Alero was a grown-up GM cousin to the Pontiac Grand Am.

▲ A 50th Anniversary Edition marked the end of the Olds Eighty Eight in '99.

◀ Oldsmobile ended production of the original Aurora at the close of the '99 model year. An evolution of its platform would return as a slightly larger model with both V-6 and V-8 power.

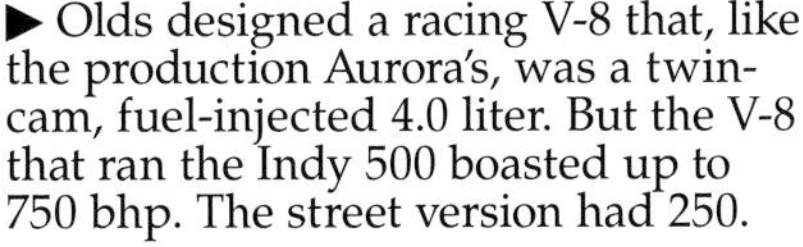

▶ Olds designed a racing V-8 that, like the production Aurora's, was a twin-cam, fuel-injected 4.0 liter. But the V-8 that ran the Indy 500 boasted up to 750 bhp. The street version had 250.

---

DaimlerChrysler continues to consolidate Chrysler-Plymouth dealers with Jeep dealers; it enters 1999 with the project about 70 percent complete, but runs into resistance from profitable dealers who don't wish to be merged

Worldwide, auto production capacity is 74 million vehicles in 1999, but projections are for 52 million sales

CarMax and AutoNation USA used-car superstores blame aggressive new-car incentives for their lackluster profit picture

Longtime Corvette modifier Callaway Cars sets its price on its ultra-performance, 440-bhp C12 version of the 1999 Corvette convertible: $211,000

Ford offers its Explorer and Windstar with an audible system that sounds a warning of objects in the way when backing up

▲ Plymouth's retro hot rod Prowler sat out the '98 season, then returned for 1999 with a new 3.5-liter V-6 of 253 bhp, 35 more than the 3.2 liter it replaced.

▲Prowler now did 0-60 mph in six seconds, not seven. It listed for $39,300. Black, yellow, or red paint added $1000.

▲ Hot-rod touches included a steering-column-mounted tachometer and central gauges in a body-colored cove.

◀ A power driver's seat was optional for the first time in the Breeze for '99. This roomy Plymouth included standard air conditioning, tilt steering, and a folding rear seatback for $15,115.

▶ Neon sedans had an abbreviated 1999 model year, as 2000 versions slid in early. This is the last of the '99 four-doors, which started at just $11,425.

One of the worst blizzards of the century hits the midwest, snarling transportation and wrecking havoc with the North American International Auto Show in Detroit. *AutoWeek* reports a snowbound Volkswagen executive takes a cab from Chicago to Detroit for the show and pays the $800 fare in cash

Wary of losing the domestic luxury-car sales race to Lincoln, Cadillac extends its 1998 sales reporting period to include vehicles sold through January 4, 1999. The move helps the GM division beat out Lincoln by 222 units for calendar 1998 and thereby preserve the title it's held since 1941

Surviving on subcompacts since its 1991 inception, Saturn prepares to introduce two midsize models, a four-door sedan and wagon based on cars built in Europe by General Motors' Opel division; they'll be "Saturnized" with selected plastic composite body panels

▲ The Pontiac Grand Am, America's best-selling compact car, was redesigned for 1999. Styling was new, wheelbase increased 3.6 inches, and overall width grew by two inches.

▲ Sedan and coupe Grand Ams returned with a standard 150-bhp twincam four-cylinder engine. Uplevel models, including this $18,970 SE coupe, got a 170-bhp 3.4-liter V-6.

◀ Anticipating a redesign for 2000, the '99 Pontiac Bonneville essentially stood pat for '99. This is the base SE model, which started at $22,800 and had a 205-bhp V-8 and standard ABS.

▶ Trans Am convertible gave Pontiac a 305-bhp rear-drive muscle car that listed for $30,245 in 1999. Its power-operated top had a glass rear window.

▲ Saturn's two-door coupes became three-door coupes during the '99 model year with introduction of a rear-opening back door on the driver's side. Coupe prices started at $12,445.

▲ Inspired by those on extended-cab pickup trucks, the new rear door on Saturn coupes eased rear-seat access, but didn't open independently of the front door.

---

Appalachian State University in Boone, North Carolina, offers a three-credit course entitled "A History of Southern Stock Car Racing"

Pontiac ditches Trans Sport and renames its minivan Montana, which had been the name of a popular options package.

Chevrolet launches a redesigned Tracker compact SUV; wagon and convertible body styles return and are again built from the same design as the Suzuki compact SUV, which is now called the Vitara

The Internal Revenue Service calculates that for the first time since 1981, the cost of owning and operating a car or truck has gone down, and it announces that the standard tax deduction or employee reimbursement for use of a motor vehicle for business will decrease from 32.5 cents to 31 cents per mile

▲ Buick's first 2000 model was the redesigned LeSabre. It was shorter overall but longer in wheelbase than the '99.

◀ LeSabre's resemblance to the Park Avenue was more than skin deep; it now shared the larger car's platform.

◀ Chevrolet returned to its big-car roots with the 2000 Impala. It could seat six, as Impalas of yore, but this was a thoroughly modern package, with front-wheel drive, standard anti-lock four-wheel disc brakes, and a choice of fuel-injected V-6 engines: a 3.4 liter with 180 bhp or a 3.8 with 200.

▲ Built on the same platform as the Impala, but with a shorter, coupe body, the new-for-2000 Monte Carlo recalled its own past with creases in its fenders and round taillights.

▲ The Monte Carlo LS (*shown*) used the 180-bhp 3.4-liter V-6. The sporty model was the SS, which had exclusive rights to the 200-bhp 3.8. Both had front bucket seats.

◀ Monte Carlo was destined for the race track as a competitor, but appeared first as a pace car. It debuted at the Las Vegas 400, but the highlight came on May 30, 1999, when slightly modified SS versions paced both the Indianapolis 500 and NASCAR's Coca-Cola 600 in Charlotte, NC.

◀ Neon made history as the first 2000 model to go on sale in the U.S. The subcompact was redesigned for the occasion, getting slightly larger dimensions, but selling again in nearly identical form at Dodge and Plymouth dealers. A coupe wasn't produced in the new design, leaving a four-door sedan with familiar styling but a one-inch longer wheelbase, a 2.6-inch longer body, and more trunk space. Base price was $12,390. The sole engine was a 132-bhp four-cylinder. Side air bags, a feature in some rivals, were not offered. But anti-lock four-wheel disc brakes were an $840 option and were packaged with traction control, a new feature for Neon.

▶ Highlight of the season was the resurrected Thunderbird. Ford dipped into T-Bird's legendary past to come up with a two-seat convertible with a removable, porthole hardtop. The reborn icon was based on the platform for the 2000 Lincoln LS, so it was a rear-wheel-drive car with a 3.9-liter V-8. Pictured is the thinly disguised show-car that provided the first glimpse of the new T-Bird. Round lights, eggcrate grille, and hood scoop were retro touches. Ford called the color "Super-8 Yellow," a hue intended to recall the pastels of the 1950s.

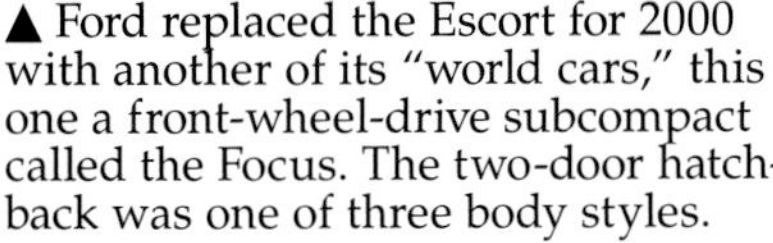

▲ Ford replaced the Escort for 2000 with another of its "world cars," this one a front-wheel-drive subcompact called the Focus. The two-door hatchback was one of three body styles.

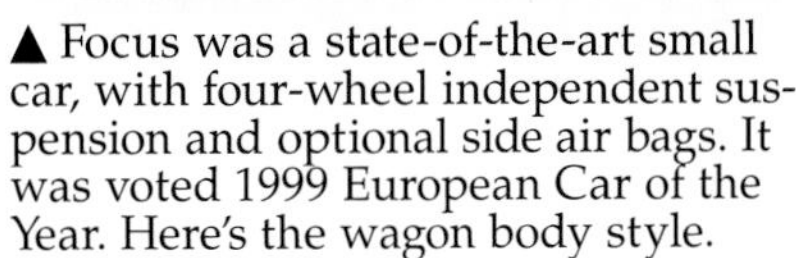

▲ Focus was a state-of-the-art small car, with four-wheel independent suspension and optional side air bags. It was voted 1999 European Car of the Year. Here's the wagon body style.

▲ Like the other body styles, the Focus sedan had a high-roof cabin that provided exceptional interior space. Focus offered two 2.0-liter four-cylinder engines of 107 and 130 bhp.

◀ Lincoln's 2000 LS was the marque's first legitimate luxury/sport sedan. Its rear-wheel-drive platform was jointly developed by Ford and its Jaguar subsidiary and was shared with the 2000 Jaguar S-Type. Accounting for 70 percent of LS sales was the top-line version with a new 252-bhp 3.9-liter V-8; it started at $35,225. Taking 25 percent was the $31,450 "base" model with a 210-bhp 3.0-liter V-6. Both these used a five-speed automatic transmission. Rounding out the line was the $32,250 V-6 model with the first five-speed manual shift in a Lincoln since 1951.

▲ Plymouth's Neon was identical to the Dodge version, except for badging. Both came with a five-speed manual transmission, but fell short of the subcompact leaders by offering an optional automatic with three speeds, not four.

▲ Pontiac's "expressive" styling carried through to the 2000 Bonneville's dashboard. Side air bags weren't offered, but the standard Head-up Display projected speedometer readings and other information onto the windshield.

◀ Pontiac launched its 21st Century lineup with the redesigned Bonneville. It rode GM's latest big-car corporate platform and retained front-wheel drive and a 3.8-liter V-6 that had 205 bhp in base tune and 240 in supercharged form. The new Bonneville changed little in size from the 1992 to '99 generation, but took styling to an even more-aggressive level, with sharper bodyside sculpting and a steeper hood and windshield rake creating a more wedge-like profile. New on the top-line SSE version was Pontiac's Integrated Chassis Control System, which employed sensors to monitor steering, wheel speed, and "yaw" (the rotation of a car around its center of gravity). The sensors talked to a computer that could apply individual brakes during sudden maneuvers, helping prevent skids or spinouts. Pontiac's theme for the 2000 Bonneville was "Luxury With Attitude for the Next Millennium."

# INDEX


Ackerman, W.K., 27
Adams-Farwell, 41
Advertising 80, 103, 141, 154, 192, 198, 205, 219, 228, 235, 252, 272, 444, 445.
Aerocar, 136, 226, 451
Air bags, 446, 472, 480, 488, 493, 504, 576, 591, 597, 598
Air conditioning, 292, 299, 304, 452, 465, 480, 597
Airphibian, 210
Airway prototype, 226
Allen, Gracie, 263
Allender, Ruben, 310, 320
Allstate, 270. *See also* Henry J.
Aluminum Corp. of America, 109
American (auto), 18, 58
American Austin, 138, 139, 153, 157, 161
American Automobile Assoc., 31, 302
American Automotive Corp., 155
American Bantam, 161, 166, 184, 190
American Bicycle Co., 19, 26
American Buckboard roadster, 304
American Electric Vehicle Co., 15
American Mors, 45
American Motor Car Manufacturers Association, 42
American Motor Co., 21
American Motor League, 14
American Motors Corp., 278, 288, 294, 303, 362, 396, 462, 496, 559
Ambassador, 415, 417, 444, 453, 471, 484, 486
Amitron electric, 442
AMX, 420, 435, 437, 444, 452, 453, 454, 462, 465
Cavalier, 420
Concord, 511, 515, 527, 532, 540
Eagle 524, 527, 532, 548, 605
Gremlin, 452, 453, 462, 480, 490, 496, 502, 504, 508, 509, 518
Hornet, 453, 462, 465, 471, 478, 480, 490, 496, 502, 508, 509, 511
Javelin, 435, 437, 444, 452, 454, 462, 465, 471, 478, 484, 486
Jeep, 434, 580, 611, 622
Marlin, 406, 407, 415, 417, 424, 426
Matador, 462, 471, 484, 486, 496, 508, 509, 511
Pacer, 490, 492, 493, 496, 502, 504, 515
profit and loss, 341, 522
Rambler, 331, 337, 341, 349, 361, 373, 406, 445
Rambler Ambassador, 337, 347, 349, 361, 372, 384, 397, 406
Rambler American, 347, 349, 354, 361, 365, 372, 378, 385, 397, 406, 415, 429, 436, 444, 445
Rambler Classic, 365, 384, 388, 397, 406
Rambler Typhoon, 401
Rebel, 415, 417, 424, 429, 436, 437, 444, 453, 455, 462, 465
Renault, 529
Renault Alliance, 532, 540, 548, 550, 553, 558
Renault Encore, 542, 548, 556
St. Maritz and Tahiti, 412
SC/Rambler, 444, 445, 451
Spirit, 515, 516, 518, 527, 540
Vixen, 420
American National Exhibition, 347
American Simplex, 55
American Underslung, 58
Anderson, Ed, 275
Andrews, Archie, 157
Anthony, Earle C., 17
Apollo, 378
Apperson, 28, 48, 55, 101
Apperson, Edgar and Elmer, 11, 28, 92
Argo, 70
Argonaut, 338, 342
Ariel, 41
Arkus-Duntov, Zora, 309, 310
Asardo, 345
Association of Licensed Automobile Manufacturers (ALAM), 32, 33, 48
Auburn, 23, 87, 108, 135, 138, 144, 147, 148, 153, 158, 161, 162, 165, 429
Autocar Co., 19, 27, 30, 36
Auto Cub, 312
Autoette, 276, 288
Autolite Lead Wedge, 441
Automobile Board of Trade, 62, 69
Automobile Club of America, 21, 27, 31
*Automobile Daily News*, 114
Automobile Industry Advisory Committee, 198
Auto. Information Disclosure Act, 329
Automobile Manufacturers Assoc., 160, 214, 308, 312, 318, 319, 339, 471
Automobile Merchants Association, 160
Automotive Council for War Production, 193, 194, 200
Automotive Golden Jubilee, 205
*Automotive News*, 511
Automotive Products Trade Act, 406
Automotor Horse patent, 15
AutoNation USA, 602, 629
Autotri, 14
*AutoWeek*, 630
Avanti Automotive Corp., 537, 538, 543, 553, 568, 585
Avanti II, 407, 445, 447, 455, 527, 532
Ayres, E.W., 17

Baker, 65
Baker, Art, 229
Baker, "Cannon Ball," 104, 106, 120, 150
Baker Electric, 23
Barber, Amzi, 19
Barit, A.E., 214, 294
Barrie, Wendy, 162
Barrow, Clyde, 159
Barthel, Oliver E., 12
Bates, M.F., 12
Beech Aircraft Co., 220
Beechcraft Plainsman, 220, 227
Bendix starter, 67
Benz, Karl, 8, 9
Bizzarrini, Giotto, 453
"Blackout" models, 190
Blake, Stephen, 537, 538
B.M.C., 269
Bobbi Motor Car Corp., 210, 218, 226
Bobbikar, 210
Bocar XP-4, 335
Bonneville (race), 282
Booth, Carlos G., 13
Bordinat, Eugene, 449
Borg & Beck, 56
Borg-Warner, 223, 256, 492
Bourke, Robert, 219, 283
Boyce MotoMeter, 64, 91, 114
Boyd, William, 290
Brayton, George, 8
Breedlove, Craig, 435
Breer, Carl, 95, 105, 123, 154
Brewster, 156
Bricklin, Malcolm, 490
Brickyard 400 race, 597, 607, 614
Briscoe, 71
Briscoe, Benjamin Jr., 33, 34, 44
Briscoe, Frank, 34
Brock, Ray, 451
Brooks, David and Steve, 525
Brown, Donaldson, 160
Brush, 55
Brush, Alanson P., 46
Bryan, Richard, 597
Bryan, Vincent, 40
Budd, Edward Gowen, 64, 102
Buehrig, Gordon, 161, 170
Buffum, 47
Buggyaut, 11
Buick, 32, 34, 36, 50, 56, 62, 74, 101, 106, 108, 118, 124, 129, 130, 207, 220, 270, 330, 401,486, 551, 569. *See also* Marquette.
advertising, 119, 202, 203, 231
Apollo, 479
Centurion, 315, 463
Century, 165, 167, 174, 182, 184, 288, 289, 298, 318, 328, 478, 482, 484,
Buick (*continued*)
496, 508, 513, 523, 533, 554, 594, 596, 601, 613 616, 619
Electra, 338, 362, 373, 398, 407, 436, 471, 491, 502, 545, 549, 551, 553, 554
Estate Wagon, 220, 231, 259, 269, 279, 298, 308, 509, 528, 581, 582
50th anniversary, 279
Gran Sport, 415
GSX, 453, 455
Invicta, 338
LaSalle II, 305
LeSabre, 268, 338, 349, 362, 407, 453, 471, 491, 496, 513, 549, 555, 559, 564, 566, 570, 575, 586, 591, 594, 598, 607, 625, 632
Limited, 328
Master Six, 109, 114, 119
Model 7, 53; Model 10, 48, 51, 55, 60; Model 16, 51; Model 19, 55; Model 22, 96; Model 24, 66; Model 25, 66; Model 26, 58; Model 34, 58; Model 38, 58; Model 39, 58; Model 43, 62; Model 50, 93, 106; Model 51, 119; Model 55, 77; Model B, 33, 36, 70, 72; Model C, 39, 42, 74; Model D, 44, 48, 77, 80; Model F, 42, 48; Model G, 45, 48; Model H, 45, 86
Park Avenue, 516, 523, 549, 581, 582, 587, 594, 596, 598, 600, 601, 613, 616, 619
races, 51, 144
Reatta, 564, 565, 575, 581
Regal, 331, 502, 508, 513, 528, 533, 538, 564, 565, 571, 581, 582, 586, 601, 604, 606, 607, 619
Regal Grand National, 533, 543, 551, 559
Riviera, 231, 233, 249, 259, 269, 298, 308, 318, 328, 348, 384, 385, 386, 397, 398, 406, 407, 415, 417, 425, 436, 453, 454, 463, 465, 472, 478, 496, 509, 516, 533, 538, 543, 551, 554, 559, 564, 566, 570, 572, 581, 591, 594, 598, 600, 601, 625
Roadmaster, 170, 186, 187, 191, 210, 231, 270, 308, 586, 587, 601, 607, 610
Sedanet, 186, 259
Series 40, 139, 162
Series 60, 148, 157, 161
Skyhawk, 491, 502, 515, 524, 533, 538, 543, 559
Skylark, 279, 280, 288, 290, 361, 362, 372, 374, 385, 396, 397, 398, 406, 407, 425, 426, 437, 472, 497, 508, 518, 523, 538, 544, 549, 570, 575, 586, 587, 597, 601, 621
Somerset Regal, 549
Special, 172, 178, 249, 269, 279, 289, 328, 361, 362, 372, 374, 397, 407
Standard Six, 118
Super, 186, 187, 203, 259, 288
Wildcat, 285, 294, 305, 372, 373, 374, 385, 397, 398, 407, 425, 436, 553
XP-300 show car, 259, 268
Buick, David Dunbar, 33, 137
Buick, Thomas, 33
Burdick Spring Motor, 14
Burman, Bob, 51, 55
Burns, George, 263

Cadillac, 23, 28, 32, 34, 37, 44, 47, 53, 62, 70, 75, 78, 128, 138, 144, 148, 182, 230, 274, 345, 569, 614, 630. *See also* LaSalle.
advertising, 198, 232
Allanté, 559, 570, 579, 586, 591, 592
Brougham, 562, 564, 582
Catera, 613, 616, 619
Cimarron, 533, 551, 553, 564, 566
Concours, 596, 602, 607, 616
Coupe de Ville, 232, 259, 308, 350, 497, 575
defense contract, 249
De Ville, 408, 415, 428, 463, 472, 503, 551, 554, 564, 572, 598, 602, 607, 613, 616, 626
Cadillac (*continued*)
Dewar Trophy, 51, 62, 66
Eight, 157
Eldorado, 280, 283, 288, 299, 308, 318, 320, 328, 329, 339, 350, 363, 373, 386, 398, 425, 428, 436, 454, 467, 491, 497, 498, 503, 516, 520, 523, 533, 543, 544, 570, 586, 587, 594, 602, 607, 619, 625
Escalade, 625
Fleetwood, 165, 178, 479, 484, 509, 556, 564, 572, 582, 586, 591, 602, 603, 610
Imperial, 124
Malcolm Baldridge Award, 582
Model B, 36; Model 51, 75; Model G, 45, 48; Model K, 45; Model S, 48
and Quadricycle, 23
Sedan de Ville, 308, 318, 491, 549, 575, 596
Series 90, 165
Seven-Passenger Car, 78, 86
Seventy-Five, 210, 222
Seventy-Two, 184
Seville, 491, 509, 516, 523, 524, 549, 566, 570, 582, 586, 587, 594, 596, 607, 619, 621, 625
Sixteen, 140, 153, 183
Sixty, 167, 174
Sixty-One, 188, 191, 221
Sixty Special, 175, 178, 182, 186, 203, 232, 249, 269, 280, 288, 350, 562, 595
Sixty-Three, 191
Sixty-Two, 184, 186, 203, 210, 214, 221, 232, 259, 280, 298, 299, 339, 363, 373
tailfins, 221
Thirty, 59
Torpedo, 67
Town Landaulet, 83
Type 59, 91; Type 61, 102
U.S. Army-Navy E Award, 200
Cafaro, J.J., 568
California (auto), 276
Californian, 211
Callaway Cars, 629
Cardiges, S. James, 601
CarMax, 602, 629
*Carrera Panamericana* (Mexican Road Race), 253, 261, 273, 282, 285, 290, 293
Carrozzeria Touring, 291
Cartercar, 40
Carter, Jimmy, 503, 510
Cassaroll, Gene, 321
Catalytic converter, 22, 468, 490, 528
Cavalier, 116
Century of Progress, 153
Chalmers, 80, 91
Chalmers-Detroit, 57
Chalmers, Hugh, 148
Chandler, 67, 93, 109, 115, 118, 128
Chapin, Roy Dikeman, 21, 27, 73, 105, 128, 153, 160
Chapin, Roy Dikeman Jr., 462
Charter Water-Gasoline car, 32
Chayne, Charles, 259
Checker, 93, 95, 97, 153, 165, 398, 408, 438, 447, 486
Marathon, 363, 408, 524, 528
Superba, 341, 352, 363
Chevrolet, 32, 58, 59, 68, 72, 84, 85, 86, 93, 105, 110, 114, 119, 124, 129, 153, 222, 233, 250, 486, 551
advertising, 93, 106, 109, 114, 124, 129, 170, 174, 191, 204, 205, 260, 270, 351, 464
Aerosedan, 204
Astro, 604
Baby Grand, 71
Bel Air, 250, 251, 280, 289, 299, 300, 309, 319, 329, 374
Beretta, 559, 560, 565, 576, 591, 598, 608
Biscayne, 305, 329, 399, 416
Blazer, 604
Camaro, 424, 426, 427, 438, 446, 453, 454, 471, 487, 503, 505, 510, 516,

Chevrolet (*continued*)
529, 533, 535, 544, 550, 551, 554, 559, 560, 566, 571, 582, 582, 587, 591, 592, 596, 598, 603, 604, 608, 614, 626
Caprice, 408, 415, 416, 422, 463, 479, 485, 492, 503, 524, 528, 555, 572, 576, 581, 582, 595, 598, 604, 608, 610
Cavalier, 533, 534, 540, 550, 555, 560, 565, 566, 568, 571, 576, 582, 587, 602, 605, 608, 626
Celebrity, 533, 534, 550, 560
CERV I, 379
Chevelle, 396, 398, 417, 425, 427, 437, 438, 446, 454, 464, 472, 473, 479, 480, 482, 487, 497
Chevelle Malibu, 408, 416, 446, 464
Chevette, 496, 499, 508, 516, 528, 529, 538, 563
Chevy II, 372, 374, 375, 386, 398, 408, 410, 428, 438, 456, 473
Citation, 518, 524, 528, 544, 550
C/K, 602, 611, 620, 628
Classic Six, 59, 67
Coach, 106, 109, 114, 144
Concours, 412, 497, 503
Confederate, 148
Corsica, 559, 565, 571
Corvair, 348, 349, 351, 352, 364, 375, 396, 398, 408, 410, 427, 438, 444
Corvair Greenbrier, 364, 410
Corvair Monza, 348, 363, 364, 372, 375, 376, 386, 399, 417, 420, 428
Corvette, 281, 289, 300, 302, 310, 320, 329, 330, 341, 348, 351, 355, 363, 375, 386, 387, 396, 399, 408, 409, 417, 427, 437, 438, 445, 447, 454, 456, 473, 476, 479, 485, 487, 492, 498, 503, 510, 513, 516, 523, 526, 529, 534, 536, 540, 544, 547, 550, 554, 558, 560, 566, 571, 572, 574, 576, 579, 583, 584, 587, 588, 591, 595, 597, 603, 608, 609, 614, 616, 620, 626, 629
Cosworth-Vega, 492, 497
Coupe Pickup, 186
Delray, 300
DeLuxe, 102, 270
Eagle, 153
El Camino, 340, 408, 510, 560
El Morocco, 310, 313, 320
Estate Wagon, 472
Fleetline, 188, 190, 191, 204, 211, 221, 233
Fleetmaster, 211, 221
Geo, 583, 600, 603, 621
Impala, 329, 330, 340, 350, 351, 386, 472, 480, 485, 498, 503, 524, 602, 610, 632
Impala SS, 348, 363, 375, 399, 409, 416, 426, 427, 437, 445, 447, 597, 598
Landau, 114, 124, 129, 509
Lumina, 575, 576, 581, 582, 587, 588, 600, 602, 604, 620, 626
Lumina APV minivan, 576, 582, 597
Master, 157, 178
Metro, 626
Model 490, 78, 83, 91, 97
Model C, 68
Monte Carlo, 453, 455, 456, 464, 472, 473, 479, 492, 498, 504, 509, 528, 529, 538, 540, 555, 558, 566, 597, 600, 603, 604, 614, 620, 626, 632
Nomad, 294, 299, 300, 319, 350
Nova, 456, 463, 479, 485, 550
One-Fifty, 319
races, 319, 326, 374
Royal Mail, 71, 76
Sebring SS, 329
Series D, 80, 82; Series H, 67, 71; Series R, 110
Silverado, 628
Special DeLuxe, 186, 187
Sport Cabriolet, 114
Sport Coupe, 139, 144
Sprint, 545

Chevrolet (*continued*)
Standard Sports Roadster, 162
Styleline, 233, 250, 260, 270
Stylemaster, 202
Suburban, 622
Suburban Carryall, 161
Superior, 114
Toronado, 401, 454
Town Sedan, 165
Two-Ten, 281
Vega, 463, 464, 467, 485, 505, 509
Vitara, 631
Chevrolet, Louis, 54, 59, 63, 71, 76
*Chevy Show*, 260
Chicago Electric, 67
Chrysler (and Chrysler Corp.), 90, 106, 114, 127, 144, 172, 180, 221, 222, 248, 249, 278, 290, 293, 309, 441, 452, 462, 464, 498, 559, 560, 562, 580, 602, 608, 609, 610, 614, 619, 627
advertising, 234, 492
Airflow, 138, 156, 157, 158, 160, 166
Cirrus, 602, 604, 621
Concorde, 592, 599, 621, 622, 627
Continental, 205
Cordoba, 456, 491, 492, 495, 498, 504, 510, 517, 524, 524, 529, 534, 539, 540
Crown Imperial, 240
Eagle, 565, 566, 572, 576, 577, 579, 584, 588, 592, 593, 598, 599, 615, 617, 625
Enforcer, 376
Executive Sedan, 539
Falcon, 305
Fargo, 136
Fifth Avenue, 571, 574
Flight Sweep, 305
Imperial, 115, 117, 148, 178, 179, 187, 260, 282, 289, 472, 486, 528, 529, 576, 583, 595, 599
K-cars, 532, 534
K-310 show car, 268
and labor unions, 214
Laser, 545, 558
LeBaron, 449, 474, 503, 513, 517, 524, 529, 534, 536, 539, 549, 550, 551, 555, 559, 560, 565, 571, 577, 583, 592, 597, 599, 603
LHS, 597, 599
Model 58, 117; Model 70, 107, 117; Model 300, 300-301, 301, 376, 400, 438, 446, 455; Model 300-B, 311; Model 300-C, 320; Model 300-E, 341, 342; Model 300-F, 352, 353; Model 300-G, 365; Model 300-H, 375, 453, 455, 456; Model 300-J, 384; Model 300-K, 398, 400; Model 300-L, 406, 408, 410; Model 300 Pace Setter, 386, 387
Newport, 363, 365, 429, 456, 473, 479, 486, 516, 517, 531
New Yorker, 178, 180, 222, 234, 250, 260, 270, 282, 289, 290, 300, 311, 321, 330, 342, 352, 365, 375, 384, 387, 400, 410, 417, 429, 431, 472, 486, 510, 516, 517, 529, 531, 536, 540, 565, 597, 599, 603, 609
New Yorker Fifth Avenue, 517, 576, 587, 595
New Yorker Salon, 592, 595
New York Special, 176
Portofino, 569
profit and loss, 124, 517, 522, 527, 538, 564, 580
races, 300, 301
Royal, 182
Saratoga, 180, 187, 260, 261, 270
Sebring, 597, 603, 609, 621, 626
75 series, 130
Silver Anniversary series, 234
Special, 270
TC by Maserati, 572, 574, 577
300M, 627
Town and Country, 188, 192, 204, 208, 212, 234, 252, 260, 536, 544, 577, 592, 609, 610, 615, 621

Chrysler (*continued*)
Traveler, 222
turbine-powered cars, 379, 390
Turboflite, 367
U.S. Army-Navy E distinction, 192
wartime production, 190, 194, 201
Windsor, 180, 234, 301, 311, 342, 363
Chrysler, Walter P., 64, 92, 95, 105, 115, 154, 158, 160, 161, 184
CitiCar, 489
Clarke, Louis S., 30
Claybrook, Joan, 503
Clean Air Act, 470, 578, 580
Cleveland Machine Screw Co., 18
Coffin, Howard, 40, 73
Cole, 77, 101
Cole, Ed, 486
*College Humor*, 125
Colt, 335
Columbia, 82
Comet Manufacturing Co., 261, 267
Convaircar, 210
Cooper, Gary, 166
Copeland, Lucius D., 8, 9
Cord, 134, 138, 140, 144, 145, 149, 165, 166, 170, 379, 402, 442
Cord, E.L., 140, 153, 165, 166
Corporate Average Fuel Economy (CAFE), 470, 510, 517, 522, 528, 539, 545, 549, 555, 578, 580, 597
Couzens, James, 33
Coyle, M.E., 222
Crawford, Robert S., 41
Crawford Automobile Co., 41
Crissman, George B., 31
Crofton Bug, 353
Crosley, 178, 184, 188, 191, 200, 202, 213, 252, 257, 271
Hotshot, 235
postwar models, 205, 208, 215
wartime production, 194
Crosley, Powel Jr., 178
Crow-Elkhart, 81
Cubster, 235
Cugnot tractor, 8
Cunningham, Briggs,
autos, 251, 261, 271
races, 271, 281, 301
Curtice, Harlow H., 154
Curtis, Frank, 211
Curtiss-Wright Corp., 190, 342, 345, 454
Cushman, 210
Cyclecars, 64, 70, 73, 75

Dagmar, 98
Daigh, Chuck, 323
Daimler-Benz AG, 619
DaimlerChrysler, 619, 627, 629
Daimler, Gottlieb, 8, 9
Darrin, Howard A. "Dutch", 184, 195, 215, 248, 263, 264, 291, 292
Davis, Gary, 235, 241
Davis Motor Car Co., 210, 211, 217, 241
Dawson, C.E., 110
Daytona 500, 255, 603, 622
Daytona Speed Weeks, 323
Dean, Hugh, 211
Dean, James, 237
Dearborn Steel Tubing, 420
De Bouteville, DeLamarre, 9
Deering Magnetic, 84
Del Mar, 240
DeLorean, John Z., 443, 532, 537
DeLorenzo, Tony, 437
de Palma, Ralph, 89
Dept. of Transportation, 416, 497, 504
Derham Body Co., 239
DeSoto, 127, 130, 135, 136, 140, 154, 171, 174, 271, 348, 353, 364, 365
Adventurer, 293, 305, 310, 311, 321, 330, 343
Airflow, 158, 160, 165, 166
Custom, 149, 162, 179, 187, 192, 206, 222, 235, 261
FireDome, 282, 290
Fireflite, 301, 302, 311, 343
Roadster Espanol, 130
Suburban, 208

DeTomaso Pantera, 464
*Detroit Tribune, The*, 36
Detroiter, 284
Detroit Automobile Co., 14, 20, 27, 28, 65
Devin SS, 335
Diamond-Star Motors, 579
Diamond T Motor Car Co., 61
Dietrich, Ray, 179, 181
Dillinger, John, 159
Doble, 71, 78, 102
Dodge, 32, 71, 72, 123, 127, 176, 207, 213, 251, 278, 409
Aries, 528, 530, 566, 572
Aspen, 496, 499, 504, 511, 526
Avenger, 597, 604, 622, 627
Beauty Winner, 166, 168
Caravan, 544, 545, 551, 561, 566, 583, 609, 610, 615
Challenger, 396, 453, 455, 456, 467, 487
Charger, 415, 417, 418, 429, 438, 439, 444, 447, 448, 455, 465, 467, 472, 480, 491, 493, 495, 498, 504, 513, 520, 535, 540
Charger II, 412
Colt, 452
Coronet, 236, 251, 271, 282, 290, 312, 321, 331, 342, 406, 409, 410, 411, 418, 419, 425, 427, 429, 438, 447, 456, 474, 486, 493
Custom 880, 187, 193, 223, 372, 388, 401, 411,
Custom Royal, 302
Dakota, 622
Dart, 349, 353, 366, 376, 377, 387, 388, 398, 401, 408, 411, 417, 427, 480
Dart Demon, 482
Dart GTS, 438, 439, 447
Dart Swinger, 448, 474, 480
Daytona, 550, 556, 558, 561, 563, 572, 579, 588, 595
DeLuxe, 158, 182
Diplomat, 503, 518, 524, 531, 537, 548, 556
DU, 162
Durango, 622
Dynasty, 565, 566, 595, 599
50th anniversary, 396
Firearrow, 294; FliteWing, 367
Hemi-Charger, 401, 409
Intrepid, 592, 593, 599, 621, 622
La Femme, 301, 302, 312
Lancer, 302, 331, 343, 361, 364, 376, 551, 551
Magnum, 511, 513, 520
Mirada, 524, 526, 530, 539
Model 330 Ramcharger, 388
Model 400, 534, 536; Model 600, 539, 540, 545, 548, 551, 555, 566
Monaco, 406, 409, 419, 427, 474, 484, 486, 487, 504, 505, 509, 577, 579, 583
Neon, 598, 599, 600, 624, 627, 630, 633, 634
New Value Six, 162
Omni, 509, 511, 520, 530, 535, 579
Omni America, 561, 563
Omni GLH, 545, 556
Polara, 353, 366, 377, 388, 401, 427, 465, 474, 480
races, 282, 290
Ram, 622
Rampage, 539
Royal, 290, 312
St. Regis, 516, 517, 531
Shadow, 559, 561, 566, 582, 583, 587, 595, 599
Shelby Charger, 539, 540, 545
Shelby Lancer, 566
Sierra, 261
Spirit, 570, 572, 577, 595, 605
Stealth, 582, 598
Stratus, 602, 604, 615
Viper, 588, 596, 598, 604, 609, 610, 615, 622
Wayfarer, 235, 236, 252, 261
Dodge, Horace and John, 33, 71, 72, 92

Dole, Elizabeth, 545
Donohue, Mark, 452
Dorris, 103
Dort Motor Car Co., 102
Doss, H.C., 31
Dreystadt, Nicholas, 207, 211
Driver's license, 20, 304
Dual-Ghia, 313, 321
Duesenberg, 89, 91, 108, 119, 133, 140, 141, 149, 159, 162, 163, 166
Duesenberg, August and Fred, 148, 161
Duesenberg, Fritz, 421
DuPont, 140
duPont, Pierre S., 92
Durant-Dort Carriage Co., 33
Durant Motors, 94, 97, 102, 103, 105, 145
Durant, William Crapo, 32, 33, 48, 50, 59, 79, 91, 92, 94, 97, 102
Duryea, Charles, 8, 11, 32, 49, 607
Duryea, J. Frank, 8, 11, 13, 15, 31, 49, 607
Duryea Motor Wagon Co., 13
Dyke, A.L., 20

Eagle. *See* Durant Motors; under Chrysler Corp.
Earl, 98
Earl, Harley, 118, 120, 122, 153, 167, 226
Earnhardt, Dale, 575
Eaton Corp., 472
Eaton, William M., 48, 50
Edsel, 278, 329, 330, 348, 353, 354
  Bermuda, 332; Citation, 332; Corsair, 343, 344; Pacer, 332; Ranger, 344, 354; Villager, 354
Edwards American, 284
Edwards, Gus, 40
Edwards, Sterling H. (auto), 291
Eisenhower, Dwight D., 201, 278, 361
Electric fence warning system, 355
Electric Fuel Propulsion Inc., 420
Electric Vehicle Co., 26, 32, 33
Electrobat, 12
Electrobile, 261
Ellerbeck, B.B., 146
Eltra Corp., 501
Empire State Motor Wagon Co., 18
*Encyclopedia Britannica,* 120
Energy Policy & Conservation Act, 493
Engel, Elwood, 388, 410
Engineering Enterprises, 211
Environmental Protection Agency, 490
Erskine, Albert R., 128, 153
Eshelman Sportabout, 291
Essex Motor Car Co., 82, 86, 87, 91, 93, 94, 98, 99, 103, 107, 115, 120, 125, 127, 131, 141, 142, 145
Essex Terraplane, 148, 154, 156
Ethyl Corp., 110
Evans, Oliver, 8
Evans, Roy S., 161
Everitt, B.F., 73
Everitt-Metzger-Flanders Co., 50, 56, 59
EV Global Motors Co., 627
Excalibur, 398, 409, 421, 458, 480, 493, 495, 520, 525, 546, 551, 573
Exner, Virgil, 219, 268, 270, 278, 282, 299, 304, 319, 421

Fageol, 81
F.B. Stearns & Co., 18, 26
Federal Reserve Board, 250
Federal Road Aid Act, 79, 85
Fiat, 210
Fibersport roadster, 284
*Field and Stream,* 40
Fina Sport, 284
Firestone, 510
Fitzgerald, F. Scott, 90
Fisher Body Co., 50, 88, 113, 119, 153, 201
Fitch, 241, 367
Flanders, Walter, 61
Fleetwood, 113
Flint Road Car Co., 102
Flint Wagon Works, 33
Ford, Benson, 237, 285, 332
Ford, Clara, 199
Ford, Edsel, 88, 99, 104, 115, 183, 196
Ford, Eleanor, 104
Ford, Henry, 11, 14, 20, 22, 23, 29, 32, 36, 39, 42, 43, 45, 63, 71, 88, 91, 95, 99, 100, 196, 199, 201, 213, 436
Ford, Henry II, 196, 199, 201, 202, 224, 237, 285, 302, 308, 332, 354, 449, 517
Fordism, 120
Ford Light Car Division, 204
Ford Motor Co. and Ford, 32, 33, 57, 60, 61, 68, 76, 88, 90, 104, 107, 111, 119, 138, 149, 154, 160, 175, 180, 230, 235, 237, 248, 271, 278, 308, 333, 420, 431, 476, 493, 501, 527, 578, 601, 609, 614, 615, 620, 626
  advertising, 40, 105, 213, 271, 354, 367, 378
  Aerostar, 550, 561
  Allegro, 390
  Arrow race car, 36, 39
  Aspire, 598, 600
  Aurora, 401
  Avant Garde, 537
  Black Pearl, 412
  Bordinet Cobra, 412
  Cockpit, 532
  Comuta electric, 431
  Continental 195X show car, 276
  Contour, 603, 605, 622
  Cougar, 379, 390
  Country Sedan, 303, 322
  Country Squire, 262, 271, 283, 313
  Crestline, 271, 283, 291
  Crown Victoria, 301, 313, 584, 588, 589, 596
  Custom, 237, 261, 262, 291, 322
  Custom Crestliner, 251, 252, 262
  Customline, 291, 312
  DeLuxe, 162, 167, 183
  Depot Hack, 72, 94
  Elite, 500, 503
  Escort, 528, 531, 535, 540, 557, 562, 566, 576, 582, 589, 596, 604, 605, 610, 616, 617, 622
  EXP, 533, 535, 566
  Expedition, 622, 628
  Explorer, 580, 602, 610, 620, 629
  Fairlane, 303, 313, 322, 333, 343, 348, 367, 372, 376, 378, 387, 389, 402, 413, 415, 418, 420, 430, 439
  Fairmont, 509, 512, 518, 540
  Falcon, 348, 349, 355, 361, 378, 387, 389, 399, 402, 409, 413, 418, 458
  50th anniversary, 279, 283
  Flair, 537
  Focus, 633
  Fordor, 111, 115, 131, 132, 159, 193, 251, 262
  and fuel-economy standards, 539, 545
  FX-Atmos, 294
  Galaxie, 340, 344, 355, 367, 372, 378, 387, 389, 403, 409, 412, 419, 430, 440
  Glideair, 334
  Granada, 492, 493, 512, 525, 531
  Gran Torino, 475, 481, 487, 493, 494
  GT40, 421
  Gyron, 367
  and labor unions, 72, 172, 186, 214
  Levacar, 345
  LTD, 406, 412, 420, 465, 475, 481, 487, 494, 505, 514, 516, 519, 526, 531, 540, 546, 551, 555
  LTD II, 503, 505
  Maverick, 444, 457, 458, 465, 467, 499, 509
  McLaren Mustang, 526
  Model A, 33, 34, 125, 126, 132, 139, 142, 144, 145; Model B, 36, 38, 40; Model C, 36, 39; Model E, 39; Model F, 40; Model K, 42, 43, 44, 46; Model 999, 23, 31, 35; Model N, 42, 43, 46; Model R, 46; Model S, 46, 49; Model T, 32, 42, 49, 50, 52, 53, 56, 60, 61, 61, 63, 66, 68, 72, 73,
Ford (*continued*)
  74, 78, 81, 84, 86, 87, 92, 93, 94, 99, 103, 104, 107, 113, 115, 119, 120, 124, 125, 330
  Mondeo, 603
  Mustang, 379, 396, 403, 409, 411, 412, 419, 423, 430, 440, 448, 457, 463, 466, 467, 473, 475, 481, 485, 492, 516, 518, 520, 521, 525, 536, 540, 542, 546, 547, 548, 551, 557, 561, 563, 566, 573, 578, 584, 589, 593, 596, 599, 604, 610, 611, 622, 628
  Mustang II, 390, 486, 487, 489, 495, 499, 505, 512, 514
  Mystere, 305
  and patent infringement, 33, 52, 59
  Paul Harvey Ford, 430
  Pinto, 463, 467, 473, 481, 482, 492, 499, 505, 510, 518, 526
  Pockar commuter car, 532
  postwar production, 201
  Probe, 571, 578, 584, 589, 592, 594
  Prove V, 553
  profit and loss, 48, 130, 203, 221, 522, 527, 554, 560, 580
  Quadricycle, 8, 9, 11, 13, 15, 19, 23
  races, 36, 39, 53, 402, 403, 421, 453
  Ranchero, 321, 322, 457
  75th anniversary, 512, 513, 514, 525
  Shuttler, 532
  Skyliner, 291, 321, 322, 344
  Sociological Department, 71
  Sport Coupe, 149
  Sportsman, 206, 208, 213, 223
  station wagons, 159, 162, 171, 193, 223, 237, 418, 465
  styling, 113, 162, 176, 191, 231, 269, 321, 354, 502, 514
  Sunliner, 322, 378
  Super DeLuxe, 187
  T2208, 553
  Taurus, 335, 554, 556, 561, 568, 570, 571, 573, 576, 580, 586, 589, 590, 594, 596, 601, 608, 609, 610, 613, 616, 620, 622
  Tempo, 541, 544, 546, 550, 555, 563, 568, 590
  Thrifty Sixty, 179
  Thunderbird, 301, 302, 310, 313, 321, 323, 331, 333, 340, 343, 344, 353, 355, 364, 376, 379, 390, 399, 402, 411, 413, 420, 428, 440, 446, 448, 470, 473, 474, 481, 486, 494, 503, 505, 512, 514, 518, 525, 526, 540, 542, 551, 562, 563, 566, 571, 573, 578, 584, 598, 600, 605, 616, 617, 633
  Thunderbolt, 402
  Topaz, 550
  Torino, 435, 439, 440, 448, 466, 470, 473
  Town Sedan, 132
  transmissions, 385
  truck, 81
  Tudor, 111, 171, 179, 206
  wages, 71, 72
  wartime production, 190, 195, 199
  Windstar, 622, 628, 629
  XL, 456
*Ford News*, 594
Ford, Paul Harvey, 430
Ford, William Clay, 237, 285, 332, 620
Foy, Byron C., 158
Franklin, 28, 29, 44, 108, 135, 141, 149
Frazer, 202, 215, 262
  Manhattan, 214, 223, 236, 238
Frazer, Joseph W., 158, 189, 196, 198, 214, 230, 238
Freewheeling, 138, 143
Frontenac, 59
Furber, Frederick, 82

Gable, Clark, 166
Gadabout, 215
Gale, Tom, 617
Galey, Thomas M., 26
Gardner, 91, 139
Gasmobile, 18
Gasoline rationing, 190, 192, 193, 199
Gasoline station (1900), 18
Gaylord, 304
General Electric, 18
General Motors Acceptance Corp., 88
General Motors Corp., 32, 48, 50, 53, 56, 59, 61, 64, 74, 78, 85, 88, 96, 114, 118, 119, 153, 177, 222, 251, 254, 278, 362, 386, 402, 431, 441, 459, 462, 464, 498, 556, 601, 608, 610, 614, 615, 620, 626, 628
  Aero, 532, 537
  Duck, 200
  Electrovair II, 420, 431
  Electrovan, 420
  EV1, 618
  50th anniversary, 330
  Firebird III, 294, 313, 325, 334, 401
  and fuel-economy standards, 539, 545
  GM-X, 401
  J cars, 533
  Lean Machine, 537
  planned obsolescence, 90, 121
  profit and loss, 76, 124, 522, 527, 570, 580
  Research Laboratories, 70, 92, 103
  Runabout, 401
  75th anniversary, 539
  Sierra, 628
  Sierra Classic, 628
  wartime production, 190, 200, 201
  X-cars, 523, 550
  XP-500, 312
  Y-Job show car, 191
General Motors Corp. Truck Co., 61
General Motors Proving Ground, 109
General Tire and Rubber, 271
George N. Pierce Co., 24, 26, 31
Geronimo, 81
Ghia, 270, 421
G.I. Bill of Rights, 197
Gilmore-Yosemite Economy Sweepstakes, 169
Glassic, 421
Glasspar Co., roadsters, 257, 304
Glidden Tour, 54, 61
*Godfather, The,* 210
Goodrich tires, 223
Goodyear-Hawley, 240
Goodyear tires, 214, 257, 390
Gordon Bennett Race, 25
Graham-Paige Motors Corp., 124, 133, 138, 140, 142, 145, 162, 163, 166, 167, 69, 179, 192, 212, 215
  Custom Eight, 154, 159
  Hollywood, 183, 188
  "Sharknose", 174, 175, 179, 181
  Special Eight, 149; Special Six, 163
Graham, Ray A., 148
Gray, John S., 32, 33, 45
Great Depression, 132, 138, 186
Gregorie, Bob, 183
Gregory, 226, 238
Grettenberger, John O., 582
Griffith, 402
Group Lotus, 556
Grove, Tom, 392
Gulf Oil Co., 69
Gulton Industries, 442
Gurney, Dan, 460

Harding, William G., 96
Hardtop convertible, 230, 231, 248
Hardtops, 240, 251, 260, 280, 356
Harroun, Ray, 62, 81
Hartford Shock Absorber, 39
Haynes, 11, 99
Haynes-Apperson, 16, 21, 28
Haynes, Elwood P., 10, 11, 101, 114
Healey, Donald, 265, 266
Heep, Uriah, 21
Heinz, Rust, 176
HELP, 407
Hendrick, Rick, 611
Henry Ford Co., 20, 23, 26
Henry J, 248, 262, 263, 272, 284 *See also* Allstate.

Herrington, Arthur W.S., 184
Hertz, 116
Hess and Eisenhart, 299
Hewitt, 47
Highway Safety Act, 416
Hiroshima, 199
Hodges, Audrey Moore, 229
Hoffman, Paul G., 161
Hoglund, William, 547
Hollowell Engineering, 420
Holsman, 28
Honda, 522, 534, 570, 576, 586, 601, 611
  Accord, 608, 613
Hoover, Herbert, 131
*Hopalong Cassidy* (TV show), 290
Hope, Bob, 204
Hoppenstand, 238
*Horseless Age, The*, 8, 13, 14
Horse, mechanical, 9
Horsepower race, 278, 288, 348, 349, 396
Horsey Horseless Carriage, 16, 21
Hudson, 32, 40, 53, 73, 116, 122, 145, 171, 175, 189, 221, 230, 278, 288, 294, 319. *See also* Essex.
  Commodore, 193, 239, 252
  Country Club, 180, 181
  Eight, 167, 214, 215
  Greater Eight, 145, 150
  Hornet, 248, 262, 263, 264, 272, 284, 292, 303, 313, 323
  Italia, 291, 292
  Jet, 282, 292
  Mile-A-Minute Roadster, 65
  Model 33, 60; Model 54, 64; Model S, 127
  Pacemaker, 155, 181, 252, 253
  Pikes Peak Special, 92
  profit and loss, 187
  races, 154, 272
  Rambler, 303, 311, 317
  Special, 112; Standard, 122
  Step-down, 224, 230
  Super Six, 78, 88, 92, 104, 116, 207, 239
  Super Wasp, 284
  Terraplane, 157, 160, 169, 171, 173, 174, 175, 177, 181
  30th anniversary, 179
  wartime production, 195, 200
Hupmobile, 32, 53, 64, 104, 116, 139, 142, 149, 150, 157, 167, 168, 174, 175, 181
  Skylark, 183, 188
Hurst/Oldsmobile, 442, 450, 477, 482, 494, 520, 541, 542, 547
Hurst Performance Products, 422
Hutchinson, B.E., 105

Iacocca, Lee, 350, 509, 517, 522, 545, 580, 602, 627
Imp, 67, 238, 241, 252, 264
Imperial, 300, 304, 314, 321, 352, 364, 376, 387, 390, 428, 450, 458, 464, 534
  Crown, 355, 379, 404, 413, 419, 439, 441
  Crown Southampton, 324, 334, 345
  LeBaron, 355, 379
IMSA Grand Touring, 565
Indianapolis 500, 59, 62, 115, 144, 154, 162
  Official Pace Car, 115, 151, 164, 168, 217, 221, 244, 260, 283, 290, 325, 386, 387, 396, 418, 440, 446, 477, 488, 510, 513, 527, 535, 554, 567, 574, 576, 586, 592, 599, 603, 609, 617, 620, 629, 632
Indianapolis Speedway, 54, 55
Indiana Toll Road, 308
Industrial Workers of the World, 72
*In My Merry Oldsmobile*, 40
*Insolent Chariots, The* (Keats), 325
International Motor Co., 61
International Race of Champions, 582
Interstate Highway, 79, 308, 350, 426
Isuzu, 464

Jackson Automobile Co., 34
Jaeger, 151
Jaguar, 578
Jaxon Steamer, 34
J.D. Power and Associates, 538
Jeep. *See* American Motors Corp.
Jeffery, Thomas B., 17, 19, 71. *See also* T.B. Jeffery Co. Jenkins, Ab, 150
Jetmobile, 272
Johnson, Lyndon B., 424
Jomar, 293
Jordan Motor Car Co., 103, 108, 122

Kaiser 202, 272, 292, 304. *See also* Frazer, Henry J.
  advertising, 240, 252, 263, 272
  Carolina, 284
  Custom, 215, 224
  Dragon, 282, 284
  Manhattan, 273, 284, 291, 302, 304
  Special, 215, 224
  Traveler, 236, 239, 264
  Vagabond, 236, 239
  Virginian, 236, 240
Kaiser-Darrin, 291, 292
Kaiser-Frazer Corp., 199, 204, 210, 212, 214, 218, 230, 253, 278
Kaiser, Henry J., 196, 214, 223, 230, 239, 288
Kaiser-Jeep Corp., 437, 455
Keating, T.H., 211
Keats, John, 325
Kerkorian, Kirk, 602
Keller, H.O., 18
Keller, K.T., 127, 161, 199, 201
Keller Motors Corp., 218, 226
Kelly, Michael, 553
Kelsey & Tilney, 15
Kelsey, Cadwallader W., 14
Kerouac, Jack, 325
Kettering, Charles F., 62, 63, 66, 70, 92, 102
King, Charles B., 8, 12, 14, 29
King Midget, 210, 268, 293
Kissel Kar, 44, 68, 75, 81
Kleiber Motor Co., 136
Kline, 75
Knight, Charles Y., 50
Knight engine, 57, 60
Knox, 23, 24
Knudsen, William S., 61, 95, 99, 109, 110, 125, 150, 182, 200
Korff, 272
Kravke, Richard, 332
Kulick, Frank, 53
Kurtis, 226, 240, 248
Kurtis, Frank, 210, 240
Kurtz Automatic, 91
Kvale, Kjell, 269

LaFayette. *See* Nash Motor Co.
Lambert, 9
Lambert, Charles, 8
Lamborghini, 560
Lampkin, Ray, 91
Landy, "Dandy" Dick, 411
LaSalle, 121, 127, 133, 142, 148, 150, 154, 163, 168, 171, 176, 179, 183
Las Vegas 400, 632
Leach Motor Carriage, 25
Lehmann-Peterson, 441
Leland and Faulconer Mfg. Co., 36, 37
Leland, Henry M., 27, 32, 70, 82, 94, 99
Leland, Wilfred, 99
Le Mans race, 251, 261, 271, 273, 275, 281, 301, 421
Lenoir, Jean Joseph Etienne, 8
Levassor, Emile, 10
Lexington, 92
Liberty, 81
Lichtenstein, Maurice, 125
Lincoln, 82, 99, 133, 134, 145, 188, 221, 252, 404, 428, 526, 569, 603, 630
  Capri, 272, 273, 285, 293, 304, 334, 345, 458
  Continental, 152, 182, 188, 194, 216, 224, 278, 364, 367, 380, 390, 412, 413, 421, 431, 441, 446, 458, 475,

Lincoln (*continued*)
  494, 512, 526, 535, 536, 565, 567, 589, 599, 600, 603, 605, 628
  Continental Mark II, 310, 314, 324
  Continental Mark III, 331, 334, 435, 439, 442, 443, 449, 466
  Continental Mark IV, 343, 345, 470, 476, 487, 500
  Continental Mark V, 356, 505, 513, 519
  Continental Mark VI, 525, 531, 535, 540
  Continental Mark VII, 544, 547, 552, 557, 568, 578, 589, 590
  Continental Mark VIII, 592, 594, 616, 621
  Cosmopolitan, 241, 265, 272, 273
  Futura, 305
  K series, 146, 164, 182; KA series, 155; KB series, 150
  LeBaron, 134, 180
  LS, 634
  Model L, 94, 104, 133
  Navigator, 614, 622, 623, 628
  Premiere, 314, 324
  races, 273, 282, 285, 293
  Town Car/Coupé, 341, 481, 531, 536, 553, 567, 576, 578, 584, 610, 623, 628
  25th anniversary, 213
  Versailles, 503, 506, 507, 513
  XL-500 show car, 285
  Zephyr, 165, 168, 172, 175, 179, 180, 183, 194
Lincoln Highway, 70, 115
Lincoln-Mercury Division, 216, 217
Lindbergh, Charles, 125
Little Motor Car Co., 58, 63, 68
Locomobile, 19, 20, 24, 25, 28, 29, 99, 102, 112
Loewy, Raymond, 149, 150, 177, 189, 395
*Lone Ranger, The*, 201
Lopez, J. Ignacio, 608
Losh, J. Michael, 547
Lotus of England, 421
Loughead, Malcolm, 85
Lozier, 40
Lustron Corp., 207
Lutz, Robert, 609, 617

Macauley, Alvan, 57, 79, 160
Macauley, Ed, 226
Maharajah of Indore, 163
Malcolm Baldridge Award, 582
Malcomson, Alexander, 29, 33, 45
Markette, 431
Markin, Morris, 165
Marmon, 38, 43, 122, 138 *See also* Roosevelt.
  Sixteen, 143, 146, 150, 155
Marquette, 133, 139. *See also* Buick.
Marr, Walter, 33
Mars II electric, 420
Martin, 130
Mason, George W., 31, 167, 225, 266, 288, 294
Maverick, 273, 284
Maxim, Hiram Percy, 16
Maxwell, 38, 40, 44, 54, 63, 67, 92, 117
Maxwell-Chalmers Corp., 106, 114
Maxwell, Jonathan, 11, 22, 29, 44
Mays, J, 615
Mazda Motor Corp., 609
McAneeny, William 145
McCuen, C.L., 154
McDonald, Marie "The Body," 204
McDonald's drive-in, 298
McKinley, William, 24
McNamara, Robert S., 333, 343, 354
McNeil, A.F., 163
Mercedes, 39, 41, 627
Mercer, 59
Mercury, 178, 180, 181, 184, 185, 194, 207, 208, 221, 242, 472
  Astron, 412
  Bobcat, 492 495, 526
  Capri, 500, 516, 519, 521, 531, 542, 547, 552, 557, 558, 584, 599

Mercury (*continued*)
  Colony Park, 335, 356, 368, 380
  Comet, 348, 349, 357, 361, 367, 380, 384, 391, 396, 399, 404, 412, 413, 415, 431, 509
  Cougar, 424, 428, 441, 450, 458, 463, 467, 476, 481, 482, 485, 487, 489, 506, 507, 526, 531, 536, 541, 547, 552, 562, 574, 584, 598, 600, 616, 629
  Custom, 293, 315
  Cyclone, 390, 399, 412, 428, 444, 448, 449, 458, 468
  Grand Marquis, 494, 513, 542, 552, 567, 584, 588, 594, 610, 616, 622
  LN7, 533, 541
  Lynx, 531, 562, 563
  Marauder, 384, 390, 399, 404, 444, 449, 450
  Marquis, 425, 488, 516, 520, 531, 542, 555
  Mermaid, 325
  Meteor, 372, 376, 391
  Monarch, 492, 494
  Montclair, 305, 315, 335, 345, 404
  Montego, 435, 470, 476, 487
  Monterey, 252, 253, 265, 274, 285, 293, 294, 315, 356, 368, 380, 391, 404, 476, 488
  Mountaineer, 610
  Mystique, 603, 605, 623
  Park Lane, 343, 345, 401, 441
  S-55, 372, 391
  Sable, 554, 557, 558, 589, 611
  Sport Sedan, 242, 253
  Sportsman, 209
  station wagon, 242, 253
  Sun Valley, 291
  Topaz, 541, 544, 547, 555, 563, 590
  Town Sedan, 184
  Tracer, 582, 594, 596, 604
  Turnpike Cruiser, 321, 325, 335
  25th anniversary, 404
  Villager, 592, 594, 616, 629
  Zephyr, 509, 513, 520, 531
Merkur, 550
Metropolitan, 257, 292, 294, 301, 315, 341, 347, 350, 361, 372, 376
Metzger, William E., 18, 73
Midgley, Thomas Jr., 96
Miller, 115, 130
Miller, Al and Chet, 154
Miller-Ford, 162
Miller, Harry, 162
Mitchell, 81, 94
Mitchell, Bill, 175, 310, 341, 350, 363
Mitsubishi Motors Corp., 464, 579
Mobile Co. of America, 18, 23
Mobilgas Economy Run, 282, 293, 378, 445
Mohs Ostentatienne Opera Coupe, 431
Moline, 38
Montalban, Ricardo, 492
Monte Carlo Rally, 173, 402
Moon, 40, 53, 104, 111
Moore, A.L., 18
Moore, Clayton, 201
Morris, Henry G., 12
Morrison, William, 9
Moskovics, Frederick, 143
*Motocycle, The*, 13
*Motor Age*, 21, 25
Motorama, 249, 279, 285, 313, 325
Motor Mart, 31
*Motor Trend* "Car of the Year," 384, 451
Motor Vehicle Manufacturers Association, 471
Mudge, Genevra Delphine, 19
Mulford, Ralph, 115
Munsey Tour, 56
Muntz, Earl "Madman," 240, 248, 265
Muntz Jet, 226, 240, 248, 265, 274, 293
Murphy, Edward M., 46
Muscle cars, 396
Mustang, 243
Myers, Billy, 323
*My Life and Work* (Henry Ford), 100